Nationalists ABROAD

Nationalists ABROAD

THE JAMAICA PROGRESSIVE LEAGUE AND THE FOUNDATIONS OF JAMAICAN INDEPENDENCE

Birte Timm

IAN RANDLE PUBLISHERS
Kingston • Miami

First published in Jamaica, 2016 by
Ian Randle Publishers
16 Herb McKenley Drive
Box 686
Kingston 6
www.ianrandlepublishers.com

© Birte Timm, 2016

National Library of Jamaica Cataloguing-In-Publication Data

Timm, Birte
    Nationalists abroad : the Jamaica Progressive League and the foundations of Jamaican independence / Birte Timm.

  p. ; cm

Bibliography: p. – Includes index.
ISBN 978-976-637-865-3 (pbk)

1. Autonomy and independence movements   2. Autonomy – Jamaica
3. Jamaica Progressive League   4. Nationalism
I. Title

320.15   dc 23

All rights reserved. No part of this publication may be reproduced, stored in a retrieval system or transmitted in any form or by any means electronic, photocopying, recording or otherwise, without the prior permission of the publisher and author.

Cover and Book Design by Ian Randle Publishers
Printed and bound in the United States

For Sven

CONTENTS

ACKNOWLEDGEMENTS ›ix

INTRODUCTION ›xv

Nationalism, Anti-Colonialism and Transnational Migration

Migration and Transnational Networks

A Note on the Sources

Literature Review

Chapter Outline

PART ONE
ORIGINS OF THE MOVEMENT FOR SELF-GOVERNMENT

Chapter 1: Nationalism in Jamaica before 1936 ›1

Chapter 2: Origins of the Jamaica Progressive League ›29

W. Adolphe Roberts and the Idea for a Movement for Self-Government

Wilfred A. Domingo and the 'Black Tropics' in Harlem

Ethelred Brown and the Harlem Unitarian Church

PART TWO
HISTORY AND INFLUENCE OF THE JAMAICA PROGRESSIVE LEAGUE

Chapter 3: Founding and First Reactions ›69

Launch of the Jamaica Progressive League in New York

First Repercussions in Jamaica

Chapter 4: Stretching Out: A Local Branch in Kingston ›86

Founding of the Jamaica Progressive League in Kingston

The Public Opinion *Debate: Calling for a Party*

'The Lid Blows Off': Activities During the Labour Protests in 1938

Chapter 5: Implementing Demands for Self-Government ›134
The Jamaica Progressive League and the Founding of the PNP
Official Representation for Self-Government before the Royal Commission
Domingo and Roberts in Jamaica 1939
First PNP Convention in April 1939
Roberts in Jamaica and the 'Jamaicanizing Jamaica' Campaign

Chapter 6: Alternative Strategies for Self-Government during the Second World War ›207
Retreat or Reinforcement: Different Reactions to the Outbreak of the War
Internationalizing Claims: The West Indies National Council and the Havana Conference
Reverberations in Jamaica
Shifting the Focus Back to Jamaica: Continued Influence on the PNP

Chapter 7: Reassuming the Struggle for Independence in Jamaica ›271
Domingo and Roberts in Jamaica in the 1940s and 1950s

Chapter 8: Opposing the West Indies Federation ›376
Early Critique against Federation
'Opposing It Tooth and Nail': The Campaign against Federation
'At the Crossroads of Destiny': The Referendum
Nationalist Stance

Conclusion ›420

Bibliography ›435

Index of Names and Organizations ›449

ACKNOWLEDGEMENTS

This book is the result of a long process that leaves me with the difficult task to thank everyone who was a part of this journey between Hamburg, Berlin, London, New York and – again and again – Jamaica. Today I am sitting here in Kingston reflecting on the countless people without whom this book would not exist, and I wish to apologize in advance to those whose names might have slipped me writing these lines. I am filled with deep gratitude for the Jamaican people, who played such a big role in pulling me deeper and deeper into the history and culture of this special island in the Caribbean, which became my second home. I cannot express how thankful I am for their hospitality, their support, their *"vibes"*, and for the many lessons they taught me. It is for them, the people of Jamaica, that this work has been done, so that they can access a missing piece in their history of becoming a nation.

First and foremost, I thank Sven Bormann. Without him, this book would simply not exist. I would never have thought of pursuing a Dissertation and I probably would not even have studied history and philosophy. It was also Sven, who introduced me to Jamaican music, and thus kindled my interest in Jamaica in the first place. His unconditional, unselfish, and tireless support along the way is what has motivated me to push through in the darkest hours of self-doubt and procrastination. This is why I dedicate this book to him.

I will forever be grateful for my doctoral advisor and mentor Professor Stefan Rinke. He believed in me and my topic from the moment I shared my idea with him. He guided and supported me throughout the years with his keen analysis and critique, as well as with positive encouragement and strong support in acquiring funding. I wish to thank the Latin American Institute at *Freie Universität Berlin*, and especially my advisory committee. Professor Nikolaus Böttcher and Professor Emeritus Reinhard Liehr provided extensive, valuable and constructive feedback on the manuscript. I also wish to express gratitude for the fruitful dialogue and close collaboration with the Department of Anthropology, especially Professor Ingrid Kummels, who was not only part of my committee, but who also became a mentor. I also thank Claudia Rauhut, who generously offered her critical and encouraging feedback; she is a wonderful colleague, and became a real friend. Although my way eventually led me to Berlin, I thank Professor Jürgen Martschukat for believing in me and my project and for opening the doors to a possibility to pursue my doctorate at the University of Erfurt.

My 'partner in crime', Rainer Schultz, was always there for me with critical feedback and Caribbean vibes, even during the longest days in the Ibero-American Institute in Berlin or at the Widener Library in Cambridge. Special thanks also to Michael Goebel und Nadia Zysman, to Franka Bindernagel, Lasse Hölck, and all my fellow colleagues in the Stefan Rinke's colloquium, who saw this project taking shape over the years and influenced its design and approach with their inspiring feedback and the example of their own scholarship.

Once I had embarked on my journey, I started to meet so many people who loved the project and encouraged me and offered support along the way. I am indebted to them for critical feedback on conference or seminar presentations, chapters or sections of my manuscript.

In Jamaica, the Department of History of the University of the West Indies, and especially its famous Friday Seminar, provided most valuable support and critical feedback. I thank in particular Professors Matthew Smith, Kathleen Monteith, Waibinte Wariboko, and James Robertson, Dr Swithin Wilmot and Sir Roy Augier for their valuable suggestions and their generous support. The late Dr Fitzroy Baptiste and Dr Glen Richards provided valuable help pointing me to sources and assuring me of the importance of my research. The Jamaica Historical Society showed great interest and offered valuable feedback to my presentation on founder Walter A. Roberts.

My heartfelt thanks to Professor Rupert Lewis, who had shown great interest and support during my research. He read the final manuscript and provided most helpful questions and suggestions. He is an admirable scholar and a wonderful mentor. He also helped to make contact with Dr Margaret Stevens, who made every effort to meet me in New York and to share valuable sources on Domingo with me.

A special thanks to Archivist, Scholar and friend John Aarons, whose father knew Roberts personally, and who showed the utmost support and generously shared his knowledge. Professor Kusha Haraksingh was always there for me with feedback, support and advice. We three became friends, and I am very grateful for that. Tony Martin always encouraged me, showed me his island Trinidad, and, despite passionate discussions about Garvey's political views, became a good friend.

I thank Professor Anne Spry Rush, who provided the most helpful and supportive critical feedback. For their time, valuable comments and suggestions, I also thank Professors Robert A. Hill, Peter Hulme, and Brian Meeks, Dr Michael Witter, Professors Colin A. Palmer, Orlando Patterson, Winston James and Anthony Bogues, Dr Robert Maxwell Buddan, Dr Edward Seaga, Professors Verene Shepherd and Anthony Harrison, Dr David Dunkley and Louis J. Parascandola. A special thanks is reserved for Professor Edward Baugh and his

Acknowledgements

wife Sheila, who always welcomed me with open hearts and provided much support.

Thanks to Jason Parker, the scholar who knew best of the significance of the Jamaica Progressive League in the international anti-colonial struggle and the research gap surrounding its history. I feel privileged that I was a part of the 9th International Seminar on Decolonization, sponsored by the National History Center, the American Historical Association, and the John W. Kluge Center of the Library of Congress, generously supported by the Andrew W. Mellon Foundation. This community of scholars helped to change my way of thinking about colonialism and decolonization, and also about the possibility of living a supportive community within academia. Special thanks to the seminar leaders, Professors Roger Wm. Louis, Jason Parker, Dane Kennedy Sudhir Pillarisetti, Phillipa Levine and Lori Watt and all my fellow participants, especially Dr Leena Dallasheh, Dr Marc Andre and Dr Charles Laderman, Dr John Aerni-Flessner, Nicole Bourbonnais and Jessica Pearson-Partel. Eric D. Duke provided unpublished manuscripts of his book and helpful feedback on a chapter draft.

Professor Frances Botkin always encouraged me to rise to the occasion and Dr Claudia Hucke and Dr Terri-Ann Gilbert Roberts not only offered professional feedback and support, but became real friends. I am thankful for the generous hospitality of Frances Botkin, Dr Kate Quinn, Sigrid Rotter, Brenda and Coltrane Campbell, Kurt and Diane Hollingsworth, Tony Screw and Lorraine, who all opened their homes without charge to facilitate my research on a student budget, whether in London, Baltimore, New York or Kingston.

I am filled with sincere gratitude for several persons outside of academia, whose life stories were entangled with the Jamaica Progressive League, and who freely shared invaluable memories, stories, material, support and offered endless encouragement. They all shared in the feeling that the time was overdue that the pioneers of Jamaican nationalism receive due acknowledgment. I know I have not done them justice, and each one of them would write a different story, but may they rest assured that I did my best trying be as objective as possible and to shed light on all different sides of the story. My heartfelt thanks to Jimmy Tucker in Kingston and Herman Thompson in New York; both were dedicated activists of the more recent past of the Jamaica Progressive League, and generously shared their time and knowledge. I was fortunate enough to speak to Richard Hart before he died, who especially held Progressive League Leaders Domingo and O'Meally in high esteem and appreciated their important support during the early years of labour and party development. It was Hart who collected most of the available original sources today that tell the different stories of Jamaica's political development. I am most thankful that I was privileged to have several long conversations with Frank Gordon at Liberty Hall before he passed, where

Donna McFarlane always welcomed me with interest and open arms. Frank Gordon's tireless activism and passion for a better Jamaica is yet to be appraised properly, his memories have been invaluable for me.

I also thank Arnold Bertram, who generously shared his knowledge on the Jamaica Progressive League and its early role in the PNP. I hope my findings can convince him that I have proof for my claims about the influence of the Progressive League.

It would not have been possible to put the pieces of the puzzle together and to tell the story of the Jamaica Progressive League and thus bring forth some missing pieces in the political history of Jamaica without the generous funding of numerous foundations and organizations. First I wish to thank the Friedrich Ebert Stiftung (FES) for a generous two-year doctoral fellowship including extensive travel funds to visit the necessary archives. I thank Judith Wedderburn, head of the FES-Kingston office, for her guidance and mentorship. Further I am thankful for a six month research grant by the German Academic Exchange Service (DAAD), a short-term research grant by the German Historical Institute in Washington, and the support to finalize my manuscript by the International Research Training Group (IRTG) "Between Spaces", FU Berlin.

The main work for this thesis has been done in several archives in Europe, the US and Jamaica. Never could this story have been told without the diligent and dedicated staff in the archives. It is not always easy to find your way through the labyrinth of the archive. But when you eventually crack open the heart of the apparently mean and disinterested archivist at the National Archives and Records Administration (NARA), who finally decides he will help you through the jungle of the State Department and Foreign Office Records, or when the staff of the library at the Institute of Jamaica, and the National Library of Jamaica go out of their way to find the last bit on the protagonists of the Jamaica Progressive League (thanks to Bernadette and Oneil) and patiently carry box after box, volume after volume, microfilm after microfilm, slip after slip, you get to know the value of the archivist. I thank the wonderful staff at the Jamaica Archives and Records Department in Spanish Town, Jamaica. I wish to thank the family of Norman Manley, who generously allowed access to the Norman Manley Papers for my research. The professional routine of the National Archives in London, Kew, offered a totally different but also pleasant research experience. The dedicated staff at the Schomburg Center for Research in Black Culture, New York Public Library, in Harlem, which is so knowledgeable of its collections, made working there a pleasure. It felt almost like time travel to walk on Malcolm X Boulevard every morning, imagining how the future leaders of the Progressive League had put up their soap boxes there during what is now known as the Harlem Renaissance, fighting against racism and colonialism. A very special thanks

Acknowledgements

to Herman Thompson for leading me to the Jamaica Benevolent Association, Harlem, which generously allowed access to its records. Special thanks are also due to Louis Moyston, who had collected some material about the Progressive League and holds some of the records in his private archive in Kingston, Jamaica. He not only shared his material generously, but also offered helpful suggestions and advice.

My heartfelt thanks to Amy Lee, Scott Harrison, and Patricia Edwards for proofreading, editing and formatting the whole or large parts of manuscript in its final stage, not written in my mother tongue. I wish to thank my harshest critics and dear friends of the proofreading crew of historians at *Der Spiegel*, Dr Thorsten Gudewitz, Dr Andreas Strippel, PD Dr Claudia Rauhut, Gesche Sager and the rest of the team. I also thank Britta Scholtys for her valuable feedback.

I thank Ian Randle Publishers for believing in the importance of this story. I dreamt of this day, and of publishing this book with IRP, from the day I first met Ian Randle in 2005 at a conference organized by Werner Zips in Vienna. Things have come full circle. Many thanks for countless hours of work on publishing this book to Christine Randle and her team. When Christine read the manuscript, she immediately decided to publish it and did much of the work on editing the manuscript herself, including giving birth to its title.

Michael Lumsden always provided most needed support in all challenging situations and reminded me that I am not alone and that everything can be achieved, one step at a time. My heartfelt thanks to Hilmar Keding and his family, who always supported me. It is only because of Hilmar's many sacrifices that the charity which he had joined me in creating during my research in Jamaica, HELP Jamaica! (www.helpjamaica.org), was able to grow while I was writing my dissertation. Last but not least, I wish to thank my parents Ilka-Dunja Timm and Jürgen Timm, my brother Steffen and his family, my grandparents Harald and Gisela Timm (who passed away at 97 while I am writing these lines) and Tante Mantje. Without the support of my family I could not have made it. I will forever be thankful that they keep me in their hearts and encourage me in all my steps, although it meant that I started a life far away from my loved ones. Finally I wish to thank Nico Szepanski. He only joined my journey of completing this book on the very last stretch, yet he has shown me what unconditional love and support means.

INTRODUCTION

On August 6, 2012, the National Stadium in Kingston was packed to capacity with a large crowd of Jamaicans, dressed in black, gold and green. When Prime Minister Portia Simpson Miller addressed the citizens of Jamaica on the occasion of the country's 50th anniversary of independence, she highlighted the historical contribution of the founder of the party she represented, the People's National Party (PNP). She proclaimed: 'One who could truly say "mission accomplished" with satisfaction was the Chief Architect of our Independence, Norman Washington Manley'.[1]

Winston Maragh, a politician affiliated with the rival Jamaica Labour Party (JLP), was quick to contradict Simpson Miller's statement in a letter to the editor of the *Jamaica Observer,* in which he noted:

> Nothing could be further from the truth, and those of us who were around at that time, as well as those of us who did history in school know this. As far back as 1957, Norman Manley declared in Parliament that his PNP government would be entering into a federation with the other West Indian islands, which they did in 1958.[2]

In contrast, Maragh emphasized the nationalist campaign against the federation in 1961 that was waged by JLP-founder Alexander Bustamante and his party, and provocatively asked:

> I am amazed that none of our so-called historians noticed anything. Was no one concerned that the writer of that speech was trying to change the history of our country? Or was it that nobody cared enough to even listen to our prime minister's message?

Indeed, after Great Britain had suggested the formation of a federated West Indies in the aftermath of the Second World War, Norman Manley and the PNP had firmly supported these plans. This position was not necessarily contradicting Manley's nationalist convictions as such, as he and many leaders of the PNP were convinced that gaining independence as part of a federated West Indies would be in Jamaica's best interest. Yet, strictly speaking, the PNP was not demanding a Jamaican nation state, but rather, a national unit of which Jamaica would be a part.

In recent discussions surrounding the independence festivities, JLP politicians like Andrew Holness tried to take advantage of portraying the JLP as the true advocate of a Jamaican nation state and referred to the referendum which the JLP had initiated in 1961.³ Maragh argued in a similar way, and indeed, it is true that the agitation against the federation led to a referendum, in which a majority of 54.1 per cent of Jamaicans decided to withdraw from the federation – a decision that led to its break-up, and Jamaica as well as Trinidad's independence as individual nation states. However, such a view omits the fact that Bustamante and the JLP had also supported the federation for several years, before the party suddenly changed its course and started a strong, populist anti-federation campaign in 1961.

Holness and Simpson Miller's speeches and Maragh's letter represent a common practice of interpreting Jamaican history from a partisan perspective. The historical narratives offered by the two political parties, PNP and JLP, apotheosize the role of their respective founders, Manley and Bustamante. The labour rebellions in 1938 and the formation of the PNP in the aftermath are usually seen as watershed events and the starting point of Jamaica's modern political history. The leading roles of Bustamante and Manley as founding fathers of the nation have become generally accepted as central to the development of nationalism and modern politics in Jamaica. These two larger-than-life figures are often portrayed in a glorified way, especially since their elevation into the status of officially proclaimed National Heroes in 1969. Despite their unquestionable importance, such a view overshadows other important figures and movements and distorts the historical course of events.

In the development of party politics in Jamaica, and in introducing demands for Jamaica to become an independent nation state, in particular, other actors played a very important, yet neglected role. The present study puts a spotlight on the Jamaica Progressive League, a transnational group formed by expatriates in the United States in September 1936, which spearheaded anti-colonial nationalism in Jamaica and exerted a great impact on the PNP in its formative years. The Jamaica Progressive League was formed by W. Adolphe Roberts, Wilfred A. Domingo, Ethelred Brown and others in New York. In 1937, W.G. McFarlane, himself a migrant who had recently returned to Jamaica, founded a local branch in Kingston that was modelled after the mother organization in New York. In pursuit of its objective to lobby for an end to colonial rule in Jamaica, the Progressive League started a massive propaganda campaign for self-government that predated the formation of the two modern political parties. The Progressive League published pamphlets and articles and toured the island addressing people in all quarters. From its inception, the Progressive League called for a political party. However, in local political circles, their ideas were often considered too radical and were received with scepticism; nevertheless, they significantly influenced the emerging political scene in Jamaica.

Introduction

This is the story of the Jamaica Progressive League and its protagonists, and their efforts to inspire an anti-colonial movement in Jamaica. It provides fresh insights into the formative stages of local party politics in Jamaica as well as into the high-level of exchange between local activists and emigrants. A special focus placed on the relationship with the PNP uncovers the important ideological and monetary support which the Progressive League provided, as well as the differences in radicalism in their nationalist expressions. The Progressive League leaders significantly influenced the formation of the early PNP, convinced its members to adopt self-government as a demand in its planks, and continued the struggle for self-government during the Second World War when the PNP had retreated from political agitation. While both parties, JLP and PNP, initially supported the federation during the 1940s and 1950s, Progressive League leaders Roberts and Domingo never abandoned their conviction that Jamaica should become an independent nation in its own right. They waged a strong campaign against federation since the early '50s, adopting an ultra-nationalist, even chauvinist position and accepted funding from Bustamante and the JLP for a series of radio broadcast against federation in the run-up to the referendum.

Despite its pioneering role, the contribution of the Jamaica Progressive League to the early political developments became nearly forgotten in public memory and is neglected in many historical accounts. The break with the PNP over the question of federation certainly contributed to the oblivion, into which the Progressive League sank in post-colonial Jamaica. There are a number of other reasons and possible explanations why the contribution of the Progressive League has been neglected in historiography as well as in public life in Jamaica in the twenty-first century. One of the most important factors is the competitive two-party-system in which both parties overemphasize their own pioneering role. Another factor is a lessened interest in what is often called creole nationalism or middle-class nationalism. In part, this is a result of the deep disappointment in the political elites that sprang from the pre-independence period and took Jamaica into independence without fundamentally challenging the colonial value system, leaving barriers based on race, class and gender largely untouched. Despite initial economic growth in post-colonial Jamaica, sections of the rural and urban unemployed poor started to voice their frustration and disappointment in the unfulfilled promises of independence. Backed by critical reflections in intellectual circles who fundamentally questioned the social order in the late '60s and early '70s, a new generation started to slowly transform society. Walter Rodney and other academic activists, for instance Rupert Lewis, Robert Hill, Trevor Munroe and George Beckford, editors of the radical newspaper *Abeng*, or Louis Lindsay, who coined the seminal phrase of the 'myth of independence', openly criticized the continued racial discrimination in post-colonial Jamaica.[4] Ever since, Jamaican historiography has put strong emphasis on the history of slavery and resistance, Black Nationalism, Garveyism and diverse forms of black spirituality, with little interest in what is often lumped together as 'creole nationalism'. Hence, even the history of the two political parties remains shrouded in legacy to a large extent, while smaller groups predating 1938, like the National Reform Association, the Citizen's Associations and the Jamaica Progressive League received very little attention.[5] Nevertheless, the histories of these organizations allow insights in the negotiations within the emerging political landscape about the future of the country and thus improve our understanding of continuities as well as ruptures within the configurations that would shape the new nation state after 1962. It is quite possible that the history of the Progressive League and its anti-colonial intervention from abroad, as well as the resistance towards these ideas in local political circles, did not suit the needs of the leaders that forged the nation-building process in post-colonial Jamaica. Later on, I will discuss these and other factors explaining why the contribution of the Progressive League was eclipsed by other narratives at greater length.

Putting the spotlight on the Progressive League and its influence in Jamaica provides a missing piece in the mosaic of political formation in pre-independence Jamaica. Yet, this focal point runs the danger of overestimating the Progressive League's influence in light of the larger developments. It is not the aim of this work to give a general account of Jamaican political history in the 30 years preceding independence, although there would be a great need for it. Through the lens of the history of the Jamaica Progressive League, this study uncovers the largely forgotten transnational roots of anti-colonial thought in Jamaica and, thus, offers a more nuanced picture of the road towards independence that usually is centred on the two main political parties.

In the recent past, Louis Moyston and Ken Jones, political activists and frequent contributors to the press, have occasionally criticized the omission of the Progressive League in the historical narrative of Jamaica's path towards independence. Although both men are affiliated with the PNP and the JLP, respectively, they both expressed concern about the way the historical narratives have been constructed to serve political purposes, while twisting the facts. In reaction to Maragh's letter to the *Observer* cited above, Moyston commended him for complaining about the prime minister's 'misguided reference' to Norman Manley as the 'father of Jamaica's political independence'.[6] Moyston emphasizes:

> This particular distortion of our country's history is something invented and unabashedly promoted by the PNP; but even Mr. Manley never claimed this authorship for himself. In fact, he was known to have acknowledged his resistance to the idea when it was proposed to him in 1938.

Introduction

Moyston further points to the ground-breaking nature of the Progressive League's intervention in local politics, underlines the crucial influence it exercised on the anti-colonial positions the PNP finally adopted in 1939, and calls founder Walter Adolphe Roberts 'the true pioneer of Jamaica's Independence movement'.

In 2011, Ken Jones had articulated similar sentiments in a series of three articles in the *Daily Gleaner*.[7] In his piece on Roberts, Jones expressed his hope that on the occasion of Jamaica's 50th anniversary, the country would reflect on 'who should wear the heroic garland for conceptualizing and initiating the march towards Jamaican self-government'. He emphasized that neither Manley nor Bustamante, but Roberts and the Progressive League originated concrete political demands for independence and called for the erection of monuments in their honour at National Heroes Park in Kingston.[8]

The findings of my research confirm that during the last three decades under colonialism, the Jamaica Progressive League was not only the first but also the most outspoken anti-colonial organization demanding that Jamaica become a sovereign nation-state. While nationalist sentiments had found earlier expression in movements like S.A.G. Cox's National Club, Marcus Garvey's People's Political Party, and the various Citizen's Associations, Poetry and Debating Clubs, a concrete political demand for a Jamaican nation state had not been the priority of any of these early groups.[9] Centuries of British rule had left a deep imprint on the mentality of the people. Scholars have increasingly paid attention to British identities and the adaption of British cultural values, diagnosing a widespread identification and loyalty to the Empire.[10] Gordon K. Lewis labelled this 'colonial ennui, colonial self-contempt, and colonial feelings of dependency – the well-known colonial mentality in West Indians themselves'.[11] The aspiring middle class, in particular, subscribed firmly to a belief system indoctrinated by the colonizers, and internalized much of the negative and often racist stereotypes that led them to believe that the majority of Jamaicans was not yet 'civilized' and fit for self-government.[12] In her insightful study on identities of middle-class Caribbeans, Anne Spry Rush has found a strong and widespread identification with Great Britain and termed this phenomenon '*imperial* British identity'.[13] Brian L. Moore and Michele A. Johnson emphasized that all sections of the society were penetrated by a strong identification with the British monarchy and many shared deep pride in being part of the British Empire.[14] For many Jamaicans this stood in no contradiction to the African cultural elements, religious practices and moral values they maintained, and which marked important areas of resistance to mental techniques of control. But in general, loyalty to the British crown was by no means exclusive to the ruling elite, who substantially benefited from the colonial system. Powerful symbols of the grandness of the Empire, impressive festivities in honour of the royal family, huge parades with pomp and glamour were an integral part of colonial reality. Patrick Bryan points to the success of such festivities that were 'aimed to produce, in Jamaicans, an unshakable loyalty to empire, and an appreciation of imperial benevolence'.[15] Also, Moore and Johnson refer to the tremendous popularity of Queen Victoria and her descendants among Afro-Jamaicans.[16] Supported by propaganda of missionaries, many perceived the abolition of slavery as a gift of the crown.

Nevertheless, opposition against colonial rule, slavery and post-emancipation misery was integral in colonial Jamaica. Yet, protest that developed in the Afro-Jamaican majority was generally motivated by the inhumane living conditions, and directed against local authority, rather than against colonialism as an abstract principle. Amongst the largely illiterate and impoverished masses, radical and potentially anti-colonial protest was largely channelled in spiritual forms of protest or retreat, for instance in Revivalism, Rastafarianism, or Pan-Africanism. If expressed in nationalist terms, visions were rather directed towards Africa than towards Jamaica. It is therefore not surprising that strong anti-colonial sentiments developed outside of the borders of the island, not amongst Jamaicans in England, but in the United Sates. Although the experience of racism in England and in the First World War had radicalized a great number of Jamaicans and inspired some degree of nationalist thought, it was a particular set of experiences in the US and encounters with other anti-colonial movements that inspired the origins of anti-colonial nationalism that were manifested with the formation of the Jamaica Progressive League.[17]

This book does not argue that the agitation of the Progressive League was the most decisive factor in gaining independence. Yet, the close examination of the Jamaica Progressive League provides an important example of the development of nationalism within a transnational migrant context and reveals its important influence on local politics. This focus questions the interpretation of decolonization in the Caribbean as a process largely directed from above. Instead, it offers evidence that the Progressive League played an important role in the orchestra of power relations that shaped Jamaica's path towards decolonization, which consisted of different players including the Colonial Office in Great Britain and its representatives in the colony, policymakers in the US State Department, local politicians in the islands, as well as migrants who pledged themselves to change the political destiny of their island home.[18] The story presented in the following chapters illuminates the transnational roots of anti-colonial nationalism and helps to interpret the configurations and experiences that triggered the development of Jamaican anti-colonial nationalism outside of Jamaica's geographic boundary.

Introduction

Nationalism, Anti-Colonialism and Transnational Migration

For a better understanding of the theoretical framework within which the Jamaica Progressive League is analysed, some clarification of terminology and understanding of concepts like nationalism, transnationalism, and a more detailed look into the configurations of race and class is helpful. Following constructivist theoreticians of nationalism like Benedict Anderson, Eric Hobsbawm and Ernest Gellner, all nations are socially constructed products of modernity.[19] Essentialist concepts of the nation are based on ethnicity or an assumed common past.[20] In contrast, constructivist approaches assert that the nation can best be described as an 'imagined community'.[21] In this concept, nationalism promotes the imagination of a specific nation and eventually leads to demands for the creation of a nation state. Eric Hobsbawm and Terence Ranger's emphasis on the importance of invented traditions, of creating national myths and historical imaginations of a shared national identity, offers a great tool for analysing the nationalist propaganda of the Jamaica Progressive League.[22]

Many Caribbean societies clearly disclose the constructed character of nationalism. The artificial and arbitrary social fabric in colonies like Jamaica, with a European minority on top of the social pyramid, a light-skinned brown middle class, and a black majority consisting of descendants of enslaved Africans, complemented by an Asian immigrant population and the absence of any recognizable indigenous population, provide a unique research field for the question of how nationalism emerges in such a colonial framework.[23] While claims to indigenous land and cultures are usually part of nationalists' legitimization for nationalist demands for an independent nation state, Jamaica provides an interesting example of how nationalism is constructed where claims to a primordial national past are impossible.

Ever since the first outsiders entered the shores of Jamaica, and since the first emigrants left the island to seek their fortune elsewhere, transnational connections and diverse influences connected the island with Europe, Africa, Asia and elsewhere. These forces have been constitutive in shaping the political, economic and social realities in the island and complicated national identity formation.[24] While the ruling elites in the Anglophone Caribbean maintained their British identity, nationalism developed in intellectual circles of an aspiring middle class that demanded more political power to expand material and educational resources. Large parts of the middle class and even many Jamaicans of African descent subscribed to ideas of belonging to an imperial collective, while African identities survived in religious and cultural practices. Most of the channels common for the dissemination of nationalist ideas were blocked by

British imperial propaganda, and none of the local political groups developed anti-colonial positions with a focus on demanding a Jamaican nation state.

A transnational research approach that takes the experiences of the emigrants and the different local configurations into account helps to explain why anti-colonial nationalism developed in intellectual circles amongst migrants in the United States. In their study on intellectuals and nationalism, Claudio Lomnitz and Dominic Boyer outlined the need for more in-depth research on nationalist leaders to improve our understanding of how nationalist thought originates.[25] By tracing the biographies of these men and women who dedicated their lives to the struggle for independence, this study on the Progressive League provides rich material for a deeper understanding of the experiences that led its leaders to abandon imperial identities and to initiate an anti-colonial movement.

These insights show that migrants integrated inspirations from various ideological streams, ranging from Lenin's theories on anti-imperialism, Woodrow Wilson's claims for self-determination, Marcus Garvey's Black Nationalism, Ghandi's anti-colonial nationalism in India, the transnational Irish nationalist movement and even Simon Bolivar's republicanism. From such a wide array of inspirations, the Progressive League crafted an original vision of nationhood, without simply replicating European nationalism.

Partha Chatterjee criticizes Anderson's analysis of nationalism as Eurocentric. He asks provocatively 'whose imagined community' is envisioned by nationalists in colonial contexts and argues that after centuries of exploitation there seems to be no space for alternative philosophies or innovative ways of organizing society.[26] He diagnoses a prolonged westernized domination and claims:

> 'Europe and the Americas, the only true subjects of history, have thought out on our behalf not only the script of colonial enlightenment and exploitation, but also that of our anti-colonial resistance and post-colonial misery. Even our imaginations must forever be colonized'.[27]

Despite the understandable scepticism, Chatterjee and other post-colonial thinkers express regarding classic forms of nationalism in a post-colonial context, Frantz Fanon reminds us of the importance of the development of national identities and describes nationalism as the main driving force in the formation of anti-colonial movements.[28] The analysis of the Progressive League and its nationalist agitation sheds light on one expression of Jamaican anti-colonial nationalism. The ideas and activities of the Progressive League, as well as the hesitation and timidity within local political circles, have been unduly neglected in historiography. Unearthing this history thus offers a more nuanced analysis of anti-colonial thought in Jamaica and of the different forces that shaped the transition from colony to nation state in the twentieth century.

Introduction

There is a special dynamic between migration, nationalism and the impact of emigrants on politics in their land of birth.[29] Various studies have shown that migrants should be thought of as individuals who often adopt multiple, and by no means exclusive, national identities, rather than as uprooted persons trying to assimilate in their host societies.[30] In many cases, anti-colonial nationalism developed in migrant circles in the metropolises of Europe or North America, or had at least a strong supporter base abroad. In the case of the Caribbean, the difference in race conceptions in the Caribbean and in the US radicalized the immigrants from the Caribbean when they encountered the bare-faced version of racism in the United States.[31]

Another important reason for this phenomenon is the encounter of the emigrants with various ideological influences and anti-colonial positions, for instance with Socialism, Black Nationalism and other anti-colonial movements. Their interaction with people from different colonial territories often inspired reflections on colonial rule and sometimes led individuals to break with imperial identities, which inhibited anti-colonial thinking in the local context. In an article published in the Jamaican weekly *Public Opinion* in 1944, Wilfred A. Domingo, vice-president of the Progressive League, describes this phenomenon from his personal migration experience:

> Like most Jamaicans I had believed in a sort of hazy manner, most of the things I had been taught at school or which had been insinuated into me by my environment and reading. As a small boy I somehow felt that the British Empire was the grandest thing in the world…I thought the English people were God's most perfect humans and we Jamaicans, being English, the best of all coloured peoples. On my arrival in Boston I was shocked out of much of this, but I still clung to some of my beliefs. But my contact with other West Indians in New York damaged my faith considerably and almost ruined it.[32]

Domingo's statement illustrates not only the transformational power of the migration experience, but also how deeply imperial identities were rooted. Although Domingo had been involved in S.A.G. Cox's National Club before he migrated, only his encounters with other activists challenged these notions of belonging to a great empire.

This observation corresponds with Richard Smith's insights from analysing the effect of the participation of Jamaican volunteers in the First World War. He concludes that despite the fledgling nationalist sentiment and the complaint about a lack of recognition for their contribution, the early nationalists that evolved from the British West India Regiment remained loyal to the king.[33]

In his study on long-distance nationalism, Benedict Anderson emphasizes the effect of migration on the development of nationalist identities, especially in societies in which racist patterns complicate assimilation and points as one example to Jamaican immigrants in London.[34] In the US, migrants from the Caribbean were confronted with the American practice of racial discrimination, which subsumes all people of African ancestry under the 'one-drop rule'. The concepts of race that developed in many colonial societies in the Americas follow a different logic and distinguish between different shades of complexion, offering more privileges to persons with lighter skin complexion. Hence, migrants who belonged to the light-skinned middle class faced forms of racism and social degradation they were not accustomed to in their home societies.[35]

Migration and Transnational Networks

Migration and the close-meshed transnational networks it produced have always been of crucial importance to the wider Caribbean region. The emergence of diverse and not necessarily mutually exclusive national, cultural and racial identities forged within these networks were constitutive in the emergence of modern Caribbean societies. Since the arrival of Europeans on Caribbean shores and the massive deportation of millions of enslaved people of African descent during the transatlantic slave trade, the region has been a place that is profoundly shaped by – voluntary and involuntary – migration and diverse flows of people, capital, goods and the fruitful encounter of different cultures. These processes affected not only those who left and profoundly changed their host societies, but also the societies they left behind, as the history of the Progressive League vividly demonstrates. After the important role of Caribbeans in the Harlem Renaissance was neglected for many years, their disproportionally high number among the most radical activists in Harlem is well documented today.[36] The fact that many activists also played crucial roles in political and social movements in their home societies in the Caribbean still deserves much more attention.

Thus the study on the Progressive League contributes to studies on transnational migration, which have produced critical insights in the role, the potential and the limitations of the nation state and contributed to a deeper understanding of the forces that link a globally interconnected world. The so-called transnational turn in historical, anthropological and sociological studies of migration has heightened our awareness towards migrants' remaining connections and involvement in private and family and also to their involvement in social, cultural and political affairs at home.[37] Nina Glick-Schiller defines transnational migration as:

> ...a pattern of migration in which persons, although they move across international borders and settle and establish social relations in a new state, maintain social connections within the polity from which they originate. In transnational migration, persons live their lives across international borders.[38]

Introduction

According to this definition, the members of the Progressive League, who frequently travelled back and forth and actively involved themselves in Jamaican politics, can be described as transnational migrants who exemplify the importance of transnational networks in the Harlem Renaissance, as well as in the developing political landscape in Jamaica.

While some scholars of transnationalism initially treated transnational networks as a recent phenomenon, the history of the Progressive League provides an example for a dense transnational network in the first decades of the twentieth century and thus supports the findings of more recent works on transnationalism.[39] One of the most prominent models emphasizing the historical connectivity within the black diaspora is Paul Gilroy's concept of the 'Black Atlantic'. He argues that 'the history of the Black Atlantic...crisscrossed by movements of black people – not only as commodities but engaged in various struggles towards emancipation, autonomy, and citizenship – provides a means to re-examine the problems of nationality, location, identity, and historical memory'.[40] More specifically, Orlando Patterson argues that high migration rates and profound cultural exchanges resulted in the formation of different regional cosmoses in the Americas. The multidimensional transfer of capital, goods and ideas produced new cultural forms, economic opportunities and political ideologies. These various interactions and exchanges closely connected the Caribbean islands with the eastern shores of the US and Central America and led to the formation of a highly interconnected space, the 'West Atlantic Regional Cosmos'.[41] In her great study on cultural exchange flows between the British Caribbean islands and the circum-Caribbean mainland, Lara Putnam distinguishes two main migratory circles within this migratory sphere in the late nineteenth and early twentieth centuries; one that connects Jamaica with British Honduras, Nicaragua, Costa Rica and Panama and one that connects the islands of the eastern Caribbean with Panama, Colombia, Venezuela and the Guianas.[42] Many migrants maintained close relations to family and friends at home and maintained cultural practices that eventually blended with cultures of the locals as well as with those of other immigrants from the Caribbean and elsewhere and created new cultural forms that influenced the cultures back home. People frequently moved back and forth between their home islands and other places, utilizing the ship routes that connected the various ports in the area. On their routes, their culture, ideas and material resources also travelled and were cross-fertilized within the transnational Caribbean space that extended far beyond the Caribbean islands into the Americas. New experiences and contact with ideas and political movements abroad often challenged traditional ways of thinking and changed the way how emigrants looked at their country of origin.

For the context of the present study, the cultural and ideological cross-fertilization that took place in Harlem in the early twentieth century is of crucial importance. In order to best capture the dynamics in which the Progressive League developed, it is helpful to see the migrant circles in Harlem and local activists in Jamaica belonging to a 'transnational space',[43] which Saskia Sassen has defined as a 'system of flows between a metropolitan center and a set of politically independent satellite countries...People, wealth, ideas, and cultural patterns move in both directions, influencing both the metropolitan centre as well as the peripheral areas, although asymmetrically'.[44] Although Jamaica was not yet an independent country, it is of special significance that it was exactly the experiences within this space that inspired anti-colonial thinking and involvement in social and political activities in the host but also in the home societies.

Such insights demonstrate that nationalism is by no means diametrically opposed to transnational experiences and that processes of globalization and migration do not diminish the importance of national identities. In accordance with recent scholarship on transnationalism and nationalism, the example of the Jamaica Progressive League exemplifies that transnationalism is no challenge to the nation state. Wherever people are on the move and their ideas transcending borders, a renegotiation of the meaning of categories like race, class and national identity is taking place – but that does not diminish the importance of nationalism. As John F. Padgett has argued in his recent book, new ways of thinking and new organizations originate whenever various networks collide.[45] From such a perspective, it is not surprising that Caribbean immigrants were disproportionally represented in political movements in the US, nor that they significantly contributed to the development of political thought in their home societies.

A Note on the Sources

I first came across references to the Jamaica Progressive League while preparing for my Magister exam in history on the end of British colonialism in the Anglophone Caribbean. I was intrigued by statements that suggested that Jamaican emigrants in New York played a pioneering and influential role in the development of anti-colonial nationalism and that the Jamaica Progressive League exerted considerable influence on the positions of the PNP.[46] On further investigation, I was surprised that no major studies, no monograph, not even a journal article was available that dealt prominently with the Progressive League and its influence on Jamaica's path towards independence.

I wondered whether the scholarly neglect was due to a lack of primary sources. Maybe the organization's material had not survived? I decided to

Introduction

find out, and embarked on a research journey that would take me to various archives in New York, Washington, London and Jamaica. This research revealed a wide array of scattered primary sources from which it was possible to recollect the history of the Progressive League and to assess its influence, mainly in the personal collections of W.A. Roberts and the Jamaica Progressive League Files at the National Library of Jamaica, in the papers of the Progressive League's life-long-serving secretary Egbert Ethelred Brown at the Schomburg Center, and in the Richard Hart collection at the Institute of Commonwealth Studies in London. The Norman Manley papers at the Jamaica Archives and Government Records in Spanish Town, Jamaica, contain important correspondence with the Progressive League, which illuminate its impact on the PNP. Numerous articles published by members of the Progressive League in newspapers like the *Daily Gleaner*, *Public Opinion*, and in African American newspapers like the *New York Amsterdam News*, were of great value. Surveillance reports from British and US authorities further provided useful insights.

The fact that the available material on the Progressive League is thinly spread between libraries and archives in Jamaica, England and the US helps to explain its neglect in practical terms. Moreover, the character of the material can best be described as patchy, limited in scope, and random in content. Unfortunately, the Progressive League in New York did not preserve its papers in any systematic way. During my research in Jamaica, I was able to locate a previously unused collection of papers from the Progressive League headquarters in New York in a private archival collection, while also the collections of Brown and Roberts contain important documents and correspondence. The branch in Kingston donated a small and fragmentary collection of papers to the National Library of Jamaica, and also W.G. McFarlane's papers can be found there. Additionally, interviews with political activists like Richard Hart, Frank Gordon, Arnold Bertram, Jimmy Tucker and Herman Thompson have been helpful in answering open questions and in pointing to further resources.

Based on this patchy material, reconstructing the history of the Progressive League resembles putting together a puzzle, in which a number of pieces remain missing. A most deplorable void in the available material is the absence of W.A. Domingo's personal papers. Although he is said to have left a collection, efforts to inquire whether family members still own material have been futile. Domingo's numerous letters to the press in Jamaica as well as personal letters that have survived in the collections of W.A. Roberts, Norman Manley and Richard Hart are only a small compensation.

Nevertheless, a thorough exegesis of the available material allows one to reconstruct the history of the Progressive League and to evaluate its influence on the fledgling political landscape and the course of decolonization in Jamaica.

However, the general scarcity of available archival material on the political history of Jamaica in the twentieth century poses a fundamental challenge to historians. Richard Hart, who collected a great amount of the material accessible today, complained that '…few contemporaries shared my enthusiasm for preserving written records of events'.[47] As an example, Hart mentions an occasion on which he 'rescued a minute book of one of the trade unions…placed in the toilet… where it was being used, page by page, for an uninspiring purpose'.[48] In addition, due to tropical climate and infestation with insects, much of the available material is already seriously damaged and in danger of decay, despite keen efforts of preservation by Jamaican libraries and archives. Limited financial resources for preserving and digitizing material seriously endanger the conservation and accessibility of archival material in the Caribbean.

The two main political parties, the PNP and the JLP have not yet made their minutes, pamphlets or manuscripts accessible to the public; it is only thanks to Hart's private donation that a substantial number of PNP pamphlets are available today. Upon researching the history of the labour movement in Jamaica, trade union specialist Jeffrey Harrods realized the scarcity of available sources and points out that 'the dangers of acquiring a mono-interpretation of events from such sources are obvious'.[49] The limited availability of original material that reflects the formation of the political parties and the development of nationalist thought makes political instrumentalization and one-dimensional interpretations more feasible.

Literature Review

In the vast literature on the decolonization of the British Empire, the possessions in the Caribbean only play a minor role. As one of the cold spots in the Cold War, the Caribbean has received less attention than other areas that transitioned from colonies into independent nation states in the second half of the twentieth century. In his reflections on the end of the British Empire in the Caribbean, Wm. Roger Louis deplores the lack of attention regarding the influence of the 'Anglo-American coalition' on decolonization and the post-war societies in the region in many historical accounts.[50] Jason Parker's studies on the US influence on decolonization in the Anglophone Caribbean not only contributed to filling this void, but also emphasized the influence of transnational actors from the Caribbean who were based in the United States. As part of a larger network of African American activists, they were able to influence the political landscape back home, but also the decision-making process in Anglo-American negotiations about the future of the region. The present study on the Progressive League testifies to Parker's claim that neglecting this transnational dimension leads to major blind spots in our understanding and knowledge of both the Cold War and the decolonization of the so-called third world.⁵¹

The British Caribbean, sandwiched between the British Empire and the United States, is an ideal case to study the dynamics of the shifting power relations between the two superpowers in light of the triangle of British officials, US diplomats and Caribbean activists in the islands and abroad.⁵² It is no coincidence that especially authors who study the process of decolonization of the British Caribbean from a transnational perspective that incorporates the United States emphasize the role of transnational activists. Examining the encounter between Caribbean immigrants and African Americans, Parker emphasizes the particular impact of this nexus on policymakers in the US, who were cognizant of the explosive mixture of African American-Caribbean radicalism in Harlem in the early twentieth century.⁵³ Parker is amongst the few scholars who acknowledge the importance of the Jamaica Progressive League, which he describes as the first group of Jamaicans 'to fuse nascent nationalism and anti-colonialism'.⁵⁴ Gerald Horne's in-depth study on the influence of US diplomacy on the labour and independence movements in the British Caribbean also emphasizes the significance of the Progressive League.⁵⁵

While many studies on decolonization focused on the Cold War era, some of the more recent studies on anti-colonialism explicitly highlight the roots of anti-colonial thought in the first third of the twentieth century. For instance, Erez Manela showed to what extent the influence of anti-colonial implications in the statements of Woodrow Wilson had radicalized anti-colonial movements worldwide when actions did not meet the hopes of many colonized peoples.⁵⁶ As in the case of some members of the Progressive League, such disappointment often motivated activists from the Caribbean to embrace Socialist ideas, encouraged by Lenin's anti-colonial positions. Others turned to increasingly popular concepts of Black Nationalism as expressed by Marcus Garvey, or tried to merge both concepts. Jonathan Derrick's study on anti-colonial movements during the interwar years in Africa shows similar influences and also emphasizes the important role of migrant circles in inspiring many of the radical organizations.⁵⁷

The Jamaica Progressive League plays no prominent role in the literature on the political formation of modern Jamaica and its pioneering contribution is often overlooked. While several authors mention its importance, a considerable research gap exists regarding the history of the organization and the ways in which it exerted its influence. Recently, Peter Hulme's work shed light on W. Adolphe Roberts and his important role in the struggle for Jamaican independence.⁵⁸ The few accounts that primarily focus on the Progressive League were written by members or sympathizers.⁵⁹ Due to their lack of critical distance and the absence of accurate references, they qualify as primary sources rather than secondary literature. W.G. McFarlane is right, when he points to the lack of appreciation of the role of the Progressive League:

> There has been a great deal of misrepresentation of the facts about the actual beginning and the promotion of the idea [of self-government] in Jamaica, by certain leaders who could not comprehend the importance of the idea when the movement first started, and even up to the present time. Some of the misrepresentations have been quite deliberate, while others result mainly from a genuine lack of information on the subject.[60]

Yet, McFarlane's own break with the PNP probably contributed to some bitterness in his opinions of the PNP.

The Progressive League's influence as a pioneer in demanding self-government is at least mentioned briefly by several scholars who looked at Jamaica's political history. James Carnegie's important study on the early political developments between 1918 and 1938 recognized its important role and its radicalizing effect. He emphasized the radicalism of the migrants in New York, especially when compared to the more moderate local scene.[61] In an article published in 1952, Alex Zeidenfelt mentions that the Progressive League was 'the first movement for universal suffrage and self-government'.[62] Zeidenfelt's study heavily relies on primary sources, and is one of the early accounts that emphasize its importance on the formation of the local political landscape: 'This propaganda efforts, introduced from the outside and nurtured largely on funds supplied by Jamaicans living in the United States, crystallized into a political party with the formation of the People's National Party in September, 1938.'[63]

The most detailed account of the Progressive League's influence is provided by Ken Post, whose important contributions to Jamaican historiography contain numerous references to the Progressive League.[64] He concludes:

> The JPL leaders in New York were thus putting forward a much more concrete and radical class programme than that of the National Reform Association in Kingston, and moreover were achieving the all-important fusion of this with a national demand for self-government, thus extending potential support for the latter far beyond a few middle class intellectuals.[65]

Gordon K. Lewis also emphasizes the importance of the Progressive League in Jamaica and its local impact, especially on the political direction of the PNP, and highlights the '...inspiration of the Harlem group of ultra-nationalistic Jamaican exiles'.[66] He further recognizes the importance of Domingo and Roberts' early and vigorous campaign against the West Indies Federation in the 1950s and early 1960s. Denis M. Benn mentions the importance of the Progressive League in the nationalist movement. Without providing many details, Benn nevertheless sees its relevance and especially its influence on the PNP, even claiming that the PNP

Introduction

'gave institutional expression to theoretical principles outlined by the Jamaica Progressive League'.[67]

Also in migration studies, scholars like Philip Kasinitz and Mary Waters clearly see the impact of the nationalist group that developed in the milieu of Caribbean and African American radicalism in Harlem. Joyce Moore Turner and W. Burghardt Turner emphasize the influence of the Progressive League in their collected edition of Richard B. Moore's work.[68] In *Caribbean Crusaders*, Moore Turner presents a detailed and rich study of a close group of Caribbean radicals in Harlem, in which not only Moore but also the future vice-president of the Progressive League, Wilfred A. Domingo, played an important role.[69] Louis J. Parascandola features Domingo in his edition of writings of immigrants from the Anglophone Caribbean who participated in what became known as the Harlem Renaissance. He points to the pioneering role of the Progressive League and highlights Domingo's influence on the PNP.[70]

Alex Zeidenfelt, who acknowledges the Progressive League as the first group demanding universal suffrage and self-government, comments that it 'originated, oddly enough, not on the island but in New York in 1935–36'.[71] Yet, given the important role of expatriates in other anti-colonial movements, the role of the Progressive League does not seem odd at all. Therefore, the Jamaica Progressive League is part of a larger phenomenon of anti-colonial pressure groups originating in exile in the early decades of the twentieth century, who often provided ideas, international channels of political influence and resources to fund the struggle in the colony. More broadly, the history of the Progressive League, with a strong focus on its main protagonists and its experience allows us to see the reciprocal effect of the migration experience that led not only to the disproportional involvement of Caribbean migrants in political activism in Harlem, but also provided fertile ground for the origins of anti-colonial nationalism and concrete political demands for the creation of a Jamaican nation state.

Chapter Outline

The book is organized in two main sections: Part I explores the origins of the Jamaica Progressive League in New York and in Jamaica. Part II examines the history of the Progressive League from the founding in 1936 to the fulfilment of its main goal, Jamaican independence in 1962. Based on a wide range of archival material, the study serves to close the existing research gap regarding the transnational roots of anti-colonial nationalism in Jamaica.

Chapter 1 sketches the historical background on society formation in colonial Jamaica with focus on early nationalist thought. After defining the use of the term self-government, a survey of nationalist organizations predating the founding of the Jamaica Progressive League in 1936 serves to legitimize one of the main theses of this book, the originality of the Progressive League's demand for self-government. By following W. Adolphe Roberts, Wilfred A. Domingo and Ethelred Brown on their journeys of political activism in Jamaica and abroad, Chapter 2 introduces three main protagonists and founding members of the Progressive League and their network of radical activists in Harlem. It accounts for the various ideological influences that shaped their political thinking and explains why and how the most outspoken and concrete political demands for self-government developed among Jamaican migrants in the US.

Chapter 3 focuses on the formation of the Progressive League in New York. Tracing the flow of ideas between New York and Kingston at this early stage, it explores how the Progressive League's nationalist push from abroad was perceived in Jamaica.

Chapter 4 analyses the obstacles that accompanied the founding of a local Progressive League branch in Kingston. It looks at the difficulties W.G. McFarlane encountered in this effort that was only met with success when founder Roberts visited the island at the end of 1937. It puts a spotlight on how the Progressive League's early call for a nationalist party in Jamaica prepared the ground for the founding of the PNP in the aftermath of the labour uprisings in May and June 1938 and portrays the League's important role in the defence of the striking workers.

Chapter 5 explores the important role that Progressive League members played in the formative stage of the PNP and outlines the close collaboration between the League and the PNP while Roberts and Domingo were in Jamaica for extended periods. By highlighting the difficulties the Progressive League encountered trying to convince the party to include radical anti-colonial demands in its platform, it acknowledges the influence of Roberts and Domingo, in particular, on the party's attitude toward self-government. A comparison of local and overseas representations in front of the Royal Commission in 1938 testifies to the more radical anti-colonial demands of the emigrants.

This difference between the migrants' views and local thought is further elucidated in Chapter 6, which analyses the different reactions of the Progressive League and the PNP to the outbreak of the Second World War and the significant macro-political changes that resulted in a fundamental shift of Great Britain's colonial policy toward the region. While the PNP immediately dropped its political agitation upon the outbreak of the war, Domingo and Roberts increased the pressure, using the changing international power relations to Jamaica's benefit. In the wake of a possible British defeat in the early 1940s, Domingo and other radical Caribbean migrants founded the West Indies National Emergency Council through which Domingo and Roberts attempted to internationalize the demands for self-government. These efforts were instrumental in altering

Introduction

the PNP's course in 1941 and laid the foundation for a continued collaboration between the party and the Progressive League.

Chapter 7 shifts the focus back to Jamaica during the 1940s and 1950s. After the PNP had changed its course, Roberts and Domingo reassumed the collaboration and intensified the campaign for self-government. In 1941, Domingo followed Manley's call for a return to Jamaica to support the PNP, but was immediately arrested and detained upon his arrival. It shows how Domingo's imprisonment, along with other pre-emptive detentions, further radicalized the local scene. It explores Domingo's nationalist propaganda activities during his involuntary sojourn in Jamaica while US authorities thwarted his wish to return to the US. Two years after Domingo was finally permitted re-entry to the US in 1947, Roberts permanently returned to Jamaica. Parallel to the examination of Domingo's nationalism, the chapter explores Roberts' activities in Jamaica and analyses his nationalist agitation.

The last chapter examines the vigorous nationalist campaign Roberts and Domingo waged against the plans for a West Indies Federation, a political entity consisting of all British possessions in the Caribbean envisioned by the Colonial Office as a means to decolonize the region. While the PNP endorsed the idea, Roberts and Domingo strengthened their critique, accepting that their agitation would play into the hands of the PNP's political opponents, Bustamante's JLP. For their uncompromising stand on nationalist principles, both men paid the high price of cutting ties with many close friends and co-workers. When the Jamaican population decided against the Federation in 1961 in a referendum, they found themselves on the winning side. With the decision of the population to leave the Federation, Jamaica abandoned the course of gradual and planned decolonization designed in the Colonial Office and achieved its independence just one year later in 1962. The primary goal of the Jamaica Progressive League was fulfilled. Starting out with a review of the reception of the Progressive League, the conclusion reveals the Progressive League's declining recognition in post-independence Jamaica. The final part offers reasons for the neglect and summarizes the main arguments of this study to demonstrate why the contributions of the Progressive League are worth remembering.

Notes

1. Portia Simpson Miller, Independence Message 2012; http://www.jis.gov.jm/news/list/31490. Last viewed, August 24, 2013.
2. Winston Maragh, letter to the editor, *Jamaica Observer*, August 30, 2012.
3. Andrew Holness (JLP), Plenary Speech at the Conference 'Fifty-Fifty: Critical Reflections in a Time of Uncertainty,' Sir Arthur Lewis Institute for Social and Economic Studies (SALISES), Jamaica Pegasus Hotel in Kingston, August 20–24, 2012.
4. Obika Grey, *Radicalism and Social Change in Jamaica, 1960–1972* (Knoxville: University Tennessee Press, 1971); Rupert Lewis, *Walter Rodney's Intellectual and Political Thought* (Kingston: The University of the West Indies Press, 1998); and Louis Lindsay, *The Myth of Independence: Middle Class Politics and Non-Mobilization in Jamaica* (Mona: Institute of Social and Economic Research, University of the West Indies, 1981).
5. The best overview is still by James Carnegie, *Some Aspects of Jamaica's Politics 1918–1938* (Kingston: Institute of Jamaica, 1973).
6. Louis Moyston, 'Walter Adolphe Roberts is True Pioneer of Jamaica's Independence Movement', *Jamaica Observer*, August 31, 2012.
7. *Daily Gleaner*, July 31, 2011; August 21, 2011; September 4, 2011.
8. Ibid., July 31, 2011.
9. Carnegie, *Some Aspects of Jamaica's Politics*, 131.
10. Gordon K. Lewis, *Growth of the Modern West Indies* (Kingston: Ian Randle Publishers, 2004), 171; see also Philip Kasinitz, *Caribbean New York: Black Immigrants and the Politics of Race* (Ithaca: Cornell University Press, 1992). Kasinitz emphasizes that this mentality was still common among many immigrants the US in recent times.
11. Lewis, *Growth of the West Indies*, 24.
12. For a contemporary description of Jamaica's 'two worlds' in 1962, the country's black majority and the middle and upper classes with their strong pro-British attitude, see Katrin Norris, *Jamaica: The Search for an Identity* (Oxford: Oxford University Press, 1962), 9ff, 93ff.
13. Anne Spry Rush, *Bonds of Empire: West Indians and Britishness from Victoria to Decolonization* (Oxford: Oxford University Press, 2011), 2.
14. Brian L. Moore and Michele A. Johnson, *Neither Led Nor Driven* (Kingston: University of the West Indies Press, 2004), 271ff.
15. Patrick Bryan, *The Jamaican People, 1880–1902* (Kingston: Stephensons Litho Press, 1991, 2000), 18.
16. Moore and Johnson, *Neither Led Nor Driven*, 271ff.
17. Richard Smith, *Jamaican Volunteers in the First World War. Race, Masculinity and the Development of National Consciousness* (Manchester: Manchester University Press, 2004).
18. The usage of the concept of Diaspora is often criticized for its unspecified meaning. While it is beyond the scope of this study to enter into a theoretical discussion, the terms Jamaican Diaspora or Caribbean Diaspora will be used to describe locations to which emigrants from the Caribbean had moved, indicating that they still engaged in the affairs of their country. For a discussion of the term black Diaspora, see Christine Chivallon, *The Black Diaspora of the Americas* (Kingston: Ian Randle Publishers, 2011).

Introduction

19. Benedict Anderson, *Imagined Communities*. 2nd ed. (London: Verso, 2006); see also Eric J. Hobsbawm, *Nations and Nationalism Since 1780: Programme, Myth, Reality*. 2nd ed. (Cambridge, New York: Cambridge University Press); see also Ernest Gellner, *Nations and Nationalism*. 2nd ed. (Oxford: Blackwell Publishing, 2006).
20. Anthony D. Smith, *Nationalism, Theory, Ideology, History*. 2nd ed. (Cambridge, Malden: Polity Press, 2001); Athena S. Leoussi and Steven Grosby, eds., *Nationalism and Ethnosymbolism: History, Culture and Ethnicity in the Formation of Nations* (Edinburgh: Edinburgh University Press, 2006).
21. Anderson, *Imagined Communities*, 6ff.
22. Eric J. Hobsbawm and Terence Ranger, eds., *The Invention of Tradition* (Canto edition, Cambridge: Cambridge University Press, 1992).
23. For a discussion of various concepts of race and class in Caribbean society see Charles W. Mills, *Radical Theory, Caribbean Reality: Race, Class and Social Domination* (Kingston: University of the West Indies Press, 2010), see especially the chapter 'Race and Class: Conflicting or Reconcilable Paradigms,' 72–99; see also Smith, Michael Garfield, *Culture, Race, and Class in the Commonwealth Caribbean* (Mona: Dept of Extra-Mural Studies, University of West Indies, 1984).
24. Violet Showers Johnson, 'Racial Frontiers in Jamaica's Nonracial Nationhood,' in *Race and Nation, Ethnic Systems in the Modern World*, ed. Paul Spickard (New York, Oxon: Routledge, 2005), 157.
25. Dominic Boyer, Claudio Lomnitz, 'Intellectuals and Nationalism: Anthropological Engagements,' *Annual Review of Anthropology* 34 (2005): 105–120.
26. Partha Chatterjee, 'Whose Imagined Community,' *Millennium. Journal of International Studies* 20 (1991): 521–25.
27. Ibid., 521. For a critique on Chatterjee's interpretation of Anderson see Neil Lazarus, *Nationalism and Cultural Practice in the Post-Colonial World* (Cambridge: Cambridge University Press, 1999), 130f.
28. See for example Fanon's chapter 'The Trials and Tribulations of Nationalist Consciousness', in *The Wretched of the Earth* (New York: Grove Press, 2004), 97–144; see also Bill Ashcroft, Gareth Griffiths and Helen Tiffin, eds., *The Post-Colonial Studies Reader* (London, New York: Routledge, 1995), see esp. the chapter 'Nationalism,' 151–57.
29. For instance, emigrants played prominent roles in anti-colonial movements in the Philippines, India, Cuba, Puerto Rico, Vietnam, Indonesia, Korea and in numerous African countries. See Elie Kedourie, *Nationalism in Asia and Africa* (New York: New American Library, 1970); Jonathan Derrick, *Africa's 'Agitators': Militant Anti-Colonialism in Africa and the West, 1918–1939* (New York: Columbia University Press, 2008), Arjun Appadurai, 'The Production of Locality,' in *Counterworks: Managing the Diversity of Knowledge*, ed. Richard Fardon (Oxon: Routledge, 1995) 208–29. In the context of Jewish studies, Shulamit Volkov points to a similarly complex relationship between internationalism and nationalism in the Jewish Diaspora: See Shulamit Volkov, 'Jewish History: The Nationalism of Transnationalism', in *Transnationale Geschichte: Themen, Tendenzen und Theorien*, ed. Gunilla-Friederike Budde, Sebastien Conrad and Oliver Janz (Göttingen : Vandenhoeck & Ruprecht, 2006), 190–201.
30. Nancy Foner, 'What's New about Transnationalism?: New York Immigrants Today and at the Turn of the Century.' *Diaspora: A Journal of Transnational Studies*

6.3 (Oxford: Oxford University Press, 1997): 355–75; Nina Glick Schiller, Linda Basch and Christina Szanton-Blanc, 'From Immigrant to Transmigrant: Theorizing Transnational Migration,' *Anthropological Quarterly* 68 (1995): 48–63; see also Peggy Levitt, Josh DeWind and Steven Vertovec, 'International Perspectives on Transnational Migration: An Introduction,' *International Migration Review* 37 (2003): 565–75.

31. Winston James, *Holding Aloft the Banner of Ethiopia: Caribbean Radicalism in Early Twentieth-Century America* (London, New York: Verso, 1998).
32. *Public Opinion*, May 3, 1944.
33. Smith, *Jamaican Volunteers*.
34. Benedict R. O'G. Anderson, *Long-Distance Nationalism: World-Capitalism and the Rise of Identity Politics* (Berkeley: Center for German and European Studies, University of California, 1992).
35. The different concepts of race in the Anglophone Caribbean and the United States are highlighted by numerous authors, see for instance Aggrey Brown, *Colour, Class and Politics in Jamaica* (Edison, NJ: Transaction Publishers, 1980); Stuart Hall, 'Old and New Identities, Old and New Ethnicities,' in, *Culture, Globalization and the World System: Contemporary Conditions for the Representation of Identity*, ed. Anthony D. King (University of Minnesota Press, 1991); Showers Johnson, 'Racial Frontiers in Jamaica's Nonracial Nationhood', *Race and Nation: Ethnic Systems in the Modern World* 155 (New York: Routledge, 2005).
36. See for instance Mary Waters, *Black Identities: West Indian Dreams and American Realities*; Irma Watkins-Owens, *Blood Relations: Caribbean Immigrants and the Harlem Community 1900–1930* (Bloomington: Indiana University Press, 1996), 94; James, *Holding Aloft the Banner of Ethiopia*; Perry Mars, 'Caribbean Influences in African-American Political Struggles,' *Ethnic and Racial Studies* 27 (2004): 565–83.
37. One instrumental step toward formulating a transnational approach was made at an international conference of the Organization of American Historians (OAH) at La Pietra, Italy, see Thomas Bender, 'Internationalizing the Study of American History: A Joint Project of the Organization of American Historians and New York University: Report on Planning Conference, Villa La Pietra, New York University in Florence, Italy, July 6-9, 1997', http://www.oah.org/activities/lapietra/report1.html (last viewed 15.10.11). See further Shelly Fisher Fishkin, 'Crossroads of Cultures: The Transnational Turn in American Studies: Presidential Address to the American Studies Association November 12, 2004', *American Quarterly* 57 (2005): 17–57.
38. Nina Glick Schiller, 'Transmigrants and Nation-States: Something Old and Something New in U.S. Immigrant Experience', *Handbook of International Migration: The American Experience*, ed. C. Hirschman, Josh DeWind, and P. Kasinitz (New York: Russell Sage, 1999), 96.
39. For a good overview see Peggy Levitt and Jaworsky, B. Nadya, 'Transnational Migration Studies: Past Developments and Future Trends', *Annual Review of Sociology* 33, no. 1 (2007): 129.
40. Paul Gilroy, *The Black Atlantic: Modernity and Double Consciousness*. Reprint ed. (London: Verso, 2002), 16.
41. Orlando Patterson, 'Ecumenical America: Global Culture and the American Cosmos', *World Policy Journal* 11, no. 2 (1994): 103–117; Orlando Patterson, 'The

Emerging West Atlantic System: Migration, Culture and Underdevelopment in the U.S. and Caribbean,' in *Population in an Interacting World*, ed. William Alonso (Cambridge: Harvard University Press, 1987), 227–60.
42. Lara Putnam, *Radical Moves: Caribbean Migrants and the Politics of Race in the Jazz Age* (Chapel Hill: UNC Press, 2013), 23.
43. Saskia Sassen, *The Mobility of Labour and Capital* (Cambridge: Cambridge University Press, 1988).
44. Orlando Patterson, 'Ecumenical America, 108.
45. John F. Padgett, *The Emergence of Organizations and Markets* (Princeton: Princeton University Press, 2012).
46. Ken Post, *Arise Ye Starvelings: The Jamaican Labour Rebellion of 1938 and Its Aftermath* (The Hague: Martinus Nijhoff Publishers, 1978); Zeidenfelt, Alex, 'Political and Constitutional Developments in Jamaica,' *Journal of Politics* 14 (New York: New York University, 1952): 513.
47. Richard Hart, *Towards Decolonisation: Political, Labour and Economic Developments in Jamaica 1938-1945*. Vol. 3. (Kingston: Canoe Preess, 1999), xvi.
48. Hart, *Towards Decolonisation*, xvi.
49. Ibid.
50. Wm. Roger Louis, *Ends of British Imperialism: The Scrumble for Empire, Suez and Decolonization* (London: I.B. Tauris, 2006).
51. Jason C. Parker, *Brother's Keeper: The United States, Race, and Empire in the BritishCaribbean, 1937-1962* (Oxford: Oxford University Press, 2008); see also Jason C. Parker, 'Remapping the Cold War in the Tropics: Race, Communism, and National Security in the West Indies,' *The International History Review* 24 (2002): 318–47.
52. Parker, *Brother's Keeper*; see also Parker, 'Remapping the Cold War in the Tropics: Race, Communism, and National Security in the West Indies,' 318–47.
53. Parker, 'Capital of the Caribbean': The African American-West Indian 'Harlem Nexus' and the Transnational Drive for Black Freedom, 1940–1948', *The Journal of African American History* 89 (2004): 98–117.
54. Parker, 'Remapping the Cold War,' 323.
55. Gerald Horne, *Cold War in a Hot Zone: The United States Confronts Labor and Independence Struggles in the British West Indies* (Philadelphia: Temple University Press, 2007).
56. Erez Manela, *The Wilsonian Moment* (New York, Oxford: Oxford University Press, 2007).
57. Derrick, *Africa's 'Agitators.'*
58. Peter Hulme, 'W. Adolphe Roberts and Jamaica', *Jamaica Journal* 34, no. 3 (2013): 14–23. See also the recently published autobiography *W. Adolphe Roberts – These Many Years: An Autobiography* (Kingston: University of the West Indies Press, 2016). The page numbers in this book refer to the original manuscript in the National Library of Jamaica.
59. Walter G. McFarlane, *The Birth of Self-Government for Jamaica and the Jamaica Progressive League 1937-1944* (Kingston: W.G. McFarlane, 1957); John S. Young, *Lest We Forget* (New York, 1981). Young joined the Progressive League in New York in the 1960s. To preserve the history of the organization, Young collected material and conducted interviews with its members. While his study provides some valuable insights, it suffers from a lack of scholarly accuracy and a reference system that would allow tracing the sources of his information.

60. McFarlane, *Birth of Self-Government*, 4.
61. Carnegie, *Some Aspects*.
62. Zeidenfelt, 'Political and Constitutional Developments,' 512–40.
63. Ibid.,' 513.
64. Post, *Arise Ye Starvelings*; Post, *Strike the Iron: A Colony at War, Jamaica 1939*–1945. 2 Vols. (London: Humanities Press, 1981).
65. Post, *Arise*, 222.
66. Lewis, *Growth of the Modern West Indies*, 184.
67. Denis M. Benn, *The Caribbean: An Intellectual History, 1774–2003* (Kingston: Ian Randle Publishers, 2004), 75.
68. Joyce Moore Turner and W. Burghardt Turner, eds., *Richard B. Moore, Caribbean Militant in Harlem: Collected Writings 1920–1972* (Bloomington: Indiana University Press, 1988).
69. Joyce Moore Turner, *Caribbean Crusaders and the Harlem Renaissance* (Chicago: University of Illinois Press, 2005).
70. Parascandola, Louis J., ed., *Look for Me All Around You: Anglophone Caribbeans in the Harlem Renaissance* (Detroit: Wayne State University Press, 2005).
71. Alex Zeidenfelt, 'Political and Constitutional Developments in Jamaica,' 512–40.

PART ONE

ORIGINS OF THE MOVEMENT FOR SELF-GOVERNMENT

CHAPTER 1: NATIONALISM IN JAMAICA BEFORE 1936

One of the main theses established in this book on the Jamaica Progressive League is the claim that the New York-based organization played a pioneering role in demanding self-government for Jamaica. In order to prove such claim legitimate, a survey of the political groups in Jamaica and their demands and positions regarding self-government in early twentieth-century Jamaica is pertinent. Hence, before we turn to the founding of the Jamaica Progressive League and the experiences that inspired the protagonists to launch an organization with concrete political demands for self-government for Jamaica, this interlude offers a historical overview of the social and political configurations of Jamaican society and the political groups and their positions.

The following survey does not offer a general examination of anti-colonial thought in Jamaica predating 1936. It is limited to nationalist political groups and serves to substantiate the pioneering role of the Progressive League. It excludes religion, for instance Myalism, Revivalism, Bedwardism and or Rastafarianism, although these religious movements often channelled protest against colonial domination and played an important role in the quest for racial equality, self-determination and autonomy in colonial Jamaica. During the Great Depression in the late 1920s and 1930s, political agitation was mainly concerned with important economic questions like land reform, skyrocketing unemployment and the horrible living conditions of the poor majority. The focus on political demands for Jamaica's autonomy as a nation state does not intend to privilege this political idea over agitation for better living conditions or other forms of anti-colonialism, for instance Pan-Africanism or ideas for a federated Anglophone Caribbean. Nevertheless, the innovative quality of the programme of the Jamaica Progressive League with its focus on self-government for Jamaican deserves to be acknowledged in the history of political development in Jamaica.

One major challenge in analysing the different political groups and actors is their often inconsistent use of the terms *self-government, responsible government* or *representative government.* Therefore, we first need to develop definitions for these terms, before we carefully analyse the ideas of the political organizations. The term self-government, as used by the Jamaica Progressive League and throughout this study, is a synonym for a nation state with full control over legislative and administrative powers, as well as over internal and external affairs. A self-governed nation-state can decide to become part of the Commonwealth of Nations, like the former British colonies Canada, Australia or New Zealand, and thus voluntarily surrender some degree of autonomy in affairs that are regulated by the laws of that umbrella body. In the context of the Commonwealth, a former colony that was granted independence and voluntarily associated with the British Commonwealth, and accepting the Queen or King as the representative head of government, is usually called a Dominion.[1]

In contrast, the term representative government refers to a colony in which the legislature consists of a majority of elected representatives, subject to the administrative powers of the Crown's representative, the Governor General. In a representative form of government, varying degrees of self-determination are possible. In Jamaica in 1959, for instance, Jamaica had internal self-government and was entitled to make decisions regarding its internal affairs, although it was still a colony.[2]

In 1655, Great Britain invaded the Spanish colony Santiago, renamed it Jamaica and turned it into a highly profitable plantation.[3] The intensified cultivation of sugar cane and other crops grown in monocultures was grounded in the expansion of the plantation system based on the brutal exploitation of enslaved Africans by a tiny white ruling class and resulted in a particular dynamic of overlapping race-class relations.[4]

Great Britain and British settlers benefited from raw materials and largely unprocessed tropical goods from the colonies in the Caribbean.[5] English settlers, mainly planters and merchants, enjoyed not only economic wealth but a great degree of political freedom in the colony. After conquering the island, the British aimed to establish a settler colony, with a political system modelled after the British parliament. For over 200 years, Jamaica had a bi-cameral Assembly with an appointed upper house and an elected lower house. Although Jamaica was ruled by a Governor, the Assembly had a great degree of autonomy over the legislature, including the right over money bills. However, the country's Afro-Jamaican majority was completely excluded from the political decision making process in the plantation society by high property qualifications.[6]

The highly intertwined categories of race and class shaped the history of Jamaica and left a strong imprint on the construction of identity. Centuries after the formal abolition of slavery in the Americas, race continues to function as a normative component of society.[7] Racism provided rationalization for the inhumane practices of colonialism and slavery and shaped the social structure of the colonial society. Racist thinking impeded granting self-government to colonies with a black majority, while many predominantly white colonies like

Australia, Canada or New Zealand were granted the status of independent nation-states within the Commonwealth of Nations from the eighteenth and nineteenth century. The belief in the inferiority of Africans, and the disregard for their traditional forms of socialization, was inextricably intertwined with a paternalistic civilizing mission based on Christianity.[8] Mental domination in the form of an internalized racial inferiority complex and indoctrination with the demand for identification with, and unconditional loyalty to, the Empire were tactics that belonged to colonial rule. The power structure in the colony, reflected in the political and economic status quo, openly displayed the prevailing racial prejudices. Even after the formal abolition of slavery in all British colonies, the majority of the population was captured in a vicious circle: excluded from the political decisions by property requirements, they remained voiceless.

During slavery, a differentiated system of racial oppression resulted in the development of a privileged middle class. This intermediate group functioned as a buffer between the wealthy white minority and the largely impoverished black majority, and played an integral role in maintaining the social order and economic status quo. This group developed and maintained a distinct social identity.[9] In contrast to the American practice of racial discrimination, which subsumes all people of African ancestry under the 'one-drop rule,' the concepts of race that developed in many colonial societies in the Americas follows a different logic and distinguishes between different shades of complexion.

In Jamaica, the population is divided into three major racial groups that are usually called whites, browns and blacks.[10] Jamaican-born Stuart Hall points to the fact that this categorization is a very generalizing approach to what is in fact a more complicated system of racialization and discrimination in Jamaica, in which social status is linked not only with the colour of one's skin, but also with other features of physiognomy like hair texture and nose shape, and is further influenced by the social background of the family.[11] Although a relic of colonial rule, this racial stratification of the society still contributes to the perpetuation of inequalities and injustices in modern Jamaica and stands in stark contrast to the widespread myth of racial harmony and equality.[12]

Since the first enslaved Africans arrived in Jamaica, acts of resistance and rebellion against the working and living conditions were part of daily life in the colony. The most prominent uprising became known as the Morant Bay Rebellion, led by Paul Bogle and George William Gordon in 1865.[13] It provoked fears among the elites that the masses could overthrow the colony and create a 'second Haiti,' a republic ruled by the black majority. The brutal and harsh reaction to the uprising is of paramount importance for the history of constitutional development.[14] Glen Richards underscores the ferocity of the British military response and concludes that together with the political, economic and social consequences of the events, the rebellion was perhaps the greatest hindrance to the development of a political movement combining race and class militancy.[15] Judging the events to be a serious threat to the stability of colonial rule, the colonial government not only reacted with a massive retaliation, resulting in the killing and imprisonment of hundreds of demonstrators, it also surrendered its far-reaching autonomy in favour of Crown Colony status.[16] As of 1866, the Crown-appointed Governor nominated all legislators, who were *de facto* prohibited from supporting any opinion opposed to the government, and had such limited influence that James Carnegie called them 'the virtual puppets of Government.'[17]

In 1884, the constitution was amended by the reintroduction of an elected element in the legislature. This, however, had little effect on the power balance in the colony. The franchise as well as the qualification to run for public office was still very restricted by high tax and property requirements; women only received the right to vote in 1919. The majority remained excluded from the political process, and less than 10 per cent of the population was able to participate in political decisions. The low voter turnout, usually between 50 and 60 per cent, was indicative of the low level of political mobilization. Grinding poverty demanded full focus on the basic means of survival; also, a high rate of illiteracy and very limited access to education were grave obstacles to political mobilization efforts. In his analysis of the plantation society and its continued influence on social and political conditions in the post-colonial states of the British Caribbean, George Beckford emphasizes that only little communication existed between the dispersed small farmers or plantation workers, whose lives were centred on the micro-cosmoses of the plantations, which impeded solidarity and political organization.[18]

At first, the political regression after 1865 was widely accepted with very little protest. But soon, some members of the Legislative Council demanded constitutional changes that would increase the powers of the elected members, while some of them demanded a return to the old constitution that would restore the great amount of freedom the Jamaican legislative had enjoyed before. However, even the most progressive members of the Legislative Council never called for an end to colonial rule.

Besides these factors, another aspect is of utmost importance in understanding the slow development of anti-colonial activism in Jamaica. The development of nationalist thought was hampered by a strong and widespread positive identification with the British Empire, deriving from indoctrination through centuries of colonial rule. Members of the Progressive League used the term *colonial mentality* to describe the difficulties they faced in arousing anti-colonial nationalism in the colony. Numerous scholars have diagnosed this mindset in

Jamaican colonial society and termed it *colonial mentality or imperial identity*.[19] Also in other colonial contexts, scholars have observed internalized feelings of inferiority of colonized peoples, widespread admiration of the society of the colonizer and deep loyalty to the colonial power.[20] Gordon K. Lewis explicitly uses the term to describe the widespread inferiority complex of Jamaicans: 'colonial ennui, colonial self-contempt, and colonial feelings of dependency – the well-known colonial mentality in West Indians themselves.'[21] Not only did the colonizers believe that Jamaicans were unable to rule themselves, many Jamaicans of all classes, but especially in the middle class, had internalized these degrading assumptions, which were intrinsically linked to racial prejudices. In 1962, on the eve of independence, Katrin Norris attests a widespread 'colonial white-bias mentality', the continued appeal of European culture and values, that complicated Jamaica's search for a national identity.[22]

In his reflections on nationalism in Jamaica, Anthony Bogues differentiates between 'brown creole nationalism' and 'black nationalism'. In explaining why creole nationalism had become hegemonic in a country with a black majority, he argues that for many black Jamaicans, social upward mobility was intrinsically connected to the acceptance of Europeanized cultural norms imposed by the colonial indoctrination.[23] He points out:

> Since consciousness is neither homogenous nor monolithic, there exists a duality in the dominated subject which sometimes allows the ideas of the dominator to find niches and resting places. This duality has enormous political consequences, particularly when the society is ideologically constructed against the majority in racial terms.[24]

In their detailed study on the reactions of Jamaicans to British cultural imperialism, Brian L. Moore and Michele Johnson also attest to such a duality. They emphasize that although African cultural elements, religious practices and moral values survived and marked important areas of resistance to mental techniques of control, the masses were largely penetrated by a strong identification with the British monarchy. The authors describe a widely shared and deeply rooted loyalty to Queen Victoria and her descendants because many Jamaicans attributed their freedom to the crown.[25] This loyalty to and admiration of the crown was by no means exclusive to the ruling elite, who objectively benefited from the colonial system. Many peasants regarded the monarchy as a benevolent protector of the people and shared pride in being part of a 'glorious Empire.' Johnson and Moore illustrate how expressions of loyalty and identification with the empire were shared by the masses. Powerful symbols of the grandness of the empire, impressive festivities in honour of the royal family, huge parades with pomp and glamour were an integral part of colonial reality. Through the involvement of children in the festivities, parades and marches, many developed a strong identification with the Empire from early on. Bryan also points to the success of such festivities, public holidays, and jubilee demonstrations in honour of Queen Victoria and the Empire that were 'aimed to produce, in Jamaicans, an unshakable loyalty to empire, and an appreciation of imperial benevolence.'[26]

From the early days of colonization, the colonizers propagandized the greatness and benevolence of the British Empire. Such indoctrination was one of the most powerful means of perpetuating colonial rule. It was actively promoted not only by the administration of the colonial state but also by churches, newspapers and schools and was partly responsible for the resistance to anti-colonial demands.[27] The channels through which the Empire disseminated its message of patriotism and its demands for undivided loyalty are similar to those through which nationalists attempted to stimulate national feelings. Bryan writes: 'The concept of nation was yet young, or at least retarded by the racially based class structure. The concept of empire was far stronger than nation. It was the concept of empire which bridged the gap between the races and classes in Jamaica.'[28] In large parts of the society, colonialism was still regarded as 'benevolent paternalism.'[29] Nationalism therefore only developed slowly. Despite an increasing critique of the Crown Colony system and demands for a return to the old constitution, many of the early nationalists remained loyal to Great Britain.[30] Carl Stone points out that this attitude existed even after the formation of the first mass-based parties in Jamaica.[31] What then were the demands of the nationalist groups in pre-1936 Jamaica? Is the claim that the Progressive League was the first group expressing the demand for Jamaica to become a nation state justified?

One example of Legislative Council members known to have radical views and advocating for the rights of the black people was Robert Love.[32] He called for adequate representation of the country's black majority. Love was born in the Bahamas in the 1830s. He had travelled extensively, and lived in the United States, Haiti and Panama, before he took up residence in Jamaica in 1890. In 1894, he launched his own newspaper *The Advocate*, after the *Daily Gleaner* refused to publish his radical letters in which he referred to the Haitian Revolution as a successful example of black liberation.[33] Yet, in the positions Love expressed as an elected member, he made no claims for expanding the electorate, much less for Jamaica to achieve independence. Instead, he demanded that those black people who were wealthy enough to meet the property qualifications should run for office; otherwise they would be guilty 'of treason to the best interests of their race.'[34] Love's emphasis was clearly on race as an organizing principle, not on nationalism.

In 1898, Robert Love and Alexander Dixon founded the People's Convention, which organized yearly anniversary celebrations in remembrance of Emancipation Day, the day when slavery was officially abolished in the British Caribbean in 1838.[35] Anthony Bogues characterizes the organization as an 'important forum for anti-colonial and antiracist views.'[36] In his speech, Love strongly condemned colonialism, slavery and the transatlantic slave trade. He claimed that Jamaica should be a full-fledged member of the British Empire and have her own government. Love insisted that only as free British citizens should Jamaicans owe loyalty to the Queen:

> In maintaining the power of the Queen, they maintained the power of the great English people. Instead of taking power from her by disorder, it was their duty to maintain that power, as it was their own power. If they owed a debt to the Queen, it was for anything she had done for them by making them free, but it was the duty that every free British subject owed to a free sovereign, and which the negro would not allow any white man to beat him at.

Statements like this prove the strong loyalty with Great Britain and the pivotal role of British citizenship that permeates Love's agitation for equal rights of black people and his demands for self-government within the Empire.

Love supported the Pan-African Association, of which the Trinidadian Henry Sylvester Williams founded a branch in Jamaica in 1901.[37] Bogues characterizes it as 'the first anti-colonial political organization of twentieth-century Jamaica.'[38] According to Rupert Lewis, it had over 500 members in Jamaica.[39] Williams's organization claimed that its mission was to communicate the problems and demands of the disenfranchised black population of the Empire to the Colonial Office.[40] Still, Williams's statements showcase a strong loyalty with Great Britain and positive self-identification as a British subject. He emphasized that the association's aims 'were in no way antagonistic to the British government; for they held that if the negro was everywhere treated in a liberal, just, and enlightened manner he would become a better, more loyal, and more valuable citizen.'[41] Williams encouraged the founding of a branch in Jamaica, but his criticism of racism was explicitly limited to South and West Africa. 'The association did not say that any oppression of the black race existed in Jamaica, but they appealed to the people of African descent in Jamaica to help to reduce the wrongs of their brethren in South Africa and West Africa.'[42] With its moderate tone, the organization attracted the support of many respected personalities, like Governor Sir Sydney Olivier, Alexander Dixon and the Revd T. Gordon Somers. Williams disclosed that the association also had 'distinguished supporters and patrons, and possessed friends in parliament'[43] in England. The Pan-African Association also reflected the strong imperial traditions in the thinking of political activists in the late nineteenth and early twentieth century.

The National Club, founded in March 1909 by S.A.G. Cox, was, as Robert Hill puts it 'Jamaica's first nationalist political organization'.[44] Like many other nationalists, Cox had studied abroad, in London, to become a barrister. Back in Jamaica, he was seriously disappointed by the limited upward mobility within the civil service. Despite his relatively light complexion, he felt that he was discriminated against on the basis of race and eventually quit the service. Subsequently, Cox began to criticize the colonial government and advocated constitutional changes toward a representative form of government.[45]

The National Club found support among prominent figures of Jamaica's political scene, like Robert Love[46] and other Legislative Council members like H.A.L. Simpson and Alexander Dixon.[47] Young and upcoming political activists like Marcus Garvey and Wilfred A. Domingo, founding member and one of the most outstanding figures in the Jamaica Progressive League, learned their first lessons in political agitation in the National Club.[48] At the inaugural meeting, H.A.L. Simpson pointed to the political apathy in the country and declared that the aim of the club was to inspire national interest.[49] Cox harshly criticized the Governor, but also the form of government itself. He alleged that the present government was unable and unwilling to change the conditions in Jamaica, especially for the working class, or to improve the inadequate education system.[50]

The founding members pledged 'to secure for the inhabitants of the island self-government, whereby we may be self-governing colonies of the great British Empire.'[51] A statement in *Our Own*,[52] the organ of the club, demanded: '...we desire a greater measure of self-government within the empire.'[53] This usage of the term self-government suggests that its leaders had representative government in mind.

This interpretation is supported by Cox's complaints about the voluntarily surrender of the old constitution in 1865 and his critique of the limited power of the elected members under Crown Colony rule. Cox accused Governor Olivier of being 'the greatest autocrat that ever visited the shores of Jamaica' who would bring in 'laws to crush the people of this country'[54] and called for protest against the government, which he called 'a monument of injustice.'[55]

Despite its radical rhetoric against the Governor and its declared nationalist goals, the National Club still exhibited loyalty to the British Empire. The members at the inaugural meeting sang the hymn, 'God Save the King' and saluted 'the flag that had liberated us.'[56] Dixon did not see nationalism and loyalty to the Empire as contradictory and stated that although he was 'ready to die with the words on his lips 'Jamaica for Jamaicans',[57] he was not opposed to the monarchy. In the following years, the Club was primarily occupied with demanding the improvement of working conditions.[58] Some of its activities were directed against the immigration of Syrians and Chinese businesses to protect native labour.[59]

After Cox's death in December 1922, the *Daily Gleaner* recalled that 'Cox swayed remarkable influence over large sections of the masses of the country.'[60] While the National Club was decidedly nationalist, it was still expressing loyalty to the Crown and exemplifies the deeply rooted imperial identity that was part of the political views of even the most outspoken nationalists at the time.

Besides the National Club, there were a few other organizations and individuals who were concerned with nationalist ideas and political issues in the first decades of the twentieth century. One important organization was the Jamaica League, founded in 1913. The Jamaica League advocated unity between Jamaicans of all classes under the banner 'Jamaica's welfare first.'[61] Personalities with moderate patriotic views, like its president, Revd T. Gordon Somers and its secretary Revd E. Ethelred Brown, future secretary of the Jamaica Progressive League in New York, gave the Jamaica League respectability. While the Jamaica League was not challenging British colonial rule in principle and expressing loyalty to the monarchy,[62] Brown criticized, 'Jamaicans were intensely loyal to the flag. Some perhaps even went too far in their loyalty in that they would not even protest against what was wrong.'[63] Brown commented,

> If patriotism means loyalty to Great Britain then the League would be assuming an unnecessary task, for as a people we are loyal even to the point of unquestioning submission. If, however, the patriotism…is love of country, and that country Jamaica, then I must confess that the work assumed by the League is not only one of necessity but one of urgency. We do not love Jamaica as we ought. The fire of patriotism burns out feebly on the altars of our hearts.[64]

This statement of Brown supports the analysis that nationalism was not yet a significant force in Jamaica, while loyalty to Great Britain was deeply rooted in the society.

One of its members, Jack Palache, stood out, expressing explicit demands for self-government. The Jamaica League's 'outstanding speaker and campaigner,'[65] encouraged Jamaicans to take an interest in their own political affairs and to question the privileges of the upper classes. He criticized the argument that the people were not educated enough to be granted a wider franchise and complained that no efforts for better education were made under the current system. Palache believed in self-government and warned: '…every one of the revolutions and violent upheavals and overturn of Empires has been due to withholdings from peoples the rights of self-government and not by conceding them to the people.'[66] However, Palache views did not represent the views of the Jamaica League as a whole.

The Jamaica League supported the election campaign of H.L. Simpson, who ran as a candidate for the Kingston seat in the Legislative Council in 1919.[67]

He demanded representative government and a return to the constitution of 1865.[68] As a reaction to Simpson's campaign, a controversy started in the *Daily Gleaner* between Edward T. Dixon, Jamaica League member and member of the Legislative Council for St Andrew; H. Vincent Hopwood, a well-known planter; and Palache about the preferred form of government. Hopwood was convinced that Jamaica was not fit for self-government and pointed to the level of education and the general apathy toward politics.[69] Palache responded that the government refused to educate the people toward responsibility for self-government and reiterated his claim that Jamaicans would have a 'right of Self-Government.'[70] Yet, even the radical Palache, who demanded a widening of the franchise, recommended a gradual process toward self-government and claimed that the elected members of the Legislative Council should, 'under our present constitution obtain all the reforms we want and ultimately, by showing our fitness and capacity to govern, obtain that full measure of self-government which as an integral part of a democratic and constitutional empire we are entitled to and will receive.'[71]

Edward T. Dixon represented the moderate position of the Jamaica League. Although Palache did not advocate immediate self-government, he felt it necessary to comment that if Palache advocated 'complete self-government for this island at a single stroke, he is either hunting a chimera, or – a revolution.'[72]

The Jamaica League's moderate position was also reflected in a proposal for constitutional change that was sent to the Colonial Office in 1920. While not speaking of self-government at all, it demanded changes in taxation, increased political responsibility and the widening of the franchise.[73] The Secretary of State for the Colonies denied the request, arguing that a strong public interest in political affairs would be necessary for changes toward a representative government. He pointed to the low voter turnout in the last general elections, in which less than half of the eligible people voted.[74] Indeed, demands for constitutional change were still limited to a small number of politically active individuals, while the authoritative political system reproduced the widespread apathy and disinterest among the people. The Jamaica League can best be described as a moderate nationalist group that aimed to change this apathy.

In the 1920s, discussions about representative government flared up again among the elected members of the Legislative Council. In part, the discussion was inspired by an increased desire for representative government in the south-eastern Caribbean and ideas of forming a federation of the islands in the region.[75] Locally, strong discontent with Governor Leslie Probyn's autocratic ruling style contributed to an increased interest in demands for representative government.[76] In 1921, two members of the Legislative Council, J.A.G. Smith and H.A.L. Simpson, started two individual campaigns for more representation.[77]

Smith was one of the few black men in the Legislative Council and very popular in his constituency, which he represented from 1916 until his death in 1942.[78] Like Cox, he was a disappointed civil servant who had studied abroad, joined the civil service upon his return and finally resigned, frustrated by the limited upward mobility.[79] In August 1921, Smith founded the Jamaica Representative Government Association to bring about changes in the constitution toward representative government. His organization found only limited support among the members of the Legislative Council.[80] Shortly afterwards, Simpson formed the Jamaica Political Constitution Reform Association. It found more support among the elected members and was more respectable in the eyes of the ruling class.[81]

These developments coincided with the visit of Major Edward F.L. Wood, Under-Secretary of State for the Colonies. As a reaction to the strong demands for constitutional change in the eastern Caribbean, Wood was on a mission to observe the political and social conditions in the British West Indian colonies. Smith and Simpson's groups both used the opportunity to present him with memoranda demanding a more representative government, similar to the pre-1865 constitution.[82]

Major Wood commented in his report that 'neither Smith nor Simpson were over-concerned with democracy, since neither suggested extended franchises.'[83] While not inclined to grant more rights to the legislature, Wood suggested in his report that Jamaica's constitution should be slowly advanced so that the elected members would be in the majority.[84] However, disunity in the Legislative Council prevented a change in the constitution.[85] James Carnegie writes: 'One consequence of this fiasco was probably that Whitehall did not, in future, tend to take Jamaican political activity very seriously.'[86] After the failed attempts to increase responsibility of the Legislative Council, no serious considerations for constitutional changes were expressed by its members in the following years. The general popularity of the new Governor Reginald Stubbs further contributed to the silence on the matter.[87]

While demands for representation occasionally flared up among the political elite, the interest in constitutional changes appeared to be low among the lower classes. Important changes in the voting laws in 1908 and 1909 that lessened the income qualifications and extended the vote to the previously completely disenfranchised women in 1919 failed to spark large interest.[88] This basic pattern would not change throughout the 1920s and 1930s. While the mass population seemed disinterested in questions of constitutional change, the demands of political representatives of the middle class did not express anti-colonial demands for self-government, while the majority of the nationalists remained loyal to the Empire.[89]

For instance, U. Theo McKay, brother of the renowned poet Claude McKay, demanded constitutional changes and more representation in the short-lived Jamaica People's Association.[90] The organization aimed to unite all those 'who were working in this colony to secure her highest good and make her worthy of her place in the great Commonwealth of Nations comprising the British Empire.'[91] The association criticized the apparent disunity of Jamaicans and of the Legislative Council in particular, and criticized the sectionalism in Jamaican society. It was by no means radical, although it proclaimed that the 'time had come when some change ought to be made in the constitution.'[92] At its first convention, the group pledged that it would 'loyally cooperate with the administration in all that makes for the advancement of Jamaica and its inhabitants.'[93] Its aims were formulated so moderately that even members of the conservative Jamaica Imperial Association supported the organization.

With the Jamaica Reform Club, founded in August 1923 by Alfred Mends[94] and S.P. Radway, a more radical nationalist organization was formed.[95] It had grown out of a splinter group of the local branch of the United Negro Improvement Association (UNIA), of which Mends had been vice president. Contrary to the UNIA's emphasis on Africa, the Jamaica Reform Club put a strong focus on local affairs in Jamaica and regarded the UNIA's aims of liberating the entire African continent as utopian.[96] It expressed far-reaching demands for adult suffrage and even 'autonomy', although the way how these goals could be achieved remained rather vague.[97] The Reform Club claimed: 'The aspiration of every son of this soil must be autonomy. Autonomy was the slogan in a population along with the cry Jamaica for the Jamaicans and it was essential that there should be a flambeau of reformation raised in this country.'[98] At the arrival of Governor Stubbs in 1926, a welcome meeting was held at which they begged that under his government, Jamaica 'may have such a Political Constitution restored to it viz: Autonomy under the British Flag.'[99] Such a statement, including the usage of the word 'restore' suggests that the Reform Club also demanded in fact a return to the old constitution. It further showed a similar ambivalence toward Great Britain which we already observed in earlier nationalist groups and explicitly assured its loyalty to the Empire:

> The Jamaica Reform Club loved liberty and loyalty to the British Crown. The British Constitution stood for Justice, but it was a pity that administrators coming out here did not get the idea imbedded in their minds. They should be missionaries and pioneers, and carry with them always the ideals necessary for British colonial expansion. Jamaica wanted unity, co-operation, co-ordination, and organization. This colony had been too long neglected by the mother country.[100]

This quote affirms that the nationalism of the Reform Club had no fundamental anti-colonial connotation, but, on the contrary, legitimized the civilizing mission of the Empire. Nevertheless, its nationalist rhetoric, for example the motto 'Jamaica for Jamaicans,'[101] during the campaign for the general elections in 1925, raised fears among conservatives, although the election results did not show any significant radicalization in the composition of the new Legislative Council.[102] Like the Nationalist Club before, the Reform Club agitated against the alien influence in the Jamaican economy, especially the Chinese retailers.[103] This xenophobic tendency is a recurring element, not only in Jamaican nationalism.

The nationalist agitation of the Reform Club was noticed and appreciated by Jamaicans in the US, including future vice president of the Progressive League, W.A. Domingo, who encouraged the Reform Club leaders in a letter to the *Gleaner*.[104] However, Domingo's hopes that the effort would be lasting would be disappointed. After the elections in 1925, only very few notes on activities or statements appeared in the press until 1933,[105] when the organization itself found an abrupt end after Radway was deported and banned from Jamaica for quackery and Mends was sent to prison.[106]

In the 1930s, a number of small nationalist groups and organizations developed, for example, the short-lived Jamaica National League (JNL) that developed out of the Kingston and St Andrews Voters League.[107] The Jamaica League encouraged communities to launch citizens associations aimed to create a national consciousness and lobbied for constitutional reform.[108] However, their claims were a mild call for patriotism, campaigning only for representative government.[109]

Another early nationalist was Rupert E. Meikle, founder of the Quill and Ink Club in Port Maria in 1932, the St Mary Debating Association and the St Mary Citizens Association.[110] The Quill and Ink Club was mainly a cultural organization based on patriotism and race-consciousness. It attempted to fight the internalized 'inferiority complex'[111] of many black Jamaicans: 'Its mission is to build up a definite back-ground of Jamaica culture, on a pride founded on the fact that its members are coloured.'[112] It prioritized patriotic education, asked the Jamaica Union of Teachers to highlight the achievements of Jamaicans in schools to counter the 'practice of discounting things Jamaican'[113] by instilling pride in Jamaican heritage. However, Meikle also believed that Jamaicans needed to educate themselves before they would be ready for self-government and advocated a gradual approach toward the 'great day to come when we shall control our own affairs like some of the other countries in our glorious Empire.'[114]

One individual stood out in his radicalism, advocating self-government, Arnold J. Lecesne of Bog Walk, who frequently sent letters to the press. In one of these letters he wrote:

> We should want to assume responsibilities of our own affairs, instead of permitting them to be taken so easily from us, gratitude for this 'goodness' tends to delay self-Government, it does not encourage the growth of a sturdy independence among us, which is what any self-respecting people aspire to; but on the contrary it intends to make us dependent, unreliable and servile.[115]

However, his viewpoint seemed not to be shared by many others, and he did not try to introduce his ideas to any of the existing political groups to press his political demands.

Two years before he would launch the Jamaica Progressive League, W. Adolphe Roberts, visited the island in 1934 and gave an interview to the *Gleaner*, in which he stated:

> It is my conviction that until the people of Jamaica start to advocate for self-Government, can they fully appreciate and understand what it means to have the National Spirit as well as a cultural background peculiar to the Country.[116]

He declared that 'Jamaica was very behind other West Indian countries in so far as her National Spirit was concerned.'[117] Carnegie claims that Rupert Meikle was 'the first man to take up Roberts' challenge and to advocate self-government publicly in the 30s.'[118] However, Meikle never abandoned his belief in a gradual development.[119] He supported the Legislative Council member C.A. Reid of Manchester, who demanded the return to the pre-1856 constitution,[120] and encouraged Jamaicans to agitate for 'representative government leading on to full responsible government.' Meikle was convinced: 'The day has passed for Crown Colony Government. I believe in the British Commonwealth, but I believe in self-government within the Empire just as strongly, and our goal as a people can only be that of full responsible government within the Empire.'[121]

Meikle blamed the government for the 'lack of national consciousness'[122] and declared that if Jamaicans were still not fit for returning at least to the constitution of 1865, 'British administration in this island has failed.'[123] He moved for a resolution in the Quill and Ink Club to support the demands for more representation in the Legislative Council.[124] In 1936, Meikle affirmed his position: 'I ardently long for the day when Jamaica[ns] will be masters in their own land, a free people, partners in an Empire of free people and not content to leave important offices of Govt. to non-Jamaicans.'[125]

Under Governor Alexander Slater, who followed the popular Governor Reginald Edward Stubbs, demands for a change in the constitution increased in the Legislative Council.[126] In 1934, Legislative Council member J.A.G. Smith claimed 'there ought to be serious agitation for a change in constitution; it was impossible...to continue as at present.'[127] Smith demanded a 'constitutional revolt to overthrow mismanagement.'[128] In June 1935, the Legislative Council referred the constitutional question to the newly founded Elected Members Association that was formed as a reaction to the increased nationalist sentiment and pressure from groups and individuals in the Legislative Council.[129] Under the presidency of J.A.G. Smith, the Elected Members Association made an effort to unite the elected members in a demand for representative government. Internal disagreements again frustrated the attempt and led Smith to retreat from the group and to distance himself from their proposals.[130] Once again, disunity in the Legislative Council impeded serious demands for constitutional change.

Let us now turn to Marcus Garvey, one of the officially declared National Heroes of Jamaica. In contrast to the early nationalists, who are largely forgotten in public memory today, Garvey plays an important role in the Jamaican public and is regarded as a pioneer of nationalism. Richard Hart, for instance, claims that Garvey '...had laid a foundation without which the organized nationalism, commencing in the late 1930s, could not have been securely built.'[131] Rupert Lewis argues that Garvey's deportation from the US back to Jamaica in 1927 '...was an important turning point in the struggle of our people against British Colonialism.'[132] According to Lewis, Garvey 'waged an intensive campaign against British colonial rule' after his return to his native island.[133] Don Robotham expresses the opinion that 'Marcus Garvey and the nationalist movement he led and then inspired after 1938, in which Bustamante and Norman Manley played central roles,' can be regarded as the 'the major attempt in the colonial period to secure this emancipation.'[134]

Without doubt, Garvey is an outstanding figure who was instrumental in fighting negative black stereotypes and internalized feelings of inferiority, inspiring pride and positive self-assertion of black people all over the world, inspiring them with his vision of an end of colonialism in Africa. At a time when racism, segregation and colonialism were vital organizational principles in post-emancipation societies in the Americas, the Caribbean, and in Africa, he developed one of the most important international mass movements of black people.[135] He certainly helped to prepare the ground for the political development in the twentieth century, not only in Jamaica, but probably even more so in Africa and the African Diaspora.[136] But was he a Jamaican nationalist? What was his vision for his native land?

Marcus Garvey started his Universal Negro Improvement Association (UNIA) in Jamaica in 1914. In 1916, he migrated and relocated the organization to New York and carried his claim to liberate Africa from colonial rule all over the Americas. His ideas spread like wildfire and inspired numerous people of African descent to fight against racist discrimination in various countries. Soon the UNIA had numerous international branches.[137]

During his years abroad, Garvey did not express any keen interest in Jamaica. In July 1922, he declared: 'I know no nationality; I know no national boundary where the Negro is concerned. The whole world is my province until Africa is free.'[138] One of the few occasions at which Garvey commented on the conditions in Jamaica occurred during a visit in spring 1921. The primary aim for his tour throughout the Caribbean was to stir up race consciousness and awareness for the UNIA's goals in the region. In Jamaica, he explained to his listeners that he aimed to:

> ...draw into one united whole the four hundred million negroes of the world for the purpose of establishing in the continent of Africa a dominion of Negroes. They believed the time had come in the history of the Negro people of the world like in the history of the White race and the Yellow race, for the Negro to pave a way and blast a way to Negro independence.[139]

His political vision was clearly directed towards Africa. Nevertheless, Garvey criticized the absence of a nationalist spirit in Jamaica and deplored widespread loyalty with the Great Britain. He declared:

> If Jamaica is to be saved, if Jamaica is to take her place among the progressive and successful nations of the world, then we must have a change of policy. Jamaica is void of that national spirit that should characterise every country, such as the nationalist spirit of Canada, Australia, South Africa, India, etc. Everybody seems to be looking to the 'Mother Country' for everything, even the black people speak of England as the motherland. I never knew black mothers were born in England.[140]

This statement shows that Garvey envisioned a nationalist future vision for Jamaica. Yet, he was convinced that the island needed a '...political awakening and it should come from within and not from without.'[141] Garvey clearly regarded himself as someone from 'without' and did not feel that a change of these conditions was his task. The *Gleaner* reported that he declared at a local UNIA meeting during his visit that '[a]ll his time, every minute of his life, every second of his life was given to the glorious and grand cause for the redemption of Africa.'[142] Garvey felt that Jamaica 'was too small a place for him. He was just wasting time here.'[143]

Garvey complained about the apathy of Jamaicans and urged: '...throughout the whole Empire men speak for their rights! You lazy, good-for-nothing Jamaicans, wake up!'[144] Garvey felt that Jamaicans themselves were responsible for their current situation: 'Men dare not talk in Jamaica! What is the matter with you men?...I have no respect for men who are too cowardly to demand their rights.'[145]

Garvey harshly criticized the Jamaican perception of race, the positive connotation of lighter skin complexion and the distinction between black and brown people that stood contrary to the racial solidarity he called for. He made clear that he had no plans to return to Jamaica. The *Gleaner* reported that 'this was probably his last visit to Jamaica as he would be proceeding to Africa where he had a big and important job and he wanted them to co-operate and improve themselves.'[146] Garvey was convinced that the people themselves were to be blamed for their conditions, and that '…there was no desire from the Governor to see that people were living in a state of starvation[,] were badly housed and poorly clad.' Garvey further encouraged the 'Negroes of Jamaica', to not allow themselves to 'remain in a process of stagnation. Arouse yourselves. Do not make fools of yourselves.'[147]

Disappointed by the reactions to his propaganda in Jamaica, Garvey wrote an open letter to the *Gleaner* after he left. 'I went to Jamaica and found a cold, callous and indifferent Jamaica somewhat, and I have left Jamaica a 100 per cent.'[148] Rather than thinking about Jamaica's future as an individual nation state, Garvey argued in May 1925 that a 'Federation of the West Indies with Dominion status is the consummation of Negro aspirations in this archipelago.'[149]

When Garvey was deported to Jamaica in 1927, he must have perceived his involuntary return as a backlash to his Pan-African mission. Contrary to Tony Martin's claim that Garvey 'promptly dominate[d] the nationalist scene,'[150] he initially did not show great interest in getting actively involved in local politics. The international UNIA and the cause of liberating Africa remained his main concern. In his first public speech in Jamaica, Garvey declared that although he was worried about the conditions in Jamaica that he, 'as President-General of the Universal Negro Improvement Association,' had 'an international duty to perform.'[151] He told his listeners that he did not intend to stay, but rather would be travelling throughout the Caribbean and Europe to broaden the support for his plans to liberate Africa. The *Gleaner* reported: 'Mr. Garvey said that he did not come to Jamaica for any local propaganda. Some people thought he was going to run for the Legislative Council, but he had no time to go there.'[152] In the *Negro World*, he promised that he would 'devote every minute of my time, from now to the grave to the great cause and your universal freedom…I shall help to save America and the world by a peaceful solution of the race problem, but anyhow, Africa must be redeemed for the Negro.'[153]

In an article which appeared in the *Daily Gleaner* one day after his arrival, Garvey assured the public, certainly aware of the heavy surveillance he would be under from the authorities: 'I respect all constituted authority; and during my stay in Jamaica I shall do everything to co-operate with the Government to help the common people.'[154] He emphasized his loyalty with Great Britain and encouraged Jamaicans to be loyal and patient.¹⁵⁵ Even the conservative editor of the *Gleaner*, H.G. de Lisser, was surprised about Garvey's meek statements.¹⁵⁶

Garvey continued to blame Jamaicans for their own situation and argued that he saw no wrong in the form of government, the constitution, or British rule in general. In a speech held in April 1928, he pointed out:

> Wherever the blame is I am going to place it without fear of consequence. But, knowing the British Constitution as I do–the Jamaica Constitution as I do–I cannot intelligently see the reason for blaming the government for the condition of the people in this country–the Home Authorities or the King–in that your Constitution both at home and abroad grants you the privilege always to organize within the law to better your own condition. If you have not done it in the past it is not the fault of the government–it is your own fault.¹⁵⁷

In 1928, he travelled to many Caribbean islands and to London, Geneva, Paris and Canada, and handed in a petition to the League of Nations in which he demanded the allotment of responsibility in South Africa to create an independent African state in West Africa.¹⁵⁸ He always wished to return to the US, until his hopes were destroyed by a landslide victory of the republicans in 1928.¹⁵⁹ Only then, Garvey decided to get involved in local politics and established the People's Political Party (PPP).¹⁶⁰ However, he still gave first priority to the UNIA and the planning of a big international UNIA convention to be held in Kingston in August 1929 that dealt chiefly with international affairs such as the 'Ten Year Plan' and the liberation of Africa.¹⁶¹

The PPP made its first public appearance at a meeting held at Crossroads on September 9, 1929.¹⁶² Garvey outlined his plan of 'sponsoring the election of fourteen men to the Legislative Council of Jamaica.'¹⁶³ He won a seat in the Kingston and St Andrew Corporation (KSAC) in October 1929, and was re-elected in 1931, but failed to become elected to the Legislative Council in the general election in 1930.¹⁶⁴ At the time of the Great Depression, Garvey's platform included 14 points that mainly addressed economic issues, demanding minimum wage, protection of native labour, land reform, higher taxation on foreign businesses, promotion of native industries and creating jobs for the unemployed. Some points referred to the need for cultural and educational development or criticized the power of the judges.¹⁶⁵

Garvey's political vision for Jamaica remained cloudy. Only one of the points dealt explicitly with the form of government. Garvey demanded that the Legislative Council should be 'filled with men who would represent the people honestly. They should not be afraid to say that they wanted to see the constitution developed.'¹⁶⁶ Garvey did not explain in detail how the constitution should be changed. In his manifesto, published in the *Gleaner*, he demanded that Jamaica

Nationalism in Jamaica before 1936

should 'secure representation in the Imperial Parliament or a larger modicum of self-government for Jamaica.'[167] It seems that a typing error occurred, because Garvey did not use the above quoted phrase consistently.[168] In the *Blackman*, the same passage demanded 'representation in the Imperial Government *for* a larger modicum of self-government.'[169] It is a significant difference whether Garvey demanded Jamaican representation in the British Government, similar to representations of the French overseas departments in the French Parliament, and regarded that as a larger modicum of self-government or whether he demanded a larger degree of self-government in the case that such representation was denied.

Some days after his defeat at the polls, he repeated the same passage from the manifesto and used the words 'for a larger modicum of self-government' and not 'or'.[170] He further argued: 'If Jamaica is to continue as a part of the British Empire, it is but right that we should have representation in the Imperial Government for Jamaica, B[ritish] Guiana and other British West Indian possessions.'[171] This supports the interpretation that Garvey requested representation in the imperial government and regarded this as a larger degree of self-government. In the case that such representation would be denied, he claimed that Jamaica should be granted Dominion status. Garvey explained:

> We do not refuse to be governed by the Mo[th]er Country, and to remain a part of the great [B]ritish Commonwealth, but we do object to be ruled and governed by ignorance...we want to remain part of the British Empire and as British subjects we think it is right for England to give us representation in the Mother Parliament, or give us Dominion status as they have given to Canada. Canada refused to be governed by the limited intelligence at home because they think they can rule themselves at home. The same is said of Australia and barbaric South Africa, and if Africa can say that I do not see why we cannot say the same thing in cultural Jamaica. The reasons for my going to the Council is to influence changes in the Constitutions, to make it that the British West Indies can be represented in the Mother Parliament of England.[172]

Amy J. Garvey cites the Peoples' Political Party (PPP) manifesto with the phrase 'for a larger modicum' and suggests that Jamaica was not Garvey's main concern. She claims that Garvey planned to form the PPP in other British and French West Indian territories and Haiti, after he 'had succeeded in Jamaica, this was his aim.'[173] But Garvey lost the elections and the *Gleaner* commented: 'The simple truth is that wherever he actively engaged in the campaign of any hitherto well-known public man, his support was actually damaging to the cause of that individual.'[174]

While Garvey claimed before the election that 'cultural Jamaica'[175] would have the same right to Dominion status as Canada and 'barbaric' South Africa, he complained after his defeat at the polls, 'I am forced to conclude that Jamaica is indeed an ignorant community; it is limited in intelligence, narrow in its intellectual concept, almost to the point where one can honestly say that the country is ridiculous.'[176] His party did not survive after the elections, although, the results might have looked different without the rigid voting restrictions based on property.[177]

In the 1930s, Garvey travelled a lot, and unsuccessfully tried to revive the UNIA internationally.[178] In 1935, Garvey left Jamaica for England and never returned to the island of his birth, not even when he travelled to other Caribbean islands in 1938. Only from far, he commented on the labour rebellions of the same year in several letters, and prepared a memorandum to the Royal Commission and welcomed Bustamante's entry into politics.[179]

Garvey's vision for Jamaica was nebulous. Africa, and not Jamaica, remained the focal point of his thinking. Such a conclusion is not meant to diminish Garvey's fundamental achievements in fighting racism and the consequences of internalized feelings of inferiority of people of African descent. His merit lies in inspiring millions of black people to take pride and self-esteem in their skin colour and heritage and to encourage them to take responsibility and action to change the societies they lived in. He was a great source of inspiration in the anti-colonial struggle of many African countries and is held in high esteem by numerous African leaders. Garvey's greatness, as Rupert Lewis states, 'lay in the massive psychological warfare that he developed to wipe out the inherited inferiority complex and the facelessness of the Negro in a white world.'[180] However, Lewis is also right when he reflects on Garvey's political involvement in Jamaica and concludes: '...Garvey's Jamaican episode left a lasting, though hidden mark upon the national spirit. He openly challenged the reigning false standards of racial values.'[181] Positive self-identification of black Jamaicans was a prerequisite to belief in the country's ability to govern itself, yet it was still a long way to go. His tremendous importance in challenging the internalized inferiority complex notwithstanding, a close examination of the sources suggests that Garvey's priority was always placed on the international sphere and that he personally regarded his time in Jamaica as an involuntarily and a rather disappointing experience in his political career. Garvey's relationship with Jamaica and Jamaicans was ambivalent and it took years after independence, before his popularity would increase in larger sections of the Jamaican population, and before he was officially recognized as a National Hero by the Jamaican government in 1969.

The survey of the Jamaican political landscape predating 1936 shows that the formation of political and cultural nationalist groups took place mainly in the educated upper and middle classes, from which most of the membership of the mushrooming political organizations, the poetry and debating societies, the book clubs and citizens associations stemmed.[182] Although membership was often small, it was in these groups that many persons who later took part in the political developments developed their oratory skills and sharpened their political views.[183] A close analysis of programmes and statements of nationalist groups and activists showed that the majority adopted a rather mild nationalist approach advocating a slow development towards more responsible forms of government. Strong identification with and loyalty to the British Empire remained largely unchallenged and limited the scope of activities of local activists. While demands for representative government considerably increased in the first decades of the twentieth century, the platforms, manifestos and programmes of the political groups did not contain demands democratic self-government. This conclusion supports Carnegie's observation: 'No local group demanded self-government before 1937....'[184]

The survey affirms the claim that the Jamaica Progressive League was the first organization with concrete political demands for self-government for Jamaica. Historian Denis M. Benn comes to the same conclusion when he argues that the propaganda of the Progressive League was '...for the first time a systematic attempt to formulate local political aspirations in terms of a positive philosophy of nationhood rather than as a negative response to Crown colony rule.'[185] The statements quoted above also support Richard Hart's explanation why Jamaican nationalism took so long to develop:

> [T]he first delaying factor was the surprisingly widespread loyalty to Britain, mentioned above in relation to the free persons of colour. This loyalty carried over into the post-1865 period and extended beyond the middle classes to the emancipated slaves and their descendants. Because of the liberal attitude of the British Government on such issues as the slave trade and the abolition of slavery, which contrasted sharply with the attitude so vociferously expressed by the slave owners, the slaves, too, had come to draw a distinction between resident whites and the people in England.[186]

Notably, many of the early nationalists shared the experience of migration. In the early political groups in Jamaica, an extraordinarily high proportion of activists in the emerging political scene, such as Norman Manley, Marcus Garvey, Wilfred A. Domingo, and many others mentioned in the survey above had either migrated or travelled abroad. It seems that their migration experiences inspired them to look at their country in different ways and to start work for social and political change.[187] In order to explore how demands for Jamaican independence developed in an organized form, we need to shift our perspective to New York and explore the experiences that helped to change the outlook of those emigrants who founded the Jamaica Progressive League.

Notes

1. Defining the term, the Encyclopaedia Britannica states: 'Although there was no formal definition of Dominion status, a pronouncement by the Imperial Conference of 1926 described Great Britain and the dominions as 'autonomous communities within the British Empire, equal in status, in no way subordinate one to another in any aspect of their domestic or external affairs, though united by a common allegiance to the Crown and freely associated as members of the British Commonwealth of Nations.' See http://www.britannica.com/EBchecked/topic/168777/dominion (last viewed November 9, 2011.).
2. See Trevor Munroe, *Constitutional Decolonization* (Kingston: ISER, University of the West Indies, 1972), 111f.
3. For a basic overview of the history of Jamaica see for example Philip Sherlock and Hazel Bennett, *The Story of the Jamaican People* (Kingston: Ian Randle Publishers, 1998).
4. For a detailed critical discussion of theories of the plantation system, society and economy as developed by George Beckford, Norman Girvan, Lloyd Best and others see Denis M. Benn, 'The Theory of Plantation Economy and Society: A Methodological Critique,' *The Journal of Commonwealth & Comparative Politics*, 12 (1974): 249–60.
5. For an overview on recent discussions of reparations in Jamaica and the rest of the Caribbean, see for example *Daily Gleaner*, August 4, 2013.
6. For a description of the British colonial administration see for instance Gordon K. Lewis, *Growth of the Modern West Indies* (New York: Monthly Review Press, 1968), 89ff.; Ronald V. Sires, 'The Experience of Jamaica With Modified Crown Colony Government', *Social and Economic Studies* 4 (1955): 150–67; Munroe, *Constitutional Decolonization*.
7. See for example Theodore W. Allen, *The Invention of the White Race*. Vol. 2. (London, New York: Verso, 1997). For the Anglophone Caribbean see esp. 223–38.
8. See Brian L. Moore and Michele Johnson, *Neither Led nor Driven: Contesting British Cultural Imperialism in Jamaica, 1865-1920* (Kingston: University of the West Indies Press, 2004), 167–204.
9. See Glen Richards, 'Race, Class, and Labour Politics in Colonial Jamaica, 1900–1934', in *Jamaica in Slavery and Freedom*, ed. Kathleen E.A. Monteith and Glen Richards (Kingston: University of the West Indies Press, 2002), 341.
10. This fact is highlighted by numerous authors, see, for instance Aggrey Brown, *Colour, Class and Politics in Jamaica* (Edison, NJ: Transaction Publishers, 1980); Stuart Hall, 'Old and New Identities, Old and New Ethnicities', in *Culture, Globalization and the World System: Contemporary Conditions for the Representation of Identity*, ed. Anthony D. King (Minneapolis: University of Minnesota Press, 1991); Showers Johnson, '*Racial Frontiers in Jamaica's Nonracial Nationhood*'. *Race and Nation: Ethnic Systems in the Modern World* (New York: Routledge, 2005), 155.
11. Stuart Hall, 'Old and New Identities', 53.
12. See Showers Johnson, 'Racial Frontiers'.
13. See Gad Heuman, *The Killing Time: The Morant Bay Rebellion in Jamaica* (Knoxville: University of Tennessee, 1994).
14. See Roy Augier, 'Before and After 1865,' *New World Quarterly* 2 (1966): 21–40.

15. See Richards, 'Race, Class and Labour', 352.
16. For an overview on the constitutional development after 1865, see Ronald V. Sires, 'The Experience of Jamaica with Modified Crown Colony Government', *Social and Economic Studies* 4 (June 1955): 150–67.
17. James Carnegie, *Some Aspects of Jamaica's Politics 1918–1938*, (Kingston: Institute of Jamaica, 1973), 15.
18. See George L. Beckford, *Persistent Poverty: Underdevelopment in Plantation Economies of the Third World* (Morant Bay, 1983).
19. See for example Spry Rush: *Bonds of Empire*; Moore and Johnson, *Neither Led Nor Driven*; Gordon K. Lewis, *Growth of the Modern West Indies* (Kingston: Ian Randle Publishers, 2004), 171; for the persistence of such identities after migration see Philip Kasinitz, *Caribbean New York: Black Immigrants and the Politics of Race* (Ithaca, NY: Cornell University Press, 1992); Anne Spry Rush, 'Imperial Identities in Colonial Minds: Harold Moody and the League of Coloured Peoples, 1931–1950', *Twentieth Century British History* 13, no.4 (2002): 356–83.
20. See for example: Michael Nkuzi Nnam, *Colonial Mentality in Africa* (Lanham: Hamilton Books, 2007), the term is frequently used in studies on the Philippines and mental health in Filipino-American migrant communities, see for example E.J.R. David, *Filipino-American Postcolonial-Psychology: Oppression, Colonial Mentality and Decolonization* (Bloomington: AuthorHouse, 2011), see for example Daniel B. Schirmer and Stephen Rosskamm Shalom, eds., *The Philippines Reader: A History of Colonialism, Neocolonialism, Dictatorship and Resistance* (Cambridge: South End Press, 1987).
21. Lewis, *Growth of the Modern West Indies*, 24.
22. See Norris, *Jamaica*, 98ff.
23. See Anthony Bogues, 'Nationalism and Jamaican Political Thought', in *Jamaica in Slavery and Freedom*, ed. Kathleen E.A. Monteith and Glen Richards (Kingston, University of the West Indies Press, 2002).
24. Ibid., 382.
25. See Moore and Johnson, *Neither Led Nor Driven*, 271ff.
26. Patrick Bryan, *The Jamaican People, 1880–1902* (Macmillan: Kingston, 2000), 18.
27. For a colourful description of the different expressions of loyalty with the British monarchy, see Moore and Johnson, *Neither Led Nor Driven*, 271–310.
28. Bryan, *The Jamaican People*, 17.
29. Carl Stone, 'Decolonization and the Caribbean State System: The Case of Jamaica', in *The Newer Caribbean: Decolonization, Democracy and Development* (Philadelphia: Institute for the Study of Human Issues, 1983), 47.
30. Lewis, *Growth of the Modern West Indies*, 171.
31. See Carl Stone, 'Decolonization and the Caribbean State System', 47.
32. For more information on Love see: Joy Lumsden, 'Robert Love and Jamaican Politics', Unpublished PhD thesis, University of the West Indies, Mona, 1987; Sherlock and Bennett: *Story of the Jamaican People*, 283–91.
33. See Bogues, 'Nationalism and Jamaican Political Thought', 379.
34. Jamaican Advocate, December 7, 1895; quoted after Rupert Lewis, *Marcus Garvey: Anti-Colonial Champion* (Trenton, NJ: Africa World Press, 1988), 26.
35. See *Daily Gleaner*, August 3, 1899.

36. Bogues, 'Nationalism and Jamaican Political Thought', 379.
37. See *Daily Gleaner*, March 30, 1901.
38. Bogues, 'Nationalism and Jamaican Political Thought', 379.
39. See Lewis, *Anti-Colonial Champion*, 30.
40. See *Daily Gleaner*, March 22, 1901.
41. Ibid.
42. Ibid., March 30, 1901, for a similar argument see also *Daily Gleaner*, March 22, 1901.
43. Ibid., March 30, 1901.
44. Robert Hill, *Marcus Garvey*, Vol. 1, 21.
45. For biographical information on Cox, see See Robert A. Hill, ed., *The Marcus Garvey and Universal Negro Improvement Association Papers* (10 Vols. Berkeley, 1983–2006), Vol. 1, 21 FN 1. For a comparative perspective on the National Club see Glen Richards, 'Race, Labour, and Politics in Jamaica and St Kitts, 1909–1940: A Comparative Survey of the Roles of the National Club of Jamaica and the Workers League of St Kitts', in *Working Slavery, Pricing Freedom: Perspectives from the Caribbean, Africa and the African Diaspora*, ed. Verene A. Shepherd (New York: Palgrave-Global Publishing at St Martin's Press, 2002), 502–23.
46. Love joined the National Club in 1909, despite the formal requirement of Jamaican birth, see Richard Hart, 'Jamaica and Self-Determination', 282.
47. See *Daily Gleaner*, March 4, 1909.
48. See Hart, 'Jamaica and Self-Determination', 282f.
49. See *Daily Gleaner*, March 5, 1909.
50. Ibid., March 4, 1909.
51. Ibid.
52. The National Club's official organ was called 'Our Own' and appeared every second month from July 1910–July 1911, see Hill, *Marcus Garvey*, Vol. 1, 21.
53. *Our Own*, July 1, 1910; quoted after Hart, *From Occupation to Independence*, 103. In his quotation, Bogues omits the words 'greater measure' and cites misleadingly that 'Our Own advocated "self-government within the empire"', Bogues, 'Nationalism and Jamaican Political Thought', 367.
54. *Daily Gleaner*, March 4, 1909.
55. Ibid., March 5, 1909.
56. Ibid.
57. Ibid.
58. See Richards, 'Race, Labour, and Politics', 510.
59. See *Daily Gleaner*, June 17, 1909; *Daily Gleaner*, June 19, 1909; see also Richards, 'Race, Labour, and Politics', 505.
60. *Daily Gleaner*, December 13, 1922.
61. Ibid., August 14, 1918; see also *Daily Gleaner*, February 15, 1919.
62. Ibid., August 3, 1918.
63. Ibid., May 7, 1919.
64. Ibid., August 14, 1918.
65. Carnegie, *Some Aspects*, 103.
66. *Daily Gleaner*, November 17, 1919.
67. Ibid., September 22, 1919.
68. Ibid., August 19, 1919.

69. Ibid., August 25, 1919.
70. Ibid., September 16, 1919.
71. Ibid.
72. *Daily Gleaner*, September 18, 1919.
73. Ibid., December 4, 1920; see also Carnegie, *Some Aspects*, 103.
74. See *Daily Gleaner*, December 4, 1920.
75. See Morley Ayearst, *The British West Indies* (New York: New York University Press, 1960), 33; see also Carnegie, *Some Aspects*, 131ff.
76. Ibid., 67.
77. See *Daily Gleaner*, January 17, 1921; *Daily Gleaner*, August 15, 1921; *Daily Gleaner*, August 24, 1921; *Daily Gleaner*, August 30, 1921; *Daily Gleaner*, September 5, 1921.
78. See Anthony Johnson, *JAG Smith* (Kingston: Kingston Publishers, 1991); See also Carnegie, *Some Aspects*, 61ff.
79. See Carnegie, *Some Aspects*, 65.
80. Amongst them labour activist Bain-Alves, Dr Oswald Anderson and Dr Penso (both to-be mayors of Kingston), the current mayor Bryant, John Soulette and Revd S.M. Jones, the president of the local UNIA, see Carnegie, *Some Aspects*, 68.
81. Ibid.
82. Ibid., 68f.
83. Wood Report, cited after Carnegie, *Some Aspects*, 69.
84. See Sires, 'Modified Crown Colony', 157.
85. See Carnegie, *Some Aspects*, 71.
86. Ibid.
87. Ibid., 162.
88. See Sires, 'Modified Crown Colony', 156.
89. See Carnegie, *Some Aspects*, 67.
90. Among them A.G. Nash, who presided over the inaugural meeting and was elected president, H.A.L. Simpson, A.A. Barclay, P. Lightbody, D.T. Wint, O. Anderson and others. See *Daily Gleaner*, March 6, 1922.
91. *Daily Gleaner*, March 6, 1922.
92. Ibid., August 3, 1922.
93. Ibid.
94. Mends had been vice-president of the UNIA in Jamaica and of the Jamaica Federation of Labour. See Carnegie, *Some Aspects*, 99.
95. Ibid., 99–101,105.
96. Ibid., 105.
97. See *Daily Gleaner*, July 14, 1924; The Gleaner criticized in a polemic way that the aims of the Reform Club were cloudy and questioned the payment of salaries of the President and the General Secretary and their trips to England to make representations.
98. Ibid., June 7, 1924.
99. Ibid., August 12, 1926.
100. Ibid., December 20, 1923; for similar expressions of loyalty, see *Daily Gleaner*, April 28, 1924; *Daily Gleaner*, August 11, 1924; *Daily Gleaner*, March 5, 1925.
101. Ibid., June 7, 1924.
102. See Carnegie, *Some Aspects*, 77, 105.

103. See *Daily Gleaner*, October 3, 1925.
104. Ibid., June 5, 1924.
105. See Carnegie, *Some Aspects*, 105.
106. Ibid., 99.
107. The leading figures were James Blackwood, a former teacher, and Williams, a returning migrant who had lived in the US, C.A. Isaac-Henry, a former teacher from Bermuda and C.G. Walker. It is notable, that many of the key figures had experiences of living in foreign countries. See Carnegie, *Some Aspects*, 97, 99, 107.
108. See *Daily Gleaner* July 9, 1934.
109. Ibid., June 11, 1936; September 12, 1934.
110. Ibid., August 1, 1936.
111. Ibid., July 26, 1933.
112. Ibid.
113. Ibid., January 28, 1936.
114. Ibid., June 8, 1935.
115. Ibid., September 2, 1932.
116. Ibid., January 20, 1934.
117. Ibid.
118. Carnegie, *Some Aspects*, 112.
119. *Daily Gleaner*, September 10, 1935.
120. Ibid., September 10, 1935; September 14, 1935.
121. Ibid., September 10, 1935.
122. Ibid.
123. Ibid.
124. Ibid., September 14, 1935.
125. Ibid., August 1, 1936.
126. See Carnegie, *Some Aspects*, 53f.
127. *Daily Gleaner*, April 13, 1934.
128. Ibid., February 26, 1934.
129. See Carnegie, *Some Aspects*, 77.
130. Ibid.
131. Hart, 'Jamaica and Self-Determination,' 283.
132. Rupert Lewis, 'Garveyism in Jamaica,' in *Marcus Garvey*, ed. E. David Cronon (Englewood Cliffs, NJ: Prentice-Hall, 1973), 154.
133. Lewis, 'Garveyism in Jamaica,' 158.
134. Don Robotham, 'The Development of a Black Ethnicity in Jamaica,' in *Garvey: His Work and Impact*, ed. Rupert Lewis and Patrick E. Bryan (Trenton, NJ: Africa World Press, 1991), 24.
135. The most important source for original material on Garvey is the giant collection of his papers, brilliantly edited by Robert A. Hill; See Hill, ed., *Marcus Garvey Papers*.
136. There is an abundance of literature available on Garvey. For an evaluation of the controversial legacy of Garvey see for example Jérémie Kroubo Dagnini, 'Marcus Garvey: A Controversial Figure in the History of Pan-Africanism', *The Journal of Pan African Studies* 2 (2008): 198–208.
137. For a list of the branches see Tony Martin, *Race First: The Ideological and Organizational Struggles of Marcus Garvey and the Universal Negro Improvement Association* (Westport: Greenwood Press, 1976), 361–73.

138. Speech at Liberty Hall New York, July 16, 1922, *Negro World*, July 22, 1922; cited after Hill, *Marcus Garvey*, Vol. 5, 729.
139. *Daily Gleaner*, March 26, 1921.
140. Ibid., June 2, 1921.
141. Ibid.
142. Ibid., March 24, 1921.
143. Ibid.
144. Ibid., March 26, 1921.
145. Ibid.
146. Ibid., March 29, 1921.
147. Ibid.
148. Ibid., August 15, 1921; see also See Eric E. Duke, 'The Diasporic Dimensions of British Caribbean Federation', *New West Indian Guide* 83 (2009): 238.
149. The *Blackman*, May 2, 1929; May 16, 1929, cited after Tony Martin, *The Pan-African Connection: From Slavery to Garvey and Beyond* (Dover, MA: The Majority Press, 1984), 116.
150. Martin, *The Pan-African Connection*, 111.
151. *Daily Gleaner*, December 12, 1927.
152. Ibid.
153. *Negro World (NW)*, December 17, 1927, quoted after Hill, *Marcus Garvey*, Vol. 7, 10.
154. *Daily Gleaner*, December 12, 1927.
155. Ibid.
156. See *Daily Gleaner*, December 13, 1927.
157. *NW*, April 21, 1928, quoted after Hill, *Marcus Garvey*, Vol. 7, 155.
158. See Judith Stein, *The World of Marcus Garvey: Race and Class in Modern Society* (Baton Rouge: Louisiana State University Press, 1986), 257f.
159. See Stein, *The World of Marcus Garvey*, 258.
160. See Hill, *Marcus Garvey*, Vol. 7, 339, FN 1.
161. See *NW*, August 24, 1929, in Hill, *Marcus Garvey*, vol. 7, 311–13.
162. Garvey's lengthy speech appeared in the issues of The *Blackman*, September 11, 1912 and September 12, 1929, see Hill, *Marcus Garvey*, Vol. 7, 328–40.
163. See The *Blackman*, September 11, 1912; September 12, 1929, see Hill, *Marcus Garvey*, Vol. 7, 328.
164. See Nicholas Patsides, 'Marcus Garvey, Race Idealism and His Vision of Jamaican Self-Government', *Caribbean Quarterly* 51 (2005): 37.
165. The *Blackman*, September 11, 1912; September 12, 1929, see Hill, *Marcus Garvey*, Vol. 7, 329.
166. *Daily Gleaner*, September 10, 1929.
167. Ibid.
168. In the manifesto that got into the hands of the Colonial Office, it reads 'or', PRO, CO 318/399, quoted after Hill, *Marcus Garvey*, Vol. 7, 401.
169. The *Blackman*, September 11, 1912; September 12, 1929, see Hill, *Marcus Garvey*, Vol. 7, 329 (my emphasis).
170. '1. Representation in the Imperial Parliament **for** a larger modicum of self-government for Jamaica.' *Daily Gleaner, February* 6, 1930 (my emphasis).
171. The *Blackman*, September 11, 1912; September 12, 1929, quoted after Hill, *Marcus Garvey*, Vol. 7, 330.

172. Ibid., 331.
173. Amy J. Garvey, *Garvey and Garveyism* (Kingston: A. Jacques Garvey, 1963), 215.
174. *Daily Gleaner*, January 31, 1930.
175. The *Blackman*, September 11, 1912; September 12, 1929, see Hill, *Marcus Garvey*, vol. 7, 331.
176. *Daily Gleaner*, February 6, 1930.
177. See Hart, *Towards Decolonisation*, 4.
178. See Martin: *Pan-African Connection*, 126f.
179. Ibid., 127f.
180. Lewis, *Growth of the West Indies*, 189.
181. Ibid., 180.
182. For example the Liberal Association of which Ethelred Brown was president before he migrated to the US (1915), the Quill and Ink Club led by Rupert Meikle (1932), the Kingston and St Andrew Literary and Debating Association (1931), the Left Book Club (1935), and the Readers and Writers Club (1937). See Carnegie, *Some Aspects*, 98.
183. See Carnegie, *Some Aspects*, 98. Prominent figures are, for example, Norman Manley, Wills Isaacs, Florizel Glasspole and A.E.T. Henry. JPL (Kingston) founder McFarlane and Ethelred Brown, secretary of the Progressive League, had also been active in debating societies.
184. Ibid., 131.
185. Benn, *The Caribbean: An Intellectual History, 1774–2003* (Kingston: Ian Randle Publishers, 2004), 75.
186. Hart, 'Jamaica and Self-Determination', 282.
187. This observation is shared by Carnegie in his survey of political developments between 1918 and 1938. See Carnegie, Some Aspects, 144f.

CHAPTER 2: ORIGINS OF THE JAMAICA PROGRESSIVE LEAGUE

Two months after Jamaica became independent, founding member of the Progressive League, Wilfred A. Domingo, reflected on the origins of the movement for self-government: 'Others had individually dreamed of achieving self-government for Jamaica, but it was left to Roberts to organize the first effective attempt for this purpose....'[1]

What had influenced the white Jamaican journalist and historian Walter Adolphe Roberts during the year of his fiftieth anniversary to dedicate the remainder of his life to the cause of liberating Jamaica from colonial rule? After extensive travels through Europe, the United States and Latin America, Roberts increasingly wondered why Jamaica silently accepted to remain a British colony, while its neighbouring countries had already achieved their autonomy from their respective colonial powers centuries ago. A trip to Puerto Rico was of special importance. There, he witnessed how the movement for independence had gained strength, and felt a strong urge to take up action to lobby for the independence of his own country of birth. The Jamaican pointed to other small but independent countries in the region in which he had travelled extensively and whose politics he found of great interest:

> When I thought of Cuba, Haiti, the Dominican Republic and Puerto Rico – neighbouring countries of the Greater Antilles – I could not believe that Jamaica would remain forever the Sleeping Princess of the fairy tale.[2]

During his travels to Jamaica in 1934 and 1936, Roberts had tried to introduce his ideas to his countrymen. To his disappointment, his anti-colonial demands did not fall on fertile ground. Especially in the politically interested middle class, identification and loyalty with the British Empire was deeply rooted. Roberts felt that it might be easier to garner support for his vision abroad amongst Jamaicans who had also travelled, and who had been exposed to different political ideas.[3]

During a visit to New York in September 1936, Roberts arranged for a meeting with the journalist A.M. Wendell Malliet to float his ideas. The latter, also a Jamaican by birth, had taken residence in New York, and wrote for the renowned African American newspaper, The *New York Amsterdam News*. Roberts was aware that Malliet and other emigrants also felt strongly about the British

Empire and subscribed to British claims for colonialism's civilizing mission.[4] Nevertheless, he felt that in the Jamaican emigrant community in Harlem, he would be able to find people who would be prepared to join an anti-colonial pressure group.

Roberts vividly remembered a 'buried note of hysteria' in Malliet's reaction to his suggestion that it was time for Jamaica to break with its colonial ties and join the British Commonwealth as an independent nation state. Roberts recalled that Malliet '...appeared suspicious of my motives, but warmed presently to the suggestion that I try out the responsiveness of our compatriots in exile'. Probably, Malliet was convinced that the Jamaican community in New York would share his scepticism and help to tone down the radicalism of Roberts' proposal. Be it as it may, he agreed that Roberts should share his vision with an audience of Jamaicans in New York and arranged an invitation for Roberts to one of the house parties of renowned Jamaican-born Judge James S. Watson in Harlem, where the who's who of the Jamaican immigrant community mingled.[5]

Among the first guests Roberts approached was Wilfred A. Domingo, a Jamaican immigrant and political activist who had risen to prominence in the circles of what became known as the Harlem Renaissance. He was well known for his sharp analysis and oratory skills, and his efforts to combine race and class-based approaches. Roberts invited those who showed interest at Watson's party to a meeting at the Jamaica Benevolent Association to discuss Jamaica's political future on July 15, 1936. In front of a group of Jamaican expatriates in New York, Roberts gave a speech on 'Self-Government for Jamaica', in which he criticized the system of Crown Colony government in Jamaica as anachronistic. Not mincing the matter, he openly complained that it benefited only Europeans and light-skinned Jamaicans, while the majority of black Jamaicans were only slightly better off than during slavery.[6] Roberts repudiated counter-arguments against self-government, for example, those presented in Major Woods's 1922 Royal Commission report, which resulted from an inquiry into the conditions on the British possessions in the Caribbean. Wood's main objection was the low interest in politics, which Roberts countered by blaming the limited political influence of the Legislative Council under Crown Colony and especially the limited franchise as reasons for the apathy. Roberts was convinced that the widespread indifference of the population toward politics would vanish once they were allowed to participate in the political process, and he strongly urged Jamaicans to take their political future into their own hands.

> It is idle for them to expect that self-government will be initiated from Westminster as a bounty. They must show aptitude for the responsibilities of liberty, or it will never be granted. They must begin to act as a people within the framework of the empire and to cease

speaking – or even thinking – as apathetic subjects under a Crown Colony system which has long outstayed its time.⁷

In contrast to Wood, Roberts did not feel that Jamaica's population was too heterogeneous to qualify for self-government and pointed to a number of independent nations with heterogeneous populations.

Roberts regarded himself as part of a nationalist avant-garde, believing that an educational campaign was of crucial importance to the movement. He hoped that waging such a nationalist campaign to popularize and encourage national culture would instil in Jamaicans feelings of national pride. In front of the expatriates, he solemnly declared that the time was ripe to start such a national movement in Jamaica: 'I set the ideal of nationalism before all Jamaicans. There is a definite sustaining and guiding strength in national sentiment, in a national consciousness, and this can be created only along the parallel lines of political action and artistic fruitfulness…I am confident that the moment in history has been reached when they are due to appear'.⁸

Roberts' powerful speech ended with an appeal to form a group in New York, demanding self-government for Jamaica. He remembered the surprised reaction of many of his listeners: 'The audience consisted mostly of practical people, who wore nostalgic expressions when I referred to the far-off island home, showed a certain incredulity at the thought that direct British rule could ever be shaken, but applauded warmly'.⁹ One of the founding members later remembered the sceptical attitude towards Roberts' proposal saying that 'maybe it was more than astonishment; it was anger and resentment'.¹⁰ These reactions illustrate how firmly most Jamaicans believed in the status quo of British colonial rule in Jamaica.

Inspired by other anti-colonial freedom movements that had manifested in exile circles, Roberts envisioned that a nationalist group of emigrants could become the body that would inspire Jamaicans to demand responsibility for their own affairs. Yet, he was convinced that nationalist thinking and concrete political organization were necessary to develop in Jamaica. Therefore, he advocated the 'immediate founding of a political party in Jamaica, pledged to work for self-government'.¹¹ These suggestions fell on fertile ground among the expatriates. Accordingly, a group of Jamaicans who had been active in political organization in Harlem readily agreed to join the movement, seizing the opportunity to give their own anti-colonial ideas a definite shape.

Wilfred A. Domingo stood out in the network of activists in Harlem and became one the greatest assets of the Progressive League. Well experienced in street oratory, journalism and political organizing, he became one of the spearheads of the group, serving as vice president of the League, and developing into one of the most visible spokesmen for self-government. In his study on the influence of immigrants from the Caribbean in the Harlem Renaissance, Winston James describes Domingo as 'one of the most influential theoreticians of the New Negro movement, authoring some of its most cogent, strategic, and programmatic articles' and claims that 'Domingo's contribution to New Negro thought is still to be properly weighed'.[12] It is equally true that his important contribution to the Jamaican movement for self-government and the early People's National Party (PNP) is likewise underrated.

Domingo was part of the small group of attendees who endorsed Roberts' ideas, and they met again on August 10 to form a committee to organize the first steps. Roberts described the group as consisting of 'men in the learned professions, merchants, and women of liberal tendencies'.[13] Many among them were hesitant as to how radically the organization should express its demands. Roberts described in his autobiography that this timidity caused disagreement about the name of the new organization.

> I wanted to call it the Jamaica Self-Government League, and I remember with some amusement that Malliet and others so feared to offend the Colonial Office by the use of the term 'self-government' in the name that we compromised on the Jamaica Progressive League. Our aims were unaffected, as may be judged by my preamble to the declaration then adopted.[14]

This anecdote highlights the novelty and boldness of Roberts' claim that Jamaica should be an independent nation. Indeed, it alienated some of the initially interested persons and caused them to withdraw from the group. Malliet was one of them, and he 'refused the nomination as secretary and dropped out of the picture'. In his autobiography, Roberts speculated that 'unfriendly critics said that he was an agent of the British Consulate General, paid to observe Jamaican activities in Harlem. If so, he had already learned enough to file his report on us'.[15]

A core group nevertheless continued the initiative. On September 1, the Jamaica Progressive League was officially launched in the hall of the Jamaica Benevolent Association and Roberts was elected president.[16] W.A. Domingo became its first vice president, and many of Domingo's fellow activists from his activist days in the Harlem Renaissance were elected to executive positions in the Board of Directors: Ethelred Brown became its long-serving secretary, and Jaime O'Meally and Theodore Burrell served as directors. In an article published in 1938, Domingo explained that the radical anti-colonialist connotation of Roberts' proposal in particular attracted the activists in Harlem, and he described the demand for self-government as:

> ...a bold challenge to the British system of colonial government that is based upon the theory of 'the white man's burden'. It is the contention

of the League that the time is long past when West Indians should tamely continue to accept and endure the anomalies of anachronistic Crown colony rule. The time has arrived when a breach must be made in the debasing and oppressive system of government which has fettered the political ambitions of a virile and civilized people for decades.[17]

This fundamental and outspoken critique of a racist and oppressive colonial government marked the foundation of the anti-colonial activities of the Progressive League.

The founding members of the Progressive League were not only men; a small number of women were among them, and some held important offices, like Ivy Bailey-Essien, the second vice president.[18] Yet, they produced no pamphlets, articles or political statements, thus, their particular impact is difficult to assess. The accepted gender roles of the time seem to have directed their activities to supportive roles, as the founding of the 'Ladies Auxiliary' in 1938 reflects. This subgroup of the Progressive League was set up with the purpose to 'identify needy projects in Jamaica, and to support them financially and morally', and organized fundraising activities like bus rides and dances, which affirms that women mainly remained in the second row of the organization, and generally were less visible than the men.[19]

The members of the Progressive League agreed upon a constitution that outlined the basic aims and goals of the new organization.[20] The analysis of this central document reveals some of the theoretical foundations on which its nationalism was based. It is remarkable that the basic nationalist principle on which the migrants developed their claims was a territorial definition of the nation. The preamble outlined the primary aim of the Progressive League:

> Firmly believing that any people that has seen its generations come and go on the same soil is, in fact, a nation, the Jamaica Progressive League pledges itself to work for the attainment of self government for Jamaica, so that the country may take its rightful place as a member of the British Commonwealth of Nations.[21]

The nationalism of the Progressive League was inspired by implications of natural law theory and religion. In an early pamphlet, Roberts stated:

> The inhabitants of Jamaica are, in fact, a people; for national entity is a gift of God to every society that has seen its generations come and go on the same soil for centuries. The awakening of a consciousness of nationality is what is needed today.[22]

This basic idea was the guiding principle on which activities were based.

The Progressive League is an early example of a transnational concept of the nation that consciously included expatriates. Its members still called Jamaica 'home', evidence that they still had a strong attachment to their country of birth.

Under colonialism, they felt national consciousness was dormant and believed that it should be awakened. This assumption legitimized the avant-garde role the Progressive League assumed and motivated its educational work. They explicitly hoped to 'stimulate among Jamaicans in the United States and other foreign countries a keen interest in home affairs'. However, Jamaicans 'at home' would not always agree with this transnational concept of the nation. Several times, the Progressive League was confronted with sentiments that it was out of touch with local opinion and that as an organization based abroad, it was not in the position to speak for Jamaicans on the island.

The first article of the Progressive League's central document aimed at democratization and demanded 'universal suffrage and the removal of qualifications for candidates for public office'.[23] This claim was directed against the restrictive voting system which excluded the majority of Jamaicans from the polls and from political positions. The next demand, 'the right of labour unions to function legally', protested against the restrictive labour legislation that provided no security for striking labourers. Prominently introduced, this second demand highlighted the Progressive League's concern for better working and living conditions for the masses as a basis for national unity between all classes. Further, the Progressive League aimed to 'study the economic and social problems of the Island and press for necessary reforms', and wished to 'foster inter-Caribbean trade and commerce, and all other relations which tend to bring about a closer union of the British West Indian countries'. This statement suggested economic cooperation between the islands, but allowed no interpretation of the advocacy of a political federation.

The third point of the declaration addressed the cultural dimension of nationalism. It aimed to 'encourage study of the history, geography, and literature of Jamaica, and give aid to all forms of artistic expression by the people'. The Progressive League regarded cultural nationalism as one of the most important tools to inspire national consciousness of Jamaicans, who had been indoctrinated with British patriotism and demands for loyalty to the Empire over centuries. Consequently, the aim to provide a nationalist education inspired many concrete actions, programmes and writings by which the Progressive League tried to incite nationalism in Jamaica.

W. Adolphe Roberts and the Idea for a Movement for Self-Government

The experience of migration and its role in the development of anti-colonial nationalism is one of the central themes of this book. Numerous scholars researching anti-colonial movements observed that important connections existed between migration experiences and the development of anti-colonial

Origins of the Jamaica Progressive League

thought and pointed to transnational influences that inspired a new way of thinking.[24] The Jamaican case provides an example for the influence of migrants who, after being exposed to different influences that impacted their thinking on race, nation and empire, started an anti-colonial movement. What exactly were these experiences that changed the attitudes of the migrants toward Jamaica? What influences inspired the migrants to challenge loyalty to the British Empire and to start thinking in nationalist terms?

A close look at the biographies of the most prominent founders of the Jamaica Progressive League illuminates the sources that inspired their nationalist thinking. One of the most important factors was their residency in the United States, a republic surrounded by other independent countries that all shared a past colonial experience. Furthermore, the contact with other Caribbeans and African Americans in Harlem, the exposure to different concepts of race and racial discrimination and the demonstration of international black solidarity in the activist circles in Harlem were decisive influences. As opposed to the imperial education system they had encountered in their island homes, the Jamaican emigrants had access to profound knowledge of black history at Harlem's street university. Further, they were exposed to Socialist ideas with a strong anti-imperialist component and to other anti-colonial movements that demanded independence for African countries, Ireland or India. All of these experiences were instrumental in shaping the outlook of those migrants who became founding members of the Progressive League in 1936, for instance Domingo, Ethelred Brown, James O'Meally and brothers Ben and Theodore Burrell.

Despite the anti-colonial positions many of the radicals of the Harlem scene had developed, the idea to form a nationalist organization to press demands for self-government in Jamaica did not develop directly within the Harlem network. While the rich experience the migrants had collected in a variety of different organizations, such as the development of analytical, writing and oratory skills, the exposure to anti-colonial ideas, fundamental critique of capitalist society, and, finally, disappointment with Socialism, Communism and Black Nationalism, had helped to prepare a fertile ground for the founding of the Jamaica Progressive League, it was W. Adolphe Roberts who initiated the Progressive League.

Although Roberts had also moved to the US in the early twentieth century, the white Jamaican had become a naturalized US citizen and was not part of the radical milieu in Harlem. He had travelled extensively and was strongly influenced by republican ideas. There is no evidence, however, that Jamaica had played any major role during the better part of his adult life, and he was already 50 years old when he launched the Progressive League.

Who was this man, the pioneer of self-government for Jamaica? What were the experiences and ideas that provided the decisive impetus for the formation of the movement demanding the decolonization of Jamaica? Walter Adolphe Roberts, historian, patriot and journalist, was born on October 15, 1886 in Kingston, but spent many of his childhood days in Mandeville.[25] He described himself as 'mainly of Celtic descent with a mixture of a little English and a little French blood'.[26] His father exercised an important formative influence on his political outlook.[27] Due to a lack of funding to send his son abroad, he homeschooled the young Roberts and instilled in him a fascination for the republics on the American continents. Further, he exposed him to the history of Latin American freedom movements, especially the independence struggle of the Cuban people. Roberts' father sympathized so strongly with the neighbouring island's fight for independence that he tried to go to Cuba to lend his support in the war.[28] Although his father's attempt failed, it inspired Roberts to write the novel, *The Single Star*, that tells the story of a Jamaican who participated in the Cuban war for independence in the 1890s.[29]

In his book *Six Great Jamaicans*, Roberts paid tribute to his father by dedicating the book to him, stating that he had been the first who 'taught me to love history and encouraged me to write it'.[30] The type of education to which Roberts' father had exposed him laid an early foundation for his high regard for men like Simón Bolívar, José Martí, and Toussaint L'Ouverture and their anti-colonial ideas.[31] Hence, Roberts was familiar with the political and historical background of the region from an early age. He developed a Pan-American outlook that made him wonder why Jamaica, surrounded by independent republics, had never demanded its own independence. His nationalist thinking was further inspired when he started to question the legitimacy of the political system of Crown Colony government in Jamaica. In 1937, Roberts recalled: 'I started in journalism on the *Daily Gleaner* of Kingston, Jamaica, my first assignment being to cover the Legislative Council. The farcical nature of the proceedings converted me to self-government for the island, and in this cause I have been interested ever since.'[32] In another speech, he referred to his disgust for the undemocratic nature of the Legislative Council under Crown Colony government and 'the idea of having nominated puppets to supply the Governor with votes to override the voices of elected representatives of the people!'[33]

Yet, since his time working for the *Daily Gleaner* from 1902 until his migration in 1904, more than 30 years would pass before his critique of the political situation in Jamaica would materialize into concrete action. In the meantime, he focused on his career as a journalist, poet and writer and was mainly concerned with his literary interests. In 1913, Roberts went to Paris and worked as a war reporter for the *Brooklyn Eagle*, for which he continued to work after he returned to the US in 1917. During this time, he edited the literary magazine *Ainslee's*, launched his own journal, the short-lived *American Parade* and published numerous poems, short stories and travel reports.³⁴

In 1930, Roberts felt compelled to write a non-fiction book about Jamaica and started to conduct research on Henry Morgan, the notorious buccaneer and Governor of Jamaica. In order to gather material for his study, he visited Jamaica after 16 years of absence.³⁵ John Aarons was right when he emphasized the profound influence of this study that inspired his nationalism and prepared the ground for his later political activities.³⁶ When the book was published in 1933, Roberts attached an appendix entitled 'Self-Government in Jamaica', that contained a first public manifestation of Roberts' nationalist perspective.³⁷ It already included many of the arguments Roberts later presented when he founded the Jamaica Progressive League.³⁸ For example, he harshly criticized the lack of responsibility in the system of Crown Colony government and complained: 'Jamaicans have worn the veneer of a superimposed northern attitude of thought unsuited to children of the tropics, and have allowed their land to be ruled as a Crown Colony far beyond the moment in history when the right to complete local self-government should have been reasserted'.³⁹

Roberts assumed a freedom-loving spirit of the inhabitants of the region that was suppressed by the acceptance of British rule. He regarded self-government as a natural right and encouraged Jamaicans to fight for it. Between May and June 1932, Roberts stayed in Jamaica to conduct research for his study on Morgan.⁴⁰ He later told a story of his visit that would foreshadow the firm opposition that his anti-colonial ideas would meet. One day in the West India Reference Library, Roberts' old friend Herbert G. de Lisser, editor of the *Daily Gleaner* and a staunch conservative, asked him about the object of his research. He remembered his response that it was 'material to buttress an argument favouring a new political movement in Jamaica…the long awakening autonomist sentiment was long overdue'.⁴¹

De Lisser's reaction was definite. He remarked: 'That is the greatest nonsense on earth…There will never be such a political party here. The people are not interested, and if the thing threatened to come up I would prevent it…I tell you, it shall not occur except over my dead body'. This offered a foretaste of de Lisser's firm resistance to Roberts' ideas. Indeed, the *Gleaner* editor was right in guessing that the idea of Jamaica becoming independent would not be received with enthusiasm in Jamaica. However, Roberts was convinced that '[t]he present period of unconcern is simply a phenomenon, an interlude. Even more than most peoples, West Indians have politics in their blood'. Yet, Roberts' romanticizing anthropological assessment of an alleged political character of the 'West Indian peoples' would not be reflected in the local reactions to the propaganda of the Progressive League.

The trip to Jamaica put the island back on his radar. Shortly before he returned to the United States, he gave an interview to the *Daily Gleaner*, in which he enthusiastically shared: 'I have been rejuvenated, and my imagination of the tropics which has been somewhat dull, has been intensified and revived during my stay here'.[42] He commented on the political situation in Jamaica, his first public remark in this direction. Roberts wondered about the low political interest of the people and the absence of many eligible voters from the elections. 'It is very astonishing to me to find this state of affairs existing here, when I think of smaller countries like Costa Rica and Salvador in Central America, where the people take an intense interest in party politics; and I hope the day is not far when Jamaicans will change their policy and take an interest in party politics'.[43]

This statement demonstrated the extent to which Roberts' views were shaped by his regional perspective. He had finally found his mission. From then on, reflections about the political condition and the form of government took firm roots in Roberts' thinking and provoked questions as to how it could be changed. And it would not be long before his thoughts would manifest into concrete political action.

In January 1934, Roberts made a short stop in Jamaica while on a cruise through the Caribbean. He used the opportunity to publicly call for self-government. In an interview with the *Daily Gleaner*, Roberts openly declared himself in favour of self-government.[44] He criticized that the planter class had voluntarily surrendered the old constitution after the uprising in Morant Bay and wondered why the people did not even protest against this curtailing of their freedom. He was disturbed that Jamaicans still accepted Crown Colony rule without serious objection. To counter the inertia he had diagnosed, Roberts encouraged nationalist education and the teaching of Jamaican history to inspire a 'National Spirit and Jamaican Culture'. He proposed that Jamaica should become a Dominion and proclaimed that he '…believed in the British Empire, but he also believed in Self-Government within the Empire, because it was only with Self-Government could the people hope to develop an intelligent National Spirit'.

Roberts argued that viewed from a regional perspective, Jamaica was far behind other countries in the region in nationalist spirit. He was critical of the fact that there was no unity among the political representatives and stated that he: '…saw no reason why some group could not take up this question of Self-Government for the island'. This statement expressed in January 1934 is the first articulation that indicated that Roberts advocated organizing such a political group. Yet, Roberts sensed that the mentality of a majority of Jamaicans could hamper such an effort. The *Gleaner* reported that Roberts '…did not believe in any radical political doctrine…knowing the loyalty of his fellow countrymen as he did. What the country needed was self-education in the practice of political rights and liberty'.

This may have been the reason why Roberts advocated Dominion status for Jamaica, and not a radical break from all ties with Great Britain. However, Roberts' regional outlook suggest that the objective of staying connected with Great Britain through the Commonwealth was rather a concession to the strong loyalty of Jamaicans to the British Empire than an expression of his personal view, in which he always saw Jamaica as an integral part of the Americas.

Roberts' early nationalist call had a first impact on Rupert Meikle, president of the Quill and Ink Club, who attempted to popularize Roberts' ideas. He admired Roberts as a 'distinguished son of this soil, well known in literary circles of the north'[45] and was convinced that it was an important task to keep 'a broad and well-fed flame of intellectual activity' and, using Roberts' phraseology, urged that the Quill and Ink Club should help to 'build up a definite cultural background peculiarly Jamaican and a National Pride'.[46]

In the 1930s, his nationalism was further inspired by the political developments in the eastern Caribbean, where calls for self-government and federation were becoming increasingly popular.[47] In an article in the renowned US journal *Current History*, Roberts presented his views on the political and social conditions in the Caribbean.[48] He approvingly referred to T.A. Marryshow in Grenada and Captain Arthur Cipriani in Trinidad and Tobago, who both led movements for more political representation and a self-governing federation of the various British Caribbean islands.[49] Roberts appreciated the impulse toward self-government and emphasized that he was glad that the movement was not linked to Socialism. The agitation in the Eastern Caribbean resulted in the appointment of a Royal Commission in September 1932 to enquire about the political situation in the island colonies in the Caribbean. The report approved the idea of a loose form of federation of the colonies in the region. However, Roberts showed no enthusiasm for the idea of federating the islands in the British Caribbean, especially not for including Jamaica in the scheme. From this early point, Roberts was opposed to Federation as a solution for Jamaica, and argued that the country, like Trinidad and Tobago, was equipped to stand alone as an independent nation state.[50]

In the course of 1936, Roberts' critique slowly transformed from theory into a concrete plan for action. Roberts was convinced that national consciousness could be aroused in Jamaica, although he was mindful of the firm opposition that could be expected.[51] Early in 1936, Roberts gave his first public speech criticizing the political conditions in the British Caribbean at the University of Puerto Rico.[52]

In the summer of 1936, Roberts decided to transform his ideas into political activism and felt that he should start by introducing his vision to launch an organization demanding self-government for Jamaica to Jamaican migrants in New York. This migrant organization should carry nationalist propaganda to

Jamaica to arouse nationalism in the island and demand an end of colonial rule. In his autobiography Roberts remembered the time shortly before the founding of the Progressive League and described it as follows:

> On my return to New York, a magazine ordered from me a long series of articles unconnected with politics. This freed me from financial worries, and I gave all the time I could spare to the question of Jamaica. I concluded that I must look for support among the thousands of the islanders living in Harlem. I had few acquaintances in that Negro center. I had paid no attention to the recent activities there of Marcus Garvey, a Jamaican by birth but a man who agitated along international racial lines. What had I to do with his dreams of a black African Empire?[53]

Indeed, Roberts' background was completely different compared to that of the other future members. Roberts regarded himself as a liberal. He had nothing to do with Garvey's Black Nationalism and knew little about the radical black Socialists in Harlem. His ideas were rooted in republican ideals, inspired by a distinctively regional perspective. Unlike W.A. Domingo, Ethelred Brown and James O'Meally, Roberts had never shown any tendency to a radical critique of capitalism.

Wilfred A. Domingo and the 'Black Tropics' in Harlem

What about those who readily subscribed to Roberts' ideas? What were the experiences that had prepared Domingo, Brown, O'Meally and other founding members to join the Jamaica Progressive League? How was life for black Caribbean immigrants in Harlem? An examination of the biographies of some of the most prominent Progressive League leaders and of the environment that stimulated their intellectual and political development shows important similarities and reveals that they were all part of a surprisingly close-knit network in Harlem in the early twentieth century.

Wilfred A. Domingo was born on November 26, 1889 in Kingston.[54] Orphaned at an early age, he grew up with his uncle. Like so many people born in the Caribbean, he decided to seek his fortune abroad. In 1910, he decided to migrate to the US and moved to live with his sister in Boston. He first intended to study medicine, but discouraged by the racial barriers in the US, he changed his mind and moved to New York to explore the lively African American scene.[55] In Harlem, he worked as a post office clerk until the 1920s. This stable employment allowed him to engage in political activities that soon became a central driving force in the direction of his life. In Harlem, Domingo developed into an outstanding and radical intellectual, who actively engaged in the 'New Negro'[56] movement, long before he would become one of the key figures of Jamaican anti-colonial nationalism. During these years, Domingo became friends with many people in whom he would find his closest allies. Among them were not only Jamaicans, but also African Americans and emigrants from other islands who would later help him to press the cause of Jamaican nationalism along lines of international black solidarity.

Domingo described Harlem as a '…Negro community of approximately 400,000 people, including immigrants from every state in the union, every island of the American tropics, as well as Africans'.[57] Attracted by the industrial growth and facilitated by improved means of overseas transportation, about 40,000 immigrants mainly from the Anglophone Caribbean had settled in New York.[58] In 1930, Caribbeans made up about a quarter of Harlem's population and their impact was so remarkable, that Franklin D. Roosevelt called Harlem the 'Capital of the Caribbean'.[59] In a later reflection in 1944, Domingo emphasized: 'West Indians are an important factor in Harlem life. Most of them have adjusted themselves to their environments. They live in all parts of a physically pleasant Black City…There are probably more Jamaicans living in Harlem than in Montego Bay, Port Antonio and Spanish Town combined'.[60]

In Harlem, not everybody was privileged to be a part of the artistic and literary scene and the glitter and glamour of nightlife in bars and cabarets. Racism and poverty affected many Harlemites. The 1920s and 1930s have rightly been characterized as a social, economic and political nadir for black America.[61] American society was still deeply permeated by racism, segregated and unequal.[62] In the black communities, churches and benevolent associations played an important role providing some degree of social security.[63]

In contrast to the experience of Roberts as a white Jamaican, the black immigrants from the Caribbean faced discrimination and even more difficulties to climb the social ladder than in the societies they had left. This disappointment often stood in harsh contrast to the expectations with which they had reached Harlem; a place that many associated with positive images of a 'Black Mecca', a 'Negro Metropolis'.[64] Disappointed in the American dream with its promise of prosperity and freedom, many African Americans and Caribbeans developed a militant response.[65] Continued outbreaks of open physical violence against black people in the United States radicalized both groups. It was in this atmosphere that a new spirit of self-consciousness developed and found expression in numerous black organizations and newspapers. To some degree, the common suffering encouraged a sense of solidarity and led to the organization of joint protest marches and a call for self-defence.[66] In the radicalization of the movement, immigrants from the Caribbean often played a decisive role.

However, not all migrants from the Caribbean reacted with solidarity. Some islanders attempted to emphasize their West Indian heritage and tried to separate themselves from African Americans. Many maintained a strong ethnic, or more precisely, national identity, as Jamaicans, Trinidadians or Barbadians. Some still clung to their feeling of superiority as British subjects. Accordingly, some of the immigrants accentuated their distinctiveness and tried to use it as an economic advantage, but in most cases, the colour line prevented them from finding employment suiting their training and education.[67] Despite the economic competition and occasionally hostile sentiments between Caribbeans and African Americans, an increasing number of immigrants from the Caribbean developed a feeling of solidarity and joined the fight against racism and discrimination. In her study on Caribbean immigrants in Harlem, Historian Irma Watkins-Owens emphasized that '...immigrants and natives of African descent...struggled to define the nature of their bonds to one another in New York during this period. In countless ways their historic encounter produced an interchange of ideas, people, and institutions that made Harlem, black metropolis, the centre of the African world'.[68]

In his famous essay, *Gift of the Black Tropics*, written in 1925, Wilfred A. Domingo pointed to the specific experience with racism in the United States that predisposed those immigrants from the Caribbean to more radical reactions:

> Unlike their American brothers the islanders are free from those traditions that bind them to any party and, as a consequence are independent to the point of being radical. Indeed, it is they who largely compose the few political and economic radicals in Harlem; without them the genuine radical movement among New York Negroes would be unworthy of attention.[69]

Although Domingo may have carried his point a bit too far, the disproportionally high number of Caribbeans among the most radical activists in Harlem is nevertheless striking. In the past two decades, scholars have increasingly highlighted the important role of the Caribbean immigrants, after it had been overlooked in earlier accounts.[70]

In his important study on Caribbean radicalism in the US in the early twentieth century, historian Winston James offers some explanation for the radicalism of the immigrants. In particular, he points to,

> ...their majority consciousness, their prior political and organizational experience, their extensive prior experience of travel and migration; a politically protected status in the United States (at least for those from the British Caribbean) as subjects of the British Crown; a somewhat lesser attachment to the Christian faith and Christian churches; and educational and occupational attainments generally beyond the reach of Afro-Americans.[71]

The experience of the harsh and openly displayed type of racist discrimination against everybody with a dark skin complexion along the 'one-drop rule'[72] stood in stark contrast to the more subtle and differentiated type of discrimination and oppression in the British colonial system. In particular, those immigrants who were of light skin complexion were used to a privileged position that derived from the gradual system of racial discrimination in the Caribbean colonies that helped to maintain the oppressive system of the white colonizers who were a minority in the population.⁷³ Domingo sums up:

> Forming a racial majority in their own countries and not being accustomed to discrimination expressly felt as racial, they rebel against the 'color line' as they find it in America...Color plays a part but it is not the prime determinant of advancement; hence the deep feeling of resentment when the 'color line' legal or customary, is met and found to be a barrier to individual progress. For this reason the West Indian has thrown himself wholeheartedly into the fight against lynching, discrimination and the other disabilities from which Negroes in America suffer.⁷⁴

While most of the immigrants tried to assimilate into the broader American society, they had to recognize quickly that assimilation meant in fact assimilation into '*black* America'.⁷⁵ These factors help to explain the general tendency to radical activism and how they contributed to challenge the imperial identity that many Jamaicans had deeply internalized and which impeded the development of anti-colonialism in the island, and which Domingo vividly recalled to have held when he arrived.⁷⁶ The contact with other African Americans, Africans and Caribbeans in Harlem, in particular, illuminated the exploitive nature of colonialism and the power of racism on an international scale. It was especially this insight that caused some to abandon positive identifications with the British Empire, inspired anti-colonial attitudes, helped overcome an initial arrogance, and lastly, inspire black solidarity.

Watkins-Owens emphasizes that due to their colonial background, the Caribbean immigrants contributed a particular 'anti-colonial/imperialist and international outlook' and paid special attention to 'interracial class and colorism issues' in their contributions to various black newspapers.⁷⁷ Domingo's writings of this period are good examples of this special contribution, as he developed a keen interest in Socialism and Black Nationalism and began to publish in many of the black and Socialist newspapers. Domingo testified to the productive exchange of ideas and strategies: 'Harlem is, as everyone knows, a great meeting place. Negroes, coloured people, or whatever you dare to call us, meet there from all parts of the world. And being a gregarious lot we fraternize and exchange experiences and opinions'.⁷⁸ These contacts, he claimed, resulted in the recognition that many of their problems were similar and that the solution would depend on a fruitful cooperation between 'the two branches of Anglo-Saxonized Negroes'.⁷⁹ In the 1940s, Domingo claimed in retrospective:

> ...both peoples, Americans and West Indians, have been the gainers and in the ultimate sense, the United States. For small though the contribution of Jamaicans must be to the sum total of Americans' civilization, a contribution has been made nevertheless. That contribution has been for the Great Republic whose destiny is now hopefully mixed up with that of Jamaica and the entire Caribbean Region.[80]

This statement signified Domingo's regional perspective and forecasts the close connectivity that developed between the Caribbean and the United States, the transnational space that Orlando Patterson describes as the 'West Atlantic Regional Cosmos'.[81]

Phillip Kasinitz supports the thesis that for many authors, poets and political activists from the Caribbean, 'nothing could have been further from their intentions than self-seclusion in West Indian enclaves; it was precisely Harlem's diversity and excitement that had attracted them'.[82] Also, James shows that there was no fundamental antagonism between West Indians and African Americans in the radical movement.[83] Domingo argued: 'Many of them [West Indian Immigrants] devoutly read the coloured newspapers and share the attitude of coloured America on racial questions. Among themselves they may criticize their American cousins, even as the latter doubtless criticize them, but on all things racial both groups instinctively close their ranks'.[84]

Conflicts among black activists were rather based on different ideological positions than on nationality or ethnicity.[85] The radical 'New Negro' movement was heavily inspired by two different currents of thought, Black Nationalism and Socialism, although some immigrants from the Caribbean tried to combine and merge the two approaches. Yet, there were fundamental differences between the two streams of thought, in particular, regarding the question on how to end racial discrimination.

Black Nationalism already had a long tradition in the US and played an important role in the formation of the New Negro movement in Harlem, preparing the ground for later separatist movements like the Nation of Islam and the Black Panthers.[86] It was fuelled by the powerful agitation of Jamaican immigrant Marcus Garvey and his mass movement, the Universal Negro Improvement Association (UNIA).[87] Garvey popularized the idea of repatriation to Africa, and slogans like 'Africa for the Africans' rose to unprecedented popularity. Black nationalists had no hope that assimilation could bring about an end to racism, and therefore, recommended black self-esteem, self-reliance, black-owned capitalist ventures and black solidarity between the classes. In sharp contrast to this analysis, Socialism highlighted the oppression of workers of all colours all over the world and demanded class solidarity above race solidarity.

The second important stream of thought, Socialism, put the emphasis on a class-based analysis of the capitalist world. Young black radical Socialists believed in an equal world order that would put an end to discrimination based on race or class. They understood capitalism and racism as linked, seeing the only cure to racism in a proletarian revolution. Anti-imperial components of Socialist theory, for example, Lenin's emphasis on the right to self-determination of all colonial peoples, was especially appealing to immigrants from the Caribbean.[88]

These different approaches of 'race first' versus 'class first' ideologies often led to bitter rivalries and personal animosities. However, the two were not as contradictory as they might have appeared at first view. A closer look reveals how intertwined the two paradigms often were, and that many activists could be found on both sides of the fence, sometimes even at the same time. In particular, the migrants from the Caribbean, including Domingo, eagerly tried to merge race and class approaches. During his time in Harlem, Domingo was not only a fierce opponent of racism and colonialism, he was also a convinced and active Socialist, like many of the Caribbean radical intellectuals of his time, and actively supported the Socialist Party of America and other leftist groups.

One of the main inspirational sources for this combination of thought was Hubert H. Harrison, who saw no contradiction between Black Nationalism and Socialism. A brilliant author, orator, educator and political activist, and described by historian Joel A. Rogers as 'one of America's greatest minds', the immigrant from St Croix, Virgin Islands, came to the United States as a 17-year-old orphan in 1900 and moved to New York City.[89] Winston James also emphasizes that Harrison was 'a major inspiration for two powerful and seemingly incompatible currents of black radicalism in Harlem: revolutionary socialism, on the one hand, and radical black nationalism, on the other'.[90] In the first decades of the twentieth century, he became a mentor for many of the political activists and pioneered Harlem's lively soap-box oratory scene.

Since 1911, Harrison was associated with the Socialist Party. However, disappointed by the party's neglect of the special situation of black people, Harrison soon turned to Black Nationalist ideas without abandoning his Socialist convictions.[91] Inspired and encouraged by Harrison's sharp analytical thinking, his excellent oratory skills and his compassionate dedication to the education of the people living in Harlem, many young radicals followed in his footsteps as orators and activists and tried to integrate both racial solidarity and Socialist elements in their thinking.

The sources do not reveal how Domingo and Harrison met, but quite likely it was at one of Harrison's fiery speeches in Harlem. Harrison, who was affectionately called the 'street professor', lectured on various subjects like the relevance of Socialism for the liberation of black people, the Socialist Party in America, on

African history, colonialism, world events and local American conditions.[92] Domingo emphasized the importance of Harlem for his personal intellectual development and used the analogy of Harlem's streets as his university:

> Harlem is my alma mater. I found it a wonderful university. There I learnt a great deal about the realities of life. It is true that I received many hard knocks while learning, but on the whole the experience made me a fuller, abler, more competent person…An important part of the education I got in Harlem was imparted to me by professors who had themselves graduated from another famous school of learning – the University of Experience.[93]

Domingo himself soon became one of Harlem's most popular street orators, as well as an organizer for the Socialist Party and an active member in various organizations. He was assistant secretary of Harrison's 'Afro-American Liberty League', which was founded in June 1916.[94] In addition, Cyril V. Briggs, founder of the African Blood Brotherhood, also gathered first organizing experiences with Harrison, and it is quite likely that Domingo and Briggs knew each other through Harrison. Around this time, Domingo met many associates and friends that soon became a close-knit network of political activists. Irma Watkins-Owens dates the meeting of the group to 1917 and states that 'those who invented the Harlem street corner speaking tradition were self-educated, mostly Caribbean immigrants'.[95]

Their ties with the Socialist Party brought them in contact with African American thinkers and organizers like A. Philip Randolph and Chandler Owen.[96] From the inception of their radical magazine, *The Messenger*, in 1917, Domingo was assistant editor of the paper. Philip Foner stresses the militancy of the publication and claims that '[i]n its militancy, the Messenger was far in advance of anything up to that point in the history of black radicalism. In fact, it was even in advance of the very Socialist Party to which it advised its readers to turn'.[97]

At the same time, Domingo became involved in the 'Independent Political Council' led by Owen and Randolph. He was also engaged in the Socialist Party's educational institutions, the Rand School of Social Science and the Twenty-First Assembly District Socialist Club and helped to coordinate the mayoral campaign of Socialist Party candidate Morris Hillquit in 1917.[98]

Despite Domingo's cooperation and friendship with African American activists, the majority of Domingo's closest friends were of Caribbean origin. Joyce Moore Turner, historian and daughter of Richard B. Moore, presents a detailed description of the 'awesome foursome' that consisted of Domingo, Richard B. Moore, Cyril Briggs and Otto Huiswoud.[99] Despite their different island backgrounds, they cooperated in their political activism in different organizations and newspapers, and for many years, their friendship lasted through theoretical and organizational differences. Despite collaborations with other Caribbean immigrants and African Americans, Domingo was also active in the Jamaican immigrant community. For instance, he was co-founder of the Jamaica Benevolent Association in 1917 which provided basic social services, and in addition, functioned as a meeting place.[100]

Domingo's 'keen, analytical mind, acerbic writing style, and gregarious manner', soon placed him in the centre of radical activism of Caribbean immigrants in Harlem, and he was often contacted by new immigrants from Jamaica.[101] Amongst them was Marcus Garvey, who arrived in New York in 1916 and soon became an icon of the Black Nationalist movement. The immigrant immediately called upon his childhood friend and colleague from their common time in the National Club in Jamaica.[102] Already well respected in the Harlem milieu, Domingo introduced Garvey to some key persons like Harrison and arranged for Garvey's first public speech in Harlem and exposed him to the scene of political activists.[103] Domingo had introduced Garvey to a printer, Henry Rogowski, who agreed to publish his newspaper, *Negro World*, and Domingo became its first editor. At its peak, it had an estimated circulation of about 200,000 copies and connected the powerful international network of the UNIA with its numerous branches in nearly every US state, Canada, many South and Middle American countries, the Caribbean, Africa and Europe.[104] Domingo participated in meetings of the UNIA, delivered speeches and contributed most of the early editorials. Despite Domingo's Socialist beliefs, which he also expressed in his editorials, he edited the *Negro World* from August 1918 to July 1919.[105] However, after one year, the ideological differences between Garvey and Domingo resulted in a split, which turned into deep personal enmity. In the midst of the anti-communist 'Red Scare' campaign, Garvey distanced himself and the UNIA from any Socialist connection. After the break with Domingo, Garvey declared that the UNIA had no political associations with other groups or parties:

> Republicans, Democrats and Socialists are the same to us – they are all white men and to our knowledge, all of them join together and lynch and burn Negroes. We are Negroes, and we want it clearly understood that persons that endeavour to use the name of the Universal Negro Improvement Association or the name of the 'Negro World' for enhancing their individual political fortunes do so without the approval of the association or the management of the 'Negro World.[106]

Garvey had no sympathy for Domingo's efforts to merge Black Nationalism and Socialism into one powerful approach. In an editorial of the *Negro World* at the end of July 1919, Domingo affirmed his racial solidarity and stressed the relevance of unified action against racial discrimination:

It may be argued that race first is racial selfishness, and as such will not remove the reasons that called it into being; but this argument loses its validity when recognition is taken of the fact that certain problems seem to suggest their own remedies...To say that because Negroes are the victims of organized race first sentiment on part of white people they should not organize along lines of race first to defend themselves is to inferentially condone their present oppression and counsel meek submission to its perpetuation...In a world of wolves one should go armed, and one of the most powerful defensive weapons within the reach of Negroes is the practice of Race First in all parts of the world.[107]

However, this reaffirmation would not change Garvey's decision to break with Domingo.

Besides Domingo, other future founding members of the Progressive League had been active in Garvey's UNIA, like James O'Meally and the Burrell brothers. James O'Meally was a teacher at the prestigious Calabar High School and the second vice president of the local UNIA in Kingston.[108] O'Meally, as a representative for the Jamaican UNIA, took part in the huge UNIA conference in New York in 1921 where he was elected 'High Commissioner'. He was part of a delegation to Geneva in 1922 to convince the League of Nations to hand over the former territory of the German colony East Africa to the UNIA.[109] In 1924, O'Meally gave up his job in Jamaica to lead a UNIA delegation to prepare a settlement scheme in Liberia; however, the group was not allowed to land, as Liberia's president King had already agreed to sell large parts of the prospected land to the Firestone Rubber Company. The failure of this mission was a big blow to the Garvey movement.[110] By January 1925, O'Meally had broken with Garvey and the UNIA and filed a lawsuit against the UNIA for outstanding salaries amounting to over US$7,600, of which he got US$3,500. In the 1930s, he worked as a salesman at Domingo's import business – most likely they also knew each other from Jamaica, as Domingo had graduated from the same Calabar High School of which O'Meally was a teacher.[111]

The brothers Ben and Theodore Burrell, also future members of the Progressive League belonged to the UNIA in New York and had organized a black history youth club in Harlem. Ben Burrell, who co-authored the UNIA's Universal Ethiopian Anthem, had worked as a reporter for the *Jamaica Times* and had come to the United States in 1917.[112] However, the brothers did not stay long in the UNIA and soon joined Domingo and Briggs in the African Blood Brotherhood in 1919.

Immediately after the split between Domingo and Garvey, Domingo officially joined Owen and Randolph's *Messenger* as a contributing editor, where he could openly articulate his Socialist views. He lauded the Russian Revolution, but also condemned racism and emphasized the international dimension of black oppression. His arguments were based on a Marxist analysis of capitalism, that the 'favored few' were dominating the 'working class – white and black – and abuse the Negro race as a whole'.[113] Domingo complained: 'It is a regrettable and disconcerting anomaly that, despite their situation as the economic, political and social door mat of the world, Negroes do not embrace the philosophy of Socialism, and in greater numbers than they do now'.[114] Domingo believed that capitalism, racism and colonialism were the inextricably connected means of controlling the world and that Socialism was the solution to poverty and inequality. Domingo recognized the parallel situation of workers all over the world, insisting that '[the employers] interests are opposed to those of their employees. And colour or race makes no difference'.[115] He concluded that many African Americans failed to understand this fact and demanded that they should join the fight of the working class.[116]

Domingo's political thought exemplifies how the seemingly contradictory concepts of Black Nationalism, Socialism, nationalism and internationalism merged together into one powerful approach. Socialism and a strong anti-racism appear as two sides of the same coin. In order to understand the ideas and philosophies of many of the black intellectuals of that period, this relation between anti-racism and anti-capitalism is important.

In practice, the effort to combine radical Socialist and anti-racist positions increasingly turned into a dilemma. Domingo's experience with Garvey showed that there was no place for Socialism in the doctrines of the Black Nationalists. Likewise, Domingo's efforts to increase the sensibility of the Socialist Party towards the particular problems of black people were in vain. In a pamphlet, Domingo argued that 'failure to make negroes class conscious is the greatest potential menace to the establishment of socialism in America whether by the means of the ballot or through a dictatorship of the proletariat, and in this must all Socialists and radicals…see their danger'.[117] Yet, when Domingo and his fellows invited Rand School director Algernon Lee to one of the weekly sessions of the People's Educational Forum,[118] Lee argued that black liberation would automatically follow the implementation of Socialism, and reaffirmed that the Socialist Party was not willing to pay special attention to race.[119] After Domingo and his comrades were called to the Socialist Party's headquarters and questioned why they had attacked Lee, the group collectively left the Socialist Party.[120]

Some years earlier, Hubert H. Harrison had already failed in a similar attempt to influence the Socialists. Harrison used a very similar argument in his essay 'Socialism and the Negro'.[121] Yet, like Harrison, Domingo and his comrades were harshly disappointed by the reactions of the Socialists.

It was a logical step for the young radicals, all sufficiently experienced in political activism and public lecturing, political organizing and writing, to launch their own organization and papers in which they could freely articulate their views. Shortly after the problems between the Caribbean radicals and the Socialist Party occurred in late 1918/early 1919, the African Blood Brotherhood (ABB) was founded under the leadership of Cyril V. Briggs in Spring 1919.[122] Moore Turner describes the ABB's efforts as the 'evolution of the movement toward an acceptance of communist philosophy while uniquely welding socialism and Black liberation'.[123] The membership of the ABB consisted predominantly of migrants of Caribbean descent; many of whom participated in the above described network. They joined forces in an effort to launch an organization that explicitly aimed to combine Socialism and the emphasis on race.[124] The organization was short-lived, yet, the experience was important for its members and deepened the friendship and collaboration between the group of immigrants.

Although there is no material evidence available that allows reconstructing how the ABB started, it is quite likely that Domingo was involved in the idea to found an organization to merge Black Nationalism and Socialism. Domingo already knew Briggs from their cooperation in Harrison's Liberty League and had cooperated with him on the *Crusader News Service*.[125] He was also involved in editing Briggs's newspaper, the *Crusader*, which became the ABB's organ.[126] The Burrell brothers, as well, were contributing editors of Briggs's *Crusader*.[127] It is remarkable that several future Jamaica Progressive League members played an important role in the Supreme Council of the ABB: Domingo as director for Propaganda and Publicity of the ABB, Theodore Burrell as secretary and Ben Burrell as director for historical research.[128] Probably the disappointment that the merger of race and class approaches was not very successful prepared them for shifting their activities back to Jamaica, when Roberts came to them and proposed the founding of an anti-colonial pressure group.

In 1920, Domingo started his own weekly magazine, the *Emancipator*, which also attempted to unite race and class consciousness. Many fellow activists of his network helped in the venture and contributed articles.[129] The paper had a clear international outlook and aimed to provide 'a scientific chart and compass' for black people 'in relation to national and international social, and political movements'.[130] It provided news on Africa, the Caribbean and the American continent and outlined its purpose in the first issue on March 13, 1920 as follows: '...to free the human family, white, brown, yellow and black, from the bonds of ignorance, race prejudice and wage slavery, to bring the Negro race in particular an emancipation more complete, more genuine, than that for which our fathers fought and died fifty years ago'.[131] The paper had a clear anti-colonial standpoint and championed 'the cause of the oppressed of all lands; the right of workers everywhere to secure the full social value of the products of their toil; the prescriptive right of native Africans to their ancestral domains'.[132] However, due to a lack of funding, the *Emancipator* only lasted a couple of months.

The direction that Domingo's paper took was indicative of his future anti-colonial activities in the Progressive League, yet a special focus on Jamaica was still missing. His radical Socialist positions came to be increasingly combined with his critique of the international dimension of black oppression and various forms of colonialism. This mix of a consequent anti-racism of international scope and a Socialist outlook following Lenin's proclamations of the right to self-determination inspired the anti-colonial nationalism that led Domingo to throw himself in the forefront of the struggle when Roberts approached him with the idea to start a group demanding an end of colonial rule in Jamaica.

Ethelred Brown and the Harlem Unitarian Church

The first issue of Domingo's *Emancipator* announced the arrival of the Jamaican, Revd E. Ethelred Brown, prominent pastor and intellectual, and future secretary of the Jamaica Progressive League.[133] Like Garvey before, Brown contacted Domingo on his arrival in Harlem at the end of February 1920, asking for help in the new country. Brown was a close friend of the family of Domingo's wife Eulalie.[134] Domingo helped the newcomer to adjust in New York and supported his effort to establish a Unitarian Church in Harlem, which became a central meeting place for the group of radical Caribbeans in Harlem.

In Jamaica, Ethelred Brown was a well-known and respected personality.[135] From his childhood days, the church played an important role in his life. He developed an interest in Unitarianism through books, although no Unitarian congregation existed in Jamaica at that time.[136] First, he chose to pursue a career in the civil service of Jamaica. After initial success as Clerk of the Treasury in Spanish Town, he was suddenly dismissed in 1907, shortly before he was to get another promotion.[137] Like others before him, the disappointment led him to criticize the Colonial Government, and it came as no surprise that his first speech at a Progressive League meeting was on racial discrimination in the civil service.[138]

After his dismissal, Brown decided to become a Unitarian minister. The president of the Unitarian Meadville Theological School admitted him, but informed him that he was required to relocate to Chicago in the US to attend the school. Again, race was an important matter. He was warned that a successful career in a white denomination would not be very likely, as there were not yet any black ordained Unitarian ministers – before Brown became the first one in 1912.[139] After his studies in the US, he returned to Jamaica and tried to establish a Unitarian church.[140] Despite the lack of financial support from the parent church in the US, Brown succeeded in establishing the Unitarian church in Jamaica, first in Montego Bay and then in Kingston. But the absence of official recognition and support hampered its success.[141]

In his years in Jamaica, Brown showed keen interest in social questions, political organization and a worldly-oriented religion, an outlook which would continually determine his faith and shape his work. Despite many obstacles, he firmly believed that religion and work for the betterment of society were two sides of the same coin. He involved himself in various political and cultural initiatives, in Jamaica as well as in the United States, among them the Montego Bay Literary and Debating Society, which he founded after his return to Montego Bay in 1912 and of which he became president.[142] Brown was deeply concerned about the living conditions of workers in Jamaica. In 1913, he wrote a letter to the Colonial Secretary, suggesting minimum wages paid for government workers to set the general standard for the wage level in Jamaica.[143] In 1915, Brown advocated a cooperative form of Socialism at a meeting of the UNIA and pointed out:

> ...one of the greatest needs of this island is the quality of co-operation. At the very outset there must be a oneness of aim and purpose. In the next place successful co-operation requires mutual confidence among the people co-operating. As a people we are too much suspicious the one of the other.[144]

Brown blamed the widespread individualism, envy and distrust in the society as the greatest obstacles to prosperity. However, despite his praise of unity, Brown himself was not free of elitist attitudes. In the Liberal Association he founded in June 1915 to discuss a wide array of subjects ranging from science to theology, politics, economy to religion and ethics, the membership was restricted to those 'educationally qualified to take part in the proceedings'.[145] Brown emphasized that the purpose of the Liberal Association was not political; its aim was 'to awaken and to cultivate in its members and others the scientific frame of mind, which enables a man to approach every subject without prejudice and with the single desire to know the truth'.[146] Among its ranks were well-known personalities of Kingston's public scene, and two future founding members of the Jamaica Progressive League were also active in the group: James O'Meally, who once gave a lecture on 'Language and Literature in Spain',[147] and Ben Burrell, who spoke on 'Democracy' and 'Thought Forces'.[148]

In 1916, Brown initiated the founding of the Progressive Negro Association (PNA).[149] Putting a strong emphasis on race, it rivalled the UNIA, but was short-lived and of rather limited influence.[150] While labour disturbances occurred in Jamaica and other islands in the region in 1918/1919, Brown championed the cause of the workers. He published a profound analysis of the 'Labour Conditions in Jamaica' in the *Journal of Negro History*, in which he criticized the low wages and the politics of the government to import indentured labourers from Asia. He deplored the unacceptable living standard of peasants and the mass migration of Jamaicans. Brown insisted that '...the labourer, living in a country much

Origins of the Jamaica Progressive League

improved in many respects, is himself no better off than his forefathers in slavery. In truth, he is still an economic slave'.[151] He argued that the exodus of Jamaican labourers to Cuba made family life impossible for the workers. He harshly criticized the local government for the 'inertness which almost amounts to callous indifference'.[152]

Brown gathered further political experience as assistant secretary of the Jamaica League, a patriotic group with strong focus on the social conditions in the country, and was instrumental in the founding of a branch of the League in Montego Bay in 1917.[153] At a convention in August 1918, Brown described the organization as a 'brave and honest attempt to unite Jamaicans of all colour, of all creeds, and of all classes, for the benefit of Jamaica'.[154] The League further rested on mild Socialist ideas and aimed to 'stimulate and foster individual and co-operative ventures tending to the intellectual, economic, social and moral improvement of the people of this island'.[155] The *Daily Gleaner* reported on a meeting of the managing committee of the Jamaica League in 1919, at which Brown explained his attitude toward politics:

> If politics meant to study conditions, to plan betterments, to inspire service, and to instruct the people in those vital principles which are necessary for the upbuilding of a prosperous future, then was he not ashamed but rather proud of his entering into politics.[156]

When Brown decided to leave the country due to the lack of support from the Unitarian Church, the numerous organizations he was involved in expressed their deep regret.[157] Yet, Brown was not to be halted on his mission to find a way to successfully combine religion and political activities and to seek his fortune in the United States. On February 27, 1920, Brown arrived in New York with a firm purpose. 'I sailed from the island of Jamaica determined to establish a Unitarian Church in Harlem and all that mattered to me in March 1920 was that the venture should be launched without delay. And it was'.[158]

With the help of Domingo, who invited his closest friends, mainly fellow Socialists and political activists stemming from the Caribbean; the founding congregation gathered on March 7, 1920, only one week after Brown's arrival.[159] Initially, the church adopted the official name Harlem Community Church; after Hubert Harrison's death it adopted the name Hubert Harrison Memorial Church in 1928; later on, it was renamed the Harlem Unitarian Church (HUC).[160]

The membership consisted of more males than females, including many left-wing radicals, many Jamaicans, some immigrants from other islands, and a few African Americans. According to Irma Watkins-Owens, the membership 'rarely if ever numbered over one hundred members', although she referred to Brown as 'one of Harlem's major religious and intellectual leaders'.[161] In his research on the origins of black Unitarianism in the US, Juan M. Floyd-Thomas speaks of 78 official members, but estimates that some big meetings attracted over 400 to 500 people.¹⁶² The small but 'vital network for social activism and radical dissent'¹⁶³ of the HUC allows further insight into the highly intertwined personal, political and organizational relationships that developed between the activists of the radical scene in Harlem. The HUC provided a 'Temple and Forum', as Brown called it, and it was a meeting place for the families of W.A. Domingo, Richard B. Moore, Otto Huiswoud, Ethelred Brown and others.¹⁶⁴

Churches played an important role in black community life in the US, providing assistance for newcomers, a variety of community services, mutual aid and, last but not least, mental counselling in a hostile racist surrounding.¹⁶⁵ Unitarianism, for Brown and his followers, embodied a useful frame for an emphasis on worldly affairs. Joyce Moore Turner describes Brown's impact as follows: 'His presence in Harlem created a different type of religious experience that combined religion with seething debate on class and race and involved the broader community in issues relevant to both Harlem and the Caribbean'.¹⁶⁶

Domingo characterized Brown's church in *Gift of the Black Tropics* as the 'only modernist church among the thousands of Negroes in New York (and perhaps the country) ....'¹⁶⁷ The HUC provided a forum for a wide range of debates and the topics of Brown's sermons illustrate its radical approach:

> Whether he was focused on an emphasis of Jesus' humanity that demanded an end to racism, sexism, and poverty or a prophetic witness against imperialism, Christian fundamentalism, xenophobia, and global warfare, Brown and his contribution to the articulation of radical Black humanism illustrates how he and the HUC consciously worked to challenge and change the status quo by bringing a new, more complex understanding of Black religiosity and social justice in the United States.¹⁶⁸

Brown was a harsh critic of dogmatic theology. He regarded religion as an 'emancipatory power' and black Unitarianism as 'an oasis of liberalism in a desert of conservatism and reaction – a light to dispel the darkness of superstition and fanaticism'.¹⁶⁹ With its emphasis on personal freedom, religious liberalism and its firm stand against orthodox beliefs and its encouragement of political activity, the HUC attracted many radical Caribbean migrants in New York.¹⁷⁰ The services often had the character of a political discussion. Brown's sermons addressed social and political topics, and sometimes, he invited guest speakers for a debate.

The members of the HUC lived according to their religious beliefs and became involved in politics. Like many of the members of his congregation, Brown joined the Socialist Party and became one of the stepladder orators in Harlem, actively supporting Socialist candidates.¹⁷¹ In 1925, the Socialist Party officially hired him as one of its campaign speakers.¹⁷² He was frequently invited to lecture at the People's Educational Forum organized by Domingo and fellow Socialists, on topics like 'Religious Liberalism and the Negro'.[173] Watkins-Owens claims that 'Brown himself was probably better known as a political leader and Harlem radical, a stepladder socialist and major figure in the Jamaican independence movement in New York'.[174] She further points to his friendly relations with other African American leaders, such as Adam Clayton Powell, Sr and Adam Clayton Powell, Jr, who at times invited him to preach at the Abyssinian Baptist Church.[175]

The mixture of politics and religion in the HUC is further highlighted by its close connections with the ABB. Not able to purchase its own building, the HUC ceremonies took place in the same building where the ABB meetings were held.[176] This was no coincidence. Not only were many of the members of the church also members of the ABB, Ethelred Brown was also the official chaplain of the ABB.[177]

The group of black Socialists formed a very close network and would meet frequently on several occasions throughout the week. Whether at one of the numerous street lectures in Harlem, at the Peoples Educational Forum, at the regular Saturday evening meetings at the home of Communist and community activist Grace Campbell, on Sundays in the HUC or at gatherings at the tailor shop of Martin L. Campbell, the activists were always dedicated to discussion and the sharing of knowledge. Thus, personal and political life of the radicals was highly intertwined. Joyce Moore Turner states that the Caribbean radicals in Harlem '…shared a common background and social concern for the plight of the victims of colonialism, and each threw himself into the fray at different positions on the barricades. Like highly energized meteorites that interacted and occasionally collided, they spread their efforts from the political international left of Marxism to the separatist Black Nationalism of Garveyism'.[178]

Despite the success of the HUC in the radical milieu, the unconventional style of ministry failed to attract a large number of followers. The lack of funds forced Brown to work in several jobs.[179] Brown described the lack of support from the AUA as his 'greatest disappointment'[180] and pointed to the obvious racism in its ranks.[181] These circumstances had a negative impact on his personal life and also his family suffered from the financial hardships. However, despite the serious problems Brown faced, the church survived. Although the Unitarian Church tried several times to remove Brown's name from the list of Unitarian ministers he continued his church for 36 years until his death.[182]

The mixture of religion and political activity was no contradiction for Domingo and many of his comrades. In 1919, even before the arrival of Brown in Harlem, Domingo employed a religious argument in favour of Socialism:

> Socialism as an economic doctrine is merely the pure Christianity preached by Jesus, and practiced by the early Christians adapted to the more complex conditions of modern life. [Socialism] makes no

distinction as to race, nationality or creed, but like Jesus it says 'come unto me all ye who are weary and heavy laden and I will give you rest.' It is to procure that rest that millions of oppressed peoples are flocking to the scarlet banner of international Socialism.[183]

Domingo's anti-colonial interpretation of Socialism is evident in his positive references to Lenin's doctrines. In the same article, he repeated the Communist leader's proclamation: 'Slaves of the colonies in Africa and Asia! The hour of proletarian dictatorship in Europe will be the hour of your release'.[184]

While anti-colonialism, Socialism and religiosity stood in no contradiction for Domingo, the membership in the HUC started to pose a problem for some of the activists who had joined the communist Workers Party. Richard B. Moore, for example, initially tried to convince the party leaders of the political character of the church and pointed to his own speeches in the church, arguing that the party would underestimate the importance of churches in African American life. However, the party leaders were not convinced and Moore eventually resigned from the HUC.[185] Likewise, Otto Huiswoud and his wife who had also been regular church attendees decided to leave the HUC and Huiswoud had adopted the view that churches in general were an 'instrument of imperialism'.[186]

Despite occasional differences, the radicals in Harlem closely collaborated as editors and contributors of the newspapers *Crusader*, *Messenger*, and the *Emancipator*. Owen and Randolph, editors of the *Messenger*, recommended reading the *Crusader* as the 'only Negro Magazine besides the *Messenger* worth reading'. When Domingo's *Emancipator* was launched, the *Messenger* dropped its subtitle: 'The Only Radical Negro Magazine in America'. In 1920, the papers offered a discount for a joint subscription of the three papers.[187] Briggs and Domingo established the *Crusader News Service*, after Domingo's *Emancipator* had to cease publication due to financial problems.[188]

The common cause, the effort to merge race- and class-consciousness, united the radicals. Yet, when the anti-imperialist slogans of the Communist Party in Russia led most of the ABB officials to join the Workers Party, Domingo did not follow them, although he had openly approved the ideas and the international outlook of the Comintern. Why had he not joined the party? Was it because he had lost confidence in leftist organizations led by whites after his experiences with the Socialist Party? In an interview with Theodore Draper, he answered that he did not join because he was no 'organisation-man'.[189] But this was no satisfactory answer as in his former and in his future life Domingo joined, founded and thoroughly influenced other organizations. In reality, the US branch of the Communist Party did not show a particular concern for the black masses. Similar to the Socialist Party, it largely neglected the black segment in its ranks and failed to pay adequate attention to their problems. The Comintern had tried to intervene, and Lenin made attempts to influence the strategy toward colonialism and racial oppression when he formulated his 'Theses on the National and Colonial Questions' in 1920, which inspired anti-colonial movements worldwide.[190] However, in the Russian Communist Party, the 'Negro Question' was always a matter of dispute, while a majority of white American Communists insisted that racism would vanish in the course of a worldwide Communist revolution.[191] It is quite likely that the party's relentless committment to a class first position was the major reason for Domingo's decision to not join the Workers Party.

In 1923, Domingo was deeply disappointed in his Socialist friends and colleagues of the *Messenger* staff. Domingo strongly disapproved Randolph's and Owen's strong anti-West Indian sentiments in the 'Garvey must Go'-campaign that black radicals waged against Garvey.[192] Although, Domingo himself had turned into one of Garvey's harshest critics after leaving his position as editor of the *Negro World*, he strongly opposed the *Messenger's* course to denounce Garvey and the UNIA with anti-West-Indian tirades. Nevertheless, Domingo himself joined the Friends of Negro Freedom, a group formed to counter the UNIA. Yet, a bitter public conflict escalated between Domingo and Owen, during which Domingo criticized the anti-Caribbean statements. Eventually, Domingo broke with Owen and Randolph and left the *Messenger* staff. Domingo regarded the new line of the *Messenger* as a betrayal of the former internationalist outlook, and its advocacy of international black solidarity.[193] He confronted Owen with the arguments that most high-ranking leaders in the UNIA were African Americans, while islanders like himself and Cyril Briggs had been among the earliest and most persistent critics of Garvey, and that many Caribbean migrants had been dependable readers of the *Messenger* and supported it with donations. Domingo felt this conflict was contributing unnecessary animosity to the racial solidarity which had evolved in the past decade between African Americans and Caribbean migrants.[194]

In an atmosphere of increasing dissent and disunity, various black organizations like the NAACP, the National Race Congress, the National Equal Rights League, the International Uplift League and the Friends of Negro Freedom issued a national call for black solidarity and unity between the organizations, mounting in the planning of a huge conference. Domingo, Moore, Briggs, and Grace Campbell participated as representatives of the ABB.[195] The outcome was an agreement signed by six leading civil rights organizations which proclaimed the aim of close cooperation and a harmonious relationship among all signing groups. Domingo signed the agreement for the ABB but soon after the conference, a split occurred, and the effort to unite the groups failed.[196]

By the mid-1920s, the enthusiasm among the radicals in Harlem was dimmed by various conflicts and disagreements. The experience with white Socialists and communists demonstrated that international working class solidarity had its limits, limits that weighed strongly for the radical black activists. The reactions to the increased disunity were diverse. Domingo chose retreat into his personal sphere where he focused on his import business with Jamaican products.[197] At around the same time, Domingo showed keen interest in political affairs in Jamaica. He noticed the strong nationalist attitude of the Reform Club in Jamaica and encouraged its leaders:

> Jamaicans living in the United States who take an interest in their country view with satisfaction the rise of a national feeling in the island and sincerely trust that it will not fade away like the National Club of S.A.G. Cox because of petty jealousy and insincerity.[198]

This intervention was to forecast the direction in which Domingo's main political focus would shift in the following years. During the Great Depression, the Central Committee declared Harlem a 'national concentration point' and appointed James Ford as a special organizer who further marginalized the black radicals. Finally, Briggs, Moore and others would be expelled from the party in 1942.[199] Although Domingo and Brown occasionally gave lectures or attended official functions, they backed away from much of their political activities during the 1930s.

About a year after the formation of the Jamaica Progressive League in 1936, Domingo recalled how the disappointing experiences with both, Black Nationalism and Socialism, had prepared a number of the Caribbean activists in Harlem to endorse nationalist ideas and to support the founding of the Progressive League: 'While the Garveyites dreamed of redeeming Africa by the sword or by persuasion, and the Socialists are working first and foremost for "the revolution", the members of the Jamaica Progressive League are working along the path that leads to nationhood, confident that once understood by the majority of their fellow-countrymen the idea will be like an irresistible tidal wave'.[200]

That such an anti-colonial organization would become like a tidal wave in Jamaica proved to be wishful thinking; yet, the Progressive League was able to provide an effective umbrella under which the different ideological streams could merge into a powerful demand for Jamaican independence. The Progressive League was able to combine Roberts' anti-colonial positions, which had derived from his regional outlook, and the anti-colonialism of the Jamaican radicals in Harlem and fuse them into a nationalist organization that was far more extreme in its anti-colonial stance than preceding and contemporary nationalist groups in Jamaica and functioned as a catalyst to the emergence of anti-colonial positions in the local political scene.

Notes

1. *Daily Gleaner*, October 10, 1962, 16.
2. Ibid., January 7, 1938.
3. For Roberts' own description of his nationalism evolved see Roberts, 'Autobiography', WAR, NLJ, MS 353, Box 2b, 7.
4. Ibid., 7ff.
5. Ibid., 7.
6. The central arguments of the speech were printed in the pamphlet W. Adolphe Roberts, *Self-Government for Jamaica* (New York, 1936).
7. Ibid., 6–15.
8. Ibid.
9. See Roberts, 'Autobiography', 7. For a similar description see W. Adolphe Roberts, *Nationalist Liberalism*, Manuscript, Article for Pepperpot, 1959, NLJ, WAR, MS 353, Box 9.
10. 'The Jamaica Progressive League of New York', *Ambassador* 2 (1952): 21.
11. Roberts, *Self-Government for Jamaica*, 6–15.
12. Winston James, *Holding Aloft the Banner of Ethiopia: Caribbean Radicalism in Early Twentieth-Century America* (London, New York: Verso, 1998), 283.
13. Roberts, 'Autobiography', 7.
14. Ibid.
15. Ibid., 8.
16. The board elected consisted of following men and women: W. Adolphe Roberts (president), W.A. Domingo (first vice-president), Mrs Ivy Bailey-Essien (second vice-president), R.J. Kirkpatrick (third vice-president), Ethelred Brown (secretary), Mrs I.A. Fraser (assistant secretary), T.E. Hanson (treasurer), Mrs T.A. D'Aguilar (assistant treasurer), See *New York Amsterdam News*, September 19, 1936, see also Young, *Lest We Forget*, 32. According to a JPL pamphlet in 1937, Mrs T.A. D'Aguilar soon became treasurer, Mrs C.A. Wallace assistant treasurer and the Board of Directors was further joined by Thomas Bowen, Theodore Burrell, Jaime O'Meally, Dorcas Thompson, R.S. Trew and Vernal J. Williams, see Jamaica Progressive League New York, 'Onward, Jamaica!' (New York, 1937), 7.
17. Wilfred A. Domingo, 'Jamaica Seeks Its Freedom', *Opportunity*, December 16, 1938, 371.
18. Ivy Bailey-Essien was the sister of Mrs Amy Bailey of Kingston, who was very active in the local political scene and among other organizations also involved in the activities of the JPL Kingston. See for instance, *Daily Gleaner*, September 19, 1939.
19. President of the 'Ladies Auxilliary' was Tessie D'Aguilar, also treasurer of the JPL. The Auxiliary supported the Big Woods Basic School in St Elizabeth, collected clothing and school books and send them to needy areas in Jamaica. It also contributed to PNP election funds, for example in the 1949 elections. See Young, *Lest We Forget*, 57f.
20. JPL NY, *Constitution and By-Laws*, September 1, 1936, SCRBC, EEB, MG 87, Box 4, Fo. 7.
21. Ibid.
22. Roberts, *Self-Government for Jamaica*, 14.
23. For this and the following quotes see Jamaica Progressive League (JPL) NY, *Constitution and By-Laws*, September 1, 1936, SCRBC, EEB, MG 87, Box 4, Fo. 7.

24. See for example Penny M. von Eschen, *Race against Empire: Black Americans and Anticolonialism –1937–1957* (Ithaca: Cornell University Press, 1997); Jonathan Derrick *Africa's 'Agitators': Militant Anti-Colonialism in Africa and the West, 1918–1939*; Horne, *Cold War in a Hot Zone*; Manela, *Wilsonian Moment.*
25. See Hulme, 'W. Adolphe Roberts and Jamaica', 14–23.
26. John A. Aarons, 'W. Adolphe Roberts and the Movement for Self-Government.' *Jamaica Journal* 16 (1983): 58–63; 58.
27. For a detailed description of his father and his influence on the young Roberts see Peter Hulmes' introduction to Roberts' autobiography, *These Many Years*, edited by Peter Hulme, 2016.
28. See Aarons, 'W. Adolphe Roberts', 58.
29. W. Adolphe Roberts, *The Single Star* (Kingston, 1956).
30. W. Adolphe Roberts, *Six Great Jamaicans* (Kingston, 1951).
31. In 1949, Roberts published a series of articles in *Caribbean Quarterly* that reflects this fascination. See W. Adolphe Roberts, 'Great Men of the Caribbean 1: Toussaint L'Ouverture', *Caribbean Quarterly* 1 (1949): 4–8; W. Adolphe Roberts, 'Great Men of the Caribbean 2: Simón Bolívar', *Caribbean Quarterly* 1 (1949/50): 4–8; W. Adolphe Roberts, 'Great Men of the Caribbean 3: José Martí', *Caribbean Quarterly* 1 (1949/50): 4–6.
32. *Public Opinion*, December 24, 1937.
33. *Daily Gleaner*, December 20, 1937.
34. Bennett presents a biographical sketch with emphasis on his literary contributions. See Wycliffe Bennett, 'W. Adolphe Roberts: A Personal Recollection', *Jamaica Journal* 16, no. 4 (1983): 54–64.
35. See Aarons, 'W. Adolphe Roberts', 59.
36. Ibid.
37. W. Adolphe Roberts, *Sir Henry Morgan: Buccaneer and Governor* (London: Covici, Friede, 1933), 293–96.
38. A pamphlet Roberts published for the JPL contained similar arguments and was based on an historical account of the constitutional developments in Jamaica. This was also the topic of his address to Jamaican migrants at the founding of the Progressive League. See W. Adolphe Roberts, 'Self-Government for Jamaica' (New York, 1936).
39. Roberts, *Sir Henry Morgan*, 296.
40. See *Daily Gleaner*, June 13, 1932.
41. This and the following, Roberts, *Six Great Jamaicans*, 115f.
42. *Daily Gleaner*, June 13, 1932.
43. Ibid.
44. Ibid., January 20, 1934.
45. Ibid., August 8, 1934.
46. Ibid.
47. See Eric E. Duke, 'The Diasporic Dimensions of Caribbean Federation in the Early Twentieth Century', *New West Indian Guide* 83, no.3–4 (Leiden, The Netherlands: KITLV, 2009): 219–48.
48. See W. Adolphe Roberts, 'British West Indian Aspirations', *Current History* 40 (1934): 552.
49. For more information on the development of nationalism in the Caribbean see for example Benn, *The Caribbean*, 65–102.

50. See Roberts, 'British West Indian Aspirations', 552f.
51. See Roberts, 'Autobiography', WAR, NLJ, MS 353, Box 2b, 4f.
52. See W. Adolphe Roberts, 'Autobiography'.
53. Ibid., 6.
54. For biographical information see Margaret Stevens, 'The Early Political History of Wilfred A. Domingo, 1919-1939', in *Caribbean Political Activism: Essays in Honour of Richard Hart*, ed. Rupert Lewis (Kingston: Ian Randle Publishers, 2012); Caribbean Reasoning Series, 118-43; Hill, *Marcus Garvey*, Vol. 1, 527-28; Moore Turner *Caribbean Crusaders*, 34; Irma Watkins-Owens, *Blood Relations*, 104.
55. See Watkins-Owens, *Blood Relations*, 104.
56. Alain Locke described the new spirit evolving among black people in the late 1910 and early 1920s in Harlem in his famous essay that provided the name for the new movement. See Alain Locke, *The New Negro* (New York: Albert & Charles Boni, 1925).
57. *Public Opinion*, February 19, 1944.
58. See Watkins-Owens, *Blood Relations*, 1.
59. Jason Parker, 'Harlem Nexus', 105.
60. *Public Opinion*, February 19, 1944.
61. See James, *Holding Aloft*, 92-100. Moore Turner had also described this period as 'the nadir of the backlash following reconstruction', Moore Turner, *Caribbean Crusaders*, 48.
62. For a good description of how the migrants reacted to the atmosphere that was determined by the separate-but-equal doctrine, the Jim Crow system, the rise of the Ku Klux Klan and frequent cases of lynching, see Moore Turner, *Caribbean Crusaders*, 48; James, *Holding Aloft*, 94.
63. See Juan M. Floyd-Thomas, *The Origins of Black Humanism in America: Reverend Ethelred Brown and the Unitarian Church* (New York: Palgrave Macmillan, 2008), 94.
64. See for example Gilbert Osofsky, *Harlem: The Making of a Ghetto*. 2nd ed. (Chicago: Ivan R. Dee, 1966); Seth M. Scheiner, *Negro Mecca: A History of the Negro in New York City* (New York: New York University Press, 1965); James Weldon Johnson, *Black Manhattan* (New York: Da Capo Press, 1930), 154-59.
65. See Moore Turner, *Caribbean Crusaders*, 16.
66. See James, *Holding Aloft*, 94 ff.
67. See Kasinitz, *Caribbean New York*, 35.
68. Watkins-Owens, *Blood Relations*, 175.
69. See Wilfred A. Domingo, 'Gift of the Black Tropics/The Tropics in New York', in *Look for Me All Around You*, ed. Louis J. Parascandola (Detroit: Wayne State University Press, 2005), 175-83.
70. In 1972, Bryce-Laporte speaks of the 'double invisibility' of Caribbean immigrants as 'blacks and as black foreigners', see Roy S. Bryce-Laporte, 'Black Immigrants: The Experience of Invisibility and Inequality', *Journal of Black Studies* 3 (1972): 29-56. Scholars like Watkins-Owens, *Blood Relations*, 94; James, *Holding Aloft*; Perry Mars, 'Caribbean Influences in African-American Political Struggles', *Ethnic and Racial Studies* 27 (2004): 565-83, helped to highlight their experiences and their important contributions to the Harlem Renaissance.
71. James, *Holding Aloft*, 50.

72. On the 'one-drop-rule' see for example F. James Davis, *Who is Black?* 2nd ed. (University Park: Pennsylvania State University Press, 2001).
73. See for instance Hall, 'Old and New Identities, Old and New Ethnicities', 53f; Showers Johnson, 'Racial Frontiers', 166f; Richards, 'Race, Class, and Labour', 341.
74. Domingo, 'Gift of the Black Tropics', 181.
75. See Kasinitz, *Caribbean New York*, 7.
76. *Public Opinion*, May 3, 1944.
77. See Watkins-Owens, *Blood Relations*, 149.
78. *Public Opinion*, May 3, 1944.
79. Quoted after Kasinitz, *Caribbean New York*, 50.
80. *Public Opinion*, March 4, 1944.
81. See Orlando Patterson, 'Ecumenical America: Global Culture and the American Cosmos', *World Policy Journal* 11, no. 2 1994:103–117.
82. Kasinitz, *Caribbean New York*, 42–43. Kasinitz mentions Claude McKay, Eric Walrond, Cyril Briggs, Frank Crosswaith, Hubert H. Harrison, Richard B. Moore and Marcus Garvey.
83. See James, *Holding Aloft*, 271.
84. *Public Opinion*, February 26, 1944.
85. See Mars, *Caribbean Influences*, 565f; James, *Holding Aloft*, 271.
86. See Theodore G. Vincent, *Black Power and the Garvey Movement* (San Francisco: Ramparts Press, 1972).
87. See for example Wilson Jeremiah Moses, *The Golden Age of Black Nationalism, 1850–1925* (Oxford: Oxford University Press, 1988).
88. See for example Mark Solomon, *The Cry Was Unity: Communists and African Americans, 1917–36* (Jackson: University Press of Mississippi, 1998); Moore Turner *Caribbean Crusaders*.
89. Good biographical sketches can be found in Wilfred D. Samuels, *Five Afro-Caribbean Voices in American Culture, 1917–1929: Hubert H. Harrison, Wilfred A. Domingo, Richard B. Moore, Cyril V. Briggs, and Claude McKay* (Boulder: Belmont Books, 1977), 51–77; James, *Holding Aloft*, 122–34.
90. James, *Holding Aloft*, 126.
91. See Samuels, *Five Afro-Caribbean Voices*, 50.
92. See Moore Turner, *Caribbean Crusaders*, 35.
93. *Public Opinion*, May 3, 1944.
94. See Moore Turner, *Caribbean Crusaders*, 49; Vincent, *Black Power*, 78.
95. Watkins-Owens, *Blood Relations*, 92. Watkins-Owens points to Hubert Harrison as the mentor of the group and mentions Richard B. Moore, Frank Crosswaith, W.A. Domingo, Grace Campbell, Elizabeth Hendrickson, Marcus Garvey, A. Philip Randolph and Chandler Owen.
96. See Watkins-Owens, *Blood Relations*, 104.
97. Philip S. Foner, *American Socialism and Black Americans: From the Age of Jackson to World War II* (Westport, CT: Greenwood Press, 1977), 277. In August 1919, the Messenger claimed to have 33,000 readers and nearly nationwide distribution.
98. See Samuels, *Five Voices*, 80; Hill, Marcus Garvey, Vol. 1, 529.
99. Moore Turner, *Caribbean Crusaders*, 58.
100. See Watkins-Owens, *Blood Relations*, 104

101. Marcus Garvey, Ethelred Brown and others contacted Domingo, who provided the new immigrants with important contacts and helped them to realize their ideas. See Moore Turner, *Caribbean Crusaders*, 35.
102. See Marcus Garvey, 'Why the Black Star Line Failed'; *Pittsburgh Courier*, February 22, 1930, in *Marcus Garvey and the Vision of Africa*, ed. John Henrik Clarke (New York: Black Classic Press, 1974), 140. Garvey mentions Domingo as one his bitter adversaries, especially influential in agitating against the Black Star Line. He referred to Domingo as a 'boyhood friend' and 'first associated with me as editor of the Negro World' who because of Garvey's success 'became jealous of me and became a communist.'
103. Floyd-Thomas, *Origins of Black Humanism in America*, 139.
104. For a list of branches and divisions around 1926 see Tony Martin, *Race First*, 361–73.
105. See Vincent, *Black Power*, 72.
106. *Negro World*, July 19, 1919, quoted after Hill, *Marcus Garvey*, Vol.1, 466.
107. Ibid., 470
108. For information on O'Meally's activities in the UNIA see Vincent, *Black Power*, 183f; Hill, *Marcus Garvey Papers*, 950, FN 1.
109. See Vincent, *Black Power*, 184.
110. Ibid., 183.
111. See Hill, *Marcus Garvey Papers*, 950, FN 1.
112. See Hill, *Marcus Garvey Papers*, 227.
113. Domingo, 'A New Negro and New Day', *Messenger*, November 1920, quoted after Parascandola, *Look for Me All Around You*, 171.
114. Domingo, 'Socialism, The Negro's Hope', *Messenger*, July 1919, quoted after Parascandola, *Look for Me All Around You*, 166.
115. Domingo, 'A New Negro and a New Day', *Messenger*, November 1920, quoted after Parascandola, *Look for Me All Around You*, 172.
116. Ibid., 173.
117. Domingo, 'Socialism Imperilled, or the Negro – A Potential Menace to American Radicalism', Revolutionary Radicalism: Its History, Purpose and Tactics, 1920, quoted after Parascandola, *Look for Me All Around You*, 174.
118. The Forum was joint effort of Briggs, Huiswoud, Randolph, Owen, Moore, Domingo and Campbell to provide an independent platform for political discussion. See James, *Holding Aloft*, 271.
119. See Samuels, *Five Afro-Caribbean Voices*, 85.
120. Ibid., 86.
121. Harrison, 'Socialism and the Negro', The Negro and the Nation, 1917, quoted after Parascandola, *Look for Me All Around You*, 137.
122. See Moore Turner, *Caribbean Crusaders*, 55.
123. Ibid., 56.
124. See James, *Holding Aloft*, 156. Members included W. A. Domingo, Richard B. Moore, and Grace Campbell, Harry Haywood, Otto Hall, Otto Huiswoud, Lovett Fort-Whiteman and Claude McKay.
125. See Theodore Draper, Interview with W. A. Domingo, The Tamiment Library and Robert F. Wagner Labor Archives, Elmer Holmes Bobst Library, NYU, New York, Tam 218, Box 1, Folder Draper.

126. See Theodore Kornweibel, *No Crystal Stair: Black Life and the Messenger, 1917–1928* (Westport, CT: Greenwood Press, 1975), 143.
127. See Hill, *Marcus Garvey*, Vol. 4, 96.
128. See Moore Turner, *Caribbean Crusaders*, 56.
129. For instance, Richard B. Moore, Cyril Briggs, Anselmo Jackson, A. Philip Randolph, Chandler Owen, Frank Crosswaith and Thomas Potter.
130. *Emancipator*, March 13, 1920.
131. Ibid.
132. Ibid.
133. Ibid.
134. In 1918, Domingo married Eulalie Manhertz from Jamaica. They had two children, Karl Marx Domingo and Yolanda Domingo. The family became close friends of Richard B. Moore and his wife. See Moore Turner, *Caribbean Crusaders*, 35.
135. Ethelred Brown was born in Falmouth, Jamaica, on July 11, 1875; see Mark D. Morrison-Reed, *Black Pioneers in a White Denomination* (Boston: Skinner House Books, 1980), 43.
136. Floyd-Thomas, *Origins of Black Humanism in America*, 32f.
137. Morrison-Reed, *Black Pioneers*, 44.
138. See Ethelred Brown, *Injustices in the Civil Service of Jamaica* (New York, 1937).
139. See Floyd-Thomas, *Origins of Black Humanism in America*, 36.
140. Ibid., 36f.
141. Ibid., 38 ff.
142. See E. Ethelred Brown, 'I Have Two Dreams', Schomburg Center for Research in Black Culture (SCRBC), E. Ethelred Brown Papers, MG 87, Box 1, Fo. 2.
143. E. Ethelred Brown, 'Labour Conditions in Jamaica Prior to 1917', *The Journal of Negro History*, 9 (1919): 349–60.
144. *Daily Gleaner*, February 11, 1915.
145. Ibid., December 28, 1918.
146. Ibid., August 8, 1919.
147. Ibid., October 10, 1919.
148. Ibid., August 28, 1916; August 30, 1916; September 30, 1916.
149. The first officers of the PNA were president, Mr J.W. Millbourne (previously UNIA treasurer), vice president Revd D.A. Waugh and Secretary Revd E. Ethelred Brown; see Hill, *Marcus Garvey*, Vol. 1, 194.
150. See *Daily Gleaner*, August 11, 1916.
151. Brown, 'Labour Conditions', 351.
152. Ibid., 352.
153. See *Daily Gleaner*, March 17, 1919 and *Daily Gleaner*, August 14, 1917.
154. Ibid., August 14, 1918.
155. Ibid.
156. Ibid., January 21, 1919.
157. See for example Liberal Association to Brown, February 4, 1920, EEB, SCRBC, MG 87, Box 1, Fo. 1.
158. Ethelred Brown, 'The Harlem Unitarian Church', September 11, 1949, Schomburg, MG 87, Box 1, Fo. 8.

159. The founding congregation consisted of Ella Matilda Brown, W.A. Domingo, Martin L. Campbell, Grace Campbell, Hayward Shovington, Frank Crosswaith, Thomas A. Potter, Richard B. Moore and Lucille E. Ward. See Moore Turner, *Caribbean Crusaders*, 69.
160. For a detailed history on the Harlem Unitarian Church, see Floyd-Thomas, *Origins of Black Humanism in America*; Morrison-Reed, *Black Pioneers*.
161. Watkins-Owens, *Blood Relations*, 62.
162. See Floyd-Thomas, *Origins of Black Humanism in America*, 87.
163. Ibid., 91.
164. Moore Turner, daughter of Richard B. Moore, describes the personal relations, friendships and various professional connections in detail; see Moore Turner, *Caribbean Crusaders*, 35f.
165. See Floyd-Thomas, *Origins of Black Humanism in America*, 81.
166. Moore Turner, *Caribbean Crusaders*, 70.
167. Domingo, 'Gift of the Black Tropics', 181.
168. Floyd-Thomas, *Origins of Black Humanism in America*, 4.
169. Ibid., 87.
170. Ibid., 85f.
171. See Moore Turner, *Caribbean Crusaders*, 69.
172. Ibid.
173. Ibid., 79.
174. Watkins-Owens, *Blood Relations*, 62.
175. Ibid.
176. See Moore Turner, *Caribbean Crusaders*, 70; Watkins-Owens, *Blood Relations*, 62.
177. See Moore Turner, *Caribbean Crusaders*, 69.
178. Ibid., 71.
179. Brown worked as an elevator operator, sporadically as speaker for the Socialist Party in America, and as secretary for 'The World Tomorrow', a publication with liberal, Socialist, pacifistic, and religious outlook. See Floyd-Thomas, *Origins of Black Humanism in America*, 87f.; Moore Turner, *Caribbean Crusaders*, 69.
180. See Floyd-Thomas, *Origins of Black Humanism in America*, 87.
181. Ibid., 91.
182. See Moore Turner, *Caribbean Crusaders*, 70; Floyd-Thomas, *Origins of Black Humanism in America*, 87.
183. Domingo, 'Socialism, The Negro's Hope', Messenger, July 1919, quoted after Parascandola, *Look for Me All Around You*, 161.
184. Ibid., 168.
185. See Moore Turner, *Caribbean Crusaders*, 165.
186. Ibid., 165ff.
187. For the quotations see James, *Holding Aloft*, 271.
188. The news service provided the news for many black newspapers, Vincent, *Black Power*, 192.
189. Theodore Draper, 'Interview with W.A. Domingo', The Tamiment Library & Robert F. Wagner Labor Archives, Elmer Holmes Bobst Library, Tam 218, Box 1, Folder Draper.
190. See James, *Holding Aloft*, 180.
191. Ibid.

192. See Kornweibel, *No Crystal Stair*, 143f.
193. Ibid., 144.
194. Ibid.
195. Ibid., 257.
196. See Joyce Moore Turner and W. Burghardt Turner, *Richard B. Moore, Caribbean Militant in Harlem*, 49.
197. See *Daily Gleaner*, January 15, 1925; *Daily Gleaner*, May 15, 1929; *Daily Gleaner*, July 19, 1930.
198. *Daily Gleaner*, June 5, 1924.
199. See Moore Turner and Turner, *Richard B. Moore*, 67.
200. *Public Opinion*, July 31, 1937.

PART TWO

HISTORY AND INFLUENCE OF THE JAMAICA PROGRESSIVE LEAGUE

CHAPTER 3: FOUNDING AND FIRST REACTIONS

Launch of the Jamaica Progressive League in New York

After the launch in September 1936, the Jamaica Progressive League organized a series of public meetings in New York to garner support for the anti-colonial pressure group in the immigrant circles. W.A. Roberts remembered: 'We now campaigned in the manner common to all agitators. We rented halls and staged mass gatherings. We lectured on such subjects as libertarian struggles everywhere'.[1] The reference to other freedom movements testifies to the inspiration the Progressive League received from transnational anti-colonial movements. For instance, the Irish Progressive League, founded 20 years earlier in New York in 1917, served as an important role model and even inspired the name of the anti-colonial pressure group. Invited to a meeting of the fledgling Jamaica Progressive League, Irish actress and radical anti-colonial activist Eileen Curran of the Irish Progressive League shared the experiences of the Irish people and underlined the importance of support from the community of expatriates.[2] In his autobiography, Roberts explained why he invited Curran and why he frequently referred to the Irish freedom movement as an example:

> She [Curran] had served her cause at home and in New York, had helped patriots with a price on their heads to escape, had pulled strings in enterprises of gun-running and the circulating of secret mail. Quietly she stood before an audience of hundreds in a Y.M.C.A. hall, told how she had worked and how it might become necessary for Jamaicans to do similar things. It was strong meat for most of her hearers. The League had always taught that peaceful means should suffice, but Eileen Curran did well to show that there could be no guarantee against bloodshed initiated by violent men on either side.[3]

This statement shows an unusual radical side of Roberts and testifies to the sincerity with which he approached his call for an independent Jamaica. The Progressive League also invited scholar and bibliophile Arthur Schomburg, the Puerto Rican immigrant who had lobbied for Puerto Rican and Cuban independence from Spain and who was instrumental in bringing together African American, African and Caribbean intellectuals in Harlem. These collaborations illuminate the tremendous importance of the inspiration the Progressive League derived from other anti-colonial movements and allude to the transnational cross-fertilization that took place among the different groups in Harlem.

Initially, the meetings of the Progressive League took place in private homes of different members in Harlem. During its formative years, it heavily depended on the financial support of its members, many of whom invested private funds to print informative material.[4] The public meetings were advertised and covered in the *New York Amsterdam News*, a popular African American newspaper.[5] The Progressive League provided a channel for Jamaicans in the Diaspora to articulate their critique of the social and political conditions in their native country. Active members frequently criticized race, class, labour and gender relations in colonial Jamaica; for instance, Ethelred Brown, who gave a lengthy speech on the Civil Service, James O'Meally on labour organization, Ivy Bailey-Essien addressed the situation of women in Jamaica, and W.A. Domingo on poverty and health. Some of the speeches were edited and published as pamphlets, like Ethelred Brown's reflections on the discriminatory legislation regarding the entry of Jamaicans into the Civil Service.[6]

The meetings were generally well attended, and the League was able to attract a growing number of supporters. Naturally, the movement was mainly supported by the Jamaican community, but some African Americans and Caribbean immigrants from other islands also endorsed the cause. Some meetings focused explicitly on wider Caribbean subjects, like one large mass meeting staged at the St James Presbyterian Church in Harlem in April 1937 with the topic 'The Fight for Liberty in the West Indies', at which many immigrants from various Spanish-speaking and English-speaking Caribbean islands gathered and discussed the political future of the region.[7]

Much of the propaganda the Progressive League spread was directed against Jamaica's colonial status, the limited franchise, racist discrimination and legal restrictions regarding the organization of trade unions. It persistently challenged the imperial mentality of Jamaicans, which they saw responsible for impeding nationalist thought. In January 1937, W.A. Roberts claimed: 'They teach our people to call old England 'home' and to belittle their native land, the only home the immense majority will ever know'.[8] To counter such propaganda, the Progressive League sponsored 'a nationalistic campaign without regard to race, class or creed'. The movement, Roberts emphasized, '...is political, and aims to win self-government for Jamaica as a full-fledged member of the British Commonwealth of Nations'.[9] In regard to the conservative tendencies in political circles in Jamaica, he readily assured that the Progressive League was 'not in any sense a revolutionary movement. It merely seeks to awaken Jamaicans to the benefits of democratic liberty'.[10]

Next to public meetings and articles in the press, the Progressive League started to spread its propaganda through pamphlets. These included Roberts' above-mentioned critique of the political system, *Self-Government for Jamaica*, Brown's uncovering of the racist limitation to the upward mobility of Jamaicans in the pamphlet *Injustice in the Civil Service of Jamaica*, the Progressive League brochure *Onward, Jamaica!* published in 1937,[11] and the elaborate outline of the Progressive League's demands and theoretical positions by Jamie O'Meally, 'Why We Demand Self-Government' in 1938.[12]

These pamphlets were widely circulated in the US and in Jamaica. Addressing the ills in the colonial society, all came to the conclusion that the only solution to Jamaica's social and economic problems was to put an end to colonial rule and to create a Jamaican nation state. Therefore, the Progressive League demanded that Jamaicans develop a nationalist outlook and claim self-government. Only then would the country be able to reform its economy and trade regulations, its educational system and all other vital areas.[13]

Remarkably, the Progressive League abstained from designing an economic programme for the time after independence. In general, the vision for political and economic organization of Jamaica after independence remained cloudy. Probably, this indicated the different economic and political positions among the Progressive League leaders that ranged from liberal to Socialist beliefs. Nationalism thus served as an umbrella providing the commonly shared belief that in a self-governed democratic Jamaica based on universal suffrage, the social evils of poverty and racist discrimination would be alleviated. The Progressive League was aware that self-government would not immediately change everything at once, yet O'Meally declared: 'but we know also that popular government contains within itself the virile and efficient means of its own progressive correction'.[14]

In the pamphlet, 'Onward Jamaica', the Progressive League clarified its theoretical position:

> The League, therefore, will agitate for self-government, petition for it, make sacrifices for it, take every legal step within its power until that supreme goal has been attained. Not only is Jamaica, in fact, a Nation; she is essentially an entity in the New World, a Western Nation. In view of this unalterable truth confronting those who now rule her, as well as those who would set her free, the League asks that Jamaica be amicably granted the political structure to which she is entitled.[15]

Despite its open concept of nationality that included Jamaicans in the Diaspora, the Progressive League leaders emphasized that legitimate claims for nationhood could only be made by Jamaicans on the island, and encouraged the founding of a local political party that would have a broad supporter base including Jamaicans from all levels of society, which should articulate strong demands self-government.[16] Roberts had made his point crystal-clear in his first speech when he addressed Jamaicans in New York. In January 1937, he reiterated that 'one phase of activity is inevitable – the founding of a party in Jamaica to agitate for universal suffrage and for self-government, and to elect candidates to the legislature upon that platform'.[17] The role the Progressive League saw for itself was as an 'auxiliary to the Jamaican end of the movement'.[18] The pamphlet 'Onward, Jamaica!' affirmed the need for a nationalist party in Jamaica that 'properly belongs to patriots who live, work and vote in the homeland' and it promised: 'But as soon as a group pledged, as we are, to the cause of self-government is formed to take political action there, the full power of the Progressive League of New York and all its branches will be ranged behind that party'.[19] In conclusion, its leaders saw the Progressive League's most important task as '…the awakening of nationalism in the hearts of our people and a fighting movement to give effect to their aspirations'.[20]

First Repercussions in Jamaica

According to its declared aims, the next logical step for the Jamaica Progressive League was to reach out to Jamaica to inspire a national movement demanding self-government. But how was the idea of self-government perceived on the island? Were Jamaicans ready for the call to form an organization to fight for self-government? The survey of early political movements in Jamaica showed that imperial mentality was prevalent in the politically active circles of society, while large parts of the population seemed indifferent towards politics, indicating that the anti-colonial ideas of the Progressive League would not be received with enthusiasm.[21]

In the 1950s, Roberts recalled that he had wrongly felt that nationalism could be easily aroused: 'My basic assumption in 1936 was that national feeling existed in Jamaica, though dormant, and though the people were inarticulate on the subject'.[22] Accordingly, Roberts sought to invigorate dormant Jamaican nationalism, arguing that self-government could improve social and economic conditions. To spread the message, the Progressive League used different means, for instance through publications of letters, interviews and articles in Jamaican newspapers and by circulating pamphlets on the ground. The reactions to its ideas were ambivalent. Individual voices welcomed the idea of nationhood, although, the majority reacted with scepticism or outright resistance. These hostile reactions tempered many of those who had initially reacted with enthusiasm, thus slowing down the pace of development of a local group advocating for self-government.

The first positive reaction came from Rupert Meikle of the Quill and Ink Club in Port Maria, who had already sympathized with Roberts' ideas when the latter visited the island in 1934.[23] Roberts saw a potential supporter in Meikle and mailed him the pamphlet 'Self-Government for Jamaica' in late 1936. As hoped, Meikle favourably discussed the pamphlet and explicitly endorsed self-government in a letter published by the *Gleaner* – the first time the Progressive League was mentioned in a Jamaican newspaper.[24] Meikle quoted at length from the pamphlet and fundamentally agreed on the necessity to form a party demanding self-government. He lauded the work of the Progressive League and blamed the present form of government for the political inertia of his fellow countrymen:

> Crown Colony Government has for so long robbed us of any political initiative that there are many Jamaicans who are too mentally and physically lazy to do anything to take a hand in running their own country. These Jamaicans abroad by forming this Progressive League... have issued a challenge to us Jamaicans at home to wake up and work for the attainment of self-government for our native land. It is the duty of the numerous Citizens' Associations and Social and Literary Clubs now springing up in this country to begin to work towards this end.[25]

This was exactly the reaction the Progressive League had hoped for. However, Meikle's enthusiasm was not shared by the Citizen's Associations and various other groups which he had hoped would follow suit.

In February 1937, Progressive League Secretary Ethelred Brown was so disheartened by the absence of concrete support from local groups in Jamaica that he even toned down the demands for self-government in a letter to the *Gleaner*: 'When the League asks for self-government for Jamaica it is really asking for a restoration of the Constitution which was surrendered in 1865'. Although the letter was officially signed by Brown as the Progressive League's secretary, this position was by no means in accordance with the official line of the Progressive League. While it is possible that Brown just acted tactically and limited demands to the common call for a return to the old constitution as a concession to local opinion, it is also possible that Brown himself was less radical than Domingo, Roberts and O'Meally. His critique on the new practices of appointing civil servants, mainly Englishmen, instead of open examinations that also allowed educated Jamaicans to enter and which were now done away with by the Governor, were quite in accordance with the feelings for upward mobility of the aspiring middle class.[26] It seems like the most recent of *arrivés* who had been firmly rooted in civil society in Jamaica were more sympathetic with the moderate approach of many his countrymen than the other Progressive League leaders. In the same letter, Brown tried to soothe possible local concern that the New York based League might have 'assumed too much' in starting the movement in New York and not in Jamaica by emphasizing that the Progressive League basically saw itself as an auxiliary to the Jamaican end of the movement.²⁷ Brown's reaction to local sentiment foreshadowed the fundamental differences between the views of the Progressive League and political groups in Jamaica. Throughout the ensuing years, Jamaicans on the island frequently argued that the emigrants were out of touch with local thought. Such differences highlighted the decisive experience of migration which had shaped the intellectual development of the migrants, while a majority of Jamaica's politically interested citizens were not prepared to rally behind anti-colonial demands.

The founding of the National Reform Association (NRA) vividly illustrates the challenges the Progressive League encountered trying to encourage the establishment of a local group with outspoken anti-colonial positions. After the first pamphlets had reached Jamaica and letters of Progressive League members appeared in the local press, Domingo decided to travel to Jamaica to garner support and to inspire the launch of a local political group or party. Although Domingo's stay is not well documented, his influence on the slowly evolving political scene is noticeable. When Domingo visited Jamaica between February 6 and March 26, 1937,²⁸ he carried a stack of pamphlets of the Progressive League and arranged meetings with young, politically-minded people urging them to get involved in the nationalist movement for self-government.

One of the first and most enthusiastic supporters was up and coming journalist, Ken Hill, who decided to launch a new political organization in Kingston. In his booklet on the Progressive League, John S. Young also states that '[t]he visit of the first vice-president, Mr. W.A. Domingo, helped in great measure to commend the League to Jamaicans at home. It aroused interest in the program, thus creating public opinion which resulted in the launching of the National Reform Association (N.R.A.)'.²⁹

Ken Hill himself testified to Domingo's influence and the inspiration he derived from the ideas articulated by the Progressive League. While Domingo was present on the island in March 1937, Hill favourably featured the Progressive League in New York in his *Gleaner* column 'Things We Need'.³⁰ He agreed with the necessity to articulate demands for self-government in Jamaica and affirmatively summarized Roberts' pamphlet 'Self-Government for Jamaica', which clearly demanded Dominion status for Jamaica. Hill stated: 'The League believes that the backwardness of Jamaica politically, economically and culturally is traceable back to the political impotence of the people'. He emphasized that Jamaicans abroad were more inclined to think in nationalist terms and asked his countrymen: 'Now is it not a disgrace that we at home have not a similar movement to represent the needs of the majority of our people?' Hill urged Jamaicans to:

> ...unite in this movement against economic servitude and social evils that oppress us daily...Because we must have a truly representative

body to speak on our behalf, to express and voice our wants, to better conditions – a body which by force of its character and organisation will command the respect of the Government and the attention we need.

Hill's choice of words allowed the interpretation to a return to the old representative form of government before 1865 – a common call amongst politically active Jamaicans.

Ken Hill immediately started to plan for immediate action and declared in early March 1937 that '[t]he movement is about to be launched. Look out for the day and let us launch it like an avalanche'. Two weeks later, another of Hill's columns testified to the influence of the Progressive League on the aspiring politician. Directly inspired by reading Brown's pamphlet on the civil service that Domingo had brought in his luggage for distribution, Hill emphasized the need for a return to competitive examination. In the column, Hill announced that he was one of the distributors for the Progressive League pamphlets in Jamaica and announced that readers could obtain their copies from him.[31]

About a month after Hill had called for the launch of a nationalist movement, he attempted to organize a group under the name 'Jamaica National Club'.[32] The advertisement for the founding meeting included a statement that the group would fight for self-government, yet this point was dropped at the first meeting. The organization that had sprung from Hill's effort chose the name 'National Reform Association'[33] and adopted a rather moderate agenda. On March 31, 1937 the inaugural meeting was attended by a large crowd.[34] Although Domingo had played an important role in inspiring the launch of the organization, he had to leave shortly before the official founding meeting took place. It is impossible to predict whether Domingo's presence would have changed the stance the group had adopted, but at least, he was able to get a firsthand report, as his wife Eulalie was present in the audience.

In his opening speech, Hill presented an outline of demands that clearly resembled the declaration of the Progressive League; in part even matching its exact phrasing:

> ...the question of universal suffrage for Jamaica, the question of protecting labour by legislation, the economic and social problems, and the necessity of social and economic reform, the question of fostering inter-Caribbean trade and commerce and other relations which would tend to bring a closer union of the British West Indies.[35]

However, the sceptical attitude of the attendees toward demands for self-government seemingly compelled Hill to adjust his proposal and to deliberately exclude the Progressive League's most important goal, the determined demand for self-government. In contrast, he claimed:

> The goal should be to make Jamaica so responsible as to be wholly worthy and entitled to a more liberal form of Government some day. That ought to come in the wake of consciousness of the fact that as a people we Jamaicans have yet a lot to learn and it is essential to learn from the right people.[36]

Hill seemed to feel that a majority of the audience, which included a wide range of renowned public figures, would not endorse radical demands for self-government.[37] He asked his listeners to be prepared for sacrifices for the common good and warned that '[t]he path of the pioneer, especially in agitation of any sort, is a rough and hard one, fraught with danger and pitfalls and deceptions, difficult to see or apprehend until perhaps too late'.[38] From this comment, we can see clearly that articulating nationalist positions was still breaking fresh ground.

Ken Hill expressed his faith in the goodwill of the authorities in England and in Jamaica and claimed that necessary reforms would be granted if the national movement would rise to strength. But even Hill's moderate nationalist positions did not find full approval of the gathering. In the discussion, one person expressed the feeling that Hill 'put something concrete before them that they could not subscribe to'. Chairman C.G.X. Henriques made it clear that 'it was not Mr. Hill's movement, it was theirs. He had only called the meeting to put his views before them, it was for them to decide what form the movement should take – how it would work'.

Apparently, the strategy Hill had adopted to form a broadly-based nationalist movement came at the cost of sacrificing demands for self-government. Although N.N. Nethersole had rejected the formation of a committee to build the organization as 'premature', a resolution was nevertheless adopted 'that this meeting whole-heartedly endorse[s] the aims and objects of the Jamaica National Movement as outlined by Mr. Hill'. The hesitant reactions foreshadowed the direction in which the NRA would go.

On April 28, the organization was officially launched, adopting the name 'National Reform Association'. It had dropped any hint of the approval of radical constitutional change in the near future and instead declared that its aim was 'to encourage and strengthen Imperial and political relationships between Great Britain and Jamaica', and also vaguely pledged to 'foster and develop a sense of public civic and political responsibility among Jamaicans'.[39] These positions were even more moderate than those Hill had proposed at the meeting. The second meeting of the NRA continued in this spirit of mild nationalist proclamations.[40] A provisional council was formed at the meeting, consisting of 24 men and women of public standing.[41]

Based on its moderate patriotic call for unity, the NRA was able to attract many politically interested persons in Jamaica.[42] Comparing the programmes of

Progressive League and NRA, historian Ken Post also arrives at the conclusion that the NRA's aims were much less radical than those of the Progressive League, recognizing that the NRA had dropped concrete demands for self-government at its first meeting.[43] Post concludes that the NRA 'could not find a form of action, or even a rhetoric, which could articulate the nationalism towards which different class elements were grouping at this time and create a new political practice'.[44] Historian James Carnegie describes Hill as an ambivalent figure between moderation and radicalism, whose ideas were too radical for the organization he had founded. Carnegie surmises correctly, that Hill promoted only 'a moderate version of the J.P.L.'s ideas'.[45] The fact that the NRA gained popularity only by sacrificing the radical claim for self-government alludes to the general scepticism in the local scene.

The adopted positions were a grave disappointment for the Progressive League. When Roberts visited Jamaica six months later, he expressed his discomfort: '[t]he N.R.A. set out an ambitious programme, but has dropped the plan, which puts the N.R.A. out of commission as far as I am concerned'. When he was asked if it would be possible for the NRA and a newly formed Progressive League branch in Kingston to merge, Roberts answered upfront: 'Yes, if the N.R.A. will pursue a definite programme for self government, instead of adopting compromises'.[46] Yet, contrary to initial hopes, the NRA was too moderate to serve as the local end of a movement demanding self-government. Hence, the Progressive League continued its propaganda, hoping to find a suitable ally on the ground soon.

In February 1937, a new weekly newspaper was launched that reflected an increased interest in Jamaica's political and cultural development. *Public Opinion* was a joint project of O.T. Fairclough, Frank Hill and H.P. Jacobs that became the mouthpiece of Jamaica's middle class and the emerging political and nationalist movement. Remarkably, two of the three founders also had migration experiences, a fact that testifies to the importance of migration in the development of nationalist thought in the colonial setting of Jamaica. Fairclough had lived in Haiti where he had been exposed to concepts of *nègritude* and upon return to Jamaica, was disappointed that he was unable to find a job that suited his level of education, while in Haiti he had worked as one of the managers of a bank.[47] Jacobs was an English liberal and had been a member of the British Labour Party, before he migrated to Jamaica in 1925 where he worked as a teacher.[48] Journalist Frank Hill was the brother of NRA founder Ken Hill.[49]

The new paper filled the void for critical journalism and became the main platform for progressive ideas. According to Richard Hart, '…it was host to expressions of the growing nationalist sentiment and to anti-imperialist ideas across a wide spectrum, from bourgeois nationalism to Marxism'.[50] It is quite telling, however, that a survey of the first issues of the *PO* clearly shows that the most radical nationalist articles were written by members of the Progessive League. Initially, *Public Opinion* covered a wide range of political, educational, economic and social topics. Parallel to the propaganda efforts of the Progressive League in Jamaica, the tone of the articles and the subjects discussed in the paper increasingly became more nationalistic. The first article that mentioned Dominion status for Jamaica was an article about the founding of the Progressive League. It quoted at length from Roberts' pamphlet and emphasized the different ideological influences on the thoughts of the emigrants. However, it offered no opinion on the outlined demands for self-government, other than that it was '... worthwhile seeing how this question of self-government appears to the Jamaican abroad'.[51] It further presented the Progressive League's argument that the political system resulted in political apathy and that Jamaicans should form a party to fight self-government to change their situation.[52] Hence, roughly a year before the first attempt to found a political party was made by Fairclough, the Progressive League's call for such a party was being presented to a wider Jamaican public.

The issue of the following week carried an outspoken editorial that referred to growing disunity between the Governor and the electives in the Legislative Council, and indicated that some of the editors appreciated the radicalized tone in nationalist propaganda.[53] The anonymous author openly complained about the lip service of some of the advocates of 'Jamaica for the Jamaicans' who would think that 'self-government is an ideal which may be realized in another 200 years' and who would be 'frightened out of their wits if they thought there was any real prospect of attaining their ideal'. The editorial advocated starting the fight for self-government now, asking its readers: 'Has India reached her present position by just saying periodically that really she must look upon full self-government as an ultimate goal? ...Has any people outside Jamaica ever obtained self-government without a struggle?'

Coinciding with Domingo's presence on the island, it is quite likely that these views were influenced by the Progressive League, probably through Ken Hill. The same issue of *Public Opinion* announced the formation of the 'Jamaica National League', the group that was to become the NRA, and announced: 'Political consciousness is to be the medium and Self-Government for Jamaica the goal'.[54] However, the announcement remained vague and contained no hint that self-government was something that was to be attained in the near future.

The following issues of *Public Opinion* carried several articles about or directly written by members of the Progressive League, for instance, 'What is Fascism' by O'Meally, a poem 'Ode to Jamaica' by Brown, an article about 'Mr. Brown and the Civil Service',[55] a report about a meeting in New York,[56] and an article by Roberts about 'Jamaica and the USA'.[57]

While there was some degree of appreciation for the Progressive League's demand for self-government by those who spearheaded the national movement in Jamaica, the Progressive League's radicalism was rejected by many of the political activists. For example, Cleveland G. Walker,[58] secretary of the Federation of Citizen's Associations, with his mild nationalist views can be regarded as a representative for many others who supported the less radical NRA. Walker strongly opposed self-government and was convinced that the masses were not sufficiently educated and responsible enough to be given full power over the affairs of the country.[59]

An editorial in *Public Opinion* commented ironically on the widespread sceptical attitude towards greater power for the people: 'Now that public feeling is definitely in favour of some change in the constitution of Jamaica, the question which inevitably arises in the mind of the Government and of half the supporters of change, is simply this: How can a change be effected without really altering anything?'[60]

But even in the pages of *Public Opinion*, the attitude towards self-government was still ambivalent. On one hand the editors claimed:

> The time has come for Jamaicans to decide whether we really intend to take our place among the nations of the Commonwealth, or whether we shall continue to be a mere chattel of an England, who has established a closed market for her manufacturers, forcing us, with our low standard of living, to support her own standard'.[61]

On the other hand, they lamented: 'But at the present we cannot claim any place at all: our exclusion is due to our demerits'.[62]

Parallel to the radicalized nationalism in the *Public Opinion* circles, the conservative section of the Jamaican society closed ranks and stiffened its resistance. In an article from 1993, journalist Terry Smith reviewed the initial reactions to the Progressive League's propaganda, and pointed to the reaction of 'the entrenched ruling class of the island, then a loyal British colony for 282 years', claiming that 'talk of self-government varied from heresy to downright treason, and this was reflected by a rather cool reception by the orthodox press, and in other high places'.[63]

Indeed, the conservative *Gleaner* was keenly observing the new tendencies and had attended the inaugural meeting of the NRA with several staff members. Afterwards, the paper immediately ceased to print Hill's column 'Things We Need', which had taken too radical a stand by approving the demands of the Progressive League and criticizing colonial rule.[64]

Unswervingly, the Progressive League continued its efforts to influence the Jamaican public. In May 1937, even the *Gleaner* carried two of the Progressive

League's cultural pieces, the poem 'Ode to Jamaica' by Brown and the 'Exile's Hymn' by Roberts.[65] In the last issue of May 1937, Roberts published his first article in *Public Opinion*, in which he shared his views about US foreign policy. He rejected frequently expressed concerns that the United States would take over Jamaica if it became a self-governed nation state. Roberts emphasized his regional perspective: 'To Jamaica, no less than to the Latin American republics by which she is surrounded, the United States of America is the 'the colossus of the North.'[66] But despite this undeniable fact, Roberts assured that he did not believe rumours that 'the United States would immediately seek to inveigle her into the Union', or would 'grab Jamaica' in the event of a new World War: 'I say that such fears are chimerical. Uncle Sam has no designs for Jamaica.'[67]

Domingo's first article appeared in *Public Opinion* in June 1937.[68] He offered a rigid critique of the traditional press for excluding progressive ideas and praised the course the new paper had taken. Domingo proved to have visionary qualities as he foresaw the upcoming World War and expected the general sentiment of the time would be in favour of further decolonization of the world. He claimed that emancipatory ideas were on the rise and expected that an increasing number of colonial people would demand and receive independence in the near future. From his internationalist perspective, he anticipated considerable changes in the structure of the British Empire. Provocatively, he asked his readers:

> Are we so sure that we had not better be studying the future status of Jamaica in the British Empire in this changing world? Are Jamaicans inferior to Filipinos, Canadians, Chinese and Hindus why they should remain passive on the question of self-government and insular nationalism?

Statements like this showcase the influence of other anti-colonial movements on the emigrants in New York.

Domingo especially welcomed the new critical journalistic voice offered by *Public Opinion* because he saw 'the journalistic opiate with which the people have been daily dosed for years' as one of the main reasons that impeded the development of nationalism. In view of such powerful indoctrination, he believed 'even so small an effort as the National Reform Association can be productive of much good'. The remark on the NRA, although trying to be encouraging, still shows Domingo's disappointment.

While mild patriotic views dominated in the NRA, the Progressive League intensified its strong advocacy for self-government on the local Jamaican scene. Another article in *Public Opinion* written by Domingo addressed Jamaica's need for self-government in an unprecedentedly outspoken manner. Domingo emphasized the important role of those pioneers who worked for the progress of the whole society. 'Man is by nature conservative', he stated, but 'all the progress of the world is a direct result of the daring of the few who blazed new trails on which the multitude later trod in comfort'.[69] He pointed to George Washington, Toussaint L'Ouverture, Frederick Douglass and Oliver Cromwell as pioneers of the 'right of all human beings to a fuller life and to participate in the governing of themselves' and claimed that without them '...mankind would still be in the feudal or the slave era of history'. This was the tradition in which he saw the pioneering work of the Progressive League. As is true for all advocates of radical changes, Domingo expected to meet obstacles. He openly claimed that race was among the main factors in deciding which colony was allowed to become a nation state:

> There are political and economic forces in Great Britain, and for that matter throughout the empire, that will leave no stone unturned to prevent any genuine democratic advance for mixed racial or non-white communities...it is not to be thought for one moment that they will be in a hurry to accord Jamaica any real self-government unless they are forced to do so.

Domingo blamed the media, schools and churches for fostering and perpetuating colonial rule. He openly criticized the racist assumptions on which Great Britain's colonial policy was based which regarded black people as not fit for self-government. To prove his point, Domingo referred to former colonies with white majorities that had been elevated into Dominion status like Canada, New Zealand or Australia. Not mincing words, Domingo continued with an outspoken analysis of the purpose the remaining colonies served within the Empire:

> Stated plainly, colonies exist as sources of raw materials, markets for capital and manufactured goods; they provide sinecures for sons of Englishmen who are later pensioned on the expense of the Colony, and in these days of militarism, soldiers to be shock troops for their imperial masters.

He referred to European roots of nationalist thought and mentioned the French Revolution and the British Magna Charta, concluding:

> ...self-government will create national pride, release new energies and stimulate the artistic and literary expression of the people who will have cast off much of the sense of colonial inferiority that a Crown Colony engenders. Our goal must be – JAMAICA A DOMINION!

Domingo's radical piece left no doubt what the Progressive League was about and allowed no mild interpretation of the term self-government. Continuing their propaganda efforts in Jamaica, Roberts continuously underlined the need for a nationalist party in Jamaica. In a reprint of an article from the Progressive League's own newssheet 'Jamaica To-Morrow'[70] that appeared in *Public Opinion* in October 1937, Roberts urged: 'Jamaica...must support an energetic Nationalist

Party and use the present limited franchise to elect persons who actually represent the aspirations of the country…Their business henceforth should be to fight for self-government'.[71]

Some reactions in the press showed that the propaganda of the Progressive League was recognized in Jamaica and had further effect on existing groups. The Poetry League, for instance, discussed Roberts' article approvingly and demanded nationalist education in schools.[72] Also, Rupert Meikle remained interested in the Progressive League's cause and discussed the pamphlets in his organizations.[73] He applauded Roberts' article in a letter to the editor of the *Gleaner* and enclosed the whole item.[74] However, Meikle seemed to believe that 'the National Reform Association is one of the best mediums through which the Jamaica of To-Morrow visualized by Mr. Roberts, can be brought about. Anyone reading the article and being moved thereby to play some effective part in working out the pattern of the New Jamaica should not fail to join the N.R.A'.[75] Willingly or not, Meikle missed the point why collaboration between the Progressive League and the NRA was impossible, unless the NRA would reconsider its take on the question of self-government.

C.A. Isaac-Henry of the NRA welcomed that even the *Gleaner* had started to become aware of the new nationalist spirit and complimented the paper for printing some of the material of the Progressive League. However, Isaac-Henry personally advocated a slow progress toward representative government, in accordance with the line of the NRA. He nevertheless positively mentioned the inspiration of Roberts and the Progressive League and also downplayed the difference between the two groups, claiming that the NRA and the Progressive League were 'having pretty much the same aims and objects'.[76]

It is difficult to judge whether Isaac-Henry and Meikle were really not aware of the gap between the positions of the moderate NRA and the radical, nationalist anti-colonial programme of the Progressive League. In any case, these first reactions affirmed that the Progressive League had inspired a discussion on the political future of the country. From the outset, the Progressive League served as an inspiring and radicalizing catalyst for even the moderate spectrum of the national movement. However, the moderate approaches of the local activists highlight the difference in radicalism between the migrants in New York and the local scene. The Progressive League quickly realized that the task to promote the demand for self-government and the aim to find a strong partner on the island to push its agenda would be rather difficult. In contrast to Roberts' optimistic assumption in 1936 quoted at the start of this chapter, he admitted in the 1950s, that his initial assumption regarding a dormant nationalism was wrong:

> I thought it possible that there would be an eager and wide response and that at all events the dynamic nature of the idea must cause it to

> spread rapidly. I counted on an entity that would see great good in a movement to obtain self-government. Events proved that I had been a doctrinaire. National feeling in Jamaica was not a dormant condition it merely was potential. A few enthusiasts could be enlisted immediately, but the general problem was, with their aid, to create a national feeling rather than to arouse it.[77]

The difficulties the Progressive League encountered during its first attempts to spread nationalist propaganda and to propose the founding of a political party to work for self-government on the island suggest that imperial mentalities, internalized inferiority complexes and strong loyalty to Great Britain enforced through centuries of indoctrination in schools and public life were still widespread and thus impeded anti-colonial nationalism. This meant that inspiring a national movement in Jamaica proved to be more difficult than expected, as the founding of the NRA exemplified. While Domingo's presence on the island stirred up some interest in small circles of politically interested Jamaicans, the indifference and at times even hostile reactions to the demand for self-government thwarted the initial enthusiasm and shed light on the limits to the transfer of ideas from New York to Kingston.

Notes

1. W. Adolphe Roberts, 'Autobiography', 8.
2. See Birte Timm, 'Caribbean Leaven in the American Loaf: Wilfred A. Domingo, the Jamaica Progressive League, and the Founding of a Decolonization Movement for Jamaica', in *Beyond the Nation: United States History in Transnational Perspective, Bulletin of the German Historical Institute*, Supplement 5, ed. Thomas Adam and Uwe Luebken (2008), 81–98.
3. Roberts, 'Autobiography', 25f.
4. See John S. Young, *Lest We Forget* (New York: Isidor Books, 1881), 35f.
5. See for example *New York Amsterdam News*, September 19, 1936; *New York Amsterdam News*, November 10, 1936; *New York Amsterdam News*, October 17, 1936; *New York Amsterdam News*, November 14, 1936; *New York Amsterdam News*, January 16, 1937; *New York Amsterdam News*, April 3, 1937 and *New York Amsterdam News* April 10, 1937.
6. See Ethelred Brown, *Injustices in the Civil Service of Jamaica* (New York: Jamaica Progressive League, 1937).
7. See Young, *Lest We Forget*, 34.
8. *New York Amsterdam News*, January 30, 1937.
9. Ibid.
10. Ibid.
11. *Onward, Jamaica!* Pamphlet published by the Jamaica Progressive League of New York, 1937.
12. Jamie O'Meally, *Why We Demand Self-Government* (New York: Jamaica Progressive League, 1938).
13. See Jamaica Progressive League NY, *Onward, Jamaica!*, 7.
14. O'Meally, *Why We Demand Self-Government*, 12.

15. Jamaica Progressive League, *Onward, Jamaica!*, 7.
16. See for instance, *New York Amsterdam News*, October 17, 1936; *New York Amsterdam News*, January 30, 1937; Jamaica Progressive League, *Onward, Jamaica!*, 4.
17. *New York Amsterdam News*, January 30, 1937.
18. Ibid.
19. Jamaica Progressive League, *Onward, Jamaica!*, 4.
20. Ibid.
21. Chapter 1, 1–28.
22. W. Adolphe Roberts, 'National Feeling,' undated [written after 1949], NLJ, WAR, MS 353, Box 9.
23. See for instance *Daily Gleaner*, August 8, 1934.
24. Ibid., December 21, 1936.
25. Ibid.
26. For this and the following quotes see *Daily Gleaner*, February 2, 1937.
27. See Roberts' statement in *New York Amsterdam News*, January 30, 1937.
28. See *Daily Gleaner*, February 8, 1937; *Daily Gleaner*, March 27, 1937.
29. Young, *Lest We Forget*, 35.
30. For this and the following quotes, see *Daily Gleaner*, March 9, 1937.
31. *Daily Gleaner*, March 22, 1937. Hill spoke of a stock of 50 copies of Roberts' *Self-Government for Jamaica* and 100 copies of Brown's *Injustices in the Civil Service* that he received from the JPL for distribution.
32. See Ken Post, *Arise Ye Starvelings: The Jamaica Labour Rebellion as of 1938 and its Aftermath* (The Hague: Martinus Nijhoft Publishers, 1978), 217.
33. *Daily Gleaner*, March 27, 1937.
34. Ibid., April 3, 1937.
35. Ibid.
36. Ibid.
37. The list of people in attendance reads like the who's who of Jamaica's public life and included C.G.X. Henriques, who initially became the NRA's president, N.N. Nethersole, who took over the position, Una Marson, Mr S.R. Braithwaite, Mr G.M. DaCosta, the Hon. Revd J.W. Maxwell, the Hon. E.V. Allen, Mr V.P. DaCosta, Mr G.R. Bowen, Mr H.P. Jacobs, Mr Frank Hill, O.T. Fairclough. Also Domingo's wife was present. Further, many future members of the JPL Kingston branch attended: H.C. Buchanan, Mr C.A. McPherson, Dr J.L. Varma, Mr P.A. Aiken, and Miss Aiken. See also Richard Hart, *Towards Decolonisation: Political, Labour and Economic Development in Jamaica 1938–1945* (Barbados: Canoe Press, 1999), 24.
38. For this and the following quotes, see *Daily Gleaner*, April 7, 1937.
39. NRA constitution, published in three parts in *Public Opinion*, April 1, 1937; *Public Opinion*, April 8, 1937; *Public Opinion*, April 15, 1937.
40. See *Daily Gleaner*, April 30, 1937.
41. For a list of names see *Daily Gleaner*, May 22, 1937. All women in the council, Mrs Amy Bailey, Mrs Morris-Knibb and Mrs P.A. Aiken later joined the JPL, Kingston.
42. See *Daily Gleaner*, May 22, 1937.
43. Post, *Arise*, 217.
44. Ibid., 219.
45. James Carnegie, *Some Aspects of Jamaica's Politics 1918–1938* (Kingston: Institute of Jamaica, 1973), 107.

46. *Daily Gleaner*, December 22, 1937.
47. See Richard Hart, *Rise and Organise: The Birth of the Workers and National Movements in Jamaica 1936–1939*, (London: Karia Press, 1989), 22; Hart, *Towards,* xv; Post, *Arise,* 215f.
48. Hart, *Rise,* 24; Richard Hart, "Jamaica and Self-Determination 1660–1970". *Race* XIII (1972):271–79, 284; Hart, *Towards,* xv.
49. See Hart, *Rise,* 21; Hart, *Towards,* xv.
50. See Hart, *Towards Decolonization,* 22f.
51. *Public Opinion,* March 20, 1937.
52. Ibid.
53. For this and the following quotes see *Public Opinion,* March 27, 1937.
54. Ibid. The announcement was not signed, but marked as 'contributed'. It is quite likely that it was contributed by NRA initiator Ken Hill, brother of *Public Opinion* editor Frank Hill.
55. All three appeared in *Public Opinion,* March 3, 1937.
56. *Public Opinion,* May 15, 1937.
57. Ibid., May 29, 1937.
58. Walker advocated self-government as a student in the US, on returning he participated in the National League and Citizens Movements, *Daily Gleaner,* July 11, 1928. He was a member of the NRA and later joined the PNP and was member of its Executive Council and secretary of the committee to draft the constitution of the party. See Carnegie, *Some Aspects,* 108.
59. *Daily Gleaner,* April 7, 1937.
60. *Public Opinion,* April 17, 1937.
61. Ibid., May 15, 1937.
62. Ibid.
63. *Daily Gleaner,* September 5, 1993.
64. A letter to the Gleaner editor, finally printed in *Public Opinion* after the Gleaner refused to publish it, harshly criticized this decision as 'imperialistic and gubernatorial', see *Public Opinion,* April 10, 1937.
65. See *Daily Gleaner,* May 18, 1937.
66. *Public Opinion,* May 29, 1937.
67. Ibid.
68. For this and the following quotes see *Public Opinion,* June 26, 1937.
69. Ibid., August 7, 1937.
70. Jamaica To-Morrow was a mimeographed magazine of which only a few issues were circulated. See Roberts, 'Autobiography', 23.
71. *Public Opinion,* October 23, 1937.
72. *Daily Gleaner,* October 27, 1937.
73. See for instance *Daily Gleaner,* August 12, 1937.
74. Ibid., October 28, 1937.
75. Ibid.
76. Ibid., October 19, 1937.
77. Roberts, 'National Feeling', NLJ, WAR, MS 353, Box 9.

CHAPTER 4: STRETCHING OUT: A LOCAL BRANCH IN KINGSTON

Founding of the Jamaica Progressive League in Kingston

Since its launch, the founders of the Progressive League insisted that the organization should be an auxiliary to a local nationalist movement. On numerous occasions, they encouraged the founding of a political party or a nationalist political group on the island. But how did the Progressive League try to reach out to Jamaica? How were the anti-colonial demands perceived by local political activists? The newspapers in Jamaica occasionally carried news about the Progressive League in New York. Soon, travellers from Jamaica would contact the group during their visit in New York, and the *Gleaner* frequently mentioned those trips.[1]

A report about the first anniversary of the Jamaica Progressive League in New York that appeared in the *Daily Gleaner* in September 1937 indirectly triggered the founding of a local branch in Jamaica.[2] Walter G. McFarlane, like so many others active in the developing political circles, was a returning migrant. The architectural draughtsman had returned to Jamaica in 1935, after he had lived in the United States for 13 years. Reading about the anniversary of the Progressive League in New York inspired him to start a branch in Jamaica.[3] Up to that date, McFarlane played no prominent role in Jamaica's emerging nationalist scene, although he was active in several organizations like the Kingston and St Andrew Literary and Debating Society. In June 1937, McFarlane had called for a more representative form of government in a letter to the *Gleaner*, although not explicitly for self-government.[4] In the pamphlet 'The Birth of Self-Government for Jamaica and the Jamaica Progressive League 1937–1944',[5] which McFarlane published in 1957, he recalled that after his return to Jamaica in 1935, he wanted to get involved in the political scene and tried to co-operate with the existing groups. However, he soon became disappointed in their approach and felt it was mainly limited to parochial matters. According to McFarlane, the existing groups rejected progressive ideas of constitutional change or the formation of a party. Like the leaders of the Progressive League in New York, he felt that the widespread identification with the British Empire impeded the development of a nationalist spirit and complained that some of his countrymen '…were trying to be more English than the English born'.

Stretching Out: A Local Branch in Kingston

McFarlane decided to initiate the launch of an organization that would be '...bold and progressive enough to join with me in forming a nucleus of the national self-government movement in Jamaica'. The idea to launch a branch of the Progressive League in Jamaica was born. He immediately contacted the Progressive League in New York and asked for permission to start a branch in Jamaica. Progressive League Secretary Ethelred Brown answered favourably: 'The Directors will be pleased to note that a League similar to ours has been organized and they will be glad to have you co-operate with us to put over our program'.[6] To make sure that the newly formed Progressive League would be in accordance with the principles of the organization in New York, he enclosed the pamphlet 'Onward, Jamaica!' as a guideline that contained the declaration of principles and a statement of the programme.[7] At the next board meeting, the directors welcomed the initiative and approved the branch in principle, but insisted that the Kingston group should first read the Progressive League's pamphlets and programmes and pledge to work according to the outlined principles before the mode of cooperation could be determined.[8]

After this encouragement, McFarlane started to scout people to join him in his efforts, but the venture turned out to be more difficult than expected:

> This task was like finding the proverbial needle in the haystack. With all the courage and determination that I could muster, I could recruit only two men between September and November 1937, who had the strength of their convictions to stand up with me at a public meeting called for the launching of the National Self Government Movement in Jamaica.[9]

This initial challenge clearly displays the cleavage between local opinion and the radical anti-colonial stance of the migrants. Finally, four persons, Dr S.W. Duhaney, C.A. Gulley, Don Messam and W.F. Campbell followed McFarlane's call and signed an invitation for the inaugural meeting to be held at the Moravian Church Hall in downtown Kingston.[10] The invitation spoke of the great success of the Progressive League in New York and argued that to ensure that its goals were realized, an active local group needed to start work in Jamaica. Anticipating that too far-reaching anti-colonial goals would alienate local activists, the invitation did not speak of self-government, and included the qualification: 'We desire to embrace, as far as practicable, the programme of the New York League'.[11] The text referred to some of the goals outlined in the declaration of the parent body and added some demands applicable to the local situation, for instance, the aim to cooperate with other citizen's organizations and the labour movement.

Members of the group were aware how much their migration and travel experiences had shaped their views and expected that people with similar experiences would be inclined to support nationalist ideas. Hence, the group pledged to assist returning migrants and to 'maintain a certain standard of sentiment and advanced opinion peculiar to persons with foreign experience'.[12] Although the high proportion of returning migrants in the political circles shows that they were indeed generally more open for nationalist and anti-colonial ideas, the statement breathes some arrogance, which might have turned off potential supporters.

The recapitulation of the founding of a branch of the Progressive League in Kingston can only be reconstructed from bits and pieces of sometimes contradictory evidence. This is indicative of the problematic nature of McFarlane's reports, which sometimes conflict with evidence from other sources and are sometimes even contradictory in itself. It is unquestionable, however, that the founding faced severe obstacles; starting with difficulties finding a meeting hall. According to McFarlane, owners shied away from the request for a meeting to be convened on their premises when they heard about the purpose of the proposed organization. Eventually, McFarlane found encouragement and approval from Reverend Walter O'Meally, pastor of the Moravian Church downtown.[13]

The next challenge was to find enough people in support of the radical demand for immediate self-government. Even some of the persons who followed the invitation indicated that they were not fully in accordance with the outlined aims.[14] The inaugural meeting was announced in the *Gleaner* to be held on Wednesday, November 24, in the Moravian Church Hall, and C.A. Reid and other Legislative Council and Kingston and St Andrew Corporation (KSAC) members were expected to attend.[15] However, at this meeting, it was not possible to successfully launch the Progressive League in Jamaica. On November 30, 1937, the *Gleaner* announced that the meeting had to be postponed due to unfavourable weather conditions and would take place in early December.[16] Yet, it seems as if the tamed tone of the invitation had attracted people who were not willing to subscribe to the radical resolution 'that Jamaica should have self-government as a member of the British Commonwealth of Nations', tabled by H.C. Buchanan, a returning migrant and left-wing trade unionist, who had lived in Cuba for several years.[17] Apparently, some persons reacted with surprise and hostility to the proposal. According to McFarlane 'a group of men and women started an uproar, declaring that they did not want self government; they wanted representative government: they did not want the Jamaica Progressive League'.[18] The incident, he continued, turned into an 'ugly scene which broke up the meeting and drove me and my small band of supports from the church after the resolution which was intended to bring the League into being was withdrawn....'[19] In 1993 in an interview with journalist Terry Smith, McFarlane claimed that a group led by Ken Hill and Alexander Bustamante were responsible for crushing the meeting.[20] Ken Hill had been among the earliest supporters when Domingo was on the island earlier, but it is possible that he saw the Progressive League as competition to the NRA. However, there is no further evidence for this claim, and given McFarlane's sometimes questionable way of skewing facts, the statement might have been intended to discredit Bustamante and Hill.

M.G. Bailey and H.C. Buchanan, who had moved the resolution to inaugurate the Jamaica Progressive League in Kingston, withdrew the motion to prevent the gathering from rejecting the proposal to bring the Progressive League into being. Accordingly, the Inaugural Meeting needed to be postponed – not because of unfavourable weather, but because of unfavourable reactions from those in attendance. Terry Smith rightly concludes: 'There was obviously a sharp divide between reform of Representative Government, and Self-Government'.[21]

In the meantime, the president of the Progressive League in New York had decided to travel to Jamaica to go on a speaking tour to promote self-government and arrived on December 2, 1937.[22] Although the inaugural meeting was scheduled for the eighth, Roberts was busy travelling the country addressing different gatherings, for instance, in Linstead and Port Maria.[23] In the above mentioned interview in 1993, McFarlane recalled that Roberts had been in contact with Buchanan, briefing him extensively before attending the meeting.[24] In a letter to *Public Opinion*, Buchanan recalled the meeting at which 'misgivings were being voiced as to the wisdom of so many organizations with identical aims'.[25] However, Buchanan was convinced that the Progressive League added an original approach. The other organization's goals, he felt, were 'shrouded in uncertainty':

> They are not backed by a sufficiently substantial body of knowledge to steer the movements clear of the difficulties that will arise. The motive force of nearly all the key figures in these movements is some individual pecuniary benefit and self-glory. Not being grounded upon the solid rock of patriotism we cannot expect anything but failure.

Buchanan held the Progressive League in New York in high regard and emphasized: 'The men behind it are patriots worthy of our support. Let us by all means have a Branch of the League here'. He affirmed his radical anti-colonial stance and declared that he was prepared to '...enter the struggle now and oppose the Englishmen tooth and nail for the freedom of my country Jamaica!' But he was aware that his views were out of touch with local opinion: 'Jamaicans are afraid of even thinking about it, to say nothing about making a start'.

Buchanan was among the first individuals who expressed full support for a branch of the Progressive League in Jamaica demanding self-government. Like McFarlane, he was also a returning migrant. He had lived in Cuba for several years and referred to the Cuban people as an inspiration for his nationalism, emphasizing their patriotism and pride. Like his friend Arnold Lecesne,

Buchanan belonged to that group of few individuals, who even favoured complete independence from Britain, but regarded self-government as a first step and therefore supported the Progressive League.

A few days after the second failed inaugural meeting on December 8, McFarlane was finally able to report to the League's secretary in New York that the Jamaica Progressive League in Kingston was officially founded on December 13.[26] At a private meeting with invited guests, the Kingston branch was launched with the following resolution:

> Whereas; it has been found necessary to inaugurate an association in Jamaica based on similar principles to the Jamaica Progressive League of New York U.S.A. and whereas, the said JPL of NY is working fearlessly and conscientiously for the National, Economic, and Educational Advancement of Jamaica; it has now become highly essential, that a similar League should be in operation here (in the homeland Jamaica) to act as a central body, for any organization operating over-seas.[27]

It is remarkable, that the resolution included no positive affirmation of the demand for self-government, although the Progressive League in Jamaica was formed privately. This founding resolution foreshadowed an undecided and inconsistent stand of the local branch, which lacked the radicalism of the mother organization in New York.

After two failed attempts and one small private meeting, the local branch of the Jamaica Progressive League was publicly launched on December 15, 1937 at a large function at Metropolitan Hall, one of the biggest and most popular venues for political debate. At the well-attended meeting, Roberts pointed out that he was glad that the new organization already found prominent supporters, among them even two members of the Legislative Council, R. Ehrenstein and C.A. Reid, and mayor of Kingston Dr Oswald E. Anderson.[28] However, most of these early prominent supporters soon disappeared from the records, either because the demand for self-government had alienated them, or because the local group was not attractive for them after Roberts left the island. During his speech, Roberts openly denounced the meek and reformist attitude of groups like the NRA and the Citizen's Associations. He brought out the need for a more radical approach and recommended the promotion of nationalist education with focus on the history of the region. The local branch of the Progressive League, he hoped, would become a lively movement in Jamaica and promised support from the overseas branch, comparing the envisioned cooperation to the Irish fight for independence, in which Irish migrants had played an instrumental role.[29] His statement highlights the inspirational role of the Irish nationalist movement for Roberts' concept of the Progressive League as a catalyst to the local nationalist movement.

Roberts' decisive role in the public launch and his well-covered presence on the island explain why historians like Denis M. Benn believe that Roberts founded the local arm of the Progressive League.[30] His prominence helped to overshadow the initial obstacles the Progressive League encountered and created a positive atmosphere of expectation. The *Gleaner* reported:

> The newly formed local section of the Jamaica Progressive League, which has its headquarters in America, had a brilliant push-off on Wednesday last. The large and enthusiastic audience at the Metropolitan Hall showed much appreciation for the inauguration of the Association, and the address given by Mr. Adolphe Roberts, and other speakers.[31]

The *Gleaner* was impressed, if not disturbed by the support the movement now received even in respectable circles. The mayor of Kingston, Oswald Anderson, the *Gleaner* reported, spoke 'strongly in favour of the idea enunciated by the Jamaican author'.[32] The *Gleaner* suspected that Roberts would return to Jamaica to continue his campaign and expected 'that the very clear-cut issue announced in the words "Self-Government for Jamaica" will win a considerable following'. At the same time, *Gleaner* editor Herbert de Lisser was confident that the idea of self-government would not arise as a practical question any time soon:

> If it should ever do so Mr. Roberts would find that the bitter jealousy which Jamaicans have for one another was a more serious obstacle to self-Government then any opposition which the Colonial Office might offer to his plan – and the Colonial Office will offer plenty.

De Lisser proved to be right; the movement would face severe challenges, and he was to throw himself in the forefront with his propaganda against self-government in the *Gleaner*.

However, while Roberts was in Jamaica, the campaign was met with great success. Another highlight was a huge mass meeting organized in a joint effort by the NRA, the Federation of Citizens Associations (FCA) and the Progressive League in Kingston, presided over by Mayor Anderson. A few days before Christmas, the Ward Theatre, Kingston's largest indoor meeting hall, was crowded, although de Lisser had lamented in an editorial it was usually not the time of the year for new political ideas and activities.[33] Yet, even de Lisser was forced to admit: 'In view of the interesting and intriguing argument employed by Mr. Roberts, and the public attention being directed to the question, it is anticipated that there will be a large and representative turn-out'.[34] However, de Lisser doubted that the radical goals would find the support of a substantial number of people and argued again that these aims were out of touch with the Jamaican people. He felt that the only reason why the ideas were taken seriously was Roberts' respectability.[35] These reactions of *Gleaner* editor de Lisser illustrate the considerable impact of the white Jamaican, the renowned historian and author who was in a position to popularize the demand for self-government in Jamaica.

The numerous lectures he gave all over the island at the turn of 1938 were organized by a variety of political groups and civil organizations and often presided over by popular public figures, mayors and Legislative Council members. Roberts left no doubt about the radical character of the Progressive League's outspoken advocacy of Dominion status and emphasized the difference from local groups that merely aimed at returning to the old constitution.[36] He frequently emphasized that he hoped the local arm of the Progressive League would become the nucleus of a political party, 'candidly calling itself national and demanding a Dominion status for the Island', and assured full support from the parent body in New York.[37]

Although the Progressive League envisioned a radical change of the political system, it pledged 'to wage its fight along constitutional lines'.[38] In order to steal the critique's thunder Roberts assured:

> ...we are not Communists and are not hatching any sort of revolutionary plot against England. Far from it. The League movement is simply an attempt to obtain Self-Government for Jamaica within the framework of the British Commonwealth of Nations.[39]

Roberts expected that Jamaica would get what it demanded if the claim was reasonably presented and referred to Great Britain's positive attitude towards self-government in other colonies that were elevated into Dominion status.[40] However, this statement stood in contrast to other occasions, at which Roberts and Domingo anticipated harsh opposition from the authorities. In front of a Jamaican audience, Roberts' statements can be seen as an effort to appease those who felt that demanding self-government would be disloyal to Great Britain. Countering such imperial thinking, Roberts encouraged Jamaicans to think about Jamaica as an independent country and demanded that school curricula should be adjusted: 'Jamaica is not a part of England. She is not a European Country. She is an entity in the Caribbean region of the North American continent and the curriculum of the schools should be based on the unalterable fact'.[41] Roberts maintained that other small countries would already enjoy Dominion status, while other colonies like India, Ceylon and Rhodesia, were clearly on their way to self-determination.[42] He tried to convince his listeners that self-government was a prerequisite to pursuing necessary economic reforms and changes, among them influence on immigration legislation, and the right to work out tariffs and trade agreements in the economic interest of the country. He insisted: 'We must have Dominion status. At all stages of the movement, therefore, we shall agitate for Self-Government, petition for it, make sacrifices for it, do everything in our power until the supreme goal has been attained'.[43]

Although the meetings were usually well attended, the reactions in Jamaica showed that doubts regarding Jamaican's ability to govern themselves still dominated the majority opinion in political circles. Roberts became increasingly aware of the transformative power of the migration experience in altering the mentality of those who founded the Progressive League abroad.[44] Reflecting on how his arguments were perceived by his listeners in Jamaica, Roberts later recalled: 'The general attitude was one of bewilderment'.[45] Ken Hill's observations support Roberts' view:

> ...Adolphe Roberts thinks only in terms of self-government for Jamaica when he thinks of Jamaica. It may even be that he is too far ahead of his fellow countrymen or most of them, but the fact remains that he loves his native land with a love that knows no bounds.[46]

Only a few enthusiasts and radicals like Buchanan and Lecesne shared demands for self-government. Roberts remembered how surprised he was when Arnold Lecesne had asked him at one of his lectures why he did not ask for Jamaica to become a republic and responded 'I had found an extremist'.[47] Although only a small minority was willing to subscribe to the Progressive League's anti-colonial demands, Roberts' presence served as a catalyst to the emerging national scene. An editorial in *Public Opinion* at the end of the year 1937 reviewed the development of a new spirit in Jamaica:

> There has been a healthy awakening to realities, and what had previously been seed...sleeping in the ground has suddenly begun to shoot up. There is a new consciousness of power and capacity. It is to this feeling that Mr. Adolphe Roberts has appealed in urging the formation of a national movement.[48]

Nevertheless, the majority of Jamaica's politically interested middle class still favoured the moderate approach of the NRA and the Citizen's Associations, like Isaacs Henry of the NRA or the Legislative Council member T.J. Cawley.[49] While generally acknowledging Roberts' ideas, they hesitated to support him on the demand for self-government and advocated less radical constitutional changes towards a system of representative government.[50] Influenced by the timid reactions, Ken Hill now also advocated a gradual approach and believed that education was necessary 'to make ourselves fully worthy of and to persuade the British government that we were entitled to a more liberal form of government if not self-government'.[51] Another letter to the *Gleaner* expressed a common argument that Jamaica was not yet ripe for self-government: 'In School, little Jamaica spent of her time in Kindergarten, yet here she is now asking for her diploma in the University of Politics. Furthermore, in Kindergarten, she never mastered the first lesson of the course, i.e., Unity in Politics'.[52]

Apparently, a number of Jamaicans started to worry about the influence of Roberts' ideas. Also *Gleaner* editor de Lisser, who represented the voice of the ruling class, made the point that the development toward greater responsibility should be gradual. He left no doubt that self-government was not at all what he envisioned for Jamaica: 'Dominion status, to put the matter frankly, means complete independence of Great Britain and its Parliament; it means absolute equality with the Mother Country, and to ask for anything of the sort seems to us to be…going beyond the limit'.[53] He was confident that demands for self-government would find no mass support in Jamaica and emphasized that only a few individuals were in support of the Progressive League's proposal, while no public figure in Jamaica had ever gone so far to demand a transition from Crown Colony status to self-government.[54]

To downplay the impact of Roberts' ideas, de Lisser frequently employed the argument that the migrants who had formed the Progressive League were in no position to see what was best for Jamaica:

> In so far as those Jamaicans have become citizens of the United States we do not see how they can actively interfere in political questions here… it will be generally admitted that long absence from any country puts the absent ones out of touch with local conditions and local thought…We must therefore discount to a large extent the activities of any group of Jamaicans elsewhere; on the other hand they can always express their views, and those views may have a certain effect upon the people of this island.[55]

In the long run, de Lisser's assessment of the mentality of a majority of his countrymen proved to be right. At the end of 1937, however, Roberts' campaign attracted a lot of public interest. An anecdote shows that he was even able to make an impression in de Lisser's circles. When Roberts was invited to address the 'Readers and Writers Club' which de Lisser had founded and of which he was president, his speech found 'enthusiastic reception'.[56] In the discussion following, de Lisser was asked for his opinion and, not surprisingly, he opposed Roberts' ideas.[57] Apparently, the members expressed more sympathy for Roberts' position, and de Lisser resigned from the position as president shortly afterwards.[58] Compassionately, Roberts commented on the incident in his biographical sketch about de Lisser in his book 'Six Great Jamaicans':

> It was gross ingratitude on the part of the group, for he had raised the funds needed to start the club and had accepted the presidency for a year because he had been begged to do so. He resigned the day after the meeting, and few members had the grace to send him personal apologies.[59]

McFarlane claimed that the founding of the Progressive League branch in Kingston triggered de Lisser's anti-self-government campaign in the *Gleaner*.[60]

Yet, a review of the editorials leaves no doubt that the main factor that led de Lisser to take up his pen against his old friend Roberts was the reception with which the latter's agitation was received. Nevertheless, mutual respect and a sense of humour was present in this and indeed in all future disputes between the two men with contradictory political views, who knew each other since their days as young journalists.

Unquestionably, de Lisser's attention helped to popularize the Progressive League's ideas. Roberts' trip had made such a public furore that news of his departure on January 7 appeared on the front page of the *Gleaner*.[61] Roberts left Jamaica satisfied with the exposure the demand for self-government received: 'Indeed, I had no cause to complain that the idea [or my advocacy of it] lacked publicity. For the ink to flow it was enough that I should be making public addresses'.[62] In a Christmas message published in 1937 in *Public Opinion*, Roberts reflected on his achievements:

> My own political ideas, more positive than the rest, and that I envisage complete self-government and Dominion status have been generously received. The Jamaica Progressive League is now established here... None of this would have been conceivable five years ago.[63]

Yet, he was aware of the strong opposition, especially from the upper class:

> Meanwhile I was seriously misunderstood in middle-class property owning circles. Most of the men I had known in my youth avoided me, trying to make up their minds, I suppose, whether I was plotting a revolution.[64]

Nevertheless, Roberts confidently declared:

> The programme of the Jamaica Progressive League calls for Dominion status now. We realise the difficulties, but we do not intend to recede from our stand. I have found gratifying support for it at all the public meetings I have addressed in the past month. Our people have begun to think politically. The apathy, the inertia, of recent decades is breaking up.[65]

On his trip, Roberts actively approached prominent Jamaicans, for instance future People's National Party (PNP) leader Norman Manley. He tried to convince the respected lawyer to get involved in launching a nationalist party demanding self-government. Yet, Manley was convinced that '...self-government necessarily would become an issue in Jamaica some day, but that it was premature to try raising it now'.[66] He refused to get involved in politics and told Roberts that his interest was limited to his legal practice and philanthropy.[67] Only the island-wide strikes and riots, which shook the whole country in May and June of 1938, led Manley to reconsider his decision.

Reflecting on his personal political development Manley acknowledged:

> I did not myself understand that we had in Jamaica, reached the stage where what we needed was to start thinking about Self-Government and making ourselves responsible for our own development. I regarded our practical problems as economic in character and ignored the considerable development of political thinking which was taking place in Jamaica.[68]

He remembered Roberts' visit and his futile effort to convince him to enter politics and commented:

> When the Jamaica Progressive League of America was founded in 1936 to work for and support Self-Government for Jamaica they sent Adolphe Roberts to tour Jamaica in 1937. He had a very poor reception here and when he came to see me I recall that I told him Jamaica's problems were economic and would not be answered by constitutional reforms.[69]

Manley's perception of Roberts' impact stands in contrast to the evidence of numerous articles in the press and the favourable statements of public figures from various political backgrounds. It is however true that his political goal, self-government for Jamaica, was not enthusiastically received and that real support for the demand was still limited to a few individuals with radical views.

Roberts' campaign did not go unnoticed by the authorities. In a 1937 report, US Consul General in Kingston, Hugh H. Watson, described how the discussion on self-government had stirred up the local political scene: 'Several bodies and gatherings have occupied themselves with it but it loses much of its force through the fact that primarily it is actively promoted by Jamaican residents in the United States'.[70] While local followers were not 'highly placed in the commercial and political life of the Island', Watson found it remarkable that 'both the *Daily Gleaner* and the *Jamaica Times*, papers which are owned and operated by Jamaicans of intelligence and responsibility, treat the matter seriously and regard change in form of government as evidentially inevitable'.[71]

The authorities in London also took notice of Roberts' trip. In his report, Governor Denham emphasized that Roberts was out of touch with the local scene and that his ideas had only limited impact. He reported to the Colonial Office:

> The President of the League, Mr. W. Adolphe Roberts, recently paid a visit to Jamaica during which he held several meetings which were I understand well attended by audiences attracted by the subjects on which he lectured but it does not appear that he made any lasting impression. Mr. Roberts is a native of Jamaica who has long been resident in the United States of America... Owing to his long absence from the Island he does not appear to be in touch with the local situation.[72]

The reflections of these officials show the extent to which the ideas of the Progressive League were shaped by their migration experience and that they could not be easily transferred to Jamaica. Nevertheless, the Progressive League had left its first footprints in Jamaica and the discussion about Jamaica's future and the call for a political party helped to prepare the country for the reaction to the island-wide labour strikes in 1938.

Roberts' popularity had helped the demand for self-government to be taken seriously. Yet, the interest in Roberts' ideas vanished soon after his departure. When the local arm of the Progressive League tried to continue the struggle, it encountered severe challenges. At times, the local group even toned down its propaganda when the leaders realized how difficult it was to find supporters. The first meetings of the Progressive League in Kingston reflected the difficulties maintaining a radical stand on the question of self-government. Disagreements about the first activities of the Progressive League occurred instantly, and rivalling fractions quarrelled whether the immediate demand for self-government was practical. The report on the first monthly meeting shows that the gathering was mainly concerned with the lot of returning migrants and plans to assist them.[73] Some members, who expected a definite focus on matters surrounding the demand for self-government, expressed their disappointment. For instance, W.A. McBean commented sarcastically: '…it was indeed unfortunate that the League was so early to be turned into a Traveller's Protection League'.[74]

McFarlane assured the members that the Progressive League would work in accordance with the parent body in New York and thus advocate self-government; '[t]here was no side-stepping the issue as far as the League was concerned and there was no compromise as they were not prepared to accept any sort of "amended Government."'[75] This position would, however, weaken soon after Roberts left the island and the leaders in New York started to doubt whether the organization that carried its name in Jamaica was the ideal vehicle to spread its ideas. The difficulties that had accompanied the founding of a branch in Kingston evince the great scepticism in the local scene towards the demand for self-government introduced by the expatriates.

The *Public Opinion* Debate: Calling for a Party

The new weekly paper, *Public Opinion*, offered a platform for political discussions in Jamaica.[76] Within a year of existence, *Public Opinion* had become the main forum for exchange about the political future of the island. In the following section, the influence of the Jamaica Progressive League on the political direction of the paper will be analysed. One discussion, in which a number of members of the Progressive League assumed a leading role, is of particular importance as it laid the foundation for the founding of the PNP.[77]

Ken Post emphasizes that 'in its early months *Public Opinion* cautiously worked toward a nationalistic position, expressing this most strongly in cultural terms'.[78] With the appearance of the Progressive League on the local scene and its strong nationalist propaganda with concrete, outspoken and radical political goals, the paper considerably changed its style and adopted a more political approach.[79] *Public Opinion* was very receptive to the League's ideas and the editors generously offered space to carry their message to the politically interested public in Jamaica. While most of them preferred a more moderate version of nationalism, as their NRA membership and the message in the majority of the editorials suggest, they were nevertheless convinced that the League's demands should be seriously considered and widely discussed.

Since its inception, the Progressive League in New York had called for a political party in Jamaica to lobby for self-government. In reaction to Roberts' call for political organization during his campaign in Jamaica at the end of 1937, a lively debate about the right form and direction of such a party and the political future of the country evolved between trade union activist and Marxist Richard Hart[80] and several members of the Progressive League in New York as well as in Kingston, namely H.C. Buchanan, W.A. Domingo, Jaime O'Meally and W.A. McBean. Domingo and O'Meally intervened from New York, while Buchanan and W.A. McBean were affiliated with the local branch. All Progressive League members demanded that self-government should be the primary goal of the future party. Ken Post rightly argues that this debate '...raised fundamental issues at the very beginning of modern politics in Jamaica'.[81] The debate is of utmost importance to the development of Jamaica's political landscape and was an important precursor to the founding of the PNP a few months later. It further allows insight into the theoretical positions of Progressive League members in New York and Kingston and illuminates their efforts of integrating Socialist and nationalist approaches.

The debate was triggered by a printed version of one of Roberts' speeches in the last two issues of *Public Opinion* of the year 1937, entitled 'Self-Government for Jamaica', in which he forcefully called for the founding of a political party and the demand for self-government.[82] Writing under the pseudonym A.R.H., Richard Hart challenged Roberts' views, but took up the demand for a political party.[83] In 'From Garvey to Roberts', Hart singled out Garvey and Roberts as the two most significant thinkers in the past decade of Jamaica's history.[84] He compared their different contributions and argued that both men failed to adopt an approach which would involve the masses. Hart argued from a Marxist perspective and felt that only a proletarian-based mass party with capable leaders could change the conditions on the island.

Hart praised Garvey for challenging the internalized inferiority complex of many black Jamaicans, but felt that when he '[h]ad fulfilled his mission in arousing self-respect in the Negro masses, his usefulness ended'.[85] Hart criticized his race-first approach and held that the Jamaican working class would not be better off if their employers would be of the same skin complexion. He further criticized Garvey for regarding repatriation to Africa as his first priority and for neglecting to make Jamaica his foremost concern.

Hart applauded Roberts for inspiring an 'awakening of political consciousness in the middle classes and the cry for self-government'. He agreed in principle with Roberts' critique of the Legislative Council and the restriction of voting rights, but expressed doubts about the practicality and even the sincerity of Roberts' demand for self-government. He suspected that even if Jamaica could reach Dominion status, the majority of the people would not benefit from the change in the political system if such changes were not accompanied by fundamental economic reforms.[86] Nevertheless, he recommended cooperation with the new movement, while proposing the establishment of a strong labour party:

> The argument that it is better to work with Mr. Roberts than to do no political work at all is unanswerable. It is perfectly true that no proletarian party has, as yet, been formed. But it is also true that we should not delay in forming one. Our readers should therefore express their opinions in a matter, and, as the first step in the right direction, explore the avenue of re-directing the policy of the Jamaica Progressive League, the N.R.A. or the Federation with the formation of a new party as the alternative.[87]

Hart's statement clearly showed that the Progressive League was making important in-roads that gave an impetus to further political development. The editors of *Public Opinion* encouraged further contributions to the discussion, and a lively and sophisticated debate developed in the following issues, discussing whether nationalism or Socialism was the best approach to combat the ills of colonialism, racism and a capitalist global economic order, and, hence, which direction and aims a future party should adopt.

Hugh C. Buchanan, Marxist and early supporter of the local branch of the Progressive League, was the next to enter the arena. He did not subscribe to the antagonism between Socialism and nationalism posed by Hart and proffered: 'Socialism by no means excludes the struggle for national self-determination, but on the contrary, is definitely bound up with it...The goal of Socialism is a free and equal association of free and independent countries, however small'.[88]

Buchanan agreed with Hart that Socialism should be the aim of the lower class, to guarantee that national independence would benefit the masses, but in contrast to Hart, he was convinced that only industrialization could be the driving factor for the development of a revolutionary labour movement. He saw no use in attempting to redirect the agendas of existing organizations like the NRA, whose indefinite stand he regarded as characteristic of the Jamaican middle class. The labour movement, however, would develop out of trade union work and develop its own leaders. Buchanan countered Hart's central argument that

> ...we shall have accomplished nothing by gaining Dominion Status while the present economic system remains unaltered. One thing at least is certain – if there is a genuine Jamaican desire for development, self-government will assist in the materialization of that desire.

The Progressive League members in New York took positive notice of the debate surrounding self-government and Socialism. Jamie O'Meally, founding member of the Progressive League, emphasized in 'Nationalism and the Masses'[89] that the League was not proposing a radical change of the economic system. O'Meally recalled that the directors had discussed the relation of nationalism and the economic advancement of the masses but had unanimously agreed that

> ...radicalism was unsuitable and not to the best interests of the island and we could not endorse or support any radical movement whose purpose was fundamentally to change the present economic system. We agreed, however, to agitate and work for self-government – for a democratic form of government – and for such reforms as would benefit the majority.

This crucial decision on the Progressive League's policy underlines that nationalism was its common denominator. No matter which political affiliations the individual Progressive League members might have held in the past, advocacy of Socialism, Communism or race-first doctrines was not part of its programme; nationalism was the banner under which its members rallied. O'Meally was sympathetic towards Socialist theories, but argued that Jamaica was no industrial nation. He felt that a proletarian class in Jamaica would of necessity be a prerequisite for the transformation into a Communist society. He stated:

> We of the Jamaica Progressive League are satisfied 'to make haste slowly' and have limited ourselves to the demand for self-government, being guided by the existing condition of its productive forces, its social development and its geographical or spatial limitations. We call for a united front of all Jamaicans regardless of race, creed or colour against the foreign oppressor.[90]

Assuredly, he felt that the members of the Progressive League were not blind to the fact that:

> self-government is no panacea for the economic evils and maladjustments which afflict the Island. In spite of its limitations, however, we believe that very substantial benefits are to be derived from self-government.

> The native bourgeoisie in its struggle against imperialism must of necessity seek the support of the masses and must pay for this support with liberal concessions which will of course improve the condition of the workers and peasants.

What O'Meally advocated here, the mutual benefit of cooperation between the middle and the lower classes, marks a central aspect in nationalist theory. While it can be questioned to what extent such cooperation would benefit the lower classes, O'Meally strongly believed:

> ...the masses cannot and should not keep aloof from nationalistic activities while waiting for the birth of their Utopia, but, on the contrary, should take most energetic part in the agitation for self-government under the direction of nationally conscious middle class leaders...Only thus can the masses ever hope to eliminate the oppressive features of British Imperialism, lay the foundation for thorough improvements in their position, and elevate their standard of living. To dream of co-operating internationally with the proletariat of all nations and of fundamentally changing the existing economic system where the conditions do not warrant it, is to postpone our freedom until the Greek Kalends i.e. forever.

This critique of the Progressive League from the Left highlights the point that it was not only the conservative section of the society, the planters, the merchants, the traditional press, that opposed the idea of forming a party demanding self-government. Nevertheless, the number of the conservative adversaries was much higher and its proponents more influential. Accordingly, O'Meally directed his next article against criticism from that section.

In 'Conservatism and the Masses'[91] he declared that conservatism in general would constrain progress. Therefore it was an important task of the Progressive League and of progressive Jamaicans 'to smash the shell of conservatism which had stifled the political growth and strangled the intellectual and moral evolution of their countrymen'. He blamed the conservative power block for the indifference of the masses and pronounced: 'Not until we have completely destroyed this passive, non-resistant indifference which causes the masses to acquiesce in THINGS-AS-THEY-ARE, will we be able to obtain that support which is essential for a strong nationalist party'.

O'Meally carefully distinguished two forms of conservatism. The first one he called 'interested conservatism', prevalent in the ruling classes and motivated by individual or class interests and directly opposed to any substantial change of the social order. It displayed, O'Meally believed, kinship to fascism and shared with it its hatred of intellectualism. The second form, 'natural conservatism', was widespread among the uneducated masses and was characterized by a lack of interest and outright passivity. He explained:

> ...the natural conservatism of the Jamaican masses is almost unconscious and certainly irrational. The term 'conservative' when applied to the masses must be considered as synonymous with ignorance and stupidity. Their unreasoning fear of the unfamiliar and untried is not of their own making...The masses have been skillfully conditioned by the authoritatively imposed habits of thought and belief inculcated by their reactionary masters, and have become more like Pavlov's dog than human beings.

O'Meally thus directs attention to the imperial identity, the infiltration of the uneducated masses with racial doctrines and feelings of inferiority. To change this condition, immediate action was necessary, and O'Meally proposed to take concrete steps, seeking remedy in nationalist education:

> If we love our country we must shake our people out of their social and political stupor, and lead them from the horrid fate of fatalistic resignation which bites deeper and deeper into mind and body, deteriorating both until utter degeneracy is reached. We must, at any cost, liquidate their illiteracy, destroy their primitive fears, superstitions, and infantile credulity, and inspire them with courage and hope for a better day under self-government.

For the middle class to assume leadership, it would be necessary to abandon its 'philistinism, its lack of intellectual curiosity, timidity, and prejudices'. O'Meally demanded: 'Progressive liberalism should be its political philosophy and not conservatism....'

His position shows that he had fully subscribed to the nationalist position of the Progressive League, and that in his view, the abolishment of the colonial system should take precedence over the fight against the local capitalist class.

The debate was in full swing and provoked Hart to answer. In 'All That Glitters',[92] he reiterated his argument that without Socialism self-government would not be of benefit to the majority. He agreed that the idea of self-government was 'sound', but emphasized what O'Meally had also admitted, that self-government in itself was no panacea and insufficient to cure the economic ills. Countering O'Meally's argument of the lack of an industrial proletarian class, he saw a similar class in the rural poor agricultural worker. He expressed his hope in a revolution on a worldwide scale and encouraged Jamaicans to prepare for that day by forming a proletarian party stating that 'the aims of the Jamaica Progressive League are better than no aims; but is all that glitters, in this case, a tolerable substitute for gold?'

Domingo now entered the debate and gave his opinion on the subject. In his article 'Nationalism and the Masses',[93] he classified Hart's views as a radical minority opinion in Jamaica, extreme in its character like the demand for complete independence articulated by Arnold Lecesne.⁹⁴ Domingo expressed sympathies with the idea of complete independence: 'But, I cannot endorse it as a practical political programme capable of rallying the masses of Jamaica to its defense. It is commendable idealistically, but romantic and inapt politically'. It illustrates that despite his personal advocacy of the idea, he supported the Progressive League's decision to compromise on the demand for self-government within the British Commonwealth. His view was based on observations he had made during his trip to Jamaica in the spring of 1937, when he realized that 'there is neither a tradition nor a popular historical belief in the necessity of separation from England extant in Jamaica, hence the projection of any such demand into the political arena at this moment is unreal and bound to fail'.

In regard to Hart's position, Domingo accused him of confusing immediate with ultimate aims. Domingo elaborated on the position of the Progressive League in a comparable manner to O'Meally affirming that the Progressive League aimed at 'political change, not social revolution'. He countered Hart's statement that self-government would not benefit the masses and pointed out the benefits of universal suffrage and freely functioning labour unions as a prerequisite for social change:

> Jamaica can initiate moves likely to benefit the masses to a greater extent than is possible under the present archaic and out-grown system of Crown Colony Government which is subject to the will of aristocratic bureaucrats and financial harpies outside the island.

He urged Jamaicans to realize that their national interests were in conflict with those of Great Britain. Hence, Domingo believed in accordance with O'Meally that developing a nationalist spirit in Jamaica was necessarily the first step:

> Jamaicans must feel that Jamaica is their country, not England; and that they have national interests which are in conflict with those of the British Empire. They must feel that they are a NATION and as such are hampered in their development because of being tied to England as a mere colony, without voice or effective part in determining the policies of the Empire, not to mention the subordination of Jamaica (sic!) interests to those of England.

Domingo's perception of nationalism supports constructivist theories of the nation like those proposed by Anderson and Hobsbawm, highlighting its imaginative character, feelings of unity among the populace, which could, and in most cases actually needed, to be stimulated and aroused.

Domingo saw this stimulation as the Progressive League's main task, to oppose the traditional identification as a colony of Great Britain. To accomplish this, he wished the other progressive organizations like NRA and *Public Opinion* cooperated with the Progressive League. Domingo emphasized that 'it seeks to create a truly national spirit to take the place of the anachronistic imperial spirit with which the people have been deliberately inoculated for decades. With the definite emergence of a genuine national consciousness, there is no telling what other political demands will find expression at the proper time'.[95]

This last sentence was designed to attract radicals like Hart who wished to see a Socialist order and the radical demands of Buchanan and Lescesne.

In this article, Domingo strongly argued against the internalized inferiority complex of Jamaicans which he blamed for the absence of anti-colonial demands:

> ...all the forces of public education in Jamaica operate to make Jamaicans belittle and despise their country, its products, history and people, whilst glorifying England and everything English. As a result, despite a deplorable social condition and a humiliating political relationship to the British Empire, there is practically no hostility on the part of the people to British Imperialism. The inhabitants are convinced that the British Empire is a benevolent organisation and that they are important units in it.

Contradicting Hart's central argument, Domingo claimed that self-government was the only way to implement radical economic changes and that it would benefit the masses because favourable changes could be made in the local context. As a colony, such a task would not only be kept in check by the local capitalist class, but by the force of the entire Empire.

In 'Premature is the Word', O'Meally countered Hart's argument within the internal logic of Marxism. To see a proletarian class in the peasants would project in them Socialist hopes that would be in vain, because structurally peasants are attached to the ownership of land, so that common ownership would never find any large support among them. The conditions were simply not applicable to a Socialist revolt, any attempt would result in bloodshed. Therefore, the Jamaica Progressive League advocated 'a practical and moderate programme of self-government, one to which every patriotic Jamaican, every lover of liberty and progress can subscribe'.[96] O'Meally, like Domingo, hoped that nationalism was the means to challenge and change the imperial identity of most Jamaicans: 'A great deal can be done under this programme if the people of Jamaica will arouse themselves from their fatalistic lethargy and develop a will to power and self-government'.[97]

Richard Hart was impressed by the arguments of O'Meally and Domingo and reconsidered his opinion in 'The Mirage and the Oasis'.[98] While he held on to his belief that the limited demand for self-government and universal suffrage were bourgeois in character and could complicate cooperation with the British Labour Party, he now agreed that cooperating with the Progressive League might be of benefit. He noted with pleasure that its members had studied Marxism and were open to its general ideas. He now saw a basis for cooperation, as long as League members would not forget that self-government would not be the final goal. They would find broad support, he believed, but still claimed that self-government was only the first step. He hoped that the Progressive League would incorporate 'in this programme a quota of Marxian education, as a constant reminder to their followers that self-government is not the complete panacea to the economic maladjustments of society'.[99]

W.A. McBean,[100] another local disputant, entered the scene and concluded the debate with an emphasis on cooperation between the progressive forces. Despite his Socialist stance, he had joined the local branch of the Progressive League and sided with Domingo and O'Meally in the debate. He generally observed common ground between all participants that they had advocated the maximum good for all and employed a scientific Socialism as a basis for their social analysis. He encouraged co-operation between the different organizations and wished to see them concert their efforts by founding a mass-based political party. McBean claimed that the absence of a proletarian class necessitated the inclusion of the middle class in this project. He believed in the unified action of NRA, Progressive League and others and declared:

> Jamaica's path to real progress [which] lies in the forging of a strong political party demanding, acquiring, and utilizing the right of Self-Government as a means of attaining the goal of Equal Opportunity for All. Such a party must be comprised of persons of the caliber of W.A Domingo, Jamie O'Meally and A.R.H.[101]

The debate shows that Buchanan and McBean attempted to bridge nationalist and Socialist positions. O'Meally and Domingo, who had subordinated their Socialist convictions under a practical nationalist approach, hoped that Buchanan and Hart would join the movement and contribute their radical views to ensure that moderate or conservative elements would not undermine the demands for self-government. Indeed, the next chapter shows how closely Hart and the Progressive League cooperated during the labour riots of May 1938. In a letter written in June 1938, O'Meally explained to Hart that their decision to downplay Socialist positions in the Progressive League was motivated by a tactical decision: 'Your philosophy and mine are not so far apart as you imagine, and in the controversy which we carried out in Public Opinion, I had hoped that you would read BETWEEN THE LINES'.[102]

Reviewing the debate, Ken Post was surprised that McBean sided with the Progressive League leaders and not with fellow Marxist Hart.[103] This is not surprising, considered that he, more than any other protagonist on the local scene, shared strong nationalist opinions and leftist ideas. He had tried to bridge both positions, similar to O'Meally and Domingo, and was a member of the local

Progressive League for several years. Post generally neglects the local branch, which was a heterogeneous pool of people from various backgrounds and with different economic convictions. What mattered and held together the Progressive League in Kingston and New York alike was a priority on nationalism. The members subordinated their particular opinions under this primary goal.

This discussion waged in *Public Opinion*, although still limited to a few politically minded intellectuals, nevertheless opened the field for the political party which would evolve in the later part of the year. The Progressive League's influence, from Roberts' inspiration to the intervention of Domingo and O'Meally, started to attract and convince local activists from the Left like Buchanan and McBean and probably left its impression on the *Public Opinion* editors Ken Hill, H.P. Jacobs and O.T. Fairclough, who would become instrumental in forming the party and who would finally succeed in what Roberts had failed: to convince Norman Manley to become the party's leader. This was the first time that such a discussion took place, and it is doubtful whether it would have appeared at this time without the Progressive League's constant nationalist propaganda and the urge that such a party was needed. Although often overlooked in historiography, these discussions helped to prepare the ground for the political development after 1938. The founding of the NRA, the local branch of the Progressive League and the debate in *Public Opinion* were precursors of the definite steps that were soon to be taken.

While the debate was still on, a *Public Opinion* editorial asked in February 1938, 'Can They Unite?',[104] and proposed a merger between the different existing organizations from NRA to Progressive League. *Public Opinion* admitted important ideological differences between the groups, but was convinced that there is no 'real cleavage whatsoever, but rather a division of labour: the J.P.L. exists to emphasise what the others assume but do not stress'. The Progressive League could contribute 'propaganda of a more political trend than that of the NRA'. The editors believed that all organizations had their specific legitimization and reflected a positive complexity of the movement. United action would be desirable and beneficial to all and Progressive League, NRA, Citizens Associations and other groups should federate into a party and find an agreement on practical policy. Yet, this view failed to take into account that the differences were more serious.

Shortly after the editorial appeared in *Public Opinion*, the NRA started an initiative to form a political party in coalition with the Progressive League.[105] The *Public Opinion* welcomed this effort in an editorial under the header 'The People's Party'. In the article, Domingo's statement in the debate that a coalition was desirable was interpreted as a 'semi-official statement' of the Progressive League from which the conclusion was drawn that 'an immediate coalition of

Stretching Out: A Local Branch in Kingston

the National Reform Association and the Jamaica Progressive League is quite possible'.[106] However, the editorial overlooked that Domingo had qualified his statement by the addition that the NRA would have to accept the demand for self-government.

The *Public Opinion* neglected this aspect and felt that such a united party, would have good expectations for the 1940 election and be able to sweep the Legislative Council. The editorial claimed:

> The formation of a party is a test of our sincerity. We may prefer to remain in little groups explaining the difference between Tweedledum and Tweedledee. But in reality the days of Tweedledum and Tweedledee are over. The imagination of the people must be fired, and at the same time their thinking must be along sound lines. Only a large idea will fire the imagination and only a great organisation will produce great leaders to direct the thoughts of the masses.[107]

The enthusiasm played down one important factor, which hampered such a harmonious coalition – the Progressive League was not willing to compromise on its principle aim, the demand for self-government. If the other organizations rallied behind this claim, then the Progressive League would be willing to merge. In regard to the proposed coalition with the NRA and other groups to form a party, Roberts warned the secretary of the Kingston branch:

> It seems that your League is contemplating entering a coalition, to form a People's Party (I quote this from *Public Opinion*). I hope that you and the other officers will weigh the matter carefully before you take any such step, and that above all you will preserve the identity of the League and its uncompromising demand for complete self-government. Co-operation with other reform elements is desirable, but not a merger. Any group which fully accepts our principles will join the League, and that is the objective you should have in view, in all your relations to other organizations. Educate them.[108]

For Roberts and the Progressive League, the matter of self-government was no question of 'Tweedledum and Tweedledee' but a necessary precondition.

While there was growing acceptance for the Progressive League's idea in the intellectual circles around *Public Opinion*, the general public displayed mixed reactions to propaganda strongly advocating for self-government. Many Jamaicans rejected the idea of self-government and openly displayed their loyalty to England. An exemplary statement of this attitude can be seen in a letter to the *Gleaner*. Directly referring to Roberts' demands, Edith Isaacs asked:

> Why should Jamaica be taught to look at England, her mother, through distorted foreign spectacles? ...There is nothing that Mr. Adolphe Roberts envisions for Jamaica under Dominion status that could not be obtained more speedily and more securely in unity with the Crown.[109]

Once again, this statement shows that the ideas of the Progressive League were often rejected as foreign ideas. Further, it illustrates the belief in Great Britain's charitable character: 'After having been nurtured, cared for and protected by mother England all these years why should Jamaica be asked to imitate the bad examples of the Dominions and seek Dominion status for herself?'[110]

Continuously, arguments against Roberts' ideas stressed the point that he was an outsider and allegedly out of touch with local affairs. NRA founding member V.R. Harry feared Roberts' agitation would stir up the minds of those people who already started to work for a change in the island:

> Some weeks ago, a gentleman, Mr. Adolphe Roberts, a native of this island, and one who lived outside for a number of years, returned, and during his short stay sowed quite a few seeds of excitement and wild probabilities, which seem to have made some kind of impression on the minds of a few of our already excited reformers. That Jamaica and her people were well ripe for Dominion Status, he believing that, is the first thought in this desire.[111]

Such reservations against the Progressive League's demands support the thesis that the experience of migration indeed played an important role in overcoming deep-seated imperial identity and developing plans for practical anti-colonial action.

Many of the initial supporters in Jamaica soon showed a tendency to retreat from their firm stand, evidencing the strong impact of the prevailing resistance to the idea of self-government. Early supporters, like Rupert Meikle, for instance, were not able to maintain their radicalism. While positively referring to Roberts' forceful condemnation of the Crown Colony system he now advocated 'full representative government'[112] instead of self-government and regarded it a necessary first step toward the ultimate goal of 'full responsible government'.[113] Quite possible Meikle's membership in the NRA which had adopted similar moderate positions on constitutional change had influenced his views.

NRA founder Ken Hill is another example of someone whose enthusiasm for self-government inspired by the Progressive League was tempered by local feelings. At the NRA's first annual general meeting in January 1937, Hill stated that Jamaica was not yet ready for self-government and declared that the NRA worked for a '…better Jamaica to which we look forward confidently by educating our people to be responsible citizens, fully able to maintain and deserving of responsible government'.[114]

While Ken Hill employed a moderate tone when he spoke as the NRA's secretary in January, he showed a remarkable re-radicalization at a speech in front of the United Aid Society in March. Hill stated: 'Jamaica's most serious problem is the economic problem and it will only be solved by attainment of self-government'.[115] In stark contrast to the statement made at the NRA founding, Hill now claimed that Jamaica was ripe for self-government and that the time for the people of Jamaica to make a definite bid for responsible government was 'now or never'. Hill proposed united action of the different political organizations 'to form a National or People's Party for the general elections of 1940'. He believed this step 'would mean that a definite start could be made toward paving the way to self-government'. He rebuked 'opponents of self-government for Jamaica and luke-warm supporters' with the argument that while it was unrealistic that full realization could be expected immediately it was still reasonable to demand immediate self-government, as it was 'idle and futile and sheer nonsense…to say that Jamaica was not fit to govern itself'. Hill insisted: 'If we are not ripe for self-government now, when shall we ever be? Every country attaining the right to govern itself had to proceed by trial and error. Why should a higher standard be set for Jamaica?'

These statements stood in stark contrast to his statements in front of the NRA. Tone and radicalism reminds of the Ken Hill before the launch of the NRA, when he had been strongly influenced and impressed by the Progressive League propaganda campaign in spring 1937. His arguments resemble the positions of O'Meally and Domingo in the *Public Opinion* debate. Probably, the debate and the perspective of a common party inspired Hill to resume a more radical position.

The *Gleaner* reported positive reactions from the audience, mentioning that Hill's speech was considered by many to be 'timely and outspoken'. F.A. Glasspole, President of the United Aid Society, 'paid a great tribute to Mr. Hill for his public spiritedness, courage and zeal' and wished 'Jamaica's young men all had Mr. Hill's independence of character and progressive views'.

Ken Hill's dilemma exemplifies the difficulties that accompanied the transfer of radical ideas from New York. The propaganda spread by the Progressive League inspired him to form an organization. It garnered the support of powerful and respectable figures well known in Jamaica's public life. The organization had been successful in its effort to provide a progressive although reformative platform for middle class discontent. But this had only been achieved by sacrificing the radical demands for immediate self-government, which had originally pushed Ken Hill to form the NRA. After Roberts' trip and the debate waged in *Public Opinion*, Ken Hill apparently felt it would be worth a try to rally support behind the more radical demands articulated by Roberts, O'Meally and Domingo, although the acceptance for the demand for self-government was still low.

The Progressive League in New York tried to encourage its partners in Jamaica not to give up and make compromises for the sake of cooperation, but to convince others that self-government was the only policy worth adopting in order to fight for a real change of the conditions of the island, because without this anti-colonial element, the fight for reform would be in vain. But even its closest cooperation partner, the local branch in Kingston, showed tendencies to compromise its radical goals in order to attract supporters. After Roberts returned to the US, McFarlane found himself confronted with opposition and difficulties to find supporters. Apparently, some of the early supporters like the Legislative Council members Ehrenstein and C.A. Reid left the group after they found out about the radical goals during Roberts' stay, which had remained cloudy in McFarlane's earlier communication.

A first sign for slow retreat of the local branch of the Progressive League from the radical demands was a letter to the *Gleaner* by McFarlane, published February 8, 1938, in which McFarlane replied to an editorial of the paper which described Roberts' aim as Dominion status which allegedly would mean 'complete independence'. The editor felt that 'Mr. Roberts was running a little too quickly, galloping furiously ahead of realities'.[116] McFarlane replied that:

> ...the Jamaica Progressive League, at no time, written or implied, past or present, advocated our separation from the British Government. Our motto has always been and still is Self Government for Jamaica within the framework of the British Commonwealth of Nations. Any other expression to the contrary does not represent the plan of the League.[117]

So far, there was no breach between the positions of the two Progressive League branches, but it was certainly not the position of the New York based League when McFarlane declared in the same letter,

> We have never been, and never will be opposed to any move or movement, to secure Representative Government for Jamaica. We have always realized, and have argued, that we might have to be satisfied with Representative Government as our first step, but we must work for self Government as our ultimate accomplishment.[118]

He continued that he desired cooperation between all progressive organizations to inspire national consciousness and to work toward a voting system based on intelligence tests. McFarlane underlined again:

> If there are expressions of unreadiness for Self Government, we are not to be blamed for their misunderstanding of our programme, because we never expected, or, gave any expressions to the effect, that Self Government for Jamaica should be an immediate accomplishment. It shall be the ultimate result, the climax of whatever change we shall be able to affect the present.[119]

This standpoint clearly diverged from a whole-hearted advocacy of self-government as an immediate goal.

Stretching Out: A Local Branch in Kingston

A two-page report from February 1938 signed by McFarlane and sent to the headquarters in New York shows that the secretary of the Kingston branch was well aware that he had changed course in the face of the massive critique the group encountered. McFarlane explained his resignation to the directors in New York:

> Our people are not at present prepared to step from Crown Colony to self Government or Dominion Status, but will appreciate agitation at present for Representative Government, as the first step, thus while there is no yielding or sacrificing of our program, we have to respect the majority opinions and speak of Self Government as our ultimate aim.[120]

It seems as if McFarlane later regretted this position and it is quite telling that page two of the report that contained this statement is missing in the version of the document that was part of the material donated to the National Library of Jamaica in the 1950s. In this collection, there is only one page, signed by McFarlane, as if the report ended there.[121] The original letter sent by McFarlane to New York can be found in the private collection of Progressive League papers in possession of Louis Moyston, which contains material collected by the Progressive League in New York. The original blatantly exposes how McFarlane tried to manipulate the evidence; here the signature is only on the second page that contains the cited statement.

Evidently, without Roberts' direct support, the local branch was not able to uphold the immediate demand for self-government. This concession to local opinion and the explicit acceptance of representative government as a first step, stood in stark contrast to the strategy of the parent body. The directors in New York reacted with astonishment and encouraged McFarlane to stick to the original policy. Answering McFarlane's doubts and complaints that the prestigious members withdrew their support, Roberts answered:

> ...you are a little disappointed at the failure of Members of the Legislative Council and other influential persons to support the Jamaica Progressive League. Do not let this discourage you. Such people never give aid to a popular movement at the beginning. They fall into line afterwards, when they realize that they are likely to lose their jobs and their businesses unless they go with the tide.[122]

Mass support was much more crucial to the success of the movement, Roberts reminded McFarlane. Roberts was convinced that the masses would finally subscribe to anti-colonial demands:

> It is bound to be successful if it is properly led, and if the ideal of liberty is firmly maintained. Otherwise, it will fail. False compromises end by repelling the masses and causing them to sink back into apathy. Remember, liberty is not a gift but a victory.[123]

Roberts requested that McFarlane would keep him abreast about local developments. However, McFarlane seemed not to be impressed by the words of the Progressive League president. In a letter to the *Gleaner* dated March 30, he declared again that he would accept a gradual transition, and advocated '…a change of the entire Government, out of the Crown-Colony class to self-government, either as our first step, or as the succeeding step from Representative Government'.[124]

It seems as if McFarlane had been asked by fellow members of the Kingston branch for material rewards for their work and carried the request before the directors in New York. Roberts insisted:

> It is absolutely essential that the League should break down the apathy of Jamaicans towards a patriotic movement such as ours. In all other countries there exists at least a minority which understands that sacrifices (financial and otherwise) must be made, if so great a boon as greater political liberty is to be won.[125]

Roberts was confident that mass support was only a question of time: 'Believe me, it is not visionary to hope that such an emotion can be aroused in the hearts of our people. All peoples are capable of it, and once it has been aroused it spreads like a flame'.[126] These statements not only show Roberts' strong confidence in the power of nationalism, they also expose the timidity of the local scene of political activists.

Roberts encouraged McFarlane to continue the work and to hold public meetings at regular intervals in order to increase the Progressive League's membership. His suggestion to delay the election of a president for the Kingston branch until his return in December testifies to Roberts' mistrust in the local leadership.[127]

While Roberts was in New Orleans conducting research for a book,[128] Brown replied with more compassion for the difficult situation McFarlane was facing on the ground in Jamaica. This shows Roberts' radicalizing influence, even on the Progressive League in New York. Brown generally lauded the activities of the Kingston branch and explicitly supported McFarlane's tactic: 'The Directors also endorse your opinion and approve your letters in the papers in regard to the need of careful consideration of all suggested changes in the Constitution of Jamaica and of the avoidance of haste in coming to conclusions'.[129] Brown further encouraged McFarlane:

> The Directors wish me also to say that they recognize that your league is doing worthwhile pioneer work of a peculiarly difficult nature, and that therefore neither you nor they should be impatient or discouraged if the results we desire do not appear as soon as we wish. Labor on with diligence, with faith, and also with patience.[130]

Stretching Out: A Local Branch in Kingston

In the first months of 1938, the Progressive League in Kingston tried to broaden its membership and attempted to exercise influence on colonial policy, especially in regard to trading regulations by demanding Jamaican representation at the Anglo-American Trade Agreement Conference in Washington.[131] The Kingston branch sent one of their directors, W.S. Duhaney as a delegate to participate in the Mayor's Economic Conference, a large conference that discussed the economic situation of the country, where he advocated increased trade with the US.[132]

However, the announcements in the *Gleaner* show that meetings were held only irregularly and dates were often postponed. It seems that there were still differences in approach and direction among the members and it took months until the constitution of the Progressive League in Kingston could be ratified.[133] While the constitution had still not been adopted, members made representations addressing the unfavourable conditions which returning migrants met in Jamaica.[134] Apparently those who favoured the group to become a 'Traveler's Protection League', as McBean had cynically commented at the first monthly meeting in January, assumed increasing influence.

While the local branch was struggling to find its direction, *Public Opinion* kept the discussion on constitutional change alive. The results from a poll on the question 'Should Jamaica Seek a More Liberal Constitution? If so, what kind? If not, why not?'[135] clearly shows the backlash after Roberts' departure. Former radical supporters like Buchanan now stated: 'I should like to see my people taking full advantage of the present constitution and struggling against its limitations before they get a more liberal one. Ask no favours, what you desire will be granted you'. Even McBean, who had sided with Domingo and O'Meally in the debate, now answered vaguely 'Maximum Representative Government'. Amy Bailey, one of the leading female political activists, expressed rather conservative views, that:

> ...by all means we are not ready yet for self-Government, but we should certainly start the ball a-rolling by having a constitution that gives the elected side a control of the finances, a voice in the preparations of the Estimates, and the majority in the Council. But until we have, by compulsory education, reduced the high rate of illiteracy in the island we will not be ready for complete self-government.

Bailey would soon join the ranks of the Progressive League in Kingston, a sign in which direction the local branch would develop.

While local opinion rarely went beyond the claim for representative government and the Progressive League in Kingston had diluted its programme, the parent body in New York continued its radical anti-colonial demands for immediate self-government. In an article in *Public Opinion*, Domingo argued that it was timely and necessary to fight for immediate self-government now. With a clear perspective on the developing crisis in Europe, Domingo denounced Great Britain's appeasement policy and pointed to the menace of Great Britain turning into a Fascist regime. Domingo concluded that achieving self-government and claiming democratic rights were the only effective way for Jamaica to react to these worrying developments. Clearly exposing the mechanisms of foreign rule and indoctrination, he emphasized:

> Self-government is the inalienable right of all peoples. No people are so superior that they have any mandate from God, Nature or Fate to govern others. Such imposition of foreign rule as exists in the world is based either upon naked or disguised Force, or is the result of a subtle inoculation of the governed with the virus of inferiority complex. In Jamaica it is a combination of both methods that is responsible for the maudlin patriotism of the people and their lack of a vigorous national consciousness.[136]

Domingo further pointed out the economic advantages of self-government deriving from more favourable trade agreements, the right to fix tariffs and to regulate immigration. Exposing the hypocrisy of the European colonial powers, who allegedly declared to fight for democracy and against fascism in Europe, he concluded: 'Self-government will place in our hands a formidable weapon of self-defense, hence the determination of those who benefit from the present situation to deny it to certain people in spite of their manifest fitness to guide their own destiny'.[137]

Statements like this exemplify the huge gap that existed between the demands from New York and local sentiment. The examination of the local reaction shows both the inspiring influence and the limits of the transfer of ideas from New York to Kingston. While the propaganda of the Progressive League had incited the political development of the emerging nationalist scene in Jamaica and inspired discussions about the formation of a political party, the attempts to unite all existing political groups into such an effort failed, because the different factions could not agree on its direction. In contrast to the local branch, the leaders in New York refused to compromise on the demand for self-government. For a few weeks, the country would fall back into its political lethargy while the enthusiasm for party organization vanished. In May 1938, island-wide militant labour protests finally shook Jamaican society out of its apathy. The events blatantly showed that large sections of Jamaica's poor were no longer prepared to accept their lot and comply with the expectations of the ruling classes. In December 1937, *Gleaner* editor Herbert de Lisser had argued:

> Our very 'strikes' are marked by orderliness and peacefulness and seem to get settled almost immediately after they have begun. The same..., moderate attitude will be displayed in our discussion of political matters. Extremism will be avoided in Jamaica. The Jamaican

is not non-progressive but, happily, he has on the whole the saving grace of judgment and balance.[138]

'The Lid Blows Off': Activities During the Labour Protests in 1938

While the discussion about Jamaica's political future had remained without practical effect, the socio-economic conditions continued to get worse across the British West Indies. Accelerating unemployment rates negatively affected wages and led to conflicts between workers and employers. Peasants and workers increasingly demanded better living and working conditions, trade unions were on the rise and a wave of strikes rocked the islands from mid-1935.[139] When massive strikes and protests broke out in Trinidad and Tobago in August 1937, *Public Opinion* criticized the inactivity of the Jamaican government regarding the deplorable living and working conditions. An editorial entitled 'A Lesson From Trinidad' asked provocatively: 'But must Jamaica wait for desperate strikes, riots, and perhaps bloodshed, before she embarks on social reform?'[140] The majority of Jamaica's political elite ignored the signs of unrest in the region and downplayed them as minor events without meaning for Jamaica, until massive strikes and unrest took hold of the island in May and June 1938 and changed the whole picture.

Early in 1938, massive strikes at Serge Island, a plantation owned by Legislative Council member Rudolph Ehrenstein,[141] foreshadowed the following events.[142] Much has been written about the labour riots at Frome and the resulting unrest which spread over the whole island.[143] This is not the place to discuss the events in detail, but a short recapitulation is necessary to provide the framework for the activities of the Progressive League, which immediately saw the chance to popularize the demands for a radical political change.

On May 7, a *Public Opinion* editorial titled 'The Lid Blows Off'[144] reported on the labour riots that occurred on May 2, 1938, at Frome Estate, owned by the West Indies Sugar Co. The editors commented:

> The unreal Jamaica of Myrtle Bank and Headquarters House crumbled to nothing on Monday. Before the rifle fire of Westmoreland, the illusions of a generation vanished. We have been told by our wiseacres that in this country there is no colour feeling, no tendency towards violence, no ill-feeling between employer and employed. Hunger, low wages, desperate want do not exist within our borders. This Fool's Paradise was destroyed on Monday, when Jamaican workers faced bullets and bayonets rather than continue in hopelessness submission to existing conditions.[145]

This illustrates how the events at Frome and the acts of violence and brutal treatment against the strikers were instantly perceived as a sign for the beginning of a new era. Post describes the incidents at Frome as characteristic of the general social conditions:

> The Frome project reproduced in a microcosmic and intensified form, therefore, the situation of the Jamaican working class – poor living conditions, exploitation, those who were fortunate enough to have jobs feeling the hot breath of the reserve-army of labour always on their necks.[146]

When the job-seekers realized that neither the demand for labour nor the pay was as high as people previously expected based on advertisements by the Estate, bitter protests and massive strikes occurred which lit the powder keg of frustration.[147] The police reacted with immense brutality and within two days, four people were killed, 13 hospitalized, and 105 strikers jailed, while large police regiments were rushed in from Kingston.[148]

Because workers were in a similar situation all over the island, many spontaneous strikes and solidarity protests flared up in the country. The labouring classes in Jamaica had increasingly been exposed to intensified labour agitation and efforts to organize into trade unions, directed foremost by the Jamaica Workers and Tradesmen's Union (JWTU). On May 2, a spontaneous protest meeting in Kingston was attended by 3,000 people. Throughout the following days, the capital was paralyzed by strikes. Dock workers and their sympathizers forced most shops downtown to close, public service was interrupted and riots occurred in the slums of West Kingston. Frustration and despair of the lower classes had found a channel to erupt.[149]

While Governor Denham waited for the situation to settle, it increasingly got out of control. Violent confrontation and shootings contributed to a rise of tension. Two men were particularly visible in these days, labour activist St William Grant, and money-lender Alexander Bustamante.[150] The latter quickly rose to unprecedented popularity, addressing large gatherings of workers, while the government decided to hand out more firearms to the police, appointed 420 additional members to the Constabulary Force and called for support from a British regiment stationed in Kingston.[151]

The members of the Progressive League in Kingston and New York agreed to assist the striking workers and to provide funds for the legal defence of the 105 imprisoned strikers. The Kingston branch called an emergency meeting on May 12 and decided to cooperate with Bustamante in his effort to raise funds for the same purpose.[152] McFarlane told the *Gleaner*: 'Mr. Alexander Bustamante...was associated with the League in this matter and they were hoping to raise a fair sum of money on behalf of the men charged'.[153]

McFarlane saw the chance that the labour unrest and especially the cooperation with Bustamante could increase the popularity of the Progressive League and wrote to New York: 'We are doing all in our power to show the worth of the League seeing the golden opportunity to do so'.[154] Indeed, the local branch got a significant boost and new members joined after the events. But as the Kingston branch still abstained from demanding immediate self-government, it continued to attract more moderate members.

The group faced obstacles in organizing legal aid for the defendants in time and unsuccessfully demanded that the trial against the workers should be postponed until the findings of the Government-appointed Riot Commission would be presented.[155] When the League hurriedly tried to find a lawyer who would take over the defence of the workers, they approached Norman W. Manley. Initially he agreed but soon changed his mind, arguing that because he held a retainer from the West Indies Sugar Company, the property under which the Frome estate fell, he could not take over the case.[156] The Progressive League in Kingston then approached a lawyer amongst its own ranks, E.R.D. Evans who was a member.[157] Evans readily accepted and immediately rushed off to Savanna-la-Mar, where the trial took place on May 13.[158]

The directors in New York welcomed the activities. They sent a first cheque for US$50 and organized a series of fundraising meetings.[159] A big protest meeting was staged on May 19, at the large Abyssinian Baptist Church of Revd Adam Clayton Powell, Jr which was attended by over 800 persons.[160] A large number of renowned speakers[161] addressed the 'monster mass meeting'. Revd Ethelred Brown presided over the meeting and complained in his speech that the striking workers were treated with disproportionate cruelty: 'For bread they asked, bullets they got'.[162] Richard B. Moore put the situation in Jamaica in perspective with events in the other islands and denounced the British colonial policy as 'ruthless suppression of the black and coloured people by British Imperialism. It is the introduction of a new brutal form of slavery'.[163]

The events in the islands reinforced anti-colonial sentiments among the migrants in New York. The Progressive League used the crisis in Jamaica to inspire public discussions abroad about the future of the island.[164] In a letter to Richard Hart, O'Meally described: 'These happenings have come upon us before we had developed the necessary machinery to handle it; but is has served as a powerful force in drawing together Jamaicans in N.Y.'[165] The Progressive League organized a number of mass meetings in big meeting halls, in part organized as a joint venture with other migrant organizations, featuring popular speakers and activists.[166] Within a short time, the migrant community around the Progressive League was able to provide the lion's share of the funds needed to defend the imprisoned workers, in total US$421.[167]

In the meantime, the authorities in Jamaica tried to restore order and imprisoned Alexander Bustamante and St William Grant on May 24, yet, this decision only added fuel to the fire.[168] Large demonstrations demanded Bustamante's release, while violent clashes with the police occurred. The Progressive League in Kingston officially sided with the workers and protested against the imprisonments and an Emergency Bill released by the Governor.[169] At the same time, Norman Manley tried to convince the Governor to release Bustamante and Grant, yet without success. At this point, he decided that his service and leadership was now needed and took over Bustamante's mediating role between strikers and employers and developed a plan for trade union organization for the time afterwards.[170]

The Progressive League in Kingston continued its work and put a special focus on the needs of the workers. One important step was supporting Agnes Bernard, a lady who had started to hand out free meals to the striking workers from her small cook shop next to the docks in Kingston.[171] Others joined her efforts and contributed whatever small donations they could spare. Agnes Bernard told a *Gleaner* reporter: 'Mrs. Manley, a few merchants and the Jamaica Progressive League came to our assistance, and so we were able to carry on till to-day'.[172] Her activities soon became very popular, Bustamante called her 'Jamaica's Joan of Arc'.[173] In July, the Progressive League staged a mass meeting in honour of the services of E.R.D. Evans and Agnes Bernard.[174] Many prominent speakers addressed the huge gathering; the audience included Bustamante and Grant.[175] At this first mass meeting after Roberts' departure, McFarlane outlined the aims of the Progressive League, but according to the *Gleaner*, he spoke vaguely of a 'better type of Colonial Government for Jamaica'[176] rather than frankly advocating self-government. Other speakers were more outspoken, for example Dr V.L. Varma, a renowned activist of the Indian minority in Jamaica, who claimed that 'every country had the right to look after its own affairs and congratulated the League in its efforts'.[177] E.R.D. Evans affirmed that he supported the Progressive League's move for self-government and encouraged others to follow his example. He declared that 'under this damned Colonial policy, we will never get anything like recognition'.[178]

The extreme atmosphere of the summer of 1938 seemed to encourage anti-colonial views. The support for the workers attracted new members, including some popular figures of Kingston's public life, for instance journalist and activist Amy Bailey, educator Mary Morris-Knibb, trade unionist Percy A. Aiken and his wife DeMena, as well as V.L. Varma, who all joined the Progressive League around this time. Many of them had been active in the trade union movement or were part of the various Citizens' Associations.

The group continued its work by protesting against various cases of police brutality. By the end of July, it moved a resolution against attempts to reward the police battalions which were involved in suppressing the uprisings.[179] It became particularly involved in defending victims of violence in Islington, St Mary and frequently made inquiries before the Riot Commission.[180] On behalf of the Progressive League, McFarlane, Evans and Duhaney went to investigate the site and interviewed eyewitnesses and the case was reopened.[181]

In the course of events, the Progressive League gained popularity and was able to inspire discussions about the country's constitution.[182] In July, it declared that it was 'preparing a programme for the launching of a Political Party, but so as not to conflict with other groups, would be quite willing to merge its ideas so as to achieve unity of action among the factions working for the political advancement of the country'.[183]

Despite the new spirit of optimism, the Progressive League continued its moderate course and launched a pamphlet advocating 'self-government for Jamaica within the British Commonwealth of Nations' as the 'Ultimate Goal'.[184] In contrast to the policy of the Progressive League in New York, it explicitly stated: 'We will be willing to accept Full Representative Government as our first step on our march to Self Government'. The Progressive League went on to encourage all Jamaicans to 'join the League and secure a better type of Government'.[185] This was exactly the opposite of the firm stand on the issue of self-government that Roberts had advised McFarlane to take.

The Progressive League in New York did not realize immediately that McFarlane was already backing off. Early in June the directors congratulated McFarlane:

> It appears as if History is now being written in Jamaica and when it is all over the Jamaica Progressive League of Kingston will be there as the organizer of the movement that came to rescue the desperate men thrown in prison as an answer to their appeal for bread. Keep up the good work. We are here behind you.[186]

From New Orleans, Roberts joined the directors in congratulating the Progressive League in Kingston: 'The League in Jamaica has risen to the occasion. Congratulations are certainly due to you and the other Directors for the way you have handled a difficult situation'.[187] Full of optimism, Roberts commented that:

> the old order has crashed to the ground in the past six weeks, and we now have a starting point for a national movement which cannot be stopped. I felt last December that this would happen, and it has proved to be so. Even the doubters must realize that such movements are based upon political action, and upon direct action as exemplified by the strikes.

Political developments took up speed and found expression in the formation of a political party in the following months – although not exactly in the way Roberts had hoped.

Roberts recognized that even the Progressive League in Kingston was still indecisive in its stance on self-government and appreciated that the branch promised not to elect a permanent president before he planned to return at the end of the year. Roberts certainly had McFarlane's hesitation in mind when he closed his letter with the phrase: 'Yours for a self-governing Jamaica'. Secretary Brown advised in another letter: 'I was instructed once again to ask you not to be over concerned about opposition and indifference. These are to be expected'.[188]

However, the local branch further departed from demands for immediate self-government. V.L. Varma, who had endorsed the right to self-government at the mass meeting in honour of Evans and Bernard, now advocated a more moderate position. Domingo commented in a letter to Richard Hart:

> It is a pity that Dr. Varma, coming from his native India which has suffered so much from the slanders of British imperialists, should have fallen for deLisser's phrase about our unfitness to govern ourselves. I presume that he advocates self-government for India. If so, how can he consistently deny similar advocacy to Jamaica when India's vastly more difficult problem (from the imperialist point of view) remains– illiteracy, diversity of languages, religions and customs; tribal and other animosities, etc.[189]

The leaders in New York felt that it would be desirable to attract more radical members to join the local branch. They had observed that young radicals like Hart and Buchanan put their emphasis on the emerging trade union movement. Especially those leaders with Socialist leanings, like Domingo, O'Meally or Brown, saw trade union work and nationalism as two sides of the same coin. From the outset, improvements of the legal situation of the unions and practical goals for improved working conditions were an integral part of the programme of the Progressive League. Its concept of nationalism was based on the hope for a strong mass-based movement in Jamaica. O'Meally and Domingo had argued in the debate in *Public Opinion* that the working class was a very important component of a nationalist movement and would benefit materially from self-government.

When Hart cabled O'Meally on May 24, asking for literature on labour organization and advice from the Progressive League, O'Meally and Domingo welcomed the contact[190] and promised help.[191] A lively correspondence between New York and Kingston developed and the three men entered into a spirited debate, sharing opinions, discussing tactics and debating the first-hand reports of the situation on the ground sent by Hart. O'Meally advised Hart to cooperate closely with the local branch of the Progressive League and the NRA in the formation of the trade unions and in very practical efforts, for example in building a worker's library.[192] He recommended that Hart should contact Buchanan who had received a stack of literature on labour organization from Domingo in 1937.[193] Domingo and O'Meally hoped Hart could strengthen the national movement and keep the local branch of the Progressive League in check. O'Meally explained:

> ...I have but one thing before me and that is Jamaica and her interests, and for that reason I should like you join the league and send me your frank opinion of the officers and their policy, always of course bearing in mind our aims and objects as outlined in our declaration. This information will be treated as extremely CONFIDENTIAL and must not be divulged to any one not even the officers of the League.[194]

This statement attests to the doubts regarding the stand of the local branch and its officers. O'Meally hoped Hart could contribute the necessary radicalism and encouraged him:

> The League in Jamaica needs militant young men to keep it in the path which we in New York have set out for it; what we are afraid of is that it will fall into the hands of men who will be more interested in commercial affairs than in politics; it is for that reason that I should like to see you and some others in the League to help keep it militant; for I fear that sooner or later a showdown will come between those who are conservatives and those who are liberals.[195]

O'Meally complained about the unsatisfactory cooperation with the local leaders of the Progressive League and encouraged Hart to contact McFarlane. He stressed the need for better communication because McFarlane 'has been very dilatory in this respect. This has impeded in many ways the speed with which we could render our assistance'.[196] These letters vividly illustrate that the Progressive League in New York was in doubt whether it had the right people on the spot. Therefore, they eagerly tried to convince radical activists like Hart that their views were not so much apart. Domingo explained three basic points of policy which he regarded as inseparably bound to each other and central for a change of conditions in Jamaica:

> POLITICAL: We must demand and work for self-government. At the same time we must fight to democratize the country and transfer power to the workers and producers of the country.
>
> ECONOMIC: The exploitation of the workers should be attacked at the point of production through labour unions and at the point of consumptions through the organization of Consumers Cooperatives.
>
> SOCIAL: Growing out of the above, and directly connected, there must be a demand for more and better education to wipe out illiteracy and superstition. Civil rights must be maintained and increased to the limit. All forms of sex, racial or other discrimination must be checked, then abolished.[197]

O'Meally encouraged the League in Kingston to support the labour unions and suggested that Hart should contact McFarlane and seek cooperation: '... show him the letter; discuss with him the points in the booklet [a C.I.O. pamphlet on labour organization] and tell him that we wish him to support the union along these lines'.[198] In the name of the directors in New York, Brown advised McFarlane to join the labour movement at this crucial stage.[199] On the other hand, O'Meally was convinced that the labour movement needed a clear political orientation. He expressed doubts whether the local union leaders had enough knowledge of trade union policies, strategy and tactics. He surmised:

> ...what we need is a militant workers union which will demand universal suffrage, and self-government. For very definite reasons we must have a militant liberal party to fall back on should labor find it necessary to retreat from its stand and save itself. This organisation is the J.P.L. the program of which is more radical than the N.R.A.'s.[200]

O'Meally further explained how the Progressive League tried to unite middle and lower classes in concerted action to change economic and political conditions, which it regarded as necessary pre-conditions for economic changes:

> The program of the J.P.L. if carried out in accordance with the intentions and socio-political philosophy of the present officers cannot but provide a suitable background and foundation for any movement designed to benefit the masses; for every move of ours will have for its objective of obtaining of more and wider rights for the people.

O'Meally shared Hart's fear that the middle class would undercut a workers movement, but insisted that a national movement needed to incorporate them, and eventually neutralize its class interests. Still he believed that the middle class played an important role in providing leadership for the movement and reflected: '...the truth is that nearly all of us who are leading or taking part in these movements are or were definitely of the middle class. We are of course more politically orientated to the historic march of things and realize that the advance of civilization lies in the hands of the workers'. But as outlined in the debate in *Public Opinion*, the Progressive League was convinced that Jamaica needed to get rid of colonial rule before its social and economic conditions would change.

However, trade union organization in Jamaica would follow another path. Under the leadership of Alexander Bustamante a waterfront workers union was formed that became the nucleus of the most powerful trade union in Jamaica.[201] After Manley's intervention, the Governor released Bustamante on May 28 and launched plans to form a Conciliatory Board to settle labour disputes in the future.[202] Bustamante involved himself in various unions that all carried his name and transformed them into one entity, the Bustamante Industrial Trade Union (BITU); H.C. Buchanan became general secretary and Ken Hill one of its vice presidents.[203]

Early attempts to put the union movement on a democratic and organized path were undermined by Bustamante's autocratic leadership style. His popularity increased after his release and he became 'Busta', the undisputed labour leader with hero status among the masses. During his steep ascendancy, he organized and governed the BITU with his demagogic and egocentric style. He accepted no advice from his officers, whom he replaced as he liked when they would not agree with his opinion. Within a short time, Bustamante had successfully taken over most of the existing unions. In the words of Historian Glen Richards, the white moneylender Bustamante who would become the most powerful leader of the movement was 'one of the most amazing developments in Jamaican labour history'.[204]

The leaders in New York were sceptical of Bustamante's way of operating the unions. O'Meally advised Hart that he should 'see it that the organization is constituted and run in the most democratic manner possible'.[205] Describing the role of Bustamante, Hart answered that 'the comet-like rise of Alexander Bustamante, Usurer, discredited officer of the Jamaica Workers and Tradesmen's Union, to the rank of deity among the masses, is nothing short of a miracle... In the space of a few short days, [Bustamante] becomes Kingston's hero, then Jamaica's hero'.[206]

In desribing Bustamante's popularity, Hart emphasized the challenge to oppose him:

> He has taught the people the strength of unity, and that unity exists in loyalty to him alone. He has the power to organize the people into unions now, and must be assisted to that end. Therefore, most of us, from the extreme left to the centre, are prepared to back him.[207]

The Progressive League agreed on a tactical cooperation to build the union movement, but only as long as he would act in line with the aims of a democratically organized union.[208] Initially, Bustamante had the support of important figures, including Norman Manley, Ken Hill, Hugh Buchanan and Richard Hart. They supported the efforts to build a strong labour movement before Bustamante's autocratic style discredited him in the eyes of the intellectuals.

When Hart informed O'Meally and Domingo that Manley planned to form a Labour Committee which should have an advisory role for the organized trade unions, Domingo reacted with scepticism.[209] He commented on Manley's new public role: 'I have watched the entry of Manley into public affairs and find it difficult gauging him. His business and professional connections place him under suspicion, although his utterances, though carefully chosen, have a tinge of nationalism in them'.[210] The following months proved that Manley's nationalism was not as strong as the Progressive League had hoped.

Domingo's comments on the development of the trade unions display another important foundation of the Progressive League's theoretical positions. He was concerned that the labour movement could develop a strong accentuation of race. Although he had always opposed all forms of racial discrimination, he warned that 'under no circumstance must the present upsurge take on a color or race aspect'.[211] Domingo explained his view:

> ...the darker sections of our mixed population will benefit most because they are farthest down socially, but any effort to help Jamaica ipso facto helps them, so it is not necessary – more it would be the limit of folly – for anyone to emphasize race or colour. The movement must be a purely labour one. It will have nationalistic implications but the other features must be avoided at all costs.[212]

This emphasis on nationalism and labour organization was characteristic of the Progressive League's approach. While many of the leaders had been active in the Garvey movement and continued to criticize racial prejudices in the colonial society, they were opposed to a race-based agitation.

Domingo approved Hart's Socialist course and encouraged him to carry his message to the masses, by issuing pamphlets in simple language and also by public speeches to reach to out the illiterates and to organize study classes.[213] He put a strong emphasis on education, as he felt that would inspire class instead of racial solidarity. 'The masses need education if they are to retain any gains that they may have made from their sanguinary sacrifices. They need enlightenment along class lines if they are to be saved from becoming tools and victims of demagogues... Left to themselves the people will be the dupes of the Tafarites and others of that stripe'.[214] These statements show Domingo's class-first position that rejected the race-based agitation of Rastafarians. In another article, Domingo reported that he used to frequent some of the meetings of the Rastafarian movement and other religious cults. He noted: 'I was struck by the desire of the masses to find a way out of their misery and the seemingly hopeless position in which they found themselves'.[215] He regarded these approaches as merely palliative and strongly believed in formal education as a means to prepare the lower classes for concerted action to change society. In his eyes, the educated middle classes played a central role in this process. Domingo underlined this in his letter to Hart:

> ...those who are enlightened owe it to their less fortunate brothers to carry the gospel of modern thought to them. In other words, the cognoscenti must come out of their ivory towers of seclusion and go to the masses who are not only hungry physically, but need intellectual food if they are to act in terms of their own class interests.[216]

In his letters to Hart, Domingo articulated his views more radically than in the official propaganda of the Progressive League that always stressed the need to act along constitutional lines:

> Like you I have no illusions about constitutional means being capable of 'turning the trick'. I always remember that liberty has to be won, not begged for...However, as you say, we must exhaust every constitutional means, and their failure to achieve the desired result will be the eloquent and effective propaganda in steeling the souls of our non-sufficiently-political people to wage relentless struggle for their 'inalienable right to liberty'. ..But time will take care of that point. The conservative elements can be depended upon to educate the people along unconstitutional lines.[217]

The exchange of letters with Hart provides crucial insights in the theoretical positions and tactics of Domingo and O'Meally, which they did not emphasize in the official propaganda of the Progressive League. It exhibits strong Socialist positions in their arguments that were in accordance with arguments Domingo had expressed during his active time in Socialist circles in Harlem. While it is possible that they used these arguments as tactic to convince Hart, it is more likely that Domingo revealed the Socialist foundation of his nationalist views more frankly than he could in the Progressive League. But whether tactically motivated or not, Hart could not be convinced to join the ranks of the Progressive League and kept a strong emphasis on Socialism. Probably the character of the Kingston officers, who showed no tendency to radicalism and rejected Socialist ideas, further contributed to his decision to abstain from joining. Yet, he held O'Meally and Domingo in high regard 'for what you both have done, and are doing for the working class of Jamaica in this first phase of awakening'.[218] Domingo accepted Hart's decision and wished 'that the good and courageous, if thankless, work you have done will bear abundant fruit to encourage you, in the path you have chosen for yourself politically'.[219]

When I interviewed Hart in 2007, he stressed the influence of Domingo and O'Meally on his own thinking. With reference to the exchange of letters between the three men in the summer of 1938 he stated:

> ...my original approach had been very misguided in thinking, was a demand for the introduction of socialist economy and that the political side wasn't so important. And certainly Domingo was very influential, and probably O'Meally as well, in making me realize that that didn't make sense; that the primary objection must be political independence. ...certainly Domingo straightened me out on that, to separate my demand for socialism from the demand for political independence.[220]

However, this view seemed to be coloured from retrospect reflections. Hart did not side with the Progressive League and kept his focus on trade union development.

The Progressive League leaders in New York were in a serious dilemma. Their positions were too radical in their anti-colonial stance for a largely conservative Jamaica and their ideas were dismissed as bourgeois by the small group of local radical leftists. The difficulties surrounding the founding of the local branch of the Progressive League in Kingston testify to the resistance against the demand for self-government in Jamaican society and exemplified how the widespread rejection of radical anti-colonial demands in the local scene tempered the early enthusiasts. The crucial role Roberts played while he was on the island in the initial stage after the founding of the Progressive League in Kingston illustrates the racially stratified order of the society. His prestige as a white Jamaican helped to provoke discussions about self-government. The conservative press could not ignore his message, but by criticizing Roberts, it even helped to raise attention for the Progressive League's demands. His views often were criticized as out of touch with local affairs, proving the originality of the idea that Jamaica should be an independent nation and showing again how alien this sounded to Jamaican ears. The fact that the interest in Roberts' ideas soon dissipated after his departure emphasizes how much the initial support was due to his popularity and his social status.

Although the radical demands found no strong local support, the Progressive League's insistence on the need for a political party that had inspired a lively discussion about political organization before the labour rebellions would eventually bear fruit. In concerted effort, the editors of *Public Opinion* resumed the idea and initiated the launch of a party that would provide an umbrella for the existing political groups. Disappointed in the leaders of the local branch who had failed to stick to a radical demand for immediate self-government, the leaders of the Progressive League in New York decided to collaborate with the new party and to try to transform it into the powerful local nucleus for a strong anti-colonial mass movement.

Notes

1. See for instance *Daily Gleaner*, August 24, 1937; September 24, 1937; September 23, 1937; June 30, 1937.
2. Ibid., September 23, 1937.
3. See Walter G. McFarlane, *The Birth of Self-Government for Jamaica and the Jamaica Progressive League 1937–1944* (Kingston: 1957), 11.
4. See *Daily Gleaner*, June 17, 1937.
5. Although it is a problematic source, containing many tendentious, fragmentary and at times inaccurate descriptions of developments, it often is the only source for some

Stretching Out: A Local Branch in Kingston 127

of the events in Jamaica. For this and the following see McFarlane, *Birth of Self-Government*, 10f.
6. Brown to McFarlane, September 25, 1937, NLJ, JPL, MS 234.
7. Ibid.
8. Ibid., October 15, 1937, NLJ, JPL, MS 234.
9. McFarlane, *Birth of Self-Government*, 11.
10. Invitation to Inaugural Meeting, November 11, 1937, NLJ, JPL, MS 234.
11. Ibid.
12. Ibid.
13. See McFarlane, *Birth of Self-Government*, 11.
14. Duhaney to McFarlane, October 26, 1937, NLJ, JPL, MS 234.
15. See *Daily Gleaner*, November 20, 1927. .There seems to be a confusion of dates in later accounts, for instance in McFarlane, *Birth of Self-Government*, 11 and *Daily Gleaner*, March 26, 1978, McFarlane dates back this meeting to the 27th. It seems as if McFarlane later mistook the 27th for the 24th, as he himself reported the meeting was held at the 24th in a letter to Brown. See Brown to McFarlane, February 18, 1938, NLJ, JPL, MS 234. There is no proof whether Reid actually attended and presided over the meeting, although he had accepted the invitation in a letter to McFarlane.
16. *Daily Gleaner*, November 30, 1937.
17. Buchanan was another returned migrant who had lived for some years in Cuba, before he returned to Jamaica. Hart calls him 'Jamaica's first active Marxist'. He belonged to a group of leftist radicals like Hart and McBean and actively involved in the trade union movement. See Hart, *Rise and Organise: The Birth of the Workers and National Movements in Jamaica 1936–1939* (London: Karia Press, 1989), 16f.
18. See McFarlane, *Birth of Self-Government*, 11.
19. Ibid.
20. *Daily Gleaner*, November 21, 1993.
21. Ibid.
22. Ibid., December 1, 1937; December 1, 1937; December 1, 1937; December 3, 1937.
23. See Roberts, Autobiography, 147; for the announcement of the meeting see *Daily Gleaner*, December 7, 1937.
24. *Daily Gleaner*, November 21, 1993.
25. For this and the following quotes see *Public Opinion*, December 18, 1937.
26. See McFarlane to Brown, February 18, 1938, NLJ, JPL, MS 234. Young dates back the meeting at Duhaney's office to December 6, 1937. See Young, *Lest We Forget*, 115.
27. Resolution, December 13, 1937, NLJ, JPL, MS 234, Mover Mr M.G. Bailey, Seconder Mr C.A. Gully.
28. Roberts claimed: 'The League keeps up a wide correspondence here. The Hon. C.A. Reid, M.L.C. for Manchester and the Hon. Rudolph Ehrenstein, M.L.C. for St Thomas are both members of the Progressive League. The present Mayor Dr. O.E. Anderson, is another with whom the League keeps in touch.' See, *Daily Gleaner*, December 22, 1937.
29. See *Daily Gleaner*, December 22, 1937.
30. Benn, *The Caribbean*, 37.
31. *Daily Gleaner*, December 22, 1937.
32. For this and the following quotes see, Ibid., December 17, 1937.

33. Ibid., December 21, 1937.
34. Ibid., December 20, 1937; December 21, 1937.
35. See *Daily Gleaner*, December 21, 1937.
36. See for instance *Daily Gleaner*, December 13, 1937; December 16, 1937; January 4, 1938; January 7, 1938; January 8, 1938.
37. See for example *Public Opinion*, December 24, 1937; December 31, 1937; December 12, 1937; January 7, 1938; January 8, 1938; *New York Amsterdam News*, February 12, 1938.
38. *Public Opinion*, December 31, 1937.
39. *Daily Gleaner*, January 7, 1938.
40. Ibid., December 20, 1937.
41. Ibid., January 7, 1938.
42. Ibid., January 7, 1938; January 8, 1938; *Public Opinion*, December 31, 1937.
43. Ibid., January 7, 1938; for similar arguments see *Public Opinion*, December 31, 1937; *Daily Gleaner*, January 7, 1938; December 22, 1937; December 20, 1937.
44. Ibid., December 16, 1937; January 8, 1938.
45. Roberts, 'The Manley Story', January/February 1960, NLJ, WAR, MS 353, Box 23.
46. *Daily Gleaner*, December 7, 1937.
47. Roberts: 'Autobiography', 12, NLJ, MS 353, WAR Box 2b.
48. *Public Opinion*, December 31, 1937.
49. See for example *Daily Gleaner*, December 20, 1937.
50. Ibid., January 8, 1938; December 21, 1937.
51. Ibid., December 20, 1937.
52. Ibid., December 30, 1937.
53. Ibid., December 21, 1937; see also See *Daily Gleaner*, December 8, 1937.
54. Ibid., December 9, 1937.
55. Ibid., December 9, 1937, for a similar argument see also *Daily Gleaner*, December 8, 1937; December 17, 1937.
56. Ibid., January 4, 1938. The Readers and Writers Club, which was affiliated with the Institute of Jamaica, came into existence early in December 1937. De Lisser had accepted the presidency, P.M. Sherlock and Una Marson acted as vice-presidents, and further members were Ken Hill, H.P. Jacobs, R. Hart, and future JPL-K members W.A. McBean, Hugh S. Burns, G.R. Bowen.
57. See Roberts, *Six Great Jamaicans*, 117; Young, *Lest We Forget*, 116.
58. See *Daily Gleaner*, February 2, 1938.
59. Roberts, *Six Great Jamaicans*, 117.
60. See McFarlane, *Birth of Self-Government*, 12.
61. See *Daily Gleaner*, January 8, 1938.
62. Roberts, 'Autobiography', 10.
63. *Public Opinion*, December 24, 1937.
64. Roberts, 'Autobiography', 13.
65. *Daily Gleaner*, January 7, 1938.
66. Roberts, 'Autobiography', 14.
67. Ibid.
68. *Daily Gleaner*, April 9, 1974.
69. Ibid.

70. Hugh H. Watson to Department of State, Semi-Annual Report, Political Developments in Jamaica, NARA, RG 84, Records of the Foreign Service Posts, US Consulate Kingston, Jamaica, Classified General Records 1936–1962.
71. Ibid.
72. Denham to Gore, March 22, 1938, PRO, CO 137/821/16.
73. Ibid.
74. *Daily Gleaner*, January 5, 1938.
75. Ibid.
76. For a great analysis of the paper see Raphael Dalleo, 'The Public Sphere and Jamaican Anticolonial Politics: Public Opinion, Focus, and the Place of the Literary'. *Small Axe* 14.2, no. 32 (Durham, Duke University Press, 2010): 56–82.
77. See Hart, *Towards Decolonization*, xiv.
78. Post, *Arise*, 217.
79. See Dalleo, *Public Sphere*, 63.
80. Richard Hart was one of Jamaica's most prominent Marxists. The son of solicitor Ansell Hart, he studied law in England and returned to Jamaica in 1936 to become a solicitor. He was heavily influenced by his friend H.C. Buchanan and was instrumental in forming a branch of the Left Book Club in 1938, of which he had been a member in England. He collected many important documents and records on Jamaica's political development and published several books and articles on Jamaican history. For more biographical information, see Post, *Arise*, 225f and various books published by Richard Hart.
81. Post, *Arise*, 225.
82. *Public Opinion*, December 24, 1937; December 31, 1937.
83. Ibid., December 31, 1937.
84. For this and the following quotations see *Public Opinion*, December 31, 1937.
85. Ibid.
86. Ibid.
87. Ibid. This comment demonstrates the view of a political activist who would become part of the radical left wing of the PNP. Already in this early stage, it becomes clear how heterogeneous the party membership was if Hart's Marxist view is seen in contrast to future party leader Norman Manley and his Socialist beliefs inspired the British Labour Party. The nationalist convictions of the Jamaica Progressive League were initially not endorsed by any of the different factions.
88. For this and the following quotes see *Public Opinion*, January 8, 1938.
89. Ibid., January 22, 1938.
90. Ibid.
91. Ibid., February 5, 1938.
92. Ibid., February 12, 1938.
93. Ibid., March 5, 1938.
94. Ibid., January 15, 1938.
95. Ibid., March 5, 1938.
96. Ibid., March 12, 1938.
97. Ibid.
98. Ibid., March 19, 1938.
99. Ibid.

100. W.A. McBean belonged to the Marxist circle around Buchanan and was selling peanuts, along with progressive books for the Left Book Club and *Public Opinion*. He also was a songwriter and a well known personality in Kingston. See Hart, *Rise and Organise*, 19; Post, *Arise*, 353. He was to become an important link between the left and the nationalist movement and was member of the board of directors of the Jamaica Progressive League, Kingston.
101. *Public Opinion*, April 16, 1938.
102. O'Meally to Hart, June 20, 1938, IOCS, R. 1, Fo. 2 (emphasis in original).
103. See Post, *Arise*, 231.
104. For the following quotations see *Public Opinion*, February 26, 1938.
105. See Post, *Arise*, 234.
106. *Public Opinion*, March 12, 1938.
107. Ibid.
108. Roberts to McFarlane, March 22, 1938, NLJ, JPL, MS 234 (emphasis in original).
109. *Daily Gleaner*, January 14, 1938.
110. Ibid.
111. Ibid., February 10, 1938.
112. Ibid., March 30, 1938.
113. Ibid.
114. Ibid., November 25, 1938.
115. Ibid., March 22, 1938.
116. Ibid., January 27, 1938.
117. Ibid., February 8, 1938.
118. Ibid.
119. Ibid.
120. McFarlane to Brown, February 18, 1938, Louis Moyston Private Collection.
121. See McFarlane to Brown, February 18, 1938, NLJ, JPL, MS 234, NLJ.
122. Roberts to McFarlane, March 22, 1938, NLJ, JPL, MS 234.
123. Ibid.
124. *Daily Gleaner*, March 30, 1938.
125. Roberts to McFarlane, May 5, 1938, NLJ. JPL, MS 234.
126. Ibid.
127. Ibid.
128. See Roberts to McFarlane, March 22, 1938, NLJ, JPL, MS 234.
129. Brown to McFarlane, May 6, 1938, NLJ, JPL, MS 234.
130. Ibid.
131. See for example *Daily Gleaner*, January 13, 1938; January 19, 1938.
132. See *Daily Gleaner*, February 8, 1938.
133. The Gleaner frequently reported that the group discussed its constitution, see *Daily Gleaner*, February 1, 1938; February 24, 1938; March 22, 1938; March 29, 1938; April 1, 1938.
134. See *Public Opinion*, April 23, 1938.
135. Ibid., April 13, 1938.
136. Ibid., April 16, 1938.
137. Ibid.
138. *Daily Gleaner*, December 21, 1937.

139. For a detailed overview about the development of labour organizations in the British Caribbean see Nigel Bolland, *Politics of Labour in the British Caribbean: The Social Origins of Authoritarianism and Democracy* (Kingston: Ian Randle Publishers, 2001).
140. *Public Opinion*, August 28, 1937.
141. See Post, *Arise*, 266. Roberts mentioned that Ehrenstein was an early member of the JPL, Kingston, see *Daily Gleaner*, December 22, 1937. Yet there is no further evidence for his active involvement.
142. See *Public Opinion*, May 15, 1938; Phelps, O.W., 'Rise of the Labour Movement in Jamaica', *Social and Economic Studies* 4 (1960): 422.
143. See Post, *Arise*; Hart, *Towards*; for an oral history account see: Patrick E. Bryan and Karl Watson, eds., *Not for Wages Alone: Eyewitness Summaries of the 1938 Labour Rebellion in Jamaica* (Kingston: Social History Project, Department of History, University of the West Indies, 2003). The most recent book was published after finalizing the manuscript of this book and could unfortunately not be included appropriately: Colin A. Palmer, *Freedom's Children: The 1938 Labor Rebellion and the Birth of Modern Jamaica* (Chapel Hill: UNC Press; Kingston: Ian Randle Publishers, 2014).
144. *Public Opinion*, May 7, 1938.
145. Ibid.
146. Post, *Arise*, 277.
147. See Phelps, 'Rise of the Labour Movement', 423.
148. See Post, *Arise*, 277.
149. Ibid.; Phelps, 'Rise of the Labour Movement', *Social and Economic Studies* 9/4 (1960): 417–86. For a detailed first-hand account on the Kingston events see: Hart to O'Meally, June 1, 1938, IOCS, RHP, R. 1, Fo. 2.
150. On Bustamante see for instance the biography by George E. Eaton, *Alexander Bustamante and Modern Jamaica* (Kingston: Kingston Publishers, 1995).
151. For a detailed description, see Post, *Arise*, 279 ff.
152. See *Daily Gleaner*, May 14, 1938. The article mentioned W.S. Duhaney (acting president), C.A. Gulley, Don Messam, C.J. Knuckle, D.A. Cooper, W.G. McFarlane (secretary). The Jamaica Progressive League, Kingston did not yet include persons prominent in Jamaica's emerging political scene, who would join the group in the aftermath of the events 1938. See McFarlane to Brown, May 13, 1938, NLJ, JPL, MS 234.
153. *Daily Gleaner*, May 14, 1938.
154. McFarlane to Brown, May 13, 1938, NLJ, JPL, MS 234.
155. See McFarlane to the Governor and the Elected Members Association, May 5, 1938, NLJ, JPL, MS 234.
156. See McFarlane, *Birth of Self-Government*, 15.
157. However, there is no evidence for McFarlane's claim that Evans was already a member of the JPL at this time, McFarlane, *Birth of Self-Government*, 16.
158. See McFarlane to Brown, May 13, 1938, NLJ, JPL, MS 234.
159. See Brown to McFarlane, May 16, 1938, NLJ, JPL, MS 234.
160. The event was widely covered, see for instance *New York Amsterdam News*, May 21, 1938; May 28, 1938; *Jamaica Labour Weekly*, June 18, 1938 (in the following *JLW*). The *New York Amsterdam News*, May 28 estimated that 'thousands' attended the meeting and $US200 were collected for the defense fund.

161. Among the speakers were Domingo, Richard B. Moore (International Labor Defense), P.M.H. Savory (United Aid for Persons of African Descent), Attorney Vernal J. Williams, Judge James S. Watson, S.A. Skinner (Trinidad Benevolent Association), Dr Lucien M. Brown, Miss Bonita Williams (Workers Alliance) and others. Even Judge Watson who earlier had been cautious to be too closely associated with the JPL condemned the 'atrocious act by a so-called civilian government'.
162. *New York Amsterdam News*, May 28, 1938.
163. Ibid.
164. See for instance a discussion at the YMCA on July 22, 1938. See New York Amsterdam News, July 16, 1938.
165. O'Meally to Hart, May 26, 1938, IOCS, RHP, Reel 1.
166. See for instance New York Amsterdam News, June 4, 1938; July 25, 1938; June 9, 1938.
167. See *Daily Gleaner*, May 20, 1938.
168. See Hart, *Rise and Organise*, 53ff.
169. See McFarlane to the Governor and the Elected Members Association, May 27, 1938, NLJ, JPL, MS 234.
170. See Hart, *Rise and Organise*, 66.
171. See McFarlane, *Birth of Self-Government*, 40.
172. *Daily Gleaner*, May 31, 1938.
173. Ibid.
174. See *Daily Gleaner*, June 7, 1938; June 13, 1938.
175. Dr J.L. Varma, Dr S.O. Anderson, Mr Karl Brandon, Mr Alexander Bustamante (who was cheered on his arrival) Mr R.C. Livingston, Mr W.G. McFarlane, Secretary of the Jamaica Progressive League, Mr Evans, Miss Bernard, Mrs P.A. Aiken, Mr E.A. Bradshaw, Mr E. Bradey, Mrs Morrison and Mr St William Grant. See *Daily Gleaner* June 13, 1938.
176. Ibid., June 13, 1938.
177. Ibid.
178. Ibid.
179. See McFarlane to Brown, July 28, 1938, NLJ, JPL, MS 234.
180. See McFarlane to Secretary of the Royal Commission, October 22, 1938, NLJ, JPL, MS 234.
181. See McFarlane, *Birth of Self-Government*, 20.
182. See *Daily Gleaner*, June 23, 1938; *Public Opinion*, July 9, 1938.
183. *Public Opinion*, July 9, 1938.
184. JPL, Kingston, 'Aims & Objects', NLJ, JPL, MS 234, see also *Public Opinion* July 9, 1938.
185. JPL, Kingston, 'Aims & Objects', NLJ, JPL, MS 234.
186. Brown to McFarlane, June 3, 1938, NLJ, JPL, MS 234.
187. Ibid.
188. Ibid.
189. Domingo to Hart, July 13, 1938, IOCS, RHP, R. 1, Fo. 2.
190. See O'Meally to Hart, May 26, 1938, IOCS, RHP, R. 1, Fo. 2.
191. Domingo and O'Meally had previously provided literature on trade unions and now supported Hart's request. See O'Meally to Hart, June 5, 1938, RHP, IOCS, R. 1, Fo. 2. See also Hart, *Rise and Organize*, 70.

192. See O'Meally to Hart, June 20, 1938, IOCS, RHP, R. 1, Fo. 2.
193. See O'Meally to Hart, June 5, 1938, IOCS, RHP, R. 1, Fo. 2.
194. O'Meally to Hart, June 20, 1938, IOCS, RHP, R. 1, Fo. 2
195. Ibid.
196. O'Meally to Hart, May 26, 1938, IOCS, RHP, R. 1, Fo. 2.
197. Domingo to Hart, July 13, 1938, IOCS, RHP, R. 1, Fo. 2.
198. O'Meally to Hart, June, 1938, IOCS, RHP, R. 1, Fo. 2.
199. See Brown to McFarlane, July 13, 1938, NLJ, JPL, MS 234.
200. For this and the following quotes see O'Meally to Hart, June 20, 1938, IOCS, RHP, R. 1, Fo. 2.
201. See Hart, *Rise and Organise*, 76ff.
202. See Hart, *Towards*, 9.
203. Ibid., 9ff.
204. Richards, 'Race, Class and Labour Politics', 359.
205. O'Meally to Hart, June 5, 1938, IOCS, RHP, R. 1, Fo. 2
206. Hart to O'Meally, June 1, 1938, IOCS, RHP, R. 1, Fo. 2.
207. Ibid.
208. See O'Meally to Hart, June 2, 1938, IOCS, RHP, R. 1, Fo. 2.
209. See Hart to O'Meally, June 1, 1938, IOCS, RHP, R. 1, Fo. 2. Hart together with E.E.A Campbell, N.N. Nethersole, W.E. Foster-Davis was appointed to form a sub-committee to draft the constitution.
210. Domingo to Hart, July 13, 1938, IOCS, RHP, R. 1, Fo. 2.
211. Domingo to Hart, May 27, 1938, IOCS, RHP, R. 1, Fo. 2 (letter 1).
212. Ibid.
213. Domingo to Hart, May 27, 1938, IOCS, RHP, R. 1, Fo. 2 (letter 2).
214. Ibid.
215. *Public Opinion*, September 16, 1938.
216. Domingo to Hart, May 27, 1938, IOCS, RHP, R. 1, Fo. 2 (letter 2).
217. Domingo to Hart, July 13, 1938, IOCS, RHP, R. 1, Fo. 2.
218. Hart to O'Meally, June 1, 1938, IOCS, RHP, R 1, Fo. 2.
219. Domingo to Hart, July 13, 1938, IOCS, RHP, R 1, Fo. 2.
220. Interview with Richard Hart conducted by the author, Brighton, July 3, 2007. Although Hart slowly started to rethink his positions, he never joined the JPL. In the PNP, he always belonged to the radical left-wing and was even ousted for his Socialist views in 1952.

CHAPTER 5: IMPLEMENTING DEMANDS FOR SELF-GOVERNMENT

The Jamaica Progressive League and the Founding of the PNP

In public memory as well as in most historical accounts, the tide of events around Frome and the subsequent founding of the People's National Party (PNP) are viewed as the birth of the decolonization movement. Carl Stone's view exemplifies this common belief:

> Although currents of social and political protest can be traced back to much earlier periods, the decolonization movement in Jamaica began essentially with the formation of the People's National Party (PNP). This party represented a coalition of members of the middle class intelligentsia which put the issue of self-government on the agenda and attempted to politicise the masses around commitment to local management of the state and a nationalist political identity.[1]

While there is no doubt that the PNP developed into one of the most important factors in the formation of the political landscape of the following decades, a close look at the available sources tells a different story and shows that to a large extent it was the propaganda efforts of the Progressive League that brought the question of political independence to the table. The Progressive League played a pioneering role in introducing and constantly pushing for the acceptance of self-government in the local political circles. The timidity of the local scene, made outspoken demands for decolonization difficult. To neglect the role of the Progressive League in lobbying for an end of colonial rule is to overlook an important aspect in Jamaican history and to dismiss the important role that the emigrants played in the developing political arena.

The following chapter analyses the course of political developments after the labour rebellions, traces the strategy of the Progressive League and reveals the influence that the expatriates exerted on local political thought and practice. The events of May and June 1938 clearly attested to the need for fundamental reform in Jamaica. A number of local activists now saw the urgent need for political organization, while the question of self-government reappeared in discussions.

In their correspondence with Richard Hart, Jaime O'Meally and Wilfred Domingo had tried to convince him of the necessity to form a nationalist party with a strong focus on labour organization, but also with a definite commitment to a strong demand for an end to colonial rule. Eventually, it was not Hart who made the first concrete steps, but O.T. Fairclough, the editor of *Public Opinion*, the weekly that had given so much space to the debate about the direction of such a party before the outbreak of the rebellions. In light of the recent outbreaks of violence, Fairclough succeeded where Roberts had failed: to convince Norman Manley to join efforts to form a political party.[2] Manley now agreed to committing himself to the organization of the emerging trade unions and the formation of a party. During the strikes, he had started to mediate between workers and employers, and had helped to form a Labour Committee.[3] Its most important tasks were 'to draw up a programme for labour reform and to try and lay a foundation for the creation of a genuine Labour Party in Jamaica'.[4] In an article entitled 'The Jamaica Labour Party', Fairclough announced on May 28, 1938 that Norman Manley would begin immediately with preparing the next steps.[5]

In June, Fairclough outlined his demand for a mass party to counter the interests of planters and merchants represented in the Legislative Council and in the powerful Jamaica Imperial Association in *Public Opinion*.[6] He emphasized that political organization in the interest of the people would be a necessary precondition for changing the economic conditions and that preparations for the next election in 1940 should start immediately. In the same issue, fellow editor Frank Hill published an unusually radical article under the header 'And Now, Self Government', in which he argued:

> ...we must press for self-government now...We must seize the opportunity of gaining, at this juncture, what we would otherwise gain in 25 nominally smooth years...It is the right moment to marshall our energies for a great burst of national consciousness.[7]

The leading activists felt a political momentum and seemed to be much more open to what the Progressive League had lobbied for in the previous months. However, Frank Hill's advocacy of self-government was still an isolated statement. Although people increasingly felt that constitutional change was necessary, there was still no strong support for demanding an end to colonial rule in Jamaican society.

The leaders of the Progressive League in New York agreed that it was crucial that they play a major role in the formation of the party to guarantee their influence on the party. They even considered making slight concessions to the new party, by not demanding too much too fast. The first priority, Domingo advised Walter McFarlane, was that 'the league must assume and hold leadership of the nationalist, labour, and democratic forces of the country'.[8] He reminded the secretary of the local branch that the support for the workers during the recent rebellions also served a tactical purpose, namely to recruit the working class for a broad nationalist movement.

Domingo's comments about Manley, Fairclough and their organizing of a political party reflected a sceptic and ironic undercurrent. He stated:

> According to the Jamaica newspapers some local men of considerable prestige and influence have at last discovered that the laborers are starving, underpaid and ill-treated and have come forward to organize a Labor or People's Party. The League cannot remain aloof. It must take advantage of the situation to press for the adoption of its programme.

Because of Manley's position as legal adviser 'of most of the big exploiters of labour in Jamaica', Domingo questioned whether he would uncompromisingly defend the workers without a bias towards those who provide his 'obviously large income'. Domingo concluded that '...the League must take the leadership not only for itself as a group of Jamaicans but to protect the real interests of the masses who toil for a living'. Domingo suggested that members of the local branch should be present at all party meetings and get directly involved in its set-up. Domingo reminded McFarlane that although labour issues seemed to be most pressing, political change was the precondition for economic change. Therefore, he argued: '...the League should press for self-government without obtruding that goal upon the Labour Party immediately'. This is the first instance, in which members of the Progressive League suggested such a concession. There is no evidence that the letter was actually sent to McFarlane. Marked as 'draft' and only part of the papers of the Progressive League in New York, it is possible that the letter had only been presented to the Board of Directors and not sent to Kingston. Be that as it may, the letter provides precious insight into the tactical considerations of Domingo and shows that at least Domingo was willing to accept a compromise in this early stage to ensure that the Progressive League would play an important role in the party.

Manley, for his part, tried to avoid confrontation in the question of self-government, attempting to unite all progressive elements in the formation of the party. When he spoke at a big meeting organized by the NRA in August 1938, he announced the building of the party, but shied away from definite statements regarding self-government:

> There are groups in Jamaica today who believe that the only remedy for this state of affairs is self-government, and I believe there is a growing opinion in this country that we should aim at self-government. There is indeed one party that has nailed its flag irrevocably to that one mast, and which demands today immediate and fully self-responsible

government. There are others who think that we are not yet ripe for it. I am not concerned tonight to debate that question one way or another. What I am concerned to do is to indicate that unless we settle here and we develop among ourselves the idea, and the technique, and the methods which belong to a political party, we will never make any progress forward.[9]

Manley's remarks testify to the outstanding radicalism of the Progressive League. His tactic was successful and his ideas were received enthusiastically by the audience. Whether directly advised by the parent body or not, McFarlane readily toned down the Progressive League's position and claimed: 'the League was not seeking self-government immediately but that was its ultimate aim'.[10] This statement demonstrated that McFarlane felt such curtailing was necessary in order to be in accordance with the other groups involved in the party founding. Whether openly communicated or not, this stand of the Progressive League in Kingston was at least expected, if not calculated, in the tactics of the Progressive League in New York to ensure that the group was involved in the party founding.

On the eve of the formation of a political party, the *Gleaner* had been busy attempting to counter the new progressive atmosphere. Since the riots in Frome, Kingston and other parts of the island had accelerated political organization, the conservative elements and especially *Gleaner* editor Herbert G. de Lisser took up their pen, trying to discredit the movement. While the events of Frome functioned as a catalyst for the progressives, de Lisser used them as an argument against constitutional change:

> From complete Self-Government for Jamaica, Good Lord deliver us! Not even Full Representative Government can be considered at a time when, to use a colloquialism, the tail is wagging the dog, and tub-thumping is practically the order of the day.[11]

He was convinced that 'an advanced Political Constitution, particularly Self-Government, is entirely out of the question when but a few weeks ago the capital of Jamaica was threatened by mob rule'.[12]

De Lisser soon realized that the general sentiment in favour of constitutional change could not be halted. He changed his strategy and started to tackle the question of immediacy instead of opposing constitutional changes per se.[13] This excerpt from a letter is a telling example of how de Lisser argued that demands for immediate self-government were alien to Jamaicans and far ahead of local opinion: '...there is not a single person of eminent intelligence and of standing in this country who is advocating or has advocated immediate self-Government for Jamaica'.[14] De Lisser's comments prove how much this radical position was linked to Roberts: 'Our friend, Mr. Adolphe Roberts, for instance, seems to have been doing so in the United States; and while he was in Jamaica at the beginning of this year, he certainly did speak of self-Government as though it might be a thing of the very near future'. Still, the *Gleaner* editor could not imagine that Roberts honestly advocated immediate self-government:

> I have known him for many years. He is a personal friend. He always was a dreamer. It is, however, the dreamers who often effect very practical changes in the affairs of their fellow men; but such changes may be for the worst as well as for the better, and we do not imagine that a man like Adolphe Roberts would become the advocate of what would amount to a sudden and drastic revolution in the whole political aspect of this country's life.

De Lisser pointed out how far Roberts and the Progressive League were ahead of local opinion.

> He will find...that a considerable proportion of our educated population will not be content with a mere hope that things will go right under the Robertian Constitution, but will want some more substantial guaranty of the country's safety and progress. In a word, we see Mr. Roberts either considerably modifying his ideas or failing altogether.

Such statements show that the Progressive League in New York was still perceived as the main force upholding demands for immediate self-government and attest to the difference. This gap between the Progressive League and local activists was a powerful tool in the arguments of the opponents of radical constitutional changes.

The Board of Directors in New York wondered about Manley's view regarding the advocacy of self-government. In a letter, Brown asked Manley to clarify his 'definite position in regards to the League's distinctive demand for Self Government'.[15] Manley promptly answered but made it clear that his statement was not intended for publication. He pledged that self-government should be the aim for which the party should start to work, but also made the point: 'I believe that in the existing state of political development and consciousness in the Island it could not now accept that responsibility and has no chance of getting it conceded'. He was convinced that the party would lay the foundation for the necessary political education of the country and stated that he had no idea of the time span this process would need.[16] Manley clearly preferred a gradual approach toward constitutional change, a view that was in accordance with many of the political activists in Kingston. His position vividly demonstrated to the leaders of the Progressive League in New York that including radical political aspirations for self-government into the party's aim would not be an easy task.

McFarlane joined the committee to prepare the party inauguration, which was appointed at a meeting of various representatives from the National Reform Association (NRA), the Progressive League and the Citizens Associations on

August 28, 1938.[17] The official launch of the party, that should carry the name People's National Party (PNP) was held at Ward Theatre on September 18.[18] In his speech, Manley acknowledged those who had earlier thought of a political party, before and during the Frome riots, and emphasized that he was not the originator of the idea. He explained that the recent events had finally convinced him, and he welcomed the new dynamics; the emerging nationalism, the development of the labour movement and the many new political organizations. He laid out the primary aims of the party and put forward a proposal for an educational campaign about Jamaica's history, the constitution and the present political conditions. He explained the party's name, and announced that 'People' had been chosen because the party represented the good for all people, and that the people were the basic element for a democratic foundation. When he addressed the term 'National', his elaborations mirrored his cautious position regarding self-government: 'I do not say that I think that Jamaica is today ripe for self-government, but I claim that we must start a movement working which will help us to become ripe for it'.[19] Manley urged that Jamaicans must develop a true national spirit before they would be prepared to carry the responsibility to govern themselves. Although Manley affirmed self-government in principle, he was still cautious and established no timeframe for this long-term goal.

A somewhat stronger advocacy of self-government came from unexpected quarters. Barrister Sir Stafford Cripps, a leading member of the British Labour Party and part of its anti-imperialist left wing, was incidentally on the island and invited to the PNP launch as a guest speaker. His speech was bolder than Manley's when he declared:

> No Imperial has ever or ever will develop the culture of colonial peoples because culture spells independence and independence spells the end of Empire. I want to see the end of Empire in the world because the Imperial method of world development has plunged us into war after war and will go on plunging us into wars until civilization itself is destroyed.[20]

However, his attitude was also undecided. At the same time, in an interview in the *Gleaner*, Cripps stated that he felt Jamaica was not yet ripe for self-government, because the people were not politically conscious enough to govern themselves.[21]

The reactions in the Progressive League regarding the positions the PNP had announced were mixed. Roberts concluded: 'A moderate constitutional advance beyond the Crown-Colony system was demanded by the P.N.P. Its ideals were plainly along the Socialist lines advocated by the British Labour Party'.[22] In his autobiography he commented that the party was 'engulfing Ken Hill's National

Reform Association, its program called for responsible autonomy – eventually'.[23] Domingo more enthusiastically welcomed the party founding a first step and advocated to support the party.[24] In his later reflections, McFarlane claimed that

> ...this phase of accomplishments close[d] the first round in the activities of the Jamaica Progressive League in its efforts to rouse a people with a strong colonial mentality, political indifference and lethargy, to a fuller life of full participation in the organizing of the first political party in the history of Jamaica and indeed in the British Caribbean.[25]

Although not solely to the Progressive League's merit, the impulse from New York nevertheless played an important role in the formation of political life of the country.

However, due to the moderate position the party adopted, the founding could only suffice as a first step for the Progressive League. Roberts remained sceptical about Manley and doubted whether he was the best choice to lead the party.

> The Chairman of the Party was none other than Manley, he who had told me that he cared mainly for philanthropy and had no wish to enter politics. I knew him to be a socialist, and Cripps support of him emphasized the point. Could a socialist be whole-heartedly for a national movement? I asked myself.[26]

Roberts anticipated that hard work on behalf of the Progressive League was needed to ensure that the demands for self-government would be accepted by a majority of the members as a definite aim.

The directors agreed on the tactic to convince individual party members of the necessity to include definite demands for self-government in the party's programme. In accordance with advice offered by Roberts, the local branch formally became an affiliate of the party, but retained a separate identity as an independent body, not willing to sacrifice its demand for immediate Dominion status.[27] In addition, many members of the local branch of the Progressive League joined the party individually. McFarlane assumed an active role in the steering committee of the party, as well as in several other committees, including the one on constitutional reform.[28] He later said that his chief concern in these committees was

> ...to further the programme of the League and to try to influence the acceptance of the entire self-government issue as the basis on which the party is to be built, knowing that by such vehicle a much shorter time will be needed to accomplish our national goal.[29]

However, there is no further evidence for McFarlane's claim that he eagerly tried to convince other members that demands for immediate self-government should be the party's primary goal. Earlier and later statements, as well as the questionable validity of his historical presentations demand the utmost caution. But whatever his personal stand was, it is likely that McFarlane's description of the committee's position was right when he claimed that the rest of the committee members advocated 'representative government' and were 'strongly opposed to the adoption of the League's programme of complete self-government.'[30] This claim finds approval in the above cited utterances of Manley and other leading figures before the PNP launch and will become even more obvious in due course.

In view of the difficulties to convince the party executives of the inclusion of demands for immediate self-government into the party's planks and the previous experience with the indefinite stand of the local branch, Roberts and Domingo decided to personally visit Jamaica to exert their influence on the direction of the newly founded party. In accordance with the Progressive League's original idea, they hoped that the PNP would become the nucleus of a strong and mass-based nationalist movement in Jamaica, which the Progressive League could support from abroad. Roberts even thought about a permanent return and to play an active role in the fight for self-government. An article in the *Gleaner* in July 1938 announced that the 'champion of constitutional reform' was planning to take up residence in the island and to reassume British citizenship.[31]

In the meantime, the Progressive League continued its propaganda efforts for self-government from New York. A review of the arguments shows how the Progressive League on one hand supported the party, while on the other hand radicalized its propaganda to push it into the desired direction. In a lengthy article in *Public Opinion* in October 1938, Domingo pointed out:

> The League stands uncompromisingly for SELF-GOVERNMENT and means to fight for it regardless of the difficulties ahead. The League is a component part of the People's National Party which is a coalition of the progressive organizations working for national improvement. Agitation is useless unless it has a definite goal, the goal of the People's National Party must be self-government.[32]

This illustrates Domingo's concerns regarding the PNP's stand while at the same time he tried to portray the party and its leaders as advocates of the common goal. Domingo publicly welcomed Manley's entrance 'into the struggle for self-government' and hoped that other prominent citizens would follow his example. He appreciated the anti-colonial tone of Cripps's speech and congratulated him for pointing to the fact that colonies had always been exploited for the benefit of the Empire and that this was the primary reason for not granting self-government, especially to non-white populations. Domingo referred to Roberts' definition of a nation outlined in the Progressive League's declaration and affirmed that Jamaica had all the characteristics of a nation: 'Independence is the logical goal of all nations whether they are large or small, rich or poor'. Interestingly, Domingo used the term independence here, suggesting that even a break from the Commonwealth was eventually possible. Perhaps he was encouraged to speak his mind after Cripps had argued in his speech at the PNP founding that Jamaica should still have a choice to remain in the framework of the Commonwealth after gaining self-government. Although he admitted that independence was currently not the pressing issue for Jamaicans and that their immediate task was to gain self-government, Domingo believed that Jamaica would one day be able to realize becoming a fully independent nation. With a view to international developments, Domingo asserted that there was an 'essential kinship of imperialism and Fascism' and pronounced that 'it is well that the middle classes of Jamaica realize this and stop dreaming'.

In another article, Domingo countered several arguments that were brought forward against self-government. He recapitulated how the propaganda of the Progressive League was initially met with 'a combination of amused amazement and contemptuous opposition'.[33] Now, since the movement had 'gained momentum' the opponents had to 'change their tactics and offer seemingly logical reasons for their position', instead of just dismissing the ideas of the Progressive League as unrealistic and out of touch with local sentiment. Pointing to other small countries, he challenged the argument that Jamaica was too small: 'Self-government is an inalienable right of all human beings who meet the definition of a nation stated above'. Racist opinions that Jamaica was not racially qualified for self-government would be 'such a devastatingly vicious attack on the mixed population that even the least self-respecting among them will be forced to show their resentment'.[34]

Domingo's rhetoric was exceptional in its radicalism in light of both his earlier statements and the articulations of the PNP. Now that a party was in existence, the Progressive League felt the need to radicalize its public statements. While Domingo's articles exemplified how the Progressive League continued to adamantly push forward their demands, the PNP reaffirmed its reservations against immediate granting of self-government. Manley made his position clear in a speech in front of the St Mary Citizens Association:

> I have said before I will say it again that aiming at self Government the People's National Party does not pretend to say that we are, at this very minute, ripe for self-government. We are not ripe for it because we have not learned unity and discipline and organisation. We are not fit for such a government until we can sweep away the stupid class prejudice and until we can unite in a common platform and until we can get cleaner and more honest politics and cleaner and more honest politicians.[35]

Fairclough, the author of an above-quoted article demanding self-government after the incidents at Frome, now underlined his reservations against demands for immediate self-government and directly addressed some of Domingo's arguments without mentioning him by name. Apparently, he felt compelled to clarify Domingo's views, that although the Progressive League was an officially affiliated body of the PNP, they should not be recognized as the party's position. Without mentioning names, Domingo and Fairclough entered into a debate in *Public Opinion* that demonstrated the difference in their positions. Fairclough described at length how the Progressive League was formed and popularized by Domingo and Roberts' visits in 1937, and he underscored its important role in sparking the founding of the PNP. However, he stressed that the PNP was a democratically organized body, so that even the four initiators, Nethersole, Fairclough, Jacobs and Manley could not dictate any policies. Nevertheless, he declared unambiguously, 'The sponsors of the Party do not believe that the people of Jamaica should *begin* by *asking* for self-government'.[36] This made clear where the leaders of the PNP stood on the question of self-government. Also, in contrast to the Progressive League's frequent references to other freedom movements, Fairclough made clear that 'the road of Ireland and the Palestinian Arabs, or possibly Ghandi's India...is not the road of the Party'. He believed that Jamaica had not yet proven that it was 'really capable of carrying out in a tolerably manner the responsibility'. Instead, he affirmed the gradual approach of the PNP:

> But Jamaica, although a Crown colony, possesses some representative institutions and a Constitution within which there is ample scope for proving to ourselves, as well to the authorities...that we are fit for the exercise of responsibility. This is the road that the sponsors of the People's National Party feel that it should take.

In the following issue of *Public Opinion*, Domingo instantly took up the challenge and responded to Fairclough's assertions. He openly exposed the exploitive character of colonialism and presented reasons why he believed that self-government was denied to colonies like Jamaica:

> It is denied, despite all the plausible camouflage shrouding the denial, for very material reasons. The people who actually rule Jamaica are not doing so for love; they are profiting from it. Colonies, it cannot be too often repeated, are very profitable, if not visibly to the Mother Country, at any rate to very important sections of its population. ... They are not held for the altruistic purpose of civilizing the 'natives' as so many naive people believe.[37]

Domingo encouraged Jamaicans to unite and to put up pressure against the oppressive system. In his eyes, the PNP were to organize groups all over the country and educate the masses: 'It must aim at educating cadres of informed adherents everywhere, so that the entire rank and file will be permeated with the ideology of the movement. Its ultimate goal of self-government for the island must be the sacred ambition of every Jamaican'. He blamed the 'journalistic opiates of the *Gleaner* for the political inertia of the masses and declared that the only hope was Jamaica's youth: 'Young Jamaicans must become infused with the lofty ideals of nationhood and self-government and rise to the occasion. They must rid themselves of the inferiority complex transmitted to them by the elders'. Jamaican teachers had a critical role to play in creating a nationalist spirit and instead of teaching about great Englishmen they should teach about Jamaica's great men, and he referred to Cox, Roberts, Manley and others. He put hope in Ken Hill and others of the younger generation who were 'determined to win a place for their country in the sun of nationhood'.

Domingo's articles openly articulated strong anti-colonial nationalist positions that were clearly ahead of the more moderate tone of statements by Fairclough and Manley and may be seen as one part of a double-edged strategy. On other occasions, in hope for a self-fulfilling prophecy, the Progressive League pretended that both organizations would basically share the same goals. In a lengthy letter to the *Gleaner*, in which Domingo reviewed the two years since the launch of the Progressive League, he lauded the newly founded PNP as a logical continuation of the Progressive League's programme and claimed that 'self-respecting Jamaicans will rally to the clarion appeal of Mr. Roberts and Mr. Manley with their ideal of self-government'. At the same time, he continued to deconstruct Fairclough's arguments against self-government. In an article about the Progressive League, Domingo recapitulated the history of the organization and outlined its main goals: '...the League lays great emphasis upon agitating for the fullest degree of autonomy within the Empire'.[38] He countered referring to Fairclough's concerns that a nationalist movement could adopt violent methods and assured that although he knew that 'mere asking will not result in the British Government granting self-government to Jamaicans....The leaders see the futility and bad strategy of encouraging any thought of Jamaicans taking the path of Ireland or Palestine'.

Domingo further criticized the political backwardness of the country and the prevalent identification with Great Britain. He demanded that the people

> ...had to be educated into the concept of their own nationhood and their true position within the British Empire had to be explained. Their inferiority complex based upon race, colour and colonial status had to be assailed in an effort to re-create them spiritually. They had to be convinced that their demand for autonomy was a natural political evolution.

Domingo advocated universal suffrage and stressed the importance of convincing the masses that a common front in the society was needed. Putting his hopes in the party, Domingo tendered: 'The People's National Party, properly organized and energetically and unselfishly led and pushed, should complete the job'. As a truly mass based organization, Domingo made it known that its leaders, who often belonged to the middle class, needed to 'be less class conscious and more nationally-minded'. He was aware of the deeply entrenched barriers within Jamaican society and perceived them as a menace to the desired national spirit:

> ...class and colour are practically identical. When a person speaks of class in his mental vision he invariably visualizes a particular type of person as representative of that class...Divisions based upon colour make for national disunity and retard progress.

Domingo pointed to a relevant argument why the middle class balked at rallying behind the demand for self-government and even universal suffrage, and that many members of the highly class-conscious group feared the loss of their privileges and thus showed a strong loyalty to Great Britain.

Still, Domingo was not discouraged by the timid reactions of Jamaicans toward the radical ideas of the nationalists abroad: 'It takes time to permeate a politically listless people with the spirit of the League'. He detailed the future strategy of the Progressive League; after it successfully stirred interest in nationalism, the next step was to focus on the upcoming elections and to engage in a political campaign. Domingo made it plain that:

> ...conjointly with the demand for self-government its advocates must take advantage of every available opportunity to utilize the existing political machinery and demonstrate its archaic undemocratic character. This the League intends doing. That explains its entry into the coalition known as the People's National Party. The advantages of both demanding and working for self-government through the existing political machinery are obvious.

If Great Britain would not grant self-government to Jamaica, the true nature of colonialism would become visible; 'it will tear the beautiful mask of benevolence from the ugly face of imperialism'.

In this instance, Domingo openly admitted that the Progressive League's decision to cooperate with the PNP was tactically motivated. Domingo spelled it out: '[T]he methods of the League are likely to be empirical. Conditions and realities alone will govern its tactics. Opposition to its ideals will necessarily fashion the future tactics of the League'. Future developments would testify to this statement, as the Progressive League always cooperated with those partners with whom they could best push forward their declared aims.

Yet, despite the evocation of unity and common goals, the PNP and the League gravely differed on the question of pace of developments for more responsibility. While both groups had tried to represent a common front against conservative opponents, they had also continued to delineate their different approaches. This difference was evident in the ambivalent character of Manley's Christmas message in *Public Opinion*. On the one hand, Manley argued with an unusual radicalism that identification with the Empire would prevent a strong national demand for self-government in Jamaica and demanded that future political leaders 'should have seen through and rejected all the false imperial philosophies...which seduce the intelligence of many otherwise enlightened persons'.[39] On the other hand, Manley himself still naively believed in the declared aims of British colonial policy:

> ...the aim of British rule is to assist the backward peoples to achieve self-government and a national status as quickly as possible. For so glorious an adventure we can indeed join forces and march forward bravely to the goal to which we are being urged. That is the loyalty of common aims shared.[40]

The contrast to Domingo's statements is clear. Domingo, who had employed a similar discourse in November, carried out his point much more forcefully:

> Jamaica is due some show of loyalty by Great Britain for her almost slavish loyalty. If England refuses self-government to Jamaica it will be necessary to conclude that Britain is devoid of gratitude and will only grant self-government when a people fight for it in the way the Irish and Boers did. Happily the precedents of Australia and New Zealand and under-populated Newfoundland furnish contrasting evidence.[41]

Despite the unquestionable loyalty with Great Britain demonstrated in Manley's statements, the idea that Jamaica should become a self-governed nation in due course had taken roots in his thoughts. However, the Progressive League realized the hesitation in the PNP's positions and remained vigilant. Roberts, therefore, brought out in his Christmas message that the struggle which the Progressive League had begun had simply entered into another stage and needed to be continued:

> [P]olitically the year 1938 has been the most momentous in the history of Jamaica since 1865. But it should not be appraised singly. Its significance lies in the fact that that it marked a long forward stride in a logical march of events since 1936. ...What of 1939? I expect to witness next year a strengthening of national consciousness, accompanied by a great increase in membership and efficiency of all the component bodies of the People's National Party. This will pave the way for the election of every candidate nominated by the nationalist coalition in 1940.[42]

While Roberts loyally supported the PNP, he put the party in perspective of the developments since the founding of the Progressive League and clearly saw it as a vehicle for a continued agitation for self-government. Domingo joined Roberts and Manley and placed an article in the Christmas issue of *Public*

Opinion. Almost as if he wanted to directly confront Manley's naive belief in the alleged aims of British colonialism, he boldly laid bare the widespread imperial mentality. Domingo outlined with ruthless clarity how an inferiority complex had been deliberately instilled into the enslaved and as a means of oppression from the first days of slavery, stating that 'the essence of slavery is the deprivation or denial of self-government to an individual'.[43] Domingo's conclusion was clear when he said: 'No people is truly free unless they govern themselves. Modern colonialism is an extension of slavery in the National political field'. Domingo further criticized Jamaicans' lack of knowledge regarding their own history, and in fact, that of people of African descent generally. It reminds of the later reflections of Fanon; he deplored that most black Jamaicans today saw Africa as 'a vast continent of "savages" who need to be "civilized". Civilization in their minds is English Christianity....Everything is judged solely from the standpoint of their European masters. Nobody is anxious to admit any connection with Africa'. It was apparent that this feeling of inferiority and shame was the main reason for lack of national consciousness, and Domingo concluded:

> National consciousness of Jamaicans is very feeble. Patriotism is not felt for Jamaica, their native land, but for England. They dream about England and their yearnings are subconsciously in that direction. There is no pride in their own country. Ironically, the average Jamaican thinks of England as 'home'...Like the chattel slave the average Jamaican does not realize his true condition. He lives in a land of make-believe. His desire for national freedom is only now being aroused.

In this most outspoken piece, Domingo presented a thorough analysis of the mindset that prevented the spread of nationalism in Jamaica, and he showed that identification with the British Empire blocked the channels through which nationalist messages could be disseminated. Therefore, he declared: 'To love Jamaica more is to love England less'.[44]

It is evident from these comments that the emigrants, in contrast to their fellow countrymen at home, were motivated by a strong anti-colonial conviction. Back home in Jamaica, in contrast, many activists hoped that slow steps toward more political self-determination and economic improvements could best be achieved by cooperation with progressive forces in England, for instance, the British Labour Party. Later on, Roberts would quote in a manuscript on the close collaboration between PNP and the British Labour Party:

> This alliance showed that Manley's attachment to the nationalist idea was not strong. It is disillusioning when a chief of an awakening people appears to forget that liberty is never a gift but a victory. Manley assuredly held that the administration of his country's internal affairs should be in its own hands, but he cared more for socialism and the welfare state than for full independence.[45]

The lack of a more dependable ally on the ground who shared the demand for Jamaica to become a nation state signified that the Progressive League needed to put strong effort in trying to embolden the party in the hope that this would finally lead to a mass-based anti-colonial movement.

The diverging positions taken by the Progressive League and the emerging PNP disclose their ambivalent relationship. While the founders of the PNP attached particular importance to a broad coalition of progressive forces, the Progressive League was forced to make temporary concessions to their conviction that the party should demand immediate self-government. This compromise served to guarantee that the Progressive League would play an integral role in the formation of the party. However, this was a mere tactical concession, as indicated by the increased radicalism of the Progressive League's propaganda and the decision that Roberts and Domingo would soon visit Jamaica for longer stays to influence the position of the party.

Official Representation for Self-Government before the Royal Commission

The events in Jamaica and other British Caribbean islands clearly demonstrated that fundamental change was necessary and that concessions would have to be made by the ruling classes in order to better the living and working conditions of the poor. Many Jamaicans from the higher echelons of society and many British residents reacted to the drama of the events of May and June 1938 with hysteria and feared for the continuance of the racially stratified social and economic order of the colony. Many turned their eyes to Great Britain and expected help from the Colonial Office.[46] Questions arose in the Colonial Office about the stability and the living conditions in the colonies of the Caribbean, and the officials reacted by sending a Royal Commission to the islands to examine the social and economic conditions and to help determine the way forward. The various political groups in Jamaica used this opportunity to directly present their demands to the Commission, which illustrated their positions clearly in direct comparison to the Progressive League's presentation.

Before the visit of the Royal Commission was announced, the Progressive League in New York had already developed a plan to try to influence colonial policy by sending a delegation to London to present its views on the living conditions and to press the demand for self-government. On Emancipation Day, they called 'a big self-government meeting in the interests of the free Jamaica that is to be'[47] to raise funds for a delegation to London to demand 'nothing less than complete self-government'.[48] Despite its formal collaboration with the PNP, Roberts declared that 'the Jamaica Progressive League marches unflinchingly

Implementing Demands for Self-Government

and uncompromisingly towards the goal of Self-Government, believing that Self-Government, and that only, will lead Jamaica into that new and real freedom which it seeks, for which it must work, and to which it is entitled'.[49] The *Gleaner* reported in a surprisingly positive tone on the mass meeting in New York:

> This forceful and definite statement was enthusiastically endorsed by the audience with prolonged cheers, and practically supported with a generous contribution. And so did Jamaicans in the City of New York led by their now acknowledged leader – the Jamaica Progressive League – celebrate the centenary of emancipation by laying the plans, the working out of which will secure a real and more complete emancipation for Jamaica and its people.[50]

The *Gleaner* now acknowledged the Jamaica Progressive League as a respectable force and the legitimate organ representing Jamaicans in New York, whereas it was precisely this outsider status the paper had frequently denounced. The events at Frome and the actions of the Progressive League had definitely improved its local recognition.

The local branch in Kingston had also discussed the plans to develop a fund for a delegation to be sent to London.[51] In August 1938, the officials around Secretary of State for the Colonies, Malcolm MacDonald, appointed a Royal Commission, headed by Lord Moyne, which made such steps unnecessary.[52] At first, some members of the Colonial Office expressed reservations about the Commission, fearing that it could inspire dangerous expectations among those who were allowed to articulate their opinions, and that financial resources were too few to follow any far-reaching recommendations it might make. Others were in favour of the Commission in that it would demonstrate that the mother country was concerned about the situation in the colonies.[53] There was also anxiety regarding the question of how the US would judge Great Britain and the stability in its colonies in view of increasing hemispheric interests.[54]

Ken Post described the decision to send a Royal Commission as the beginning of 'a new phase of colonial policy, which was to have an effect not only on those territories but more widely in the British Empire'.[55] The official mission statement outlined by Malcolm MacDonald initially called for investigations into social and economic matters only, before it was modified to include possible questions about the constitution.[56] MacDonald cabled Charles Campbell Woolley, the acting Jamaican Governor, informing him that the 'Commission may also wish to hear evidence about the Jamaican constitution and the organisation of local government so far as may be necessary to elucidate social and economic problems'.[57]

The Progressive League and other organizations welcomed the step, seeing it as their chance to present their views directly to the Colonial Office. Richard

Hart warned the Progressive League in New York that its local branch might not provide the representations to the Royal Commission that the nationalists in New York expected, especially in regard to self-government. Domingo responded:

> I don't know the Jamaican officers at all. Roberts met some of them when he was there, but to me they are unknown personally, so I cannot gauge their calibre. Even if they were the best of persons imaginable there is certainly nothing amiss for us at this end to continue the work that we started by making the necessary representations in cooperation with the people on the other side.[58]

The Progressive League was aware that for the time being, this meant direct and committed involvement from New York. Roberts remembered, 'I felt that it was an opportunity for the Jamaica Progressive League to go on record officially and I urged that our secretary, the Rev. Ethelred Brown, should be sent to Kingston to state our demand to the commission'.[59] Before Brown left for Jamaica, the Progressive League organized another big fund-raiser for this mission.[60] The news quickly reached Kingston that Brown would come on a six week trip to Jamaica to represent the Progressive League before the Royal Commission; at the same time, he planned to stop in Panama to address the Jamaican overseas community there.[61]

An article in the *Gleaner* emphasized Brown's popularity, and recalled his early social and political activities in Jamaica.[62] The League equipped its secretary with two memoranda to the Royal Commission outlining its strong demand for self-government. One was entitled 'Social and Economic Programs for Jamaica' and contained minimum requests to improve the living and working conditions in Jamaica.[63] The second, 'Self-Government for Jamaica', dealt exclusively with political demands. The first document listed various demands under topics like Civil Liberties, Labour, Education, Health, Water Supply, Reforestation and Parks, Land Settlement, Franchise, Census, Immigration, Civil Service. The introductory remarks left no doubt about the purpose of its representation; '...to submit its Social and Economic Programme to the Commission and to advocate the larger issue of complete Self-Government. Without Self-Government, we cannot hope for any permanent healing of our ills'.[64]

The second memorandum 'Self-Government for Jamaica', further explained the demand for immediate self-government:

> ...the point in the political life of the island has been reached at which the Secretary of State for the Colonies should be asked to grant it the status of a Dominion and thus permit it to venture forth on the great experiment of self-government. The Directors, being thus convinced, herby request His Majesty's Royal Commission now in session assembled to recommend that the Island of Jamaica be granted the right

to govern itself as a Dominion-member of the British Commonwealth of Nations.[65]

The Progressive League contended that its demands were legitimate because in Jamaica the desire for self-government 'exists to-day in such measure and in the minds of so many persons who know what they want politically and why they want it'. This assertion was clearly exaggerated, as the comparison with the petitions of other groups demonstrated.

In the memoranda, the Progressive League presented numerous arguments for self-government and openly questioned the ability of the present administration to address the grave social and economic problems because it was out of touch with the needs of the people and unable to fulfil the present legitimate aspirations of Jamaicans. It stipulated the request for responsible government, i.e., Dominion status, 'a Prime Minister and a Cabinet responsible to a popularly elected Legislature, and the right and the responsibility to do all such things as are done by other Dominions included in the British Commonwealth of Nations'. The high rate of illiteracy was no reason to deny the request, they averred, because of the high standard of education and intelligence of the middle and upper classes. Aware of the fact that Jamaica would be the first Dominion in the British Empire with a black majority, the Progressive League proclaimed that 'a great and unique experiment will be launched – an experiment which will afford Jamaica the enviable opportunity of demonstrating to the world that non-white citizens are fully qualified to govern themselves'. Statements like these evidenced the racism with which the power structure within the Empire was interwoven.

On October 23, 1938, Brown arrived in Jamaica after an 18-year absence to bring these radical demands before the Royal Commission. On the day of his arrival, he gave an interview to the *Gleaner* in which he affirmed that he represented the claims of 500 members of the Jamaica Progressive League in New York. Brown reported to the *Gleaner* that anti-colonial sentiment was strong amongst Jamaicans overseas; 'the majority of Jamaicans in the United States feel the time is ripe that this colony be granted self-government, and that his visit to the colony was primarily for advocating that end....'[66]

Regarding the local branch in Kingston, Brown indicated doubts as to whether it was ready to push goals of the parent body in New York: 'The object of the League in New York is to get the central body here strong enough to carry out the work and then they will act as a kind of outside dynamo to the mother League in Jamaica'.[67] Upon his arrival, Brown was met by a delegation of the Kingston branch.[68] They organized a welcome meeting at which Brown was the principal speaker. In his address, which the *Gleaner* called 'fiery and outspoken', Brown stressed the novelty of their demand and boldly referred to race as a factor that seemed to determine which colonies would be granted Dominion status: 'If you give it to these, who are whites, and refuse it to us, who are not whites, then the only answer is that you still believe that black men are different and inferior'.[69] Brown denounced the internalized inferiority complex of many Jamaicans and criticized their imperial identity: 'You are not English – By God you're not! Englishmen laugh at you when you say you are English. You are not English – you are Jamaican'. Jamaican identity, Brown claimed, had precedence over other identifications and related his personal perception: 'I was a Jamaican when I was British. I am still a Jamaican now that I am American. I love England but I love Jamaica more'.

Brown's words provoked critical remarks from reactionaries, and similar to the reactions to Roberts' agitation, some Jamaicans who opposed the demand for self-government, questioned his competence to speak for Jamaicans due to the fact that he lived abroad.[70] Yet, in the understanding of the Progressive League, Brown felt as a legitimate mouthpiece '…of Jamaicans in America but also of Jamaicans at home'.[71]

Brown's request to be heard at an early session to elaborate on the demands of the Progressive League was not granted, however, he was invited to a session together with the Jamaica Deputation Committee, which consisted of representatives of different local groups. In the beginning, Brown appeared satisfied with this decision.[72]

In line with the strong demands for self-government in front of the Royal Commission, Domingo provided a number of outspoken articles in the local press to popularize the positions of the Progressive League among Jamaicans at home.[73] Domingo conveyed:

> The RC [Royal Commission] must be made to understand quite clearly that Jamaicans object to their present inferior status in the British Empire. It must be told without the slightest equivocation that Jamaicans are civilized according to every Western Standard and as such entitled to self-government as a natural right. It must be informed that the right of self-government will be prosecuted relentlessly regardless of consequences. The timorous ones must be silenced and the bolder spirits given the floor. No people deserve freedom unless they are willing to struggle for it. Freedom is a victory, never a gift.[74]

Subscribing to the belief in civilization as a requirement and a basis for self-government, Domingo seemingly accepted the colonizers' standards and their definition of progress and development. However, he used this argument to turn things around, fighting against colonialism utilizing the colonizers' own weapons.

After a meeting with the NRA and other associations, the local branch of the Progressive League had joined forces with other local organizations, instead of siding with the Progressive League in New York. The outcome was the Jamaica Deputation Committee (JDC) with the goal of preparing a common memorandum for submission to the Royal Commission.[75] One original memorandum and one supplement contained various social and economic recommendations on education, social matters, political reform, taxation, industries, health, agriculture and land settlement. The JDC memorandum put forth that it would be 'expressing through its programme of Self-Government for Jamaica, the Political thought of the majority of the thinking People of Jamaica at present'; however, no such statement was included in the text itself.[76] In the section about 'Political Reform', it called for adult suffrage with the restriction of a literacy test. While the Progressive League in New York had decided not to propose specific constitutional changes except for a general demand for self-government to avoid detailed discussions that would defer from the principal goal, the JDC memorandum listed numerous detailed suggestions for constitutional changes. Among them was a call for the enlargement of the Legislative Council, a removal of property qualifications for candidates seeking public office, the right of nominated members to vote according to their convictions, and a majority of elected members. Instead of advocating self-government, it asked for better representation through an enlarged Legislative Council with more responsibility and greater influence of the elected members. In fact, this was not different from what local politicians had asked for under the slogan to return to the old constitution prior to 1865. In the hearings before the Royal Commission, the JDC only touched on constitutional questions in passing. In contrast to McFarlane's later claim that it had demanded 'Complete Self-Government for Jamaica as a member of the British Commonwealth',[77] the archival records do not provide evidence for such demand.[78]

Oral evidence was scheduled to be presented before the Royal Commission on November 17.[79] Now, the responsibility for demanding self-government rested on Brown's shoulders, as he was the appointed spokesman of the delegation for questions regarding political reform. However, circumstances were not favourable for Brown. Lord Moyne opened the session with the declaration that the Royal Commission had restricted its examination to the two memoranda handed in by the JDC. Obviously, the Royal Commission chose to avoid discussing radical demands for self-government. Brown then missed his chance to incorporate the Progressive League's demands. He tried to make clear that he was not the representative for the JDC's position, and outlined the Progressive League's position: 'The Jamaica Progressive League, which I represent, have decided it would not be wise for us to enter into details as to how the constitution should be framed, and to leave that for a later date and for an expert committee to go into details'.[80] Before Brown could further elaborate the demands for self-government outlined in the Progressive League's memorandum, Lord Moyne readily grasped the chance to stop the discussion: 'If you are not pressing that, I will leave it'.

This outcome was not Brown's intention, yet, he had missed his chance to direct attention to the Progressive League and its demand for self-government. Brown made another attempt at a later point during the hearing, when Sir Walter Citrine asked for further explanation of the point in the JDC memorandum that the president of the Legislative Council should never be the Governor. Brown tried to draw attention to more far-reaching constitutional changes:

> The whole scheme we have in mind is of having a more responsible Government in this colony than now, and therefore the Governor would cease to be in the Council at all. We would have a Speaker elected by the Legislative Council.

When Citrine replied by asking whether the Governor would not conduct his responsibilities properly, Brown saw the chance to outline the demand for self-government:

> The great thing we are trying at last to get away from is being under tutelage of England, as we are to a great extent, and having more opportunity of governing ourselves. We felt, as in other Dominions, the Governor General is not on the Council at all, so we in Jamaica – if we are to make a move at all – ought just to have a Governor as a link and not as a ruling power in the Legislative Council.

While Brown tried to bring out the important point that Jamaicans would gain experience to govern themselves and thereby object to the idea of having a governor, Citrine closed the discussion on the subject and went on to other topics. Citrine realized that Brown held a 'more progressive view than perhaps your colleagues', and deliberately went on to discuss the JDC memorandum in detail. When the discussion came back to constitutional questions, McPherson acted as spokesman, and Brown never again got the opportunity to intervene. Dissatisfied with the proceedings, Brown endeavoured to speak to Lord Moyne directly after the session closed, but Moyne refused his request.

The hearings show that not only had Brown missed the chance to discuss the memoranda of the Progressive League in New York, but it also testifies to the more diffident attitude held by the members of the JDC. Whether it was strategically planned or not, the Royal Commission cleverly avoided any serious discussion about demands for Dominion status and readily dismissed it as more advanced and ahead of local opinion. Brown was disappointed. On the same day of the hearing, he wrote a letter to the chair of the Royal Commission in which he asked for a separate hearing, explaining that he '…had some important statements to make in clarification of our demand for self-government'.[81] The Royal Commission rejected Brown's application, answering in a formal letter that there was no time to hear him again and recommended a written statement to clarify the views of the Progressive League.[82]

Implementing Demands for Self-Government

Even the *Gleaner* noted with surprise that Brown had not articulated a more radical position:

> [Brown] behaved with remarkable restraint. He refused to enter into details of the prime American contention that Jamaica should have self government in the immediate future, and tactfully refrained from expressions of opinion on matters which have transpired during the many years he has been absent from the island – for the Rev. Brown came here recently and chiefly to meet the Royal Commission.[83]

This statement is not wholly accurate, due to the fact that Brown had tried to put the matter before the Royal Commission and had even attempted to converse with Lord Moyne afterwards, albeit unsuccessfully. However, it was certainly a disadvantage for the League that Brown was not allowed the opportunity for a personal hearing. Lumped together with the JDC, it was easier for the Royal Commission to dismiss more radical demands.

Brown was anxious about the reactions from New York and asked the Royal Commission, 'I wish I could be authorized to report to the members of the League in America that our memorandum so fully and clearly set out the grounds of our demand for self-government that there was no necessity to supplement the written evidence with oral amplification'.[84] The secretary of the Royal Commission answered that the proposed statement could not be authorized, but 'that the conclusion is allowed that since the Commission had the memoranda and did not ask further questions there seemed to be no necessity for further questions'.[85]

In comparison with all other groups, the Progressive League articulated demands for constitutional change more strongly than the rest. Some of them did not speak to the political conditions at all, while those who did advocated slow steps toward a larger degree of responsibility. The most far-reaching demands for constitutional reform came from abroad, notably, from a joint memorandum from the League for Coloured People, the International African Service Bureau and the Negro Welfare Association all based in the UK.[86] Although it did not ask for immediate self-government, it questioned the sincerity of British claims that the colonies would be granted self-government if they were fit. It called for responsible government as a first step toward a desired Federation of the British possessions in the region with Dominion status.[87]

The PNP was still in its infancy and did not present a memorandum. Norman Manley handed in two memoranda on behalf of the Jamaica Welfare Ltd, and led a delegation consisting of other influential figures such as D.W.E. McCulloch, N.N. Nethersole, H.P. Jacobs and May Farquharson. Both memoranda were mainly concerned with the question of social and economic reorganization of the country. They presented a detailed land settlement scheme, offered recommendations concerning rural practices of work, as well as an elevation of the social living standard of industrial and rural workers. One of the memoranda mentioned that the present constitution also played a role in the existing political corruption and did not adequately provide responsible leadership. It explained:

> ...a stage of social development is reached in which political leadership is essential. Government cannot supply that leadership and indeed its own efforts are stultified in the impossible task of trying to make a semi-dictatorial organisation function without any effective means of propaganda or consultation with the people. The social regeneration of this Colony is not possible under the present form of Government and the difficulty is going to increase not abate.[88]

During the hearings held on November 14, Manley had the opportunity to clarify his views on the constitution. Although Lord Moyne had taken the stance that he preferred to ask Manley about his views on constitutional questions *in camera*, Morgan Jones brought up the question regarding the ills of the present government. When asked if a different franchise would alter the personnel in the Legislative Council, Manley answered: 'The major evil is that of having no responsibility and having powers that can only be used for destructive criticism. Whatever your personnel that method produces political irresponsibility'.[89] Despite his harsh condemnation of the present constitution, Manley refused to propose a specific form of government but advocated greater responsibility of the elective element. When Sir Walter Citrine posed the question whether 'Self-Government could be conferred in any full sense, at the present time', Manley answered: 'It is my opinion that it should not be conferred immediately'. He went on to advocate the widest possible franchise but at the same time he was 'prepared to see it based on a literacy test'. When the Royal Commission members brought up the dangers of a literacy test, his rejoinder was, 'I would be quite content to see adult suffrage without any test', but emphasized that this was 'an entirely individual opinion that is contrary to the majority of opinion at present in Jamaica'.

Despite Manley's careful statements, the *Gleaner* tried to scandalize Manley's answers and alleged that he had advocated 'self-government in a little while preceded by adult suffrage'.[90] However, Ken Post correctly concluded in his review of the various memoranda, that 'it was left to the Jamaica Progressive League of New York, the pioneer of Jamaican nationalism and sponsor of the PNP, to make the most direct demand for self-government, sending its Secretary, the Rev. Ethelred Brown to Kingston to do so'.[91]

Although Brown had failed to powerfully articulate the entreaty for Jamaican self-rule in the Royal Commission hearings, the Progressive League had placed its memoranda and Brown used the occasion to convey the Progressive League's

Implementing Demands for Self-Government

goals to the people at various meetings and interviews while he was on the island.[92] In particular, he tried to attract the working class to nationalistic goals and demonstrated the Progressive League's solidarity with the situation of the workers. Once more, he denounced the prevalent inferiority complex which he saw manifested in the rejection of the demand for self-government. In his speeches, Brown was emphatic: 'We held meetings in America and were glad to see that Jamaica was waking up at last. It is indeed a good sign, and there is a lot of stirring up to be done'.[93] This shows that Brown was conscious that there was not much support for the position of the Progressive League and that 'the struggle for self-government had just begun'.[94]

On November 18, a farewell meeting was held for Brown, organized by various groups including the Progressive League in Kingston.[95] After a round of appreciative speeches by barrister E.R.D. Evans, now Deputy Mayor, and others, Brown addressed the meeting and reiterated that radical change in the constitution was needed in order to alleviate the social and economic situation of the country.[96] While the *Gleaner* reported that Brown was full of the highest praises for Manley and had urged Jamaicans to follow him as their leader, he also made the Progressive League's diverging position regarding the speed in which independence could be achieved clear, arguing that '...a man would never learn to swim unless he got into the water'.[97]

In a short interview which Brown gave to the *Gleaner* before his departure, he concluded: '...I leave Jamaica convinced that self-government is now a live political issue and that the clear cut demand made by the Jamaica Progressive League will be answered earlier than some expect in the granting of an appreciable measure of responsible government'.[98] He further announced that he would leave the island on November 20, for Panama 'to succeed with the plan to establish a branch of the Jamaica Progressive League there'. Panama was one of the major receiving countries for Jamaican migrants, especially during the construction of the Panama Canal.[99] Brown's trip to Panama was successful and resulted in the founding of several branches of the Progressive League. Each of the new branches could claim more than 60 members.[100] Clearly, the migrants in Panama were more receptive to the ideas of the Progressive League. This observation further supports the thesis that migration changed and transformed the outlook of many Jamaicans who had left the island.

The Royal Commission hearing attracted some interest in the question of self-government even in the United Sates where the *Pittsburgh Courier* carried a story entitled 'Are Jamaicans Ready to Govern Themselves?'[101] The article portrayed Brown's testimony before the Royal Commission in contrast to Alexander Bustamante's evidence. It cited Bustamante declaring in front of the Royal Commission that no Jamaican should be put in positions of responsibility in the government because 'these Jamaicans invariably acted as brutes to their fellowmen'.[102] The article also pointed out that Brown 'took the opposite view' because he and the delegates of the JDC advocated that Jamaicans 'should become head of all Government departments and that native legislators be permitted to hold a majority of seats in the local Council'.[103] This was indeed the position that the JDC took, but it was certainly not the radical posture the Progressive League attempted to project.

Nevertheless, Brown was positive when he took stock of his mission after his return from Panama. In a letter to the secretary of the local branch, W.G. McFarlane, he expressed his satisfaction:

> I was pleased that in spite of the fact that things in regard to my appearance before the Commission did not go of as we expected, everybody seem to have fully grasped the situation and were satisfied. Personally I do not feel that my visit was in vain. We surely left something with the Commission even in regard to self-government.[104]

He lauded the work of McPherson and McFarlane: 'I was indeed glad to meet you and to find out in person how interested you are in our program and to feel that in you we have a capable and energetic man on the spot'.[105] The more moderate Brown seemed to have fewer doubts regarding the local branch than Roberts and Domingo, who decided to go to Jamaica in December to give further support to the movement.[106]

At a mass meeting staged by the Progressive League in New York to celebrate Brown's return, he complained again about the widespread identification of many Jamaicans with Great Britain and the difficulties resulting from this mindset for the Progressive League's efforts to promote its demands in Jamaica. He stated that 'my first job when I arrived in Jamaica was not to convert Englishmen but Jamaicans to the idea of self-government for the island'.[107] Undeniably, Brown was optimistic after the trip, stating that he believed that in five years the country would have self-government and placed all of his hopes in the newly founded PNP.

The Royal Commission certainly stimulated thinking, discussions and new considerations for constitutional change in many quarters of Jamaican society and provided a first opportunity for the actors to place their stipulations before the authorities in Great Britain. In his semi-annual report, the US Consul remarked that in view of the demands for constitutional change: 'The general feeling is that the Commission discovered nothing new which was not already known. It did, however, centre the limelight upon several notable deficiencies besides bringing new into debate some highly controversial matters'.[108] This last point clearly recognized the innovative position of the Progressive League. The Consul, however, was convinced that most of the suggested changes were impractical and would overstrain the available budget in the colony.

Implementing Demands for Self-Government

The comparison of the representations to the Royal Commission sheds light on the political visions of the different actors in the decolonization process in Jamaica. The authorities were not particularly concerned with the political situation in the colonies. The local actors' viewpoint, including the local branch of the Progressive League, was to advocate gradual constitutional changes towards representative government. The Progressive League in New York was the only organization to demand an immediate end to colonial rule, although its representative missed a window of opportunity to lobby for the expressed aim. However, the Progressive League's demand for self-government was clearly the most forward, which markedly differentiated the migrants' position based on their overseas experiences and local thought. The course of events had encouraged Roberts and Domingo in their decision to personally go to Jamaica for extended stays to attempt to influence the position of the PNP in this crucial formative stage and sway party leaders that aspirations for a genuine change of living conditions in the country were inseparable from full political self-determination.

Domingo and Roberts in Jamaica 1939

Shortly after Brown's trip to present the Progressive League's memorandum before the Royal Commission, Roberts and Domingo arrived in Jamaica for lengthy stays to continue the fight for self-government. The question was whether they would be able to accomplish what they set out to do, such as influencing those who were involved in creating the new party policy, or expressing their more radical propositions without alienating the party founders. The strategy of the Progressive League was a dual one: to fully lend support to the newly founded PNP while trying to push it in the desired direction, and at the same time, maintain the individual identity of the Progressive League while continuing its strong propaganda for immediate self-government.

Domingo arrived in Kingston in mid-December 1938, followed by Roberts in early January 1939. Roberts' stay in late 1937 had left a deep footprint, and the way the *Gleaner* styled him as the well-known 'father of the idea of Dominion status for Jamaica'[109] once more testifies to the originality of the demands for self-government. The *Gleaner* correctly expected that Roberts returned to actively work toward that goal. Looking back at this important stage of the movement, Roberts later reflected in his autobiography:

> The year 1939, or at least the first eight months of it, was the outstanding period of my connection with Jamaica's struggle for a new regime. I landed in Kingston on New Year's Day and found myself to be regarded as one of the three principal leaders....Alexander Bustamante as head of the inchoate labor agitation, Norman W. Manley as chairman of the People's National Party, and I with the League that sought total autonomy, were the men who commanded active vanguards. We might

later be pushed aside as individuals, but the advance of the things for which we stood could not be halted.[110]

In autobiographies, authors sometimes over-emphasize their own recognition, and Roberts' may be no exception. However, the course of events in the following months clearly shows the important influence the Progressive League had on political and trade union development. Roberts and Domingo in particular, exerted considerable influence, especially on the PNP and its leaders, a point that is frequently overlooked in the historiography of this period.

Roberts recalled that one of their main tasks was to ensure that the PNP would not '…relax into a welfare, reform organization as advance word about it indicated might be the case. We wanted a frankly autonomist party with an aggressive programme, and we believed that the P.N.P….could be stimulated into becoming one'.[111] This was even more important after the disappointing experience with the local branch of the Progressive League and its lack of courage to adopt a firm stand in regard to the self-government question. Roberts and Domingo now focused on convincing a majority in the new party that the fight for immediate self-government should be commenced without delay and firmly included into the party's programme. Hence, the Progressive League stressed unity and cooperation on the one hand, while on the other hand maintaining a distinct identity pushing for immediate self-government. Brown outlined this strategic approach in a letter to the *Gleaner* in December 1938: 'There is no necessary antagonism between the Jamaica Progressive League and the People's National Party; neither is there need for a merger. Both organizations should continue to operate as separate bodies each complementary to the other'.[112] Brown reassured the public that the League had always hoped for a nationalist party in Jamaica and pledged uncompromising support. Especially in hindsight of the upcoming elections in 1940, the leaders of the Progressive League aimed to build a common front of progressive forces. Brown declared that the hesitant approach of the PNP would not pose a problem to the Progressive League, as the cause of self-government would be 'appreciably advanced'[113] after successful election to the Legislative Council in 1940.

In accordance with this strategy, Roberts and especially Domingo lent their full support to the emerging party. Roberts remembered:

> W. A. Domingo had preceded me by arrangement, this enthusiast having resolved to jeopardize his business by leaving it to itself while he campaigned for self-government. He had proved himself a much better stump speaker than I, and his aid would be invaluable to me.[114]

Domingo's ability to reach the masses put him in the forefront to be of utmost value not only for the League, but also for the PNP, which initially lacked powerful mass orators in its ranks.

Upon his arrival in December 1938, Domingo threw himself heavily into party work, especially in the Kingston division of the PNP, the Metropolitan Group.[115] Roberts' opinion on Domingo's importance was correct and reflected by the fact that the group elected him as its vice chairman. In the *Gleaner*, Domingo expressed his pleasure about the privilege of being 'so closely connected with the party after being back in Jamaica the matter of a week' and pledged to 'do everything he could to help increase the party's usefulness'.[116] In Domingo's eyes, the PNP had the potential to become a strong nationalist mouthpiece. Accordingly, Domingo put his main focus on nationalist propaganda.

He published various articles in which he presented the position of the Progressive League, belabouring the demand for self-government. His writings provide valuable insights into the theoretical background of his understanding of nationalism and his explanations for the lack of national consciousness in Jamaican society. Domingo blamed the prevailing imperial mentality and complained that instead of loyalty and love for Jamaica most Jamaicans still felt strong loyalty to England and regarded themselves as inferiors.[117]

Domingo's analysis and rhetoric benefited largely from the experience of innumerable rhetorical lessons he had learned and practised during his time in Harlem. He unmasked the internalized inferiority complex of Jamaicans as a result of British strategy to legitimize slavery and colonialism. Over many generations, European characteristics like light skin colour and a straight hair texture had been associated with positive attributes while curly hair and dark complexion had a negative connotation. He argued that this perception had facilitated the development of a privileged light-skinned middle class and complained that 'until this day Negro mothers regard themselves fortunate to have children who are not physically handicapped through possession of the 'bad' characteristics of her race'.[118] Domingo blamed the nexus of race and class to be the main restraint of the development of a nationalist thinking in Jamaica. He was convinced:

> ...men and women of all races will be freed from the humiliating and erroneous belief that some races are innately inferior to others. It is a mental house cleaning that should go hand in hand with agitation for the development of a healthy national consciousness in a country like Jamaica'.[119]

Such arguments marked the core of the Progressive League's analysis of Jamaican society and pointed to a central theme: that the middle and upper classes in Jamaica were obsessed with an apotheosis of everything British, while they perceived Jamaican and especially Afro-Jamaican characteristics as being inferior. As a result, this mentality prevented the growth of a radical national and anti-colonial movement in Jamaica. In contrast, the migration experience, the contact with different concepts of race, the inspiration of racial solidarity and the study of other countries in the hemisphere had triggered anti-colonial ideas of the emigrants who now threw themselves into local political developments with the firm goal for Jamaica to obtain self-government.

Roberts arrived in Jamaica shortly after Domingo and supported him in his efforts to launch a broad and radical nationalist campaign and to work with the PNP, trying to influence the party's policy. During their stay, both men closely collaborated with Norman Manley, who appeared as one of the main speakers at the welcome meeting for Roberts in January 1939.[120] In his speech at the meeting, Roberts demanded that Jamaica should aim for the immediate granting of self-government and also noted that other small countries of non-white and mixed populations would enjoy Dominion Status within the Commonwealth. In response to a critique in the *Gleaner* that the Progressive League would not fully understand the changes, Roberts contended with similar arguments like Domingo:

> Let me assure you that I and the other officers of this organization are perfectly well aware of the meaning of Dominion status. We did not need the horrified comments of the Daily Gleaner to inform us that the change would promote Jamaica to equality with England in councils of the Empire and to a certain extent in councils of the world. We deplore the inferiority complex that causes such an idea to seem overweening and scandalous to some Jamaicans.[121]

On his arrival, Roberts was met by Domingo and some of the officers of the local branch of the Progressive League.[122] At this time, Roberts was considering to permanently return to Jamaica after his extended stay. The *Gleaner* announced: 'Mr. Roberts is making Jamaica his headquarters to further the idea of the league, for self-government in Jamaica'.[123] Roberts confirmed his plans in an interview before he left the island and stated that he planned to go back to New York for business and then return to permanently settle down in Jamaica.[124] He announced that he aspired to establish a number of branches of the Progressive League in the countryside and was thinking about regaining his British citizenship as he considered pursuing a political career and becoming a member of the Legislative Council in the future.

At the welcome meeting, Domingo emphasized his own Jamaican identity: 'Even in the U.S.A. where the term West Indian was insular, he had always been Jamaican first, last and all time'.[125] He went on to declare that he was ready to render his service for his country and wished to inspire a strong self-government movement to fight against the deeply entrenched inferiority complex. Like Manley and Roberts, he accentuated the need for concerted action; the progressive forces had to close ranks. He explained that was why the Progressive League supported the PNP and became affiliated with the party. Domingo further stressed the

Implementing Demands for Self-Government

importance of the party's appeal to the working class: 'They could not afford to disassociate this national movement from the cause of labour, for labour today was the champion of democracy'.

For now, close cooperation with the PNP was the order of the day. The Progressive League tried to present itself as willing to compromise, but without abandoning its anti-colonial stance. In contrast to earlier statements, Roberts promised they would accept the granting of a more representative system as a first step. This clearly demonstrated the concession to the PNP. But although Roberts expressed hope that the Royal Commission would suggest such constitutional changes, he left no doubt that the Progressive League would always continue its agitation for immediate self-government. He explained:

> ...at all times, we shall be positive instead of timid and procrastinating. If, by some miracle, complete self-government were offered to Jamaica to-morrow, the League would take the stand that it must be accepted instantly. We feel that this country has the right to learn by experience, to make mistakes if these cannot be avoided, but at all events to function at the earliest possible moment as a nation among nations.

Like Brown and Domingo, Roberts did not regard the differing views of the Progressive League and PNP to be irreconcilable. He explained that:

> ...the party is by no means committed to immediate self-government, but in advocating its own more radical policy the League is not being disloyal with the party. We are one of the members of a coalition and in the elections of 1940 we expect to offer a united front to the forces of reaction.

The Progressive League's wish to cooperate with the PNP was shared by the party leaders. Manley regarded the Progressive League as a radical spearhead that could help to inspire a nationalist movement in the country and heartily welcomed Domingo and Roberts back on the island. In Manley's speech at the welcome meeting, he also emphasized unity and warned that a split between the PNP and one of its affiliated bodies or the labour movement would be the 'greatest tragedy'.[126] He stressed the need for organized party politics, the building of a national spirit and finally the demand for self-government which he described as an 'inevitable corollary' to the steps now being made. Aware that this would be a 'hard and serious fight', he welcomed Roberts' arrival because the party would need 'men of courage, men who were fighters, men who were not going to compromise'.

Manley went on to openly admit that he was not the architect of the idea to form the PNP and even less, that he had considered the demand for self-government. He pointedly paid tribute to Roberts for having exposed him to the idea:

> ...when Mr. Roberts was last in Jamaica he had done him the honor of calling on him in his chambers to discuss his ideas about self-government for Jamaica. And he must be perfectly frank. A year ago he had not seen it. He had travelled in his own mind a long way in 12 months, but he felt he had travelled with the country and not away from it.

Manley was surely right that his own approach was more in congruence with the sentiments in Jamaican society. Manley affirmed that 'the PNP...had not put in first place the immediate demand for self-government. What it had put was a demand for organization....'[127] He went on to aver that the 'ultimate aims and ambitions' of the PNP would not digress from those of the Progressive League and that he 'was glad that in that body there was leadership to put that demand in a naked and uncompromising form'.[128] Manley welcomed the alliance between the two groups and hoped that the Progressive League's radicalism would help to accelerate the developments.

In this time of collaboration, Domingo and Roberts spoke at various meetings all over the country and, in accordance with their strategy, frequently claimed that the PNP shared the same basic goal. Domingo, for instance, announced at the newly founded Left Book Club that self-government was not only the Progressive League's aim but also the PNP's 'chief aim'.[129] Also at public PNP meetings, Domingo frequently claimed that self-government was the common aim, while concealing the contrasting views on the alacrity with which it was to be achieved.[130]

Manley supported this tactic, affirming that the demand for self-government was the party's ultimate aim. This was the basis on which cooperation was possible, and the Progressive League pledged its support for the PNP candidates in the next general elections.[131]

The collaboration worked out well, despite all differences. Domingo gained some prominence in the PNP, especially in the Metropolitan Group, where he often presided over the meetings and was frequently announced as one of the main speakers or was asked to raise funds for the party.[132] Oftentimes, Domingo and Roberts accompanied Manley on his propaganda tours throughout the country, often chairing those meetings or giving one of the main addresses at newly founded groups.[133] Thus, they helped to organize the party at the grassroots level and to establish its country branches. The three men formed a great team. With Manley's prestige, Domingo's appeal to the masses and Roberts' popularity as an author of some merit who embodied the idea of self-government, they had no problem drawing a crowd. Manley delivered eloquent and elaborate speeches, appealing to the intellectual elite, while Domingo's rhetorical ability was useful to inspire the people.[134]

It was an intense time, during which foundations for friendship and mutual appreciation were laid, and in which the leaders of the Progressive League were able to exercise profound influence on Manley and the PNP. However, the close cooperation also revealed some relevant differences. Roberts remembered the many conversations with Manley on the drives to and from country meetings:

> His type of socialism disturbed me a little, though he stopped short then of preaching that the party should be socialist. On the question of national independence I was more radical than he was, on other matters less so. Manley wanted labor unionism to be firmly established and allied, as I understood him, with the self-government movement. He also wanted universal suffrage without a literacy test.[135]

In the time they spent together, Manley and Domingo were probably more in agreement in regard to the question of labour organization and universal suffrage, particularly in light of the efforts of Domingo and O'Meally to unite the labour movement with a broad national movement demanding self-government. Roberts' approach was different: 'We had not meant unions to be tied in with political activities, and I now feared that if they should be, they might become the dominant factor'.[136] However, all these differences were compromised for a common strong nationalist campaign in the hope that the PNP would become the nationalist force and cooperation partner the Progressive League desired to have on the ground.

Yet, the Progressive League maintained a separate identity to ensure that its demand for immediate self-government was not watered down by cooperation with the PNP. Accordingly, Domingo and Roberts did not only speak at PNP meetings but also to Trade Unions and youth groups to further promote the idea of self-government for Jamaica.[137] To demonstrate the Progressive League's different opinion on the self-government question and to test the popularity of the idea, the Progressive League nominated its own candidate in a special election in January 1939 for the seat for Kingston and St Andrew in the Legislative Council. The candidate of choice was E.R.D. Evans, the solicitor who had defended the workers in the Frome trials and who had become vice president of the local branch of the Progressive League. Roberts emphasized that Evans was not running the campaign as an individual candidate or as someone who would later accept the manifesto of the Progressive League, but instead, as a candidate who represented an organization and sincerely stood for its most vital demand, the claim for immediate self-government for Jamaica.[138] The PNP did not nominate its own candidate, but many PNP members supported the rivalling E.E.A. Campbell, who held more moderate views on constitutional change.[139] Domingo and Roberts gave full support to Evans, for instance, in speeches at PNP meetings.[140]

When Evans officially announced his candidacy on January 5, 1939, he outlined three main planks of his programme: a new census, a land settlement scheme and self-government.[141] He employed an economic argument to justify this claim, stating that 'Self-Government must be immediately sought, if we are to have freedom in market manipulations'.[142] Evans and the Progressive League officially started the electioneering campaign, and Evans was formally sworn into the programme of the Progressive League, the fight for self-government and the preamble of the Progressive League.[143] The *Gleaner* reported on the meeting of the League and quoted Evans's statements: 'it was time for the colony to be cut off from apron strings of the Colonial Office. He felt the island was fit for self-government and that if a deputation had to go to Downing Street they must get it'.[144] Evans's candidacy was not only remarkable in the sense that he was the Progressive League's first and last appointed candidate for political office, but it was also the first time in Jamaican history that a political candidate ran on a platform for self-government.

A comparison of the official programmes of Evans and Campbell shows that Evans's first two aims were complete self-government and universal adult suffrage. Further goals included the creation of a department of labour, effective means against unemployment, prison reform, the demands for a local broadcasting station and a Jamaican university. In contrast, Campbell advocated a majority of elected members in the Legislative Council and argued that nominated members should be able to vote according to their conscience. The Federation of Citizen Associations (FCA) also listed a number of practical aims, but was comparatively restrained in regard to political issues.

The reports about the election meetings suggested that Evans was more able to attract supporters from the lower classes, who sometimes showed their loyalty through crude methods like trying to disturb or break up meetings. At one point, the Progressive League saw the necessity to come out against the violence and push 'for better behaviour at street meetings'.[145]

Reports about Evans's campaign suggest that the demand for self-government had started to take root in Jamaican society, especially in the lower class, where Evans's programme was seemingly received with enthusiasm. The *Gleaner* stated: 'Mr. Evans does not fear competition of the platform offered by his opponents. His own platform rests on the vital issue of self-government, and the enthusiastic popular reception which has greeted every mention of this subject convinces him that victory is certain'.[146] One of Evans's meetings in a poor area of West Kingston even suggested that self-government was the most well received aspect of Evans's planks.[147]

Evans's popularity even seemed to have temporarily influenced the position of his rival Campbell. At a PNP meeting on January 23, Campbell and Evans

Implementing Demands for Self-Government

appeared and spoke on the same platform. After Evans affirmed his faith in self-government, Campbell, the *Gleaner* reported, 'declared his firm belief in Self Government and the party'.[148] Campbell then continued in a populist manner and stressed the responsibility of the wealthy to assist the poor, but there was no evidence that Campbell was very serious about these aims. Possibly, he simply wanted to impress those PNP members who sympathized with the lower classes or with the demand for self-government. In his programme, there was only a vague reference to constitutional change, but no concrete demand for self-government. After the elections, the *Gleaner* praised him for his campaign against the demand for universal suffrage and self-government.[149]

Evans's campaign attracted different forms of criticism. There was not only critique of those who genuinely opposed his declared aim of self-government, but also those who questioned Evans's sincerity. O.E. Anderson, for example, who supported Campbell, accused Evans of being a 'ventriloquist dummy'[150] of the Progressive League, an accusation to which Evans answered 'my ventriloquist is God'.[151] In a series of articles published in the *Gleaner*, Evans was portrayed negatively and accused of being a populist who was 'ready and willing to stand for anything he thinks the public will fall for'.[152]

There seemed to be a grain of truth in the accusation of opportunism, as Evans was also accused of detouring from the firm advocacy of self-government. The author of a letter to the editor who signed it as 'Frome Victim' complained that Evans was

> ...toning down on that plank of his platform because he fears that to advocate self-government will do him harm from the capitalist class to which he is pandering in his attacks of Mr. Campbell and the Clerk's Union. Is this the kind of candidate Kingston is to have and the Jamaica Progressive League is supporting?[153]

Later, McFarlane indicated as well that Evans had sometimes forgotten that he was campaigning for a cause and had been overwhelmed by the massive criticism in the press and from his opponents.[154] Evans himself would condemn the idea of self-government in his later career when he ran as a candidate of the Jamaica Labour Party in the 1944 elections.[155] However, the reports about his campaign in 1939 indicate that Evans mainly declared himself as a firm supporter of the idea of immediate self-government and that this was what he was perceived to stand for by the public. At the end of the campaign, one article in the *Gleaner* reported on Evans pledging again that he stood firm behind the platform of the Progressive League and self-government in particular, possibly because of doubts as to his firmness on this part of his planks.[156] At another meeting, attended by more than 300 people, Evans was reported to have declared that he believed that 'the country was ripe for self-government'.[157]

Evans's campaign showed that the middle and upper classes were still strongly opposed to the demand for self-government, yet at the same time, the idea gained some degree of popularity among those on the lower strata of society. The outcome of the election supports this conclusion. The voters, who qualified despite the high property qualifications, decided for Campbell and against Evans in a landslide victory.[158] The first political campaign for self-government was lost. Notably, while the majority of those who enjoyed voting rights opposed the idea, some sections of the disenfranchised apparently showed more support.

Progressive League Secretary McFarlane later commented that the organization had questioned Evans's chances for a victory from the beginning, 'but we considered the opportunity as being ideal in now being able to carry the self-government issue to a wider audience with a greater measure of self-confidence and drive'.[159] McFarlane blamed the defeat mainly on the limited franchise, the property qualification as well as the novelty of the idea:

> We realized how impossible it would be for a people who nearly three hundred years were satisfied to be regarded as being loyal British subjects, to suddenly become converted to a new and strange method of thinking especially in the midst of consistent denunciation by the Press, the opposing candidate and his platform speakers. Our candidate too, being himself a new convert, finally got caught up in the web of strong opposition, began to whimper, forgetting that at the moment, he was representing a 'Cause' and not simply campaigning to win a seat in the colonial legislature.[160]

Again, this highlights how revolutionary and unpopular the idea was of cutting ties with England, but the Progressive League was satisfied that it had 'fought the very first political battle in the British Caribbean colonies on a national self-government platform'.[161]

After Evans's defeat in the elections, the leaders of the Progressive League continued their dual strategy to support the PNP and concurrently to continue their propaganda for self-government. An article by Roberts that appeared just after the election advised that 'the first step is to support the People's National Party, either by acquiring direct membership or by joining the Jamaica Progressive League, an affiliated body which is privileged to maintain a common front with the party in the fight that is ahead'.[162]

Similar to the reactions garnered by Roberts' preceding visit, the agitation for self-government provoked criticism from the conservative elite. In light of the cooperation between the PNP and the Progressive League and the possibility of a strong nationalist movement, prominent conservatives like Esther Chapman and de Lisser tried to denounce nationalist propaganda with different strategies. Chapman, for instance, used exaggeration and alleged that the spokesmen of the self-government movement would work for secession from the Empire and

Implementing Demands for Self-Government

claimed that Jamaicans were not fit to govern themselves. Domingo exposed her arguments as hysterical and alarmist and openly blamed the race-class conjunction in Jamaica and the advantages of the upper class for the desire to protect the status quo: 'The temporary advantages enjoyed by some people (including those of Mrs Chapman's racial stock) at the expense of the Jamaican masses should not blunt their humanity or cloud their common sense'.[163] Domingo asserted that to oppose self-government in a country with a black majority, the opponents would always point to Haiti as an example of failed self-government, instead of looking at Nazi-Germany, fascist Italy or the Balkan states as bad examples of nation states with a white majority. Race, Domingo was convinced, should not be a hindrance for the nationalist aspirations of Jamaica. He elaborated:

> Jamaican self-government is now the ideal of a minority but it will sooner or later become the irresistible demand of all the people. Jamaica is a nation composed of people of various racial strains and admixtures, but a nation nonetheless – a nation of many bloods like the United States. As a nation Jamaica deserves and demands a status in the British Empire similar to that of New Zealand.[164]

Domingo firmly denounced racist arguments to counter conservative fears of granting responsibility to colonies with large black populations.

The *Gleaner* presented the claim for self-government not only as unrealistic but as against the wishes of the majority of the people:

> Nobody imagines that we shall have Dominion status 5 years hence as Mr. Adolphe Roberts demands; we doubt if there are more than a dozen persons in Jamaica seriously demanding this and we are certain that Mr. Roberts does not expect his demand to be conceded. But as soon as a candidate in any parish talks about Dominion status, the other candidates opposing him will do likewise; none of them may take the matter very seriously, but none would wish to give the other the slightest advantage over him.[165]

This statement contains internal inconsistencies. If it was true that nobody wanted Dominion status, it does not appear to be logical that advocating for said status would have been of advantage in any election campaign. Similar to his earlier critiques, de Lisser underscored the respectability of his friend Roberts who simply happened to have the wrong political views, which he assumed were partly due to his unfamiliarity with the local scene. He stated that 'Mr. Adolphe Roberts is the advocate of immediacy, but then Mr. Roberts has spent many years in a country of speed and hustle and does not yet know about Jamaica as those of us who have lived here do'.[166]

Reflecting on the conservative reaction to the recent election campaign, Roberts claimed:

> In troublesome times, a favourite method of reactionaries is to belittle all popular movements, and to accuse the leaders of not meaning what they say, and to credit the rank and file with vocal enthusiasm. It amounts to asserting that the revolt against the existing order is illusory.[167]

He warned that the influence of de Lisser, the 'old master and chief practitioner' of this tactic, should not be underrated. Roberts directly answered two columns the editor published during the election campaign in which his name was called. Contrary to de Lisser's claim that the programmes of the contesting candidates had not been much different and the election was more a matter of personalities, Roberts argued that Evans had been defeated particularly because he ran on a platform for self-government. However, he felt the idea itself had not been defeated. In light of the voting restriction, he declared that:

> ...about one-third of the apathetic ten-shilling voter on the old registration list exerted themselves to come out and vote at all. A majority of the handful evidently were hostile. They defeated the Jamaica Progressive League candidate. A Pyrrhic victory maybe, but still a victory. But the voters of tomorrow under universal suffrage, which is bound to come, flocked to Evans's meetings and cheered every mention of self-government.[168]

This is positive testimony of the demand for self-government in the lower classes. Therefore, Roberts was optimistic that a united front of PNP and Progressive League could stand against the conservative elements of the society which the *Gleaner* represented.

> We have here a cohesive, island-wide movement, growing stronger every day and positive about its objectives. The founders of the P.N.P. already have declared for self-government, universal suffrage and justice to labour. They have met with a reception which can only be described as a popular revolution – from the ground up.[169]

The PNP and the Progressive League continued their cooperation after the by-election. Roberts and Domingo continued to speak at numerous party meetings all over the country and actively participated in membership drives for the PNP, showing full support for the party.[170] At one meeting, Roberts stated: '...any Jamaican who failed to join would be a disgrace in his own eyes and the eyes of his country'.[171] Roberts also encouraged the members of the local branch of the Progressive League to join the PNP, which many did and, 'which would not of course mean dual allegiance but a stronger pulling together for the national advancement of Jamaica'.[172]

While Roberts and Domingo continued to stress the demand for self-government in the earliest possible time, Manley's statements at this time also emphasized the need for self-government, although his utterances lacked any urge for immediacy.

> National spirit was a great unifier of the people of a country, led to a pride in the country and in their own great men and in their own history and in teaching of their children of their own great men in their own history. That was why the party believed in self-government, because unless people believed in their own power to rule themselves they would not be a real people. Self-government was no movement of disloyalty or disunity. It was the inevitable growth of a people.[173]

Manley's statement is indicative of the fact that the Progressive League's constant push had started to bear fruit and had its effect on the party leader.

While closely cooperating with the PNP, Roberts tried to turn the local branch of the Progressive League into the stronghold for the forceful demand for immediate self-government. One important step in that direction was his own re-election as president at the first annual meeting of the local branch.[174] Upon election, Roberts explained the relationship to the PNP, and emphasized that:

> The League was an affiliated body [of the PNP] with Self-Government for Jamaica as its main objective. By retaining its identity, the League had the power towards that objective no matter what other things the party might advocate for Jamaica.[175]

Roberts urged that unity was much needed but '[t]here is no reason why we, who first put forward the idea of Self-Government, should not retain our identity'.[176]

However, not all members of the local branch of the Progressive League uncompromisingly supported the demand for self-government. For example, P.A. Aiken and C.A. McPherson, who also held memberships of the FCA, participated in the committee designing the election programme for Evans's rival, Campbell.[177] At this time, the dual membership in political organizations started to become a potential for conflict. When Progressive League member Mary Morris-Knibb[178] announced her candidacy for the Kingston and St Andrew Corporation (KSAC), some fellow Progressive League members complained that the organization should not support her, because she had not supported Evans in the recent campaign, but had supported Campbell. Roberts used this occasion to complain about a lack of loyalty to Evans from the ranks of the League and demanded group loyalty and firm support in the future. He stated: 'Any time the League is doing anything as an individual body or co-operating with the party as an affiliated body it is the duty of every member to come forward and support the action of the board of directors of the League as a political body'.[179]

When Morris-Knibb announced her candidacy in the *Gleaner*, she claimed to have the support of the Progressive League.[180] After harsh criticism from

Progressive League members, she declared publicly that she regretted the misunderstanding and explained that the Progressive League would not be in support of her candidacy. She made it clear that she was a member of two organizations, the FCA and the Progressive League, and underlined her belief that she had made use of her personal freedom to choose a candidate by conscience in the recent by-election and that the choice was more a matter of personality since she did not see much difference in the programmes.[181] This statement indicates that Morris-Knibb did not put much emphasis on the crucial difference regarding the question of self-government, or that she even rejected the idea. The support for the demand for self-government was still limited, even within the ranks of the local Progressive League.

While demands for self-government were still not deeply rooted in the politically interested middle class, Domingo tried to introduce nationalist ideas to the working class in order to plant the seeds for a strong mass-based national movement. The organization of a more cohesive trade union movement was one important corollary of the Frome riots. Ken Post emphasizes the contradiction of working class activism and the nationalism emerging in the middle class.[182] But for Domingo, there was no contradiction in the effort to create synergies between the trade unions and the nationalist movement, and he had already advocated for such collaboration in the exchange of letters between Domingo, O'Meally and Hart.

In 1939, Domingo attempted to create unity between the newly formed labour unions and the nationalist movement. He believed that the working class would benefit the most from an end to colonial rule, and expected that a strong supporter base could be recruited. Self-government, Domingo had declared in the debate in *Public Opinion* in early 1938, was the prerequisite for any change of the economic conditions.[183]

A valuable opportunity for the Progressive League to specifically address the workers occurred when H.C. Buchanan and Stennett Kerr-Coombs, the editors of a new weekly newspaper, the *Jamaica Labour Weekly*, which had developed in the aftermath of the labour rebellions in May 1938, were imprisoned.[184] Because of an article about police brutality, both men were charged with seditious libel in October 1938 and sentenced to six months in prison.[185] The editors needed support to continue the paper, and thus Buchanan approached one of the contributors, Progressive League member and fellow Socialist W.A. McBean.[186] McBean, similar to Domingo, believed in a symbiosis of labour and national movement and had already written in the *Jamaica Labour Weekly* about the special responsibility of the workers as voters and citizens.[187] Richard Hart also agreed to join the effort to continuing the paper and it resumed publication in December.[188]

Implementing Demands for Self-Government

With his experience of editing the *Negro World* and the *Emancipator*, Domingo seized the opportunity to join the editorial staff of the *Jamaica Labour Weekly* and also contributed various articles. Domingo's influence is best reflected in the paper's changed attitude toward nationalism and the demand for self-government. Since he had joined, the orientation toward nationalism changed remarkably. Before the imprisonment of the editors, the newspaper mainly circulated news relevant to the working class and was dedicated to a Marxist approach. Focusing on class solidarity, its emblem showed a black and white hand in the foreground of a map of Jamaica.

After Domingo got involved, a number of articles featured topics the Progressive League frequently addressed, for example, the reopening of entrance into the civil service to all Jamaicans.[189] In contrast to the first issues, an increasing number of articles discussed the demand for self-government; in most cases Domingo was the author. He advocated universal adult suffrage and reminded the workers of their numerical power, which they should use in order to change political and economic conditions. In line with the principles of the paper, and also with those of the Progressive League, the vice president stressed that inequality was not a matter of race but of class.[190]

The *Jamaica Labour Weekly* featured enthusiastic reports about some of the mass meetings at which Roberts and Domingo spoke in favour of self-government, for example, one on January 8 at Race Course, attended by approximately 4,000 people. One article called Roberts and Domingo 'Jamaica's foremost fighting nationalists' and commented: '…it is perhaps the first time that the truth about Imperialist Exploitation has been so forcibly brought before such a large audience'.[191] In an editorial, the demand for Dominion status was combined with the critique of those who opposed self-government, who were called 'zombies' and 'animated corpses most of whom never saw England in the flesh, but whose souls long since were transported there'.[192]

The paper actively promoted the Progressive League's vision of a strong, united national movement:

> The fact that the revolt of labour and the self-government movement were practically simultaneous here has deep significance. Both are symptoms of the passing of that moral servitude and political apathy which in generations set Jamaica apart from her neighbors. The dual awakening spells National consciousness, a state of mind which gives sustaining and guiding strength to a people in struggle for liberty.[193]

The *Jamaica Labour Weekly* was a valuable new platform for the propaganda of the Progressive League, with better outreach to the working class, especially in contrast to the middle-class based *Public Opinion*. When both original editors were released,[194] the staff organized a big welcome meeting on April 3, at which

Domingo was master of ceremony.[195] However, a split occurred between Kerr-Coombs, who owned the press, and the rest of the editors, because the team had continued the paper without his approval. After Kerr-Coombs' release, he continued the paper alone.[196] The last issue on which Domingo, McBean and Hart had influence appeared on April 15, 1939. In this issue Domingo urged the workers to develop more class loyalty. He argued from a Marxist position and saw the Jamaican labouring class on the path of a fundamental struggle for hegemony. He nevertheless warned, without directly naming Bustamante: 'Labour loyalty should be to the class and not to the individual. Men will come and men will go, but classes will exist until the end of the capitalist system'.[197] Domingo still held Socialist views, but his nationalism had taken precedence.

Domingo and Roberts were offered another chance to influence the labour movement during their stay on the island. In February 1939, they were involved in the formation of the Trade Union Advisory Council (TUAC), out of which the PNP-affiliated union, the Trade Union Council (TUC) developed. The founding of the TUAC had been a recommendation of Sir Walter Citrine, who had suggested such a body as a reaction to the findings of the Royal Commission.[198] The TUAC was intended to work closely together with the Committee for West Indian Affairs (CWIA), which was formed in the House of Commons in November 1938.[199] The goal of the latter organization was to support British West Indian political and industrial growth and make representations on behalf of labour unions in the West Indies before the Colonial Office.[200] However, the immediate catalyst for the formation of the TUAC was a general strike called by Bustamante, who had solidified his firm grip on the trade unions.[201] While the workers had only reluctantly supported the sudden call for the strike, the reaction of the Governor was drastic. He immediately called a State of Emergency on February 14, 1939, banned all public meetings and marches, threatened to arrest Bustamante and declared that he would only lift the Emergency Regulations when the strike was ended. As a corollary, the TUAC was formed in the following days, to bring the situation under control. Largely based on a statement by Manley in the *Gleaner* in June 1939, Post and Hart describe how a meeting was held on February 17 between Manley, Domingo, Campbell, Ken Hill, J.A.G. Edwards and Bustamante with a plan to act along Citrine's advice of forming an advisory council for the unions.[202] Neither Manley nor the two historians mention the important role Roberts and Domingo played in convincing Bustamante to accept the proposal and to bring the TUAC into being.

Domingo presents a more detailed version of the story that shows the impact of the leaders of the Progressive League. In an article in *Public Opinion* in 1945, he reviewed the development of the labour movement and repudiated the widespread perception that the TUC was initially formed by the PNP. Domingo remembered that after the Governor had issued the State of Emergency on February 14, L.P. Waison approached Domingo, suggesting that they convince Manley 'to find a way out to save the young unions from what seemed to be certain destruction'.[203] Subsequently, they approached Manley, who in turn tried several times to convince the Governor to lift the State of Emergency. Richards' demands were difficult to meet, as he required Bustamante to call off the strike, democratize his unions and make peace with rivalling labour organizer, Coombs. Manley then decided to send a delegation to Bustamante to convince him to cooperate in order to save the young union movement.

Roberts described how he, Domingo and E.E.A. Campbell made their way to Bustamante's office after earlier approaches by Manley had failed. The group put the proposal in front of Bustamante that Manley and the Governor had agreed upon. Roberts remembered that when the idea was explained to Bustamante that he should call off the strike, democratize the unions and accept the advice of an Advisory Council, he showed a strong physical reaction, shivering and rolling his eyes. According to Roberts, Bustamante answered: 'I am beaten this time and I will have to give in....'[204] However, he proclaimed that he alone 'controlled the masses and if ever he were crossed again there would be terror' and threatened 'I can cause Jamaica to run with blood'.

Roberts remembered how Domingo tempered him down: 'Mr. Bustamante, you do wrong even to think of violence in this country. There is no necessity for it, and if it got out of hand it would be punished by massacres of our people'. According to Roberts, Bustamante assented giving a 'scarcely perceptible nod'. This concession set the stage for the founding of the TUAC. Bustamante accepted all the requirements, except to drop his own name from the union's name.

Domingo's important role is confirmed by one A. Cawley. In a letter to the *Gleaner* in August 1943 answering allegations of Bustamante's co-worker Pixley against Manley and Nethersole that they had not been politically active before 1938, he pronounced that:

> Mr. Pixley might not know where Mr. Manley and Mr. Nethersole were before 1938, but Mr. Bustamante knows where they were both in 1938 and in 1939 when they and Mr. Domingo rescued him and his union in the general strike which he rashly called to the detriment of labour.[205]

After Bustamante had acquiesced, the Emergency Regulations were called off and the TUAC was officially established on February 17, 1939, with Nethersole as president and Domingo as one of two vice presidents.[206] The significant influence of Roberts and Domingo is reflected in the fact that both men were elected as members of the newly formed body. A huge mass meeting at Race Course on February 21 was attended by about 10,000 people.[207] It was staged by the PNP and some trade unions and was chaired by Domingo with Roberts seated on the platform next to Bustamante.[208] The Progressive League was applauded for the help it provided during the labour disturbances in 1938.[209] Another TUAC meeting was held at Race Course on February 26, at which Manley lauded the new unity in the labour movement.[210] On Domingo's announcement, Bustamante publicly shook hands with his arch rival A.G.S. Coombs.[211] Roberts used the opportunity to encourage Jamaicans to think in terms of unity and nationalism, and even used a populist and chauvinist approach to popularize the Progressive League's position:

> If you wish to shut out any more Chinese immigrants from this country – even those who come from the British-owned territory of Hong-Kong – you ought to have the right to do it. You ought to have the right to shut out the Syrians if you think that there are too many of them. You don't have that right, and you never will have that right until this country becomes self-governing.[212]

This xenophobic element propagated by the Progressive League, had also been part of the nationalist agitation of earlier political groups.

In the remaining time he spent in Jamaica, Domingo kept close relations with the TUAC. As its vice chairman, he was involved in solving a dispute involving the Shipping Association and helped to bring that union under the umbrella of the advisory body. Not surprisingly, a conflict between Bustamante and Domingo soon arose. Bustamante wrote a letter to Manley in which he complained:

> Rightly or wrongly the workers are forming an opinion that Mr. Domingo is intended to cause disloyalty to the Bustamante Union, and as a matter of fact Domingo may be in for a very hard time owing to his utterances. ...I am quite capable of self-defense; still I feel as he is connected with the Labour Party and the Advisory Council you should if you feel it wise ask him what it was all about.[213]

Manley wrote a handwritten note next to the sentence: 'no truth in this'.[214] At this juncture, the argument could have been settled. Nevertheless, Bustamante remained doubtful. Indeed, Domingo openly criticized Bustamante's autocratic style to run the unions. According to his strategy to inspire close cooperation between the labour movement and anti-colonial nationalism, Domingo tried to minimize Bustamante's influence. These incidents foreshadowed a more serious conflict between the two men in the following years.

Domingo threw himself into the field of trade union work, but Roberts was sceptical of the success of the TUAC: 'There were optimists who believed that the labour movement had been lastingly put on a sane basis at that meeting. I doubted it myself, and I did not prove to be wrong'.[215]

Bustamante withdrew from the TUAC at the end of April 1939. Subsequently, the organization changed its name into Trade Union Council (TUC) and developed into a PNP-affiliated umbrella organization for all unions not willing to associate themselves with the BITU, and thus turned into a rival organization.[216] Roberts, who stayed in Jamaica after Domingo left the island in April, received an official request to become a co-opted member of the TUC, but refused the offer. He felt it was inappropriate 'to sit on a body representing only one wing of the labour movement of Jamaica, and…that the new Council needed the service of trade union experts rather than of persons like himself who were pledged to a political program'.[217]

In the three-part series 'Jamaica As I See It', published in the *Gleaner*, Roberts outlined his views on the political and labour developments in Jamaica.[218] He criticized Bustamante's 'personal dictatorship' which could not be 'prolonged indefinitely'. While lauding the efforts trying to unify the trade unions, he explained the patriotic reasons why he declined to serve for the TUC: 'It is not that I lack sympathy with orderly unionism, but simply that as an advocate of self-government for this country I feel it would be improper even to appear to taking sides in a temporarily disunited labour movement'.

The split in the trade union movement turned out to be irreconcilable and Bustamante proceeded to agitate against former members of the TUAC denouncing them as Communist.[219] Manley repudiated these allegations in a long statement which appeared in the *Gleaner*, and it became a major task of the PNP in later years to build the TUC as a strong umbrella for all unions that refused to affiliate with the BITU and promote the organization of the workers in a democratic fashion along internationally accepted standards of trade unionism.

Thus far, it has been shown that the mutual support and close cooperation between the PNP and the Progressive League in the development of party politics and trade union organization have been the dominant feature of the relationship between the two groups. Nevertheless, the differences regarding the political aim of self-government remained, as the proceedings of the first Annual Party Convention demonstrate. The major differences between the radical vanguard of the Progressive League and the still hesitant PNP would resurface, particularly when Domingo and Roberts undertook to convince the party to adopt the demand for immediate self-government in its platform.

First PNP Convention in April 1939

The excellent cooperation between the Progressive League and the PNP reflected in their joint activities, could not mask the fundamental differences in their views regarding self-government. Particularly in Manley's case, he frequently made his position known that the party stood for a gradual approach to constitutional changes. The party's first general convention, at which a definite programme was expected to be resolved, was therefore of utmost importance to the Progressive League. How did Domingo and Roberts try to convince the PNP of the inclusion of the demand for self-government in the PNP's planks? Would they be successful in integrating the Progressive League's policy into that of the party? The events at the convention give another example of the influence the Progressive League leaders exerted on the PNP in this crucial formation stage, and it also depicts the hesitant attitude of influential figures in the party toward the demand for self-government as an immediate goal that had not yet fundamentally changed during the time of close cooperation with the leaders of the Progressive League.

Notably, the Progressive League's chances to influence the party's position had tremendously increased through the popularity Domingo and Roberts had gained in party circles in the months they stayed in Jamaica and helped the PNP to get off the ground. Domingo's reputation in the party, in particular, is evidenced by the active role he played in the Metropolitan Group. When the group determined who was to be the representative to attend the first annual party conference, Domingo was the man of choice.[220] Roberts was confident that their efforts would meet with success. He later recalled:

> I had faith that our drive to arouse national consciousness must win a following capable of becoming a majority within the P.N.P. and forcing the latter to take a more positive stand. A good many lower middle-class people supported me on this, and when I explained the idea at meetings volunteers seldom failed to speak up.[221]

But while Roberts believed in the possibility to influence the party in the desired way, he also knew that the enthusiasm for the more radical goals of the Progressive League was limited to a small number of citizens, stating:

> A marked readiness to catch fire existed among the young, but the number that could be enlisted in a practical sense was limited. Since we did not favor violence, there was no immediate action that could be asked of them. I urged them to study the island's past, to think and discuss so as to make a patriotic elite of themselves.[222]

From these observations, two different strategies evolved. On the one hand, the Progressive League put a strong focus on the PNP convention and the persuasion of individual PNP members to embrace a definite advocacy of self-government. On the other hand, the group planned an educational nationalist campaign to spread nationalism in the wider society. Based on the experience with the undecided attitude of McFarlane and the Progressive League in Kingston, the directors of the Progressive League anticipated that their own active involvement in the party formation would be decisive. The task to convince the PNP would not be an easy one, and headwind was to be expected.

Implementing Demands for Self-Government

McFarlane who was actively involved in varied party committees recalled the obstacles he had encountered during the founding stage of the PNP. Often, he felt as if he was the only one who pressed for the demand for self-government, '...the lone voice in a wilderness on this issue'.[223] McFarlane claimed that it was his idea to call on the leaders of the Progressive League in New York. Whether the directors of the Progressive League decided on McFarlane's call to come to Jamaica or on their own, they saw the necessity for their personal involvement and decided to attend the first annual party convention in April 1939.

While supporting the PNP in the necessary groundwork, Roberts and Domingo simultaneously began to work behind the scenes to convince individual members of the need to make the stipulation for self-government a central point in the party programme. McFarlane reminisces that they personally convinced some PNP members and that the leaders of the Progressive League dominated the lively discussions on the subject at the conference. When the proposals for either immediate self-government or representative government were put to vote, McFarlane recalled that the 'majority of the delegates voted in favour of immediate self-government for Jamaica with universal suffrage, thereby defeating the proposals coming from Manley and his supporters'.[224]

What really happened on the conference floor of the PNP convention that took place between April 12 and 14, 1939, attended by more than 100 delegates from all parishes?[225] Unfortunately, the available evidence is shrouded by contradictory reports and statements, and it therefore requires a more in-depth examination. Certainly, there was much public interest in the event. Various articles in the *Gleaner* and in *Public Opinion* reported on the conference and published extracts from the party planks that differed from each other in a few but crucial points. Remarkably, the agreed policy in regard to the demands for constitutional change appeared in different versions. A copy of the minutes in the Walter Adolphe Roberts papers reveals interesting details of the discussions. The published versions in the press were diluted from an outright demand for self-government to vague phrases on representative government and stood in contradiction to the agreement fixed in the minutes and as outlined in Manley's closing remarks.

At the beginning of the conference on April 12, Manley expressed his position on the question of self-government in the morning session that was open to the public. In his statement, Manley affirmed his timid approach and pointed out the obstacles the young party had experienced:

> We have made a beginning, and considering the difficulties of rousing political interest in Jamaica and the wall of opposition and lethargy one was bound to find, I think we have made a great beginning. ...Our next greatest task is the task we are embarking on – getting to grips with

our own understanding of the vital aims of the party, and how these aims might be translated into realities, and to give practical effect to the realities in the object clause of the constitution.²²⁶

This characterization of the present condition of the country led Manley to propose a hesitant position regarding the demand for self-government, recommending a slow pace for the envisioned political changes:

It has to be remembered in all political thinking that the immediate programme and the ultimate policy are two parts of the same whole. The fundamental thing is to discover the basic policy, because after that the rest becomes a matter of elaborating the details, bearing in mind what is immediately possible. It is very easy to draw up a utopian programme and then discover that the achievement proposed is altogether beyond the financial possibilities that might be opened up before in the next century.²²⁷

This was a clear rejection of any immediate demand for self-government. The party founder compared the developments to the building of a house: '[i]t may take generations to complete but each generation will see it nearer to completion and each year will see a pattern emerging from the foundation'.²²⁸ With that metaphor, Manley encouraged his comrades to have patience and exercise unity, urging cooperation of all party members to develop a common policy.

In the afternoon session, Manley noted that the debate on constitutional reform was scheduled for the first day 'by reason of its great importance for the policy of the Party'.²²⁹ He proffered a gradual approach: 'The Party certainly did not envisage to stopping short at representative government, but from that stage would look forward to full responsible government'.²³⁰ Although Manley continued to advocate a Jamaican civil service and full adult suffrage, his comment on constitutional development could not satisfy the leaders of the Progressive League, who advocated that the demand should be for immediate self-government and not a slow-moving development implemented in stages.

Despite Manley's emphasis on its importance, the discussion about constitutional change was postponed on the motion of C.A. Ross and H. Cooke. This meant that agricultural and industrial development would be discussed on the first afternoon with the explanation that on the Sunday, when the agricultural session had been originally scheduled, many delegates would have been on their way back home to the countryside.²³¹ This move supports Post's conclusion that the country was indeed 'still concerned with agrarian problems'²³² and not particularly interested in questions of constitutional change.

Nevertheless, the representatives of the New York based Progressive League were able to exert their influence on the first day of the convention. While McFarlane was on the platform with McPherson, Arnett, Fairclough and others, Domingo and Roberts both gave speeches. The *Gleaner* reported that Domingo 'exhorted delegates to conduct deliberations with a feeling of nationalism'[233] and praised Manley, whom he lauded as a most able leader. Domingo claimed that Manley was so much inspired by patriotism that he made his fellow countrymen abroad feel proud of him. Roberts elaborated on the position of the Progressive League and, in strong contrast to the meek remarks of Manley, pronounced that he believed it was 'possible to have self-government in Jamaica in five years'.[234] He accentuated the need for a new constitution, especially in the event of another World War, which he predicted was coming in the near future. Jamaica should be politically prepared, he said, as such a war would accelerate the decolonization process. He congratulated his compatriots 'that their political activity had reached a point already before that war where they had a foundation as that represented in the launching of a party with definite aims'.[235]

Roberts and Domingo also addressed individual delegates throughout the conference, trying to win support for the Progressive League's position in the constitutional debate. According to the minutes of that debate, Manley finally drew attention to the issue of constitutional reform, but chose not to delve into details without 'expert advices and study'.[236] Unmistakably, he declared: '[U]nlike one of the Party's affiliated organizations – the Jamaica Progressive League – the Party never advocated immediate Self-Government'. He explained that he was convinced the country would need political education first, and that it was the party's duty to work toward that end. Hence, the logical conclusion was a development in steps. The first one should be '...Representative Government which should mean Legislative Control, and that would lead to Executive Control of full Self-Government. The period of Representative Government should be a period of transition to Self-Government'. Yet, Manley warned:

> There should be a time however to build up political responsibility, intelligence and organization; to develop a class of persons able to tackle the job, to make the transition. Without this preparation, by getting too much they might fail where they should never fail.

Manley's proposal tried to offer a compromise to satisfy those who advocated immediate self-government, because it included a definite and positive demand for responsible government and adult suffrage, but at the same time, the qualification that the first step should be representative government would attract those who advocated a return to the old constitution, more representation and increased influence of the elected members in the Legislative Council.

However, Manley's plan was made without Roberts and Domingo's approval, and subsequently, both men entered into a lively discussion in which they 'insisted that nothing short of Self-Government should be asked for'. They were supported by Frank Hill, P.L. Miller, G.C. Atherton, S. Davidson and O. Munroe. Ken Hill, the early but unstable advocate of self-government also came out in support for the position of the Progressive League: 'The masses of the country, above all others, had shown a desire to follow true leadership, honest leadership, and shown a willingness to unite. Self-Government had to be fought for'. Others like Amy Bailey, O.H. Cameron, V.P. DaCosta, T.J. Cawley, S.E. Brooke and Victor Bailey supported Manley's moderate position. When the decision was put to a vote, the more radical position Domingo and Roberts suggested received a majority of votes. Manley, whose proposal had been outvoted, then suggested the following text for the resolution, which was met with approval: 'The Party advocates and will work for the claim of Jamaica to achieve responsible Government as a National unit within the British Commonwealth of Nations'. Full adult suffrage was made a necessary pre-condition to bringing about a fundamental change in the form of government.

In his closing address which was printed in the *Gleaner*, Manley stated that the session on the constitution was one of the 'finest, keenest and most inspiring debates he ever heard'.[237] Summing up, Manley affirmed the position regarding the demand for Dominion status and vowed:

> They [the PNP] did not believe that it was right to stop short at a claim for what was called representative government. The difference between Representative Government and Responsible Government were explained...there had been representative government in this country before, it ended in a rebellion (laughter) Representative Government involved legislative control; Responsible Government meant executive control.[238]

The adopted position at the end of the discussion as recorded in the minutes and in the final remarks of Manley shows that the leaders of the Progressive League successfully convinced a majority to accept a definite advocacy of self-government. However, the statements regarding the adopted policy in the aftermath of the conference were somewhat less definite. In a PNP pamphlet that outlined the programme and policy adopted at the conference, the first two demands read: '1. Adult Suffrage and 2. The achievement of representative and responsible Government within and as a Unit of the British Commonwealth of Nations'.[239] In contrast to the original phrase used in the minutes cited above, the crucial word 'national' was missing in front of the word 'unit', and instead, the word 'representative' had been included.

Under the point, 'Constitutional Reform', the pamphlet explicated: 'The Party advocates and will achieve the claim of this country to a **representative** form of Government as a Unit of the British Commonwealth of Nations'.[240] This phrasing lacked the word responsible and was allowed to be read as advocating internal self-government, not necessarily Dominion status. This stood in contrast to the more definite avowal of '**responsible** Government as a **National** unit

Implementing Demands for Self-Government

within the British Commonwealth of Nations',[241] as democratically agreed on at the Party conference. Even the statement that the PNP advocated 'a parliamentary democracy on the lines which obtain in other self-governing units of the British Commonwealth'[242] was no definite declaration for full self-government and is open for interpretation in both ways. Given Manley's opposition to a policy that advocated immediate Dominion status, it seems as if the changes from the original agreement were no mistake, but a sophisticated representation of the agreement at the conference that left room for a more moderate interpretation.

The way the *Public Opinion*, which was quite close to the PNP, published the 'P.N.P. Basic Outline of the Party's policy as decided by the Convention of Groups'[243] provides further evidence suggesting that these changes were not made accidentally. In *Public Opinion*, the aim of the PNP's policy was described as 'representative and responsible Government', while language regarding Jamaica becoming a 'national unit' of the Commonwealth was completely absent. Additionally, the statement emphasized that nothing should be rushed: 'much that is advocated and will be worked for will have to wait achievement at a time when the resources of the country will allow....'[244]

The sources do not provide enough information to judge how these remarkable changes occurred. One thing was obvious; the Progressive League would have to continue its work on the ground forcefully to safeguard that the PNP would not refrain from the positive demand for self-government, like the NRA and the local branch of the League had done before and acquiesce to powerful sections in Jamaican society which rejected the idea of Jamaica achieving self-government any time soon.

The phrasing was so cleverly chosen that the subsequent changes from the agreement of the conference remained largely unnoticed. There is no evidence that the leaders of the Progressive League protested against the way the results were published. Regarding the policy of the PNP adopted at the party conference, Roberts declared:

> The League is advocating immediate and complete self-government; in short, Dominion status. The P.N.P., at its convention of party groups held in April, stiffened its original demand for a gradual approach to responsible government and promised, without qualifications, to work for the claim of Jamaica to become a "National unit within the British Commonwealth of Nations". Except for its silence in the matter of immediacy, the P.N.P. now occupies exactly the same ground as the League on this major principle. A country cannot be a "National unit within the British Commonwealth of Nations" unless it is a Dominion.[245]

Roberts used the phrase from the original minutes, without mentioning the different versions that appeared afterwards. Roberts adhered to the original conclusion that the conference had agreed on and regarded it as the basis for fruitful cooperation. There is no evidence to prove whether or not Roberts was aware of the subsequent changes, but, in any case, the gap between the two organizations was bigger than he would openly admit.

In his autobiography, Roberts claimed that their attempt to implement their position into the party's planks was successful and that his and Domingo's influence was crucial in this endeavour. He commented that:

> ...the demand would still have been for something less than complete self-government if Domingo and I had not fought for this principle from the floor. Support flocked to us, persuading Manley, who having once taken the advanced standpoint adhered to it firmly. Naturally this seemed to me the most valuable outcome of the convention.[246]

The sources prove this claim legitimate. The minutes of the PNP conference support Roberts' view on how important their role had been on the question of self-government in the party's programme. A statement by McFarlane suggests that certain elements in the party were not happy about this influence:

> At this juncture, we were no longer the lone advocate of the self-government idea, but we became aware of the fact that we still have the responsibility for seeing to it, that the entire programme was carried forward without adulteration and not becoming bogged down by those persons who were forced by circumstances to adopt it.[247]

Surprisingly, the only author who acknowledges Domingo and Roberts' influence on the party's programme is Zeidenfelt. He states: '[T]he party accepted the suggestion of Mr. Roberts and Mr. Domingo that direct demands be made on the British Government for full self-government and universal adult suffrage, and laid the groundwork for the later development of its program and principles'.[248]

Most authors who present a detailed account on the political developments of this time do not mention the significant role of the Progressive League at this conference. Hart dismisses the crucial influence of the leaders of the Progressive League on the formation and direction of the early PNP in general. To the contrary, he suggests that there was ready acceptance of the Progressive League's pioneering advocacy of self-government in this period, while he admits that he himself had objected to the goal initially.[249]

Domingo left the island shortly after the conference, so that the task of safeguarding that the PNP would keep in line was left to Roberts and the local branch of the Progressive League. Before he left, Domingo was honoured with a mass meeting at Metropolitan Hall and a following reception presided over by Manley.[250] At the public meeting, Domingo promised to act as a PNP ambassador in New York and guaranteed he would return to support the general elections in 1940. Prominent members of the party praised Domingo's significant work and his value, especially for the Metropolitan Group, in glowing terms. Domingo

Implementing Demands for Self-Government

replied that ever since he had left the island in 1937, he 'had hoped to return to take part in bettering the conditions of his countrymen'.[251] Manley and Roberts paid tribute and Manley called attention to the fact that Domingo had arrived at an opportune time to help his country. Roberts called Domingo a tower of strength in Jamaica and New York.

At the reception that followed, Manley reflected on the influence of the migrants and the reasons for their different approach to the politics of the island. 'He had always wondered why it was that Jamaicans who had been abroad were far more appreciative and devoted to Jamaica than they who had spent their lives at home'. Manley saw the main reasons in the migrant's perspective on political conditions in the country and their exposure to a comparison with other countries, resulting in a more international perspective. This observation testifies to the importance of the migration experience and the important influence of the Jamaican migrants in the US on the development of politics in their home country.

The Progressive League, Manley emphasized, was 'an organization which had unquestionably played and continues to play a very important part'. He also lauded Roberts as the founder of that movement and continued to describe the PNP as a logical progeny of the Progressive League: 'There was no doubt that the party had come precisely at the right time to develop the movement which the Progressive League foresaw long ago. He was only too willing to give the League the fullest credit for their anticipation'. Manley openly pointed to the important influence of the two men and his gratitude for their work in the first months of existence of the party:

> To that beginning, however, courageous and active work contributed an enormous amount because it was not a time for talk and jaded accents it was time for perfectly clear and plain speaking. And whatever Mr. Domingo might have lacked he certainly did not lack the ability to call a spade a spade. He personally could never give enough thanks to him and to Mr. Roberts for the courageous and steadfast help they gave to the party, and for throwing in their lot with their real idea of true party loyalty and the loyalty of persons working for a common aim. He did not know what the party was going to do without Mr. Domingo that was one of the reasons why he looked forward to his speedy return before the 1940 elections.

This comment proves how much Manley valued the input of the Progressive League and particularly Domingo's work for the party. The PNP leader was deeply impressed by Domingo's skills as an orator and his appeal to the masses. Manley knew the value of the loyalty the Progressive League exhibited to the party, despite their varying positions on self-government. In this early phase of the PNP, the role of Roberts and Domingo was much more powerful than the historical accounts suggest. Manley was very aware of this influence and he regretted the return of both men to New York, whom he would have preferred to have in his local team on the ground. Although he personally advocated a gradual approach, it seemed as if he valued their agitation as a radical spearhead to jumpstart the national movement and propel it forward. Manley would indeed soon send for Domingo to support the PNP in the election campaign, but the Second World War would change the whole picture, delay the elections and also Domingo's return. In the remaining weeks, Roberts stayed in Kingston after Domingo's departure; he focused his activities on the local branch of the Progressive League and continued the mission to launch a nationalist campaign in order to popularize the demand for self-government in broader sections of the populace.

Roberts in Jamaica and the 'Jamaicanizing Jamaica' Campaign

The first PNP conference openly displayed the differences of opinion between a moderate group around PNP leader Norman Manley and the Jamaica Progressive League as to how quick self-government could and should be acquainted. For the Progressive League, this meant an emphasis on its independent approach and the continuation of its uncompromising nationalist campaign.

After Domingo returned to New York, it was now Roberts' task to balance the particular views of the Progressive League and the PNP. Roberts publicly lauded the work of the PNP and congratulated Manley for doing his best to provide the masses with an education in politics. He felt that in order to bring about the envisioned change, a close cooperation was necessary. In fact, Roberts demanded, 'the Jamaica Progressive League must identify itself with the P.N.P.....'[252]

Motivated by the hope that the party would soon become the political force for a strong nationalist demand, the Progressive League was willing to cooperate, despite the differences. Nevertheless, the Progressive League developed an alternative strategy and pursued a division of labour with the PNP. While the PNP campaigned for political development, the Progressive League complemented the effort by preparing the groundwork for a more deeply-rooted nationalism by putting a strong focus on nationalist education. Accordingly, Roberts shifted his focus on the Progressive League in Kingston and the promotion of cultural nationalism, although he still supported the party's work and gave speeches at PNP meetings. Local secretary McFarlane also affirmed the unity between the Progressive League and the PNP and repudiated allegations that the Progressive League had become inactive, and that the PNP had stolen its programme. In a letter to the editor of the *Gleaner*, he averred:

Implementing Demands for Self-Government

> ...we do not accept the statement that the PNP has taken away our programme for self-government. The League, being affiliated with the party, has decided to work in complete harmony and concord with the larger organization, realizing that the cause which we advocate can only be successful if we practice the doctrine of co-operation in its true sense. In addition, we have been able to over-come the disease of petty jealousy and the vanity of 'We were the first in that particular field'. We believe in the diction 'All for One and One for All.'[253]

Despite the officially declared unity, Roberts frequently drew attention to the one crucial difference: 'We are advocating Dominion status for Jamaica as quickly as possible, and make a definite demand for its immediate adoption'.[254] While aspiring to the same goal, the PNP advocated an educational period.[255] However, this difference was crucial. Roberts affirmed that the Progressive League refused to consider any interim solution or to compromise its quest for immediate Dominion status. The president of the League explained how he envisioned the proposed division of work:

> I regard the work of the People's National Party in organising the political life of the people as the most important work which could be done in the island at present, there being no such organization before. For that reason the Jamaica Progressive League has subordinated their own programme for the present, and are confining their activities to the sponsoring of a cultural programme which we describe as 'Jamaicanizing Jamaica'.[256]

In order to highlight the unity between both groups, Roberts declared that the Progressive League would not appoint its own candidates in the coming elections, but would rather support those of the PNP.

Gleaner editor de Lisser readily attempted to take advantage of Roberts' statement and claimed a few days later that the Progressive League had subordinated its programme and deliberately ignored the maintenance of its definite advocacy of immediate Dominion status. Once again, de Lisser tried to downplay Roberts' radicalism, claiming that he was a lofty idealist and 'not really a politician'.[257] The Progressive League was indeed committed to support the PNP, at the same time, it was misleading to argue that it had abandoned its convictions of demanding immediate self-government.

The Progressive League regarded the tactical subordination under the umbrella of the new party as the best way to reach the outlined aims, given that both organizations would focus on different areas of agitation. For now, it would leave the task of working for the political development of the country to the PNP. It would primarily promote cultural nationalism to change outlook and self-perception of the Jamaican society to break the strong loyalty with England, and to replace it with Jamaican patriotism. To convince the party leaders to adopt a more outspoken anti-colonial attitude, the leaders of the Progressive League believed that the country's population needed to become more nationalist in the first place.

The means by which the Progressive League tried to promote cultural nationalism was by means of an educational campaign. The local branch of the Progressive League launched a 'Jamaicanizing Jamaica' campaign at the end of April 1939, shortly after the PNP conference.[258] This strategy enabled the organization to continue its work to popularize nationalist feelings without interfering with the political work of the PNP. As Roberts pointed out, the campaign was 'frankly nationalistic and outside the scope of the normal activities of the P.N.P.'[259] He explained that while the party was purely political, the aims of the Progressive League were much wider, including the cultural and educational aspects. At their monthly meeting, Roberts officially launched the programme and further clarified the strategy of close cooperation during the founding period of the PNP. He assured:

> ...to press any of the policies of the League at the expense of the party would have been a tactical mistake. Hence the League had eased up their activities a little to affiliate with the Party and joined the coalition towards getting responsible government for the country.[260]

However, Roberts declared that now was the time for the Progressive League to resume its independent activities.[261] In the first announcement of the campaign, the League made it plain that it was based on its basic belief that Jamaica was '...already, in fact, a nation' and hence prudent 'to arouse that consciousness in the minds of all our citizens'.[262]

During the tide of PNP activism, the Progressive League had lost the power to attract even its small circle of supporters and the monthly meeting for March was cancelled because of scant attendance.[263] This suggests that most of the members of the local branch were busy helping the party to get off the ground. Given their undecided stand on the issue of self-government, some members may even have felt more comfortable with the more moderate nationalism of the PNP.

The campaign therefore not only served the obvious purpose of promoting nationalism, but also provided a distinct identity for the local branch of the Progressive League as an independent organization.[264] Concerning the relationship with the parent body in New York, Roberts tried to empower and transform the local group into the spearhead of the nationalist movement: 'The Kingston organization is not a branch of the League in New York. It is the vanguard of the movement, and New York willingly accepts the position of an auxiliary body'.[265] Such a design was in accordance with the role the Progressive League envisioned for the local branch since its inception. Furthermore, the renewal of this pledge reflected Roberts' decision to return to Jamaica permanently at the end of 1939 to lead the national movement as president of a strong Progressive League in Jamaica.²⁶⁶

In an article in *Public Opinion* in May 1939, Roberts outlined the strategic plan of the campaign.²⁶⁷ A historian himself, Roberts was aware of the instrumental role that historical memory played constructing a nation, and importantly, one of the cardinal points in the programme was an emphasis on Jamaican history. The Progressive League insisted that the glorified history of the Empire be replaced and instead the focus be put on history written from the perspective of the country. In accordance, the League formed a research committee to rewrite Jamaican history and correct faults propagandized in schoolbooks by publishing leaflets and giving lectures. To instil patriotic feelings among the people, the Progressive League planned to highlight the lives of famous Jamaicans and to organize public functions in their honour. Children and adults were encouraged to study the history and culture of the country. Jamaican creative artists were encouraged to produce nationalist literature, music, dancing, drama, etc. The Progressive League further proposed to rename all villages, towns and places with Jamaican names, and in addition, demanded an increase of consumption of local products. The Progressive League summarized the purpose of the whole campaign as follows: 'The Jamaica Progressive League is firmly of the opinion that training along the lines of this programme will help to equip future citizens for the responsibilities of self-government'.²⁶⁸

The first object of study of the research committee, consisting of Varma, McBean and McFarlane, was the Jamaican politician and editor, Edward Jordon. The group presented and discussed its findings at the regular meetings of the Progressive League in Kingston.²⁶⁹ The Progressive League in Kingston decided to lay down a wreath on the anniversary of Jordon's death on February 8, 1940 and to publish a pamphlet about his life.²⁷⁰ Roberts published the findings in the booklet 'The Patriot', in which he lauded Jordon's patriotic service for Jamaica.²⁷¹ The Progressive League highlighted this early Jamaican politician as a positive role model who fought against slavery and acted in the more responsible political environment of the constitution before 1865 to inspire Jamaicans to strive for assuming political responsibility. One year later, Domingo published an article on Jordon in which he argued that the campaign was primarily directed to 'aid in making Jamaicans proud of their country and help them to get rid of their inferiority complex'.²⁷²

McFarlane later stressed a very similar argument in his review of the campaign. However, more than Domingo, he accentuated the racial aspect and drew a direct line from Marcus Garvey to the attention of the local branch of the Progressive League:

...as a people many people have been very badly brainwashed into regarding the colour of the other person's skin to be the chief factor for superiority, provided that skin is not black. Knowing too well that Marcus Garvey had been struggling almost in vain with this said subject, the League of Kingston instituted a programme aimed at the positive recognition of our racial and national statue based on self-respect and the accomplishment of fellow Jamaicans past and present.[273]

In addition, McFarlane postulated that 'the average Jamaican in all strata of our society needs to be orientated on the question of racial and national consciousness, two basic requirements in the making of a nation'.[274]

The apogee of the campaign was a public function in honour of Jordon, with Dr Varma, officer of the local Progressive League, as master of ceremonies. The event garnered some amount of public interest and the Progressive League secured the support of prominent politicians like Kingston's Mayor and Norman Manley, whom Domingo later called 'the Jordon of today'.[275] Manley gave the keynote speech, stressing the role of education in the development of a national spirit. He encouraged Jamaicans to have pride in themselves and in the history of the country and hoped that the Progressive League would continue other cultural and historical projects on other important Jamaican figures in the future. In his speech, Manley again publicly paid tribute to the Progressive League's pioneer work for Jamaica: 'The Jamaica Progressive League as you know is the first organization to raise a strong voice for self-government for Jamaica. It is the first organization to demand that we try to develop a national spirit in this country'.[276]

The 'Jamaicanizing Jamaica' campaign with its focus on cultural nationalism was quite successful and found wide coverage in the press.[277] The support of influential and respected people like Manley gave the local branch the desired push and attracted some popular, albeit moderate political activists, for example, Clare McFarlane, Mary Morris-Knibb, and Amy Bailey. Some of them strongly sympathized with the Progressive League's activities and joined the organization, like Amy Bailey, who supported the campaign in her column in the *Gleaner*[278] and later became vice president of the local Progressive League in the early 1940s.[279]

The strategy of continued cooperation between the Progressive League and the PNP with a separation of their fields of action worked well for the time being. The months leading up to the Second World War were a time of unity, at least on the surface. Early in January 1939, the PNP tried to initiate discussions about a new constitution and presented a proposal, which the group had worked out before the founding of the party.[280] The paper proposed a two-chamber system like that of Great Britain and suggested a gradual increase of responsibility and power of the electives and a ministerial executive. This was exactly the position taken by the group around Manley. They believed the country was not yet

Implementing Demands for Self-Government

ripe for self-government but should be educated and given the chance for a development in stages. The Progressive League did not raise its voice to criticize the proposals of the PNP. Nevertheless, whenever constitutional matters were discussed internally, the differences between the two groups concerning the prospected timeframe in which self-government could be achieved were visible. The PNP and the Progressive League were not the only bodies directing their interest to the question of constitutional change.

The developments after the events of Frome, the founding of the PNP and the constant propaganda for constitutional change had also forced members of the Legislative Council to change their conservative attitude toward Jamaica's political future. A first reaction of the Legislative Council was a resolution in December 1938 that demanded universal suffrage, although even Governor Arthur Richards felt this claim was half-hearted and merely a 'face-saving device'.[281] Richards mentioned a conversation with veteran Legislative Council member J.A.G. Smith in which the latter admitted his concern when Richards suggested that universal suffrage was about to be implemented. Smith was quick to bring up the point that he never believed that this should be realized any time soon because he felt the people were not ready for it.[282]

In April 1939, J.A.G. Smith, presented his idea for a new constitution that threatened the progressive direction into which the country moved after the founding of the PNP. The Progressive League and the party united in a broad front against Smith's conservative proposal that suggested even less responsibility than the pre-1865 constitution. Smith's idea included a bi-cameral legislature consisting of House of Assembly with 14 elected members and a Legislative Council consisting of 10 nominated members, appointed by the Governor.[283] From both organs, an Executive Committee was supposed to be formed consisting of five members elected by the Assembly, three officials and two nominated members by the Governor. The draft was approved by a majority of members in the Legislative Council on June 15, 1939.[284]

The Progressive League in Kingston rejected the constitutional changes proposed by Smith and launched public protests. At a public meeting Roberts criticized the proposal in detail. A resolution of the Progressive League especially disapproved of the inadequate size of the House of Assembly as too small, objected to the centralizing of authority in the Executive Committee without the safeguard of public criticism and criticized the property requirement of £50 for candidates who ran for public office citing it would violate the principles of democracy. The resolution further expressed a 'total lack of confidence in the honourable J.A.G. Smith and the other seniors of the majority report because the constitution proposed by them is a retrograde step and a veiled threat to the liberties of the Jamaica people'.[285] The Progressive League staged a mass meeting against the Smith proposal, chaired by E.R.D. Evans, at which Roberts appeared as the main speaker. He denounced the proposal as an 'attempt to introduce in this country an out-moded form of government that does not even have the merit of the old constitution'.[286] He further argued that the changes would not lead to responsibility but stopped short at a representative form of government. He emphasized again that even responsible government would not be what the Progressive League desired and that it would always continue to demand Dominion status for Jamaica. V.L. Varma and Amy Bailey also raised their voices against the proposal.[287]

Numerous letters in the press not only show that the proposals were unpopular, but also how much Roberts and Manley had become authorities on the question of constitutional change. One writer, Z. Scarlett-Munroe, suggested that patriots like Manley, Evans, and Roberts should be appointed to draft a new proposal.[288] *Public Opinion* joined the protest and called the proposals a 'Travesty of Reform'.[289] Even the FCA rejected the Smith proposal and advocated presenting a memorandum on it and sending a delegation to London with different suggestions. Such a delegation should consist of Manley as the representative for the PNP and Roberts for the League.[290] The League discussed the proposal and suggested a joint strategy with PNP and FCA to carry the protest to London.[291] Although this delegation never came about, the FCA's proposals reflect Roberts' authority on constitutional questions.

The *Gleaner*, not surprisingly, was favourable toward Smith's ideas. The editor did not miss the chance to urge a slow pace and to reject any idea of Jamaica becoming a Dominion. Again, de Lisser tried the tactic to belittle Roberts' political ideas and assumed that '...self-government is not a practical proposition either now or within the next five years and we doubt very much whether such self-government is being seriously demanded even by our friend Mr. Adolphe Roberts'.[292]

Another example of unanimity between the Progressive League and the PNP in this period was the protest against a new 'Public Meetings Law', designed to curtail the progressive atmosphere in the country. It was first introduced on the parish level by the Parish Board in St James in 1938; it was immediately met with protest by the League in New York.[293] The directors criticized the law as an 'unwarranted interference with the privilege of free speech' and an 'inexcusable infringement of the constitutional right of the people freely to assemble and to state their grievances and seek redress therefore'.[294]

When it became public that the bill was to be introduced on a national scale, the Progressive League and the PNP organized their protest in concerted action. Together with other organizations, they planned a major protest meeting, presided over by Roberts who was also one of the main speakers.[295] He denounced the anticipatory power given to the police by this law and accentuated that there was no justification for such a law, as Jamaica would develop on a legal road to political and labour organization without any attempts or signs of disorder or upheaval.[296] The meeting was well attended and found support in letters to the press in which both the Progressive League and the PNP were congratulated on their protest against the law.[297]

While the Public Meetings Law found wide approval in the Legislative Council, Roberts sharpened the rejection of the proposal into a strong argument for self-government. He stated:

> ...the sole effective answer is to wage the fight for self-government with redoubled energy. Britain understands that argument. ...this island cannot be sure of freedom from such ignominies as the Public Meetings Law until there is an all Jamaican legislature on guard for the voters that elected it and watched in turn by them.[298]

The Progressive League in New York supported the local protest and sent a resolution to the Secretary of State for the Colonies.[299] Overseas, the protest found wide support in Caribbean migrant circles, for instance, at a protest mass meeting at the YMCA, organized by the Progressive League. Domingo organized the meeting at which he and other prominent figures like Richard B. Moore, Max Yergan and Hope Stevens and members of the Progressive League gave speeches to express sympathy with the protest in Jamaica.[300] The meeting denounced the new law as 'wholly unnecessary, unduly repressive and flagrantly violative of the elementary and fundamental rights and privileges of the people of the Island of Jamaica, namely, the long established and sacred rights of free speech and free assembly'.[301] The solidarity crossed island borders and gives another example of the close network of migrants in New York, illuminating the transnational ties between the anti-colonial activists. It shows how the Progressive League served as a medium between the islands and the mainland that guaranteed that developments in the islands would have repercussions abroad.

The New York-based Progressive League members readily used the protests against the law as an argument for self-government and utilized the pages of *Public Opinion* to reach out to the Jamaican populace. Domingo made a strong case for self-government in an article provocatively entitled 'Not Slaves'. He compared the acceptance of the law by the members of the Legislative Council with the action of their forefathers who had voluntarily surrendered the constitution in 1865. He harshly criticized the law as being on the 'thin edge of facism' and argued:

> ...the British Empire boasts of being a democracy, but the world is gradually recovering from the opium of self-serving British Imperial propaganda and realizing that in the so-called colonies there has never

been any democracy for 'natives' and that it is the tendency to curtail such political rights as the inhabitants may have long enjoyed. ...Every reduction of political rights is a step away from the goal of self-rule that has been the aspiration of all intelligent and progressive peoples. Instead of surrendering part of their rights, politically conscious colonial peoples should be fighting to increase them.[302]

One week later, O'Meally warned in a similar manner that only a tyrannous and despotic government would use such means to curtail freedom of assembly and freedom of speech. He condemned the members of the Legislative Council and denied them the capacity to speak for the people. O'Meally advised Jamaicans to look to the judicial and political system of the US for inspiration, where freedom of speech was seen as a basic and unchallengeable democratic right.[303]

McFarlane later remembered the uniting and radicalizing effect of the protest against the Public Meetings Law.

> The regulations were particularly irksome to that section of the society which hitherto remained snug and complacent because they thought they were immune to any restrictions, being loyal British subjects. Eventually, there were signs of a state of national unity taking shape on all sides and the people began to see the urgent need for a change in the type of government under which we were living so contended before these 'Acts' became the law of the country.[304]

McFarlane points out that despite the fact that scepticism regarding the radical conclusion resulting in a demand for self-government did not find approval from all those who rejected the law, the call for changes in the constitution became loud in 'all quarters of the country'.[305]

Yet, Roberts and the Progressive League insisted on their uncompromising demand for self-government. When rumours reached Jamaica in August 1939 that based on the findings of the Royal Commission, it was recommended that the country be reconstructed with a welfare plan amounting to £10,000,000, Roberts declared in an article in *Public Opinion* that if the Progressive League were acting alone, it would oppose accepting any grants offered by England. He declared: 'A nationalist movement which demands complete and immediate self-government could hardly solicit grants in aid, though there would be no objection to its accepting them if proffered on a basis of friendly co-operation'.[306] Roberts' main criticism was that constitutional change should precede any fundamental grants. Alternatively, he proposed that the country could decide how to use the money and continue on the road to responsible government: 'If we fail to fight for the point, we may take it for granted that there will be no broadening of the Constitution until the last penny of the £10,000,000 has been dispensed'.

Although the general attitude toward the PNP was a closing of ranks, the Progressive League continually emphasized its first priority. In an article in the same issue, on the upcoming election campaign in 1940, Domingo wrote demanding commitment to self-government and Jamaican nationalism from all candidates for public offices and the elected members. He stated that each person should publicly declare, 'whether they believe in self-government for Jamaica or in a continuance of the present constitutional arrangement...Elected members should be made to declare whether they are for Jamaica first or for the Empire first'. Domingo criticized in his characteristically outspoken manner that the press would actively instil an inferiority complex in Jamaicans by promoting the belief that only those who colonized the country, those who Jamaicans were supposed to regard as their superiors, could adequately govern Jamaica. He blamed this belief to be the reason why the masses had no interest in politics and were not demanding adequate representation. Domingo was convinced that to counter this mentality, it was necessary to arouse the political consciousness that had been dormant because of 'many decades of paralyzing political indifference' and the 'conscious propaganda of those who employ political means, open or secret, for the achievement of class or personal ends'. This article testified that Domingo was compromising neither his class-consciousness nor his radical anti-colonial agitation, and that he unceasingly continued to criticize the imperial identity that he saw as the root for the political inertia the Progressive League criticized since 1936.

However, the Progressive League's wish of building a broad nationalist coalition was reflected when Domingo not only pointed to their pioneering work in New York, but also hailed the work of the NRA, the Citizens Associations and the PNP. Domingo lauded the courageous men and women who 'decided that Jamaica was just another country in the world...they studied the situation and resolved that what the country needed was organized politics and a definite policy for the future'. He acknowledged the harsh rejection with which these new ideas met initially and congratulated the PNP for carrying out the nationalist message to all corners of the country. The election campaign was now on, and Domingo declared: 'The People's National Party is solemnly charged with the duty of Jamaicanizing Jamaica politically through the safeguarding of existing rights whilst struggling for the acquisition of complete political power'.

In this atmosphere of close cooperation between the Progressive League and various groups in Kingston, Roberts had attracted even more attention than on his previous visits. The list of renowned personalities who gathered to attend his farewell luncheon reflected this. Among the speakers were prominent men like Roberts' respected friend and dearest enemy, de Lisser, who presided over the meeting, along with many prominent members of the League and the PNP.[307]

Roberts used the opportunity to counter some of the arguments which were brought up against him during this intense time of political agitation. He distanced himself from Communism and underlined:

> ...in certain circles – circles which should know better...I am suspected of three things: It has been hinted that I am a communist; that I am a paid agent of the United States Government come to Jamaica to bring about the annexation of the island to the United States; that I came here for revolutionary purposes; to incite rebellion in Jamaica.[308]

To these allegations he replied that he would not support the usage of violent means and repudiated that he was a Communist. He contended:

> [A] great many people believe that I am a communist: and they appear to be serious. I can assure you that such political views that I hold that are radical are socialistic and certainly not communistic. I am not a communist. I do not agree with the communist conception. It does not appeal to me.

This is a rare occasion at which Roberts claimed to have Socialist views. However, like the PNP, Roberts used the term following the lines of the British Labor Party, advocating some degree of control of state ownership over public businesses and legal rights for workers to struggle for better working conditions, as opposed to the usage of the term in the Russian context. Roberts' political and economic views suggest that he was a liberal, advocating social improvement for the country as a whole and convinced that democracy was the political form of government for Jamaica.

Even de Lisser came out in support of Roberts and made it clear that he never believed Roberts was a Communist. He attested that Roberts was a charming personality, an 'idealist', and he still hoped that Roberts would become more of a realist one day. He lauded the respectful manner with which Roberts treated his political adversaries and cited their own friendship as the best example for this attitude. De Lisser emphasized:

> ...when he spoke of Roberts as a friend, few people realized that it was not just a conventional term. It was a very real friendship. He had known him since they were lads, and a close personal friendship existed between them. There were no differences between them, except one, namely that he thought that anyone who held Mr. Roberts' political beliefs should be taken out and shot.

H.P. Jacobs stated that he also never saw Roberts as a revolutionary but rather lauded his literary and his political work. Jacobs put special emphasis on the influence deriving from Roberts' glowing patriotism, his agitation against the feeling of inferiority and his wish to change the outlook of Jamaicans toward their own aspirations. Concerning the political developments of the past two years, he emphasized Roberts' immense contribution: 'Many thought they had come to a definite crossroads, heralding the start of something new, and they would all agree that Mr. Roberts had done a great deal in changing their attitude towards certain things'.

Roberts' rejection of Communism, his warning that the domination of the proletariat would often cause civil war and would estrange the ruling classes from the country, seemed to please and calm some of his opponents. However, it earned him harsh criticism by one of his co-workers in the local Progressive League. W.A. McBean expressed in *Public Opinion* how Roberts' comments on Communism disturbed him and described them as 'misguided rhetoric' and 'hopeless phrase-mongering'. Although McBean claimed '…it is with great regret that I find it necessary to lift my pen against him', the harshness with which he attacked Roberts is surprising. McBean alleged that the president of the League 'simply does not understand the system on which he assumed to speak with such an authority and which he regards with intense disfavor'.[309] The reaction of McBean again testifies how different the ideological framework of the members of the Progressive League was and, in turn, how much cohesive force nationalism was able to provide.

During Roberts' stay in Jamaica, the wish to permanently return to his country of birth took shape and he confided before he left: 'I have definitely decided to settle in Jamaica and although each year I hope to make periodic visits abroad I shall certainly spend the greater part of my time at home'.[310] He departed for New Orleans on August 20, for three months to finish his next book, and then planned to come back for good and to give full support for the PNP's election campaign. He even stepped back from his position as president of the League in New York and focused on his presidency of the Jamaican branch.[311]

However, the Second World War changed all plans and although thousands of kilometers away, had a grave impact on the developments of the emerging political landscape in Jamaica. The elections expected in 1940 were postponed, and the war forced Roberts to delay and reconsider his plans for the immediate future. As a US citizen engaged in the politics of the island, he would have been an easy target for British authorities under wartime emergency regulations. The war would also have an unexpected influence on the PNP, which felt inclined to renew its loyalty to Great Britain. Therefore, Roberts and Domingo decided to stay in the US and observe the developments. In the meantime, both leaders of the Progressive League entered into a lively exchange of letters, from which they derived ideas for the next steps and even the founding of a new organization to carry out the goal of pushing Jamaica and the West Indies further toward political independence.

Notes

1. Carl Stone, 'Decolonization and the Caribbean State System', 47.
2. See Roberts, 'Autobiography', 14.
3. See *Daily Gleaner*, May 27, 1938; See also Hart, *Towards Decolonisation*, 31; Post, *Arise*, 364. Director of the Labour Committee was V.L. Varma.
4. *Daily Gleaner*, May 27, 1938.
5. *Public Opinion*, May 28, 1938.
6. Ibid., June 18, 1938.
7. Ibid.
8. For this and the following quotes see Domingo to McFarlane, undated letter draft, Louis Moyston Private Archive; The letter does pose some problems as a source because there is no evidence whether the letter was ever mailed to Jamaica or not.
9. *Daily Gleaner*, August 12, 1938.
10. Ibid.
11. Ibid., June 20, 1938.
12. Ibid.
13. Ibid., January 27, 1938; June 20, 1938; August 22, 1938.
14. For this and the following quotes see Ibid., August 22, 1938.
15. Brown to Manley, September 7, 1938, Jamaica Archives and Records Department, Norman Manley Papers, 4/60/2B/2 (in the following: JA, NMP).
16. See Manley to Brown, September 15, 1938, JA, NMP, 4/60/2B/2.
17. The Committee consisted of Manley (chair), Fairclough (secretary) and O.G. Penso, H.P. Jacobs, H.F. Cooke, N.N. Nethersole and W.G. McFarlane.
18. See *Daily Gleaner*, September 19, 1938, see also Post, *Arise*, 365ff.
19. *Daily Gleaner*, September 19, 1938.
20. Cited after Hart, *Towards*, 32.
21. See *Daily Gleaner*, September 19, 1938.
22. Roberts, *The Bustamante Story*, November/December 1959, WAR, MS 353, Box 23.
23. Roberts, 'Autobiography', 24.
24. See *The Opportunity*, December 16, 1938.
25. McFarlane, *Birth of Self-Government*, 24.
26. Roberts, 'Autobiography', 24.
27. Ibid.
28. Consisting of Manley, N.N Nethersole, O.T. Fairclough, H.P. Jacobs, H.F. Cooke, O.G. Penso, V.A. Bailey, O.H. Cameron, W.J. Tomlinson, R.O. Bell, C.G. Walker and W. G. McFarlane. See PNP Pamphlet 'The People's National Party. Report of the 1st Annual Conference'.
29. McFarlane, *Birth of Self-Government*, 23.
30. Ibid.
31. See *Daily Gleaner*, July 25, 1938.
32. For this and the following quotes see *Public Opinion*, October 15, 1938.
33. Ibid., November 5, 1938.
34. Ibid.
35. Ibid., November 7, 1938.
36. Ibid., November 12, 1938 (emphasis in original).
37. Ibid., November 19, 1938.

Implementing Demands for Self-Government

38. Ibid., December 17, 1938.
39. Ibid., December 24, 1938.
40. Ibid..
41. Ibid., November 5, 1938.
42. Ibid., December 24, 1938.
43. Ibid.
44. Ibid.
45. Roberts, *National Feeling*, NLJ, MS 353, WAR Box 9.
46. See Post, *Arise*, 307ff.
47. *Daily Gleaner*, August 12, 1938. The meeting featured popular speakers like Archbishop William Ernest (Archbishop of the African Orthodox Catholic Church) who spoke on loyalty and criticized the prevailing colonial mentality in Jamaica. Ben Burrell spoke on 'Why celebrate this day?' and urged not to stand still at thankfulness about giving back of rights after abolition of slavery, but to continue and demand self-government, Roberts spoke about the 'The free Jamaica that is to be'.
48. *Daily Gleaner*, August 12, 1938.
49. Ibid.
50. Ibid.
51. Ibid., July 22, 1938.
52. The Commission was not a homogenous group. At least two of its members, Sir Walter Citrine (TUC) and Morgan Jones (BLP), sympathized strongly with the working class. See Phelps, 'Rise of the Labor Movement', 433; See Hart, *Rise*, 98; Post, *Arise*, 328ff.
53. See Post, *Arise,* 329, 331; Hart, *Rise and Organize*, 98.
54. Post, *Arise,* 329.
55. Ibid., 332.
56. Ibid., 335.
57. Ibid.
58. Domingo to Hart, July 13, 1937, IOCS, RHP, R. 1, Fo. 2.
59. Roberts, 'Autobiography', NLJ, WAR, MS 353, 22f.
60. See *New York Amsterdam News*, October 1, 1938; October 8, 1938; October 15, 1938.
61. See *Daily Gleaner*, September 12, 1938.
62. Ibid.
63. See Jamaica Progressive League of New York, 'Social and Economic Programme for Jamaica', PRO, CO 950/73.
64. The *Gleaner* published parts of the programme including the radical preliminary remarks. For this and the following quotations see *Daily Gleaner*, September 30, 1938.
65. For this and the following quotes see Jamaica Progressive League New York, Memorandum to Royal Commission, PRO, CO 950/73. The memorandum was also printed in the *Gleaner*, November 2, 1938.
66. Ibid., October 24, 1938.
67. Ibid.
68. Ibid..The delegation consisted of E.R. Dudley Evans (Deputy Mayor), Dr S.O.G: Johnson, W.G. McFarlane, Dr W.S. Duhaney, C.J. Knuckles, B. Durham and P. Aiken.
69. *Daily Gleaner*, October 28, 1938.

70. Ibid., October 29, 1938; November 1, 1938.
71. Brown to Chairman of the Royal Commission, November 3, 1938, PRO, CO 950/73.
72. See Brown to Secretary of the Royal Commission, October 26, 1938, PRO, CO 950/73; November 13, 1938, Brown to Secretary of the West Indies Royal Commission, PRO, CO 950/73.
73. See for instance *Public Opinion*, October 29, 1938; November 5, 1938.
74. Ibid., October 29, 1938.
75. The JDC listed the delegates, many of whom were associated with the Kingston branch of the Progressive League, with their special responsibilities for the various topics as follows: Chairman C.A. McPherson (Taxation), Mary Morris-Knibb (Social Service), E.R.D. Evans (Agriculture, Land Settlement, Industry), O.A. Anderson (Health), and Ethelred Brown (Political Reform). See *Daily Gleaner*, August 17, 1937; McFarlane to Royal Commission, November 6, 1938, PRO, CO 950/111.
76. For this and the following quotes see Memorandum of the Jamaica Deputation Committee, PRO, CO 950/11; Supplementary Memorandum, Jamaica Deputation Committee, under the Auspices of the Jamaica Progressive League, presented to the West Indies Royal Commission 1938, SCRBC, EEB, ScMG 87, Box 4, Fo. 7.
77. McFarlane, *Birth of Self-Government*, 19.
78. See *Daily Gleaner*, October 4, 1938; see also Minutes of the Royal Commission Hearings of the Jamaica Deputation Committee, PRO, CO 950/111.
79. See Carstairs (Assistant Secretary of the Royal Commission) to McFarlane, November 10, 1938, PRO, CO 950/111, see also *Daily Gleaner*, November 15, 1938.
80. For this and the following quotes see Minutes of the Royal Commission Hearings of the Jamaica Deputation Committee, PRO, CO 950/111.
81. Brown to Secretary of the Royal Commission, November 17, 1938, 1938, CO 950/73.
82. See Secretary of the Royal Commission to Brown, November 18, 1938, CO 950/73.
83. *Daily Gleaner*, November 18, 1938.
84. Brown to Secretary of the Royal Commission, November 20, 1938, PRO, CO 950/73.
85. Lloyd to Brown, November 21, 1938, PRO, PRO, CO 950/73.
86. See the joint memorandum and minutes of the hearing, CO 950/30. See also Post, *Arise*, 374; John G. LaGuerre, 'The Moyne Commission and the Jamaican Left', *Social and Economic Studies* 31 (1982): 62f.
87. See the joint memorandum and minutes of the hearing, CO 950/30.
88. Memorandum Rural Reconstruction in Jamaica prepared by Manley, Nethersole, McCulloch, PRO, CO 950/86; see also *Daily Gleaner*, November 15, 1938.
89. *Daily Gleaner*, November 15, 1938.
90. Ibid.
91. Post, *Arise*, 373.
92. See for instance *Daily Gleaner*, November 10, 1938; November 11, 1938; November 17, 1938; December 5, 1938.
93. Ibid., November 21, 1938.
94. Ibid.
95. Ibid.
96. Ibid., November 18, 1938; November 19, 1938.
97. Ibid., November 21, 1938.
98. Ibid., November 19, 1938.

Implementing Demands for Self-Government

99. See for example Julie Greene, *The Canal Builders: Making America's Empire at the Panama Canal* (London: Penguin, 2009); see also Putnam, *Radical Moves*, 23.
100. See for instance *Daily Gleaner*, November 28, 1938; December 5, 1938; December 7; December 15, 1938; February 1, 1939. The branches adopted the programme of the Progressive League including the demand for self-government. See also the epistolary exchange between the Progressive League and the new branches in Panama that can be found in the Louis Moyston Private Archive. However, the material is patchy and allows no in-depth description of positions and activities of the branches.
101. *Pittsburgh Courier*, December 3, 1938.
102. Ibid.
103. Ibid.
104. Brown to McFarlane, December 15, 1938, NLJ, JPL, MS 234.
105. Ibid.
106. Ibid.
107. *New York Amsterdam News*, December 17, 1938.
108. Watson to Department of State, Semi-Annual Report, January 5, 1939. NARA, RG 84, Records of the Foreign Service Posts, US Consulate Kingston, Jamaica, Classified General Records 1936–62, (1936–41 All Files), Box 1.
109. *Daily Gleaner*, November 1, 1938.
110. Roberts, 'Autobiography', 27.
111. Ibid., 26.
112. *Daily Gleaner*, December 21, 1938.
113. Ibid.
114. Roberts, 'Autobiography', 26.
115. *Daily Gleaner*, December 28, 1938.
116. Ibid.
117. See *Public Opinion*, December 24, 1938; December 31, 1938.
118. *Public Opinion*, December 31, 1938.
119. Ibid.
120. See *Daily Gleaner*, January 6, 1939; January 9, 1939. The meeting was chaired by S.O.G. Johnson, Roberts, Manley, Domingo and Varma addressed the gathering.
121. *Daily Gleaner*, January 9, 1939.
122. E.R.D. Evans, W.G. McFarlane, George Bowen, B. Wilson, W.A. McBean.
123. *Daily Gleaner*, January 4, 1939.
124. *Daily Gleaner*, August 14, 1939.
125. Ibid., January 9, 1939.
126. *Daily Gleaner*, January 9, 1939.
127. Roberts, 'Autobiography', 28.
128. Ibid.
129. *Daily Gleaner*, January 17, 1939.
130. Ibid., January 18, 1939.
131. Ibid., January 13, 1939.
132. Ibid., January 21, 1939; January 23, 1939; January 24, 1939.
133. See Roberts, 'Autobiography', 30. See for instance *Daily Gleaner*, January 18, 1939; January 21, 1939; January 26, 1939; February 2, 1939; March 2, 1939; March 15, 1939; March 3, 1939.

134. See Roberts, 'Autobiography', 31.
135. Ibid.
136. Roberts, 'Autobiography', 31.
137. See for example at the Builders and Allied Trades Union, *Daily Gleaner*, January 6, 1939 or the Jamaica Youth Congress, *Daily Gleaner*, January 9, 1939.
138. Ibid., January 24, 1939. The other men contesting for the seat were C.C. Campbell, Clifford Rae and barrister E.E.A. Campbell (FCA).
139. See for example *Daily Gleaner*, February 1, 1939.
140. Ibid., January 28, 1939.
141. Other goals included national industrial development, the revival of the West India Regiment, a prison reform and municipal industrial schools. Further he demanded reconciliation of labour and capital, a fixed minimum wage and an increased salary for long-time civil servants, see *Daily Gleaner*, January 5, 1939.
142. Ibid.
143. Ibid., January 10, 1939; January 11, 1939.
144. Ibid., January 12, 1939. At the meeting, Duhaney, Roberts, Domingo and A.R. Mends were on the platform.
145. Ibid., January 24, 1939.
146. Ibid.
147. Ibid., January 28, 1939.
148. Ibid., January 24, 1939.
149. Ibid., February 8, 1939.
150. Ibid., January 28, 1939.
151. Ibid., February 1, 1939.
152. Ibid., January 28, 1939.
153. Ibid., January 30, 1939.
154. See McFarlane, *Birth of Self-Government*, 21.
155. At an electioneering meeting in 1944, Evans reportedly '…compared the programme of the Labour Party with that of the other Parties pointing out that the People's National Party was offering self-government, socialism and communism, the sort of things which would not work in Jamaica and which would steer the islands towards ruin.' *Daily Gleaner*, November 14, 1944.
156. Ibid., January 14, 1939.
157. Ibid.
158. Ibid., February 2, 1939. In Kingston and St Andrew 2, 299 voters participated of which 1, 443 voted for Campbell, 552 for Evans, 197 for C.C. Campbell, and 49 for Rae, 58 votes were invalid.
159. McFarlane, *Birth of Self-Government*, 21.
160. Ibid.
161. Ibid., 22.
162. *Public Opinion*, February 4, 1939.
163. Ibid.
164. Ibid.
165. *Daily Gleaner*, February 6, 1939.
166. Ibid., February 8, 1939.
167. *Public Opinion*, February 18, 1939.

Implementing Demands for Self-Government

168. Ibid.
169. Ibid.
170. See for instance *Daily Gleaner*, February 4, 1939; February 8, 1939; February 11, 1939; February 13, 1939; February 14, 1939; February 15, 1939; March 2, 1939; March 4, 1939; March 15, 1939; March 20, 1939; March 30, 1939.
171. Ibid., February 15, 1939.
172. *Daily Gleaner*, February 15, 1939.
173. Ibid., March 6, 1939.
174. See *Daily Gleaner*, January 28, 1939. Officers elected: Roberts (president), E.R.D. Evans, McPherson (vice president), McFarlane (secretary), D. Bethune (assistant secretary), Varma (treasurer), Board of Directors: Johnson, Duhaney, C.G. Nuckle, I. E. Davis, W. McBean, W.A. Domingo.
175. Ibid.
176. Ibid.
177. Ibid., January 07, 1939.
178. Mary Morris-Knibb, pioneer female politician and was first woman elected to the KSAC in 1939.
179. *Daily Gleaner*, January 28, 1939.
180. Ibid., January 25, 1939.
181. Ibid., January 27, 1939.
182. See Post, *Arise*, 407.
183. See *Public Opinion*, March 5, 1938.
184. The first issue of the left newspaper *Jamaica Labour Weekly* appeared on May 14, 1938. See Post, *Arise*, 278; Hart, *Towards*, 11ff.
185. See *Jamaica Labour Weekly*, July 20, 1939.
186. Ibid., August 6, 1938.
187. Ibid.
188. Ibid., December 17, 1938; see also Hart, *Rise*, 123f.; Hart, *Towards*, 17.
189. *Jamaica Labour Weekly*, March 11, 1939.
190. Ibid., January 14, 1939.
191. Ibid.
192. Ibid., January 28, 1939.
193. Ibid.
194. Ibid., April 1, 1939.
195. Ibid., March 25, 1939.
196. See Hart, *Rise and Organise*, 123.
197. *Jamaica Labour Weekly*, April 15, 1939.
198. See Post, *Arise*, 395.
199. The committee consisted of Arthur Creech Jones, Peter Blackman, Stafford Cripps, Reginald Bridgeman, John Jagger, Alex Gossip, Dudley Collard, H.B. Morgan and Dr C.B. Clarke; See Post, *Arise*, 405f.
200. See Hart, *Towards Decolonization*, 25.
201. Ibid., 24ff.
202. See *Daily Gleaner*, June 10, 1939; Hart, *Towards*, 25; Post, *Arise*, 400.
203. *Public Opinion*, February 12, 1945.
204. For this and the following quotes see Roberts, 'Autobiography', 38f.

205. *Daily Gleaner*, August 24, 1943.
206. The leadership of the TUAC consisted of Nethersole (chairman), Anderson und Domingo (vice-chairman), R. Hart (secretary), A. Bustamante, H.C. Buchanan, G.E. Valentine, E.E.A. Campbell, A.G.S. Coombs and J.A.G. Edwards, see Post, *Arise*, 401.
207. See *Daily Gleaner*, February 21, 1939; Post, *Arise*, 401; Hart, *Towards Decolonisation*, 26.
208. See *Daily Gleaner*, February 23, 1939. The article alleges that the Advisory Council was set up by Bustamante.
209. Ibid.
210. Ibid., January 28, 1939.
211. Ibid., February 27, 1939.
212. Ibid., January 28, 1939.
213. Bustamante to Manley, JA, NMP, 4/60/2B/3.
214. Ibid.
215. Roberts, 'Autobiography', 40.
216. See Post, *Arise*, 409.
217. *Daily Gleaner* May 16, 1939, see also Roberts, 'Autobiography', 41.
218. For this and the following quotes see *Daily Gleaner*, June 3, 1939.
219. Ibid., June 10, 1939.
220. Ibid., April 1, 1939.
221. Roberts, 'Autobiography', 36f.
222. Ibid.
223. McFarlane, *Birth of Self-Government*, 24.
224. Ibid.
225. See *Daily Gleaner*, April 14, 1939.
226. Ibid., April 13, 1939.
227. Ibid.
228. Ibid.
229. Minutes of People's National Party Convention of Groups, April 12–14, 1939, NLJ, WAR, MS 353, Box 20.
230. Ibid.
231. See *Daily Gleaner*, April 12, 1939.
232. Post, *Arise*, 409.
233. *Daily Gleaner*, April 13, 1939.
234. Ibid.
235. Ibid.
236. For this and the following quotes see, Minutes of People's National Party Convention of Groups, April 12–14, 1939, NLJ, WAR, MS 353, Box 20.
237. *Daily Gleaner*, April 17, 1939.
238. Ibid.
239. PNP pamphlet, Outline of Policy and Programme of the People's National Party, WAR, NLJ, Box 20.
240. Ibid. My emphasis.
241. Minutes of People's National Party Convention of Groups, April 12-14, April 1939, NLJ, WAR, MS 353, Box 20. My emphasis, BT.
242. PNP pamphlet, Outline of Policy and Programme of the People's National Party, NLJ, WAR, MS 353, Box 20.

Implementing Demands for Self-Government

243. *Public Opinion*, April 15, 1939.
244. Ibid.
245. *Daily Gleaner*, June 10, 1939.
246. Roberts, 'Autobiography', 4; for a similar statement see also Roberts, 'National Feeling', NLJ, WAR, MS 353, Box 9.
247. McFarlane, *Birth of Self-Government*, 24.
248. Zeidenfelt, 'Political and Constitutional Developments', 515.
249. Hart, *Towards Decolonization*, 30.
250. See *Daily Gleaner*, April 20, 1939.
251. Ibid., April 24, 1939.
252. Ibid., May 16, 1939.
253. Ibid., September 26, 1939.
254. Ibid., August 14, 1939.
255. Ibid.
256. Ibid.
257. Ibid., August 17, 1939.
258. Ibid., April 27, 1939.
259. Ibid., June 10, 1939.
260. Ibid., May 1, 1939
261. *Public Opinion*, April 22, 1939.
262. *Daily Gleaner*, April 22, 1939.
263. Ibid., March 31, 1939.
264. *Public Opinion*, May 13, 1939; September 9, 1939.
265. Ibid., May 13, 1939.
266. Ibid., August 14, 1939.
267. Ibid., May 13, 1939.
268. Ibid.
269. Ibid., September 25, 1939; October 25, 1939; see also McFarlane, *Birth of Self-Government*, 26.
270. *Daily Gleaner*, October 30, 1939.
271. Edward Jordon was active in the Anti-Slavery Society in the 1820s. He was editor of the *Watchman* and was fought by the authorities for the messages he spread. He later gained recognition and became member of the Assembly and became mayor of Kingston. He served as speaker of the Assembly and was part of the Executive Council. See W.A. Roberts, 'The Patriot' (Kingston 1939), NLJ, JPL, MS 234.
272. *Public Opinion*, February 8, 1941.
273. McFarlane, *Birth of Self-Government*, 26.
274. Ibid.
275. *Public Opinion*, February 8, 1941.
276. *Daily Gleaner*, February 9, 1940.
277. See *Public Opinion*, April 22, 1939; *Daily Gleaner*, April 22, 1939; May 1, 1939.
278. See *Daily Gleaner*, August 26, 1939.
279. Ibid., October 7, 1941.
280. *Public Opinion*, January 7, 1939.
281. Hart, *Towards Decolonisation*, 40.
282. See Hart, *Towards Decolonisation*, 41.

283. Ibid.
284. Ibid.
285. *Daily Gleaner*, May 26, 1939.
286. Ibid., June 12, 1939.
287. Ibid.
288. Ibid., May 30, 1939.
289. *Public Opinion*, May 27, 1939.
290. See *Daily Gleaner*, August 2, 1939.
291. Ibid.
292. Ibid., June 17, 1939.
293. See *Public Opinion*, August 13, 1938.
294. Ibid.
295. *Daily Gleaner*, July 4, 1939.
296. Ibid., July 7, 1939.
297. Ibid., July 12, 1939.
298. *Public Opinion*, July 15, 1939.
299. See Brown to Secretary of State for the Colonies, July 21, 1939, CO 137/838/10.
300. See Domingo to Roberts, July 21, 1939, NLJ, WAR, MS 353, Box 2b; Chicago Defender (NE) July 29, 1939; *New York Amsterdam News*, August 5, 1939.
301. *Daily Gleaner*, August 3, 1939.
302. *Public Opinion*, August 5, 1939.
303. *Public Opinion*, August 12, 1939.
304. McFarlane, *Birth of Self-Government*, 27.
305. Ibid.
306. For this and the following quotes see *Public Opinion*, August 19, 1939.
307. See *Daily Gleaner*, August 21, 1939; other speakers included H.P. Jacobs, O.T. Fairclough, S.O.G. Johnston, E.R.D. Evans, Clare McFarlane, Ken Hill, W.G. McFarlane.
308. For this and the following see *Daily Gleaner*, August 21, 1939.
309. *Public Opinion*, August 26, 1939.
310. *Daily Gleaner*, August 14, 1939.
311. Ibid.

CHAPTER 6: ALTERNATIVE STRATEGIES FOR SELF-GOVERNMENT DURING THE SECOND WORLD WAR

Retreat or Reinforcement: Different Reactions to the Outbreak of the War

The outbreak of the war impeded the movement for self-government in Jamaica, which had just taken up speed triggered by the constant agitation of the Jamaica Progressive League. However, the weakening of the British Empire during the course of the war caused a power shift between the declining British Empire and the rising superpower USA, which accelerated the decolonization of the British colonies in the Caribbean. Yet, developments were not only a bilateral constellation, as Jason Parker correctly emphasizes.[1] The Caribbean actors in the US as well as in the islands played an active role in the negotiations about the future of the colonies.

During these months, the impact of Adolphe Roberts and Wilfred Domingo spearheading nationalist thought is particularly visible. The examination of their efforts in looking for new allies in the fight for self-government not only testifies to their outstanding role but shows how they reacted to the macro-political changes which they regarded as an opportunity, while most other activists retreated into inactivity.

The previous chapters showed that the leaders of the Progressive League were optimistic that the new party would become the main vehicle for continuing the propaganda for self-government in Jamaica, although they kept a close eye on the PNP leaders and put emphasis on the Progressive League's separate identity. Domingo and Roberts were confident that they would be able to continue to influence the party, especially on their return to Jamaica, as both men intended to do when they left. But the Second World War changed everything.

On many levels, the war had grave impacts on the course of decolonization worldwide and the power relations between the European Empires, their colonies and the new superpower in the West. In regard to Britain's territorial possessions in the Caribbean, the war had various effects. While it slowed down the pace of the self-government movement in Jamaica, it increased the speed with which the power shifted from the economically and politically declining British Empire to the new world power of the United States. Great Britain's resources were stretched thin, overstrained with the effort of fighting the menace of Nazi Germany and its allies in Europe. On the other hand, the United States was rapidly gaining economic and military influence throughout the world. It was in this climate of political change that the decolonization movement gained some room to manoeuvre. Historian Claus Füllberg-Stollberg, analysing the Caribbean in the Second World War, concluded that:

> ...military activities went hand in hand with the general interest of the United States in this region and reinforced its dominance, accelerating the process of decolonization and preparing the ground for economic and cultural penetration of the region during the post-war period.[2]

The US strategists wanted to take measures to defend the region around the Panama Canal, including the Caribbean islands with their strategically important raw materials like bauxite for aluminium production, but they hesitated to get militarily involved in the Second World War.[3] These interests motivated the decision to establish a neutrality zone at the Pan-American Conferences in Panama in 1939 and Havana in 1940.[4] The trading of outdated war vessels for the granting of land-leases in the Caribbean to erect US military bases or the Conference of Havana, at which 21 American nations adopted a defence strategy for the hemisphere, were obvious signs of the shifting power relations between Great Britain and the US.[5] Roberts and Domingo developed their own strategies to contend with these events, but an examination of local reactions in Jamaica is necessary to fathom why Domingo and Roberts felt forced to undertake independent action.

After war broke out, the PNP decided to retreat from outdoor meetings and political agitation, especially regarding constitutional change, to show its loyalty to Great Britain.[6] This marked a serious setback for the movement for self-government, which had only just started to gain a foothold after the massive nationalist propaganda campaign of the Progressive League and its influence on the party. Such setbacks were proof that the demand for self-government at the time was not firmly rooted in the party, especially as the party had been quite hesitant about including the demand for self-government in its party platform at the party conference in April 1939. Louis Lindsay interprets the PNP's retreat from anti-colonial agitation as a sign for the strong anglophilia that was still a dominant line of thinking in the party, despite all its rhetoric for self-government.[7]

In September 1939, Roberts wrote to Norman Manley and inquired whether the party would adjust its policy and how it planned to continue the struggle despite the war and censorship regulations.[8] Manley replied that he believed that no elections would be held during the war, and that he had limited all party work to educational and internal activities. Despite his loyalty, Manley opposed the subscription of Jamaicans to fight in the war, although he felt that it would

Alternative Strategies for Self-Government

find support among Jamaicans, because many still had strong sympathies and remained loyal to England.⁹

Even after the French and British defeat in Flanders in the summer of 1940, the PNP was still in a 'sort of coma', as Domingo put it, and unable to develop a programme in the event that the British lost the war.¹⁰ Domingo was disturbed by the fact that the PNP and its leaders still seemed to be confident of Great Britain's success, while even British officials started to worry about the outcome of the war and increasingly sought help from the US.

Roberts and Domingo, who had pinned their hopes on the PNP becoming the main force in the fight for self-government in Jamaica, were disappointed by the party's decision. Both men's reactions were similar and they strongly disapproved of the stand the PNP took. Straight away, both leaders began to exchange ideas as to how best to adjust their policies, where to find new allies in the fight against colonialism, and how to take advantage of the changing geopolitical situation.

The next blow on the course of the Progressive League, due to the impact of the war, was the interruption of Roberts and Domingo's plans to return to Jamaica in 1940. Domingo was keeping an eye on the war developments and still planned to return to Jamaica as soon as it was possible.¹¹ Roberts wrote to Edna Manley in early October 1939, saying that 'at the moment, it does not seem practicable for me to return to Jamaica as soon as I had intended. I do not feel that, under existing conditions, I could be of much service in the political movement'.¹² His US citizenship put him in danger under war conditions. However, although he decided not to return during the war, it was Roberts who proposed increasing the activities in New York to compensate for the local inactivity on the island.

Like in 1936, Roberts provided the impulse for decided anti-colonial action. At the time, he was in Washington, DC, working on a book on the history of the Caribbean region when he wrote to Domingo to discuss the impact of the war and to outline a possible strategy for continuing their work. He was worried that the 'war has wrecked our political movement' and doubted that, given the withdrawal of the PNP, the partnership between the Progressive League and the party was to endure during a long war.¹³

Furthermore, Roberts feared that England and France stood to lose the war if the US did not become involved. He advised Domingo that they needed to be prepared for all circumstances:

> If the British Empire falls, the only rational step for Jamaica may be to declare her independence. She cannot do so effectively, cannot obtain recognition from the United States and Canada, unless there is leadership and a machine ready for taking over the Government in an intelligent way. The thing should be planned for, as a contingency.¹⁴

Roberts suggested that the best way to prepare was to form a 'secret society, to be composed of wholly reliable persons'. He asked Domingo if he would support him in that endeavour and what persons they should consider asking to join, adding: 'The fewer the better. Yet we should not exclude any Jamaican of the *right sort*. In Roberts' opinion, the Progressive League should abstain from too radical a propaganda for self-government, but continue to secretively prepare for a worst case scenario. He proposed that a circle of Progressive League members form a committee to implement the proposed strategies.

Domingo agreed that the developments demanded immediate action. One of his major concerns was about the future of Jamaica if England would lose the war, especially in light of Britain's policy of appeasement toward Nazi-Germany, a policy which led him to doubt the intent and sincerity of Great Britain in the war against Germany.[15] Domingo agreed with Roberts' proposal and turned first to the Progressive League in New York to solicit support for the emergency plans. While Roberts was in New Orleans, Domingo assumed his responsibilities as vice president and tried to influence the attitudes of the members toward the war. At a public meeting on September 24, 1939, which was attended by some 200 people, Domingo presented various resolutions he had drafted, and which were adopted as the official position of the Progressive League. These resolutions included: England and the self-governing parts of the Empire should be the first to send out soldiers; that black troops should be regarded as equal to white troops; and that Jamaica should be granted self-government as a proof of Great Britain's sincerity in its advocacy of democracy.[16] In contrast to the PNP, the Progressive League declared that it would not:

> ...abate its campaign or abdicate its right to struggle for self-government for Jamaica in order that the people of the island may enjoy some of the political blessings for which they [the British] are willing to make the supreme sacrifice in behalf of others.[17]

Taking the declared British war aims at their word, the Progressive League demanded that self-government and democracy should not only pertain to European countries but also to the colonies. Although Domingo was able to convince the majority of Progressive League members to formally commit to a continuation of the struggle for self-government during the war, at the same time, he was hesitant to share what he and Roberts really thought – even with the directorate. He was under the impression that the directors and the majority of the members would not endorse the idea to form a clandestine organization 'ready to press our demand and take over in case England is defeated and the future of Jamaica is imperiled'.[18] Domingo shared his doubts in a letter to Roberts. At a director's meeting, he was asked what position the Progressive League would assume in case of England's defeat. His response was:

Alternative Strategies for Self-Government

> ...nobody envisaged bold action. Reid [acting Progressive League president] suggested, and his view prevailed, that we should bide our time and shape our course according to circumstances. That is, follow an opportunistic policy. Having in mind the seriousness of your proposal I said nothing. Yes, secret action is necessary, but the job will be to find the right sort of human material.[19]

Domingo decided firstly to approach only O'Meally. Although O'Meally firmly approved of their ideas, he and O'Meally were not able to proceed with the plans during the winter months. In a letter to Roberts in April 1940, Domingo reported that due to serious health problems of O'Meally and also of himself, as well as business problems during the war, he had not succeeded in making any concrete steps. Nevertheless, he admitted:

> But those are only excuses. The truth of the matter is that we lack experience in the matter you spoke of and the censorship in Jamaica makes it next to impossible to feel out the opinion of even the most militant ones in Jamaica. Since you left I thought the matter over several times, but don't even know how to start. I agree with you that world events forebode ill for the British Empire and we ought to be prepared, but we are so woefully ignorant and ill-equipped for undertaking such serious moves. We need guidance.[20]

Domingo was desperate and at loose ends with the situation. He felt he could not share the secret plan with the board of directors of the Progressive League. Roberts reacted with understanding and agreed that the Progressive League lacked the experience to carry out secret actions of such magnitude. Yet, once again, it was Roberts who persisted in developing a plan of action.

> But Jamaicans will pay a steep price for unpreparedness when the crisis does arrive. It has always been so with nationalist movements in the adolescent stage. I had hoped that our country might be spared the misery – or at least some of it – which is certain to occur unless there is a group of unselfish leaders ready to take over, with a plan already worked out. Yet I myself cannot see how this can be accomplished unless some of us go to Jamaica, found an organization much more resolute than any existing now, and establish a secret liaison with New York. I need scarcely add that service in Jamaica on such a mission would be extremely dangerous under war conditions.[21]

The war clearly galvanized Roberts into thinking about this clandestine plan. The statement also reflects his grave disappointment with all local groups, including the branch of the Progressive League in Kingston. In every letter, Roberts and Domingo discussed recent war developments and shared their concerns with one another. Roberts strongly felt that England and France would not be able to win the war alone and came to the assumption that the US would eventually intervene, taking over the duty of defending the hemisphere. He believed that if a strong movement for independence existed in Jamaica at the time, it was possible that sovereignty might be; however, he warned that at the slightest sign of trouble, a US invasion could be the result. He also made these assertions in the last chapter of his book, *The Caribbean*,[22] that he was in the process of finishing at the time. He stated that these ideas 'are likely to be unpopular with pro-English Jamaicans. But I believe they will turn out to be approximately correct. They constitute one of the reasons why we should be ready with a shadow government'.[23]

Domingo shared Roberts' concerns. Even more so than Roberts, he emphasized his concern for all non-white populations in the colonies, fearing that a pro-fascist regime could take control in England. He sincerely hoped for a victory of the allies, in spite of the opportunity that might present itself for the self-government movement in case of a defeat. He was less confident than Roberts that there would be enough support in Jamaica:

> ...from any angle it seems to me that we are caught in a difficult and dangerous situation. Unfortunately, there seems to be no way of rousing our people to any of the likely consequences. They are blindly confident of England's invincibility and so even the intelligent ones refuse to take an interest in peering into the future where their country is concerned.[24]

Domingo blamed 'the seemingly incurable inertia of the Jamaican masses respecting matters that should be of intimate political interest to themselves' for the difficulty in finding dependable partners for action in Jamaica. He assured Roberts that he and Brown were doing their best to try to 'orientate the minds of our countrymen here and at home towards the fundamental problem of developing a healthy national sentiment'.[25]

This was no easy task. The reaction of the directors of the Kingston branch of the Progressive League to the war developments affirmed for Domingo and Roberts that they could not rely on their local partner. One of the founding members, W.S. Duhaney, wrote a telling letter to the press, shortly before the war, lauding Chamberlain's policy at a time when Domingo was highly critical of his appeasement policy.[26] It was evident from the announcements for meetings and the resolutions passed by the local branch that it continued to maintain a course of promoting a mild cultural nationalism, addressing matters of local interest, like the reorganization of the Parochial Boards.[27] When the Progressive League supported the Governor in preventing the post of the income tax commissioner to become vacant in the present war situation, Domingo bluntly shared his and Brown's opinion of secretary McFarlane in a letter to Roberts:

Alternative Strategies for Self-Government 213

> McFarlane's position is tantamount to saying that only an Englishmen can be trusted to be diligent enough to collect the tax. The clear implication of inferiority or corruption implied in the Governor's and McFarlane's position is inescapable. As you said once we have to educate the leaders. I think we have the task of making men out of them.[28]

What made the situation even worse was McFarlane's harsh criticism of the Progressive League in New York. He claimed that Roberts and Domingo 'practically gave the League to the PNP against the advice of the people on the spot'.[29] Domingo was disgruntled and stated in a letter to Roberts:

> Of course, you and I know that the League in Jamaica was less than a shade when we got there and decided that because of that fact and the superior personalities and facilities of the P.N.P. it was far better to infect that group with our ideals than let the whole thing die of stagnation as it seemed doomed to do under the conditions that we found.[30]

The differences between Domingo and McFarlane testify to the ideological gap between the two organizations. While the leaders in New York had hoped to find dependable support to push for self-government in Jamaica, the group around McFarlane was not sufficiently radical to meet their expectations. McFarlane apparently felt left out, although he had openly protested against allegations that the PNP had taken away the Progressive League's programme and underlined the need for close cooperation.[31] Once more, McFarlane's volatility and his tendency to present the 'facts' as he felt convenient becomes visible; and likewise, the fundamental difference in perspective between the branches of the Progressive League in New York and Kingston.

Roberts agreed with Domingo in his judgment about the Progressive League in Jamaica and complained that its members 'have no political sense and are wishy-washy characters to boot. I am disgusted with W.G. McFarlane, and I keep in touch with him and try to arouse some firmness in him for the sole reason that it is necessary to maintain a link for the future'.[32] The local branch had again disqualified itself as a serious partner in the eyes of Roberts and Domingo. The cooperation between both groups was merely a stopgap for the Progressive League in New York in its search for dependable partners in Jamaica.

In the face of Great Britain's disastrous situation in the military crisis in the summer of 1940, Roberts and Domingo agreed that immediate action was necessary: 'The situation for colored peoples in both the United States and the West Indies is as you say, extremely gloomy. The spread of Fascism to this country is to be anticipated'.[33]

After the French defeat, the scenario of a possible German victory over Great Britain was not as improbable as it appears today. For the anti-colonial movement it certainly had a dramatic effect. Roberts recommended changing the strategy in Jamaica and proposed alerting Jamaicans of the dangers that would accompany a fascist take-over. Roberts suggested that Domingo should write an open letter to the Jamaican public to alert the populace, hoping that it would overcome its inertia to save the country. Reflecting the converging lines of race and class, Roberts held the paternalistic view that only the middle class around Manley was able to assume responsibility to protect the black majority from a fascist take-over:

> ...the mulattoes of Jamaica are indeed the only class there who could quickly set up a political structure capable of running the island under autonomy. If they have the least grain of sense, they will rally behind Manley and the bolder self-government advocates, so as to establish in Jamaica at least a small bulwark against the oppression of the Negro race – if for no other reason.[34]

Roberts recommended that such a letter should be phrased in such simple terms as Domingo would use in a public address. He recommended that it should not contain open critique of England or predictions about the Empire's defeat. Instead, it should serve to introduce the likelihood of US domination in the course of the war and insist on the need for Jamaicans to lay the groundwork to demand their own nationhood before the developments caught them unprepared. This letter should be secretively smuggled into the country, somehow bypassing the censor, Roberts advised.[35]

Domingo was sceptical about the possibility of convincing Jamaicans of the need for prompt action. The only support in Jamaica, Domingo felt, could be expected from the editors of a new newspaper, the *Worker and Peasant*.[36] He argued: 'It is very left and strongly nationalist. Every article bears witness to the propaganda we let loose in the island'.[37]

In the meantime, the situation in Jamaica was deteriorating, as Governor Richards extensively used his right to overrule decisions of the Legislative Council under the 'Paramount Importance Clause'. The Progressive League in New York decided to protest against Richards' autocratic style of governance by sending a cable to the Secretary of State for the Colonies, demanding the limitation of the Governor's constitutional powers and the recall of Governor Richards.[38] Richards reacted promptly; he answered his superiors, trying to belittle the influence of the Progressive League by pointing out its outsider status and dismissing its primary goal:

> The Jamaica Progressive League operates in New York and largely represents Jamaicans who have left their country for their country's good. Their general principle is to be against the Government. They have no influence in Jamaica other than the mutual support which all

Alternative Strategies for Self-Government

subversive elements are apt to give each other. They stand essentially for self-government by the unfit.[39]

This episode shows how closely the Progressive League followed local developments and how boldly and promptly it reacted. Furthermore, this conflict is significant in explaining the relationship between Richards and the Progressive League in the years to come.

A few weeks later, Governor Richards introduced an 'Undesirable Publication Bill' to keep subversive literature out of the country, which was passed by the Legislative Council in May 1940.[40] This action was not only protested against by Manley and even by stalwart conservative journalists like de Lisser and Natty Parker, it also resulted in speedy action by the executives of the Progressive League who feared that the bill was expressly directed against the League and designed to keep its propaganda out of the country.[41] The Progressive League launched a broad protest and published a resolution against the bill in the *Gleaner*.[42] Another letter, written by Domingo under the pen name 'Proletariat', was printed two days later. He employed arguments similar to those he used in a signed open letter to the members of the Legislative Council, which appeared the following day.[43] In both letters – written before the bill was passed by the Legislative Council – Domingo articulated the feeling that the law was specifically directed against the import of propaganda by the Progressive League and condemned the bill as an undemocratic violation of the freedom of speech. He even compared it with methods used by the Nazis. Once again, Domingo juxtaposed the supposed British war aim, namely the fight for democracy and the undemocratic methods of governance in its colonies. After the Legislative Council passed the bill, Domingo commented bitterly in a letter to Roberts: 'Poor fellows, they are devoid of manhood and common-sense. They work against their country's interest, but I suppose, in favor of their personal fortunes'.[44]

Analysing the reasons why the country's elected officials were able to pass the bill without provoking massive protest in all sections of society, Domingo blamed the class division that divided the country along racial lines:

> The handful of whites on top (including the Jews who should think of their fate under Fascism) feel that they have nothing to lose. They fear the rise of the black masses for they realize that they will have to make many concessions to them. The people of obvious mixed ancestry are jealous of their preferred position in the commercial life of the country and their dominance of the Civil Service and fear to yield any ground to the blacks whom most of them despise; and the blacks for the most part are too uneducated and sodden with ignorance, superstition, and religion to comprehend the situation, so there we are.

Domingo's analysis of the society reflects the race-class nexus in the colonial society and is indicative of the Progressive League's prioritization of classical forms of nationalism. Shrugging off any radical potential within the black majority, the Progressive League adopted a typical nationalist position that focused its hope and agitation on the middle class, expecting that it would advance into a nationalist avant-garde that would eventually be able to convince the masses. Domingo shared Roberts' hope that the middle class had the educational background and the power to rule the country, if they were willing to make concessions to the dark lower classes. Furthermore, they had serious reasons to fear a loss of their privileged position in the case of a fascist victory in England. If they saw that danger more clearly, Domingo hoped, they would 'cease dreaming and get down to business'.

Like a mantra, Domingo continued to intone that:

> Our only hope is to fight like the devil for autonomy so that even if we come under America with or without our consent they will find us with a strong demand for self-government. But it will not do for us to accept our status under the British as a Crown Colony and then make demands for self-government if the Americans take our country. Our position would be ridiculous.

Roberts responded post-haste. He was in full accord with Domingo's analysis of the crisis. He commented on the recent 'Blitzkrieg' success in the Netherlands, Belgium and France, which reaffirmed his prediction that '[t]he British Empire will fall'.[45] Roberts expected that should England win the war with help of the allied forces, the days of the glorious Empire would be numbered and her colonies would be taken over by a powerful and victorious US. He stated that:

> Jamaica's problem, therefore, is largely of her future relationship with the United States. Your contention that we should fight hard for self-government now is absolutely correct. We must have the best standing possible as an incipient nation when the United States stretches out her hand on Port Royal and when the peace settlement is made.[46]

Although Roberts' belief that the US would take over the colonies proved to be wrong, he was correct in his prediction that US policy and pressure would catalyze the decolonization process and that the new superpower would tighten its economic and political grip on the islands and increasingly expand its influence.

In a situation where a British defeat became more likely day after day, politicians and military strategists were not the only ones in a rush to come up with new solutions. Expecting the worst, Domingo was apprehensive that Jamaicans could be affected by the fascism that could take hold in Great Britain and the US or by a direct take-over by Germany in the event of a British defeat.[47]

In order to prevent such a scenario, Domingo resumed his efforts to form an organization in New York that could compensate for the lack of radicalism in Jamaica. These efforts resulted in the founding of the West Indies National

Emergency Council (WINEC). In the literature, information about the WINEC and how it came into being is scarce and shrouded. Richard Hart identified the 'JPL led by Domingo'[48] as the inspiring force behind the founding of WINEC. The letters between Roberts and Domingo show clearly that it was these two men's initiative to develop a new group as a substitute for the lack of radicalism in the existing groups, including the Progressive League. Both men stood out in their boldness, their dedication and their undeviating agitation for Jamaica as a national entity.

Again, the spearheads of anti-colonialism were forced to look for potential supporters in New York rather than in Jamaica. However, Domingo was unable to find sufficient Jamaican migrants willing to make provision for a possible British defeat. Disappointed, Domingo decided to reach out to the broader Caribbean community in New York. The ties that held together the network of Caribbean radicals in New York still functioned. In June 1940, a small group of people from the Caribbean came together and founded the WINEC. However, Domingo was quick to assure Roberts that the Committee would not be in favour of a political federation of the British West Indies.[49] Although the organization's design as well as the cast of characters was a compromise, the WINEC became the interim instrument for Roberts and Domingo to continue the fight for self-government and attract some degree of international interest.

The time was particularly opportune for an organization that aimed to popularize the claim for independence for the British colonies in the Caribbean. While the course of the war in Europe became more disturbing after Germany's victory over parts of France, the US and many Latin American countries reacted by immediately scheduling a conference in Havana with the intent to consolidate the defence strategy of the region.[50] While US public opinion was still against military entry into the war, sensitivity toward the vulnerability of the Panama Canal Zone, due to its proximity to European possessions in the hemisphere, grew. In a letter to a friend in Jamaica, Domingo analysed the hemispheric dimension of the war in Europe as follows:

> The position of the West Indies is giving America plenty bother. France, defeated and cowed is virtually Fascist. If she continues to hold her West Indian colonies not only will the inhabitants of those colonies be under Fascism but Germany will in reality have a basis for attacking the Panama Canal. The same thing will be true if England is beaten. Jamaica will be under English Fascists, which will be bad for the people and for America.[51]

A poll in the US, conducted shortly before the Havana Conference, revealed that many Americans shared Domingo's fear. Eighty-seven per cent of the US population was in favour of taking over the European colonies in order to secure the Panama Canal and, in fact, the hemisphere.[52] In reaction to the war developments, a conference of 21 American republics was scheduled to take place in Cuba with the aim to adopt a common security strategy for the hemisphere. This was the background of the founding of the WINEC.

Domingo saw the conference as a potential chance to carry the claims of Jamaicans to an international audience of diplomats. He wrote to Roberts suggesting drafting a declaration which would proclaim the right to autonomy of the European possessions in the Western hemisphere. He explicated his strategy:

> To be clear, I mean we should try to win our autonomy by winning the sympathy of Latin America and playing those countries against the United States. If we can win Latin American countries to the principle (which I think they have already enunciated) that there should be no transfer of colonies, and they push the corollary out of sheer opposition to the United States, namely, that every country is entitled to self-determination, we will have played a trump card.[53]

The plans were in tandem with Roberts' concepts. He had argued for many years that Jamaica and the rest of the Caribbean islands should belong to the Pan-American family of nations and should be independent units within that framework. Domingo was increasingly influenced by this approach and now attempted to utilize it in support of anti-colonial action. Domingo invited fellow Caribbean activists and approached A.M. Wendell Malliet, who held a key position at the *New York Amsterdam News*. Malliet was soon won over by Domingo's plan and published an article in the *New York Amsterdam News*, which outlined the recent efforts to launch a new movement demanding autonomy of the British colonies in the Caribbean.[54]

An emergency conference was announced, to be held within the following 10 days. The conference, the article stated, 'will discuss principles and policies to save the West Indies as a national unit under the control of the native population, in case of a Hitler victory or a barter scheme between the British and United States Governments'.[55] This indication that a 'national unit' would be desirable was either a misunderstanding or a deliberate misinterpretation by Malliet, who, in contrast to Roberts and Domingo, was in favour of the idea of a federation of the British colonies in the Caribbean that was being considered in the Colonial Office. Domingo, as seen above, had clearly repudiated such a scheme. However, it is also possible that Domingo did not distance himself openly from the concept at this time, since he was desperately in search of new allies. Richard B. Moore, who was an integral part of WINEC, was later surprised and harshly disappointed when Domingo published his first pamphlet against the Federation, which suggested that Domingo did not openly oppose Federation in that committee.[56]

In view of the menace of fascism, Domingo reiterated the need for racial

Alternative Strategies for Self-Government 219

solidarity between African Americans and immigrants of Caribbean descent and concluded: 'Conceding the possibility of a German victory, it is the duty of West Indian and American Negroes to give serious consideration to their future. More than ever, the fate of American and West Indian Negroes seems linked together'.[57]

While the dramatic international crisis had a motivating effect on Roberts and Domingo, these developments had the opposite effect in Jamaica. In reference to a letter from Edna Manley, Roberts reported: 'Opinion in Jamaica has become chaotic now as a result of the disasters in Flanders. Mrs. Manley writes me today that the P.N.P. leaders are sunk in gloom and frantic with uncertainty'.[58] Domingo was deeply disappointed by the reaction of the PNP and hoped that the party leaders around Manley would open their eyes to the developments and help educate the masses about the possible consequences of the war.[59] In the hope that she would be able to inspire a different attitude in the PNP, Roberts cautiously shared his and Domingo's plans with Edna Manley:

> The question of future relations with the United States is about to come up, if I am correctly informed, and it behooves the leaders to prepare for this. We ought not to allow ourselves to be taken by surprise. We should have ready a policy and a programme with which to counter anything that might prove a set-back to the essentials of our movement.[60]

Roberts mentioned that he would soon be in Washington, DC to lobby for Jamaica's case and expressed his hope that the PNP would resume propaganda activities and articulate a strong demand for self-government in Jamaica. Concurrently, he persevered in putting the pressure on Domingo to get the new group off the ground, asserting that 'the real crisis is almost upon us. Jamaicans – and West Indians generally – will be infatuated dupes if they fail to realize that the British Empire is going to fall, and that if self-government is not claimed now it may be impossible to get it for another generation'.[61]

The lack of support from the PNP led Domingo to increase his efforts, but the new group developed slowly, and two weeks passed before the first meeting took place. Blaming the prevalent loyalty with Great Britain amongst West Indians in New York, Domingo explained his challenge:

> ...the problem before me is to move this inert mass here into action. I hate to admit it, but West Indians generally are about the most lethargic people one could find in matters pertaining to politics. They have been so long accustomed to English men thinking for them that they seem incapable of thinking for themselves. Then, too, in this particular emergency they seem incurably sure of the British being able to muddle through. I mention the foregone to let you know that I am not having easy sailing getting the Committee into motion.[62]

It is evident that many migrants still adhered to a strong loyalty to Great Britain, especially during the war. Domingo elaborated on how he would use the uniting power of nationalism to approach members of all angles of the migrant community, including 'liberals, reactionaries, communists, pro-Allies etc.'[63]

Finally, Domingo attained success, and a first meeting was held on June 15, 1940. The meeting was attended by roughly 20 people who agreed on a planning committee chaired by Domingo to draft a declaration and define the committee's policy.[64] Still, Domingo was concerned whether he had found the right set of people: 'Truth to tell, the only ones who have shown any great amount of interest so far in cooperating with me are the fellows from the other islands and they are mostly left-wingers. I would naturally prefer to deal with people less identified with extreme views on political questions, but one must work with the material available'.[65]

This was no surprise, as Domingo had strong roots in the radical Left milieu of Caribbeans living in Harlem, and held strong Socialist positions himself. Numerous names of former associates were among the members of the committee.[66] Such a composition was certainly not the ideal that Roberts and Domingo initially had in mind. Not only did left-wingers from other islands comprise a large proportion of the members, some members of the Progressive League in New York also joined, who Domingo had not envisioned as part of the inner circle in the first place as he questioned their willingness to adopt radical anti-colonial action.

At this point, Domingo had put aside his Socialist ideas in favour of a decidedly nationalist outlook, a tendency that would become stronger throughout the years. His partners on the committee did not share the same approach. Domingo reported:

> I have a difficult job keeping the fellows to one line – laying the basis for self-determination and nationhood. I want the statement to be clear and unequivocal on that question, hence I am doing my best to keep out everything that is controversial or extraneous.[67]

Despite the Socialist leanings of some of its members, he was successful in preventing Socialist connotations from being included in the three basic principles of the WINEC:

> SELF-DETERMINATION (no change of sovereignty without the consent of the peoples involved), DEMOCRACY (to insure an appeal to American ideals, and for the application of them), AUTONOMY (the legitimate goal of all peoples which had been attained by every member of Pan-America).[68]

While Roberts was happy to see that the committee had finally been formed, he was concerned about the leftist tendency and urged Domingo to 'eliminate the Communist note, as much as possible, from resolutions and documents. This

Alternative Strategies for Self-Government

is no time to compromise the cause of self-determination with visionary and unpopular internationalism'.[69]

Domingo agreed. He then prepared a 'Declaration of Rights of the Caribbean Peoples to Self-Determination and Self-Government',[70] which was revised by R.B. Moore.[71] According to Domingo:

> I did the original work and was aided by a committee in having the language refined, but the essential ideas are mine and I did everything possible (and I think I succeeded) to exclude anything of a red aspect from the document. But my principal aides are known Left Wingers, so there's the rub. The others are indifferent, befuddled, or cowardly. I will have to trust to the intrinsic value of the document and the consequent publicity and the attendant embarrassment to the governments involved to bring the desired result.[72]

Although the declaration claimed to represent the peoples of the Caribbean, Domingo assured Roberts that it 'bulks with Jamaican references'.[73] Like the original declaration of the Progressive League from 1936, the document was based on the assumption of a basic right to self-determination of all peoples. The opening phrases quoted the US Declaration of Independence 'in order to confront Americans with their own language', Domingo claimed.[74] The declaration argued from a Pan-American perspective and laid special emphasis on the point that Caribbean peoples shared a common destiny and similar interests with the other nations on the continent. Regarding the US security interests threatened by the war developments, he expressed:

> But any such menace can best be removed only by integration of the West Indian peoples into the Pan-American family of nations strictly on the basis of the right of self-determination. Only by this will it be possible to create an enduring foundation for genuine 'Good Neighbor' relations.

Again, the reference to declared aims of US foreign policy is apparent. However, while the declaration claimed to support the protection of the hemisphere, it clearly opposed the sale, transfer or the establishment of military bases without the consultation of the people, who would have an 'indefeasible right to a dominant voice in the shaping of their own destiny'. The document described self-determination and democracy as underlying principles of all Pan-American nationality. If these rights were denied to the Caribbean peoples, it would 'weaken, undermine and destroy the democratic structure' and destabilize the region. The American countries were reminded that their very own nationality was an achievement of anti-colonial struggle. For these reasons, the WINEC expected the countries to support Caribbean demands for independence and nationhood, to which they were not only entitled, but for which they were sufficiently prepared. The principal right to freedom and self-determination, so the declaration stipulated, had been affirmed by the US in various declarations and presidential statements, and had recently been reaffirmed at the hemispheric conference in Panama, where the Mexican delegate had presented a statement in which he affirmed that no case of change in sovereignty of one of the European colonies in the Americas could be tolerated without consultation of the peoples to decide over their own political destiny. The declaration finally urged that:

> The Committee appeals to all who uphold democracy and to every true lover of liberty in all the Americas and indeed throughout the world to support the rightful claims and just cases of the peoples of the West Indies and the adjacent Caribbean areas to self-determination and self-government.

As promised, Domingo attested that in all references to nationhood and self-government, he was referring in particular to Jamaica. While working with the Committee 'on the general West Indian question' he divulged that it would 'not preclude me and the Progressive League from working for Jamaica specifically'.[75]

Malliet became enthused by the developments, probably pushed by Domingo's convictions. He supported Domingo in his emphasis on Jamaica's interest.

Domingo proposed in a letter to Roberts:

> We think it wise for the League to prepare and file a statement on Jamaica's behalf immediately. He [Malliet] thinks someone should go to Jamaica to see Manley and the others for action NOW. ...He is anxious to lay the claim for Jamaica as a nation.[76]

Domingo was determined to continue to lobby for Jamaican self-government and had fully adopted Roberts' argumentation of Jamaica being a part of a Pan-American region. He believed in the economic and strategic interest of the US in the area and expected this interest to support Jamaica's claim for independence.[77] Accordingly, Domingo encouraged Roberts to draft a resolution specifically demanding self-government for Jamaica. Roberts immediately agreed and advised that it should be officially signed by the Progressive League and as many Jamaicans in the US as possible.[78]

The Jamaican declaration that Roberts drafted firmly opposed any transfer to another power without consent of the Jamaican population: 'The status of an independent nation is the only status that should automatically follow the demise of British imperial authority'.[79] Like Domingo before, Roberts used references to US foreign policy, invoked the Monroe Doctrine as well as statements from US officials who had advocated that the colonies become self-governing units within the Western hemisphere. In a blatant exaggeration, the Jamaica Declaration charged that the demand for self-government was already firmly rooted:

Alternative Strategies for Self-Government

> The extreme of local nationalist sentiment has been manifested in the legitimate aspiration of the Jamaica Progressive League, and other forces, to Dominion status within the framework of the British Commonwealth of Nations.[80]

The document declared that if British rule should cease as a corollary of recent international developments, Jamaicans would demand to be consulted about their political future. It further stated, 'Jamaica is an entity in the Western World' and therefore, its interests 'will be identical with those of the countries in the Pan-American Union'. As part of that framework, it would be Jamaica's duty to provide necessary aid in the defence of the region, for example, by providing military naval and air bases. It ended with the demand that 'we shall not be contented, under any new order that may emerge out of the present war, to be less than free citizens in our native land'. Approved and signed by all its officers, the Progressive League sent the document, together with the memorandum that Brown had presented to the Royal Commission, directly to the secretary of the Pan-American Congress in Havana and to US Secretary of State, Cordell Hull, who was asked to present it to the US Congress.[81]

Domingo continued his propaganda efforts and published a lengthy letter in *Public Opinion*, in which he repudiated arguments articulated in Jamaica that England should sell the islands in the Caribbean to the US in exchange for arms to secure Germany's defeat. Some voices expressed their belief that such an attachment to the US would be economically beneficial to the masses in Jamaica.[82] Donald A. Draughon, US Marshall in Puerto Rico, affirmed this feeling when he observed the serious economic situation on a visit to Jamaica and reported that the masses would welcome US annexation, while the coloured upper class was opposed to it, fearing racism and class degradation based on the specific system of race discrimination in the US.[83] To counteract arguments that US domination would lead to prosperity, Domingo pointed to the case of the US colony Puerto Rico as a negative example and described it as 'still poverty-stricken' and lamented: 'The masses of the people are landless and their standard of living unbelievably low'.[84] He criticized the lack of patriotism in Jamaica and accused the leaders of lying about the actual state of affairs in the war.

Domingo further warned of the danger of race discrimination if Jamaica came under US rule, pointing to the different concepts of race in the US and in Jamaica:

> The majority of Jamaicans – black brown, mulatto, quadroon – are Negroes in the American use of the term, and under American rule they would suffer severely as men and women accustomed to a more or less tolerant attitude where race and colour are involved.[85]

Domingo encouraged Jamaicans to demand support for Jamaica's pursuit to become an independent nation. He felt that this was a realistic effort, because the majority of US citizens would not 'be unanimously anxious, even in the name of national security, to adopt over a million more Negro step children to add to the 14,000,000 on the mainland'.[86]

The negotiations at the Havana Conference would prove Domingo right, at least on the point that the US had no interest in annexing Jamaica or other islands in the Caribbean. In Domingo's view, Jamaica should at least have the status of a Dominion within the Empire, so that no one could think of trading the islands, including their populations. Yet, he left no doubt about his position:

> ...if Jamaica is destined to lose British Sovereignty it must not be in exchange for rule by the United States. In such a situation, Jamaica should have the right to membership in the family of Pan-American nations as a full-fledged autonomous unit like Canada and Newfoundland. And as such she would gladly contribute her quota to all measures that are necessary for making this continent secure against Fascist invasion.[87]

This was also the line of argumentation the WINEC would adopt at the Havana Conference and which led to a small diplomatic success and unexpected publicity for Jamaica's case.

Internationalizing Claims: The West Indies National Council and the Havana Conference

In light of a possible British defeat in the summer of 1940, 21 republics on the American continent convened a conference in Havana in order to agree on a security strategy for the hemisphere. The debates about the destiny of the British possessions in the Caribbean that took place in the Cuban capital August 21–30, provided an important chance for the newly founded WINEC to place its demand for autonomy before an international audience. But how would the representations of the British colonies in the Caribbean be received at the conference? Would the American republics assume the role of powerful advocates in the decolonization process, as Roberts and Domingo hoped they would?

Shortly before the conference, rumours appeared that the US strategists would advocate a trusteeship solution if Britain's colonies were threatened with occupation by Fascist forces. Domingo was disappointed because he had anticipated sympathy and support for the anti-colonial movements in the region. He criticized the idea of a collective trusteeship on the following basis:

> I presume the idea is to hurdle the legal difficulties and mollify and flatter Latin-American sensibilities. I have a suspicion that many Latins

Alternative Strategies for Self-Government   225

> will fall for the plan since it will make them appear important and equals of the U.S.A. There is where the danger lies, I think. The Latins, falling under American propaganda, may feel that because the majority of our people are colored we are unfit to assume the role of a self-governed people.[88]

Race discrimination and feelings of superiority, Domingo feared, would slow down the march toward independence. While accepting the US as a real superpower, Domingo refused to accept that the islands should come under the rule of Latin American countries, which he believed were not authorized to shape the destiny of the Caribbean people. In a condescending manner, he claimed in a letter to Roberts that Jamaica was not backwards, compared to most Latin American countries: '...it will be an insult and an injustice to place our country under a trusteeship made up of people not our superiors, and in some cases, not our equals in civilized developments'.[89] This statement exemplifies a dangerous tendency in nationalist approaches; the tendency to super-elevate one's own culture in comparison with others. This argument was accompanied by a strong Western civilizing model of progress. Such a view stood in contrast to Roberts' fascination for the Latin American republics.

Although Domingo rejected the trusteeship idea, he looked forward to the Havana Conference, which offered a completely new platform to place the demand for self-government before an international audience. Domingo felt that timing and circumstances were favourable for a solution granting self-government, because the interests of the islands coincided with those of the US:

> ...the U.S. can avoid offending anti-imperialist sentiment here, meet the objection of those who don't want more Negroes under the flag, legally obtain needed air bases etc., by aiding our movement for autonomy. If that can be impressed upon those in authority, then there should be comparatively easy sailing now for England needs America at this crucial moment.[90]

To place their demands before the conference, Roberts and Domingo decided that the WINEC should send an unofficial delegate to present the two declarations at the conference, one on the principal right to self-government and the other on the fitness of the islands to decide about the region's destiny. Domingo believed that neither Roberts nor the WINEC's declaration could offend anyone, as both documents carefully avoided suspicious and revolutionary anti-British passages. In correspondence to Roberts he wrote:

> ...they say in effect, if England wins the political status quo remains. If, though, America sincerely desires to control the Caribbean area for strategic reasons against even a victorious England then we are giving her an excuse for supporting us since we promised to work with her in defending the continent.[91]

The basic idea was to take advantage of the specific military and economic interests of the US, so that the superpower – in its own interest – would become a catalyst in the anti-colonial struggle. The strategy rested on the observation that the US had acknowledged strong national movements in countries like Cuba, the Philippines and Panama. Likewise, Domingo hoped that the US would consider strong nationalist demands in the considerations about the Caribbean's future.[92] Therefore, the WINEC delegate should also hand out the memorandum which Brown had presented to the Royal Commission to prove that the movement for self-government antedated the current critical international crisis.[93]

After the strategy was agreed upon, a suitable delegate needed to be chosen. Roberts advised Domingo to be very careful: '…No communists, for God's sake! Yourself or O'Meally would be ideal'.[94] Domingo promised to choose a man without Communist leanings and finally the young attorney Hope Stevens from Nevis[95] was selected for the task.[96]

Before Stevens went to Cuba, the WINEC organized a public meeting to raise funds for the passage, at which US$150 was collected. Domingo complained that Malliet, who had withdrawn his support for the WINEC, had given the meeting no publicity in the *New York Amsterdam News*.[97] Malliet remains a dubious figure and his role in the nationalist movement in the exile milieu in New York is not entirely clear. Malliet had resigned from the WINEC as suddenly as he had from the Progressive League. At first, he was fully involved in setting up the organization, only to silently disappear from the scene after its inception. It is possible that the leftist leanings of some individuals in both organizations had alienated him.[98]

Domingo tried to avoid spreading any open anti-British propaganda at the meeting. He successfully intervened after the first two speeches contained strong anti-British connotations. No speaker made Communist remarks, Domingo assured Roberts.[99] The night before the conference, the WINEC staged a second huge mass meeting, attended by more than 2,000 people and at which Hope Stevens gave a speech before he went to Havana on July 21, 1940.[100]

At the beginning of the conference, US Secretary of State Cordell Hull outlined the proposed strategy in regard to the threat that the European war would reach America's shores. He proposed that in case of a British defeat, the American republics would take the European colonies under a collective trusteeship:

> …we have no desire to absorb those possessions or to extent our sovereignty over them, or to include them in any form or sphere of influence. We could not, however, permit these regions to become a subject of barter in the settlement of European differences, or a battleground for the adjustment of such differences.[101]

Hull suggested the establishment of a 'collective trusteeship, to be exercised in the name of all American republics'. Such a trusteeship should end 'as soon as conditions permit'. Further, 'the reign should be restored to its original sovereign or be declared independent when able to establish and maintain stable self-government'. This proposal for a trusteeship, although admitting the possibility of self-government eventually, was not what the WINEC and the Progressive League had hoped for.

It was now Hope Stevens's task to distribute the declarations among the delegates and to convince them to oppose the US proposal. It was particularly Roberts' Jamaica declaration that came to the attention of some of the Latin American delegates, notably, Leopoldo Melo from Argentina. He was impressed by the documents and saw the chance to use the statements to criticize the US approach in order to demonstrate the power of the Latin American republics. According to Roberts, Melo reported to his government that the proposal, '...would wound the sentiments of certain units as cultured as, for example, Jamaica'.[102] Accordingly, the Argentine delegation drafted a protest note that opposed the idea of an imposed trusteeship. The *New York Times* reported: 'The Argentine draft called attention to the position of Jamaica, a British colony, which has already gone on record that it can attend to its own affairs without Pan-American resistance'.[103] This was certainly a considerable success for the strategists of the Progressive League.

Hull was quick to vouchsafe that no serious disagreement between the US and other delegations existed, although this was a partial truth.[104] However, Melo failed to find support for his position, and the US proposal was eventually accepted.[105] Nevertheless, important changes were made in the final Act of Havana that differed in some crucial points from Hull's original proposal. The phrase 'trusteeship' was replaced by 'provisional administration' and it was added that 'such territories shall either be organized into autonomous territories, should they appear capable of constituting or maintaining themselves in such a state, or be reinstated to the former situation'.[106] This small but remarkable victory for the WINEC and the Progressive League at least offered the potential that the politically advanced colonies would be transformed into independent units in case of a British defeat.

Both groups got some exposure after the conference. Melo published a report in Spanish in which he detailed Hull's proposal before and after the Argentine delegation's intervention, quoting from the Jamaica declaration, and explicitly complimenting the Progressive League and the WINEC for their contributions.[107] Domingo welcomed the changes in the Act and felt the agitation from New York was responsible for the 'democratic nature of the act insofar as the rights of West Indians go'.[108]

Domingo and the Board of Directors of the Progressive League decided to thank Melo officially and to encourage him to continue lending his support in the fight for self-government. At the same time, Domingo was aware that Melo's actions were not fully disinterested: 'he did so not so much to help us but to block American hegemony over the islands and to promote Latin American interests in opposition to those of the Colossus of the North'.[109]

Melo felt flattered by the praises of the WINEC and promised Domingo that he could,

> ...rest assured that I will continue working with all my strength in favour of the achievement of these ideas and purposes, and you may count me among those who are fighting for the realization of the ideals which the West Indies National Emergency Committee is defending so courageously.[110]

Melo wrote a similar letter to the Progressive League in which he stated his appreciation of their memorandum and reported that the representation had impacted the final version of the Act of Havana, which now acknowledged the right of the politically advanced to determine their own future.[111]

Despite this small diplomatic success, the WINEC was not satisfied with the outcome. In a document signed by Ivy Bailey-Essien and H.P. Osborne, the WINEC criticized the statement and articulated disappointment that the colonies might possibly return to the European colonial powers.[112] Nevertheless, Domingo felt the formation of the WINEC and the representation at Havana was a first step in the right direction. He was convinced that without Roberts' foresight and his own 'seizing the psychological moment to form the Committee nothing would have been done and America would have been able, if the necessity arose, to impose her will upon us without the slightest consideration for our wishes'.[113]

The Havana declaration is often interpreted as a reaffirmation of the Monroe doctrine.[114] Indeed, the policy objected to tolerating more European colonies in the Pan-American hemisphere, albeit implicitly accepting the existing possessions and promising non-interference as long as hemispheric interests were not threatened. Ken Post judges that the Act should rather be interpreted as a precursor to the changes which would follow the Second World War on the macro-political level: 'More than giving the peoples in the Caribbean a voice in their own affairs, the Act of Havana demonstrated the new influence of the US in the Caribbean and reflected the powershift of the British Empire in favour of the new western superpower'.[115]

Jason Parker called the Havana declaration an 'implicit acknowledgement of imperial weakness' that 'offered activists a potential weapon against the British, and was an opening through which the longer-term question of Caribbean freedom might be raised before the world'.[116] Parker's view is congruent with the

Alternative Strategies for Self-Government 229

self-assessment of the protagonists. The tiny diplomatic victory in changing the tone of the document towards the direction of self-determination of the islands allowed Roberts and Domingo to pursue their strategy. Although they originally had hoped for more, they decided to make the best use out of it.

Roberts lauded their successful efforts and the subsequent support of the Argentine delegation and reckoned that without this impact the Act of Havana would not have principally acknowledged the colonies' right to self-determination and the islands might even have been annexed. Now, their voices had at least been heard on the international floor.[117]

Post supports Roberts' view and underlines the impact of the Caribbean activists. 'Jamaica thus suddenly leaped into prominence in Havana, and this represented a notable propaganda coup for the expatriates in New York, who had thus managed to project their view, and that of the PNP, as the opinion of the whole island'.[118] Roberts circulated the outcome among his diplomatic contacts in Washington. The fact that a principal right of the colonies to determine their own future had been acknowledged by the nations that gathered in Havana would provide a 'strong point of departure'.[119] Roberts declared that '[f]rom now on, we can argue our case with the certainty of being heard by the American foreign offices'.[120] While Roberts probably overstated the impact on the foreign offices, the Act of Havana was certainly a strong push for the decolonization movement in New York as well as in Jamaica.

In the case of a British defeat, Roberts advised that Jamaica should promptly declare its independence. According to the Havana declaration, a commission would then investigate the fitness for autonomy. Therefore, Roberts urged, the leaders of the PNP in Jamaica had to be convinced to work out a Jamaican Declaration of Independence. He expected that,

> ...an unbiased inquiry by the commission would show that there are Jamaican leaders perfectly capable of forming a stable Government, and we might be able to get the point conceded at a stroke. With the possible exception of Trinidad, no other British West Indian unit could hope to do so. We must not fumble the opportunity, if it arises.[121]

To be prepared, the Act of Havana had to be circulated as widely as possible in the US, in the Caribbean and especially in Jamaica. Roberts believed that Jamaicans were beginning to lose confidence in the Empire and that the time was ripe to stir 'definite anti-British sentiment'.[122] Roberts was convinced that 'Jamaica's future is not with England, but in the Pan-American combination, as an independent or semi-independent country. This always has been inevitable'.[123] Roberts' comment exemplified his strong regional perspective. It is remarkable that he even considered the possibility that Jamaica could be a 'semi-dependent' country within that framework, although he did not expound further on what he meant by the phrase. He wrote Domingo:

> Jamaica stands to gain by the defeat of England, whereas victory for the latter would serve to hold us in political bondage. It is time for the leaders to admit this and shape policies accordingly....We must gamble everything on obtaining liberty under the principles laid down in the Act of Havana.[124]

This letter made it perfectly clear, how much Roberts was radicalized by the turn of events, and he employed even more radical arguments than Domingo, who had always stressed that British victory would still be desirable.

Domingo's judgment of the Act of Havana was ambivalent. Although he criticized aspects of it, especially the right to extend the trusteeship period, he also valued the outcome and lauded the work of the young and still inexperienced WINEC:

> Of course, I know that when our utter unpreparedness is considered and our real strength is realized, it must be conceded we accomplished a great deal in forcing, through skillful timing, publicity, and maneuvering, Cordell Hull of Tennessee to concede to colored peoples in the West Indies the fundamental right of self-government.[125]

Despite its shortcomings, Domingo agreed with Roberts that the Act of Havana could become the 'Magna Charta of our future should England be beaten'.[126] Domingo was proud that 'at one stroke, and without shedding a drop of blood, the peoples of the West Indies have been guaranteed more rights than they now enjoy. Of course, everything depends on the result of the war'.[127]

In his frequent letters to his friend M.L. Campbell in Jamaica, former fellow companion in the Harlem circles, Domingo communicated the outcome of the conference as a victory and a great success.[128] After the first disappointment directly after the conference, Domingo became more appreciative. In the middle of August, 1940, he declared:

> ...the more I read the Act the more I am convinced that if put in operation, despite its obvious flaws, our status would be immeasurably better than the present one, not overlooking the fact that the Act implicitly recognizes our right to independence. Maybe I am over enthusiastic and have read into the Act things that are not in it, but even if England wins we can use it to show Jamaicans just what Americans think we are deserving of now.[129]

Domingo was convinced that the document would be an inspiration and a stimulant to self-government. In a letter to Campbell, he expressed confidence that Jamaicans at home would soon see the value of the Havana Conference and appreciate the service of the migrants in New York in securing the freedom of the islands in case of a British defeat.[130]

Alternative Strategies for Self-Government 231

More important than the diplomatic victory was the publicity for the demand for self-government. Domingo actively promoted the outcome and aimed to attract the solidarity of African Americans. He approached other organizations, for example the NAACP, to ask for their support for the cause of freedom for the colonies. He wrote to NAACP Secretary Walter White, sent him material on the Act of Havana, the PNP and on the WINEC, and underlined not only the international dimension of the freedom struggle of the colonies in Caribbean, but also the historical significance:

> I think it safe to say that this is the first time in the history of the Western World since the Haitian Revolution that a group of Negroes, without the backing of a state, succeeded in influencing an international gathering along the lines they desired. The fact and its logical consequence, the possibility of creating new black nations in the Caribbean should be of the highest significance to American Negroes, especially with Fascism looming over the United States.[131]

Many African Americans and fellow Caribbeans shared Domingo's enthusiastic perception and emphasized the anti-colonial implication the coup had for other movements. The *New York Amsterdam News* carried a lengthy article about the Havana Conference and called the WINEC declaration a 'historical document' which was 'said to be one of the most straightforward and significant state papers ever drafted by West Indians'.[132] Numerous leading black public figures expressed their sympathy and support. For example, George Padmore commended the WINEC on its work in a letter to the editor of the *New York Amsterdam News* and suggested that further actions should be directed toward building an autonomous federation of British and French West Indian islands and recommended seeking US support in return of the granting of bases.[133] Adam Clayton Powell Jr expressed his appreciation of the WINEC and its efforts toward self-government for the peoples of the Caribbean. He suggested that the WINEC should internationalize its efforts and organize a world conference of colonial peoples:

> I cannot fail to see the importance of this struggle to the complete freedom of all the Negro peoples everywhere. Greater unity is the need of the hour between American Negroes and the West Indians, and among all the darker peoples of the globe who are battling for independence and the right to share equally in the world wealth and culture.[134]

Other prominent African Americans like Max Yergan, Prof. Charles Houston, former Dean of Howard Law School, and Prof. Charles Wesley, Dean of the History Department at Howard University, also expressed their appreciation.[135] Furthermore, a few reports and letters in the Cuban Press had been very favourable toward the Progressive League expressing their sympathy with the demand for self-determination of the neighbouring islands.[136]

However, instead of putting emphasis on the international dimension of the colonial question, Domingo and Roberts seized the moment to approach officials in the US to stress Jamaica's claims.[137] Domingo directly approached Roosevelt and sent him a copy of the WINEC Declaration and suggested:

> ...history had presented him [Roosevelt] with the opportunity to complete the work begun by George Washington, forwarded by Toussaint L'Ouverture and greatly extended by Simon Bolivar by freeing the remaining remnants of European domination in this hemisphere.[138]

These statements illustrate not only the effect of the Act of Havana in African American circles, but also the radicalization of Domingo and Roberts' stance toward Great Britain. From the demand of self-government within the framework of the British Empire, the claim had now changed to independent nationhood within the Pan-American hemisphere.

Despite the ideological success, the WINEC faced financial difficulties.[139] Domingo suspected that Malliet had been instrumental in not giving the fundraising meetings enough publicity. 'Malliet occupies the position of "guardian of the gate" on that paper and he is a very pity and spiteful individual, as you doubtless know'.[140] In a letter to Roberts, he affirmed that Malliet withdrew his support because of the left wing tendencies and suspected he became alienated because he was not given the prominence he felt he deserved.[141] Despite a successful welcome meeting for Stevens,[142] Domingo was disheartened by the lack of support and unsure if his original decision to transfer the emergency committee into a permanent council would be worthwhile.[143] Domingo reflected on the inertia of large sections of West Indians in New York:

> The local professionals of West Indian origin, with a few honorable exceptions, are either the biggest jackasses politically or they are so ignorant and self-centered that I despair at ever penetrating the thick shell of indifference with which they surround themselves.[144]

Reverberations in Jamaica

After the Havana Conference, Domingo and Roberts shifted their focus back to Jamaica. Already in early August 1940, Domingo declared that he would now exclusively devote his energies to Jamaica. He assured Roberts: 'my whole program is one of back to the J.P.L.'[145] This decision reflected Domingo and Roberts' priority on the decolonization of Jamaica, but it also was a reaction to the lack of support from the Caribbean community in Harlem. Domingo decided to eventually 'let the Committee fade away, since the few of us carrying the burden cannot continue to do so any longer without the support of the masses'.[146]

Alternative Strategies for Self-Government   233

In October, Domingo stated: 'The Council is marking time and seemingly dying from financial strangulation'.[147] However, he was still willing to 'keep its skeleton going in order to be prepared to meet any new crisis'.[148] These statements once more exemplify the gap between the intellectuals and the masses that were not prepared to engage in radical anti-colonial agitation.

In this situation, Roberts emphasized the need for more agitation and clarification about the dangers ahead and advised Domingo to convince fellow Jamaicans to develop a fund for the case of a British defeat.[149] Roberts believed that the time for a decision was near and expected 'our fate as a people will be in the balance very, very soon'.[150] Domingo fully agreed with Roberts and was able to report that the Progressive League had successfully started to raise funds.[151]

The next important step was to wake the political leaders in Jamaica from their apathy. Roberts and Domingo hoped that the Progressive League in Kingston would be helpful in popularizing the merits of the Havana Conference in Jamaica, where the conference did not yet have great publicity. Roberts believed that strong propaganda was now a necessity:

> The League should press the point home at every opportunity, for some day – perhaps sooner than we realize – the real leaders of the League are going to be called upon to take part in the forming of a Jamaican Government.[152]

While the Progressive League in New York tried to prepare for assuming responsibility in the case of a British defeat, the local branch in Jamaica once more failed to implement the strategy of the Progressive League in New York. Shortly before the Havana Conference, the following statement appeared in the *Gleaner*:

> From the League's – not the organization which exists in New York and whose affairs are directed by a directorate – viewpoint, it is desirable that Jamaica should strive to become a province of the Dominion of Canada, to be governed from Ottawa, and with representation in the Dominion parliament.[153]

The local branch even questioned Jamaica's fitness for self-government openly when it commented: '…realising the impracticability of any small nation standing isolated, the League desires that this island be granted the status of a federal state of the Dominion of Canada'.[154] This position stood in stark contrast with the position of the Progressive League in New York. Of course, conservative elements in Jamaica were happy that the local Progressive League had stopped its agitation for self-government and substituted it with a demand for attachment to Canada.[155]

Roberts had already rejected attachment to Canada when de Lisser came up with the idea in June 1940. When de Lisser went to Canada on a special mission to sound out possibilities of a potential annexation, Roberts saw the trip as proof to the seriousness of the situation. De Lisser 'has a good deal of political sophistication, and he will certainly not let the future go by default, as other prominent Jamaicans are inclined to do',[156] Roberts commented. However, he strongly opposed annexation by Canada and believed that Jamaica's situation would be even worse than as an English colony.

Upon hearing about the proposals of the local branch, Domingo suggested writing to McFarlane strongly disapproving the step.[157] Roberts sent a letter forthwith to McFarlane stating that his idea was an unrealistic dream and that he did not see any chance that Jamaica's status could be anything more than that of a colony of Canada, to which he was firmly opposed.[158] In the name of the Progressive League in New York, Brown also wrote a letter to McFarlane in which he explained why a strong demand for self-government was considered to be the appropriate strategy at this crucial point in time. He asked McFarlane to consider the approach of the WINEC and requested that the local Progressive League should in the meantime abstain from any further action.[159]

The letters of the Progressive League in New York had the desired results. On September 2, 1940, the local Progressive League issued a statement in the *Gleaner* in which it withdrew its desire for annexation to Canada and pledged to continue to fight for self-government for the island.[160] Right after the local division returned to a policy that was in congruence with the Progressive League in New York, it tried to adorn itself with borrowed plumes, boasting of the results from the Havana Conference as if it was by their own merit. Quite simply, they had overlooked the fact they had recently demanded annexation with Canada while Domingo and Roberts had worked on the conference and on getting publicity for its results.

Without recognizing the logical break in strategy, an article in the *Gleaner* went so far as to claim that the founding of the WINEC was inspired by the Canada-resolution of the local branch.[161] It seems as if the reporter had been deliberately misinformed in a way that the uninformed public must have believed all action was inspired by the local arm of the Progressive League and only carried out by the Progressive League in New York. In a letter to *Public Opinion*, McFarlane even quoted from a letter that Melo had addressed to him:

> As a result of our activities and the far-reaching effect of such foresight and thought, the following letter was received by me from the representative of the Argentine Delegation: "Leopoldo Celo [sic!] presents his compliments to the Jamaica Progressive League, representing the noble Jamaican people, and takes pleasure to establish in the proposals presented by the Argentine Delegation, its due Rights to freely decide its future destiny."[162]

Alternative Strategies for Self-Government 235

Believing that unity existed between the two branches, Melo had indeed addressed a letter to the local branch to express his appreciation.¹⁶³ He could not know that McFarlane and the local branch of the Progressive League were on a completely contrary course during these months when Domingo, Roberts and even the Argentine delegation were vigorously struggling to present the claim for self-government to an international audience.

This episode marked another chapter in the history of the local branch's veering between different courses toward the goal of self-government. We see again how McFarlane often claimed others' merits to be his own, and the inaccuracy with which he presented historical facts, always in a direction that put him in a positive light. It is quite possible that Domingo was right in his speculation about the reasons for McFarlane's decision to abandon the Canada plans and to resume his original stance: 'I suppose he feels flattered by Melo's praise although he knows full well that it was intended for us over here'.¹⁶⁴ Roberts and Domingo were disgusted by the indecisive stand of the Progressive League in Kingston and by McFarlane's dishonesty in particular. In a letter to Roberts, Domingo ranted:

> They are such spineless asses. They say it is impracticable for a small nation to stand alone. I wrote McFarlane a personal letter on the matter pointing out that the 21 American countries do not think Jamaica too small to stand alone since provision is made for exactly that circumstance in the Act of Havana.¹⁶⁵

In another letter, Domingo called the officers of the Kingston branch a 'stupid lot'.¹⁶⁶ Roberts shared Domingo's aversion and called them 'a collection of numbskulls and weaklings'. 'When we return to Jamaica, I think we shall be compelled to shove them aside and found a new organization'.¹⁶⁷

In general, the reactions to the Act of Havana in Jamaica were mixed. According to Domingo, the *Gleaner* '...ignored our work and the Act of Havana except to state that Jamaica's interest in the conference was academic'.¹⁶⁸ The *Gleaner* indeed tried to play down the relevance of the Act and affirmed Jamaica's loyalty to Britain, claiming that no one in Jamaica would even wish to separate its ties from the mother country.¹⁶⁹ In a letter to Campbell, Domingo stated plainly: 'If England loses, the Act of Havana will be applied and not all the DeLissers in the world can alter its clauses'.¹⁷⁰

Domingo felt that too many of his compatriots in Jamaica as well in New York remained overconfident of a British victory. Domingo harshly condemned such an attitude as 'blind unreasoning loyalty or wishful thinking'.¹⁷¹ To popularize the Act in Jamaica, Domingo published an article in *Public Opinion* in August 1940, in which he encouraged all Jamaicans to get familiar with its content and to compare it with the original proposal from Hull:

> If England wins, as I hope she will, then we can forget all about the Havana Conference and resume our fight for self-government within the British Empire, but if she loses, the Agreement will be of supreme importance to the people of the West Indies and only then will they be able to appreciate the value of the work done by the Committee.[172]

While the *Gleaner* tried to belittle the achievements of the WINEC at the conference in Havana, the events had a very significant effect on the course of the PNP, which decided to resume its political activities upon realizing the significance of Roberts and Domingo's activities. Before the Havana Conference, the two leaders of the Progressive League were disappointed by Manley's inactivity in Jamaica. Nevertheless, they could not help but put all hope in him. A few days before the conference Domingo wrote to Roberts: 'I wonder what Manley is doing now? He is the only man out there with the vision, courage, and patriotism to act along our lines now; besides, he has the training and ability. The others cannot be trusted'.[173]

Domingo and Roberts frequently updated Manley on their activities in New York, the conference in Havana and their concerns about the turn of events. Eventually, Manley was so inspired that he decided to redirect the course of the PNP. A few days before the conference at Havana, Manley contacted Domingo to inform the Progressive League that he and the party had now also started to doubt the military success of England and made preparations for a possible British defeat by resuming its policy of advocating Socialism and self-government.[174] Manley expressed his appreciation for the work done by the WINEC and the Progressive League, which he had followed 'with great interest'.[175] Manley promised that after a stiff, slow year for the party, he would now discuss the achievements of the WINEC at the upcoming annual Party conference and propose a shift in policy.[176]

Domingo immediately seized the opportunity and prepared an open letter on behalf of the WINEC to the delegates of the PNP. In this letter, Domingo encouraged the party to continue its efforts in Jamaica in a similar spirit as the WINEC in New York.[177] During the PNP conference in September 1940, Manley referred to the Act of Havana, encouraging the delegates to fight against any form of trusteeship and to resume the fight for self-government. After the conference, PNP Secretary V.L. Arnett informed the WINEC that a resolution was resolved that expressed 'deep appreciation of the services rendered by the progressive movement in the colonies particularly in regard to their national aspirations, by the West Indies National Emergency Committee and further declares its entire agreement with the policies outlined and the steps taken by them'.[178]

The resolution sheds light on the significant influence of Roberts and Domingo. The following *Gleaner* report about the conference proceedings exemplifies how much the agitation at the Havana Conference now influenced the position of the PNP:

> It is therefore the duty of the party to resume its propagation of the idea of self-government...where any colonial territory loses its connection with the European country to which it belongs it should claim the right relative to American interest to be treated as independent and consulted in any arrangement that may be made in regard to its future politically or economically and that all such arrangements should derive force from freely negotiated agreements.[179]

For Manley, the return to a declared demand for self-government was also a prerequisite for the new economic policy of the party, which now declared to be Socialist: 'It is self-evident...that one cannot develop any true Socialist policy without having local autonomy'.[180] Manley felt that the new PNP policy was in line with that of Great Britain. Work for self-government, so Manley, was not in contradiction with the interests of the British Empire,

> ...since it is the declared aim of the British Empire to secure self-government for its constituent elements and it is the aim of the Labour Party which now shares in the government of England to create a SOCIALIST society after the war.[181]

Manley made the point that 'Self-Government should mean complete local legislative executive control embracing financial and economic matters'.[182] However, the way Manley defined 'Self-Government' could also apply to internal self-government. Nevertheless, Manley wrote a letter to Domingo in September 1940, in which he claimed that the policies of the WINEC and the PNP were basically the same:

> Please convey to the Committee my sincere appreciation and the sincere appreciation of the party for their magnificent work. We pledge ourselves to continued cooperation and whatever can be done on our end we will do. So far I can definitely state that in regard to all matters that have arisen we see almost exactly eye to eye with the Committee.[183]

Additionally, the PNP had begun to prepare a memorandum to the Governor and the Elected Members Association and planned to utilize the Act of Havana for its propaganda.[184] Moreover, the PNP restarted to convene public meetings discussing the issue of self-government, for example, one meeting in cooperation with the local branch of the Progressive League featuring several renowned speakers.[185]

In *Public Opinion*, the work of the WINEC in Havana was also enthusiastically praised.[186] Domingo commented: 'The editorial very closely associated the P.N.P. with the work we did from here. I don't mind it'.[187] The same issue featured an extract of the Jamaica Declaration by Roberts.[188] In a lengthy review in *Public*

Opinion, Manley lauded the WINEC and congratulated the 'far-sighted and loyal West Indians'[189] for having been the only British Caribbean representation at the conference. Manley congratulated the migrants for successfully pressing for adjustments to the Act that now acknowledged the right to self-determination of the islands in principle, as well as the existence of democratic forces and nationalist movements. Manley concluded with a strong urge to resume the agitation for self-government, self-determination, a truly Jamaican civil service and the right to free economic development and trade in the interest of Jamaica – and not in the interest of Great Britain.[190] All these demands were original claims of the Progressive League expressed in its declaration from 1936. The PNP was obviously back on track.

Domingo was glad about the turn in PNP policy and satisfied that Manley 'has acted quickly on the suggestions I sent him through our Committee to use the terms of the Act and the Convention as dynamite to press home the demand for self-government....'[191] Domingo felt that PNP leaders were now more convinced of self-government and credited that change of mentality to the propaganda of Roberts and himself.[192]

Domingo wholeheartedly endorsed the policy outlined in the PNP pamphlet 'Plan for Today', including the adoption of Socialism; 'Personally I agree with you that socialism is the only base on which to work for the betterment of our people. Capitalism offers them no future'.[193] In various letters to Manley and PNP Secretary Arnett, Domingo commended the party on the new policy and the return to the fight for self-government.[194] Domingo wrote to Roberts:

> One thing you and I did when we were in Jamaica and that was to wake up even the leaders to the necessity for demanding self-government. Today they emphasize that point. The Plan begins and ends on that dominant note.[195]

Domingo valued Manley's new emphasis on nationalism and was pleased about the PNP's approval of the WINEC's work.[196] It was not only important for the continuation of the struggle in Jamaica, but also to silence sceptics in the migrant community in New York.

> We are using that to prove to the Doubting Thomases among us (and they are legion) that our effort was not actuated by disloyalty, but by the highest patriotism and that it has received approval from Jamaica, as instanced by Arnett's letter and the attitude of P.O.[197]

The statement shows that even many Jamaicans abroad regarded the continuation of the campaign for self-government during the war as disloyal. Roberts felt relieved that the PNP had finally begun to make preparations for a possible British defeat by resuming its fight for self-government.[198] The PNP's

Alternative Strategies for Self-Government 239

appreciation of Roberts and Domingo's unflinching work during the war and the redirection of the PNP policy provided a new basis for close cooperation.

Shifting the Focus Back to Jamaica: Continued Influence on the PNP

After the PNP returned to a nationalist and explicitly anti-colonial course, the leaders of the Progressive League readily shifted their attention back to Jamaica. Domingo and Roberts were pleased that their efforts to influence the PNP, their numerous letters to Norman and Edna Manley, had finally fallen on fertile ground. In this time of renewed close cooperation, Domingo and Roberts could exercise a great deal of influence on Manley and the PNP, for example, in regard to the concern about US bases on the island.

At this time, Edna and Norman Manley started to beg Roberts and Domingo to return to the island to give the movement a well-needed push. These requests coincided with tactical considerations by Domingo and Roberts as to whether one of them should return to Jamaica during the war to launch an energetic campaign for self-government. The developments of the war forced them to come up with creative ideas and new strategies.

After the Havana Conference, bad news from Europe continued to dominate the headlines. The French colonies had fallen under the Vichy government and posed a vital threat to the security of the hemisphere. The Italian entry into the war in June 1940 and the successful continuation of the German 'Blitzkrieg' aggravated the situation. Great Britain's industrial centres were under heavy attack from the air and expected naval attacks made the fortification of the British coast necessary. When German U-boats started to trouble Caribbean waters, it became obvious that Great Britain was no longer able to grant the security of the hemisphere and its colonial possession, and US military strategists reinforced their plans to erect military bases.[199] Earlier efforts to acquire bases in the Caribbean antedated the occasion and first agreements had been signed even before the outbreak of war. Eventually, the so-called bases-for-destroyers deal was officially signed on September 2, 1940, and granted the US the right to establish eight military naval and air bases on British transatlantic territory in exchange for a handful of old destroyers from the era of the First World War.[200] The agreement was generally interpreted as a sign of weakness of Great Britain and an approval of the Havana declaration. According to historian Denis Benn, it reflected the fact that the Caribbean had become 'the focus of joint Anglo-American defense strategies'.[201]

Domingo interpreted the bases-for-destroyers deal as a sign of Britain's weakness and believed:

> The Blitz that Hitler unleashed upon England yesterday should cause our chronic optimists to revise their opinions as to the possibility of a British defeat. Churchill coolly proposes to give American naval bases in any part of the West Indies in exchange for a few old destroyers. That shows England's position is serious.[202]

Domingo still called Great Britain, 'the lesser of the two evils',[203] and hoped that it would not be defeated. However, he was prepared to make use of Britain's weakness to lobby for Jamaica's quest for self-government. When Domingo heard of a statement made by Churchill stressing the fact that the bases were granted voluntarily and acknowledging that any shift of sovereignty would only be possible with the consent of the colonies, he felt this position was a result of the Havana declaration.[204] In a letter to Manley, Domingo emphasized that this was the first time that the will of colonial peoples was acknowledged by a British Prime Minister. He suggested the time was ripe for diplomatic activity to press for the right to self-determination of the colonies.[205]

Domingo charged that the lease of island property without the consent of the population in the colonies could be interpreted as a violation of the Act of Havana. Similar to the strategy at the conference, he tried to arouse concern among the Latin American countries regarding the unilateral activities of the US regarding the bases. Domingo suggested sending a statement to the various foreign offices, claiming that the bilateral negotiations between Great Britain and the US would be 'a betrayal of the spirit of the conference'.[206] Domingo asserted that the turn of events revealed that Great Britain's avowal of fighting a war for democracy was merely lip-service if the colonies were allowed to be ruled by autocratic governors with emergency powers, and were not given the right to determine their own future, nor were consulted in long-time lease agreements for military bases.[207]

With such arguments, Domingo secured the support of civil rights organizations in the US, for example the Women's International League for Progress and Freedom (WILPF), which had excellent contacts to diplomatic circles in Washington. The WILPF made a representation to President Franklin D. Roosevelt and argued along the suggested line that the granting of bases would be a violation of the Act of Havana.[208]

Just after the bases deal became public, Domingo wondered how Jamaicans would react. His comments show that he did not expect much from his countrymen:

> I know how dead they are above their shoulders, but they should realize that England is thinking of herself first and will sacrifice every colony and disregard the basic rights of the people in order to save herself. I do wish our people would think of themselves first, last and all the time, but that would be expecting them to really think. If they

Alternative Strategies for Self-Government

try to think they would probably have hemorrhage of the brain or what passes for their brains.[209]

Domingo's strong contempt for the lack of nationalism as well as the frustration over the restrained attitude of his countrymen in Jamaica is markedly exhibited in that statement.

Domingo wrote a letter to the PNP, in which he listed points that needed to be safeguarded to protect the population from negative impacts resulting from any future US base. He insisted on the need to continue the fight for self-government with full power and encouraged the PNP to try to arouse public protest in Jamaica.[210] In an open letter to the PNP, Domingo pointed to the examples of Newfoundland and India, which had been consulted in the question of granting bases to the US, whereas the inhabitants of the possession in the Caribbean had been left out in the negotiations. In a letter to Manley, Domingo suggested that local groups should agitate for the building of a committee to influence the regulations on the bases and to demand that black Jamaicans from local political organizations should be included in the negotiations.[211]

Even months before the bases deal was solicited, Domingo had tried to encourage Jamaicans to become involved in the discussions about land leases to the US by organizing a plebiscite. That, he suggested, would have allowed them to bargain with the US and demand control of their destiny, in harmony with US interests.[212]

In an open letter to the delegates of the annual PNP conference, Domingo resumed his arguments and concerns regarding the bases and its possible negative impacts on Jamaica.[213] He offered numerous suggestions as to what Jamaica should demand, including a law that would prohibit US forces from entering the country with firearms, soldiers would underlie local laws and customs when leaving the bases, and that the import of labourers be limited to skilled labourers unavailable in Jamaica. In regard to practices in the Panama Canal Zone, he demanded that racial discrimination should explicitly be interdicted. These demands should be made publicly as to safeguard the implementation of regulations to protect Jamaican citizens against the 'virus of American race prejudice'.[214]

In letters to Manley and PNP Secretary Arnett, Domingo shared his concern about potential discrimination on the bases and stressed that the status of extraterritoriality on the bases must be prevented.[215] The PNP valued the material and prescriptions offered by Domingo. Arnett thanked him and pronounced that it was 'extremely useful [and] provide quite a storehouse for future action'.[216] The party promised to study the lease agreement carefully and to launch the necessary action. Indeed, the PNP took up the advice to make representations to colonial officials, and Arnett was happy that he could inform the WINEC that he had already written to the Colonial Secretary protesting against the bases and requesting Jamaican representation at the negotiations.[217]

The activities of the PNP resulted in a first success when the Governor promised the PNP to ensure the rights of citizens. Still, Domingo made his reservations known in a letter to his friend Campbell:

> So the Governor promised that the points raised by us through the PNP relative to the bases and the people's right will be granted. I prefer to see it before I believe. I don't trust our officials a bit.[218]

In contrast to a widespread favourable attitude toward the establishment of bases in Jamaica, Domingo shared his view with Roberts that any material benefit would only be temporary and short-lived.[219] However, many Jamaicans expected that naval bases in the West Indies would result in influx of capital into the colonies.[220] In general, US observers noted a strong loyalty with Great Britain and its war efforts in the population, but even greater sympathy toward the United States. This sentiment was developed to a degree, that the US officials felt it could be embarrassing for England.[221] The semi-annual report from the US consulate in Kingston testified to the high expectations for material benefit and warned of possible riots resulting from differences between wages on the bases and the local wage level. While noting a general approval of the bases, the report went on to point out that only the PNP, mislead by nationalist sentiment, was the only dissident.[222] Apparently, the propaganda of the Progressive League and the WINEC continued to bear fruit and its influence on the PNP at this time was clearly noticeable.

In New York, Domingo continued to raise awareness of the situation in the West Indies in public lectures and frequent articles.[223] Both, the WINEC and the Progressive League, prepared letters to officials to prevent negative impacts of the erection of bases and to demand representation of the people in the negotiations.[224]

The answers were all general affirmations of official policy. For instance, Cordell Hull, Secretary of State in the Roosevelt Administration, answered declaring that the decision for the bases was conducted in full cooperation with other Latin America countries and in harmony with policies adopted at the hemispheric conferences of Lima, Panama and Havana. He assured that the US intended to attempt the lowest possible degree of interference with local life on the islands and emphasized that the erection of bases would be of economic benefit to the colonies.[225] However, the numerous representations unquestionably helped to raise awareness in official circles that there were various groups testifying to Jamaica's claims for independence. In Domingo's answer to Hull, he firmly stated that he expected that granting of the bases would in turn accelerate the decolonization process:

> The people's involved, knowing full well the perils, sacrifices, and burdens which will inevitably be theirs and finding themselves standing at the outer bastions of the Western World in the defense of democracy are confident that, as a corollary, their own democracy and Self-Government will be speedily realized.[226]

In a letter to Manley, Domingo called Hull's statement a 'trump card', but only if the population would be vigilant and closely observe the impacts of the bases. Still, Domingo was disillusioned regarding the local sentiments:

> If we could only rouse the intelligent middle class of our country to realize that the future of their children and themselves is being decided now, I have no fear at all but that they would courageously demand proper consideration of all their rights, but unfortunately most of them are seemingly under the influence of a strong narcotic. They are fast asleep where their rights are concerned.[227]

In New York, Domingo tried everything to solicit support for Jamaica's claims and approached his contacts from the Harlem days. He contacted the NAACP and suggested arranging concerted action. Domingo demanded that African Americans should join the protest against possible discrimination on the bases and support the Caribbean peoples in their demand for self-government.[228] NAACP Secretary Walter White answered sympathetically and assured Domingo that the NAACP had already tried to find support for the position of the West Indies in Washington.[229] Domingo had also been successful in securing support from the Socialist Party. Norman Thomas pledged: 'I am thoroughly sympathetic with the demand of the West Indian people for self-government and with their immediate protest against segregation etc. in areas occupied by US, military and naval bases'.[230] Domingo further tried to stimulate public discussion with letters to the press in which he warned of Jim Crow practices in areas under US influence.[231]

After a long illness during the winter of 1940, Roberts resumed his public agitation and supported Domingo's efforts with lectures on the possible impact of the bases.[232] This campaign showed that the Progressive League in New York was successful in giving the matter of the bases in the Caribbean some publicity and raising awareness for the claim for independence. As for the Progressive League in Kingston, it was back on track and supporting the leaders in New York and the PNP in their course regarding the bases, after it abandoned its Canada plans. In October 1940, it came to a resolution with exactly the points Domingo had suggested.[233] The renewed solidarity is especially remarkable, as concerns about US bases were rare and a majority of Jamaicans welcomed the idea and expected economic advantages.

In the following months, the PNP and the Progressive League in Kingston joined forces in articulating concerns against the bases and in popularizing the national movement. For instance, Manley was the principal speaker at the annual meeting of the Progressive League in 1941, at which Roberts was re-elected president, despite his prolonged absence.[234] In Manley's speech, a new radicalism was evident when he made a 'clarion call for Jamaicans to unite in an immediate effort for self-government'.[235] He paid glowing tribute to the pioneering work of the Progressive League, and especially to Roberts. Manley reminded the audience that many of the present day progressives had regarded Roberts' idea as 'crazy' when he 'first started speaking on self-government'. He complained that in Jamaica, nobody had been interested in the conference of Havana and lauded the WINEC for filling that gap and representing the interests of Jamaica and the other islands in the Caribbean. Now all political groups must show unity, he charged, because 'only Jamaica matters', and double their effort in demanding self-government.

At this time, Manley clearly valued the Progressive League's persistence in the demands for self-government. The work of Domingo and Roberts in particular incontestably served as an inspiration for the PNP leader and resulted in a reconsideration of the party's political course during the war. Domingo and Roberts were glad that their partners in Jamaica had realigned themselves and the anti-colonial movement clearly picked up speed. Domingo involved the PNP when he suggested a 'major move' to make a direct request for self-government to the British Government. He referred to the example of India, which had made a similar demand before independence was granted for the time after the war. Domingo drafted a similar demand for Jamaica, requesting universal suffrage and other democratic rights after the end of the war. He shared his tactic with Roberts: 'The idea is to put England on the spot. If she makes a satisfactory statement, we win; if she does not, then we will use the fact to expose her to West Indians, the Americas, and the world'.[236]

Domingo encouraged Manley to support this demand.[237] He felt that Jamaica's case as the largest island would be strong enough to be heard in England, especially as the Labour Party now dominated the parliament in Great Britain and suggested arguing along following lines:

> Although fighting a war for democracy for over a year, the British Government has not uttered a word suggesting the introduction of genuinely democratic government in the West Indian colonies. The long loyalty of the inhabitants and their contributions in money and man to England's many wars including the present one, entitles them to definite consideration.[238]

In formulating this strategy inspired by the national movement in India, the strong international influence on Domingo is unmistakable. Since his political

Alternative Strategies for Self-Government

activism in New York, he was always inspired by other international anti-colonial movements and had a great interest in developments on the international tribune.

Triggered by the desperate situation Great Britain was in, rumours frequently surfaced in the US and the Caribbean press during 1940, about a possible transfer of sovereignty of the islands by selling them to the US.[239] In a letter to Campbell, Domingo expressed his frustration about the strong British loyalty in Jamaica and the affirmative attitude of many Jamaicans of being taken over by the US:

> The people in Jamaica are such a dead lot and one cannot hope for much from them. They believe that any and everything the English do is perfect. They are such fools that they are willing to sacrifice themselves for dear old England, even to the point of seeing their country sold (and them with it) to the Americans.[240]

Domingo commenced organizing a massive protest, trying to counter this mentality. He contacted Manley and spurred the PNP to prepare for a firm demand for self-government in that eventuality: 'Better we insist that we assume responsibility for ourselves then for our colored population to be brought under horrors of American Jimcrowism'.[241] In a letter to the party's secretary, he called the prospective sale a 'real estate deal'[242] because it would ignore the wishes of the people and protested against a transfer of sovereignty without their consent. He was emphatic that people shouldn't be 'sold like cattle',[243] suggesting that the PNP resolve a protest resolution and announce Jamaica's right to self-determination.

The West Indies National Emergency Council (WINEC), which had changed its name to West Indies National Council (WINC) after the Havana Conference, joined the protest and published a flyer against ideas of selling the British West Indies.[244] Together with the Progressive League and other organizations, it organized a protest mass meeting.[245] In the above-quoted letter to Roosevelt, Domingo requested a firm statement against any US desire to take over the islands.[246] Notwithstanding the action in New York, Domingo always laboured the point of the need for action in Jamaica itself:

> Blocking any such backstair deal involving the political fate of the peoples of the islands will depend to a large extent on the peoples concerned. If they sleep, then they must not be surprised if they wake up one morning to discover that they have become second-rate Americans without their consent.[247]

When the discussion about selling the West Indies ceased and the US clearly declared that its interests were satisfied with the granting of military bases in the region, Roberts tried to see the benefits of the US presence in the island. He saw a chance to cooperate with the US and influence policymaking in the region. He made reference to the PNP's responsibility:

>...whether she [the US] operates through local parties will depend absolutely on the readiness for responsibility of those parties. Eventually there will be autonomy: in a few years if the PNP and ourselves display intelligent statesmanship; otherwise in a far-distant, unpredictable future.[248]

Roberts demanded that the Progressive League would press for self-government at every occasion and expressed fervent hope that the League leaders would soon play a part in forming a Jamaican government and asserted: 'The more authoritative the propaganda now, the larger the part tomorrow'.[249] This demonstrates how much importance Roberts attached to his own and to Domingo's role. He was not alone in this assessment. Manley also held both men in high regard, which can be seen in his request for them to return to Jamaica in order to aid in the struggle.

In return, Roberts' appreciation for the Manleys is evident in the dedication of his book, *The Caribbean: The Story of Our Sea of Destiny* to them, published in 1940.[250] In the last chapter of this outstanding history of the region, Roberts anticipated the establishment of US military bases in the region. The book was published even before the bases-for-destroyers-deal was solicited, and many reviewers in Jamaica and the US were impressed by Roberts' foresight and the timeliness of his book.[251] Bridget Brereton emphasizes that Roberts' book was one of the first works that pioneered a shift towards a decidedly Caribbean perspective in regional historiography.[252]

In the book, Roberts made observations on the impact of the war on the Caribbean and underlined that the destiny of the islands was at stake. He felt serious changes were about to take place and that even independence had become a tangible possibility. Not surprisingly, Roberts strongly advocated the latter, referring to the already existing nationalist movements pioneered by the Progressive League but existent also in other islands, the Monroe Doctrine, and a statement of Ulysses S. Grant in 1869 that had affirmed the colonies' right to self-government and self-determination.[253] Roberts concluded his book with the following statement:

> One thing is sure: The Caribbean is the Mediterranean of the West and, if the present war reaches the New World, or totalitarianism dominates the Old, the sea's strategic importance will be greater than at any time in the 448 years since the coming of Columbus.[254]

This line of argumentation clearly demonstrates the continuity in Roberts' regional perspective.

Even two editorials in the *Gleaner* were in part sympathetic to the book and accentuated its timeliness, although they criticized Roberts' position in regard to the demand for self-government and disliked the predicaments of the last chapter.[255]

Alternative Strategies for Self-Government

Others acknowledged how the developments had changed the tides of the time. H.P. Jacobs in his review, for instance, underscored that the new ideas of the Progressive League, that had sounded so strange to many Jamaicans who had proudly identified with Great Britain, now appeared in a different light: 'Few British West Indians had ever seriously thought that British world-power could be shaken. The British Empire had seemed to most of them a thing immutable and eternal'.[256] Jacobs explained how they have always seen the mother country as the 'embodiment of moral principles' and 'racial equality'.[257] This widespread mindset was only now starting to become cracked and the faith in an invincible and victorious Great Britain slowly began to vanish.

De Lisser's opinion was that Roberts' book was written from an 'ultra-liberal American point of view', and that the author did not understand the feelings of his countrymen:

> ...we fancy he does not even now realize, after his recent visit to this island, the strong British feeling of Jamaica, a feeling entirely to the credit of the Jamaica people. But on this topic we can not embark at the end of an article which we have intended to be one of high appreciation for what we consider to be the best book that has yet come from the pen of our old friend Adolphe Roberts.[258]

However, in an editorial, he critically commented on Roberts' views on self-government and his neglect of loyalty to Great Britain.[259]

The Manleys were proud and felt honoured by Roberts' dedication. In September 1940, Edna Manley wrote to Roberts: 'Norman is most enthusiastic, genuinely & sincerely impressed'.[260] Norman Manley also expressed his deep appreciation in a letter to Roberts, highlighting the important influence on his own thinking: 'Since I have known you I have found your approach to the things with which I am now concerned a real source of inspiration'.[261] Manley even took up his pen against de Lisser and criticized his review in the *Gleaner*. Manley told Roberts that he had mixed feelings writing the letter of protest because of the friendship between the two men.[262] But the friendship between Roberts and de Lisser was never a reason for them not to openly fight against each other's political views. Manley accused the editor of giving a wrong impression of the book and misunderstanding its aim as political, whereas it was mainly a historical account with a timely analysis of the present situation. He repudiated de Lisser's argument that the book was written from an American perspective and insisted on Roberts' nationalist pioneer role:

> [Roberts] toured Jamaica almost alone and very much misunderstood in a campaign to rouse us out of our unambiguous sloth to the cause of freedom and democracy and its corollary, the demand for self-Government, can hardly be accused even by implication of having forgotten the land of his birth. It is indeed well-known that he plans to

settle here and is willing to devote his time, his talents, and his energies to the cause he has espoused.²⁶³

In turn, Manley accused de Lisser's editorial to be 'obsessed with its own insularity', failing to see the importance of the Caribbean region in the geopolitical hemisphere. Manley then presented an interesting comparison:

> It is as if a history of the Mediterranean were to be criticized on the ground that is was written from the point of view of England, Greece, Italy and Spain and did not appreciate the real feelings vis-a-vis British Imperialism of Gibraltar, Malta, and Cyprus.

This regional approach toward the Caribbean that Manley shared with Roberts was still rare, and overshadowed by historical approaches dominated by the borders of empires. Manley claimed that instead of being bothered by Roberts' speaking out unloved facts, Jamaicans should better be proud of a patriot like Roberts with his sense of love and attachment to his country of birth 'which is unhappily all too rare among her own successful sons, even those who stay at home'. Domingo noted with pleasure that Manley generally came out in support of Roberts and was pleased to see how the PNP leader was 'roasting the editor' and paid 'tribute to you [Roberts] besides actually reviewing the book and putting over some propaganda for self-government'.²⁶⁴

Manley's observations further illuminate the lack of nationalism in Jamaica and shed light on the great impact that Roberts and the Progressive League had on Manley's thinking. Roberts and Domingo's agitation was clearly key among the influences that caused Manley to come out radicalized and in full strength advocating the Progressive League's demand for self-government with even more vigour than before, thus ending the period of silence and despair among the leadership of the PNP during the war.

Manley frequently commended Roberts and Domingo on their achievements and promised that 'we are doing our best to play it up as hard as we can in Jamaica. I have written on it [the Havana Conference] and we are getting out the pamphlet on it'.²⁶⁵ Particularly, the conference at Havana had played a major role in rekindling the PNP's nationalist stance and in invigorating the demand that both men should come back to support the party. At the same time, Domingo and Roberts had come to the conclusion that it would be best if one of them could return to Jamaica to support the PNP in its resumed fight for self-government and the next elections. Shortly after the outbreak of the war, Norman and Edna Manley had expressed their disappointment about Roberts' decision to postpone plans to return to the island. In November 1939, Edna Manley insisted:

> ...you _must_ come back and please persuade Mr. Domingo, that it is now that we are at war, that Jamaica will notice if he turns his back. We miss you so much too.

She complained about the low level of reflection in the Jamaican populace and remarked that the PNP needed Domingo 'more than ever before'.[266]

From this early point, it seems as if the Manleys imagined Domingo as a potential candidate to spearhead the labour movement. Edna Manley shared Roberts' concerns regarding Bustamante's leadership: 'The Union wants to be landslide into other more honest & more capable hands'. She also made clear that Roberts' presence would be equally desirable 'not only for *Public Opinion's* sake, but because it is now that people with your mind and your talent are needed'.

Roberts promised to think about her suggestions and discuss them with Domingo. He agreed that Domingo 'would be the best possible successor to be in the labour movement. That is my opinion, and I think it is what you meant'.[267] However, the dangers of political agitation during the war combined with the disappointment about the initially meek attitude of the PNP to be silent on constitutional matters during the war had caused Domingo and Roberts to feel that they could lend better service to the cause from New York, and hence concentrated on the WINEC and the Havana Conference.

Still, Domingo, a powerful orator with mass appeal, was sorely missed as evidenced in a futile by-election campaign for Nethersole for a seat for Kingston and St Andrew in the Legislative Council in January 1940. It was obvious that while the PNP was attractive to intellectuals, it still lacked appeal to the masses.[268] Another problem became visible during the election campaign – the split of the progressive forces and rivalries between organizations like the PNP, the Progressive League and the Citizen's Associations. During discussions whether one of the Citizen's Associations should nominate its own candidate, the multiple memberships in various organizations of men like Varma and McPherson became a problem and conflict occurred regarding the question of exclusive membership along with a demand for more distinct programmes.

Varma, for instance, was treasurer of the Progressive League in Kingston, president of the FCA,[269] and member of the PNP executive. He was harshly criticized for his support of PNP candidate Nethersole and his recommendation to abstain from nominating another FCA candidate, while a group around E.E.A. Campbell wished to keep more individuality and wanted to nominate Oswald Anderson.[270] At a meeting of the FCA executive, Campbell and others proposed that multiple memberships should be prohibited.[271] Consequently, Campbell disconnected his affiliation with the PNP and came out in strong support for Anderson, who was now nominated as the FCA's candidate.[272] When Nethersole was officially nominated as the PNP's candidate in the by-election, the Progressive League supported his candidacy.[273] However, the problems and rivalries continued and ran across the adopted lines of the organizations and their candidates, despite various claims that there should be no grave disunity between the progressive forces in the country. After Anderson won the election, Domingo encouraged the PNP members not to be too disappointed and concluded that they had done a great job to compete against Campbell and Anderson.[274]

Reflecting on the campaign, Edna Manley complained in another letter to Roberts in May 1940 about the lack of an effective mass orator: 'But we are a handful of intellectuals without a single mob orator. Domingo could make a world of difference to us, but we never even hear from him these days'.[275] Roberts took the cry to heart and encouraged Domingo to return, quoting Edna Manley.[276] Shortly after the Havana Conference, Norman Manley wrote to Domingo assuring him:

> I need hardly tell you that we miss you not less but more every day. We have a very devoted band of propaganda workers who has stood up to severe tests but we do need men of experience and knowledge of organization. I still look forward to the day when you will return because I feel that the future is full of possibilities which will want all the best people to help to realise them.[277]

Slowly, both men started to give the idea of a return to Jamaica new attention. However, financial concerns plagued Domingo and prevented him from moving to Jamaica which would have had to be at his own expense. Not only was the WINC in financial strains, Domingo had personally suffered a great loss of money from his import business as a result of the war.[278] Roberts likewise suffered from the financial burden their work demanded:

> I note your statement that you cannot afford a trip to Jamaica. I wish you could. The day may be close upon us when financial sacrifices will seem a small matter, indeed, compared with the tangible things at stake. Personally, I have spent money so freely in connection with our cause during the past two years that my bank account is in a sad state.[279]

Roberts suggested that the Progressive League should raise funds to send Domingo to Jamaica.[280] Domingo agreed that someone should journey there to continue the fight and to support the PNP.[281] The Manleys continued trying to convince the two leaders of the Progressive League to return. In September, Norman Manley mentioned internal problems within the party with its radical left-wing and stressed again how much Roberts' presence would be desirable: 'We miss you a lot and the day I feel we can no longer do without your help I am going to cable you.'[282]

Edna Manley was aware that the return to the policy advocated by the Progressive League bettered the chances for a return of Roberts and Domingo:

> We want you so badly, won't you come back now that the fight for self-government is on again. The Left-Wingers are doing their best to wreck everything, for the sake of their holy bible and its holy prophet.

Alternative Strategies for Self-Government

> ...We need you every way I can think of & we need Domingo with his powerful appeal to the masses.[283]

She further encouraged the two prime leaders of the Progressive League that the time for agitation for self-government was good, as she felt that '...funnily enough people are much less hysterical over self-government then they used to be. At least they have gotten used to the word'.[284] While Roberts' liberal views were well known, Edna and Norman Manley did not fear that Domingo could side with the left-wingers. Despite Domingo's sympathies for Socialism that he had portrayed in the controversy in *Public Opinion* in 1937/38, he had developed into an ardent nationalist, while his Socialist leanings, although not vanished, were less visible.

Both men appreciated Manley's compliments and were glad to know that they had a strong partner in Jamaica to carry on the political work.[285] While Domingo was ready to go to Jamaica if the PNP covered his expenses, Roberts hesitated, fearing intimidation by the authorities.[286] But whatever the situation, Roberts felt that if Manley called for him, he would regard it 'virtually as a mandate'.[287]

Other members of the PNP, like Secretary Arnett, had also been in close contact with Domingo and constantly exchanged views and strategies.[288] The letters from New York were circulated among the PNP executives, testifying to the influence of the Progressive League leaders.[289] Arnett's letter showed that it was not Manley's idea alone that Domingo should return: 'your name is often in the lips of PNP folk and we do long for the very real help you are so capable of giving'.[290] Domingo felt flattered and answered with an emotional, nationalist pledge:

> It is a real pleasure to be assured that I am not forgotten out there. My only regret is that I cannot be there now but as long as I have breath I will be in the frontline fighting for the right of Jamaica to be a self-governing unit of the British Empire and if the fortunes of history wills it that there is to be a change of sovereignty our country should be independent.[291]

With the dawn of 1941, Domingo's return became a question of time. Roberts lauded the influence which the propaganda of the Progressive League had begun to attain in Jamaica and encouraged Domingo:

> Fine as your work has been here, I believe you can exert a still greater influence at home, that you are in fact indispensable to Jamaica's struggle right now. Too few leaders have been developed on the spot. You are needed.[292]

After several letters had been exchanged between Kingston and New York, the PNP decided to pay for Domingo's ticket to Jamaica and to offer him the same salary the local executive earned.[293] On February 14, 1941, Manley officially invited Domingo to work for the party and called attention to the fact that his services were especially needed in the areas of journalism and trade union work. Referring to his time in Jamaica in 1939, he added: '...it would give an enormous amount of personal pleasure and satisfaction to myself and to a host of others who so admired the work you did whilst you were in Jamaica'.[294] Manley pledged that despite the desperate finances of the PNP, Domingo's salary would be guaranteed for at least a year, since a large amount would be paid out of his private pocket.[295] It is evident that Manley valued Domingo highly for the party.

Domingo readily agreed to Manley's offer:

> The period through which the world is passing convinces me that all lovers of Jamaica must be prepared for almost anything. Whatever the outcome of the war, Jamaicans must be ready to defend their interests and work for the advancement of their country. Holding those views I regard your invitation as a call to duty, one that a real patriot cannot ignore or refuse. The salary offered entails a sacrifice on my part but I know it means one from you as well, so it is accepted.[296]

Roberts congratulated Domingo and made clear the significance that he attached to Domingo's decision:

> From my standpoint, this marks an important advance in the entire self-government movement. You are a natural leader, a good and tireless orator. You will know how to lift the campaign above the level of a fumbling provincialism, how to make our people proud of their Jamaican nationality and willing to fight for it. Your grasp of the international aspect is larger than Manley's. Jamaica is fortunate to have you at this time and you are to be congratulated for giving yourself wholly to her cause. I believe you will also accomplish much in straightening out the Labour Unions.[297]

Obviously, Roberts considered the PNP and the labour unions to be promising fields of engagement, and there was no mention of the Kingston branch of the Progressive League. The turn of events early in 1941 made the two leaders of the Progressive League feel that Domingo's presence might become important and useful. In Jamaica, discussions about constitutional changes were again on the agenda. For the executive of the Progressive League, it seemed opportune to have someone on the ground in Jamaica to safeguard appropriate action.

The question of constitutional change had been a contentious issue since the Frome riots and the subsequent recommendations of the Moyne Commission in 1939. The war caused a pause in the constitutional debate, which had been lively during 1939. One important factor was certainly the PNP's voluntary retreat from political agitation. After the party returned to demanding self-government and started to question the defence regulations, the relationship with

Alternative Strategies for Self-Government

the government turned sour. Governor Richards, with whom Manley had shared a respectful and friendly relationship now started to discredit the PNP for their disloyalty.[298] Not too long ago, he had asked Manley to prepare a memorandum with recommendations for Constitutional Change.[299]

Domingo was happy to hear about the conflicts, as they proved the successful influence of the Progressive League's propaganda in Jamaica:

> Unquestionably the self-government pot is boiling and that is more than the English rulers can stomach. Really we did good work in Jamaica when we converted Manley to the need for self-government. The J.P.L. has revolutionized the thinking of our people and cannot be stopped unless Fascism overwhelms us.[300]

Indeed, developments could not be halted. In January 1941, the Governor suddenly left for a trip to London, and the PNP and the Progressive League suspected that it was in relation to proposing minor constitutional changes to temper the demands for self-government which had flared up so vigorously.[301] The PNP immediately invited other organizations to a joint meeting, to demonstrate that minor changes would not be accepted as sufficient, demanding internal self-government that would 'gradually lead to and automatically introduce at the end of a specified period of time full Self-Government within the framework of the British Commonwealth of Nations'.[302]

Although the proposal was in contrast to the Progressive League's demand for immediate self-government, evidence suggests that this immediate action on behalf of the PNP was again inspired by the Progressive League's representatives in New York. When rumours about a Governor's trip to London occurred and the PNP intensified its agitation for self-government, an extraordinarily high number of letters were exchanged between Domingo and the party executives, in which Domingo told Manley that the Governor was requested to come to London to discuss the outline for a new constitution.[303] Except for the point of immediacy, all of Domingo's suggestions were included in the ratified resolutions. In the meantime Domingo prepared a pledge for self-government to the Secretary of State for the Colonies articulating the same demands. The document, officially signed by WINC secretary Osborne, but written by Domingo, claimed the right to self-government for Jamaica.[304]

Seemingly, the strained relationship with Richards and the activities in New York pushed Manley further. In a *Gleaner* interview on January 9, 1940, Manley advocated immediate self-government with unprecedented radicalism:

> We, the party, stand uncompromisingly on our demand for the grant of immediate self-government. We know that self-government cannot be taught or approached in stages. But we feel nonetheless that others in the invited groups who do not go so far, at least go as far as this: that they

feel that any constitution will be useless which does not make positive provision for the actual training which is supposed to be necessary in preparation for self-government, and which does not provide for the achievement of self-government in an actually defined time.[305]

A letter from Manley to Domingo, written shortly after the Ward Theatre meeting, further testifies to the influence from New York: 'You will doubtless have seen from communications already made to you that we took action exactly along the lines suggested by your Council as soon as the Governor left for England'.[306]

An article in *Public Opinion* suggests that the meeting attracted immense attention and that a growing part of the populace was now convinced that self-government was the only solution to Jamaica's problems. But the editors carefully pointed to the fact which Manley had only insinuated; there was 'not yet real unanimity in the island at large upon the speed of the change over'.[307] The editors encouraged every Jamaican to think about this question and warned that a transition period might bring minor improvements and then it was possible that the 'old apathy re-appear'.[308]

In his semi-annual report, US Consul General Watson remarked on the present atmosphere and stated that the PNP was far ahead of local opinion and that nobody would take their demands for self-government seriously. He felt that whereas there was little to say against internal self-government, Jamaica was still too dependent for real autonomy.[309] The Consul's remarks highlighted that large sections of the populace, and the political circles in particular, did not support the demands for the attainment of self-government.

However, the Progressive League was grateful about the new line adopted by the PNP. Domingo viewed the new developments in Jamaica with enthusiasm and immediately started campaigning for the PNP and for self-government and freely offered his advice on tactical approaches. In an article in *Public Opinion*, Domingo lauded the PNP for accepting the inheritance of the Progressive League, which initially started to shake the country out of its lethargy in 1936. Domingo noted with satisfaction: 'On the whole, the leaders and pioneers of Jamaican self-government can feel gratified that their efforts are bearing fruit'.[310] Domingo pointed again to the alleged self-declared fight for democracy in the Second World War and used it as an argument in favour of Jamaican autonomy: 'If the Empire wins the war the insistent demand of Jamaicans for control of their affairs must gain consideration and receive satisfaction unless England is to repudiate the ideal for which she is supposed to be fighting'.[311] In a letter to the PNP, Domingo pushed the party leaders to adopt arguments along these lines to put Great Britain on the spot by underlining the right to self-government and democracy of the colonies.[312] Domingo foresaw that the US officials would closely observe Great Britain's colonial policy after the war. In regard to the

Alternative Strategies for Self-Government

new constitution, Domingo clearly objected to the acceptance of any 'makeshift, ersatz, fake, shadow constitution' and was convinced: 'The time has come for a showdown between the Colonial Office and the people of Jamaica. It is either our interest first or theirs'.³¹³ Domingo explicitly lauded Manley and Nethersole's speeches at the Ward Theatre that contained 'none of that colonial psychology that is unwilling to discuss England and Englishmen freely. None of that stupid awe in dealing with Englishmen as if there are tin gods in possession of all the virtues and the representatives of an unchallengeable type of intellect'.³¹⁴ The outspoken speech of a visiting British politician, Henry Brinton, was of special moral importance, Domingo felt. In view of the prevailing admiration for everything British and the almost natural respect shown for their positions, he stated: 'It opens the eyes of Jamaicans to the fact that all is not well with their country and that some Englishmen of education and influence agree with them'.³¹⁵ In order to reach out to the majority of Jamaicans and to change their mindset, Domingo advised the PNP to spread its propaganda for self-government through means of a massive oral campaign in the countryside. Given the high degree of illiteracy, he felt this would be a powerful strategy.

The reactionary *Gleaner* tried to counter the reinforced self-government demand with its usual tactic – by downplaying the renewed interest: 'As a matter of fact we do not believe that 50 persons in Jamaica anticipate complete self-government within the next 20 years, or even really desire it'.³¹⁶ It is difficult to estimate how much the *Gleaner's* suspicion matched the facts. The *Gleaner* editor certainly had a point when he reflected on the consciousness of the masses:

> We are thinking of course of those in Jamaica who are the people that, in matters like this, must really count. They did not originally advocate immediate Dominion status or the immediate granting to Jamaica of Responsible Government; they do not talk about dominion status even now.

The *Gleaner* affirmed the Progressive League's influence, and tried to show that the most radical demands were actually made overseas and espoused that Roberts '…was the original leader in this business', the idea originated in New York among people of whom many had accepted US citizenship. The PNP, the *Gleaner* pointed out correctly, had not initially advocated immediate self-government. In its claims about the current atmosphere in Jamaica toward self-government, the paper was possibly closer to the truth than the PNP and the Progressive League, whose judgments might have been influenced by wishful thinking. This might even be true for the *Gleaner's* suspicion that the party's demands for immediate self-government were tactical and that even within the party a majority still favoured a gradual development.

However, there was more sympathy for the goals of the Progressive League than ever before. The local branch, now that self-government had become more popular, turned into a fierce advocate of 'immediate and complete Self Government'.³¹⁷ In a letter criticizing the *Gleaner* editorial quoted above and defending the Progressive League, McFarlane recognized that,

> The membership of the Jamaica Progressive League is much more than 50 persons and each member has definitely and completely accepted the declaration quoted by you. Furthermore, there has been nothing in the expressions of the League for the past three years of its activities in Jamaica, to imply or to suggest to anyone that we had an indefinite period in view.

Additionally, McFarlane claimed that the PNP's membership ran into thousands and that more than 50 per cent of PNP members demanded instantaneous and complete self-government. This, however, seems to have been an optimistic estimate. While McFarlane was a little over-confident, he now presented himself to be wholly in line with the Progressive League in New York and felt he had to defend it in the 'crusade against our legitimate demand for self-government' that was put forward by the *Gleaner*.

As Domingo suspected, resulting from the recommendations for constitutional change by Lord Moyne and accompanied by the pressure of increasing nationalist sentiments in the society, the Colonial Office proposed some minor constitutional changes in March 1941.³¹⁸ The proposal included an increase in the number of elected members and nominated members, and an increase in the powers of the Governor. The greatest democratic concession was the granting of universal suffrage. The proposal suggested that the changes would be introduced as a second step after taking a census and the structure of local government fundamentally reformed.³¹⁹

The elected members in the Legislative Council reacted with scepticism and opposed the proposal; officially because they rejected the increase in power of the Governor. The reality, Richard Hart believes, was their adamant opposition to universal adult suffrage, having an uneasy sense of the fact they would not be elected should the vote be cast among the masses. Domingo suspected the same: 'They really fear Universal suffrage'.³²⁰

Domingo's initial reaction to the proposal was positive, based on reports that Jamaica had received a constitution for self-government, and without knowing details of the proposal. He commented in a letter to his friend Campbell that although he felt that universal suffrage was 'no panacea, no end in itself, it is a means for forcing the pace of political development in Jamaica'.³²¹ Domingo regarded the proposal for constitutional change as a direct result of the activities of the Progressive League in New York and its influence in Jamaica:

Alternative Strategies for Self-Government

> The British Government could not withstand the barrage for self-government emanating from Jamaica and from this side. The double attack placed the British on the spot. I had involved Americans and Latins. I sent the propaganda everywhere and although the newspapers ignored us we were able to reach influential people in this country. The agitation at home was powerful and combined with our propaganda was very effective.[322]

In a letter to Manley, he repeated this claim and applauded the PNP for the powerful propaganda campaign that was part of the united effort that resulted in the present changes in the constitution.[323] But Domingo was not so naive as to believe that the constitution would not contain any pitfalls. He assured Roberts: 'If the new Constitution is tricky (as I expect it will be) then it must be rejected and the fight for self-government resumed with greater energy. It will then be our job to expose the British as tricksters'.[324] Domingo wrote to Campbell in a similar spirit. In a fiery manner and in view of the pressure of the anti-colonial movement in India, he warned:

> If England wants another India, this time at the door of the United States then we should be prepared to let her have it. English Statesmen pretend to believe in democracy, but it is such an exploded lie that hardly no one outside of a lunatic Asylum or a home for the feeble minded believe any such Anancy story.[325]

Manley's reaction to the proposal was ambivalent. Correcting Domingo's initial perception, Manley informed him that the proposal was for representative and not for responsible Government and asked for Domingo's advice. While he opposed the increased powers of the Governor, he felt,

> ...to reject it now would be to set back for an unknown number of years the best prospects of the development of the Party. Naturally the situation presents difficult tactical problems. I should be very glad to hear your views.[326]

Manley suspected that the Legislative Council would reject it because of the granting of universal suffrage and believed that the PNP should fight for its acceptance.

In this new situation, Manley was especially glad that Domingo had accepted his call for duty. He promised to send his steamship ticket as soon as possible, because he felt that now was the right time for Domingo to come and support the PNP in its fight to improve the constitution.[327] Domingo agreed in principle with the PNP's position, and hoped that through universal suffrage, the PNP would have a majority in the Legislative Council in the next elections.[328]

In a letter to Campbell, Domingo shared his concerns a bit more openly than in his letter to Manley, but nevertheless recommended accepting the proposal because it granted universal suffrage: 'My instincts and temperament are for rejection, but I don't think we here should be too far ahead of the masses out there'.[329] He felt that the Governor's powers would not be greater in practice than at the present time, but the changes would certainly inspire party organization and politicization in Jamaica.

Initially, Roberts objected to the PNP acquiescing to the proposal if it did not contain responsible government, although he felt that the offer of a new constitution was a good sign and resulted from the united efforts of the Progressive League, the PNP and the WINC.[330] However, after careful reading of the proposal and reflecting thereupon, Roberts offered insight that universal suffrage was a valuable gain, although he still felt the general document was not satisfactory. He advised a different tactic for the different organizations:

> The P.N.P. probably should accept this Constitution, with reservations. But the J.P.L. should not. The League delegates should fight the point in the party conference, the way we fought for self-government plan in 1939. If voted down, the League could go along with the party, while always reserving the right to take a more positive stand when the time is ripe.[331]

In Roberts' view, the Progressive League should use its separate identity as a means to strongly advocate self-government. In a similar manner to the party's first convention, the members of the Progressive League should press for a radicalization of the PNP. Roberts was convinced that Domingo's presence would help immensely.

In order to make sure that the local branch in Kingston would stick to the line proposed by the Progressive League in New York, Brown wrote McFarlane and enclosed the Progressive League's positions on the proposed changes of the Constitution.[332] But the Progressive League in Kingston did not react in the desired way and had already embarked on a different road. McFarlane and his colleagues attempted to build a broad front with other local organizations and convened a round table conference inviting a wide range of organizations.[333] The meeting resolved that the proposal for a new constitution should be accepted, including universal suffrage and an enlarged Legislative Council with elected majority.[334]

The result represented the type of representatives at the meeting and did not even include the explicit demand for self-government. Instead, it generally accepted the proposal by the Colonial Office. The conference decided to convene again on April 9 and renew the invitation to those who could not attend. The second meeting confirmed the decisions of the first one. One more time, the local Progressive League exhibited its undecided stand and its tendency to follow local opinion instead of spearheading a radical anti-colonial movement.

Alternative Strategies for Self-Government 259

In contrast, the PNP took a more critical posture. At a special PNP conference on the constitution in May 1941, the proposals of the joint conference were accepted only as a minimum requirement.[335] In the pamphlet *Forward March*, which resulted from the conference, the PNP's critique of the proposed constitutional changes was explicated in detail. The PNP decidedly advocated 'immediate self-government' and declared that Jamaica was indeed ready and fit for immediate grant of responsibility.[336] Unequivocally, tribute was paid to the pioneering work for self-government by the Jamaica Progressive League.[337]

According to Roberts' recommendation, the Progressive League in New York criticized the proposal in detail. In a resolution, the Progressive League stipulated:

> ...the proposed Constitution, stripped of the concession of the demand for Universal Suffrage, denies to the people of Jamaica any effective control of their own affairs and is foreign to the traditions and political conscience of the Western Hemisphere.[338]

The Progressive League pointed to the contradiction between the enlarged powers of the Governor and the granting of universal suffrage, and that the spirit of the constitution would contradict the agreement of Havana, ignoring the right to self-determination. It protested against the delay in reform because of proposed changes in parochial administration, and the increased powers of the Governor were criticized. For the elected members, the Progressive League suggested travelling allowances and a salary, while property and income restrictions for Legislative Council members should be removed. With these qualifications, the Progressive League concluded, the constitutional changes should be accepted as a step toward self-government which Great Britain would finally be forced to grant because of its assertion to fight for democracy worldwide.[339]

At the height of the constitutional debate and after exploiting all options in the US for attaining support for their goal that Jamaica become a nation, Domingo and Roberts decided that the time was ripe to resume active agitation in Jamaica. Shortly before Domingo went to Jamaica, Roberts emphasized Domingo's crucial role in the emerging political system and hoped he would run for public office in the next elections.[340] Roberts also encouraged him to join the editorial staff of *Public Opinion* and to continue his propaganda through that channel. But whatever the Progressive League leaders had planned for Domingo and his influence in Jamaica, the story would take a different turn.

Before Domingo finally sailed to Jamaica on June 13, 1941, the WINC organized a large testimonial dinner with 85 guests to honour him for his service.[341] An illustrious range of organizations with which Domingo was in close contact sent representatives, among them the Progressive League, whose secretary Brown was the Master of Ceremonies, the *New York Amsterdam News*, the YMCA, the WILPF, the Council of Pan-American Democracy, and various other organizations.[342] Clearly, Domingo had become one of the outstanding activists in the Caribbean and New York and – so it seemed on the eve of his departure – was destined to continue to serve the cause of his country at home among the rank and file of the nationalist elite, into which Manley and his colleagues had developed. Equipped with a wristwatch he had received from the WINC as a gift and US$21 for a new typewriter for the PNP, Domingo headed into an unpredictable future.[343]

Notes

1. Jason C. Parker, *Brother's Keeper: The United States, Race and Empire in the British Caribbean, 1937–1962* (Oxford: Oxford University Press, 2008), 8.
2. Claus Füllberg-Stollberg, 'The Caribbean in the Second World War', in *General History of the Caribbean: The Caribbean in the 20th Century*. Vol. 5., ed. Bridget Brereton (London: Macmillan Publishers, 2003), 83.
3. Denis Benn, *The Caribbean: An Intellectual History, 1774–2003* (Kingston: Ian Randle Publishers, 2004), 86; Ken Post, *Strike the Iron: A Colony at War: Jamaica, 1939–1945*. Vol. 1. (Atlantic Highlands, NJ: Humanities Press, 1981), 114; Parker, *Brother's Keeper*, 57ff.
4. Benn, *The Caribbean*, 84.
5. The bases-for-destroyers deal will be more closely analysed in the following chapter.
6. *Daily Gleaner*, December 23, 1939; Manley to Roberts, September 26, 1939, NLJ, WAR, MS 353, Box 2b.
7. Louis Lindsay, *The Myth of Independence: Middle Class Politics and Non-Mobilization in Jamaica*. Reprint ed. (Kingston: SALISES, 1981), 17.
8. Roberts to Norman Manley, September 21, 1939, NLJ, WAR, MS 353, Box 2b.
9. Manley to Roberts, September 26, 1939, NLJ, WAR, MS 353, Box 2b.
10. Domingo to Roberts, June 24, 1940, NLJ, WAR, MS 353, Box 2b.
11. Domingo to Campbell, January 1, 1939, JA, NMP, 4/60/2A/2.
12. Roberts to Edna Manley, October 3, 1939, NLJ, WAR, MS 353, Box 2b.
13. Roberts to Domingo, September 20, 1939, NLJ, WAR, MS 353, Box 2b.
14. Ibid.
15. Domingo to Roberts, September 28, 1939, NLJ, WAR, MS 353, Box 2b.
16. Domingo to Campbell, October 1, 1939, JA, NMP, 4/60/2A/2.
17. Resolution Jamaica Progressive League, September 24, 1939, NLJ, JPL, MS 234, see also *Daily Gleaner*, October 12, 1939.
18. Domingo to Roberts, September 28, 1939, NLJ, WAR, MS 353, Box 2b.
19. Ibid.
20. Domingo to Roberts, April 24, 1940, NLJ, WAR, MS 353, Box 2b.
21. Roberts to Domingo, May 8, 1940, NLJ, WAR, MS 353, Box 2b.
22. W. Adolphe Roberts, *The Caribbean: The Story of Our Sea of Destiny* (Indianapolis: Bobbs-Merrill, 1940).
23. Roberts to Domingo, May 8, 1940, NLJ, WAR, MS 353, Box 2b.
24. Domingo to Roberts, May 20, 1940, NLJ, WAR, MS 353, Box 2b.
25. Ibid.

Alternative Strategies for Self-Government 261

26. *Daily Gleaner*, May 12, 1939; see in contrast Domingo to Campbell, September 20, 1939, JA, NMP, 4/60/2A/2.
27. *Public Opinion*, September 9, 1939; November 4, 1939. See also the exchange of letters between the JPL, Kingston and numerous Parochial Boards, NLJ, JPL, MS 234.
28. Domingo to Roberts, May 20, 1940, NLJ, WAR, MS 353, Box 2b.
29. Ibid.
30. Ibid.
31. *Daily Gleaner*, September 26, 1939.
32. Roberts to Domingo, May 23, 1940, NLJ, WAR, MS 353, Box 2b.
33. Ibid.
34. Ibid.
35. Roberts to Domingo, May 23, 1940, NLJ, WAR, MS 353, Box 2b.
36. The *Worker and Peasant* first appeared on April 1, 1940 and was the organ of the leftist Negro Workers Education League (NWEL), chaired by Cecil Nelson and was rooted in the circles of Jamaican Marxists like Buchanan, McBean and Hart. See Post, *Strike the Iron*, Vol. 1, 94f.
37. Domingo to Roberts, May 27, 1940, NLJ, WAR, MS 353, Box 2b.
38. *Daily Gleaner*, April 27, 1940. See also Post, *Strike the Iron*, Vol. 1, 98.
39. Post, *Strike the Iron*, Vol. 1, 98.
40. Ibid.
41. Roberts to Domingo, May 20, 1940, NLJ, WAR, MS 353, Box 2b.
42. *Daily Gleaner*, May 18, 1940.
43. *Daily Gleaner*, May 20, 1940; May 21, 1940.
44. Domingo to Roberts, June 4, 1940, NLJ, WAR, MS 353, Box 2b.
45. Roberts to Domingo, May 23, 1940, NLJ, WAR, MS 353, Box 2b.
46. Ibid.
47. Domingo to Roberts, May 27, 1940, NLJ, WAR, MS 353, Box 2b.
48. Hart, *Towards Decolonisation*, 95.
49. Domingo to Roberts, May 27, 1940, NLJ, WAR, MS 353, Box 2b.
50. For details on the shifts in US policy toward the West Indies around the Havana Conference see Fitzroy Baptiste, *War, Cooperation, and Conflict: The European Possessions in the Caribbean* 1939–1945 (Westport: Greenwood Press, 1988), 39–49.
51. Domingo to Campbell, June 29, 1940, JA, NMP, 4/60/2A/2.
52. Hart, *Towards Decolonisation*, 95; Post, *Strike the Iron*, Vol. 1, 114.
53. Domingo to Roberts, May 27, 1940. NLJ, WAR, MS 353, Box 2b.
54. *New York Amsterdam News*, June 1, 1940.
55. Ibid.
56. Moore Turner and Turner, ed. *Richard B. Moore*, 85f. For a more detailed discussion, see chapter 2.
57. *New York Amsterdam News*, June 8, 1940; for a similar argument see *New York Amsterdam News*, June 1, 1940.
58. Roberts to Domingo, June 1, 1940, NLJ, WAR, MS 353, Box 2b. Roberts referred to an undated letter written end of May 1940, Edna Manley to Roberts, NLJ, WAR, WAR, MS 353, Box 2b.
59. Domingo to Roberts, June 4, 1940, NLJ, WAR, MS 353, Box 2b.
60. Roberts to Edna Manley, June 11, 1940, NLJ, WAR, MS 353, Box 2b.

61. Roberts to Domingo, June 14, 1940, NLJ, WAR, MS 353, Box 2b.
62. Domingo to Roberts, June 4, 1940, NLJ, WAR, MS 353, Box 2b.
63. Ibid.
64. Domingo to Roberts, June 17, 1940, NLJ, WAR, MS 353, Box 2b; Ivy Bailey-Essien attended as representative of the Jamaica Progressive League (JPL).
65. Ibid.
66. The committee consisted of Hope R. Stevens (chairman), Ivy Bailey Essien (vice chairman), H.P. Osborne (secretary) and Dr F. Theo Reid (treasurer). Other members included R.B. Moore, Dr C.A. Petioni, Archbishop Ernest, Reginald Pierrepoint, Arthur E. King and others. Further members of the League were Revd Ethelred Brown and R. Samuel Trew. See, for example, Domingo to Roberts, July 20, 1940, NLJ, WAR, MS 353, Box 2b. After his initiating role and as head of the planning committee Domingo did not aspire to assume any official position within WINEC at first. However, when the Committee was reorganized into the permanent organization West Indies National Council (WINC) in September 1939, Domingo was elected as president.
67. Domingo to Roberts, June 17, 1940, NLJ, WAR, MS 353, Box 2b.
68. Ibid.
69. Roberts to Domingo, June 20, 1940, NLJ, WAR, MS 353, Box 2b.
70. WINEC, 'Declaration of Rights of the Caribbean Peoples to Self-Determination and Self-Government', NLJ, MS 353, WAR Box 9.
71. Moore Turner and Turner claim that the declaration was 'largely the work of Moore'. See Moore Turner and Turner, eds., *Richard B. Moore*, 75. However, they present no source for this claim and there is no hint that they consulted the letters between Roberts and Domingo. Hence they described the founding of the WINEC inadequately as a result of an accidental meeting of Domingo and Moore on Lenox Street.
72. Domingo to Roberts, June 24, 1940, NLJ, WAR, MS 353, Box 2b. Domingo repeated this version in a letter to Campbell, see Domingo to Campbell, August 8, 1940, JA, NMP, 4/60/2A/2.
73. Domingo to Roberts, June 24, 1940, NLJ, WAR, MS 353, Box 2b.
74. Domingo to Roberts, June 17, 1940, NLJ, WAR, MS 353, Box 2b.
75. Ibid.
76. Ibid.
77. Ibid.
78. Roberts to Domingo, June 20, 1940. NLJ, WAR, MS 353, Box 2b.
79. Ibid.
80. For this and the following see 'Jamaica Declaration', June 20, 1940, 1940, NLJ, WAR, MS 353, Box 2b.
81. Domingo to Roberts, undated [end of June or early July], WAR, MS 353, Box 2b.
82. *Public Opinion*, June 22, 1940.
83. Draughon to Warren, June 17, 1940, NARA, RG 59, 844D.014/9.
84. *Public Opinion*, June 22, 1940.
85. Ibid.
86. Ibid.
87. Ibid.

Alternative Strategies for Self-Government

88. Domingo to Roberts, July 8, 1940, NLJ, WAR, MS 353, Box 2b.
89. Ibid.
90. Domingo to Roberts, undated [end of June or early July], NLJ, WAR, MS 353, Box 2b.
91. Domingo to Roberts, July 8, 1940, NLJ, WAR, MS 353, Box 2b.
92. Domingo to Roberts, undated [end of June or early July], NLJ, WAR, MS 353, Box 2b.
93. Domingo to Roberts, June 24, 1940, NLJ, WAR, MS 353, Box 2b.
94. Roberts to Domingo, July 6, 1940, NLJ, WAR, MS 353, Box 2b.
95. Hope Stevens was a young attorney, born in Nevis. He was very active in the network of Caribbean activists in New York around Domingo, Moore, Pierrepoint, etc., and had also participated at several meetings of the Progressive League. See Moore Turner, *Caribbean Crusaders*, 226.
96. Domingo to Roberts, July 8, 1940, NLJ, WAR, MS 353, Box 2b.
97. Domingo to Roberts, July 16, 1940, NLJ, WAR, MS 353, Box 2b.
98. Malliet was later reported to be active in the counter organization to the WINEC, the American West Indian Association on Caribbean Affairs, which clearly repudiated any leftist tendencies and in which also members of the JPL had been engaged (including Ethelred Brown, who was member of the board of directors, T.E. Hanson, Lucien M. Brown and others). See 'Dossier American West Indian Association on Caribbean Affairs', Hoover to Berle, August 2, 1944, NARA, RG 59, CDF 1940-44, 844.00B, Box 5058.
99. Domingo to Roberts, July 16, 1940, NLJ, WAR, MS 353, Box 2b.
100. *New York Amsterdam News*, July 20, 1940, see also *Pittsburgh Courier*, July 20, 1940. Other speakers included Domingo and other prominent Caribbeans and Latin Americans, for instance Dr P.M.H. Savory, R.B. Moore, Theo J. Alcantara, Charles Petioni, Revd E. Elliott Durant and Adam Clayton Powell.
101. WINEC, 'Statement on the Address Delivered by Secretary of State of the Unites States of America, Cordell Hull, To the Pan-American Foreign Ministers' Conference at Havana, Cuba, July 22, 1940 in Respect to the Status of European Possessions in the Western Hemisphere', SCRBC, Richard B. Moore Papers (RBM), MG 347, Box 8, Fo. 2.
102. Roberts, 'Autobiography', 52.
103. Quoted after Post, *Strike the Iron*, Vol. 1, 115.
104. Post, *Strike the Iron*, Vol. 1, 115.
105. *New York Times*, June 28, 1940.
106. Ibid., June 30, 1940.
107. Domingo to Roberts, 23.12.1940, NLJ, WAR, MS 353, Box 2b.
108. Ibid.
109. Domingo to Roberts, 06.08.1940, NLJ, WAR, MS 353, Box 2b.
110. Melo to Domingo, 28.09.1940, WAR, MS 353, Box 2b, also NMP, 4/60/2A/2.
111. Melo to Brown, 28.09.1940, Library of Congress (LOC), Manuscript Division, The Records of the NAACP, Group 2, Box A332, Folder 9, Labour British West Indies, 1940–1949.
112. WINEC, 'Statement on the Address Delivered by Secretary of State of the Unites States of America, Cordell Hull, To the Pan-American Foreign Ministers' Conference

at Havana, Cuba, July 22, 1940 in Respect to the Status of European Possessions in the Western Hemisphere', SCRBC, RBM, MG 347, Box 8, Fo. 2.
113. Domingo to Roberts, August 14, 1940, NLJ, WAR, MS 353, Box 2b.
114. Hart, *Towards Decolonization*, 95 ff. See Post, *Strike the Iron*, Vol. 1, 15ff.
115. Post, *Strike the Iron*, Vol. 1, 116.
116. Parker, 'Harlem Nexus', 104.
117. Roberts to Domingo, August 18, 1940, NLJ, WAR, MS 353, Box 2b.
118. Post, *Strike the Iron*, Vol. I, 115.
119. Roberts to Domingo, August 2, 1940, NLJ, WAR, MS 353, Box 2b.
120. Ibid.
121. Roberts to Domingo, July 29, 1940, NLJ, WAR, MS 353, Box 2b.
122. Roberts to Domingo, September 15, 1940, NLJ, WAR, MS 353, Box 2b.
123. Ibid.
124. Roberts to Domingo, September 15, 1940, NLJ, WAR, MS 353, Box 2b.
125. Domingo to Roberts, August 6, 1940, NLJ, WAR, MS 353, Box 2b.
126. Domingo to Campbell, August 8, 1940, JA, NMP, 4/60/2A/2, for a similar statement, see Domingo to Roberts, August 6, 1940, NLJ, WAR, MS 353, Box 2b.
127. Domingo to Campbell, August 8, 1940, JA, NMP, 4/60/2A/2.
128. Domingo to Campbell, July 29, 1940, JA, NMP, 4/60/2A/2; Domingo to Campbell, August 2, 1940, JA, NMP, 4/60/2.
129. Domingo to Roberts, August 14, 1940, NLJ, WAR, MS 353, Box 2b.
130. Domingo to Campbell, July 29, 1940, JA, NMP, 4/60/2A/2.
131. Domingo to White, November 6, 1940, LOC, Manuscript Division, NAACP, Group 2, Box A332, Fo 9.
132. *New York Amsterdam News*, August 3, 1940.
133. Ibid., August 10, 1940.
134. Hoover to Berle, September 22, 1944, enclosed article by Powell in *The Peoples Voice*, NARA, RG 59, 844D.00/9-2244.
135. Domingo to Campbell, November 8, 1940, JA, NMP, 4/60/2A/2.
136. Domingo to Campbell, August 29, 1940, JA, NMP, 4/60/2A/2.
137. Domingo to Roberts, August 14, 1940, NLJ, WAR, MS 353, Box 2b.
138. Ibid.
139. Domingo to Roberts, August 6, 1940, NLJ, WAR, MS 353, Box 2b.
140. Ibid.
141. Ibid.
142. Domingo to Campbell, August 29, 1940, JA, NMP, 4/60/2A/2.
143. Domingo to Roberts, August 6, 1940, NLJ, WAR, MS 353, Box 2b.
144. Ibid.
145. Ibid.
146. Ibid.
147. Domingo to Roberts, October 3, 1940, NLJ, WAR, MS 353, Box 2b.
148. Ibid. End of September 1940, the organization changed its name to West Indies National Council, with Domingo as president, Moore, Petioni, Baily-Essien and Chalwell served as vice-presidents, Arthur E. King was the treasurer.
149. Roberts to Domingo, June 1, 1940, NLJ, WAR, MS 353, Box 2b.
150. Ibid.

151. Domingo to Roberts, August 14, 1940, NLJ, WAR, MS 353, Box 2b.
152. Roberts to Domingo, December 25, 1940, NLJ, WAR, MS 353, Box 2b.
153. *Daily Gleaner,* July 3, 1940.
154. Ibid., September 2, 1940.
155. Ibid., July 4, 1940.
156. Roberts to Domingo, June 1, 1940, NLJ, WAR, MS 353, Box 2b.
157. Domingo to Roberts, June 17, 1940, NLJ, WAR, MS 353, Box 2b.
158. Roberts to McFarlane, June 18, 1940, NLJ, JPL, MS 234.
159. Brown to McFarlane, June 22, 1940, NLJ, JPL, MS 234.
160. *Daily Gleaner*, February 2, 1940, see also McFarlane to Brown, September 14, 1940, NLJ, WAR, MS 353, Box 2b.
161. *Daily Gleaner*, September 30, 1940.
162. *Public Opinion*, October 5, 1940.
163. Melo to McFarlane, July 31, 1940, NLJ, WAR, MS 353, Box 2b.
164. Domingo to Roberts, October 12, 1940, NLJ, WAR, MS 353, Box 2b.
165. Domingo to Roberts, September 13, 1940, NLJ, WAR, MS 353, Box 2b.
166. Domingo to Roberts, September 16, 1940, NLJ, WAR, MS 353, Box 2b.
167. Roberts to Domingo, September 15, 1940, NLJ, WAR, MS 353, Box 2b.
168. Domingo to Roberts, September 9, 1940, NLJ, WAR, MS 353, Box 2b.
169. See *Daily Gleaner*, September 2, 1940,
170. Domingo to Campbell, September 11, 1940, JA, NMP, 4/60/2A/2.
171. Ibid.
172. *Public Opinion*, August 17, 1940.
173. Domingo to Roberts, June 17, 1940, NLJ, WAR, MS 353, Box 2b.
174. Manley to Domingo, August 16, 1940, JA, NMP, 4/60/2A/2; August 18, 1940, Roberts to Domingo, NLJ, WAR, MS 353, Box 2b.
175. Manley to Domingo, August 16, 1940, JA, NMP, 4/60/2A/2.
176. Ibid.
177. Domingo, 'Open Letter to the Delegates of the PNP Annual Conference', August 26, 1940, NMP, 4/60/2A/2.
178. Arnett to Osborne, September 10, 1940, NLJ, WAR, MS 353, Box 2b.
179. *Daily Gleaner*, August 30, 1940.
180. Ibid., August 29, 1940.
181. Ibid., August 30, 1940.
182. Ibid.
183. Manley to Domingo, September 18, 1940, JA, NMP, 4/60/2A/2.
184. Ibid.
185. *Daily Gleaner*, January 15, 1940; Manley, Campbell, Brinton, Nethersole, Shirley, Amy Bailey.
186. *Public Opinion*, August 3, 1940.
187. Domingo to Roberts, August 14, 1940, NLJ, WAR, MS 353, Box 2b.
188. *Public Opinion*, August 3, 1940.
189. *Public Opinion*, September 21, 1940.
190. Ibid.
191. Domingo to Roberts, September 20, 1940, NLJ, WAR, MS 353, Box 2b.
192. Domingo to Roberts, September 9, 1940, NLJ, WAR, MS 353, Box 2b.
193. Domingo to Manley, August 23, 1940, JA, NMP, 4/60/2A/2.

194. Domingo to Manley, August 23, 1940, JA, NMP, 4/60/2A/2; Domingo to Arnett, December 2, 1940, JA, NMP, 4/60/2A/2; Domingo to Campbell, December 4, 1940, JA, NMP, 4/60/2A/2; Domingo to Arnett, December 19, 1940, JA, NMP, 4/60/2A/2.
195. Domingo to Roberts, December 23, 1940, NLJ, WAR, MS 353, Box 2b.
196. Domingo to Campbell, September 11, 1940, JA, NMP, 4/60/2A/2; Domingo to Roberts, August 14, 1940, NLJ, WAR, MS 353, Box 2b.
197. Domingo to Roberts, August 14, 1940, NLJ, WAR, MS 353, Box 2b.
198. Roberts to Domingo, August 18, 1940, NLJ, WAR, MS 353, Box 2b.
199. Baptiste, *War, Cooperation, Conflict*, 51ff, see also Füllberg-Stollberg, 'The Caribbean in the Second World War', 83.
200. The security interest of the US and the power shift between the US and Great Britain is widely discussed in literature. With special reference to the bases-for-destroyers deal see for example: Baptiste, *War, Cooperation, Conflict*, 51ff; Füllberg-Stollberg, 'The Caribbean in the Second World War', 91; Parker, *Brother's Keeper*, 31ff.; Charlie Witham, *Bitter Rehearsal: British and American Planning for a Post-War West Indies* (Westport: Praeger Publishers, 2002); Anthony P. Maingot and Wilfredo, Lozano, *The United States and the Caribbean:Transforming Hegemony and Sovereignty* (New York: Routledge, 2005).
201. Benn, *The Caribbean*, 84.
202. Domingo to Campbell, August 16, 1940 [mistakenly dated 1941], JA, NMP, 4/60/2A/2.
203. Domingo to Campbell, September 6, 1940, NMP, 4/60/2A/2.
204. Domingo to Manley, August 23, 1940, JA, NMP, 4/60/2A/2.
205. Ibid.
206. Domingo to Roberts, August 19, 1940, NLJ, WAR, MS 353, Box 2b.
207. Domingo to Campbell, December 4, 1940, JA, NMP, 4/60/2A/2.
208. Bussey to Roosevelt, December 17, 1940, NLJ, WAR, MS 353, Box 2b.
209. Domingo to Campbell, August 16, 1940 [mistakenly dated 1941], JA, NMP, 4/60/2A/2.
210. Domingo to Delegates of Annual PNP Conference, August 26, 1940, NMP, 4/60/2A/2.
211. Domingo to Manley, September 5, 1940, NMP, 4/60/2A/2. He named the FCA, PNP and the Legislative Council (LC) as organizations and suggested men like Manley, Nethersole, Campbell or Anderson.
212. Domingo to Roberts, June 4, 1940, NLJ, WAR, MS 353, Box 2b.
213. Domingo to Delegates of Annual PNP Conference, August 26, 1940, NMP, 4/60/2A/2.
214. Ibid.
215. Domingo to Manley, January 28, 1941, NMP, 4/60/2A/2; Domingo to Arnett, January 24, 1941, NMP, 4/60/2A/2.
216. Arnett to Domingo, March 27, 1941, NMP, 4/60/2A/2.
217. Arnett to Osborne, September 19, 1940, NMP, 4/60/2A/2.
218. Domingo to Campbell, October 23, 1940, JA, NMP, 4/60/2A/2.
219. Domingo to Roberts, December 23, 1940, NLJ, WAR, MS 353, Box 2b.
220. Hull to Roosevelt, Telegram, December 5, 1940, NARA, RG 59, CDF 1940–1944, Box 3790, 811.34544/308. The information was based on an enclosed telegram of

Charles W. Taussig after his trip to the Caribbean to observe the local situation.
221. Ibid.
222. Watson to Department of State, Semi-Annual Report, January 9, 1941, NARA, RG 84, UD 2882, Classified General Records 1936–1941, Box 1.
223. *New York Amsterdam News*, January 4, 1941; *New York Times*, November 24, 1940.
224. Domingo to Roosevelt, December 25, 1940, LOC, NAACP, Group 2, Box A332, Fo. 9; Brown to Cordell Hull, February 20, 1941, NARA, RG 59, CDF 1940-1944, Box 3790, 811.34544/612; See Osborne to Lord Lloyd, January 9, 1941; JA, NMP, 4/60/2A/2; Osborne to Lord Moyne, February 20, 1941, NLJ, WAR, MS 353, Box 2b.
225. Hull to Domingo, February 15, 1941, NLJ, WAR, MS 353, Box 2b.
226. Domingo to Hull, February 21, 1941, LOC, NAACP, Group 2, Box A332, Fo. 9.
227. Domingo to Manley, February 26, 1941, JA, NMP, 4/60/2A/2.
228. Domingo to White, February 7, 1941, LOC, NAACP, Group 2, Box A332, Fo. 9.
229. White to Domingo, February 21, 1941, LOC, NAACP, Group 2, Box A332, Fo. 9.
230. Domingo to Arnett, March 20, 1941, JA, NMP, 4/60/2A/2.
231. *New York Amsterdam News*, November 23, 1940; *New York Amsterdam Star News*, March 15, 1941 (The New York Amsterdam News changed its name for a few months and will accordingly be abbreviated NYASN).
232. *New York Amsterdam Star News*, January 25, 1941.
233. JPL, Kingston Resolution, McFarlane to Secretary of State, October 14, 1940, NLJ, JPL, MS 234.
234. *Daily Gleaner*, January 23, 1941; January 25, 1941. The officers of the JPL, Kingston were McPherson (president acting); Amy Bailey (2nd vice-president), trustees: J.C. Chisholm, Don Messam; Board of Directors: W.S. Johnson, Clifford Rae, Revd Cooper and W.A. McBean.
235. *Daily Gleaner*, January 25, 1941.
236. Domingo to Roberts, September 9, 1940, NLJ, WAR, MS 353, Box 2b.
237. Domingo to Manley, August 23, 1940, JA, NMP, 4/60/2A/2; Domingo to Manley, October 11, 1940, JA, NMP, 4/60/2A/2.
238. Domingo to Manley, October 11, 1940, JA, NMP, 4/60/2A/2.
239. Domingo to Arnett, December 2, 1940, JA, NMP, 4/60/2A/2; *Public Opinion*, June 22, 1940.
240. Domingo to Campbell, November 26, 1940, JA, NMP, 4/60/2A/2.
241. Domingo to Manley, November 25, 1940, JA, NMP, 4/60/2A/2.
242. Domingo to Arnett, December 2, 1940, JA, NMP, 4/60/2A/2.
243. Ibid.
244. Domingo to Roberts, December 23, 1940, NLJ, WAR, MS 353, Box 2b.
245. *New York Amsterdam News*, December 30, 1939.
246. Domingo to Roosevelt, December 25, 1940, LOC, NAACP, Group 2, Box A332, Fo. 9.
247. Domingo to Arnett, December 19, 1940, NMP, 4/60/2A/2.
248. Roberts to Domingo, December 25, 1940, NLJ, WAR, MS 353, Box 2b.
249. Ibid.
250. Walter Adolphe Roberts, *The Caribbean. The Story of Our Sea of Destiny* (Indianapolis, New York: Bobbs-Merrill, 1940).

251. *Daily Gleaner*, September 3, 1940; The *Washington Post*, September 4, 1940; *New York Times*, January 19, 1941; *New York Amsterdam News*, June 21, 1941.
252. Bridget Brereton, 'Recent Developments in the Historiography of the Post-Emancipation Anglophone Caribbean'. *Beyond Fragmentation: Perspectives on Caribbean History* (2006): 187–209.
253. Roberts, *The Caribbean*, 337.
254. Ibid., 342.
255. *Daily Gleaner*, September 3, 1940; August 24, 1940.
256. *Public Opinion*, September 7, 1940.
257. Ibid.
258. *Daily Gleaner*, September 3, 1940.
259. Ibid., September 10, 1940.
260. Edna Manley to Roberts, September 1940, NLJ, WAR, MS 353, Box 2.
261. Manley to Roberts, September 23, 1940, NLJ, WAR, MS 353, Box 2b.
262. Ibid.
263. *Daily Gleaner*, September 11, 1940.
264. Domingo to Roberts, September 20, 1940, NLJ, WAR, MS 353, Box 2b.
265. Manley to Roberts, September 23, 1940, NLJ, WAR, MS 353, Box 2b.
266. Edna Manley to Roberts, undated, [November 1939] NLJ, WAR, MS 353, Box 2b.
267. Roberts to Edna Manley, November 29, 1939, WAR, MS 353, Box 2b.
268. *Daily Gleaner*, December 4, 1939. The election campaign committee consisted of men from the top ranks of the PNP: Manley, William Seivreight, V.L. Arnett and also some people from the JPL Kingston circles like Amy Bailey or McPherson.
269. *Daily Gleaner*, January 23, 1940.
270. Ibid., December 7, 1939.
271. Ibid., December 11, 1939.
272. Ibid., December 21, 1939.
273. Ibid., December 16, 1939.
274. Domingo to Campbell, January 26, 1940, JA, NMP, 4/60/2A/2.
275. Edna Manley to Roberts, Undated [April 1940], NLJ, WAR, MS 353, Box 2b.
276. Roberts to Domingo, May 8, 1940, NLJ, WAR, MS 353, Box 2b.
277. Manley to Domingo, August 16, 1940, JA, NMP, 4/60/2A/2.
278. In a letter to Roberts, Domingo claimed he had lost more than US$14,000 since the outbreak of the war, Domingo to Roberts, August 6, 1940, NLJ, WAR, MS 353, Box 2b.
279. Roberts to Domingo, August 2, 1940, NLJ, WAR, MS 353, Box 2b.
280. Ibid.
281. Domingo to Roberts, August 6, 1940, NLJ, WAR, MS 353, Box 2b.
282. Manley to Roberts, September 23, 1940, WAR, MS 353, Box 2b.
283. Edna Manley to Roberts, undated [September 1940], NLJ, WAR, MS 353, Box 2b.
284. Ibid.
285. Domingo to Roberts, October 3, 1940, NLJ, WAR, MS 353, Box 2b.
286. Roberts to Norman Manley, September 29, 1940, NLJ, WAR, MS 353, Box 2b.
287. Ibid.
288. Domingo to Arnett, January 21, 1941, JA, NMP, 4/60/2A/2; Manley to Domingo, January 18, 1941, JA, NMP, 4/60/2A/2; Domingo to Arnett, January 21, 1941, JA, NMP, 4/60/2A/2; Arnett to Domingo, January 21, 1941, JA, NMP, 4/60/2A/2.
289. Domingo to Arnett, January 21, 1941, JA, NMP, 4/60/2A/2.

Alternative Strategies for Self-Government   269

290. Arnett to Domingo, December 11, 1940, JA, NMP, 4/60/2A/2.
291. Domingo to Arnett, December 19, 1940, JA, NMP, 4/60/2A/2.
292. Roberts to Domingo, February 9, 1941, NLJ, WAR, MS 353, Box 2b.
293. Domingo to Roberts, February 14, 1941, NLJ, WAR, MS 353, Box 2b; Roberts to Domingo, February 15, 1941, WAR Box 2b; Roberts to Edna Manley, February 16, 1941, WAR Box 2b.
294. Manley to Domingo, February 24, 1941, NMP, 4/60/2A/2.
295. Domingo to Roberts, March 3, 1941, NLJ, WAR, MS 353, Box 2b.
296. Domingo to Manley, March 3, 1941, NMP, 4/60/2A/2.
297. Roberts to Domingo, March 5, 1941, WAR, MS 353, Box 2b.
298. Hart, *Towards*, 111.
299. Ibid., *Towards*, 42f.
300. Domingo to Roberts, January 2, 1941, NLJ, WAR, MS 353, Box 2b.
301. Hart, *Towards*, 111.
302. Ibid., 114.
303. Domingo to Manley, January 2, 1941, JA, NMP, 4/60/2A/2.
304. Osborne to Lord Lloyd, January 9, 1941, JA, NMP, 4/60/2A/2; See Domingo to Arnett, January 29, 1941, JA, NMP, 4/60/2A/2.
305. *Daily Gleaner*, January 10, 1941.
306. Manley to Domingo, January 18, 1941, JA, NMP, 4/60/2A/2.
307. *Public Opinion*, January 18, 1941.
308. Ibid.
309. Watson to Department of State, Semi-Annual Report, January 9, 1941, NARA, RG 84, Records of the Foreign Service Posts, Jamaica, U.S. Consulate Kingston, Classified General Records, 1936-1941 All Files, Box 1.
310. *Public Opinion*, January 18, 1941.
311. Ibid.
312. Domingo to Arnett, January 15, 1941, JA, NMP, 4/60/2A/2.
313. Ibid.
314. Domingo to Arnett, January 21, 1941, JA, NMP, 4/60/2A/2.
315. Ibid.
316. *Daily Gleaner*, January 29, 1941.
317. Ibid., February 7, 1941.
318. Hart, *Towards*, 115.
319. Ibid.
320. Domingo to Campbell, March 8, 1941, JA, NMP, 4/60/2A/2.
321. Ibid.
322. Domingo to Roberts, March 12, 1941, NLJ, WAR, MS 353, Box 2b.
323. Domingo to Manley, March 12, 1941, JA, NMP, 4/60/2A/2.
324. Domingo to Roberts, March 3, 1941, NLJ, WAR, MS 353, Box 2b.
325. Domingo to Campbell, March 13, 1941, NMP, 4/60/2A/2.
326. Ibid.
327. Domingo to Campbell, March 13, 1941, JA, NMP, 4/60/2A/2.
328. Domingo to Manley, March 25, 1941, JA, NMP, 4/60/2A/2.
329. Ibid.
330. Roberts to Domingo, March 16, 1941, NLJ, WAR, MS 353, Box 2b.
331. Roberts to Domingo, March 25, 1941, NLJ, WAR, MS 353, Box 2b.

332. Brown to McFarlane, April 23, 1941, NLJ, JPL, MS 234.
333. *Daily Gleaner*, March 19, 1941.
334. Minutes of Conference on Constitutional Proposal, March 20, 1941, NLJ, JPL, MS 234.
335. *Daily Gleaner*, May 22, 1941.
336. PNP, 'Forward March', undated [1941].
337. *Daily Gleaner*, May 22, 1941, see also Hart, *Towards*, 117.
338. Progressive League Statement, March 1941, NLJ, JPL, MS 234.
339. Jamaica Progressive League-Statement, March 1941, NLJ, JPL, MS 234.
340. Roberts to Domingo, May 9, 1941, NLJ, WAR, MS 353, Box 2b.
341. Domingo to Roberts, June 3, 1941, NLJ, WAR, MS 353, Box 2b.
342. *New York Amsterdam News*, May 31, 1941.
343. Domingo to Roberts, June 3, 1941, NLJ, WAR, MS 353, Box 2b.

CHAPTER 7: REASSUMING THE STRUGGLE FOR INDEPENDENCE IN JAMAICA

Domingo and Roberts in Jamaica in the 1940s and 1950s

The Detention of W.A. Domingo

The Jamaica Progressive League attempted to influence the changing course of decolonization and played an active role in the interplay of power relations between Great Britain, the US, the transnational activists, and the local groups in Jamaica. The combination of pressure from US diplomats, who demanded a signal from the British Empire toward decolonization, and increased demands for self-government in Jamaica, forced the Colonial Office to implement a series of liberalizations to mollify US diplomats and anti-colonial activists alike. While officials in London considered possible changes in the Jamaican constitution, Governor Arthur Frederick Richards continued to rule with a heavy hand, provoking widespread protests in Jamaica, the US and Great Britain. His actions were in direct opposition to the Colonial Office's new policy toward the region, especially his decision to detain Wilfred Domingo under the Defense Regulations. What was the result? Did it have the desired effect of preventing further radicalization or did it rather fuel the flames of anti-colonialist action?

Before Domingo reached Jamaican soil on June 17, 1941, he was given a surprise reception. Instead of encountering a big reception committee consisting of friends and co-workers, the Jamaican authorities arrested Domingo on board the ship. The following day, the *Gleaner* reported on the front page that the authorities '…apprehended Wilfred A. Domingo, well known both here and among West Indian circles in New York as one of the most outspoken champions of self-government for the West Indies. Under order of the Governor, Domingo has now been detained in Up Park Camp'.[1]

This drastic decision of the Governor shows how much power and influence Domingo was believed to have exerted on the already destabilized society in Jamaica. Anti-colonial and Communist literature found in his luggage further corroborated the fears of the authorities.[2] The Jamaican government, which had noticed Domingo's untiring propaganda efforts for self-government and the recent radicalizing influence of the WINEC and the Havana Conference on the People's National Party (PNP), had anticipated his arrival with anxiety.

The detention, although surely a shock, did not blindside Adolphe Roberts and Domingo. Domingo suspected that his letters to Jamaica were being steamed open to keep him under close observation while giving him the impression that he could speak his mind frankly in his letters to friends and colleagues in Jamaica.[3] Domingo was a bit nervous: 'It looked as if they had set a trap and were waiting to catch me. That is my real fear', he admitted in a letter to Roberts shortly before he left for Jamaica. But he was prepared to meet the consequences.[4] In numerous letters to his friend M.L. Campbell, Domingo repeated his suspicion:

> I am not a reckless person by nature; I am usually cautious; but when it comes to my political opinions I prefer to be frank, regardless of the danger. Of course, that does not mean that I will walk up to the prison, open the gate, walk in and slam it behind me. It does mean that I refuse to be terrorized when I believe I am right.[5]

Roberts was likewise aware of Great Britain's praxis to closely observe subversive movements. Accordingly, he proposed a secret code shortly before Domingo's departure to ensure that both men could continue their open exchange about developments and strategies.[6]

The developments in Jamaica were indeed alarming. Governor Richards' autocratic ruling style, the harsh Defense Regulations and the launch of the Undesired Publications Law contributed to the tense atmosphere. Between September 1940 and May 1941, several activists were arrested under the Defense Regulations, among them Bustamante Industrial Trade Union (BITU) leaders Alexander Bustamante and W.A. Williams, as well as Samuel S. Marquis, propaganda secretary of the PNP, and *Gleaner* journalist G. St C. Scotter.[7] The reasons for their detention orders were based on vague accusations about inflammatory, defeatist and anti-British statements. While Bustamante's verbal attacks on the government had reached a level that was hardly tolerable, some of the other detentions appeared to be out of proportion, and civic protest slowly started to become vocal. This time, it was not Bustamante's arrest that spurred a wave of protests. A representative of the country's upper class, Leslie Ashenheim, a *Gleaner* director, started to protest against what he felt was a deliberate violation of civil rights in the guise of the Defense Regulations, which were in fact more strict than those in England. The arrest of Scotter in particular, one of the *Gleaner's* top sport journalists, and, in the words of Richard Hart, 'an innocuous and probably very loyal Englishman',[8] stirred the *Gleaner* director's anger, which he expressed in several articles in the *Gleaner*.[9]

Scotter's detention had an ironic touch. In May 1940, Scotter had supported the Defense Regulations, while the PNP had organized protests against them.

He claimed: 'Millions of Empire citizens have gladly surrendered all their "civil rights and liberties" for wartime services needed, to keep those very civil rights and liberties in existence among mankind....'[10] It is questionable whether he still subscribed to that opinion while he was incarcerated.

With the detention of W.A. Domingo, public dismay reached its climax. Hart averred: 'His arbitrary imprisonment contributed to awakening public opinion in Jamaica and among Jamaicans in the U.S.A as to the extent of the Governor's autocratic and dictatorial rule'.[11]

The subsequent reactions highlight the importance as well as the high esteem Domingo enjoyed in Jamaica and in the US. Norman Manley was appalled when he heard what had happened. He felt guilty for having sent for Domingo and admitted in an interview on the *Gleaner*'s front page:

> I have never been more shocked and amazed in my life at any act done by this Government and I feel a terrible sense of responsibility because it was entirely of a result of my urgent personal appeals to Mr. Domingo that he made the great sacrifice of coming here.[12]

Manley testified that he had spoken with Domingo on 'hundreds of platforms and never heard him say a word that I could consider undue or extreme'. He recalled the hysterical reactions to Roberts and Domingo's propaganda while they were in Jamaica in 1939, when 'the wildest and most ridiculous stories' circulated and even Roberts, with his decidedly liberal and anti-Communist views, was accused of being a Communist. Referring to Roberts' liberal views, Manley stated: 'Mr. Domingo can be no dangerous man and remain a friend of Mr. Adolphe Roberts. You know men by the company they keep'. Manley personally vouched for Domingo, promising that he was loyal to Jamaica and that he defended Great Britain in the war, pointing to various public debates in New York, in which Domingo publicly supported the war. His detention was so shameful and unjustifiable that it must have been an error, Manley concluded. He was sure that Domingo's work would be of supreme value to the party, although, he admitted, it might cause some embarrassment for the authorities. He assured that Domingo would stir up no racial antagonism but strictly conform to the PNP's policy. Therefore, Manley felt, Domingo's detention was an arbitrary abuse of powers by the authorities.

In the same issue of the *Gleaner*, the PNP published a long and detailed statement protesting the detention. The statement lauded Domingo's work for the Progressive League and WINEC, his successful efforts at the Havana Conference and called him a 'liberal with mild socialistic leaning'. In regard to Domingo's work in Jamaica, the statement claimed: 'Thousands of people can testify to the fact that Mr. Domingo's work as a public speaker in Jamaica was distinguished by candour and moderation....' The PNP's statement explicitly referred to Domingo's service for the trade unions and recalled his important role in intermediating in the serious labour disputes of spring 1939 when Bustamante's stubbornness paralyzed the country,

> ...though this is not well known his [Domingo's] assistance freely given to the Trade Union Movement after the General Strike of 1939 proved of great use and his wise and prudent counsels and practical assistance did much to restore harmony and to pave the way for the peaceful elimination of conduct which was eventually achieved.

Similar to Manley's letter, the PNP expressed great sorrow about having 'unwittingly betrayed Mr. Domingo into the situation' and apologized to his friends and family in the US and in Jamaica. The PNP further complained that the government had not yet provided reasons for Domingo's detention.

Two days later, Manley published another statement:

> The facts about his recent career which can be proved and established will show that so far from being detained he should have had a public welcome for exceptionally valuable service to the cause of the West Indies and to the cause of Britain in this war.[13]

Manley emphasized that Domingo held no anti-British positions, but supported the war, mentioning that Domingo's only son was serving in the US army. Manley pointed out that Domingo's attitude toward the war had caused strong disapproval in African American circles and some of the more radical leftists even accused him of having pro-British tendencies. In regard to suspicions that he came with intentions to stir up racial antagonism, Manley recalled that it had been on Domingo's initiative that the Progressive League kept out racial connotations from its propaganda for self-government. He assumed that 'the whole island of Jamaica will regard this case as an acid test of what this Administration stands for'.[14] And this was exactly what happened; the Governor's action provoked a wave of protest, not only in Jamaica.

When the news reached the US, the WINC and the Progressive League immediately launched press releases stating their sympathy with Domingo, testifying to his innocence and demanding his immediate release.[15] The WINC resolved a protest resolution and sent it to Governor Richards, demanding the release of the 'stalwart champion of democratic rights'.[16] Furthermore, Domingo's detention started to involve organizations like the NAACP and encouraged them to send cables to Richards, Lord Moyne and Lord Halifax in protest of the 'undemocratic and Hitler-like act' and to give wide publicity to the matter.[17] The statement claimed that Domingo strictly advocated non-violent measures for reform of political and social conditions and that he would actively oppose defeatist positions.[18]

Roberts was in New Orleans when he heard about Domingo's detention. He contacted the officers of the League right away and sent a manuscript which he advised was to be read at a protest meeting, its conclusion demonstrating the need to invigorate the agitation for self-government:

> For members and supporters of the Jamaica Progressive League the lesson is plain. The struggle for self-government must be waged with more energy than ever before. Domingo is the League's first martyr. He is an object lesson of what can happen to any Jamaican so long as we do not control our own destinies.[19]

The Progressive League sent a cable to Lord Moyne, Secretary of State for the Colonies, that detailed the inconsistencies in Great Britain's foreign policy, protested against the Governor's 'tyrannical use of arbitrary powers provocative of disorder and revolt' and claimed that Great Britain 'cannot fight Hitler in Europe and support him in Jamaica'.[20]

This cable highlights the contradiction between the ideals of democracy with which Great Britain explained the war against Germany and the undemocratic methods the Empire's officials used to govern the colonies. An emergency protest meeting was scheduled on July 14, 1941, organized in cooperation with other Caribbean organizations in New York.[21] The report about the first of a series of mass meetings was enthusiastic. Ten speakers addressed the gathering at the Renaissance Casino, among them Ethelred Brown, who denounced the British policy as hypocritical: 'The greatest menace to the peace of Jamaica is not Wilfred Domingo but Sir Arthur Richards. He is goading the people to start a rebellion so that the soldiers may have a chance to shoot them down'.[22] Ivy Essien-Bailey, Progressive League member and Director of the Board of Strategy of the WINC, emphasized the unifying effect, saying that 'Domingo is a symbol of true democracy. We sink all differences that we may have had with the man during the course of his life here'. A resolution demanding the immediate release of Domingo was resolved.

Domingo's co-workers showed their sympathy and expressed their concern. In addition, the wider African American and Caribbean scene was very disturbed by the course of events in Jamaica and many came out in support of Domingo. On June 28, 1941, a lengthy article on Domingo's incarceration appeared in the *New York Amsterdam Star News*, which used expressions from the Second World War, drastically taken out of context, to exemplify the disgust about the detention of 'nationalist leader' Domingo:

> Crushing down with the might and ruthlessness of a Hitler blitzkrieg, the British Government in Jamaica last week-end moved to suppress further agitation for self-rule by Jamaicans, when it ordered the arrest of W. A. Domingo, leading advocate of independence for the West Indies,

on his arrival...Domingo was not allowed to land or communicate with friends or relatives, but rushed off to the concentration camp....[23]

This exemplifies increasing awareness of the antagonism between British ideals of democracy and imperial practice that provoked comparisons with fascist methods. The author of the article appreciated the protest that was immediately launched by organizations like the WINC and commended its members for sending out cablegrams to Lord Moyne, Governor Richards and various members of Parliament in England criticizing the Governor's 'tyrannical rule' under the Defense Regulations under which he would have 'more power than Hitler, Stalin and Mussolini combined'.[24]

Even the US authorities reacted with incomprehension and 'considerable anxiety'[25] to Domingo's detention. The State Department speculated about the reasons for the unwise actions of the Governor and disapproved of the recent detentions made under the Defense Regulations and complained that the detainees were 'not pro-Nazi or even anti-British, but simply against the Jamaican Government'.[26]

Domingo's detention provoked widespread protest in Jamaica and the US. Domingo's co-workers in the Progressive League and in the PNP deplored the violation of civil rights by the pre-emptive detention. Several individuals of Jamaica's elite who were traditionally loyal to Great Britain, for example, L.E. Ashenheim and Ansell Hart, were worried about the increasing contradiction between ideals and practice of the Empire and launched a massive civil protest in Jamaica. Roberts later commented on the positive effect of the Governors extreme act:

> For the legal profession, including even its most conservative members rallied together in protest against the imposition of defense regulations in a form that had been rejected by the English House of Commons as undemocratic. In June a Jamaican Council for Civic Liberties was launched, with L. E. Ashenheim as chairman. It proved to be a powerful factor in forcing the release of the detainees and, incidentally, in ending the rule of Richards.[27]

The prominent and respected attorney Ansell Hart, father of Richard Hart, felt that Domingo's detention was 'a case in which the lovers of freedom should not remain silent'.[28] Although he did not know Domingo personally, Hart senior stated that he was 'profoundly impressed by the method, quality, judgment, and moderation evinced by his writings'. He felt that the arrest was in connection with the service Domingo planned to render to the island in its political development. He was very disturbed by the course that the government was taking and complained openly about the arbitrary abuse of the extraordinary powers granted to the government since the outbreak of the war: 'Today it is Scotter or

Domingo, tomorrow it may be Manley or anyone – you or me.' Concluding, he encouraged his compatriots to unite in the effort to defend liberty and freedom, not only because of personal fears, but motivated by a real spirit of unity for a political change.

Hart and Ashenheim's voices were heard, and the protest against the Governor and the curtailing of civil liberties found its first repercussion in a huge 'Civil Liberties Meeting' organized by the PNP, aimed at establishing a National Civil Liberties Council, similar and affiliated to the powerful Council in England.[29] The meeting was well-received and described on the front page of the *Gleaner* as 'one of the largest, most representative and enthusiastic meetings ever held in this island'.[30] The list of renowned speakers from various corners of the society, for example Ashenheim, Manley, Henry Brinton and H.M. Shirley of the BITU, proves Hart's wish for a uniting effect to have come true. Like its role model in England, the Civil Liberties Council was dedicated to compelling British authorities to grant amendments of the Defense Regulations in Jamaica in order to prevent abuse by the Governor. Accordingly, the gathering resolved a protest resolution and decided to send a direct petition for amendments of the regulations personally to the King.

It was frequently criticized that Great Britain had already amended and changed its Defense Regulations in England, while the more restrictive Regulations were still valid in Jamaica. In his speech, BITU officer H.M. Shirley emphasized that Domingo's detention was a violation of civil rights and claimed:

> The removal of Mr. Domingo from that ship would always be remembered in the heart and lives of all the people of Jamaica irrespective of color or class or creed, because after all it was nothing short of a cutting off completely of the liberties of His Majesty's subject.[31]

Manley lauded the new unity in the society and hoped that this spirit would prevail.

While not everyone was convinced that Domingo's arrest was a mistake, and a *Gleaner* editorial played down the differences in English and Jamaican Defense Regulations to counter the united spirit,[32] an increasing number of Jamaicans became aware of the contradictions in British imperialism and protested against the curtailment of civil rights and personal freedom.[33] Even in the reactionary Legislative Council, the demand for an amendment of the Defense Regulations was favourably discussed, accusing the Governor of excessively misusing his power.[34] However, the Governor appeared to be unmoved by the united spirit and refused the motion.[35] Although Domingo's detention resulted in an impressively broad wave of protest in Jamaican society, most members of the Civil Liberties Council were not adopting a radical anti-colonial attitude, but were rather interested in eliminating the open contradictions in the Empire's policy by bringing the Defense Regulations in accordance with those in Great Britain.

Nevertheless, Manley and the PNP were further radicalized by the Governor's attitude and tried to support Domingo in the most effective manner possible. Manley arranged for N.N. Nethersole to serve as Domingo's legal counsel, and he immediately got in touch with various organizations in the US and requested to gather as much material as possible to contribute to the evidence he needed to defend Domingo.[36] Manley and his wife Edna frequently visited Domingo at the detention camp and kept in close contact with the WINC and the Progressive League, reporting that Domingo met the situation 'with courage as those who know him would expect'.[37]

Preparing Domingo's defence was hindered by the fact that the Governor had still not presented official reasons for the detention. In July, the Colonial Secretary in answering an inquiry by the League, presented vague accusations and declared that the detention of Domingo was meant to prevent him 'from acting in any manner prejudicial to public safety and defence'.[38] Yet, as a result of the massive protest, the Defense Regulations were amended in August and brought in line with those in Great Britain.[39] Domingo and the other detainees were now entitled to a hearing and an explanation of the reasons for their arrest.

Hence, in September, the Governor was forced to present official reasons. He informed Domingo that the government 'has reasonable cause to believe that Domingo has recently been concerned in acts prejudicial to the public safety or the defense of the realm, or in the preparation or instigation of such acts'.[40] One day later Domingo was given a detailed list containing a number of charges against him that were neither based on his public utterances in New York or Jamaica, nor on his numerous articles in *Public Opinion*. Instead, as previously suspected by Domingo, they were based on secretly intercepted letters between himself and M.L. Campbell, Norman Manley, V.L. Arnett and E.E.A. Campbell. The charges included four major points:

- a) to promote and foster anti-British sentiments and to embarrass and impede the policy of the Imperial and local Governments in relation to the war effort;
- b) to foster defeatist sentiments;
- c) to excite opposition to the policy of the Imperial Government allowing the United States to establish defense bases in Jamaica and to embarrass and delay the rapid execution of plans for establishing such bases; and
- d) to promote and foster amongst the coloured population of Jamaica feelings of colour prejudice and racial animosity, in particular by alleging the existence of those feelings amongst officers and men of the United States Forces, likely to be stationed in Jamaica.

The PNP then published a pamphlet to counter the charges. It painted a very positive and balanced picture of Domingo and repudiated every single accusation. It argued that the charges would not provide justification for a detention because they were based on private letters that could hardly qualify for propaganda. Only the letters to Campbell contained statements with the potential to offend the authorities, the PNP argued, but in these Domingo only shared his private views with a friend who played no active role in Jamaican politics. Lengthy examples of content and tone of the letters followed, reviewing the details of his unfair trial. The pamphlet concluded:

> The letters do show that Domingo loves his own race more than he does the English or any other European race – they do show his dislike of all forms of Imperialism, they do contain some hurt and bitter statements. But, and this is the whole point, he is not supposed to be locked up for his private likes and dislikes. He is locked up on specific charges of acts done or intended to be done. A fair and impartial study of all the known facts disproves, absolutely disproves all the charges. False in spirit they are and false in fact. Domingo is a victim of fear and prejudice.

The following trial was unfair; hearings were often postponed; only a few persons were questioned, and a number of witnesses proposed by Domingo were denied the chance to speak. At the important hearing of M.L. Campbell, Domingo was excluded, so that this hearing remained obscure.

Domingo prepared his own lengthy statement, answering all allegations. Domingo denied that he would 'promote and foster anti-British and defeatist sentiments'.[41] The contrary was true, he claimed; he had supported Great Britain in the war, as his position in many public debates would prove. In the US, he was even alleged to be a 'British apologist'. He had bought US defence bonds, his son served in the US army and, so he asserted, he was saying nothing different than British officials who would now start to see for themselves how serious the situation was. Domingo disclosed: 'My opinions on the military situation fluctuate with the undisputed actualities and represent my wishes no more than the forecasting of hurricane by the local meteorologist represents his wishes'.

Against the charge that he would 'embarrass and impede the policy of the Imperial Government in relation to the war effort', he answered:

> My intended short stay in Jamaica under the conditions of my coming could not by any stretch of the most elastic imagination achieve what is charged. How could any one person, short of a superman, on a three or four month visit to the island, under the constant control of Mr. Manley and the other executives of the People's National Party and the watchful eyes of the police and its secret agents succeed in embarrassing and impeding the war Policy of the local Government, let alone the Policy of the Imperial Government?

Domingo and his supporters claimed that all charges were without foundation, and that Domingo was neither anti-war, nor defeatist or opposed to the bases. However, what really was Domingo's attitude toward the war and Great Britain during this time? The following survey of Domingo's positions will answer this question and serve to further explore Domingo's theoretical and political positions during the Second World War.

In August 1940, Domingo explained his position in a nutshell. 'If I am anything at all it is anti-Fascist, anti-imperialist and definite Pro-Jamaican. That defines my patriotism'.[42] Indeed, his strong opposition to fascism and imperialism and a clear demand for the independence of Jamaica can be regarded as the essence of his attitude toward Great Britain during the war. While some of the letters on which the charges were based contained harsh verdicts on the menace of fascism and racism in Europe, the US, and also Great Britain, Domingo's views can hardly be described as defeatist. Domingo frequently expressed that he hoped for a British victory over Germany and encouraged black West Indians and African Americans to give their full support to the war; although he admitted:

> I am not the least bit concerned about the outcome of the war from the standpoint of Europe or Europeans. They and their continent and civilization would sink in the ocean without evoking a tear from me, but I must think of Africa and my people.[43]

In a letter of April 1941, he affirmed this position and explained:

> My position is one of pure racial selfishness and working-class consciousness in relation to world realities. Above all, I do not want Russia or Negroes to rush headlong into the struggle and pull England and France's chestnuts out of the fire. I want Germany beaten, but for racial and proletarian reasons.[44]

This testifies to the foundations of Domingo's thought in Socialism and black international solidarity. In face of the menace of fascism, Domingo's arguments show a special emphasis on race and racial unity, showing again how much his nationalism was part of an international black emancipation project. Although the first quote has a strong anti-British connotation, Domingo expressed that to prevent a British defeat, black people needed to uncompromisingly support Great Britain in any war against fascist powers. He feared that the Empire could openly become fascist and argued that takeover by a fascist regime would consequentially reduce Jamaica's chances to become self-governed.[45]

Although Domingo generally supported Great Britain in the war, he did not hide his true opinion about Great Britain and his anti-colonial convictions. Especially in the letters to Campbell, Domingo did not mince words. Employing the race argument again he stated:

> I hope that the British will win because of our future as a race, but ordinarily I would derive quite some satisfaction from the spectacle of the two great exponents of white racial supremacy exterminating themselves. I would enjoy the circus best if despite the severe retribution inflicted upon the murderers of Africans and other unarmed colored peoples the British emerge victors.[46]

Statements like this surely contributed to the allegations that Domingo would foster anti-British sentiments, despite his advocacy of supporting Britain in the war.

Domingo's frequent attacks on the censor probably contributed further to the anger of the authorities. In many letters he wrote to Campbell and Roberts, Domingo commented on the censor and compared the practice with fascist methods: 'That is why the British are so disliked everywhere. They pretend that they believe in democracy while as a matter of fact they are the worst tyrants on earth save the Fascists whom they so closely resemble and whom they long antedated'.[47]

However, while Domingo harshly criticized Great Britain for its imperialism and fascist tendencies, he was more anti-colonial than genuinely anti-British. Only around the time of the Havana Conference did Domingo consider how the anti-colonialist cause could benefit from a possible British defeat and saw the chance that the Act of Havana provided a great chance for the timely achievement of independence in Jamaica.[48] Nevertheless, Domingo still welcomed the entry of the US and Russia into the war. On the one hand he hoped that a united effort of the Allies would be able to prevent a fascist take-over of Europe, on the other, he felt that the two countries would support a democratic and anti-imperialist solution for the colonies at the peace talks.[49]

In order to encourage African Americans and fellow Caribbeans to support Great Britain in the war, Domingo gave numerous speeches and participated in various public debates.[50] His views stood in stark contrast to the opinion held by most African Americans and black Caribbeans in New York, among them many of his close friends and associates, many of which supported George S. Schuyler's Negroes against the War Committee.[51] They opposed any participation in a European war between imperialist and fascist nations and condemned Great Britain's concept of democracy as racist and hypocritical, since it did not include non-white nations. Domingo's position, being pro-Britain in the war and being pro-Russia was a minority position, shared only by A. Philipp Randolph, Domingo claimed.[52]

In a letter to Campbell, Domingo admitted that on a theoretical level he shared the scepticism of most African Americans regarding Great Britain's sincerity in the question of war aims. Nevertheless, he was convinced that supporting Great

Britain was necessary to stop the fascist forces and stated his view in public. At a meeting attended by various Caribbean nationals from different islands at which the majority advocated non-participation of islanders in a 'white man's war or an imperialistic war',[53] he publicly declared that as long as one side of the combatants advocated fascism, black people should support the other side. On behalf of the League, he rejected subscribing to a resolution against participation in the war that was adopted by the meeting. For this stand, Domingo was harshly criticized by a majority of the audience, including his close friends Huiswoud and Moore. In a letter to Campbell, Domingo explained his position:

> ...we hate fascism more than we do British Imperialism, although in my case I dislike both intensely as the stranglers of the legitimate aspiration of our people in Africa and elsewhere to control their own affairs in their own interest.[54]

This disagreement between Domingo and his friend Richard B. Moore led to the idea of a series of public debates. In December 1939, the 'battle royal'[55] between the two icons of radical Caribbean activism in Harlem took place on the question: 'Should British Colonial Negroes Support the British Empire in the Present War?'[56] Although he knew that Moore's position was more popular, Domingo encouraged his listeners to support the war without abandoning the fight for independence: 'Yes, fight for your right, fight Britain for self-government but beware that you don't jump from the British frying pan into the Nazi fire'.[57]

Domingo lost the debate, but felt that Moore did not win by his arguments. In a letter to Campbell, he propounded:

> ...He did not debate the question at all. He simply ranted about the wrongs England had inflicted upon Negroes for centuries and about the possibility of British colonies in Africa and the West Indies revolting. I demanded that he should cite a single colony with Negro population that is prepared psychologically, militarily, politically to follow his mad advice and he could not show one.[58]

Several intellectuals from the audience attested that Moore was not able to present convincing arguments to prove his point but instead appealed to emotions.[59] The public debate on the highly controversial subject was a big success and a series of similar debates followed, sponsored by different organizations.[60] However, while Domingo and Moore were fierce opponents in the debates, Joyce Moore Turner calls attention to the fact that despite their opposite opinions in regard to the war, both men shared a 'deep friendship' and an 'ardor for forensic forays'.[61] Moreover, Moore and other associates would change their minds during the course of the war. Moore Turner states: 'As the war progressed, Moore, Briggs and Huiswoud found themselves on Domingo's side, favoring support for the Allies. They began to appreciate that the war would aid their cause against

British and Dutch colonialism....'⁶² This change of mind illuminates Domingo's influence and shows the importance of the WINC and the anti-colonial hopes the Havana Conference inspired.

However, the Governor was neither interested in the fact that Domingo wanted to see Great Britain win the war, nor did he feel that private letters should not qualify as propaganda. He decided that Domingo was guilty and imprisoned him until the end of the war and, similar to the charges, explained that Domingo had recently been involved in acts '...prejudicial to the public safety or defense, or in the preparation or instigation of such acts. Evidence is available which indicates that Mr. Domingo has been engaged in defeatist and anti-war propaganda, including propaganda designed to stimulate opposition on racial grounds to the establishment of United States Bases in the West Indies'.[63]

An assessment of his position reveals that Domingo's general attitude toward Great Britain was far more complex than the Governor would admit. However, it is also undeniable that the letters contained strong anti-British statements. Domingo was not against the bases in general, but he was rather more concerned about a possible transfer of American standards of race discrimination based on the one-drop rule, and he objected to the fact that the island's population was not consulted in the negotiations of such far-reaching decisions.

The wider public in Jamaica, in the US and even in Great Britain regarded Domingo's conviction as unjustified and disproportional. Hence, Domingo's imprisonment caused exactly the reactions the British officials feared: defeatist, anti-British, anti-colonial outbursts in the US press and even among liberals in England. The decision was grist to the mills of those who were already sceptical toward the honesty of Great Britain's motives in the war, and various individuals, prominent figures and institutions rallied behind Domingo.

Domingo had successfully prepared for the machinery of protest to commence immediately. Shortly before he left for Jamaica, he told Campbell:

> [O]ne never knows what the shining knights of democracy in control of Jamaica may attempt. I will naturally arrange my affairs here so as to give the British some very unwelcome publicity of a persistent kind if I am unduly bothered. It is the kind of publicity that will not do them any good, even in this country.[64]

Domingo had done well. Numerous articles and statements testify how much Richards' style of governance and especially Domingo's detention were able to provoke anti-British sentiments. A letter to the *New York Amsterdam Star News* exemplifies this effect in a powerful way:

> This man Richards is serving the ends of the subversive forces which would destroy the British Empire because his acts are such as tend to raise a battle cry of freedom in the hearts of the people of Jamaica.

> He is doing his best to bring about another 'Morant Bay Rebellion' and make of men like Manley, Nethersole, Bustamante and Domingo, 'George William Gordons'. The cause of self-government and social reform in Jamaica, and the West Indies for that matter, is closely allied to the imprisonment of Domingo. If he is allowed to remain in a concentration camp until the end of the war, it will mean a victory of the forces of oppression; the continued degradation of the black race in the West Indies, and a step that will take us back to the dark days of chattel slavery.[65]

An editorial of the *New York Amstredam Star News* also condemned Domingo's detention and regarded the act as a 'severe blow to the cause of democracy and small nations'.[66] Criticizing the detentions under the Defense Regulations as fascist and dictatorial, the editorial concluded that the detentions would not appease the situation, but rather have an opposite effect and provoke harsh critique on Great Britain.

National Association for the Advancement of Colored People (NAACP) Secretary Walter White shared the feeling that Governor Richards' attitude was dangerous. In a letter to Franklin D. Roosevelt's advisor for the West Indies, Charles Taussig, he made known his regrets:

> I think the arrest is exceedingly unwise if not stupid as it is, in the first place, useless, and in the second, will increase suspicion of the integrity of the British War aims far more than would any speeches or other acts by a dozen Domingos.[67]

White contacted Secretary of State Hull to draw his attention to the matter and to express his 'very great resentment'.[68] White's reactions highlight how the African American-Caribbean solidarity was able to bring the resentment of the activists to the attention of US officials.

Roy Wilkins, also of the NAACP, wrote in his column: 'Another evidence of British stupidity and cruelty is found in the arrest of W.A. Domingo, militant West Indian leader who has lived in New York for many years'.[69] Metz T.P. Lochard of the *Chicago Defender* denounced polemically:

> Britain is using the Gestapo method to intimidate and discourage British subjects who look too critically at John Bull. It is not necessary for them to say or do anything of a truly seditious character. If they frown or raise their eyebrows at King George's picture on a postage stamp, they are not likely to enjoy their personal freedom very long.[70]

One article in the *New York Amstredam Star News* called Domingo's detention the 'Dreyfus case' of the British West Indies.[71] These sentiments impressively show how his detention fortified anti-British sentiments. Also, renowned isolationist organizations like the America First Committee used Domingo's case as another example of the fascist methods used by Churchill and renewed its counsel that the US should not enter the war and become a close ally of Great Britain.[72]

Various individuals believed in Domingo's innocence and started to approach influential persons in the hope that they could petition the US officials on his behalf. Among them were millionaire and Socialist Alfred Baker Lewis, who encouraged White to pressure the US authorities,[73] journalist and member of the isolationist 'America First Committee' Oswald Garrison Villard,[74] and Socialist Norman Thomas.[75] Lucille B. Millner, Secretary of the American Civil Liberties Union, petitioned the State Department to intervene in the matter.[76] In Consul Watson's semi-annual report to the State Department, he also questioned the wisdom of Richards' decision with similar arguments.[77]

The various reactions show that the matter created a considerable public stir, reaching the highest offices of the US. Yet, all these efforts were in vain. The officials argued that there was nothing they could do to interfere in British matters, asserting that Domingo was not a US citizen. Even Walter White's contact in the State Department promised to see if he could be of help,[78] but a few days later the legal advisor of the State Department answered White: '… Mr. Domingo is not an American citizen, it would not be appropriate for the Department to take any action with respect to this matter'.[79] White still did not drop the subject matter and expressed his deep concern. Alluding to the discontent of African Americans, he suggested that the State Department should continue its investigations and exert its influence on the British officials.[80] Other organizations, like the Society for the Americas, emphasized the legitimacy of the Jamaican fight for freedom. Its president, D. Stockton Stevens, sent a letter to Sumner Welles, Undersecretary of State, promising to send representations to the 21 American republics to increase pressure on Great Britain and asked him to lend support for the 'colonial champion of self-government'.[81] However, the attitude of the State Department remained the same: since Domingo was not a US citizen, there was nothing that the officials could do.[82] There was more behind the State Department's stance, namely the fact that they were not terribly keen about Domingo's return to Harlem. US officials feared a radicalizing effect on the African American–Caribbean milieu.

The strong reactions in the US were of course noticed by British officials. Reginald Pierrepoint quoted one official at the British Embassy in the US:

> Sir Arthur is a fool to use such high handed methods as boarding an American ship and seizing a passenger and imprisoning him without trial. We are straining every effort to convince the American people of our democracy. The silly ass should let the man go and blow out his own brains. This thing can do irreparable harm to our cause in America.[83]

In England, the detention also provoked critique of colonial rule. The Council for Civil Liberties resolved a protest note, signed by David Adams, A. Creech Jones and H.B. Morgan.[84] In the resolution, debates in the House of Commons about Domingo's case were mentioned in which his excellent reputation was emphasized. In the debate, Creech Jones 'paid a tribute to the integrity of Domingo and his excellent work in the United States'.[85] Various members of the British Labour Party strongly protested against Domingo's detention, while conservatives like Sir Leonard Lyle of the sugar empire 'Tate and Lyle' defended the action of Governor Richards.[86]

The Colonial Office felt uneasy about the international reactions Richards' action provoked. Undersecretary of State for the Colonies, George Hall, went personally to Jamaica to investigate the situation. An article in *New York Amsterdam Star News* interpreted this decision and reflected that Domingo's detention and the following reactions were a 'source of unusual embarrassment to the British Government'.[87]

The support for Domingo was overwhelming and widespread. However, the unity and unqualified support did not last long. Remarkably, it was from within the inner circle of the Progressive League that doubts started to arise whether Domingo's arrest was possibly not fully unjustified. This is particulary important as it proves that the radical anti-colonial position held by Domingo and Roberts was not shared by all members of the Progressive League.

Initially, Progressive League Secretary Brown supported the common approach; he pledged his full and unequivocal support, denounced Richards' actions as 'atrocious, un-English and arbitrary' and boldly declared that 'tyrants can only be defeated by resistance'.[88] In July 1941, Brown still argued that Domingo's detention was purely preemptive and while today Domingo was arrested, tomorrow it could be himself or somebody else.[89] He suspected that some informers from New York had supplied misleading information to the officials and pledged: 'Knowing Domingo as I do, as a friend and as a political co-worker for 21 years I am sure that any information which could justify his arrest and detention was false and malicious'.[90]

Yet, slowly, Brown's statements became more cautious and distanced. In a naive way, he seemed not to be able to believe that Domingo's fight for self-government was exactly the reason for his detention. In a letter to the *Gleaner*, Brown quoted from a conversation with the Colonial Secretary in which he assured that the Progressive League directors would believe in:

> ...the British ideal of justice and the British tradition of fairplay, they confidently cherish the hope the deliberate and solemn assurance of the bona fides and absolutely patriotic intentions of Mr. Domingo will serve to correct the false information which presumably led his

Excellency to assume that Mr. Domingo's arrest and detention are necessary, and thus secure his early and honorable release.⁹¹

After the charges had been made public and Domingo's detention been officially prolonged, Brown and some of the directors withdrew their support. In a letter to Cordell Hull, Brown asserted:

> The directors wish to assure you that in spite of the indiscrete and improper remarks contained in letters written by Mr. Domingo, which would justify his arrest and detention, he had no intention whatever to engage in any subversive activities either here or in Jamaica. He may be likened to a dog who barks but never bites.⁹²

This statement was a severe blow to Domingo. Not only the offending statement which compared Domingo to a harmless dog, but particularly Brown's concession that the content of Domingo's personal letters was of an incriminatory nature was a hurting insult for Domingo.⁹³ To make matters worse, the Progressive League executive decided to officially disassociate from Domingo. In an FBI report about a meeting in January 1942, Brown was reported telling the audience:

> ...at a recent meeting of the board of directors, it was decided that they should drop all work pertaining to the Domingo case as they thought in this way they would better serve the interest of the organization. He stated that they were not ready to give an answer for their change of policy at the present time, and requested them not to discuss the subject or ask any questions concerning the case, but to leave it to the discretion of the board of directors to act for them.⁹⁴

However, the Progressive League was seemingly split over the matter. At a meeting in the following months, Arthur King, treasurer of the WINC and member of the Progressive League, harshly criticized the stand of the Progressive League, 'pointing out that the West Indies National Council is continuing to work for the release of Domingo and accused the Progressive League of taking a cowardly stand'. Some Progressive League members reportedly sided with King, and Brown was forced to defend his decision. He explained that the board had decided on the basis of the material relating to Domingo's case which had been handed over to them by Manley. The letters to Campbell in particular had caused grave concern among the directors:

> ...they were shocked by their contents. He stated that they arrived at the conclusion that the Governor of Jamaica was justified in holding Domingo. He stated that in some of these letters, Domingo mentioned that after his arrival in Jamaica, there would be a revolution at the very gateway to the United States, and that if England wanted another India in the West Indies she would get it after he arrived in Jamaica. He stated that Domingo also condemned all of the democracies and entered into considerable name-calling of various British and American officials. He

also advised the audience that there were other things in his letters which he was ashamed to read to them.

The arguments mentioned by Brown were outright misinterpretations and quoted out of context.

Roberts was stunned and wrote to Manley, sharing his disgust about the decision of the directors of the Progressive League to withdraw their unqualified support for Domingo: 'Indeed, I was fully as shocked by the action of the Jamaica Progressive League here as you were'.[95] Roberts mentioned an incriminating letter from Brown addressed to Domingo, about which Manley had informed him. From Brown's standpoint at the meeting and Robert's reaction, it is reasonable to conclude that Brown had informed Domingo that the Progressive League had distanced itself from the content of his letters to Jamaica and that some members would have some degree of understanding for the Governor's reaction. Roberts emphasized:

> At all events, I disassociate myself from his [Browns] letter. I am not now a member of the board. ...That Brown and others here should have accepted, even temporarily, the Jamaica Government's contention in preference to yours was a stupid and scandalous blunder.[96]

Roberts assured Manley that he harshly criticized Brown and encouraged him to repair the damage. In a letter to Edna Manley, he called the Progressive League decision an 'outrageous blunder' and wondered whether it had 'prejudiced our friend's case'.[97]

The cracks within the Progressive League's ranks reflect a more fundamental disagreement over ideologies and programme. Obviously, the more conservative members of the Progressive League were increasingly concerned about Domingo's cooperation with renowned Communists in the WINC. At a meeting on May 4, 1942, Brown reportedly stated:

> ...some of the members had evidently felt the League was somewhat Communistic as a result of their fight for Domingo and had stopped attending their meetings. He stated for that reason they had decided to adopt a new constitution to explain their demand for self-government in Jamaica and to drop the Domingo case temporarily.[98]

The sources do not give further information on the atmosphere in the Progressive League. However, in a personal conversation with two FBI informants in April, Brown explained his change of mind. First, Brown argued that Domingo appeared to be in favour of the Axis powers in the letters. Second, he formerly believed that Domingo had been opposed to any Communist position. Now 'he had changed his opinion of Domingo somewhat and was not quite sure of his stand'. Brown described his own position as opposed to Communism and readily declared that his earlier sympathies, for example, in the Davis campaign, were motivated by anti-racism.

The position of the Progressive League directors indicated a decided shift to the right. The disassociation had at least one desired result; the concluding FBI report summarized: 'Inasmuch as the activities of this organization do not appear to be of a nature inimical to the United States at the present time, this case is being closed'.[99]

The ideological differences between the Progressive League and the WINC were evident, but now the factions within had also become more visible. Without the leadership of Domingo and Roberts, the Progressive League drifted toward an increasingly conservative and conformist attitude. Interestingly, Roberts and Domingo's relationship had become even closer, although Roberts had been an exemption without any Socialist sympathies in his biography, whereas many of the early members had been active in Harlem's leftist circles. In comparison with Domingo, Brown had been much more moderate from the start. With his recent attitude, Brown had alienated himself from the radical stand Domingo and Roberts were prepared to assume to reach the predominant goal: independence for Jamaica.

The ideological differences that became visible over the question of support for Domingo even led to the founding of a splinter organization to the WINC.[100] In March 1944, the American West Indian Association on Caribbean Affairs was founded on the initiative of Jamaican-born businessman Herbert Simeon Boulin. The FBI report reveals that Ethelred Brown was part of the board of directors. Other Progressive League members like T.E. Hanson and Lucien M. Brown were part of the 'group of conservative Negroes of British West Indian ancestry' who founded the new organization with the aim 'to oppose the alleged Communist influence of the West Indies National Council'.[101] However, the organization was short-lived and could not find much support in New York, while the WINC continued its strong and unrestricted support for Domingo. In contrast to the Progressive League's meek and undecided stand, the WINC celebrated its president as a martyr for the anti-colonial cause and declared: 'Domingo's imprisonment is a cause of all oppressed peoples. He is the Nehru of the West Indies and like Nehru, can be rescued from prison by the people'.[102]

In mid-1942, Domingo's re-entry permit to the US would expire, hence Domingo and his supporters tried to convince the authorities to release him, promising that he would immediately leave Jamaica. Among those who tried to convince the authorities were Brown,[103] Manley,[104] George S. Schuyler, Roy Wilkens and Walter White of the NAACP,[105] Alfred Baker Lewis[106] and WINC secretary H.P. Osborne.[107] However, the Governor had grave concerns:

> I presume it is fully realized that if Domingo is released to go to the U.S.A., he will immediately start a virulent anti-British campaign in America and will no doubt be clever enough to keep under cover himself. I have the gravest doubt of the wisdom of letting him go, even if the U.S. authorities were unexpectedly to agree to receive him.[108]

Richards' decision to keep Domingo behind bars stirred further trouble when he released Bustamante on February 8, 1942. Immediately, Bustamante launched a vigorous campaign against the PNP, after its officers had helped to keep the BITU alive during his incarceration.[109] Bustamante felt betrayed by Manley and threatened by Domingo's presence in Jamaica, accusing Manley of trying to sabotage him, to infiltrate the BITU and to install Domingo as a rival to replace him. In a long statement in the *Gleaner*, Bustamante claimed that Manley had actively decreased the speed of his release, and in the meantime had tried to split the BITU. Bustamante claimed to know the correspondence between Domingo and Manley and claimed that it contained statements that the PNP had asked Domingo to return to Jamaica to run the unions.[110] On another occasion, Bustamante claimed that even earlier he had been suspicious about Domingo:

> Manley once told me, 'You must keep your eyes on Domingo. He is a great man'. I smiled, but I said to myself: I will keep my eyes upon Domingo and upon you.[111]

Right after his release, Bustamante dismissed the BITU leadership around H.M. Shirley, who had closely cooperated with the PNP and TUC during his detention.[112] Bustamante's hatred reached a bizarre peak with a symbolical 'burying' of Manley and Shirley's 'bodies' at a BITU mass meeting in April, while the gathering was intoning funeral songs.[113]

Was there a grain of truth in Bustamante's allegations? Did Domingo intend to involve himself in the trade unions? In 1969, *Gleaner* editor Theodore Sealy encouraged the West India Reference Library to collect as much personal collections as possible to answer some of the unanswered questions in Jamaican history. As an example for those questions, he mentioned the reasons why Domingo came to Jamaica in 1941.[114]

While Manley more likely had the impact on the trade unions in mind when he called for Domingo, Domingo and Roberts pursued their unshakable goal of self-government. Roberts felt sure that the reasons for Domingo's detention laid in his agitation for self-government and his active role in the Progressive League and the WINC. He explicitly stated:

> We now know to what length the British Government intends to go, to silence voices that demand real self-government. Let us not be deceived. The arrest of Domingo is due not to the fact that he was entering Jamaica to work for the PNP, but to his connection with the Jamaica Progressive League and the West Indies National Council.[115]

An article in the *New York Amsterdam Star News* also saw the reasons for Domingo's detention related to his 'activities on behalf of self-government' and his agitation against 'racial discrimination in connection with the aerial and naval bases'.[116]

However, Manley felt immediately that the detention was connected to the service that Domingo intended to render to the PNP and also to the trade unions. Manley emphasized that Domingo came only because of the party's invitation and that he was supposed to be engaged especially in fields of education and the trade unions.[117] But while Manley admitted that the PNP supported union members who wished to democratize the unions, he firmly rejected Bustamante's suspicion that he had called for Domingo to take over the leadership of the unions to weaken Bustamante's leadership while he was detained.[118]

Yet, Bustamante was not the only one who felt that Domingo came to challenge his leadership role. While both men were still imprisoned, Legislative Council member C.A. Reid asked provocatively in a letter to the *Gleaner*: 'I should like to know whether there is any truth in the rumor that Domingo was being brought out here to take Bustamante's job? Because that is the rumor since Bustamante has been away and must of necessity be quiet'.[119] Manley reacted immediately and condemned the 'very discreditable attempt made by Mr. Reid to create friction between the Bustamante Trade Union and myself'.[120] He then still felt sure that the officers of the BITU, including Bustamante, would firmly reject the allegations; 'he is attempting the impossible when he tries to propagate a type of lie designed to set the progressive forces in this country at each other's ears'.[121] Manley suspected that class interests were the motives to bring about a split in the working class, fearing the power of the masses under universal suffrage. Ex-BITU vice president Shirley approved Manley's statement and protested against the attempt to spread rumours about animosity between the PNP and the BITU.[122]

When discussions came up in September 1941 that Bustamante's case would be revised, the *Gleaner* actively spread the rumour that Domingo had come to take Bustamante's place:

> The most recent detainee was W.A. Domingo, who came to Jamaica on an invitation of the People's National Party to do work in connection with the Labour Union. Should Bustamante be released he will be in a position to perform the task himself.[123]

Others, for example, Benjamin B. Wilson,[124] complained about the article and speculated: 'it will certainly have the effect it was intended to create among those who view all such matters with a jaundiced opinion' and was convinced that 'Mr. Domingo...harbours no ambition of leading labour or superseding anyone'.[125]

These statements show that the split between the BITU and the PNP was definitely in the interest of the ruling cases and that Domingo's case was exploited to bring about animosity.

The PNP tried to rebut the allegations. N.N. Nethersole, president of the PNP-affiliated trade union, Trade Union Congress (TUC), defended Domingo against Bustamante's allegations and reminded that in spring 1939, Domingo had been 'one of the persons who exercised the greatest influence in saving the labour movement, saving the Bustamante Union'.[126] Manley personally answered Bustamante's accusations in a public speech at the PNP headquarters at Edelweiss Park and called the attack on Domingo 'mean and despicable',[127] after Bustamante pretended friendship with Domingo when they were in neighbouring cells at Up-Park Camp. He denied allegations that he had called for Domingo to take over the labour unions, although he admitted that he had hoped that Domingo would lend his support to the labour movement. Instead of any rivalry, he urged unity and progress of the labour unions and openly criticized the autocratic style in which Bustamante had organized the worker's movement.[128]

It is difficult to decide whether Manley deliberately wanted to install Domingo as a rival to the powerful Bustamante to unite the working class behind the PNP. His efforts to repudiate the allegations do not convincingly disprove that he had hoped that Domingo could help to push the process of democratization of the unions and thereby help to lay the foundation for a strong mass-based national movement. A review of Manley's correspondence further supports this interpretation. In a letter to WINC Secretary Osborne, written shortly after Domingo's detention, Manley referred to the reasons that had motivated his decision to call for Domingo:

> ...I wanted him to do work in connection with Union Organisation. Domingo realized certain weaknesses in Union structure which he observed in Jamaica and which are unnecessary for me to discuss and I think that his gift for organization would have been invaluable at a time when the movement is at a critical stage of development.[129]

In December 1942, Manley admitted in a letter to Harold Stannard of the British Council that he had called for Domingo 'to do the Trade Union work that was absorbing all my time',[130] while the question about Jamaica's political future had been reinforced by the Havana Conference and amidst sugar strikes and the threat of serious labour unrests. In a conversation between Manley and Roberts in 1949 about the ambitious PNP politician Wills O. Isaacs, Roberts also had the impression that 'Manley saw Isaacs as Bustamante's opposite number, and that he somewhat regretted that this role not have been filled by Domingo'.[131]

In 1939, Domingo had written to Manley about the importance of labour organization, complaining about the inadequate leadership of Bustamante, criticizing his autocratic style and worrying about the damage he could do to the national movement. He then had pledged: 'You can depend upon me to fight with my last breath for the extension of the rights of the masses, especially the toilers who are today almost without leadership of a useful kind'.[132] Written shortly before the outbreak of the Second World War, Domingo indicated that he personally could imagine getting involved in local politics and promised to 'be back in time for participation in the ensuing elections'.[133] Statements like this indicate that Domingo was available for the task to weaken the position of the BITU and to strengthen the mass base of the PNP.

The sources suggest that the Governor consciously tried to sow seeds of discord to prevent cooperation between the PNP and the BITU. On the cusp of being granted universal suffrage, such a scenario that could have led to the creation of a strong and radical mass-based nationalist and anti-colonial movement, was obviously threatening. Richards' report to the Colonial Office in June 1942, provides illuminating insights into the Governor's motivations. It openly reveals the split between Manley and the Governor after Domingo's detention and indicates that Bustamante's release was indeed meant as a direct attack on the PNP. In his report, Richards frankly admitted that the country was in a grave crisis. The labour movement was on the rise, radicalized and politicized by the influence of the PNP while Bustamante was detained. His comment on the dispute between the PNP and Bustamante after his release is telling: 'the Labour Leader's release spoiled their little plan to capture the entire labour movement for their political purpose'.[134]

At the same time, the Governor left no doubt that his sympathies with Bustamante were tactically motivated:

> Bustamante is a damned nuisance, admittedly, and he too is stirring up trouble all over the island. The difference is that he is first and last out for Bustamante and Bustamante's credit. He is not fundamentally anti-Government and his activities are sporadic and incoherent. On the other hand the Manley group is fundamentally anti-government and subversive.

In the eyes of the Governor, Bustamante was still the lesser of the two evils: 'Nuisance, though Bustamante is, there is no doubt that had he not been released or had he gone in with Manley, the situation would be far more serious than it is'. The Governor was further disturbed by the Socialist course the PNP had adopted and feared that Manley aspired to erect a Socialist despotism.

Bustamante's release was indeed meant to disturb the success of the PNP. Richard Hart supports this interpretation, arguing that Bustamante was released because he entered in an agreement with the Governor to fight the PNP and the demand for self-government which had gained increasing popularity among the workers.[135] While Hart does not mention the accusation about Manley's vision to install Domingo as a new leader for the unions, he nevertheless supports the claim that there was more behind the Governor's decision to release Bustamante while Domingo remained in detention.

The detention of Bustamante, whose agitation had reached an unusual level of radicalism and critique of the government, was designed to bring stability to the colony that was increasingly destabilized by a worsening economic crisis, by the PNP's radicalized demands for self-government and by a growing degree of restiveness in the labour movement, which was accelerated by the construction of US military bases. After the Havana Conference, the PNP's extreme approach to the question of self-government had taken on an increasingly outspoken anti-colonial tone. Because of this situation, Domingo's arrival on the island was most unpleasant to the Governor, who feared that Domingo's presence could inflame both the labour and self-government movements and eventually even bring about the merger of both. It was exactly this mixture of local and expatriate radicalism that threatened the stability of the colony in these troublesome times of war and anti-colonial upheavals throughout the Empire.

It is less clear if trade union activism was what Domingo and Roberts had in mind when they decided that Domingo should return to Jamaica. While Domingo had emphasized the need of a strong nationalist labour movement in his earlier writings, for example, in the *Public Opinion* debate with Richard Hart, he gradually directed more attention to a nationalist propaganda that was appealing to all classes, trying to prove that self-government was in the best interest of the whole society.

The correspondence between Roberts and Domingo suggests that the decision for Domingo to return was motivated by their shared feeling that the time was ripe to support the PNP's resumed campaign for self-government. Domingo and Roberts continued to act strictly along the tactical lines they derived from their unchanging priority on nationalism. Domingo's actions after his release, to be examined later, do not suggest he was particularly interested in labour organization, but that he was guided by one overarching aim, the gaining of independence for Jamaica.

After Bustamante was released, the prolonged detention of Domingo chafed and had a motivating effect on Manley and the PNP. In December 1942, Manley stated in a letter to Stannard:

> The detention was the most flagrantly unjust thing. I appealed to the Governor in vain. I was ready to pledge my own liberty that he would do no wrong and would obey party orders or go back to the states. The Governor was adamant. This single act, more than anything else, set the party on a line of final opposition of Government and its ways.[136]

It expressed itself in the PNP's decision to launch a forceful self-government campaign. At the party's Annual Conference in September 1942, the party declared that the days of patience were gone:

> The cornerstone of our economic recovery and stability is the immediate transfer of responsibility and power to the people of Jamaica....Full self-government for Jamaica becomes a necessity the delay of which increases the hardships and sufferings which our people are forced to bear day after day.[137]

During the campaign, various articles appeared in *Public Opinion* and numerous public meetings were held. At one big meeting, the party started a petition demanding self-government and universal suffrage.[138] The PNP pronounced: 'Self-government is not a prize for successful nations, it is a natural right of all peoples. It is not the goal of political development, but its beginning'.[139] After a month of campaigning, most PNP groups declared that the successful campaign should continue, and the executive decided to prolong the campaign until December 31.[140] In an article in *Public Opinion*, Manley expressed his confidence that Jamaicans would be entitled to achieve self-government and claimed that this was in accordance with the Empire's declared policy. He openly accused the government of clinging to its unjust privileges by preventing further steps toward self-government.[141] The PNP's campaign testifies to the profound effect Governor Richards' actions had on the population. His decision to detain Richard Hart, Arthur Henry, Ken Hill and Frank Hill, four of the most prominent leftists in the PNP, on November 3, 1942, further estranged the PNP.[142] The radicalized atmosphere in Jamaica, combined with pressure from the US, forced the Colonial Office to reconsider its attitude toward Jamaica. The proposal of a new constitution for Jamaica, accompanied by Domingo's release and Governor Richards' relocation to Nigeria, was the first manifestation of significant changes in the colonial policy.

Shifts in Colonial Policy: Domingo's Release and the Granting of a New Constitution

This section examines the reactions to the changes in colonial policy, to the granting of the new constitution and to Domingo's release. A close analysis of Domingo's agitation during his forced stay in Jamaica will help to understand Domingo's nationalist thinking and to analyse his strategy for influencing the further course of decolonization. It further explores the reasons for Domingo's coming to Jamaica, as his writings and actions, in contrast to Bustamante's allegations, do not suggest that he intended to focus on challenging his leadership position in the trade unions. Instead, his main concerns remained the promotion of nationalism, support for the PNP and tireless advocacy of self-government for Jamaica. Before Domingo's activities are analysed more closely, it is necessary to outline the important changes that were taking place internationally that compelled Great Britain to alter its colonial policy, thus providing the framework that set the stage for the actors.

Local and international reactions to Domingo's detention speaks to the fact that Governor Richards had carried things too far. After the PNP resumed its anti-colonial propaganda, the effects of the Second World War on the national movement in Jamaica were more radicalizing. In 1941, Domingo wrote in a letter to his friend Campbell:

> I am not surprised that self-government should be in the air. It was bound to be understood and taken up by the people. The war and its hardships and the attitude of Richards served to stimulate the latent nationalism of the people.[143]

The Governor's actions provoked exactly the opposite effect of what he had intended. Rather than preventing an alleged dangerous influence, the detentions of Domingo and other PNP members fortified a general trend toward further radicalization. It provoked a strong campaign for self-government by the PNP in November and December of 1942 and had brought even traditionally loyal citizens in opposition to the government. On an international scale, it had roused harsh criticism which increased the pressure on the Colonial Office. The British officials were not pleased about the developments that filled the void of political development imposed by the war.[144] The break between Manley and the Governor, the strong opposition to the detentions that led to the formation of the Civil Liberties Council, the fortified demands for self-government and the attraction of international attention in a situation in which the US closely monitored the conditions in the colonies caused grave concern. The changing power relations between Great Britain and the US during the crisis of the war, the increased security interest and recent bauxite findings in Jamaica had whetted the appetite of the US to gain more control in the region.[145]

Through instruments like the Anglo-American Caribbean Commission (AACC) that was established in March 1942 to meet the security and supply crisis in the Caribbean, the US was able to exert influence on the course of the colonial policy in the British West Indies.[146] Since both partners had possessions in the region, comparisons between the conditions in Puerto Rico and Jamaica further helped to bring about steps toward more self-government.[147] Jason Parker emphasizes the special influence of race in the course of events.[148] Strong ties between African Americans and Caribbean immigrants in the US caused all matters related to racial discrimination in the transnational black community on the 'Kingston-Harlem-axis',[149] to reverberate on the mainland, whether they happened in the AACC when black Caribbeans demanded representation, on the islands or on the military bases.[150] Thus, the network in Harlem with excellent connections to the AACC and to think tanks of the State Department was able to exert some influence on the course of decolonization the British West Indies.[151]

A combination of factors resulted in a shift in the Colonial Office's policy, including the disheartening course of the war in Europe, US influence and the increasing demands for self-government in Jamaica in the face of events in India where uncompromising demands for independence gained momentum. Colonial Secretary Oliver Stanley admitted that the situation in Jamaica was most dangerous, especially in view of the heavily politicized Jamaican community in New York under the leadership of the Progressive League. Creech-Jones pointed to the fact that Governor Richards' behaviour was contributing largely to the US concern and intensified President Roosevelt's wish to see more self-government and a larger franchise.[152]

The first manifestation of changes in the colonial policy in the direction desired by US strategists was the offering of a new constitution to Jamaica with universal suffrage and a significantly increased influence of the legislative.[153] After the relationship between Richards and Manley turned cold following Domingo's detention, the Colonial Office was worried whether or not the PNP would accept the proposal for a new constitution and arranged for a meeting between the two men. To 'sweeten Manley's mood', as Ken Post puts it, and to ensure the cooperation of the PNP, Domingo was finally released on February 19, two days after the meeting between Manley and Richards and a few days before the proposal was presented to Jamaica.[154]

Upon his release, Domingo complimented his supporters in Great Britain, such as George Padmore and several members of the British Labour Party. He clearly saw that US influence driven by the interest of democratizing the region played a crucial role in his release and recognized the coincidence of events. Domingo later claimed: '...ultimately, President Roosevelt intervened, as many persons in Jamaica know, and under pressure the British Government released me a few days before Jamaica got its new constitution'.[155]

Domingo's detention was certainly a matter of consideration in the formation of the constitution. In a parliamentary debate about Jamaica's new constitution, Arthur Creech Jones[156] lauded the proposal as a 'real step forward in regard to both representative government and responsible government'.[157] Creech Jones emphasized that Domingo's internment exemplified the excessive use of powers by the Governor and stated: 'The long imprisonment of Domingo seems to me to be completely indefensible from the point of view of any standard of civil liberty'.[158] The increasing local protest against Richards' authoritarian style of governance, combined with strong disapproval of his actions in the press in Jamaica, the US and Great Britain had considerably weakened the Governor's stand and finally forced the Colonial Office to intervene. A few weeks later, Richards, who had done so much to prevent the strengthening of the nationalist forces and blocked all attempts toward a greater degree of self-government, was relocated to a new appointment as Governor of Nigeria, and was replaced by Governor John Huggins in the summer 1943.[159] Historians like Cary Fraser and Ken Post agree that the removal of Richards, who was 'a symbol of an anachronistic order',[160] signalled the 'end of an era'.[161]

The authorities in England felt uneasy that Domingo's release and the announcement of the constitutional changes could be perceived as being more than merely a coincidence. T.K. Lloyd expressed his concern: 'As regards to the question of timing, it will, I imagine, be desirable to avoid any linking of Mr. Domingo's release with the constitutional changes now under consideration'.[162] But Lloyd's wish was in vain. For instance, the *New York Amsterdam News* expressed its belief that both events were significantly connected:

> The release is believed to have been inspired by very important moves to come in the British Caribbean, as it came almost simultaneously with announcements regarding large-scale expenditures for the development of social welfare and economic adjustment programmes and a grant of a new constitution with other political reforms.[163]

In the following months, intellectuals like George Padmore claimed that the high-handed acts against Bustamante and Domingo contributed to Richards' unpopular stand. His removal, Padmore argued, would 'pave the way for greater cooperation between the British government and Jamaicans in applying the new constitution'.[164] Lucius C. Harper, editor of the *Chicago Defender*, likewise emphasized the connectivity of events:

> Domingo comes out a martyr to the cause for the British have granted Jamaica universal suffrage and a new constitution, giving its black subjects a voice and vote in its own affairs, an experiment, which, if successful will clear the way for the extension of democracy throughout the British Empire's subject lands. Sir Arthur Richards, once Jamaica's demagogic ruler has been handed his walking papers and is on high seas searching for another political job.[165]

Such statements testify to the way in which the events were seen as intertwined, while Domingo's significant role was emphasized by many observers.

When Domingo was released, Manley immediately informed the Progressive League via telegram.[166] The front page of the *Gleaner* announced his release and advertised a big welcome meeting under the auspices of the PNP.[167] Domingo's release was greeted with cheers from all corners. The positive reactions to Domingo's release show that the detention did not damage his reputation, but to the contrary, had increased his popularity. His important role in the early days of the formation of the party was frequently highlighted, for example, in the announcement for the welcome meeting.[168] With over 3,000 people in attendance, the welcome meeting was overwhelmingly well-received.[169] Chaired by Wills O.

Isaacs, it featured various notable speakers and co-workers of Domingo, among them Norman Manley, W.G. McFarlane, Dr J.L. Varma and even respected attorney Ansell Hart.[170]

Manley's speech showed how much the detention had worried him personally and praised the patience with which Domingo had accepted his lot. He emphasized the large degree of Domingo's influence on his thinking, especially in regards to constitutional reform.[171] In his own speech, Domingo thanked all his friends and supporters and emphasized the tireless efforts of Norman and Edna Manley to secure his release and the splendid hospitality he enjoyed at their house. Domingo encouraged his listeners to close ranks and follow their leaders who had fought for the new constitution and to disappoint those who wanted to see it fail.[172]

The proposal for the new constitution suggested a bicameral legislative system with a House of Assembly elected on the basis of universal adult suffrage and a Legislative Council with five elected members from the Assembly, three officials and two appointed members. The powers of the Governor were limited to some extent and it was suggested that the constitution would be revised after a five-year trial period.[173] The report of US analyst Paul Blanshard[174] called the proposal 'probably the most important step toward democracy in the whole history of the British West Indies'.[175] Blanshard expected that the ministerial system could develop into a responsible government after the five-year trial period and welcomed the granting of universal suffrage. Possibly this assessment was too optimistic. Hart doubts that 'in 1944 there was anyone in the Colonial Office who envisaged that more would ever be conceded to Jamaica, or any other colony in the region, than internal self-government'.[176]

Answering anti-colonial demands of President Roosevelt, Winston Churchill had declared in November 1942 that he would not 'preside over the liquidation of the British Empire'.[177] However, the proposal unquestionably was a first manifestation of the shift in the colonial policy of Great Britain, designed to appease both local and international demands for more self-government in the region.

While Blanshard noted a widespread favourable attitude toward the proposal, even in the conservative section of society, he also pointed to another important aspect which needs to be kept in mind in order to understand the development of the following years. Large parts of Jamaica's populace were still not interested in politics, especially in the countryside, and many people were neither aware of the content of the new nor of the old constitution.[178] Ken Post also emphasizes this point and concludes that the proposals had no significant impact on the people at large.[179] These observations demonstrate again how limited and small the circle of politically interested persons was. Much political ground work still needed to be done and accordingly, the granting of universal adult suffrage for the upcoming elections was a radical step.

In regard to tempering the radicalized demands for self-government, the offering of the new constitution had the desired effect. In a report about the political situation in Jamaica in the run-up to the elections, Blanshard observed: 'one major development stands out and that is the temporary subordination of imperialism vs self-government as an issue in local politics. Until the granting of the new constitution this issue overshadowed every other economic and political problem'.[180]

Although Domingo did not stop his agitation for self-government, he welcomed the proposal and especially the granting of universal suffrage. He recommended that the Progressive League and the PNP accept the proposal, although it did not fully grant what he had demanded in the past years.[181] In a letter to a personal friend in the US, he called the proposal a step in the right direction and argued that the pressure from the US, combined with the united front that demanded constitutional changes in Jamaica, had forced the Colonial Office to offer such far-reaching changes. However, Domingo had regrets:

> Tactically, it would have been better if we had asked for more but the elected members are a timid lot and have no conception of genuine political progress. They are a conservative lot and committed to a program of conservatism. I really think that they were surprised when they got as much as they did.[182]

In a letter to Progressive League member Ivy Bailey-Essien, Domingo alleged that the proposals were designed to silence those Americans 'who have been pointing to the anomaly of England fighting avowedly for freedom of countries under her own rule'.[183] While he felt that the Progressive League should keep up its uncompromising demand for self-government, he decided to support the People's National Party in accepting the proposals.

Domingo's position exemplifies the often employed strategy to regard the Progressive League as a spearhead for more radical demands of self-government, while the PNP was utilized as a suitable instrument for more moderate and practical steps in the political arena in Jamaica. In the election campaign, Domingo assumed a double role. While he continued his agitation for self-government in his writings, he fully supported the PNP campaign, thus silently accepting the measure of improvement that was granted.

Manley judged the proposal as the offering of a real step toward self-government and appreciated that Domingo was released and present in Jamaica at this particularly important time.[184] Roberts told Manley that he hoped Domingo would use the extraordinary chance to exert his influence in Jamaica:

> ...I find it in my heart to hope that he will decide to stay in Jamaica. Circumstances have given him authority as a leader which he might not otherwise have had. Jamaica badly needs such men. His opportunity, really, is unique. I think he could be elected to the new Assembly, where his voice would be a potent one. Tell him that I feel this way, if you see fit. I should not like him to think that I am trying to influence his affairs unduly, but I cannot escape the conviction that he has an appointment with destiny and that New York is not the rendezvous.[185]

When the PNP started to plan its election campaign, Manley also hoped that Domingo and even Roberts would take over active roles and tried to convince Roberts to return for the campaign.[186] When Domingo's request for a visa was refused by the US authorities, Manley and Roberts hoped that Domingo would run for a seat in the new House. Although Roberts had tried to lobby in the State Department for Domingo's permission to return, he admitted in a letter to Manley:

> From the standpoint of our fight in Jamaica, I cannot help feeling glad that you are not to lose the valuable help that Domingo can and will give. He must be elected to the assembly.[187]

Domingo himself clearly saw the great chance and the potential influence he could exert on the course of political developments in Jamaica. In his first article in *Public Opinion* after his release, he called the simultaneity of his release and the offer for a new constitution a 'significant augury'.[188] Domingo appreciated that he was able to attend the debate on the constitution in the Legislative Council as one of the PNP's delegates.[189] Domingo declared that he had recovered from the detention experience and announced that he would resume his propaganda efforts: 'I shall devote myself to the task of doing my best to promote the ideals of the People's National Party which I am absolutely convinced represent the aspirations of the vast majority of our people'.[190]

However, Domingo's commitment to support the PNP in all possible ways and to lend his support in the country's fight for self-government was not strong enough to take precedence over his personal wish to return to the US as soon as possible, so he refused to run for public office.[191] After the forced 20-month stay at Up-Park Camp, Domingo never felt the desire for a long stay in Jamaica again. In a letter to his son Karl, he described his feelings: 'It has been a terrible experience and it has left me with one great desire – to get back to New York as quickly as possible'.[192] However, the US authorities refused to grant Domingo a visa so that his wish would remain unfulfilled for the next four years.

Something had changed in him during his detention. Despite Manley's initial optimism that the detention had made Domingo 'a bigger man',[193] he was disappointed that he abstained from running for a seat in the Assembly and later told Roberts: 'Domingo had shown a sort of psychic hypochondris, had found nothing good in Jamaica thereafter, he had in fact thrown away a great prestige'.[194]

Nevertheless, Domingo used his stay for continued propaganda and maintained a close working relationship with the PNP. With some degree of pathos, he declared that he was committed to fight for democracy 'not in Europe, but right here in Jamaica where I was born, where I am and where my ancestors sweated and bled'.[195] Accordingly, Domingo significantly contributed to the political and journalistic life of the country, making the question of constitutional change and the promotion of nationalist ideas his main objective.

Domingo was aware of the fact that with the offering of far-reaching constitutional changes, Jamaica was the centre of attraction for everybody who closely followed the political developments in the region and the colonial policy of the Empire. Initially, he expressed concern about the widespread perception that the developments in Jamaica would now influence the destiny of other British colonies with a black majority: 'Whatever the result, other peoples should not be judged by us. After all Jamaica is no guinea pig for the other colored peoples'.[196] However, Domingo soon changed his mind, realizing the significance of Jamaica's case for the course of decolonization of the British West Indies and, in contrast, admitted:

> Jamaica is to be the constitutional guinea pig of the African and other predominantly coloured colonies. That imposes on the Jamaican people a great, if unjust responsibility. We must make good. We cannot afford to fail. If we fail, not we alone will suffer, but millions of people who had no part in the experiment. Jamaicans are to be the political cross-bearers of the British colonial world.[197]

Roberts shared Domingo's perception that Jamaica served as a 'testing ground for the granting of self-government to non-Aryan peoples, and in particular to Negroes'.[198] Indeed, Jamaica played a crucial role in the design of post-war colonial diplomacy. Without question, the racist assumption that black people were not fit for self-government that guided the paternalistic colonial policy was still effective. Domingo warned the country of those who discredited the Jamaican people by not believing in their ability to live up to greater responsibility and encouraged his listeners to unite in support of the leaders to prove those sceptics wrong.[199] The experiences with the new constitution in Jamaica would therefore have implications on the course of decolonization in the region. The outcome of the upcoming elections, the first under universal suffrage, would be of utmost importance.

Domingo's attitude toward the constitution was in congruence with the PNP's position. The party decided to accept the proposals, which Domingo saw as a result of the PNP's radical campaign for self-government of the past months.[200]

Although Manley saw a potential for dispute and deadlock in the proposals and did not regard them as 'the last word either in progress or political wisdom', he nevertheless felt that the changes would be 'a great stride forward' and saw the proposals' 'historic importance to the whole Colonial Empire'.[201] In the *Gleaner*, Manley emphasized the fact that for the first time, the Colonial Office offered proposals for a new constitution for Jamaica that principally acknowledged that a guided process and a definite time frame toward self-government were needed.[202]

Roberts agreed that the PNP should accept the proposed constitutional changes. For the Progressive League, he recommended that it should also support the new proposal in the hope that internal self-government could be obtained after the five year trial period. At the same time, he felt the League should continue to forcefully demand Dominion status. Accordingly, the Progressive League prepared a memorandum which made clear:

> ...if it were not for the promise to review the Constitution at the end of five years to determine 'the justification for further advance' it [the Progressive League] could not endorse it since it does not grant full self-government and fails to give her rightful place as a free and equal partner in the British family of nations.[203]

Roberts valued the opportunity to demonstrate that countries like Jamaica were ready for self-government. Nevertheless, he felt that 'ballots for all, without a literacy test, is undeniably a radical and surprising concession to a country like Jamaica'.[204] But at this time, Roberts believed that 'the Jamaican peasant is a level-headed type'[205] and was therefore confident that the experiment would work out satisfactorily.

While a broad front of PNP, Progressive League and other organizations advocated accepting the proposal, conservative circles eagerly opposed the far-reaching steps.[206] De Lisser was once again in the frontline of the critics. He was now forced to admit that by accepting the proposals by the Colonial Office, the country was inexorably moving toward a more responsible form of government.[207] Interestingly, de Lisser again emphasized Roberts' influential role in the movement for self-government that had gained a first victory now:

> ...even if Manley were silent on the subject of Dominion Status – absurd though that would certainly be for the next quarter of a century at least – Adolphe Roberts would not be silent. And those persons here who are inclined to belittle the future influence of Adolphe Roberts may simply be considered as arrant fools.[208]

De Lisser emphasized Roberts' pioneering role as 'the first man to advocate Dominion Status or self-government for Jamaica'[209] and expected Roberts to return to Jamaica after the war to resume the fight for immediate self-government. In a personal letter to Manley, de Lisser admitted that the political dynamics could not be halted: 'Frankly I think that the self-Government people are likely to win the next toss to a certain advanced extent; that is the indication of the time and that indication will become clearer as the years go by'.[210] Not surprisingly, he promised that despite his bad state of health: 'Naturally, I shall fight a rearguard action against them if I am alive. What is the use of being a reactionary if you do not live up to the reactionary standard?'[211] However, despite de Lisser's unrelenting attitude, there was a degree of acceptance that even the most reactionary opponents of self-government were now forced to acknowledge that changes toward more responsibility were inevitable.

For Domingo, the PNP was the instrument of choice to move forward to self-government. As the logical inheritor of the nationalist inspiration that derived from the League abroad, giving political expression to its ideas, it was clear that the PNP needed to win the first elections under universal suffrage in order to guide the country along its way toward independence.[212] Since the PNP had resumed its agitation for self-government, Domingo saw no reason to highlight the timidity the PNP frequently showed during the first years of the movement. Rather, in his writings, he drew a direct line from the political aspirations of Love, Cox, Garvey, the Progressive League, and the NRA to the founding of the PNP.[213]

Nevertheless, Domingo emphasized the crucial role the Progressive League had played, inspiring anti-colonial nationalism with their 'burning desire to see their country rise to the full dignity and stature of nationhood'.[214] At one meeting he recalled the important impact of migration and the inspiration deriving from living in the US:

> It was Jamaicans…who had gone abroad and had learned the ideals of freedom in real democracies, who, fired with these things, and with a sense of patriotism towards their own country; and above all desiring to see the fruits of that freedom, accruing to the people of this country, who have initiated a national movement which was to find its roots in Jamaica with the formation of the People's National Party.[215]

He recalled how the PNP developed out of the labour uprisings in 1938 and pointed out that while it was '…mothered by the militancy of the masses', it was 'nursed by Jamaicans in New York City who had boldly raised the cry for self-government'.[216] Nevertheless, he was convinced that national consciousness had to develop in Jamaica.[217] He averred that the PNP had successfully popularized and channelled the demands for self-government in Jamaica and was now 'indisputably the leading and most vital political force in the British West Indies' that had become the 'spearhead of British West Indian national movements'.[218]

The PNP, in turn, held Domingo in the highest esteem. Domingo's outstanding reputation was reflected in the fact that he often chaired meetings and oftentimes appeared as one of the main speakers, along with Manley.[219] His presence at a PNP conference on the Constitution was recognized as 'a specially inspiring feature'[220] and he was appointed as one of the PNP's delegates to attend a joint conference of the PNP, the Elected Members Association and the Federation of Citizens Associations on the constitutional proposals.

Although he was not prepared to take over an official position while waiting for permission to return to the US, he was rewarded with a special honour at the annual PNP conference in August 1943:

> As a mark of Mr. W. A. Domingo's great worth and value to the Party, the conference unanimously passed a resolution declaring that as long Mr. Domingo remains in Jamaica he shall be entitled to an ex-officio seat on the general Council of the Party.[221]

Domingo fully supported the PNP's election campaign and spoke alongside many PNP candidates, such as Wills O. Isaacs, N.N. Nethersole, Victor Bailey and Norman Manley.[222] Although an abundance of evidence highlights Domingo's exposed position as a speaker during the first national election campaign of the PNP, his contribution is not recognized in the official historiography of the PNP.[223] However, Domingo's contribution to the election campaign was so remarkable that even the Jamaican expatriate W.A. Malliet, a journalist with a strong pro-British attitude who had earlier criticized Domingo for his Socialist leanings, recognized Domingo's importance. In an article on the political rivalry, he stated that the PNP was 'led by Manley and Domingo'.[224] The subtitle under Domingo's picture claimed that he was: 'the most outstanding leader in the People's National Party'.[225]

When the election campaign started, the political landscape was not yet firmly established. The upper classes, which had largely benefited from the limited franchise, only hesitantly tried to organize within the framework of a democratic party system based on universal suffrage.[226] With a vast majority of black people belonging to the lower classes, their chances to win significant votes were not very promising. All parties were inclined to present themselves as mass-based parties and much agitation circulated around issues of race and class.[227]

While the PNP had been around since 1938, some new parties developed since the first announcements of elections based on universal suffrage.[228] The conservatives were not able to channel their interests into one strong party. The Jamaica Democratic Party (JDP) led by T.H. Sharp and Abe Issa was the party of the upper middle class and mainly interested in protecting their status. But neither the JDP nor the even smaller Jamaica Conservative Party (JCP) was able to recruit a noteworthy following, although the JDP was able to attract potent financiers. The prospects of universal suffrage wrecked all hopes for success at the polls of any party with a decidedly conservative programme.

Therefore, conservatives tried to aggravate the campaign of the PNP, accusing it of advocating nationalization in a Communist manner, heavily utilizing the daily press, which they still dominated. The ruling classes feared that their privileges were at stake and accused the PNP of overemphasizing questions of race and class.

Domingo was in the forefront of those PNP members who took up their pen defending the party against such allegations. Because of his importance as one of the PNP's most prolific journalists, prominent conservative writers started to answer directly to his articles. For instance, with English-born Esther Chapman, Domingo argued about whether or not racism was a continual problem in Jamaica.[229] In several articles, Domingo proved the affirmative and criticized Chapman for her objection toward nationalism and self-government and accused her of holding racist views.[230] Chapman alleged that Domingo was prejudiced and obsessed with the idea that Jamaicans are the victims of racism and offended Domingo in several columns in the *Gleaner*.[231]

When other politicians discovered their solidarity with the black masses, Domingo pointed to the hypocritical nature of their newly developed concern. He harshly criticized E.E.A. Campbell, who had recently started to denounce race discrimination in his election campaign, and reminded the public that in 1939, he had opposed the Progressive League proposal for a reopening of the examinations for civil service entry for all Jamaicans.[232]

The economic position of the PNP was another major point of critique for the conservatives. Many feared that the PNP aspired to establish a Communist economic system and would expropriate the wealthy classes and nationalize the economy.[233]

In his articles, Domingo had indeed criticized the social injustice that the capitalist economic system produced all over the world and had warned of an uncritical apotheosis of 'free enterprise'.[234] Walter Lewis, Secretary of the Jamaica Conservative Party, attacked the PNP and especially its leader Manley and alleged that many of the PNP leaders, including Domingo, were Communists.[235] Both men entered into an outright debate, while Domingo countered Lewis's arguments and pointed out that he never considered himself to be a Communist.[236]

The most dangerous opponent of the PNP was the charismatic Bustamante with his strong mass base among the workers and peasants and support from the conservative elites, who sympathized with his anti-Socialist views. In the campaign, Bustamante used race-based arguments and frequently denounced self-government, declaring it would mean 'brown-man-rule' and a return to slavery. He warned that the PNP would pursue Socialism and the nationalization of small land properties.[237] While Bustamante himself was opposed to the idea of self-government, he saw the signs of the time and announced that he was about to form a political party in August 1942. He was sure that under self-government, there was no question that he soon would be voted into power. Bustamante emphasized that his party would be autocratically organized like his union and especially appealing to the working class.[238]

Domingo dedicated much energy to criticizing Bustamante. He condemned the autocratic way in which he ruled the Jamaica Labour Party (JLP) and called him a devotee of fascism, pointing to the potential embarrassment for Jamaica if he was elected in democratic elections.[239] He complained that the 'Labour Leader' had such a low opinion of his fellow countrymen that he did not believe they could master self-government.[240] Domingo further tried to discredit Bustamante by exposing his undemocratic attitudes toward the organization of labour and questioned his integrity. He pointed to the fact that Bustamante often spoke about black people in condescending terms and tried to style himself as white and suspected that Bustamante's 'opposition to self-government in Africa and Jamaica is based on race'.[241]

Domingo emphasized the significance of the upcoming election, the first under universal suffrage and with the chance for wider rights and more self-determination, if the trial period proved to be successful. He warned that class distinctions and the perpetuation of the discrimination of the masses by a lack of education would leave them vulnerable for the propaganda of 'cults and demagogues'.[242] He encouraged all Jamaicans to rise in united spirit against Bustamante's propaganda, to prevent Jamaica from becoming the 'international laughing stock' after electing Bustamante. He was however aware that to defeat Bustamante at the polls would not be an easy task:

> Let there be no underestimation of the virulence and vitality of Bustamanteism. It has precious little brains, but it has vast energy and devotion. To meet the horrible thing we must be patriotic, which means that we must be willing to fight to our last drop of blood for our country, if needs be.[243]

In view of a lack of viable alternatives, there was a general trend among conservatives to support Bustamante.[244] With his strong opposition to the PNP and to any demands for Socialism or self-government, he appeared to be the lesser evil and many conservatives decided to support the JLP. Political observer Paul Blanshard noticed that many conservatives and businessmen would be willing to support Bustamante in order to prevent further steps toward self-government and Socialism.[245] Like Domingo, Blanshard feared:

> If Busta through the use of conservative money and his own considerable record of achievement in winning improved conditions for labor should gain control of the new legislature, the whole democratic experiment

would be set back at least a decade. He will make the island a joke by his eccentric dictatorship. He would ostensibly represent labour, but his record this far indicates that he would be a pliant tool for shrewd business manipulators in handling complex problems of government.[246]

Blanshard was further concerned about the rise of political violence at the party meetings and observed several attacks on the PNP by 'the Busta gangsters'. *Public Opinion* also reported on occurrences of violence at election meetings.[247] Blanshard commented that the trend of uniformed guards in the JLP would lead to 'fascist tactics'.[248] The increased tension at the party meetings became a regular feature of many election events, a characteristic that accompanies Jamaican elections until today. With his appeal to the masses, Domingo was reported to be able to maintain order and control at the campaign meetings. For example, at one meeting in Morant Bay, the *Gleaner* reported that an effort to break up the gathering by rivaling JLP supporters 'failed dismally under the tongue-lashing of Messrs. Moyston and Domingo'.[249]

Not only did Domingo give wholehearted support to the PNP's election campaign, but the Progressive League provided the lion's share of the desperately needed funds to carry out the election campaign.[250] In October 1943, Manley wrote to Roberts asking whether he saw any possibility that the Progressive League in New York would be able to contribute financially.[251] Roberts agreed and advised: 'Aid to the PNP in its pre-election campaign is the greatest service we can render at the moment to the cause of self-government'.[252] Accordingly, the League frequently sent donations to Jamaica, totalling up to the remarkable amount of US$840.[253] The Progressive League had successfully raised funds at numerous well-attended meetings with 500 and more participants, supported by some non-Jamaicans like African American Adam Clayton Powell, and Richard B. Moore from Barbados, who spoke alongside the Progressive League speakers at some of the fund-raising meetings.[254]

Manley and the PNP were thankful for the much needed support of their first election campaign on a national scale:

> I have been hearing with great pleasure of the successful effort to raise funds in New York for the party. I can assure you that this is our critical need to date. Now that the Democratic Party has got into action nearly everyone who has money to spare has gone over to that body.[255]

Manley affirmed: 'I would like you to know how much we appreciate the help that is being given to us and how useful it is proving'.[256] Also members from the local branch of the Progressive League actively supported the PNP. Many members of the Kingston branch, for example McFarlane, Amy Bailey and P.A. Aiken held double memberships and actively supported the campaign and spoke on various platforms.[257]

Five months after the first announcement of the constitutional changes, the final proposal was presented in the middle of the election campaign. The new constitution contained a lesser degree of power granted to the elected element as promised, and accordingly, the PNP leaders were harshly disappointed. At a huge mass meeting chaired by Domingo, the PNP presented its objections against the final proposal.[258] The PNP complained about the five months of secrecy during which they lost valuable time to lobby against the changes. The PNP then worked out a detailed memorandum criticizing the shortcomings of the proposed constitution.[259]

Nevertheless, Domingo and the PNP were forced to accept the proposal that was presented in the middle of the election campaign. He was not surprised that the final proposal was not as far-reaching as promised. The British never make concessions without pressure, he reminded, and a real transfer of power could not be expected to be granted voluntarily. Domingo pointed to other examples within the Empire and concluded that everywhere hard struggle was needed to secure steps toward more self-determination.[260]

Right before the election, the PNP organized a huge 'On-To-Victory Meeting'[261] at which Domingo was among the main speakers. Several goodwill messages appeared in the *Gleaner*, including a telegram from the Progressive League.[262] However, the atmosphere of optimism and confidence that the PNP would win the election proved to be premature. On Election Day, December 14, 1944, thousands of Jamaican labourers, peasants and unemployed had the right to vote for the first time in their lives. The JLP came out as the victor at the polls, 29 JLP candidates were elected, 19 of the PNP, 9 of the JDP, 4 of other small parties, and one of the FCA.[263] However, only slightly more than half of the population (52.7 per cent) made use of this opportunity and casted valid votes. The low turnout was a sign of the general indifference of the masses toward the political development. It probably reflected the high degree of illiteracy and a deep-rooted feeling of impotence and scepticism whether the politicians would be willing and able to bring about a real change of living conditions.

For the advocates of self-government, the election result was a source of distress. As brought out before the election by Domingo and Blanshard, Bustamante was a destabilizing factor in the country's political development and thus a trump card for everybody who argued that the country was not yet ripe to govern its own affairs. The election showed that advocating self-government did not attract the majority of voters. This fact is embodied in the success of E.R.D. Evans, who first ran on a self-government platform for the Progressive League in 1939. Now, he won his seat in the new House of Representatives, but not by advocating self-government, but on the ticket of the JLP which was clearly opposed to any such demand.[264]

The PNP worried about the development toward self-government with Bustamante as the head of the country. The election results caused similar concerns in England and in the US. In his report Paul Blanshard expressed his uneasiness about Bustamante's victory and his 'arrogant personal dictatorship'.[265] In his post-election report, Blanshard reaffirmed the suspicion that the release of Bustamante was a conscious tactical move of the Governor to weaken Manley and the PNP: 'So, in essence, the present ascendancy of Bustamante over Manley is a triumph of Machiavellian colonial policy'.[266] The American analyst further blamed the conservative press for having fuelled the fears toward the PNP's Socialist positions and for having supported Bustamante and accused them of deliberately ignoring his unfitness to lead the country in the next deciding years toward greater freedom for Jamaica.

In Domingo's first reaction to the elections, he defended the ideal of universal suffrage, despite the disappointing outcome.[267] He pointed to the attacks from the press, the conservative parties and the Labour Party and deplored that many were taken in by the belief that Bustamante truly stood for labour and would act in the interest of the small people. He regretted that able politicians like Manley and Nethersole did not receive a mandate and promised that the PNP would 'continue its work of education and organization undaunted'.[268] A close analysis of the results led Domingo to see hope for the PNP, as the numbers of votes for the PNP were promising. Often the PNP candidate only slightly lost his seat to a candidate from the JLP or to an independent.[269] Ken Post, discussing the election results, also pointed to this fact that the Westminster system caused a disproportion between votes and seats.[270]

Domingo and the PNP felt encouraged when thousands of people turned out to a post-election meeting at the PNP headquarters at Edelweiss Park, at which Domingo addressed the huge gathering.[271] Domingo eagerly tried to create an optimistic atmosphere and countered arguments that the voters were ungrateful to the PNP for winning them the right to vote. In public, he reaffirmed that the demand for self-government and universal adult suffrage logically belonged together and hoped that voters would soon become more experienced.[272] He felt confident that the voters would soon realize that the PNP genuinely stood for labour as a truly democratically organized party, while Bustamante appealed to emotionalism and many of his candidates had never articulated any sympathy for the cause of the labouring class.[273]

However, Domingo shared his genuine views in a private conversation with Manley that the party leader then shared with Blanshard:

> After it was all over, W. A. Domingo, the most prolific writer for the P.N.P. and a determined optimist concerning black democracy, confessed: 'The masses are desperately ignorant and greatly superstitious. Almost

anything is believed by them. The simple principles of logic, of cause and effect, and of human activity in its simpler fields are alien to the thought processes of the majority of Jamaicans.[274]

Blanshard further remarked that roughly 10 per cent of ballots were invalid. He felt that for the next election a literacy test would be advisable.[275] While no such statement is contained in Domingo's utterances, Roberts reversed his optimistic attitude toward universal suffrage. Even before the elections, Roberts had expressed his surprise about the granting of universal suffrage, given the low level of literacy in the country:

> Ballots for all, without a literary test, is undeniably a radical and surprising concession in a country like Jamaica. A million votes may now be cast, as compared with fewer than 50.000 under the old regime. One fourth of the voters may have to be helped at the election booths to distinguish the printed names of candidates.[276]

However, he was then convinced that universal suffrage would work out successfully.[277] In retrospect, he claimed that his opinion on the question '...was, and is, liberal rather than radical. I believe that the franchise should be modified by a literacy test'.[278] Obviously disappointed by the outcome of the elections, Roberts doubted whether universal suffrage was a useful basis on which to ground elections. In the late '50s, he argued:

> The primitive human being is not individualistic. He moves in packs, or herds, and blindly follows a leader. Political parties under manhood suffrage can create blocs by organizing the ignorant and swamping the literate by mere tally of noses.[279]

Roberts' old opponent de Lisser was somewhat right when in 1938 he mockingly said that Roberts was,

> ...talking about Prime Ministers and Ministers of Finance (which is quite characteristic of our old Adolphe Roberts); but when he come to grips with his subject he will find that his idea of a Prime Minister maybe very different from that of the peasant voter who after all is the dominant figure in most of our elections today.[280]

Bustamante as head of Jamaica was certainly not what Roberts and many others had wished. Nevertheless, although many officials were not satisfied with the election results and had wished for Manley as a partner in the developments of the upcoming years, they did not reverse the course they had started by granting first steps toward more responsibility. Colonel Stanley, Secretary of State for the Colonies, paid the island a personal visit and underlined in a speech at the Ward Theatre that the country was indeed on a path toward self-government and encouraged cooperation between the parties to guarantee the success of the venture.²⁸¹ After the elections, Stanley declared that the coming years would reveal if self-government would work out in Jamaica.

Domingo articulated his concern and stated that it would be unfair to judge this question since the country now had a leader who did not believe in Jamaica's capacity to become an independent nation.²⁸² However, as the main beneficiary of universal suffrage, Bustamante suddenly saw the potential of the new situation. Because it meant a substantial increase of his powers, he quickly changed his view and, for the time being, turned from a fierce opponent to an ardent supporter of self-government.²⁸³ Domingo pointed out the paradoxical situation and criticized Bustamante's change of mind as hypocritical.²⁸⁴ Also Blanshard noted with surprise: '... Bustamante, who had been less than enthusiastic about self-government, felt impelled to climb on the bandwagon and express his own support of the idea of self-government'.²⁸⁵

The representatives of the Progressive League, as well as the officials, had to accept the voter's decision. Domingo continued his propaganda efforts with the same zeal, heavily publishing in Jamaican newspapers. Despite the great disappointment, Domingo kept on supporting the PNP and tried to spread optimism after the disappointing election. He regarded the PNP's victory in a by-election in February 1945 as a sign of hope.²⁸⁶

Since his release, Domingo eagerly tried to get a visa to return to the US. But the officials were much concerned about his left leanings and his propaganda against race discrimination. A memorandum prepared by the FBI on Domingo's activities repeated the official reasons for his detention given by Governor Richards. They described him as a Communist, involved in racial propaganda and someone who had been very critical of the US effort to establish the bases.²⁸⁷ The report mentioned an alleged trip to Moscow in 1931 as proof for his Communist world view and pointed further to the wave of support of several prominent leftists who had lobbied for Domingo's release.²⁸⁸ Although the State Department had recognized that Domingo supported the British war effort, contrary to the majority of African Americans and Communists who harshly opposed the war, they worried about a statement by Domingo that his real loyalty was with Russia and that Great Britain was only the lesser of two evils. The report quoted Domingo commenting on Russia as 'the hope of all oppressed colonial peoples, especially those of the colored races'.²⁸⁹ Statements like this made Domingo even more suspicious to US authorities, especially given increased fears of possible conjunctures between Communism and anti-racism in the colonial world as well as on the mainland.

In the middle of the 1940s, US-based organizations of Caribbean migrants like the WINC and the Progressive League had increasingly come under heavy surveillance. The Communist leanings of some of its members were a cause of grave concern to the FBI, which was aware of the explosive potential that derived from African American-Caribbean connections.[290] The evidence gathered by the State Department highlights that the particular mixture of anti-colonialism, anti-racism and alleged Communist positions in Domingo's thinking led the officials to the conclusion that his presence in New York could be dangerous. The FBI believed he could do less harm while he was in Jamaica and advised the American Consulate in Jamaica not to issue a visa to Domingo because they feared that Domingo, 'if admitted into the United States, would engage in activities likely to arouse undue racial consciousness and to promote and foster racial animosity in this country'.[291] When the Consulate in Jamaica attempted to gather further evidence to prevent Domingo's return, they could not find any 'evidence that Domingo has either been associated or sympathised with any political group or organisation contemplating the overthrow of any Government by force or violence'.[292] However, the officials in Washington as well as in Kingston, remained adamant that Domingo should stay in Jamaica.

When Roberts wrote to NAACP Secretary White, asking him to do all in his power to influence the decision in favour of Domingo, he also mentioned that he himself had been excluded from visiting Jamaica, while Domingo now was denied the opportunity to return to the US. Roberts suspected that there was 'some sort of agreement on policy, between Great Britain and the US, regarding travel by advocates of autonomy for colonies'.[293]

White pledged that he had utmost faith in Domingo's integrity and recommended that he should be allowed to return to the US and tried to confront the US officials with the paradoxical nature of their decision:

> ...he was guilty of no crime safe that of seeking independence and freedom for his people, it was most extraordinarily that he should be punished for that during a war presumably being fought for freedom. Inasmuch as the denial of re-entry to the United States seems to have in some fashion been connected with that persecution, I hope he will now be permitted to return to the United States and his family.[294]

Manley tried to seek help from Charles W. Taussig, Co-Chairman of the AACC and President Roosevelt's advisor for Caribbean affairs, and repeatedly asked him to intervene.[295] However, despite the support of high-ranking personalities in the US with good links to the State Department, the authorities were not yet prepared to let Domingo return.

At the end of 1946, Taussig felt embarrassed and pointed out that now, after the end of the war, 'there might be no objection to granting him a visa'[296] and instructed an assistant to contact the State Department. The State Department then inquired at the US Consulate in Jamaica about the advisability of granting a visa to Domingo. US Consul Kemp answered: 'I know of no specific act on which to base a refusal for a visa, on the other hand I would consider a visa highly inadvisable'.[297] Domingo, he claimed, was openly 'pro-American', but 'violently anti-British', and Kemp suspected that when he was back in New York Domingo would 'continue his propaganda against British rule in the West Indies and in the African colonies, to our possible embarrassment'. Kemp suspected that Manley's intervention was driven by the motive to increase the popularity of the PNP in the US and argued:

> With Domingo's prestige increased by his internment in Jamaica in 1941, added to certain natural abilities as a propagandist, he might be very much of a headache to the Department. While I do not feel it is our business to protect British interests, I have always been opposed to allowing aliens to use the United States as a base for subversion of their home governments.

For now, Domingo was trapped in Jamaica. Kemp agreed with the State Department's concern in regard to the explosive force that might result from a combination of African American and Caribbean radicalism. This nexus, which had been integral to Domingo's political agenda and was in part responsible for the US efforts to bring about democratization and decolonization in the Caribbean, now played against Domingo's wish to return to New York as soon as possible.

Writing Back: Domingo's Anti-Colonial Agitation in Jamaica

How did Domingo react when he realized that his stay in Jamaica was to be even further prolonged? How did he attempt to influence the further progress toward self-government? Domingo's writings after his release from prison serve to provide deeper insight into his theoretical thinking and political tactics.

A combination of factors led to disengagement and 'inertia in US-Caribbean affairs',[298] the most important being the end of the war, Roosevelt's bad state of health, and the disappointing results of the Jamaican elections, in which Jamaicans had voted against the PNP with its strong demand for self-government. As a result, US diplomats lessened their efforts to put pressure on Great Britain for further steps toward decolonization of the Caribbean.[299]

Nevertheless, Domingo increased his nationalist propaganda while he was forced to stay on the island. He contributed heavily to *Public Opinion* and the *New Negro Voice*, of which he took over the editorship after his release.[300] In his remaining time in Jamaica, Domingo continued to provide a particularly international perspective, conjuring up the international solidarity of all colonials and black people in particular. He tried to capitalize on the tensions between Great Britain and the United States in regard to their respective colonialisms, keeping a close eye on Puerto Rican affairs. Even more than in the months before the election, he emphasized the relationship between race and class in Jamaica, but always appealed to Jamaicans of all classes and origins, trying to convince them that self-government would be beneficial to all.

He stood out in his radical nationalism and concentrated on flooding his readers with nationalist propaganda:

> ...I have given more emphasis to the need for Jamaican self-government than to any other theme. I have treated the subject from almost every conceivable angle. Nothing has ever shaken my conviction that autonomy of my country is the primary desideratum if we are to make any kind of progress which people of my way of thinking envisage for Jamaica.[301]

Domingo was conscious about the fact that he still spearheaded the production and dissemination of nationalist propaganda and that his agitation was not appreciated by all. Reflecting on his on his own role, he stated:

> Since somebody has to speak with embarrassing and unwelcome bluntness at time, I might as well take over the thankless task. It can't make my local reputation any worse. One advantage I have is that no one is likely to try and take my job away. My monopoly is as complete as that of the local match factory.[302]

The statement suggests that Domingo's radical nationalist propaganda was still isolated. Still, on other occasions Domingo showed himself more optimistic about the nationalist disposition of his fellow countrymen. One year after his release from prison he declared:

> Today Jamaicans are thinking of their country first, and not of other countries and other peoples. Call it narrow nationalism if you please but the path to healthy nationalism lies in the direction of a decent and natural love of one's country.[303]

In fact, both assessments seem to be exaggerated. While nationalist feelings had considerably grown during the past years, radical claims for immediate self-government were still not shared by a majority.

A review of Domingo's writings in the middle of the 1940s shows that his nationalism rested on three major interconnected pillars: anti-colonialism, anti-racism and an increasingly regional perspective of Pan-Americanism. However, the most dominant, over-arching concern was the demand for Jamaica's independence. It was based on the strong belief that all peoples should have a natural right to govern their own affairs and should not be ruled by another country. Nationalism was, Domingo claimed, 'the logical development and expression of all subject people, of all colonials'.[304] Domingo rejected the colonialist justification that colonies would first need to become ready for self-government or that Englishmen would be better suitable for the top positions in the country's administration and civil service.[305]

Domingo's definition of a nation still resembled the phrasing of Roberts in the original declaration of the Progressive League and combined elements of a territorial, cultural and historical legitimization. Domingo declared: 'Any people with a community of economic, political, cultural and historical interest and who have existed on a particular soil for generations, are a nation. National progress develops out of national self-realisation'.[306] He continued to prove why Jamaica would qualify as a nation, citing different definitions, based on a shared territory, a common language or a common history. Domingo further pointed to various small nations and dominions to counteract arguments that size was a relevant factor for nationhood. Domingo concluded that Jamaica, 'a nation by every accepted standard',[307] would legitimately demand to become a self-governed nation within the framework of the British Commonwealth of Nations.

Domingo was conscious about the role that print media played in the development of nationalism, an assumption which had been popularized, for instance, by Benedict Anderson.[308] One of the difficulties to create an 'imagined community' in Jamaica and to arouse nationalism was the dominance of the press by the conservative elites. Since 1938, the monopoly was broken to some extent by *Public Opinion*; yet, its circulation was much smaller and it appeared only on a weekly basis. Domingo therefore welcomed its conversion into a daily newspaper in 1944.[309] He promised that it would continue to advocate the rights of the oppressed and explicitly stated that it would represent the patriotic Jamaica as a balance to the conservative daily papers which had controlled the press landscape for centuries, promoting loyalty with the Empire and thus helped to cement the status quo. Further explicating the reasons why nationalism was so difficult to arouse, Domingo described colonialism as an exploitive system, in which the so-called mother country benefited from economic exploitation of the colonies. He described the psychological tactics as the main instruments with which the colonial power could legitimize and ensure the continuation of such a parasitic relationship:

> Jamaicans, like other colonial peoples, are subjected to a continuous barrage of subtle influences intended to induce them to identify their interests with those of their ruler. The reason for this is plain. If a subject people think in terms of their own interests they lose the sense of inferiority deliberately infused in them by their alien political masters.[310]

Domingo deplored the absence of a national consciousness and felt nothing did more to retard the progress of Jamaica. He described how the lack of unity was prevented by a strong positive identification with Great Britain, indoctrinated by the colonizers, stigmatizing the African roots of the populace, by glorifying the history of the colonizers and by neglecting the country's own complicated past. Lacking control over educational institutions and the press, the populace was easy to manipulate. He criticized:

> An important part of the technique of control is to encourage the colonial peoples of an empire to lose their identity in the whole. All questions are supposed to be viewed imperially, which is really from the point of view of the interests of the dominant section of the Empire.[311]

With striking clarity Domingo described why national consciousness was so difficult to arouse in colonies. He understood perfectly well how the Empire occupied the channel through which community was imagined in independent countries: 'Colonials are taught and encouraged to believe that the Empire is the nation. It commends their first loyalty'.[312]

Domingo exposed the internal contradiction within the Empire, which claimed to be a Commonwealth of Nations, while in fact it exploited its colonies by indoctrinating feelings of inferiority instead of accepting them as independent and equal nations.[313] Domingo's analysis is reminiscent of of what Frantz Fanon and other anti-colonial theoreticians so prominently criticized: an inferiority complex of colonial peoples, loyalty and identification with the mother country and a disregard for the cultural heritage of the enslaved Africans and their descendants.[314] Accordingly, he called for a nationalist spirit to overcome what he called 'national inertia'.[315] He diagnosed a natural tendency in mankind to accept negative situations, accept oppression and to label reformers and progressives as revolutionaries and radicals and deplored: 'We are the slaves of ignorance, poverty, political servitude, superstition', and asked: 'Can we rise above these and emancipate ourselves? The task belongs to all of us. Let us put our shoulders to the wheel and achieve a better Jamaica for ourselves and our progeny'.[316]

From his analysis, Domingo derived the conclusion that only nationalism was an 'antidote of the national inferiority complex of colonials'.[317] This insight directed Domingo's propaganda efforts throughout the years. Domingo tried to break the loyalty and identification with the so-called mother country, a very euphemistic term, by exposing Great Britain's racist behaviour, the economic exploitation and the psychological tactics the Empire employed to manifest its domination. Domingo's nationalist propaganda was designed to counter this mentality and to instil nationalism in the population that would result in a strong demand for self-government.

The means by which Domingo tried to inculcate nationalism was education. He recalled how he himself had a negative self-conception and admired the British aristocracy. He recalled that only when he came in contact with literature about the British Labour Party and learned about class conflicts within British society did his worldview slowly start to change.³¹⁸ In their conservatism, Domingo claimed, Jamaicans were even more imperialistic than the British and 'they regarded it as impertinence for anyone to assert that one man was as good as the next regardless of colour, race, or class. This was sacrilege, almost blasphemy'.³¹⁹ However, Domingo showed optimism and pronounced: 'Today an increasing number of Jamaicans have come to hate everything the Conservatives of England and their Jamaican camp followers stand for; Imperialism is under attack'.³²⁰

This was probably wishful thinking, rather than a realistic assessment. The disappointing election results had clearly revealed that nationalism was not at all firmly rooted among the masses and anti-colonial demands were still not very popular. In classical nationalist manner, Domingo tried to inspire interest in the country's history and to engender pride in being Jamaican to counter the widespread admiring of an ostensibly benevolent Empire that in fact ruthlessly exploited its colonies. Promoting cultural nationalism was Domingo's strategy to counter the connotation of inferiority that was attached to everything Jamaican. Therefore, Domingo encouraged Jamaicans to study the country's history, and to take pride in its achievements.³²¹

With this step, Domingo tied in with the promotion of cultural nationalism which the local Progressive League had started before the Second World War. In several articles and letters to the press, Domingo shed light on the country's neglected past. Like Roberts in 1939, Domingo highlighted the Jamaican politician Edward Jordon and explicitly lauded the Progressive League campaign 'Jamaicanizing Jamaica' in 1939.³²² These mild forms of nationalism had proved to be especially attractive to the middle class in 1939, when the campaign had attracted broad interest. Domingo pointed to three main channels: music, literature and art, through which 'the distinctive thoughts and emotions of a nation are transmitted to the world'.³²³ When the nation was not free, it could not develop its distinct culture, so Domingo was convinced, and compared it to a bird which tried to learn to fly in a cage. He especially encouraged teachers to inspire a positive attitude toward the history and culture of Jamaica in their students. He frequently addressed the Jamaican Union of Teachers, as he had also done on his earlier visits, and outlined their special significance for the national development of Jamaica.³²⁴

Domingo claimed: 'National culture is natural culture. It emanates from national consciousness and reflects the spirit of a nation'.³²⁵ Domingo's understanding of Jamaican culture rested on a belief in desirable progress of mankind toward civilization. He believed that the rural African traditions would vanish and be replaced by genuinely Jamaican habits and expected that the dialect patois would finally be replaced by Standard English, so that the inhabitants would be better able to communicate with the rest of the world. Which cultural influences would become dominant, Domingo openly admitted, he was not able to foresee. However, it would be genuinely Jamaican culture, Domingo claimed, and condemned the ignorant attitude of many conservatives, criticizing for example, that Esther Chapman was appointed to the board of directors of the Institute of Jamaica, without being Jamaican or even embracing Jamaican culture or political freedom.[326]

For Domingo, cultural nationalism was inextricably tied to political demands. Domingo was aware of the class divisions that were closely linked with racial stigmatizations. He regarded this nexus as a major impediment toward the development of a broad nationalism. The interest of the many, Domingo felt, should always take precedence over the material interest of the few.[327] In this regard, Domingo described illiteracy and poverty of the lower classes as impediments toward nationalism in Jamaica and advocated an improved educational system open for all Jamaicans.

Domingo was convinced that economic conditions in a democratic, self-governed Jamaica would automatically benefit the masses.[328] However, his statements in the 1940s show a shift from a particular concern for the working class; his statement now revealed grave disappointment in the masses that blindly followed the demagogic leader, Bustamante. While nationalist thinking grew stronger and took precedence over Socialist ideals, Domingo increasingly emphasized unity between the classes, demanding that in order to heal the country from the negative consequences of colonial rule all classes should unite in a strong demand for self-government. In 1941, he had outlined how each class would benefit from independence:

> The development of a national outlook is the prerequisite to self-government. Jamaicans of all classes must develop a passion *for their country*. If Jamaican capitalists are to break the bonds which limit their investments and their enterprise, they must support the movement self-government. The middle class, regarded from any definition of the term, have a paramount interest in attaining control of the political life of their country. They, like all other patriotic Jamaicans, have a country to win.[329]

Like many nationalist theories, Domingo attributed a special role to the middle class in the emergence of national movements. He argued that as a result of conditions deriving from colonialism and slavery, their status was 'shot through with all sorts of contradictions'.[330] He complained about the society's division 'along social and colour lines'[331] and urged that the middle class was in need of internal unity and solidarity with the country's lower classes. He hoped they would join with the country's masses in a common aspiration for self-government to change the economic and social conditions, which would in fact be in accordance with their own class interests. Yet, he complained, large sections of the middle class were strongly opposed to the demand of self-government and eagerly sought to prevent the upward mobility of the masses.

Domingo also appealed to the upper classes and advocated local manufacturing and industry. He encouraged Jamaican capitalists and businessmen to think more locally and argued that self-government would increase local consumption and would thus benefit the local manufacturers and the Jamaican economy in general.[332] Free trade in the region, profits from the recently discovered bauxite resources in the island[333] or revenues from the US-leased bases could have contributed to Jamaica's development instead of serving Great Britain's interests.[334]

Domingo exposed complaints of British officials about the 'financial burden' the colonies would impose on the 'mother-country' and denounced them as hypocritical. He pointed to the exploitation and mismanagement of overpaid colonial officials, while self-government and local economic efforts were constantly and deliberately suppressed.[335] Domingo explicitly approved the theses of Eric Williams, who had outlined in his book, *Capitalism and Slavery*,[336] how much slavery and colonialism had contributed to the rise in power and wealth of the British Empire and that slavery was only abolished when it ceased to be economically advantageous.[337]

Similarly, just as Domingo advocated unity among all of Jamaica's classes in a strong national movement, so he also advocated racial unity. This claim was of special importance in a society based on a racist ideology. Over centuries, imperialists justified colonization with overlapping racial and class distinctions and thus defined the social fabric in Jamaican society. In a society in which the majority of the population suffered from racial discrimination, the demand for racial unity under a nationalist umbrella was necessarily accompanied by contradictions.

On one hand, Domingo criticized racial discrimination against the black majority. On the other hand he demanded racial unity and subordination under the nation and neglected claims for representation of other racial minorities. This topic involves complex questions about race, ethnicity, and nationalism and points to the core of how nationalism operates, how nationalists define the population and whether the national concept was based on diversity or homogeneity.

From Domingo's time as a soapbox speaker in Harlem, the fight against racial oppression was one of his main concerns. In the 1940s, Domingo still exposed race discrimination, whether in Jamaica, Great Britain or the US. For example, Domingo reflected on the racist ideology and the double standard with which matters were discussed and treated in the Empire. He criticized the discrimination of Great Britain's black 'colonial subjects' that motivated the colonial policy toward countries with a black majority.³³⁸ Domingo condemned the 'double standard in the empire'³³⁹ that was based on a feeling of racial superiority with which Englishmen justified inequalities, for example the more drastic Defense Regulations in Jamaica, the unequal treatment of black and white prisoners in detention or the toleration of the existing colour line in the Jamaican police force.³⁴⁰

Domingo strongly believed in the right of self-determination of all peoples, he deprecated all forms of racial oppression and criticized racism as a powerful instrument of imperialism. Anti-racism and anti-colonialism were closely connected in Domingo's concept of nationalism. In Domingo's eyes, racial oppression was one of the main factors for the apparent lack of national unity: 'Discrimination weakens patriotism and breeds resentment'.³⁴¹ Domingo advocated a Jamaican nation with equal rights for all citizens, regardless of their racial or ethnic background.

However, what provides equal opportunities for all in theory can determine disadvantages and discrimination against minorities in reality. A conflict that led to the withdrawal of one of the members of the local branch of the League helps to exemplify the problem. It had adopted Domingo's position that all Jamaicans, regardless of race, class or creed should subordinate all other allegiances under their national loyalty and patriotism. Right after the proposal for the new constitution, the question of whether or not racial minorities needed special representation caused a major conflict and points to the weaknesses of a radical nationalist approach.

Dr J.L. Varma, a well-known personality in Kingston, Secretary of the East Indian Progressive Society,³⁴² and Progressive League member from the early days of the Kingston branch and its representative in the PNP's Executive Committee, believed that racial minorities should be granted some form of representation in the Nominated House.³⁴³ Indian-Jamaicans formed the island's largest minority. The majority consisted of descendants of indentured workers who were brought to Jamaica after the abolition of slavery. Many still worked as unskilled labourers in low-paid sectors. Yet, the majority within the local League and the PNP was convinced that 'such minorities suffered no legal disabilities and any such representation would be the means of disuniting the Jamaican nation instead of welding the people into one united whole'.³⁴⁴

Varma was harshly disappointed by this stand of his political co-workers and decided to resign from both the Progressive League and the PNP.³⁴⁵ As secretary of the East Indian Progressive Society, Varma further explained his decision in the press and claimed to represent the 'entire Indian community of Jamaica'. He argued that only by representation in the Nominated House, the racial minorities in Jamaica would have a fair chance to present its particular point of view.

Although Varma declared that the 'East Indians of Jamaica consider themselves as Jamaicans', he was convinced: 'If true democracy is to be applied to Jamaica then the principle of self-determination...of the different racial groups must be accepted. To do otherwise would be a negation of principles of democracy'.[346]

To prove his point, Varma referred to various cases of discrimination against the Indian minority. Aside from some legal discriminations, for example in the marriage law by which descendants of Indians were still considered migrants and needed special approval by the Governor to marry, he cited several occasions of discrimination, for example when they were excluded from the contingent of Jamaicans who were allowed to work in Panama or the US, or when Indians were barred from attending government schools because they were not Christians. Indian candidates who ran for public office, Varma claimed, would never have a fair chance of being regularly elected and thus were entitled to have a voice in the Nominated House. With reference to the US he pointed to the gap that often existed between a theoretical affirmation of equal rights and practical discrimination, from which, for example, African Americans suffered.[347]

Domingo firmly rejected Varma's demand from a nationalist standpoint and challenged his assumptions, claiming that there was no discrimination against Indian-Jamaicans.[348] Domingo was convinced that if discriminating laws existed they should be abolished, but there should be no special consideration of the position of the 'racial minorities' in the country's political organs. In contrast to Varma, he denied that there was a 'racial minorities question' in Jamaica and claimed that the economic success of minorities in Jamaica, such as the Chinese or the Syrians, would attest to the 'extraordinary racial tolerance of the majority'. The few existing cases of discrimination or aggression against minority groups were rather based on class differences and linked to economic advantages that the particular groups had acquired. Black Jamaicans, who formed the majority group, were still economically disadvantaged, while the minorities were still overrepresented in government jobs, as employers, and in the wholesale and retail business. Domingo insisted that any special representation was counterproductive and would rather impede the national development. Therefore, all Jamaicans should be regarded equal and should have the same rights and duties.

Regarding Varma's statement on the right to self-determination, Domingo answered that the term was originally meant to be political, not racial:

> Self-determination does not mean, and never was intended to mean that every small racial or religious minority in a country was entitled to determine its own political future. It is an abuse of the terms to imply that self-determination means political fragmentation.

While Domingo affirmed the Indians' right to their particular cultural heritage, he claimed 'were the Indians not stimulated to consider themselves as distinct from the rest of the population they would in time assimilate and become average Jamaicans. Individual Indians themselves will decide the question'.

From this statement it is clear that Domingo personally advocated assimilation and strongly believed in nationalism that subordinates religious, cultural and racial distinctions. He objected to the building of separate institutions, for example, schools and hospitals, fearing they would tend to 'perpetuate differences in the island'. Domingo explicated: 'It was my understanding', pointing to Varma's own statement, 'that Indian-Jamaicans were "true Jamaicans" and I assumed their point of view would be Jamaican (national) not racial'.

Yet, the question was not settled for the East Indian community in Jamaica. With a letter to *Public Opinion*, I.N. Fyzullah, Secretary of the Jamaica Indian Conference, resumed the discussion. Presenting similar arguments like Varma, he claimed that Indians and other minorities would suffer from discrimination and also compared the situation of Indians as a racial minority to the situation of African Americans.[349] Domingo and Fyzullah exchanged their arguments in several articles, while the organized Indian-Jamaicans eagerly tried to reach their goal of political representation. An All Island East Indian Conference lobbied for support from the Indian as well the British government. Domingo rejected Fyzullah's representation of particular minorities, fearing that through the agitation of groups like the East Indian Society, they would gain a 'disproportionate amount of political power and influence under the New Constitution'.[350] He argued that this would de facto mean that that group would 'enjoy an advantage over the other races, thereby undermining the growth of political democracy in Jamaica'.[351] Recalling the history of the East Indians who came to Jamaica mainly as unskilled indentured labourers, Domingo was not surprised that they still belonged to the working class. He claimed that class belonging, rather than racial or cultural particularities, would be responsible for the chances of an individual. From this standpoint, all working class Jamaicans were in fact disadvantaged: 'Only a liar or a fool will claim that there is equality of opportunity, or anything near it, for the masses of any capitalist country'.[352] Indian workers would share the same lot with the rest of the Jamaican workers and should therefore identify themselves with the national movement. Domingo was convinced: 'The real cure for the conditions of the Indian minority (as it is for the black masses) is for it to cast its lot with those liberal and national movements in Jamaica which are dedicated to lifting the living standards of all the workers'.[353]

Domingo went as far as to accuse the East Indian leaders of purposely exaggerating the 'implied racial "suffering" of their people and are working to make political and other capital out of the exaggeration'.[354] Fyzullah rejected such accusations and replied that Domingo was ignorant toward the problem Indians would face in Jamaica.[355] Fyzullah argued that contrary to the original contract on which Indian immigration was based, the repatriation into their homeland had not been provided for by the British. He accused Domingo that he would not accept cultural and racial diversity and visualize 'a solution of the racial problem only in the merging of all the racial groups from which will ultimately emerge a new physical type of humanity'.[356] In contrast, Jamaica's Indians would believe in 'each racial group developing its own particular genius and contributing the same to the welfare of all'.[357]

To back his position, Fyzullah quoted a letter from a Chinese-Jamaican, who full-heartedly supported the demands of the East Indian Progressive Society that Indians should be granted a permanent seat in the nominated house, and claimed other minorities should be granted the same.[358]

Because Domingo felt Fyzullah 'has been guilty of some gross misstatements' in regard to his opinion, he answered once more. With an undeniably aggressive undertone, Domingo alleged:

> The campaign of the organized East Indians as to their treatment in Jamaica is a slander of the masses of the Jamaican people and should not be allowed to go unchallenged. Falsehood, like a fire, is capable of attaining uncontrollable proportions.[359]

In regards to his alleged advocacy of miscegenation, Domingo answered:

> It is ridiculous for anyone to 'advocate' race mixing in the Western World where human beings are not mated like animals. Unlike in some Eastern countries people who live under Western culture and ideals select their mates by free choice. They are not married in their infancy by their parents. Hence, it would be nonsensical and futile for anyone to 'advocate' miscegenation in a country like Jamaica.

In this comment, a certain chauvinist neglect of the Indian's cultural and religious practices is undeniable. However, the question of how much assimilation a nation state can and should require and to which degree religious and cultural rites that differed from the moral standards of the majority is not easy to answer and concerns many immigrant societies until today. For Domingo, the answer was clear. Although Jamaican society was a 'composite', he believed in a common 'national pattern'. He further elaborated what this pattern meant: 'language, traditions, peculiarities of speech, habits, customs, and maxims etc.' Domingo explicitly denied that the language or traditions of small minorities should be actively preserved. Domingo saw 'no need for the creation of little islands in our midst for the preservation of customs and languages which have as much chance of permanent survival in Jamaica as the proverbial snowball has in Hades'.[360]

When the Colonial Office rejected the demand of the East Indians for representation in the House of Representatives, Domingo was glad about the decision.[361] With similar arguments like in the question of East Indian representation, Domingo also rejected the idea of special platoons, for example, Chinese or East Indian platoons, in the Jamaican military forces.[362] Domingo summed up his position:

> ...I believe in unqualified racial equality, because I am irrevocably opposed to this or any future government of Jamaica giving preference to any group, be it of the black, brown, yellow or white race or any of their mixtures, or it is a majority or minority of the population. I stand uncompromisingly for absolute human equality. For anyone to believe otherwise is for such a person to reveal that he is a Fascist who believes in the theory of 'superior' and 'inferior' races.[363]

Domingo's position toward racial minorities in Jamaica was guided by a firm belief in human equality. His nationalist convictions allowed no form of separation or segregation. In his eyes, the cure for the social and economic problems of Jamaica was national unity and loyalty, regardless of phenotypic or cultural differences. His nationalism, however, neglected the particular problems of other non-white racial minorities, especially Indian descendants who still belonged to the country's lowest classes.

Domingo was aware that his position provoked some people to feel that he was 'anti-Chinese, anti-Indian, anti-Semitic, anti-British and anti-God alone knows what'.[364] Repudiating such allegations, Domingo stated: 'as a person of socialist belief I believe in tolerance and human equality'. Although nationalist arguments dominated Domingo's statements in the 1940s, it is interesting to see that Domingo traced back two of his guiding principles, tolerance and belief in human equality, to a fundamental belief in Socialist values. Domingo made his position plain that his nationalism was still dominated by the category of class:

> I want to make it clear that I am anti-none of the peoples mentioned. I admit that I am anti-lies, anti-injustices, anti-inequality, anti-imperialist, anti-race and colour prejudice. If by being against these things I collide with some people who profit from them, then the blame is theirs not mine. I am very definitely pro-Jamaican and that is important. And by Jamaica I mean all the people who inhabit this and regard it as their home and the place of their first loyalty. Those who consider me against them because I object to them being enjoying privileges denied the masses or because I insist on telling the naked truth and sometimes ruthlessly expose the dross we have taken for gold should ask themselves if I am right. The criterion of judgement should be truth.

In Domingo's interactions with the country's minorities, he exhibited a bias in favour of the black masses of the country. His conviction that nationalism could unify the population and that all classes, including the poor masses, would automatically benefit from political autonomy highlights the notion that nationalism tends to highlight the existing class differences and inequalities in a society and often leads nationalists to underestimate them. Although certain Socialist values were still present in Domingo's mindset, a strong anti-colonial nationalism had become the determining influence in his thinking. Although he appreciated Russia's entry in the war, anticipating a positive anti-colonial impact at the peace table, he was no longer convinced that the world was quickly developing toward a global Socialist revolution.[365] Domingo's motivation was rather anti-colonial, feeling that the Soviet Union would have a democratizing effect at the peace table and would help decolonization in the post-war period.[366]

Remarkably, Domingo did not speak to the question of how the interests of the upper and the lower classes, or the majority and the different minorities could practically be brought in accordance after the nation state was founded. Hence, Domingo's nationalist ideals were somewhat short-sighted and guided by a nearly naive belief in equal opportunities for all in the new nation-state he desired Jamaica to become.

During his involuntary stay in Jamaica, Domingo often shared his insights and reflections on international developments with his Jamaican readers. He focused on topics he felt were useful to inspire nationalist feelings and support the demands for self-government. Numerous radicalized anti-colonial movements were an additional source of inspiration and provided an encouraging example for Jamaica. While many colonies supported the British war effort in the name of democracy, they now asked a weakened Great Britain why they would not be granted the same democratic rights they helped to defend. Domingo claimed that most of the recruits from the colonies had in fact 'fought for their own countries'[367] and would now expect to be supported in their demands for independence, democracy and freedom.

Domingo closely observed other anti-colonial movements in Africa[368] and Asia. Especially with the defeat of Japan, the anti-colonial movements in Asia gained even more strength. Domingo recognized with appreciation: 'In Southeast Asia the flame of freedom is burning fiercely'.[369] He pointed toward developments in India, Burma, Japan and Indo-China, that he felt were inspired by the decolonization of the Russian empire and US proposals to offer independence to the Philippines.[370] Especially after the harsh disappointment of the election, Domingo increasingly asked his compatriots to look outside of Jamaica for inspiration, instead of worshipping the autocrat Bustamante. He encouraged his countrymen to take other colonial countries like India, Burma, Korea, Puerto Rico or Nigeria as an example for the fact that 'nationalism precedes everything else, if all sound and real progress is to be achieved'.[371] Domingo was convinced:

> The crusade for national independence will spread and engulf the entire colonial world. Gone are the days when cringing 'natives' make

low salaams to their European overlords. Economic forces and political examples in the Philippines and the Soviet Union are undermining the foundations of imperialism.[372]

Statements like this testify to Domingo's international perspective from which he derived much of his anti-colonial fervour. Domingo was sceptical toward the apparently generous offers made by Churchill toward a greater degree of self-government for India and Burma.[373] Domingo suspected that the steps were designed to please the US and to continue on the road of slow development toward self-government within the Empire to prevent increasing demands for autonomy and international sympathy toward such claims. Hence, India's decision to reject lukewarm offers toward more self-government by the British Government with an 'unequivocal demand for independence'[374] found Domingo's full approval.

In general, India was of special importance to Domingo and had influenced his nationalist thinking from early. Domingo remembered how as young man he became an 'Indian nationalist sympathiser',[375] after he read about India's nationalist aspirations in various articles in English periodicals. These sympathies intensified the more he learned about Mahatma Ghandi, M.N. Roy, Tegere and Jawaharlal Nehru.

Despite his endorsement of the nationalist movement in India, Domingo doubted that its independence would automatically lead to further decolonization of the British African or West Indian colonies with a black majority. Although advocating for an end of colonialism in all countries, he warned that the independence of some British colonies might even lead to an intensification of exploitation of the colonies in Africa.[376] The West Indies, he indicated, would still be a special case because of their proximity to the US and the embedding in a Pan-American context, which will be more closely examined in the latter part of this chapter.

From the 'chess board of history', Domingo drew the following conclusion: 'Imperialism is being checkmated at every turn and that this spells a brighter day for the enslaved colonial peoples'.[377] When he realized that many Jamaicans did not pay attention to these developments, Domingo stated: 'It was hard for me to believe that that there were people alive who were not conscious of the rising spirit of freedom in the various British colonies'.[378] While Domingo was optimistic regarding the anti-colonial developments in the world, he diagnosed that Jamaicans were still unaffected by this international drive. Such a conclusion suggests that loyalty with England was probably stronger than in other colonies.

Still, Domingo felt anti-colonial sentiment in Great Britain could make up for the lack of radicalism of Jamaicans. With a view to the British Labour Party, Domingo felt sure: 'Eventually there will be a tie-up between the colonial peoples and the radical elements of England'.[379] At the same time, he did not naively believe in British benevolence.[380] Based on earlier historical experiences, he did not expect that the colonial policy would radically change even when Labour came into power in 1946. He only expressed cautious hopes, no enthusiasm.[381]

Domingo's suspicions proved to be true. The new Labour Government did not undertake radical steps toward self-government and Domingo soon complained about the colonial policy of the 'avowedly Socialist, and for that reason theoretically anti-imperialist'[382] British Government. Domingo soon recommended looking for allies outside of England and expecting to find them 'in nations whose political and economic interests coincide, in one way or another, with those of the Indians and other colonial masses'.[383] In Jamaica's case, the most powerful potential partner was certainly the US, but also other neighbouring republics. Domingo encouraged studying the conditions in surrounding states to affirm his thesis that these nations were better off than the British colonies.[384] He felt that Jamaicans needed to change their negative attitude toward the neighbouring republics and start to recognize the potential of the fact that their own country was closely embedded in the region.[385]

While the war came to an end in Europe, delegates from 50 nations came together in Dumbarton Oaks, San Francisco, in June 1945 to found the United Nations (UN). This event was observed closely by Domingo, because he hoped that the conference would officially support the demands for independence of all colonies, especially those that had supported the war efforts of the Allies. At the same time, US foreign policy had lost interest in the Caribbean and shifted toward more urgent questions like those of mandates and trusteeships resulting from the end of the war.[386] Thus, Domingo's hopes were harshly disappointed, when the position of Russia and China, 'our two champions',[387] who advocated the abolition of all colonial regimes at the conference in San Francisco, found no approval. The US did not support the demands for independence of all colonies and rejected the assumption of responsibility for the colonies in the region by taking them under a temporary trusteeship. Ken Hill, who attended the conference as a journalist and observer, reported that the US would be ready to back British colonial interests and advocated only internal self-government for the colonies and not 'ultimate independence'.[388] The recent election of Bustamante might have contributed to feelings that the region was not ready for full self-government.

Domingo argued that the US position contradicted the Havana declaration of 1940. Indeed, Hull had then advocated a trusteeship solution, but it seems as if Domingo blanked out the fact that the arrangements were made for the case of Great Britain's defeat. While Domingo had initially objected to the trusteeship idea at Havana and had advocated for immediate independence for Jamaica in a case of British defeat, he now advocated 'international supervision' during a transitional period.[389]

In reaction to the disappointing conference, Domingo advocated a strong united demand for the independence of all colonies:

> Colonial peoples must aim at complete autonomy within the shortest time possible or write themselves down as fools or inferior-minded. Lacking the material means for achieving freedom with arms, and recognizing the unlikeliness of freedom being conferred on them by those who profit from its denial, colonials must think clearly and advocate: 1. That colonial control be taken from any one nation and vested in a concert of nations. 2. A definite time limit should be set for colonial autonomy.[390]

Domingo's comments regarding the San Francisco conference were again a clear sign for the radicalization that can be observed in his statements and writings in the mid-1940s. After his release from prison, he showed a tendency to increasingly use the words republic, independence and autonomy when discussing Jamaica's future, instead of self-government within the Commonwealth. It is therefore no surprise that Domingo showed sympathy for the effort of Canada to advance from Dominion status to full independence.[391] In addition, he cited Cuba as a positive example for Jamaica as a prospering republic in the region.[392]

Although Domingo did not advocate armed anti-colonial uprising to bring about the desired political change in Jamaica, he commented favourably on a statement in which Ghandi prophesized a bloody war if India was not granted independence after the Second World War.[393] He showed sympathy with other nationalist movements that used violent means, for example, pointing toward events in Indonesia, where the declaration of independence in August 1945 was the start of a bloody conflict between the natives and the Dutch colonial regime. The Indonesian case would demonstrate to Domingo, that 'freedom is never given; it has to be won'.[394] To support his argument, Domingo pointed to the fact that the Pan-African Congress had recently acknowledged that colonials would have the right to use all means at their hands to fight for their legitimate right for national freedom. Domingo underlined the benefit of international cooperation between people of African descent against racism and imperialism:

> Our job should be to internationalise our problems. We must show up our local tyrants to the world. Contact with democratically-minded brothers in the neighbouring islands and in the United States, as advocated by Mr. Manley, will bring us valuable allies in our struggle against imperialism and native fascism.[395]

Certainly, the end of the war and the disappointment about the outcome of the conference in San Francisco had radicalized Domingo and reinvigorated his internationalist outlook.

Yet, despite the disappointing attitude of the US diplomats at the founding conference of the UN, Domingo remained convinced that the US had a strong interest in a decolonized Caribbean. He preferred a strong US influence over British control of the resources. Quite conscious about the shift in power relations on a macro-political level, he speculated that this could become another reason for the US to increase the pressure on Great Britain and help to facilitate Jamaica's decolonization: '...the Americans have a powerful weapon – they can aid Jamaicans in their present struggle for national freedom'.[396] In this context, the strategic importance of the bauxite findings at the end of 1942 in Jamaica is noteworthy. Parker notes that despite its strong influence on the relation between Great Britain and the US, the local activists hardly mentioned the subject.[397]

At least Domingo was an exception and addressed the matter in several articles.[398] From his nationalist perspective, he deplored the fact that the government had kept the discovered mineral resources a secret, in fear it might 'affect the war effort',[399] but had in the meantime granted a monopoly to the Canadian company Alcan. Domingo pointed out that the government was 'not inclined to make the industry a national one'[400] and demanded that Jamaicans should at least have a say in the granting of mining rights. Competition would benefit the seller, he claimed, and explicitly wished that Reynolds, a US company, be allowed to bid on the remaining available lands that were not yet granted to Alcan. Domingo was convinced that under self-government, Jamaicans would have been able to secure better prices and thus the deal would have benefited the country more.

Domingo was right to assume that the US had a great interest in the discovered bauxite mines in Jamaica. The large country on the mainland lacked access to satisfactory resources to meet the needs of the crucial resource for alumina production, especially in the wartime industry.[401] Hence the finding of large amounts of bauxite in Jamaica put the West Indies even more in focus of US strategic interests. In view of the strong hesitations of Great Britain to grant permissions to US companies to mine Jamaican bauxite, it was only reasonable to speculate that the US would now become an even more powerful catalyst of the decolonization process.[402] This development supported Domingo in his approach to look for the US as a potential ally in the fight for the decolonization of Jamaica. Like Roberts, Domingo was sure that Jamaica would naturally belong to the Pan-American hemisphere. He argued that the political future would be more connected with the US than with Europe: 'The logic of history and the strategic needs of the hemisphere point to a day when all the people of this continent will be part of one whole – the Pan American Union'.[403]

Domingo's perspective was recognized and even shared by Amy J. Garvey, who often disagreed with Domingo:

> The future of this area is of vital concern to the U.S.A. ...The viewpoint Mr. Domingo expresses is the voice and feelings of the people of these islands from the standpoint of good common sense, security in the future, and economic stability.[404]

Domingo tried to capitalize on the increased economic and political interest of the US in the region and the vision of a decolonized world, which the US proclaimed to be the future of the post-war world.[405] In his eyes, economic imperialism was still the lesser of the two evils of imperialism and colonialism.[406] Colonialism, Domingo explained, was both political and economical dominance, while the possibility to determine trade agreements and economic exchange based on the self-interest of the country would be economically beneficent for Jamaica, even if the economic power of the US was dominant.[407] Domingo did not worry about frequent rumours about US interests to annex the islands and pointed to statements of President Roosevelt to counter such fears.[408] Free trade and military bases in independent countries in the region would be sufficient to satisfy US economic and safety interests. These arguments supported Domingo's conclusion that the US was a potential ally in Jamaica's struggle for self-government:

> The wise and democratic course for America to pursue so as to obtain national security and immunize the continent from automatic involvement in non-American wars is to assist West Indians to get a status similar to that of Canada as quickly as possible. ...England would be placed in an awkward position resisting a democratic move which coincides with her own professions, serves the strategic interests of the United States and the hemisphere and achieves the political aims of the West Indian peoples.[409]

With a good perception of the delicate relationship between the US and Great Britain, Domingo capitalized on comparisons between the colonial policies of Great Britain and the US and the respective economic and social conditions in Puerto Rico and Jamaica. He was convinced that Puerto Rico was better off and blamed the exploitive nature of British colonialism for this difference.[410] Indeed, Puerto Rico and Jamaica had become, as Parker puts it, 'unquestionably the pawns in a game of competitive colonialism'.[411]

While exposing the wickedness of British colonialism, Domingo increasingly showed a clear pro-American bias.[412] Domingo's pro-American attitude was recognized and harshly criticized by Richard Hart and other leftists in the PNP. The Cold War reached local politics in Jamaica. The leftists preferred international connections with Russia and feared the economic and political imperialism of the US.[413] However, Domingo's opinion was guided by the assumed positive effects which US interests could possibly exert on the way toward decolonization. In a very US-friendly series of articles, he reviewed the foreign policy of the United

States toward its neighbours and argued that the US would have a genuine economic interest in Jamaica becoming a self-governing unit in the hemisphere.[414]

Closely comparing the social, economic and political conditions of both islands, Domingo concluded that while in Puerto Rico illiteracy rates were declining, they were increasing in Jamaica. Domingo claimed that Puerto Rico had a much stronger nationalist movement and lacked the 'self-abasing expressions of gratitude'[415] that Jamaicans showed toward Great Britain. He felt that the substantial difference in the colonial policies of the US and Great Britain was reflected in the status of democratic developments in their respective territories.[416] While the US pictured full autonomy as the desired status for all their dependencies, Britain would grant self-government only within the Empire. He claimed: 'to the British self-government means going along the road they map out for you'.[417] Domingo saw the reasons for the different approaches in the 'insistent demand for freedom and certainly because of the genuinely democratic attitude of President Roosevelt and recent Governors'.[418] In a short time, Puerto Rico had achieved a larger degree of self-determination than Jamaica had gained during the past centuries, Domingo argued. He insisted that a comparison of the different forms of US and British colonialism would successfully challenge false beliefs about the benevolent character of the British colonialism and prove that its effects were even worse than US imperialism.[419]

Paul Blanshard came to similar conclusions when he presented a report on conditions in Puerto Rico in August 1946, concluding that Puerto Ricans were economically and politically better off than colonial peoples in the British and Dutch Caribbean.[420]

Nevertheless, these evaluations stood in contrast to Domingo's own views that he articulated around the time of the Havana Conference in 1940, when he objected to a transfer of sovereignty to the US. Back then, he had cited Puerto Rico as a negative example, when he argued that it was 'still poverty-stricken. The masses of the people are landless and their standard of living unbelievably low'.[421] In 1941, Domingo also criticized US racism on military bases in Puerto Rico and Haiti more harshly and warned of Jim Crow practices on the US bases that had been granted in the bases-for-destroyers deal.[422]

It is hard to discern whether the more positive light in which Domingo now portrayed Puerto Rico and US foreign policy was motivated by strategic considerations in regard to a possible US influence on the speed of Jamaican decolonization or tactical reasons to please US officials who still refused him a visa to return to the US. Most likely, it was a mixture of both. In every case it shows a certain tendency of Domingo to use arguments in the way that best served his nationalist claims.

Domingo's positive attitude toward the US in this time went so far, that he downplayed evidence of racism, for instance when the US advertised jobs on the military bases explicitly for whites. When critique mounted in Jamaica, Domingo argued that the US had not invented this form of racist job advertisement and pointed to earlier examples in the Jamaican press. He claimed that Jamaicans needed to address the race prejudices in their own society before they criticized racism in the US.[423] He argued in a similar way when addressing occurrences of racism in the US, arguing that Jamaicans would do better to address British and even Jamaican forms of race discrimination than to limit their complaints to cases of US racism.[424] Domingo, for example, criticized the prevailing racism in the British Army, again pointing out the better treatment of Puerto Ricans in the US army and provocatively asked if Jamaicans would feel they were inferior to Puerto Ricans because they accepted inferior treatment.[425]

Domingo still criticized all forms of racism, like racial discrimination against Jamaican seasonal farm workers in the US.[426] However, his pro-American bias and the downplay of racism in the US in comparison with British racism was recognized and criticized by a number of African Americans.[427] Among them were some of his friends, who felt that he had become anti-British and bitter during his imprisonment and that he had lost 'all sense of proportion in dealing with conditions in Jamaica and those in the United States'.[428]

When Domingo heard about the critique, he was very disturbed and responded with a lengthy series of articles in which he reflected about his own attitude toward the US and affirmed that he strongly condemned racism in every form and in every country.[429] He felt that he had simply argued from a Jamaican perspective and justified this approach with his strong Jamaican nationalism. In the articles, he highlighted the different practices of race discrimination in Jamaica and the US and felt that while the more open form of race discrimination in the US was often shocking for immigrants from the islands, this was no reason to downplay Jamaican or British forms of racism. To further counter accusations of overlooking US racism, Domingo published a number of articles in which he expressly criticized discrimination in the United States.[430] For instance, he pointed out racist connotations in US movies like *Gone With The Wind*, and feared a negative influence on Jamaican spectators as well.[431] He also criticized racism in the US army, stating it was as bad as in Great Britain,[432] and strongly denounced all forms of segregation and discrimination. However, Domingo showed a tendency to view the US more favourably, a fact that was noted by the US authorities in various reports.[433] It is quite possible that this was part of his motivation, while he renewed his efforts to return to the US.

In 1945, Domingo asked Walter White to support a renewed visa application. He expressed his lack of understanding for the decision of the US authorities to keep him out of the country. He wondered how his ardent Jamaican nationalism, the advocacy of self-government from which the US would benefit and his general pro-American attitude could be offensive. Even in regard to race discrimination in the US, he had tried to paint a more balanced picture than many Jamaicans:

> It is, I suppose, fair to say no man has done more to give a balanced picture to Jamaicans of the true condition of coloured Americans. I have done this not in order to cowtow to anyone or to curry favour with Americans, but because it is my candid opinion.[434]

However, despite Domingo's notable pro-American attitude it still took until August 1947 before he was finally admitted re-entry in the US.[435] The State Department still felt that Domingo's pro-American attitude was motivated by 'nostalgia' and expected it to change as soon as he was allowed to return.[436]

Only after Nethersole returned from a visit to London where he got the chance to read some of the confidential information filed against Domingo, he started to understand why the US government was concerned. Domingo was 'unable to recognize himself'[437] in the reports and complained that Governor Richards had sent out false statements to the US government that now provided the basis on which the US officials grounded their decision.

However, in face of the massive support for Domingo and a lack of evidence for Communist leanings or criminal records, it became increasingly difficult finding good reasons to keep Domingo out of the country. A handwritten note on a letter from the consulate to the State Department indicates that the Immigration and Naturalization Service of the Department of Justice issued a petition to grant a visa to Domingo.[438] Somehow, Domingo learned about the petition. Based on the rumours that his visa had been granted, a farewell party was organized by the PNP.[439] However, this celebration proved premature and was cancelled accordingly. The final granting of Domingo's visa was delayed for another few months. However, the situation had become very difficult for the US Consulate. Vice Consul Kelly cabled to the Secretary of State to come up with a quick decision: 'Embarrassing situation as Domingo knows of petition here'.[440] The State Department was still hesitant and advised the Consulate to delay the visa until a definite decision was made in the US.[441] Acting Secretary of State Dean Acheson answered reluctantly that he did not regard the petition of the Immigration Service as binding. Nevertheless he had to admit: 'If however you have no further information, Department would appear to have little basis for disagreement if you should find that favourable action is not warranted'.[442]

Kelly replied with a long letter, now supporting, to grant a visa to Domingo. He provided the results of further investigations and announced that Domingo was no Communist, never a member of the Communist Party, and that there was no evidence for a trip to Moscow. He explained that while Domingo sympathized with Communism after the First World War, hoping that it would bring the desired end of oppression of black people, he soon became disappointed by the Communist policy. His position in the PNP and as a close associate of Manley would give further proof of his political stand:

> ...far from being a radical Domingo has the rather anomalous position in Jamaica of not being a good socialist – according to those who consider themselves good socialists...and is accused of being too nationalistic.[443]

Kelly emphasized that Domingo was mainly a nationalist, advocating an independent Jamaica 'with an economy directed towards the United States, as opposed to a close tie-up with the British Empire'. Although Domingo would be strongly anti-imperialistic, 'there is no evidence to point to his being anti-British in spite of his desire to see Jamaica freed of British control'. Kelly explained that Domingo started to believe that elements in the US were trying to work against his wish to return. He then concluded:

> While this office is reluctant to do so, it must admit that to refuse an immigration visa to Domingo at this time would be purely arbitrary and legal dishonesty on the part of the responsible consular officer, unless new evidence of a material nature is presented.

Finally, after more than four and a half years during which many high-ranking and popular personalities in the US lobbied for Domingo's permission to return, his wish was granted in August 1947. In an interview shortly before his departure, Domingo declared that he would not desire to be actively engaged in politics in the United States, but 'always have the interest of Jamaica at heart'.[444] In a letter to Vice Consul Milton C. Walstrom, Domingo declared:

> At my age (nearing 58) I am not disposed to take any active part in politics of any sort, unless it affects Jamaica adversely. In such a case I would return to Jamaica, regardless of the risk, just as I did in 1941.[445]

Indeed, there would be one last heavy involvement in Jamaican affairs. Although he would not physically return to Jamaica to wage the fight, he would bitterly oppose the West Indies Federation, regardless of risks, loyalties and old friendships.

Close examination of Domingo's propaganda elucidates the old lines of argumentation, such as the critique of racist oppression and economic exploitation, the widespread imperial identity, the need for education, encouragement of patriotism, critique of class and colour barriers in Jamaica, and the demand for self-government as the only solution. Domingo increasingly commented on the changing political background on the international scale and pointed toward international developments like other anti-colonial movements or Jamaica's relationship to the US. In the following years, a fortified nationalism that was less interested in the fate of other colonies determined Domingo's thinking and guided his opposition toward the plans of the Colonial Office to federate the British West Indies. But before delving into the campaign of Domingo and Roberts against the federation in the 1950s, the next section examines Roberts' efforts to return to Jamaica, and his nationalism.

Roberts Return: Promoting Nationalism in Jamaica

When Roberts decided to visit Jamaica in 1945, he wrote to Manley, asking him to investigate whether the officials had reservations regarding his visit, bearing in mind that he was a naturalized US citizen.[446] The Governor assured Manley that there was no objection to Roberts' visit. Hence Manley and Roberts both were astonished to learn that the Jamaican authorities had turned down Roberts' request for a temporary visa in March 1945.[447] In his answer to Roberts, Manley expressed his surprise:

> I know how sensitive authority is about political activities but it must be well known that your only political activity was your past connection with the Jamaica Progressive League which initiated a Movement for Self-Government in Jamaica and thus can rightly claim to have acted in accordance with Imperial policy as now established here.[448]

It appears to be somewhat naive that Manley did not take into consideration that these activities in particular could have been the reason why Roberts was barred from returning to Jamaica. After Roberts asked Manley to investigate if there was a misunderstanding,[449] Manley went on to inquire into the situation and put in a word for his 'personal friend'.[450] In a letter to Governor John Huggins, Manley lauded Roberts' integrity and his outstanding contributions. He mentioned his distinction as an author, as a historian of the region and as a journalist. Manley pointed out that Roberts' political views were in no way extreme. Manley described Roberts as 'politically a mild liberal with no other interest but his interest in the development of Self-Government'.[451] Manley again pointed to the pioneer character of the Progressive League, 'the first Body to seek to develop the idea of Self-Government for Jamaica',[452] but emphasized that it adhered to the moderate aim of achieving Dominion status within the British Commonwealth.

Manley felt it would be helpful to prove that his views had been in accordance with those of the PNP: 'He became a member of the People's National Party entirely because the party had adopted self-government as one its aims'.[453] Manley asked the Governor if there was anything he could do to aid in the situation. In strong words, he assured the Governor:

> Speaking with all sincerity and being convinced that I have the fullest and most direct knowledge of Roberts and his status politically and

otherwise I am entirely at loss to understand the reason for a refusal to allow him to come to Jamaica.⁴⁵⁴

In Manley's eager efforts to prove that Roberts was no threat to the political stability of the island, Manley's own high esteem for Roberts is evident. He tried in vain, however, the Governor informed Manley that the denial of Roberts' visa was not his own high-handed decision but that he had referred the question to the Executive Council.⁴⁵⁵ This meant, in fact, that Bustamante and the men he nominated for the Council had decided that Roberts was not welcome in his country of birth. To Manley this seemed to be a mean trick and he suspected that the Governor deliberately delegated the decision to the Executive Council, knowing quite well that Bustamante would reject the request.⁴⁵⁶

The Jamaican public reacted with indignation and the incident became what Roberts called a 'cause célèbre'.⁴⁵⁷ In the forefront of the protests were PNP heavyweights like Norman Manley, W.A. Domingo, Florizel Glasspole, Seivreight, Dr Ivan Lloyd and other prominent PNP members.⁴⁵⁸ Glasspole suggested making political capital out of the issue, but Manley feared that further political confrontation between the JLP and PNP would not serve Roberts' interest.

However, the PNP still tried to reverse the decision. In the House of Representatives, Dr Ivan Lloyd, declared the ban as unconstitutional and asked for referral of the question to the Privy Council, but the request was voted down.⁴⁵⁹ As a reason for Roberts' exclusion, Frank A. Pixley, one of Bustamante's closest intimates, declared:

> Suffice it to say, as a part of the government of this country I decided that it was not in the best interest of the progress of the new Constitution to have Mr. Roberts in this country, because this government intends to see that this Constitution succeeds and we have no intention of allowing persons to come from abroad to affiliate themselves with any socialist group.⁴⁶⁰

This phraseology, with its slight touch of cold war argumentation, shows that the political climate between the PNP and JLP was so embittered that even a liberal like Roberts was accused of being a Socialist because of his loyalty to the PNP. Given the enmity between the JLP and the PNP, there was some justification in Manley's recommendation that the Civil Liberties Council or the Press Association should deal with the matter.⁴⁶¹

The tenor of the various statements protesting against the decision of the Executive Council was similar and again highlighted Roberts' outstanding reputation. Numerous articles by Domingo and others appeared in *Public Opinion*, protesting against the ban of Roberts from his native land and rebutting accusation that he would be a Socialist as outright nonsense.⁴⁶² Also the conservative press from the *Daily News* to the *Daily Gleaner* could not see 'the existence of reasons for banning him from entering the country',[463] and pointed to Roberts' great reputation and his contribution to Jamaican society. The *Gleaner*, a very dependable opponent of self-government in the past, now stated:

> Like so many Jamaicans who have breathed the free air of a virile, young democracy in the United States, unquestionably Mr. Roberts was one of the earliest to be associated with the movement for self-government in Jamaica. But in that he is of like persuasion with the present leaders of the British Government. So that if the barrier to his entry is linked with his political concepts, it could only be in regard to his methods and not his principles.[464]

The statement not only pointed to the migration experience into a free republic which inspired nationalism, but also showed how much the idea of self-government had soaked into the society, so that even its fiercest opponents now started to accept a slow development toward it as it had become official colonial policy. De Lisser assured his readers that, knowing Roberts personally, he could testify that he advocated neither revolutionary nor violent methods. The *Gleaner* wondered how the Jamaican government could ban Roberts from his native land, while the US government held Roberts' talents in high regard and had asked him to write a book on the US navy. The *Gleaner*, usually in support with the government, now asked for an explanation of the rationale behind the decision and warned: 'great harm can be done to domestic and international confidence in the purposes of our administration by acts such as this, in which the justice and wisdom of the decision are not obvious and not even apparent'.[465]

Domingo put the arbitrary act in one line with the constructed evidence that was presented as reason for his detention.[466] He recalled the history of the Progressive League, the pioneer role of Roberts and stressed that it always operated exclusively with legal and constitutional measures. He argued that given the heavy surveillance by the British and US secret services under which it stood at times, any violation would have immediately caused serious problems. Domingo emphasized Roberts' patriotism and declared that, unlike other successful Jamaicans, Roberts had never forgotten his land of birth: 'If America is his wife, Jamaica is his mother'.[467]

The new constitution, Domingo claimed, 'stemmed directly from the work Roberts had initiated in Jamaica in 1937', and was brought about by the aid of the British government, the pressure of the public opinion in Jamaica, England and the United States, and the support by President Roosevelt. Domingo emphasized:

> But for the work and sacrifices [of] Roberts, who is now barred from the island, there would have been no new constitution or an Executive Committee, as yet. The responsibility for banishing him from his

country would then have been the responsibility of the Governor and his Privy Council. To their eternal shame Jamaicans elected by the people under a franchise largely the result of Roberts' devotion to freedom, participated in excluding their benefactor from paying a temporary visit to his native land.[468]

Blanshard and the US consulate in Kingston also observed the matter with concern, noting that not one newspaper article appeared in support of the decision by the Executive Council. In his observations, Blanshard openly questioned Bustamante's capacity to provide stability for Jamaica.[469]

Nevertheless, the widespread disgust about the decision and unanimous assurances about what a fine and unquestionable patriot Roberts was could not help to reverse the decision. Roberts finally decided to let the matter rest and postponed his trip. After Manley heard about Roberts' decision he wrote a letter in which he assured him:

> We here have done all we can. The matter has been mentioned at public meetings, a Resolution was moved in the House of Representatives and I have dealt with it literally at dozens of small indoor meetings that I have been holding over the last six months.[470]

The reactions to the barring clearly show the respectability and popularity that Roberts had gained over the past years. Even his advocacy for self-government had become socially acceptable and some of his old friends who politically disassociated themselves in the pioneer stage of the movement now expressed their disapproval of the decision. Bustamante, the recent convert to self-government, had just found out how the new powers could contribute to an affirmation of his political position. With Roberts supporting the PNP, he feared that his position could be weakened and his sincerity as a politician and his motives for his recent advocacy for self-government questioned.

The effect of Bustamante's decision to ban Roberts proved to be even more harmful to his own reputation than what Roberts could have done while visiting the island. Roberts saw the positive aspect clearly when he reflected in his autobiography:

> He provided me with a vast local publicity, which has been useful to me in view of the fact that I had been absent during the war. I had always been critical of Bustamante; my fresh distaste, if any, was caused by the foolish terms in which he tried to attack but could not harm me.[471]

The impressive unity in disapproving the Executive Council's decision in all corners of the society proves Roberts' statement to be right.

Roberts' popularity was also reflected by the enthusiastic reception he received when he eventually came to the island in 1946. This time he did not bother to apply for a visa and suddenly appeared at the airport, flying in from Cuba. Roberts was on a tour to write a travel book about the Caribbean islands. At this time, he did not experience difficulties in entering Jamaica. In his autobiography, he remembered how a polite immigration officer welcomed him with a friendly advice:

> I could land as a tourist...for six months. But he warned me not to make political speeches, because the police might think my ideas subversive and report me to higher authorities. Various security rules were still in force, and under them an alien could be deported. I thanked him, smiling, for giving me such valuable information, and he smiled back.[472]

The return of Roberts was a widely celebrated event. He gave a number of speeches and interviews and was honoured at numerous receptions. For example, the Poetry League, of which he was the first vice president, gave a luncheon in his honour,[473] and the Jamaica Press Club organized a reception at which Roberts spoke about conditions in Cuba and encouraged his listeners to visit the neighbouring free republic.[474] The 'highwater-mark of my political prominence in Jamaica', as Roberts himself described it, was an honorary dinner at the prestigious Myrtle Bank Hotel on August 6, 1946. The celebrity affair was crowded with high ranking guests from politics and society. Among the speakers were Norman Manley and N.N. Nethersole for the PNP, W.A. Domingo and W.G. McFarlane for the two branches of the Progressive League, Philip Sherlock, *Gleaner* editor T.E. Sealy, and Hugh Paget who represented the Jamaica Historical Society that had recently been formed.[475] An extensive report gave detailed information about the event filled with patriotic spirit in honour of Roberts.[476] All speakers praised the contributions of Roberts in a variety of fields; including history, poetry, journalism, and politics, as well as his pleasant and sincere character. Manley especially emphasized his patriotic contribution, including the special role he played in Manley's own political and ideological development. The *Gleaner* reported him as saying:

> To Mr. Roberts he owed his first serious and deliberate consideration of the subject of a national outlook and life for Jamaica by means of self-government, and from him he had derived his first and most lasting inspirations about it. That was a heroic venture of his. At the time single-handed, like some strange prophet in the wilderness travelling this comparatively sleepy country from one end to the other, speaking to half a dozen sleepy and skeptical sets of persons, perhaps, but always undaunted and determined. He believed then the time had come when the people of the West Indies should be brought together encouraged to go forward to achieve a destiny of their own, and now he was witnessing the first-fruit of that movement that he started 10 years ago in the U.S.A.[477]

Reassuming the Struggle for Independence in Jamaica

Manley's glowing tribute testifies to the tremendous influence that Roberts and the Progressive League exerted on the development of the local political scene. Roberts gave a speech addressing the historical and political development of Cuba, where he had just stayed for three weeks before coming to Jamaica. Roberts argued from a strong regional perspective that marked a cornerstone of his thinking. He pointed to the independent countries in and around the Caribbean as positive examples and complained that people in Jamaica would feel closer to New York and London than to their immediate neighbours Cuba and Haiti and were neither reading their neighbour's newspapers nor studying the history or the political conditions.[478]

During this visit, Roberts did not actively engage in political affairs and the meetings he attended were seemingly apolitical. But, at a second look, the subjects of his speeches that were primarily concerned with other countries in the hemisphere were highly political. By pointing to the inspiring potential of the neighbouring independent countries, Roberts tried to give a new push the movement for self-government in Jamaica. In his autobiography, Roberts elaborated on his tactic:

> I made a good many speeches which assuredly could not have been called non-political. My approach was to announce that I was a tourist, and then to appraise conditions in terms of mock innocence. At times I dispensed with the irony. It would have suited me to have the Government cap my tour with an arrest and more publicity. But they let me alone. Policemen on duty at my meetings went out of their way to be friendly.[479]

When Roberts left to continue his trip throughout the Caribbean[480] and his return to the US, he planned 'to go back to Jamaica as soon as possible and to arrange my work so that I could live there'.[481] However, his work on a historical novel on the Cuban War of Independence[482] interrupted his plans, before he could return permanently at the end of 1949.

Before Roberts would return to Jamaica, Domingo's wish to return to the United States and finally end his involuntarily prolonged stay in Jamaica was finally granted. In the months before, the Progressive League in Kingston had increasingly edged away from the PNP. During the duration of Domingo's stay in Jamaica, he was only loosely associated and not actively involved in the affairs of the local branch. The sources provide no definite statement, but it does not seem as if Domingo was involved in conflict between the PNP and the local Progressive League.

At the end of 1946, the Progressive League in Kingston issued a resolution complaining about the increasing feuds and personal conflicts among the parties that would endanger the proper working of the political system under the new constitution.[483] McFarlane blamed the PNP and particularly its leadership for a loss of confidence of the Jamaican populace in the party and in the political system as a whole. Political quarrels with the majority party, the JLP, were futile and the country would be tired of the conflicts, McFarlane complained. He claimed that a particular group of Communists in the party would cause the problems and urged Manley to 'make a definite choice, either to be a part of this irresponsible group of hot-heads in the Party, and you stick to them, or you are part of the level-headed sober group of members and supporters of the Party at home and abroad'.[484]

Manley answered that he could not understand what McFarlane was complaining about, completely disagreeing with his views. Instead of feeling forced to take any sides in a conflict that he did not even see, Manley stressed that he embodied the interest of the party as a whole.[485] He repudiated the allegation that there were Communist elements in the party and that he would side with them. Instead, he made it clear that the only disagreement between McFarlane and the party was 'over your suggestion that the party should be used to favour and advance individual members of the party in affairs which affected members of the public at large'.[486]

As a reaction, McFarlane wrote a statement to the PNP, declaring that the local branch of the Progressive League had decided to 'discontinue the affiliation'[487] with the PNP. As reasons, McFarlane cited that the party was not nationalist enough and only criticized Bustamante and the Labour Party. In addition, he claimed, the party would not consult the members of the Progressive League in important matters. Deliberately misquoting Manley's statement, he alleged that Manley had declared in a letter to him that he supported that faction, while, on the contrary, Manley had denied that any such factions existed within the party. Further, McFarlane complained that he had not been given enough speech time at the last PNP conference.[488]

In his answer to McFarlane, PNP Secretary Arnett responded that he regretted the decision of the Progressive League in Kingston and that he could not understand the reasons for the step.[489] The PNP was a democratic party, he attested, and he was surprised that the Progressive League did not make use of opportunities to influence its policies. The accusation that there were Communist elements in the party's executive was a complete falsehood, and he expressed his feelings that McFarlane's personal issues with the party were the motive behind the decision.

In a letter to Duhaney, president of the Progressive League in Kingston, long time member and Treasurer P.A. Aiken supported McFarlane.[490] McFarlane answered Arnett in clear and harsh words:

> Your letter is so full of mis-statements, inaccuracies, and mis-representations, which has become the greatest proof of the wisdom of our belated decision to severe our connection with your Party. Our great regret is that those of us who influenced the decision of our League to become entangled in your web in 1938 have now to bow our heads in shame to a minority, who were opposed to the affiliation. That group was right.[491]

McFarlane then decided to take the division even further and personally ran as a candidate in the next election to the Kingston and St Andrew Corporation (KSAC).[492] Although a futile effort, this episode marked the break between McFarlane and the PNP.

When McFarlane asked for financial support in the campaign, in which he was a direct competitor of PNP candidate Ken Hill, the Progressive League in New York left no doubt where its loyalty was.[493] Instead of supporting McFarlane, it continued to raise funds for the PNP's election campaign, while McFarlane was forced to advertise his campaign in the classified advertisements of the *Gleaner*.[494] The decision of the Progressive League in New York caused further resentment when Ken Hill tried to take advantage of the lack of support for the Kingston branch while instead rallying firmly behind the PNP.[495] McFarlane was quick to point out that the Progressive League in Kingston was not a branch of the Progressive League in New York.[496] This statement stood contrary to what he claimed in July 1947, when he repudiated an allegation by Bustamante that the Progressive League in Kingston was a tiny group of Communists. McFarlane then had answered that the Jamaica Progressive League with its branches in New York, Kingston and Panama have thousands of members and was not Communist.[497] McFarlane was upset and replied:

> The fact that the branch of the League did not send me a contribution for my campaign fund, is no reflection on my sincerity, honesty and ability to be of much greater value to the community if elected as a Councilor than Hill. This fact does not prevent me opposing Hill and Co. who are known to be the element of destruction in the PNP and my fight against that gang goes on even if I am not elected. The success of self-government cannot be achieved under the guidance of political hot-heads.[498]

McFarlane tried to appear as the saviour of the national movement.

> I am not in fact opposing the PNP as an organization, because my personal contribution to the building-up of that Party is well known to a large section of our island's population, but I am forced to oppose the candidate of the PNP in an effort to save the basic principles of our progressive national movement from further ruin.[499]

In reality, it became evident that not only the Jamaican society but also the Progressive League in New York had turned away from the local Progressive League and from McFarlane in particular. Without the support of the Progressive League in New York, the branch in Kingston was doomed to failure.

The PNP felt relieved that the Progressive League in New York continued the crucial upkeep of the party, especially in face of growing political disagreements.[500] Brown was instrumental in mediating between the party and factions of the Progressive League.[501] When the PNP gained its first electoral victory in 1947, the Progressive League congratulated heartily and both groups were optimistically looking forward to the 1949 general elections.[502] Manley frequently asserted the crucial importance of the support of the Progressive League for the funding of the election campaign.[503] Throughout the following years, the Progressive League continued to be one of the most important financiers of the PNP, despite the differences.

The relationship between the two branches of the Progressive League never improved again. Throughout years of cooperation, the relation had been frequently dulled by disappointments about the unreliability of the local Progressive League, its indecisive stand regarding the declared aim of self-government and its opportunistic behaviour. When Roberts returned to Jamaica in 1949 to settle in his land of birth, he saw no benefit in keeping the group alive. Although the sources do not illuminate the reasons for Roberts' decision, the recent disaffiliation from the PNP certainly was one of them. In June 1950, Roberts met with several officers of the Kingston branch, namely McFarlane, Duhaney, Messam and Aiken. A picture appeared in the *Gleaner*, without an article, but naming the officers and their function and crediting them to be the 'Pioneers of the Self-Government Movement in Jamaica and other West Indian Islands'.[504] This last sign of appreciation was followed by an announcement in the *Gleaner* in the following week that the 'local branch has closed down'[505] and that correspondence and other papers were handed over to the reference library of the Institute of Jamaica. This was the silent end of the local branch of the Progressive League in Jamaica. Shortly after independence, McFarlane tried to revive the group, criticizing the government's use of public funds and trying to promote nationalism, but the efforts attracted no great attention.[506] In 1989, Jimmy Tucker and the late W.G. McFarlane tried to renew the Progressive League, demanding a new constitution and a complete break of the ties with Great Britain, but these efforts never found notable support.[507]

After the Progressive League in Kingston was dissolved, Roberts faced the dilemma of not having a suitable organization through which to channel his activities. Although Roberts never objected to a close cooperation with the PNP, his own relationship to the party was ambivalent. Initially, Roberts had shared the hopes that the PNP was a suitable partner to promote nationalism in Jamaica. However, when the PNP adopted Socialism as one of its main pillars in 1940, Roberts strongly disapproved of the decision and felt that this would be 'dimming the lustre of the word "Nationalist" in its name'.[508] In 1940, he had advised the Progressive League to continue its support nevertheless.[509] However, when Roberts finally returned to Jamaica in October 1949, he was not at all pleased with the course the PNP had taken:

> The socialism it had embraced in 1940 had grown to be, at least superficially, a revealed religion. The clenched-fist salutes which had irked me in 1948 had multiplied to the point of seeming an exhibitionist mania. I found the rank and file to be chiefly trade unionists and district politicians. Devotees of the old idea of an independent Jamaica were rare among them.[510]

Roberts was firmly opposed to the 'leftist air'[511] that prevailed in the party. In the *Gleaner* interview, Robert unmistakably declared: 'Communism is an absurdity in an agrarian country such as Jamaica. Communism is bad anywhere, and I am unalterably opposed to it…anyone who holds that communism is good for Jamaica is either a visionary, or a dupe'.[512] Roberts even regarded the moderate British type of Socialism as 'too extreme'.[513] This was a fundamental difference between Roberts and Domingo, who frequently expressed sympathies with the PNP and its Socialist course.[514]

Accordingly, Roberts abstained from active involvement in the PNP's election campaign. The PNP, in turn, did not ask him to appear on their platforms. Roberts pointed out:

> In contrast with the early days when they welcomed any patriotic expression they had become cautious, perhaps on the grounds that I might utter some social heresy, perhaps fearing that in a post-war atmosphere their opponents might make an issue of my United Sates citizenship.[515]

Nevertheless, Roberts hoped for a win for the PNP and promised Manley that he would soothe 'rising doubts of the Progressive League in New York and tell it to go on collecting money to aid Manley'.[516]

Roberts deeply regretted that Domingo was not in Jamaica to exert an influence.[517] He felt that Domingo had 'suffered morally to the verge of a nervous breakdown while held in the internment camp'[518] and understood his wish to go back to New York. Hence, it was Roberts' turn to decide how best to exert influence on the local political scene.

Both parties provided no acceptable basis for active involvement of the liberal Roberts. In his eyes, none of them was nationalist enough: 'Neither of them [Bustamante and Manley] gets radically away from the colonial mentality', he argued and complained: 'The P.N.P has worked from the outset for what was called Home Rule in the Irish struggle and beyond which an awakened Ireland went far'.[519] This admiration for Great Britain had been visible from the PNP's very first days, Roberts remembered. He argued that this shortfall was visible from the close cooperation between the PNP and British Labour Party:

> This alliance showed that Manley's attachment to the nationalist idea was not strong. It is disillusioning when a chief of an awakening people appears to forget that liberty is never a gift but a victory. Manley assuredly held that the administration of his country's internal affairs should be in its own hands, but he cared more for socialism and the welfare state than for full independence.[520]

Roberts deplored that Bustamante was 'condemning self-government on illogical grounds' and suspected that he feared that such radical claims could 'hamper his programme'. The efforts of the Progressive League to transform the labour protests in 1938 into nationalist aspiration, as seen, for example, in the discussion with Richard Hart in *Public Opinion*, remained in vain. Roberts regretted: 'Nothing could have been more harmfully (sic) to the growth of national feeling than the ten-year ascendancy of Bustamante'. The following split between the PNP and the JLP had forced the PNP to start its own labour organization, Roberts concluded, and led to a situation in which both of the political parties were 'too closely allied with labour unions and subjects to the latter's needs'.[521]

In view of the upcoming elections in December 1949, Roberts briefly considered filling the political void by the founding of his own nationalist party. Although Roberts had publicly declared that he went to Jamaica without plans to get actively involved in politics,[522] he remembered in his autobiography:

> Certain persons – a larger number than I have ever admitted publicly – came to ask me whether I would back a new party based on the principles of the Jamaica Progressive League. This could not be shrugged aside and I gave serious though to it.[523]

Roberts' papers even contain a basic outline for a platform for such a nationalist party which reflects his principal political goals, as well as the seriousness he attributed to the consideration of founding a party:

> 1. Dominion Status; 2. Free enterprise, but acceptance of certain major socialist reforms; 3. A strong agricultural policy; 4. Loosening of the European connection, with orientation toward the Pan-American Union; 5. A Caribbean customs union, to include the republics; 6. A literacy test for the registration of voters; 7. Encouragement of literature and art.[524]

However, Roberts feared that such a party would mainly attract voters from the PNP and thus indirectly help Bustamante and the JLP, so Roberts decided against this step. He preferred the PNP to win the elections, as he expected Manley to become a great statesmen and no leftist extremist when he got into power. In retrospect, Roberts reflected that the combination of the Second World War, the war regulations, his US citizenship and the Socialist course of the PNP 'cut short my active leadership in the movement…I thought of founding my own party but decided against it, and the initiative passed for me'.[525]

Hence, Roberts chose to stick to his promise to support the PNP's election campaign by organizing financial support for its campaign from New York and encouraged the Progressive League, which also started to have serious concerns about the Socialist course of the PNP, to organize mass meetings to raise funds.[526]

Such support was urgently needed, as Manley, Arnett and Glasspole pointed out in various letters.[527] In a letter to Brown, Manley reminded him of the vital importance of the election for the course of decolonization of the region and explained that while the Progressive League was supported by the local capitalists, the PNP was under heavy pressure:

> It is indeed the most critical period that we face and to anyone who knows conditions out here to-day and can appreciate what threatens us it is impossible to over-emphasize the gravity and importance of this present crisis.[528]

When Glasspole asked the Progressive League to arrange a tour for him, he announced: '…it is a matter of life and death to us here in this struggle'.[529] The Progressive League agreed and organized a two-week tour to support the campaign with several other mass meetings. Due to the successful fund-raising efforts, the Progressive League was able to significantly contribute to the election fund.[530]

When the PNP lost the election by a very narrow margin on December 20, 1949, Roberts approached Manley on the following day and shared his feeling that 'a straight nationalist programme would have been better understood and would probably have triumphed', still, 'Manley mused over this and said he did not agree'.[531] Roberts felt that England's mild attitude and the Socialistic welfare policy of the PNP had hampered local feeling.[532] In his eyes, the granting of a 'half-way-constitution' was a gift instead of a victory that was readily accepted. Nevertheless, despite the lacking of a 'tightly-knit nation that a period marked by sacrifices might have brought into being',[533] Roberts believed in continuing to try to arouse nationalism by putting all factional issues aside:

> I concluded that my future work lay along those lines. I would not resume British citizenship and seek office. It was later than ever for me to lead a new party; the answer plainly must be No. History, local culture and the story of liberty were already my themes, and I must make the most out of them.[534]

During his time in Jamaica, Roberts started to coin a term for his understanding of nationalism, *Nationalist Liberalism*.[535] In the remaining part of this chapter, the main features of the theoretical background of his thinking highlight the continuity in the approach of the Progressive League founder and shed light on the determinants of his thinking:

> It is not enough, however, for nationalism to announce itself as a generalisation. What sort of government is advocated? What is the ideal? Personally I would not have endorsed neither a Tory nor a Leftist extreme, though nationalism can be based honestly upon either of them'.

He advocated a democratic republic, based on the values of freedom and liberty. He defined that Nationalist Liberalism, was not to be understood,

> ...in the sense of any nineteenth–century liberal parties, but associated with freedom of choice and generosity of outlook. Deriving from the key word – liberty. The stand was that the future Jamaica would be against coercion, that it would be democratic; in truth, if not in name at the beginning, it would be republican.

For Roberts, the main goal was an independent democratic nation. He regarded the desire to form such a state, national consciousness, as the legitimate aspiration of any people: 'Freedom is a supreme end, and it is more valued if it comes as a victory instead of a gift. Self-Government ranks ahead of good government. There is a sustaining and guiding strength in national consciousness. Until it appears a people is not adult'.

Roberts admitted that the absence of a widespread nationalist consciousness in Jamaica was in contrast to his more optimistic view in 1936, when he believed that such a feeling could be aroused by nationalist propaganda.[536] Over time, the Progressive League agitators were forced to realize: 'There was little or no aspiration already ardently held. The movement could be compared to a bringing to birth, seriously delayed but inevitable unless the end were to be death'.[537]

The basic assumption of all nationalists, that their people were in fact a nation with a right to an independently governed state, was also shared by Roberts. In his view, the assumption that Jamaica was a nation was a given fact: 'That Jamaicans form a recognizable people is not to be disputed. Why? Because men who have clung to a land isolated by the sea, or by fixed frontiers, develop traits which inevitably make of them a people'.[538] This territorial argument can be traced back to the preamble of the Declaration, the central document of the Progressive League, and was frequently referred to by the Progressive League members. Such an understanding of the nation necessarily was combined with anti-colonialist convictions against the power that prevented the assumed nation from its teleological end of creating a state.

Hence, the lack of national consciousness needed an explanation. Analysing the reasons for the absence of a strong nationalism, Roberts blamed the 'paralysis caused by the long rule of outsiders' and demanded that it 'must be replaced by a feeling of political entity in the world, or my country would be unworthy of having the great name of Liberty evoked in connection with her'.[539]

Roberts saw one of the main reasons in the dynamics of the colonial hierarchies and the deeply entrenched racism in the society. In his eyes, the ruling class missed its opportunity to demand autonomy at a time when many other colonies in the hemisphere demanded and successfully fought for their independence. Instead, Jamaicans voluntarily surrendered the Assembly in 1865 after the Morant Bay Rebellion. Roberts recalled how present the turn of events in Haiti was in the consciousness of the planters and quoted Governor Edward Eyre warning the Assembly of Jamaica of 'being turned into a Second Haiti'.[540] The subsequent voluntarily dissolution of the Assembly and acceptance of Crown Colony rule was a watershed event that plays a key role in Roberts' nationalist argumentation. In another manuscript, Roberts commented: 'The entire planter class, rich and poor, was purblind. It should have regarded true autonomy as the island's destiny, yet it looked to support from Britain to keep it in power, and it would not even see that the basis of control had to be broadened'.[541] Roberts blamed the voluntary dissolution and the subsequent crown colony regime for prolonging the endurance of colonialism and for driving the country apart from its independent neighbours in the hemisphere. Roberts clearly saw the dynamics of race contributing to such a decision: 'The whites wanted mainly to check the coloured. Professing to fear new uprisings and massacres by the Negroes, the whites asked paternalism and they got a good long dose of it'. Roberts attested that colonial rule had enforced a 'colonial humility' that was nourished throughout the centuries and that had sunk in deeply into the mindset of Jamaicans; Roberts deplored: 'he [the Jamaican] willingly accepts the conditions of a retainer in exchange for that of a serf'.

Yet, in his concept of the nation, race did not play any significant role. From the outset, the Progressive League had repudiated racial approaches in its nationalist propaganda, although this would have possibly attracted many in a country with a vast majority of African descendants and strong tradition of racial discrimination. For Roberts and the Progressive League, the criterion for belonging to the Jamaican nation was purely territorial. Roberts believed that all Caribbean nations would share a 'Caribbean character' and believed that Jamaicans would share more attributes with, for example, Cubans than with either Africans or Europeans.

Racial descriptions of the 'typical Jamaican' were 'meaningless and harmful' in Roberts' eyes. 'National cultures are not founded upon race, but upon a synthesis of the strains involved', Roberts claimed. 'Let us leave it to the Hitlers to attempt to revive the myth of race as a unifying virtue'. Jamaica was neither a black nor a white country, 'Jamaica is itself'. Roberts firmly believed in a Jamaican nation that would be able to overcome all race discriminations. As a white Jamaican, he possibly was over-optimistic in regards to the realization of such ideals.

In his teleological perspective in which the nation state was the focal point:

> A people cannot just lose a hundred years without showing that its case has been one of arrested development. All our republican neighbours were astonished that Jamaica should still be a colony in the late 1930's. They said unflattering things about us. Who can blame them?

Roberts' strategy to promote nationalist feelings arose from his belief that the majority of Jamaicans lacked national consciousness. He used the traditional means that nationalists have at hand: the recurrence on national role models, the construction of common legacies, shared experiences and shared expectations in the future. The historical examples of the former colonies that had turned into free republics played a major role in his arguments. Remarkably, his nationalism sprung from a decidedly internationalist perspective that heavily influenced his thinking.

At first glance, Roberts' decision to abstain from involvement in party politics appeared to be apolitical. While he was mainly recognized as a 'distinguished Jamaican-born novelist and historian' with a strong patriotism, a bohemian character, an 'intellectual with a twinkle in his eye, a palate for good wine, a zest for living and an eye for pretty women',[542] his message was highly political. As a historian and journalist, he continued to promote the demand for self-government in a more subtle way, actually continuing his emphasis on cultural nationalism. In most of his activities, Roberts pursued his mission either as a historian trying to counter colonial history with local and regional history, or by highlighting the history of the neighbouring independent countries. He always encouraged Jamaicans to take a similar stand. As an author of books on the Cuban War of Independence and the history of the Caribbean islands, as a journalist with reflections on the nature of nationalism and Jamaica's rightful place in the hemisphere, and by founding a Bolívarian Society in Jamaica, he proved himself to be a multifaceted political thinker.

For Roberts, history carried a political message. He regarded national history, and in fact regional history, as opposed to colonial history. This aspect marks one of the cornerstones of his anti-colonial nationalism. Roberts was convinced that pride in Jamaica's history and inspiration from the surrounding countries could activate the nationalist feelings and contribute to a strong demand for autonomy. Therefore, it was only logical that Roberts joined the Jamaica Historical Society, and even became its president, to popularize Jamaican history.[543]

Roberts showed a special interest in the history of Jamaica that was inextricably connected with a political perspective. The appendix traced back the history of Jamaica, criticized the voluntarily abolition of the Assembly in 1865 and ended with a clear advocacy of self-government.[544] In fact, Roberts was interested not only in the history of the whole region, but especially in the political conditions.

During his trip to Jamaica in the summer of 1949, Roberts met his friend and fellow historian Philip Sherlock,[545] who was heavily involved in the development of the University of the West Indies. He gave him a tour of the future Mona campus, which recently had been a camp for Gibraltar and Maltese refugees. Sherlock asked Roberts if he would help to build the university by giving extra-mural lectures on Caribbean history before a regular history department was built and staffed.[546] Roberts agreed and immediately started to give the first of his numerous lectures on Caribbean history, colonialism and the liberation struggles of the Latin American countries all over the island.[547] After relocating to Jamaica, Roberts continued his service for the university by giving weekly extra-mural lectures and continued to see in them a valuable chance to take the history of the region to the people.[548] In these lectures, Símon Bolívar, José Martí, and Toussaint L'Ouverture were often singled out as 'liberators and champions of the Republic idea',[549] hoping that the admiration for the efforts to demand independence of the free Latin American and Caribbean republics that had inspired the founding of the Progressive League back in 1936 would now serve as nationalist inspiration to his countrymen. This aspect displays a strong continuity in Roberts' thinking and provides a key to understand his theoretical framework.

Roberts frequently claimed that in regard to temperament and customs, the typical Jamaican had more in common with his fellow Caribbean neighbours than with Englishmen or North Americans. He was convinced:

> The temperament of the Jamaican people was Caribbean...The problems that came up here were those in other countries around us, therefore, to understand best how to guide our craft we should not look to Europe or North America, but to the countries that were near us and learn from their experiences.[550]

In comparison with the independent neighbours, Roberts felt Jamaica was a politically backward Caribbean example. At a conference on the Caribbean at the University of Florida in 1959, Roberts presented a paper on 'Pan-Americanism and the West Indies'.[551] In the lecture, he strongly argued for a regional perspective on the Americas including the Caribbean:

> Pan-Americanism is the most far-reaching and effective political doctrine ever formulated for the guidance of the New World. A natural balance of power obtains between the United States of America to the

north and the Latin countries to the south. The axis upon which this resolves is the Caribbean region, not merely because the inner sea lies with admirable exactitude at the geographical center, but because great interests are concentrated there. The Caribbean is the lobby between the Atlantic and Pacific Oceans. Trade routes converge from all points of the compass and are served by the vitally important Panama Canal.

Roberts understanding of Pan-Americanism was largely inspired by Simón Bolívar's vision of free republics on the continent, bound together in form of a confederation.[552] Although Roberts disapproved a federation of the British West Indies as a merger, he embraced Bolívar's idea of a 'nation of republics', 'not a union or a federation...but a looser alliance, a confederacy, the members of which would be republics not provinces, yet be held together by a bond of obvious destiny'. In particular, Roberts emphasized that Bolívar was adamant that the Antilles, Cuba and Puerto Rico would belong to the Pan-American sphere and also referred to early ideas in the colonial Office about a West Indian Federation of their colonies. Roberts went on naming other advocates of the idea[553] and cited the Puerto Rican philosopher, educator and nationalist Eugenio Mariá de Hostos with a statement from 1868: 'Because I am an American, because I am a Puerto Rican, I therefore am a federalist. From my island I see Santo Domingo, I see Cuba, I see Jamaica, and I think of a confederation'.

While a nationalist and anti-colonial spirit had inflamed the Spanish colonies in the nineteenth century, the British, French and Dutch colonies remained silent, due to a more rigid colonial rule, Roberts supposed. As an example, Roberts referred to the Morant Bay Rebellion in Jamaica and the drastic reprisals in its aftermath during which the leaders and more than 439 peasants were killed, 600 men and women flogged and over 1,000 homes burned down. Most Caribbean territories remained under firm grip of European powers, while the free states on the continent moved more closer together, for example, in the International Union of American Republics[554] that was founded in Washington in 1890, which, as Roberts saw it, 'gave reality to the dream of Simón Bolívar'. Roberts pointed to the historic importance of the Caribbean region, from the Panama Canal to the more recent decisions about safety measures in the region at the Havana Conference.

In general, Bolívar played a central role in Roberts' thinking. Roberts was inspired by the nationalism of the Latin America liberator. His article in the *Gleaner* about Nationalist Liberalism started by quoting Bolívar: 'Let us found a fatherland at all costs, and all the rest will be bearable'.[555]

The tremendous importance of Bolívar on Roberts is reflected in the fact that he even formed a Bolívarian Society in Jamaica.[556] For Roberts, who was elected president of the Society, Bolívar's zeal for a break of colonial ties of the Spanish colonies made him a role model for all other colonies in the hemisphere. Roberts was convinced that Bolívar 'furnishes an excellent approach to our problems'.[557] Yet, it was not only the nationalism and anti-colonialism of Bolívar that inspired Roberts, but also his Pan-American outlook. Roberts favourably quoted from Bolívar's famous 'Jamaica Letter', written from his exile in Jamaica in September 1815, in which he advocated a free American hemisphere consisting of republics and federal units, free from European control and oppression. Throughout the next years, the Bolívarian Society staged a series of public events, exhibitions and functions to keep the memory of Bolívar alive and to serve as an inspiration for the nationalist cause in Jamaica.[558]

Another example of Roberts' inspiration deriving from the free Latin American countries was his fascination with the neighbouring islands, Haiti and Cuba. In his capacity as lecturer at UWI's extra-mural department and as president of various organizations, he often put the history and the literature of those countries in the spotlight, for example, when he organized a lecture by Jean-Ferdinand Brierre, a Haitian poet and author, who was a fierce of opponent of the US occupation and contributed to the negritude movement in the francophone Caribbean.[559]

Roberts had a very special passion for Cuba and especially valued Jose Martí's historic contribution to Cuban nationalism.[560] At a reception on his first visit after the war, Roberts dedicated a speech to Cuba. Roberts closely observed the political landscape in Cuba and commented on Batista's revolt, whose efforts to tackle crime he appreciated. However, he was sceptical about the autocratic tendencies the new Cuban leader showed.[561] In 1962, he expressed scepticism about Castro's Socialist views.[562]

Roberts visited Cuba frequently, for example when he attended the 50th anniversary celebrations in 1952. When Roberts travelled to Cuba, he was awarded with the prestigious 'Order of Merit'.[563] Roberts mentioned that it was his 12th visit in 22 years.[564] In 1949, Roberts published his historic novel about a Jamaican who went to Cuba to take part in the War of Independence against the Spanish.[565] In 1953, he published a portrait about Havana.[566] When Roberts opened an art exhibition on Cuban art, he lauded the Cuban-Jamaican friendship and was 'happy to realise that the two countries were growing closer together'.[567] He was invited to the ceremony when the Cuban government donated a bust of Antonio Maceo to Jamaica, and gave an address at the public function. Over time, Roberts had become an authority on Latin American and Caribbean history in Jamaica.

By the middle of the 1950s, Roberts' ideas and the nationalism the Progressive League promoted since 1936 had seeped into the mainstream society. Global developments drastically impacted Britain's attitudes toward its colonies in the

West Indies, facing powerful claims for independence in the course of the war, for example, in India where these claims resulted in the independence of India and Pakistan in 1947. Consequently, the Colonial Office was forced to undertake fundamental changes, as increased discussions about decolonization flared up in Africa, the West Indies and South Asia. In the post-war design for the Caribbean, the idea of a West Indian Federation gained increasing popularity among British officials and provided the basis for colonial policy. At the same time, Great Britain continued to grant further constitutional development in Jamaica, where the constitution was amended in 1953, providing for a cabinet of elected ministers.[568]

In 1955, the city of Kingston honoured some of its citizens, among them Edna Manley and Roberts. Messages of greetings were printed in the *Gleaner*. Roberts was especially honoured for his various contributions highlighting Jamaica's rich history which was directly put into relation with the nation-building process that was taking place. He was lauded: 'Sir, as Jamaica advances towards full nationhood, we are conscious of the magnitude of the contribution made by patriots like yourself to the fostering of that national pride which is a first ingredient in the composition of a nation'.[569]

Not only was Roberts recognized for his historical contributions, in the middle of the 1950s he had become an honoured citizen, well respected for his liberal views, his patriotism, his historic and literary contributions. Roberts had not only become an expert on the history of the region, but during the 1950s he presided over numerous organizations like the Bolívarian Society and the Jamaica Library Association. He became the first honorary member of the Pen Club and was not only part of the Board of Directors of the Institute of Jamaica but also served as its chairman from 1960 on.[570] In 1960, he was awarded O.B.E, Officer of the Most Excellent Order of the British Empire, for his contributions as a poet and author.[571]

The great prestige that Roberts accumulated was reflected by awards like the Gold Musgrave Medal of the Institute of Jamaica.[572] Upon receiving the honour, Roberts elucidated the motive behind his interest in the history of the region:

> ...to show Jamaica in its proper perspective, unalterable a unit of the Western Hemisphere, though long governed as an appendage of Europe. To do this I had to establish the American and then the global significance of the Caribbean region where Jamaica lies. It was necessary to tell far more about the region than about my own island.[573]

His statement makes plain the importance of the regional perspective in Roberts' nationalism and explains the comparatively small amount of works that exclusively dealt with Jamaica.

Roberts' popularity and prestige were further reflected by the illustrious guests at events like his 70th birthday celebration in 1956, among them the consuls of

Haiti and Cuba. The president of the Poetry League, Clare McFarlane, highly praised Roberts' literary contribution as well as his contribution to the political development of the island and claimed: 'So long as we can consider ourselves a nation, the name Walter Adolphe Roberts will never die for to him has fallen the task of introducing this young nation to itself'.[574] McFarlane credited Roberts for his pioneering nationalism and drew a direct line from his ideas to his ban:

> The new outlook is due to Walter Adolphe Roberts. Yet what he said in thirties was considered so far-fetched that when he sought to return here he was not allowed to land. That was because Roberts was not understood. His kingdom was not of this world. Today he sees being put into practice ideas he had disseminated. He is not, I believe, looking in disdain at the mess we are making, but it is with compassion he sees the mistakes we are making.

In his own speech, Roberts again brought out that: 'In studying history and writing history, I have indulged a certain ambition to influence the history of the future by arousing Jamaica to creative action based upon her pride in the past'.

In contrast to the post-independence period, Roberts' particular contributions to the nationalist ideas and the political developments were frequently mentioned and appreciated in the 1950. For example, at a Pen Club Dinner where Roberts was invited as a guest of honour, one speaker pointed out that when Roberts started to agitate for self-government, he was a 'lone voice crying self-government in Jamaica'[575] and the founding of the Progressive League marked the 'nucleus of the national movement in Jamaica'.[576] When Roberts was presented with the Gold Musgrave Medal in 1954, a prestigious award that only two persons had been honoured with before, Edna Manley, who was herself one of the awardees, underlined Roberts' patriotism: 'W. Adolphe Roberts is an intense patriot. He was one of the first to utter the hope for self-government for Jamaica, even though at that time a resident of the United States'.[577]

Although Roberts' nationalist ideas did not result in the formation of a strong mass movement, they were now widely appreciated among the intellectual elite, as his growing prestige showed. Even the conservative *Gleaner*, now commented favourably on his ideas: 'Mr. Adolphe Roberts was one of the first advocates of what may be called the National idea for Jamaica and of the self-government which was its inevitable corollary'.[578] Nevertheless, the *Gleaner* still emphasized Roberts' outsider status and that his theories had evolved in the US. The *Gleaner* emphasized that the 'conception [was] clearly influenced by his long residence in the United States. Consequently, his "Jamaican nation" has no more to do with race or colour than Suisse nationhood has to with language or Belgium nationhood with religion'. It is quite remarkable that the *Gleaner* underlined this aspect of a colour-blind nation that made it easier for the privileged to embrace a nationalist doctrine. The following conclusion supports this claim:

> Mr. Roberts regards his national idea as a solvent; it is the existence of race and colour discrimination which calls for the national idea, and to make race or colour the basis of the national idea is simply to reject Mr. Roberts' medicine.

In his column in the *Gleaner*, Thomas Wright appreciated the paper's editorial, especially the fact that that it was a reminder of Roberts' particular contribution and his neutrality in the two-party system in Jamaica:

> ...Mr. Roberts was one of the first people to advocate, and think seriously about, the means of our independence and nationhood. While working for our independence he has maintained his own. While others dashed into violent partisan action, grabbing hungrily at each end of the intellectual bone that he had tossed them he remained, and still remains the aloof and impartial observer. This is not to say that he does not in his own way, work for the things he considers good. It is to say that he approaches his and our problems with the non-attachment which is appropriate to the civilized man.[579]

The column was an impressive laudation, singling out Roberts as the national hero the country truly needed:

> It is sad enough that Jamaica should be a country in search of a hero, but it is even sadder that she is looking in the wrong places. Jamaica has produced many fine men, and one of the finest of them is W. Adolphe Roberts.[580]

This was the time for historical reflections, for example, the lengthy review on the 'The self-government movement' by H.P. Jacobs. The stalwart PNP member pointed out that the theoretical foundations for the local movement were laid by the Progressive League. With a reference to a widespread British identity he pointed out:

> Those who held the theory of political action believe that the co-operation of all able Jamaicans with an administration controlled by the Colonial Office was unnatural. Faced with the argument that the Colonial Office represented Britain, and 'We are British, aren't we?', they were forced develop the 'national' theory – that is the view that the Jamaican people, having had a continuous historical existence for over two centuries, was a nation. The theoretical formulation of this view was influenced by the Jamaica Progressive League of New York, and in particular by such members of it as Adolphe Roberts, the founder; W. A. Domingo, and Ethelred Brown.[581]

Roberts' views on the political landscaped were also appreciated by the US consulate. On one of his reports to the Department of State, Consul General Duke commended Roberts as an excellent source of information, a close observer, 'personally acquainted with leading members of both parties and although he is evidently pro-PNP, he maintains a high degree of objectivity and does not permit this to seriously influence his judgement'.[582]

Roberts' ideas were recognized and appreciated in intellectual circles. Gordon K. Lewis, renowned Caribbeanist and professor at the University of Puerto Rico, commented:

> If any definite philosophy has emerged in the region since 1937 it is that of middle-class nationalist liberalism. It can be seen in the historical novels of Adolphe Roberts, as well as in his plea...for Pan-Americanism which fails to see that the United States, for example, are no longer a dynamic revolutionary force in the New World but rather a conservative capitalism that has lost even the mild reformist drive.[583]

Lewis highlights an important point. The positive light in which the US was portrayed in both Roberts and Domingo's writings are a clear sign for the expectations the Progressive League leaders attached to the neighbour in the north to support the claims for autonomy in the Caribbean. Their nationalism caused them to estimate the potential menace that a strong US influence would mean for the region, for the economic situation as well as for racial relations. This is even more surprising in regard to Domingo, who initially held strong Socialist ideals and a decided racial consciousness. The liberal Roberts never shared these beliefs, but articulated classic middle-class positions and a sometimes naïve hope in self-government as a panacea for all problems in the colonies.

Even stronger than Domingo, Roberts argued from a regional, Pan-American perspective that had also been the foundation of his idea to form a movement demanding Jamaica's independence. While Roberts referred to the neighbouring independent countries as a positive inspiring example, Domingo sometimes uttered chauvinist remarks in regard to other Latin American countries, as we have seen at the Havana Conference.

In regard to Roberts' regional perspective, fellow historian Hugh Paget stated that:

> ...every country should realise that its history had dignity and importance to it and was worthy of the people's study and consideration, and Mr. Roberts chief contribution to the study of our history was that he had shown with commendable objectivity the importance of the relationship between West Indian history and the factors of West Indian geography.[584]

At first glance, it might be surprising that Roberts developed into such a staunch nationalist and one of the most powerful opponents to the idea of a West Indian Federation. He saw Jamaica as an equal member of the Pan-American family of nations. In Roberts' view, the strategic importance of the region, the availability of important raw materials and the tremendous wealth that was extracted out of the colonies, combined with a strong colonial rule based on a rigid race-class division had not only caused the fragmentation of the region but also caused a longer duration of colonialism than in the rest of the hemisphere. However, Roberts was optimistic, 'This hampered the development of Pan-Americanism at the heart. Only hampered, for the march of so inevitable a destiny could not be stopped'.[585]

In regard to the future of the colonies, within or without the context of a federation, which Roberts rejected, he was convinced: 'Autonomy, in one shape or another, must follow for the remaining colonies. The new nations can scarcely fail to come within the orbit of Pan-Americanism'.[586]

Notes

1. *Daily Gleaner*, June 18, 1941.
2. They found the 'Manifesto of the Communist Party', a picture of Lenin, and several books and pamphlets like 'Colonies: What Africa Thinks', 'The Decline and Fall of the British Empire' and 'Do We Have a Stake in the War' in Domingo's possession. See FBI Report, undated, SCRB, West Indies National Council Papers, MG 666, Box 1.
3. W.A. Domingo to Campbell, January 23, 1941, NMP, 4/60/2A/2; Domingo to Roberts, May 21, 1941, NLJ, WAR, MS 353, Box 2b.
4. Domingo to Roberts, May 21, 1941, NLJ, WAR, MS 353, Box 2b.
5. Domingo to Campbell, April 9, 1941, JA, NMP, 4/60/2A/2; Domingo to Campbell, August 16, 1940 [mistakenly dated 41], JA, NMP, 4/60/2A/2; Domingo to Campbell, May 8, 1941, NMP, 4/60/2A/2.
6. Roberts to Domingo, May 20, 1941, NLJ, WAR, MS 353, Box 2b.
7. Richard Hart, *Towards Decolonisation: Political, Labour and Economic Developments in Jamaica 1938–1945* (Barbados: Canoe Press, 1999), 80ff.
8. Hart, *Towards*, 90. Hart assumes he was arrested because he was reported to have uttered defeatist statements in a bar in Kingston.
9. Ibid.
10. *Daily Gleaner*, May 15, 1940.
11. Hart, *Towards*, 90.
12. *Daily Gleaner*, June 21, 1941.
13. Ibid., June 23, 1941.
14. Ibid.
15. See for instance Jamaica Progressive League, 'Statement on Domingo's Arrest', June 28, 1941, Louis Moyston Private Archive; WINC Press Release, LOC, NAACP, Group 2, Box A332, Fo. 9.
16. WINC Press Release, LOC, NAACP, Group 2, Box A332, Fo. 9.
17. Osborne to White, June 28, 1941, LOC, NAACP, Group 2, Box A332, Fo. 9.
18. Jamaica Progressive League 'Statement on Domingo's Arrest', June 28, 1941, Louis Moyston Private Archive; WINC Press Release, LOC, NAACP, Group 2, Box A332, Fo. 9.

Reassuming the Struggle for Independence in Jamaica 359

19. W.A. Roberts, 'The Internment of W.A. Domingo', July 1, 1941, NLJ, WAR, MS 353, Box 2b.
20. *Public Opinion*, July 5, 1941.
21. Ibid.
22. *New York Amsterdam Star News*, July 19, 1941.
23. Ibid., June 28, 1941.
24. Ibid.
25. Department of State, Division of European Affairs to Hickerson, July 30, 1941, NARA, RG 59, CDF 1940-1944, Box 6058, 844D.00/42.
26. Ibid.
27. Roberts, 'The Manley Story', NLJ, WAR, MS 353, Box 23.
28. *Daily Gleaner*, June 23, 1941.
29. Ibid., June 24, 1941. The Civil Liberties Council in England consisted of renowned figures like Henry Nevinson (president), Aldous Huxley, A.A. Milne, H.G. Wells, Bertrand Russell and various other prominent writers and journalists as well as other professionals.
30. *Daily Gleaner*, June 25, 1941. In attendance were for instance J.A.G Smith, H.G. de Lisser, E.E.A. Campbell, May Farquharson, Ansell Hart and numerous other prominent Jamaicans including PNP executives.
31. Ibid.
32. Ibid., June 27, 1941.
33. However, L.A. DaCosta would later make the accusation that the Council for Civil Liberties lost its interest after the release of Scotter, while Domingo and Marquis were still interned. See *Daily Gleaner*, June 9, 1942.
34. *Daily Gleaner*, June 25, 1941.
35. Ibid., June 27, 1941.
36. See for instance Nethersole to White, June 27, 1941, LOC, NAACP, Group 2, Box A332, Fo. 9.
37. Manley to Osborne, June 28, 1941, JA, NMP, 4/60/2A/2.
38. Colonial Secretary to JPL, July 12, 1941, LOC, NAACP, Group 2, Box A332, Fo. 9 (Answer to letter by Jamaica Progressive League, July 2, 1941).
39. *Daily Gleaner*, August 8, 1941.
40. PNP, 'The Case of Domingo', (Kingston: PNP, undated), 5–10.
41. Domingo, undated manuscript, [Summer 41], JA, NMP, 4/60/2A/2.
42. Domingo to Campbell, August 8, 1940, JA, NMP, 4/60/2A/2.
43. Domingo to Campbell, November 21, 1939, JA, NMP, 4/60/2A/2.
44. Domingo to Campbell, April 9, 1941, JA, NMP, 4/60/2A/2.
45. Domingo to Campbell, November 21, 1939, JA, NMP, 4/60/2A/2.
46. Domingo to Campbell, September 11, 1940, JA, NMP, 4/60/2A/2.
47. Domingo to Campbell, August 23, 1940, JA, NMP, 4/60/2A/2.
48. Domingo to Campbell, August 8, 1940, JA, NMP, 4/60/2A/2.
49. Domingo to Campbell, April 18, 1941, JA, NMP, 4/60/2A/2.
50. *New York Amsterdam News*, November 11, 1939.
51. Domingo to Campbell, April 18, 1941, JA, NMP, 4/60/2A/2.
52. Domingo to Campbell, September 11, 1940, JA, NMP, 4/60/2A/2; Domingo to Campbell, April 18, 1941, NMP, 4/60/2A/2.

53. Domingo to Campbell, October 20, 1939, JA, NMP, 4/60/2A/2.
54. Domingo to Campbell, November 21, 1939, JA, NMP, 4/60/2A/2.
55. Domingo to Campbell, December 8, 1939, JA, NMP, 4/60/2A/2.
56. *New York Amsterdam News* announced the first debate sponsored by the Caribbean Union for December 17, 1939 at Renaissance Casino. See *New York Amsterdam News*, December 9, 1939.
57. Domingo to Campbell, December 15, 1939, JA, NMP, 4/60/2A/2.
58. Domingo to Campbell, December 18, 1939, JA, NMP, 4/60/2A/2.
59. Ibid.
60. Moore and Domingo debated five times, and Moore won all of the debates. See Moore Turner and Turner, eds. *Richard B. Moore*, 76.
61. Moore Turner and Turner, eds., *Richard B. Moore, Caribbean Militant in Harlem: Collected Writings 1920-1972* (Bloomington: Indiana University Press, 1988), 76.
62. Ibid.
63. *Daily Gleaner*, October 8, 1941.
64. Domingo to Campbell, May 8, 1941, JA, NMP, 4/60/2A/2.
65. *New York Amsterdam Star News*, July 12, 1941.
66. Ibid.
67. White to Taussig, July 14, 1941, LOC, NAACP, Group 2, Box A332, Fo. 9.
68. White to Hull, July 16, 1941, NARA, RG 59, DF 1940-1944, 344D.1121. Domingo, W.A./2.
69. *New York Amsterdam Star News*, July 19, 1941.
70. *Chicago Defender* (NE), September 27, 1941.
71. *New York Amsterdam Star News*, November 29, 1941.
72. *Chicago Defender* (NE), October 4, 1941.
73. Alfred Baker Lewis to White, December 4, 1941, LOC, NAACP, Group 2, Box A332, Fo. 9.
74. O.G. Villard to White, January 8, 1942, LOC, NAACP, Group 2, Box A332, Fo. 9.
75. Norman Thomas to White, January 24, 1942, LOC, A. Philip Randolph Papers, Box 1.
76. Lucille B. Millner (American Civil Liberties Union) to Green H. Hackworth, July 9, 1941, NARA, RG 59, DF 1940-1944, 344D.1121. Domingo, W. A./1.
77. Watson to Department of State, July 16, 1941, NARA, RG 59, CDF 1940-1944, Box 6058, 844D.00/42.
78. Duggan to White, July 31, 1941, LOC, NAACP, Group 2, Box A332, Fo. 9.
79. *Daily Gleaner*, August 4, 1941, see also Hackworth to White, NARA, RG 59, DF 1940-1944, 344D.1121.Domingo, W.A./3.
80. White to Hackworth, July 28, 1941, LOC, NAACP, Group 2, Box A332, Fo. 9.
81. Stevens to Welles, October 28, 1941, NARA, RG 59, DF 1940-1944, 344D.1121. Domingo, W.A./5.
82. See Sumner Welles to Stevens, November 4, 1941, NARA, RG 59, DF 1940-1944, 344D.1121.Domingo, W.A./5.
83. *Chicago Defender* (NE), October 4, 1941.
84. National Council for Civil Liberties, undated [mid to end July1941], JA, NMP, 4/60/2A/2.

85. *Daily Gleaner*, August 11, 1941.
86. Ibid., September 22, 1941.
87. *New York Amsterdam Star News*, September 13, 1941.
88. Ibid., July 19, 1941.
89. Ibid., July 12, 1941.
90. Ibid., July 26, 1941.
91. *Daily Gleaner*, August 14, 1941.
92. Brown to Hull, March 27, 1942 NARA, RG 59, DF 1940–1944, Box 3029, 800.20201. Domingo, W.A./3.
93. When he returned to New York, Domingo stated that he went to the JPL's executive meeting and 'greeted Mr. Brown cordially, despite the unfortunate letter while I was in camp'. See Domingo to Manley, August 15, 1947, JA, NMP, 2/60/2B/12.
94. FBI report by Special Agent Torrens, April 10, 1942, NARA, RG 59, CDF 1940–1944, Box 3083, 800.00B.Jamaica Progressive League.
95. Roberts to Manley, April 19, 1942, JA, NMP, 4/60/2B/6.
96. Ibid.
97. Roberts to Edna Manley, April 12, 1942, NLJ, WAR, MS 353, Box 2b.
98. Hoover to Berle, June 1943, NARA, RG 59, CDF 1940–1944, Box 3083, 800.00B Jamaican Progressive League/5.
99. Hoover to Berle, May 20, 1943, NARA, RG 59 CDF 1940–1944, Box 3083, 800.00B Jamaican Progressive League/5.
100. See Hoover to Berle, March 22, 1944, FBI Dossier on American West Indian Association on Caribbean Affairs, February 15, 1944, NARA, RG 59, CDF 1940–1944, Box 5058, 844.00B.
101. Hoover to Berle, March 22, 1944, FBI Dossier on American West Indian Association on Caribbean Affairs, February 15, 1944, NARA, RG 59, CDF 1940–1944, Box 5058, 844.00B.
102. *New York Amsterdam Star News*, March 28, 1942.
103. Elliot Coulter to Brown, April 16, 1942, NARA, RG 59, DF 1940–1944, Box 3029, 800.20201.Domingo, W.A./4; Brown to Elliot Coulter, August 21, 1942, NARA, RG 59, DF 1940-1944, Box 3029, 800.20201.Domingo, W.A./6.
104. Lord to Department of State, May 28, 1942, NARA, RG 84, Records of the Foreign Service Posts, US Consulate Kingston, Jamaica, Classified General Records 1936–1962, 1942 All Files, Box 2.
105. White to Osborne, August 19, 1942, LOC, NAACP, Group 2, Box A332, Fo. 9.
106. Lewis to White, August 13, 1942, LOC, NAACP, Group 2, Box A332, Fo. 9.
107. Osborne to White, August 17, 1942, LOC, NAACP, Group 2, Box A332, Fo. 9.
108. Governor Richards, 'Memorandum', September 30, 1941, SCRBC, WINC, MG 666, Box 2.
109. Hart, *Towards*, 155.
110. *Daily Gleaner*, February 27, 1942; April 1, 1942.
111. Ibid., April 1, 1942.
112. Hart, *Towards*, 155.
113. *Daily Gleaner*, April 1, 1942.
114. Ibid., April 20, 1969.

115. Roberts to Brown, June 21, 1941, NLJ, WAR, MS 353, Box 2b.
116. *New York Amsterdam News*, June 28, 1941.
117. *Daily Gleaner*, June 21, 1941.
118. Ibid.
119. Ibid., July 29, 1941.
120. Ibid., August 4, 1941.
121. Ibid.
122. Ibid., August 13, 1941.
123. Ibid., March 3, 1941.
124. Co-Founder of the National Defender Committee, a nationalist group whose activities were mainly directed against the Chinese minority and its economic monopoly of the grocery retail. See Carnegie, *Some Aspects*, 111, 119.
125. *Daily Gleaner*, April 4, 1941.
126. Ibid., March 6, 1942.
127. Ibid., March 3, 1942.
128. Ibid.
129. Manley to Osborne, June 28, 1941. JA, NMP, 4/60/2A/2.
130. Manley to Stannard, December 21, 1942. JA, NMP, 4/60/2B/6.
131. Roberts, 'Dinner with N.W. Manley at Drumblair', July 21, 1949. NLJ, WAR, MS 353, Box 9.
132. Domingo to Manley, July 28, 1939, JA, NMP, 4/60/2A/2.
133. Ibid.
134. Richards to Downie, June 1, 1942, PRO, CO 137/854/14.
135. Hart, *Towards*, 151f. Hart quotes from PNP Secretary Arnett's memoirs, who also supports the thesis that Richards released Bustamante with the clear plan to seek his support in the fight against nationalist and anti-colonial ideas.
136. Manley to Stannard, December 21, 1942, JA, NMP, 4/60/2B/6.
137. *Public Opinion*, October 31, 1942.
138. Ibid., November 21, 1942.
139. Ibid.
140. *Public Opinion*, December 12, 1942.
141. Ibid.
142. Hart, *Towards*, 199.
143. Domingo to Campbell, February 28, 1942, JA, NMP, 4/60/2A/2.
144. Post, *Strike the Iron: A Colony at War, Jamaica 1939–1945*. Vol. 2 (London: Humanities Press, 1981), 298.
145. For more information on the changing macro-political background see for example Jason C. Parker, *Brother's Keeper: The United States, Race, and Empire in the British Caribbean, 1937-1962* (Oxford: Oxford University Press, 2008), 52ff; Cary Fraser, *Ambivalent Anti-Colonialism: The United States and the Genesis of West Indian Independence, 1940-1964* (Westport, CT: Greenwood Press, 1994), 69ff.
146. On the Anglo-American Caribbean Commission see for example Fraser, *Ambivalent Anti-Colonialism*, 69ff; Parker, *Brother's Keeper*, 52ff.
147. Parker correctly emphasizes the special role of Puerto Rico as a direct comparison of colonial administration in the Caribbean. See Parker, *Brother's Keeper*, 44ff. Domingo clearly saw the power of such comparisons and frequently presented thorough analyses of conditions in both countries. These will be more closely examined in the following chapter.

148. Parker, *Brother's Keeper*, 41ff.
149. Ibid., 53.
150. As one example, Parker points to a spontaneous but well-attended solidarity meeting in Harlem held for Domingo when he was detained in 1941. See Parker, Ibid., 43.
151. Ibid., 41ff.
152. Ibid., 49f.
153. On the background to the offering of a new constitution in Jamaica see for example Trevor Munroe, *The Politics of Constitutional Decolonization: Jamaica 1944–1962* (Kingston: ISER, University of the West Indies, 1972), 26ff.
154. Post, *Strike the Iron*, Vol. 2, 298.
155. *Daily Gleaner*, August 25, 1960.
156. Arthur Creech Jones was a member of the British Labour Party, member of the Colonial Office's Educational Advisory Committee and shaped colonial policy even before he became Secretary of State for the Colonies.
157. *Daily Gleaner*, April 28, 1943.
158. Ibid.
159. Post, *Strike the Iron*, Vol. 2, 326.
160. Fraser, *Ambivalent Anti-Colonialism*, 77.
161. Post, *Strike the Iron*, Vol. 2, 325.
162. Memorandum on Domingo's Release, March 8, 1943, PRO, CO 968/86/6.
163. *New York Amsterdam News*, March 6, 1943.
164. *Chicago Defender*, July 3, 1943.
165. Ibid., July 17, 1943.
166. Telegram, Manley to Brown, February 19, 1943, JA, NMP, 4/60/2B/7.
167. See *Daily Gleaner*, February 20, 1943.
168. Ibid., February 23, 1943.
169. Ibid., March, 1943; *Public Opinion*, March 6, 1943; *Public Opinion* even spoke of over 4,000.
170. *Daily Gleaner*, March 1, 1943.
171. See *Public Opinion*, March 6, 1943.
172. Ibid., March 1, 1943.
173. For a review of the constitution see Hart, *Towards*, 213f; Richard Hart, *Time for A Change: Constitutional, Political and Labour Developments in Jamaica and Other Colonies in the Caribbean Region, 1944–1955* (Kingston: Arawak Publications, 2004), 1ff; Munroe, *Constitutional Decolonization*, 45.
174. Paul Blanshard was advisor to Charles W. Taussig, especially appointed to observe the developments in Jamaica, see Post, *Strike the Iron*, Vol. 2, 327.
175. Blanshard Report, March 9, 1943, NARA, RG 59, 844D.011/6.
176. Hart, *Time for a Change*, 1.
177. Cited after Post, *Strike the Iron*, Vol. 2, 342.
178. Blanshard Report, March 9, 1943, NARA, RG 59, 844D.011/6.
179. Post, *Strike the Iron*, Vol. 2, 323. A report prepared on the basis of censored letters showed that only in 11 letters out of 17,000 the proposals for constitutional change were mentioned, the majority of references was sceptical or opposing.
180. 'The Political Situation in Jamaica', Blanshard Report, September 20, 1943, NARA, RG 59, 844D.00/56.
181. *Public Opinion*, March 27, 1943.

182. Hoover to Berle, May 18, 1943, NARA, RG 59, CDF 1940–1944, Box 3029, 800.20201.Domingo, W.A./14.
183. Ibid.
184. Manley to Roberts, March 12, 1943, NLJ, WAR, MS 353, Box 2b.
185. Roberts to Manley, March 28, 1943, NLJ, WAR, MS 353, Box 2b.
186. Roberts to Manley, August 25, 1943, NLJ, WAR, MS 353, Box 2b; Roberts to Manley, October 4, 1943, Roberts, NLJ, WAR, MS 353, Box 2b.
187. Roberts to Manley, December 8, 1943, NLJ, WAR, MS 353, Box 2b.
188. *Public Opinion*, February 27, 1943.
189. Ibid. See also Hoover to Berle, Memorandum, May 18, 1943, NARA, RG 59, CDF 1940–1944, Box 3029, 800.20201.Domingo,W.A./14.
190. *Public Opinion*, February 27, 1943.
191. *Daily Gleaner*, February 23, 1943.
192. Hoover to Berle, May 18, 1943, NARA, RG 59, CDF 1940–1944, Box 3029, 800.20201. Domingo,W.A./14.
193. Manley to Roberts, March 12, 1943, NLJ, WAR, MS 353, Box 2b.
194. Roberts, 'Dinner with N.W. Manley at Drumblair', July 21, 1949, NLJ, WAR, MS 353, Box 9.
195. *Public Opinion*, August 8, 1944.
196. Hoover to Berle, May 18, 1943, NARA, RG 59, DF 1940-1944, Box 3029, 800.20201. Domingo,W.A./14.
197. *Public Opinion*, April 3, 1943.
198. Ibid., August 7, 1943.
199. *Daily Gleaner*, March 1, 1943.
200. *Public Opinion*, February 27, 1943.
201. Ibid.
202. *Daily Gleaner*, March 1, 1943.
203. Ibid., April 30, 1943. The memorandum was also sent through Manley to the *Public Opinion* and printed on May 15. See Manley to Brown, May 1, 1943, JA, NMP, 4/60/2B/7.
204. *Public Opinion*, August 7, 1943.
205. Ibid.
206. *Daily Gleaner*, March 1, 1943. See also Blanshard Report, March 9, 1943, NARA, RG 59, 844D.011/6.
207. Ibid., March 11, 1943.
208. Ibid.
209. Ibid.
210. De Lisser to Manley, March 16, 1943, JA, NMP, 4/60/2B/7.
211. Ibid.
212. Domingo explicitly named self-government, universal suffrage and the right of labour unions to function legally as the original contributions of the JPL and claimed that the PNP had 'crystallised them into a coherent and living programme', *Daily Gleaner*, February 23, 1943.
213. *Public Opinion*, March 22, 1942; April 3, 1943; August 8, 1944.
214. Ibid., August 8, 1944.
215. Ibid.
216. Ibid., December 24, 1943.

217. Ibid., August 8, 1944.
218. Ibid., December 24, 1943.
219. Ibid., April 7, 1943; April 21, 1943.
220. Ibid., March 11, 1943.
221. Ibid., August 23, 1943.
222. Ibid., August 17, 1944; October 9, 1944; October 10, 1944; October 11, 1944; October 17, 1944; October 27, 1944.
223. The PNP's website only mentions the Progressive League as a fore-runner of the PNP, but does not emphasize its further influence. The short paragraph on the Progressive League includes inaccurate information and errors. See http://www.pnpjamaica.com/index.php?option=com_content&view=article&id=209&Itemid=62 (last viewed November 19, 2011).
224. *New York Amsterdam News*, February 5, 1944.
225. Ibid.
226. Post, *Strike the Iron*, Vol. 2, 353.
227. Parker, *Brother's Keeper*, 55.
228. For a thorough analysis of the political landscape and particular attention to race-class connections see Post, *Strike the Iron*, Vol. 2, 307ff; Munroe, *Constitutional Decolonization*, 36ff.
229. *Daily Gleaner,* March 29, 1950.
230. *Public Opinion,* October 16, 1944; October 17, 1944; October 18, 1944.
231. *Daily Gleaner,* October 18, 1944; October 20, 1944.
232. *Public Opinion,* October 23, 1944.
233. *Daily Gleaner,* November 2, 1944.
234. *Public Opinion,* January 22, 1944.
235. Ibid., October 17, 1944.
236. Ibid., October 12, 1944; *Daily Gleaner,* November 8, 1944.
237. George E. Eaton, *Alexander Bustamante and Modern Jamaica* (Kingston: Kingston Publishers, 1995), 89.
238. Ibid., 84ff.
239. *Public Opinion,* January 22, 1944.
240. Ibid., October 19, 1944.
241. Ibid., October 25, 1944.
242. Ibid., October 27, 1944.
243. Ibid.
244. Post, *Strike the Iron*, Vol. 2, 356.
245. Blanshard Report, Taussig to Department of State, September 20, 1943, NARA, RG 59, 844D.00/56.
246. Ibid.
247. *Public Opinion,* October 17, 1944.
248. Blanshard Report, Taussig to Department of State, September 20, 1943, NARA, RG 59, 844D.00/56.
249. *Daily Gleaner,* February 26, 1944.
250. Parker, *Brother's Keeper*, 57.
251. Manley to Roberts, October 16, 1943, NLJ, WAR, MS 353, Box 2b.
252. Roberts to Brown, November 5, 1943, NLJ, WAR, MS 353, Box 2b.
253. *New York Amsterdam News*, October 7, 1944.

254. Ibid., February 19, 1944, Brown to Manley, 06.06.1944, JA, NMP, 4/60/2B/9; Hoover to Berle, 08.05.1944, NARA, RG 59, 844D.00/59.
255. Manley to Brown, January 26, 1944, JA, NMP, 4/60/2B/9.
256. Ibid.
257. *Daily Gleaner*, October 20, 1943.
258. Ibid., July 3, 1944.
259. PNP Memorandum, July 3, 1944, PRO, CO 137/859/18.
260. *Public Opinion*, July, 1944.
261. *Daily Gleaner*, December 13, 1944.
262. Ibid., December 12, 1944.
263. For a detailed account on the election results see Post, *Strike the Iron*, Vol. 2, 490ff.
264. Ibid., 498.
265. Blanshard Report, January 23, 1945, NARA, RG 84, US Consulate Kingston, Jamaica, Classified General Records 1936–1962, Reports and Related Records of Paul Blanshard, UD 2823.
266. Ibid.
267. *Public Opinion*, December 16, 1944.
268. Ibid.
269. Ibid., December 18, 1944.
270. Post, *Strike the Iron*, Vol. 2, 483.
271. *Daily Gleaner*, December 22, 1944, *Public Opinion*, December 23, 1944; *Daily Gleaner*, December 27, 1944.
272. *Public Opinion*, December 19, 1944.
273. Ibid., December 20, 1944.
274. Blanshard Report, January 23, 1945, NARA, RG 84, US Consulate Kingston, Jamaica, Classified General Records 1936–1962, Reports and Related Records of Paul Blanshard, UD 2823.
275. Ibid.
276. *Public Opinion*, August 7, 1943.
277. Ibid.
278. Roberts, Manuscript, Article for Pepperpot, 1959, NLJ, WAR, MS 353, Box 9.
279. Ibid.
280. *Daily Gleaner*, August 22, 1938.
281. *Public Opinion*, January 6, 1945.
282. Ibid.
283. Ibid., January 8, 1945.
284. Ibid.
285. Blanshard Report, January 16, 1945, NARA, RG 84, US Consulate Kingston, Jamaica, Classified General Records 1936–1962, UD 2823, Reports and Related Records of Paul Blanshard.
286. *Public Opinion*, February 10, 1945.
287. Hoover to Berle, February 24, 1943, NARA, RG 59, DF 1940–1944, Box 3029, 800.20201.Domingo, W.A./12.
288. Ibid. See also Holmes to Lord, February 12, 1945, NARA, RG 84, US Consulate Kingston, Jamaica, Classified General Records 1936–1962, 1945 All Files, UD 2822, Box 5.

289. Holmes to Lord, February 12, 1945, NARA, RG 84, US Consulate Kingston, Jamaica, Classified General Records 1936–1962, 1945 All Files, UD 2822, Box 5.
290. Parker, *Brother's Keeper*, 56. Next to Parker who frequently stressed the importance of these connections, see also Fraser, *Ambivalent Anti-Colonialism*, 77.
291. Holmes to Lord, February 12, 1945, NARA, RG 84, US Consulate Kingston, Jamaica, Classified General Records 1936–1962, 1945 All Files, UD 2822, Box 5.
292. Henderson to Lord, March 1, 1945, NARA, RG 84, US Consulate Kingston, Jamaica, Classified General Records 1936–1962, 1945 All Files, UD 2822, Box 5.
293. Roberts to White, July 7, 1945, LOC, Manuscript Division, The Records of the NAACP, Group 2, Box A332, Fo 9; Roberts' attempts to return to Jamaica will be discussed in the following chapter.
294. White to State Department, June 22, 1945, LOC, NAACP, Group 2, Box A332, Fo. 9.
295. Parker, *Brother's Keeper*, 57.
296. Borrjes to Kemp, November 8, 1946, NARA, RG 84, Classified General Records, UD 2822 1946, Box 6.
297. For this and the following quotes see Confidential Letter, General Consulate to Borrjes, November 12, 1946, NARA, RG 84, Classified General records, UD 2822, Box 6.
298. Parker, *Brother's Keeper*, 61.
299. Ibid.
300. *Public Opinion*, October 9, 1943.
301. Ibid., November 23, 1945.
302. Ibid., April 22, 1944.
303. Ibid., March 25, 1944.
304. Ibid., August 8, 1944.
305. Ibid., May 25, 1944.
306. Ibid., July 31, 1944.
307. Ibid., March 29, 1941.
308. Benedict Anderson, *Imagined Communities*. 2nd ed. (London: Verso, 2006), 37ff.
309. *Public Opinion*, April 4, 1944.
310. Ibid., July 31, 1944.
311. Ibid., March 29, 1941.
312. Ibid.
313. Ibid.
314. Franz Fanon, *Black Skin, White Masks* (New York: Grove Press, 1994), 83ff.
315. *Public Opinion*, January 29, 1944.
316. Ibid.
317. Ibid., July 31, 1944.
318. Ibid., August 26, 1944.
319. Ibid.
320. Ibid.
321. Ibid., January 22, 1941.
322. Ibid., February 8, 1941.
323. Ibid., September 23, 1944.
324. Ibid., June 12, 1944; August 7, 1944.
325. Ibid., September 23, 1944.

326. Ibid., September 25, 1944.
327. Ibid., April 15, 1944.
328. Ibid., July 3, 1944.
329. Ibid., March 1, 1941.
330. Ibid.
331. Ibid.
332. Ibid., September 18, 1944; October 6, 1944.
333. Ibid., August 15, 1944; October 14, 1944; October 20, 1944.
334. Ibid., November 9, 1944: November 10, 1944; November 11, 1944.
335. See *Public Opinion*, November 21, 1944.
336. Eric Williams, *Capitalism and Slavery* (Chapel Hill: University of North Carolina Press, 1944).
337. *Public Opinion*, January 12, 1945.
338. Ibid., January 8, 1944; February 6, 1944.
339. Ibid., February 5, 1944.
340. Ibid.
341. Ibid., July 14, 1944.
342. The term East Indian was frequently used to describe migrants of Indian descent in the Caribbean.
343. *Daily Gleaner*, April 24, 1943; June 1, 1943.
344. Ibid., April 15, 1943.
345. Ibid., April 24, 1943.
346. Ibid., June 1, 1943.
347. Ibid., June 1, 1943.
348. For the following quotes see the two-piece article in *Public Opinion*, June 12, 1943; June 19, 1943.
349. Ibid., July 31, 1943.
350. Ibid., May 8, 1944.
351. Ibid., May 9, 1944.
352. Ibid., May 8, 1944.
353. Ibid.
354. Ibid., May 9, 1944.
355. Ibid., June 7, 1944.
356. Ibid.
357. Ibid.
358. Ibid.
359. Ibid., July 1, 1944.
360. Ibid., March 5, 1945.
361. Ibid.
362. Ibid., August 21, 1943; November 20, 1943; May 1, 1944.
363. Ibid., August 21, 1943.
364. Ibid., May 31, 1945.
365. Ibid., August 4, 1945.
366. Ibid., February 12, 1944; June 3, 1944.
367. Ibid., October 6, 1945.
368. Ibid., March 11, 1944; March 18, 1944.

369. Ibid., October 6, 1945.
370. Ibid.
371. Ibid., January 13, 1945.
372. Ibid., October 6, 1945.
373. Ibid., June 25, 1945.
374. Ibid., October 6, 1945.
375. Ibid., April 24, 1944.
376. Ibid.
377. Ibid., February 12, 1944.
378. Ibid., May 6, 1944.
379. Ibid., August 26, 1944.
380. Ibid., June 23, 1944; August 29, 1944.
381. Ibid., August 4, 1945; June 6, 1945; August 8, 1945.
382. Ibid., October 6, 1945.
383. Ibid.
384. Ibid., July 4, 1944.
385. Ibid., July 5, 1944.
386. Parker, *Brother's Keeper*, 64.
387. *Public Opinion*, May 28, 1945.
388. Ibid., April 25, 1945.
389. Ibid., May 29, 1945.
390. Ibid.
391. Ibid., August 30, 1945.
392. Ibid., September 17, 1945; November 23, 1945.
393. Ibid., November 23, 1945.
394. Ibid.
395. Ibid., October 30, 1945.
396. Ibid., October 20, 1944.
397. Parker, *Brother's Keeper*, 57.
398. *Public Opinion*, August 15, 1944; October 14, 1944; October 20, 1944.
399. Ibid., August 15, 1944.
400. Ibid.
401. For a detailed description of the American efforts to secure mining rights in Jamaica see Parker, *Brother's Keeper*, 57ff.
402. Finally, Jamaica became the largest supplier of bauxite for the US and the American company Reynolds one of the largest employers in Jamaica. See Parker, *Brother's Keeper*, 59.
403. *Public Opinion*, April 1, 1944.
404. Wilfred A. Domingo, 'Anglo-American Interests – How they affect the Caribbean Islands', in *The African, Oktober* (*Public Opinion* Reprint), 1994; Kopie, SCRBC, MG 87.
405. *Public Opinion*, June 29, 1944; June 30, 1944; August 24, 1944.
406. Ibid., November 23, 1945.
407. Ibid., May 17, 1944; August 19, 1944; January 26, 1945.
408. Ibid. August 19, 1944; August 21, 1944.
409. Ibid., August 24, 1944.

410. Ibid., February 5, 1944; August 3, 1944; August 4, 1944; October 3, 1944.
411. Parker, *Brother's Keeper*, 53.
412. *Public Opinion*, October 9, 1943; October 16, 1943; October 23, 1943; November 6, 1943; November 13, 1943; November 20, 1943; November 27, 1943.
413. Post, *Strike the Iron*, Vol. 2, 431.
414. *Public Opinion*, November 6, 1943; November 13, 1943; November 20, 1943; November 27, 1943.
415. *Public Opinion*, October 9, 1943.
416. Ibid., October 23, 1943.
417. Ibid., June 25, 1945.
418. Ibid., October 9, 1943.
419. Ibid., July 28, 1944; July 29, 1944.
420. Ibid., September 10, 1946.
421. Ibid., June 22, 1940.
422. Domingo to Arnett, January 24, 1941, JA, NMP, 4/60/2A/2.
423. *New York Amsterdam News*, March 25, 1944.
424. *Public Opinion*, August 17, 1944; October 13, 1944.
425. Ibid., July 13, 1944.
426. Ibid., April 27, 1944; April 28, 1944; April 29, 1944.
427. *New York Amsterdam News*, April 8, 1944.
428. *Public Opinion*, June 15, 1944.
429. Ibid.; June 16, 1944; June 17, 1944; June 19, 1944; June 20, 1944.
430. Ibid., April 19, 1945; April 20, 1945.
431. Ibid., September 30, 1944.
432. Ibid., March 20, 1945.
433. See for example Blanshard Report, March 12, 1945, NARA, RG 84, US Consulate Kingston, Jamaica, Classified General Records 1936–1962, Reports and Related Records of Paul Blanshard, UD 2823; Kemp to Secretary of State, July 8, 1946, NARA, RG 59, CDF 1945–1949, 844D.00/7-846 and Department of State to Consul General, August 26, 1946, NARA, RG 59, CDF 1945-1949, 844D.00/7-846.
434. Domingo to White, June 13, 1945, LOC, NAACP, Group 2, Box A332, Fo. 9.
435. *Daily Gleaner*, August 8, 1947.
436. Borrjes to Kemp, November 8, 1946, NARA, RG 84, Classified General Records, UD 2822, 1946, Box 6.
437. Kemp to Secretary of State, 'Jamaica Notes 3', May 25, 1946, NARA, RG 84, Classified General Records, UD 2822, 1946, Box 6.
438. Confidential Letter, General Consulate to Borrjes, November 12, 1946, NARA, RG 84, Classified General Records, UD 2822, 1946, Box 6.
439. *Daily Gleaner*, November 16, 1946.
440. Telegram, Kelly to Secretary of State, February 11, 1947, NARA, RG 84, Classified General Records, UD 2822, 1947, Box 7.
441. Secretary of State (acting) to American Consul, March 10, 1947, NARA, RG 84, Classified General Records, UD 2822 1947 Box 7.
442. Acheson to Kelly, March 20, 1947, NARA, RG 84, Classified General Records, UD 2822, 1947, Box 7.
443. For this and the following quotes, see Kelly to Secretary of State, May 2, 1947, NARA, RG 84, Classified General Records, UD 2822, 1947, Box 7.

444. *Daily Gleaner*, August 8, 1947.
445. Kelly to Secretary of State, May 2, 1947, NARA, RG 84, Classified General Records, UD 2822, 1947, Box 7.
446. Manley to Roberts, March 28, 1945, JA, NMP, 4/60/2B/10.
447. Roberts, 'Autobiography', 64 (492) (For the later part of the Autobiography, two different page numbers appear in the original, both will be presented).
448. Manley to Roberts, March 3, 1945, JA, NMP, 4/60/2B/10.
449. Roberts to Manley, April 11, 1945, JA, NMP, 4/60/2B/10.
450. Manley to Huggins, April 14, 1945, JA, NMP, 4/60/2B/10.
451. Manley to Governor Huggins, April 14, 1945, JA, NMP, 4/60/2B/10.
452. Manley to Richards, April 14, 1945, JA, NMP, 4/60/2B/10.
453. Ibid.
454. Ibid.
455. Manley to Cyrus, April 30, 1945, JA, NMP, 4/60/2B/10; Manley to Huggins, May 12, 1945, NMP, 4/60/2B/10.
456. Manley to Cyrus, April 30, 1945, JA, NMP, 4/60/2B/10.
457. Roberts, 'Autobiography', 65 (494).
458. *Public Opinion*, May 2, 1945; May 3, 1945; May 17, 1945; August 2, 1945; *Daily Gleaner*, June 20, 1945; *Daily Gleaner*, July 25, 1945; *Daily Gleaner*, October 4, 1945.
459. *Daily Gleaner*, July 25, 1945.
460. Lord to Secretary of State, July 27, 1945, NARA, RG 84, US Consulate Kingston, Jamaica, Classified General Records 1936–1962, 1945 All Files, UD 2822, Box 5. The report contains a summary of the debate; see also Roberts, 'Autobiography', 66 (495). In an enquiry of American Consul Lord, government officials stated that Roberts was suspected to contact subversive elements which was regarded as dangerous because the new constitution was in its infancy, see Telegram, Lord to Secretary of State, July 5, 1945, NARA, RG 84, US Consulate Kingston, Jamaica, Classified General Records 1936–1962, 1945 All Files, UD 2822, Box 5.
461. Manley to Glasspole, May 5, 1945, JA, NMP, 4/60/2B/10.
462. *Public Opinion*, May 17, 1945; May 2, 1945; May 3, 1945; August 2, 1945.
463. *Daily Gleaner*, May 11, 1945. For a short press review see Blanshard and Lord, 'Jamaica Weekly News Letter', May 12, 1945, NARA, RG 84, US Consulate Kingston, Jamaica, Classified General Records 1936–1962, Reports and Related Records of Paul Blanshard, UD 2823.
464. *Daily Gleaner*, May 11, 1945.
465. Ibid.
466. *Public Opinion*, May 2, 1945; May 3, 1945.
467. Ibid., May 2, 1945.
468. Ibid., May 3, 1945; one of those members nominated by Bustamante and selected from the House of Representatives was E.R.D. Evans, one of the founding members of the Progressive League, Kingston, who had joined the Jamaica Labour Party.
469. See Blanshard and Lord, Jamaica Weekly News Letter, May 12, 1945, NARA, RG 84, US Consulate Kingston, Jamaica, Classified General Records 1936–1962, Reports and Related Records of Paul Blanshard, UD 2823.
470. Manley to Roberts, August 13, 1945, JA, NMP, 4/60/2B/10.
471. Roberts, 'Autobiography', 65 (494).

472. Ibid.
473. *Daily Gleaner*, July 27, 1946.
474. *Daily Gleaner*, July 27, 1946.
475. Roberts, 'Autobiography', 67 (496).
476. *Daily Gleaner*, August 9, 1946. The menu reflected the patriotic spirit of the event and consisted of local specialties like ackee and saltfish, roasted breadfruit, pepperpot, old harbour bay lobster cocktail, blue mountain coffee, planters punch and rum swizzles, while the quotations of the discussions about Roberts' ban in the House of Representatives were printed on the back.
477. *Daily Gleaner*, August 9, 1946.
478. Ibid.
479. Roberts, 'Autobiography', 67 (496).
480. Puerto Rico, the Lesser Antilles and Trinidad and Tobago, the Dominican Republic, Haiti, Cuba. See Roberts, 'Autobiography', 69 (498).
481. Ibid.
482. Roberts, *The Single Star* (Kingston: Pioneer Press, 1956).
483. *Daily Gleaner*, November 13, 1946.
484. McFarlane to Manley, February 20, 1947, NMP, 4/60/2B/12.
485. Manley to McFarlane, March 3, 1947, NMP, 4/60/2B/12.
486. McFarlane to Manley, February 20, 1947, JA, NMP, 4/60/2B/12.
487. McFarlane to Manley, April 30, 1947, NLJ, JPL, MS 234.
488. Ibid.; see also Walter G. McFarlane, *The Birth of Self-Government for Jamaica and the Jamaica Progressive League 1937–1944* (Kingston: 1957), 25.
489. Arnett to JPL, Kingston, July 10, 1947, NLJ, JPL, MS 234.
490. Aiken to Duhaney, July 22, 1947, NLJ, JPL, MS 234.
491. McFarlane to Executive Committee of the PNP, July 25, 1947, NLJ, JPL, MS 234.
492. See *Daily Gleaner*, October 6, 1947.
493. Ibid., October 16, 1947.
494. Ibid., October 21, 1947.
495. Ibid., October 16, 1947.
496. Ibid., October 13, 1947; October 30, 1947.
497. Ibid., July 21, 1947.
498. Ibid., October 22, 1947.
499. Ibid., October 13, 1947.
500. The sources unfortunately do not speak to the reasons, but the uneasiness is obvious in the correspondence. One reason for conflict surely was the pro-Federation course the PNP adopted, while Domingo and Roberts strongly opposed the idea. This conflict will be closely examined in the following chapter.
501. Manley to Brown, September 20, 1947, Louis Moyston Private Archive.
502. Brown to Manley, November 25, 1947, JA, NMP, 4/60/2B/12; Manley to Brown, November 28, 1947, JA, NMP, 4/60/2B/12.
503. Manley to Brown, November 28, 1947, JA, NMP, 4/60/2B/12.
504. *Daily Gleaner*, June 23, 1950.
505. Ibid., June 30, 1950.
506. Ibid., January 3, 1963; See also JPL, Kingston, The Jamaican Nation, NLJ, W.G. McFarlane Papers (WGMcF), MS 1893, Box 2.

507. Jimmy Tucker, *Developments in the Renewed Jamaica Progressive League* (Kingston: The League, 1992). See also Interview by the Author with Jimmy Tucker, December 12, 2006. Tucker expressed the hope that a study on the JPL and its aims might renew the discussions about turning Jamaica into a republic.
508. *Daily Gleaner*, May 4, 1958.
509. Roberts, 'Nationalist Liberalism', 1959, NLJ, WAR, MS 353, Box 9.
510. Roberts, 'Autobiography', 81 (512).
511. Ibid., 69 (198).
512. *Daily Gleaner*, February 7, 1948.
513. Ibid.
514. Ibid., November 29, 1949.
515. Roberts, 'Autobiography', 81 (512)f.
516. Ibid.
517. Ibid., 82 (513).
518. Ibid.
519. *Daily Gleaner*, April 4, 1958.
520. W. Adolphe Roberts, 'National Feeling', undated manuscript [after 49], MS 353, NLJ, WAR, MS 353, Box 9.
521. *Daily Gleaner*, May 4, 1958.
522. Ibid., February 7, 1948.
523. Roberts, 'Autobiography', 81 (512).
524. Roberts, 'The Platform', NLJ, WAR, MS 353, Box 17.
525. Roberts, Manuscript, undated, NLJ, WAR, MS 353, Box 9.
526. Roberts, 'Autobiography', 80 (511).
527. Glasspole to Brown, August 23, 1949, Louis Moyston Private Archive; Manley to Brown, December 13, 1948, Louis Moyston Private Archive; Arnett to Brown, August 25, 1949, Louis Moyston Private Archive; Glasspole to Brown, October 11, 1949, Louis Moyston Private Archive.
528. Manley to Brown, December 13, 1948, Louis Moyston Private Archive.
529. Glasspole to Brown, Louis Moyston Private Archive.
530. Brown to Glasspole, December 14, 1949, Louis Moyston Private Archive. See also *Daily Gleaner*, November 16, 1949.
531. Roberts, 'Autobiography', 82 (513).
532. Roberts, 'National Consciousness', undated [late 50s], NLJ, WAR, MS 353, Box 9.
533. Roberts, 'Autobiography', 85 (515).
534. Ibid.
535. *Daily Gleaner*, April 4, 1958.
536. Roberts, 'National Feeling', undated, NLJ, WAR, MS 353, Box 9.
537. Roberts, 'Nationalist Liberalism', 'Manuscript for Pepperpot', 1959, NLJ, WAR, MS 353, Box 9.
538. Roberts, 'Analysis of the Jamaican', NLJ, WAR, MS 353, Box 9.
539. Roberts, 'Nationalist Liberalism', 'Manuscript for Pepperpot', 1959, NLJ, WAR, MS 353, Box 9.
540. *Daily Gleaner*, May 10, 1955.
541. Roberts, 'Analysis of the Jamaican', undated, NLJ, WAR, MS 353, Box 17.
542. Roy de Coverley, *Candid Portraits, What's on in Jamaica*, July 24, 1950, NLJ, WAR, MS 353, Box 17.

543. *Daily Gleaner*, February 28, 1957.
544. Roberts, *Sir Henry Morgan: Buccaneer and Governor* (London: Covici, Friede, 1933).
545. Sir Philip M. Sherlock was the first Director of the Extra-Mural Department, involved in establishing the UWI, and later pro vice chancellor of the University of the West Indies, St Augustine campus.
546. Roberts, 'Autobiography', 70 (499).
547. *Daily Gleaner*, June 1, 1949; June 15, 1949; June 29, 1949; July 20, 1949.
548. Ibid., January 12, 1950.
549. Ibid., July 20, 1949.
550. Ibid., August 9, 1946.
551. Roberts, 'Pan-Americanism and the West Indies' (University of Florida, Gainesville Florida), NLJ, WAR, MS 353, Box 23.
552. On Bolívar's vision of a united Pan-America see Simon Collier, 'Nationality, Nationalism, and Supranationalism in the Writings of Simón Bolívar', *The Hispanic American Historical Review*, 63 (1983), 37–64.
553. Roberts mentioned the two Puerto Ricans Dr Ramón Emeterio Betánoes and Juán Diego; Gregorgio Luperón from the Dominican Republic; Amténor Firmin from Haiti and the Cuban Francisco Aguilera.
554. The organization had been transformed into the Organization of American States, of which also the independent states in the Caribbean became members.
555. *Daily Gleaner*, May 4, 1958.
556. The first public meeting of the Bolivarian Society was held on the premises of the Pen Club in September 1952. Varma, prominent JPL, Kingston officer and advocate of Indian Independence was vice-president. See *Daily Gleaner*, September 18, 1952.
557. Roberts to Domingo, September 10, 1952, NLJ, WAR, MS 353, Box 2b, (emphasis in original).
558. *Daily Gleaner*, August 17, 1954; September 6, 1955; February 3, 1956; June 17, 1957; July 19, 1957.
559. Ibid., January 29, 1953.
560. Ibid., March 13, 1953.
561. Ibid., May 24, 1952.
562. Ibid., July 6, 1962.
563. Ibid., April 8, 1950.
564. Ibid.
565. Roberts, *Single Star*.
566. W. Adolphe Roberts, *Havana, Portrait of a City* (New York: Coward-McCann, 1953). To launch his book, Roberts travelled to Cuba in 1953, *Daily Gleaner*, May 5, 1953.
567. *Daily Gleaner*, August 6, 1953.
568. For an overview on the constitutional development see Hart, *Time for a Change*, 300ff and Munroe, *Constitutional Decolonization*.
569. *Daily Gleaner*, December 29, 1955.
570. Ibid., March 29, 1960.
571. Ibid., December 31, 1960.
572. Ibid., March 25, 1955.
573. Ibid.

574. Ibid., December 22, 1956.
575. Ibid., November 27, 1953.
576. Ibid.
577. Ibid., March 12, 1954.
578. Ibid., July 8, 1954.
579. Ibid.
580. Ibid., July 17, 1954.
581. Ibid., May 10, 1955.
582. Duke to Department of State, November 25, 1957, NARA, RG 84, Classified General Records, NND 959049, 1956–1958, Box 11.
583. Roberts, 'Nationalist Liberalism', Manuscript for Pepperpot, 1959, NLJ, WAR, MS 353, Box 9.
584. *Daily Gleaner*, August 9, 1946.
585. Roberts, Pan-Americanism and the West Indies, Speech for 'Conference on the Caribbean' (University of Florida, Gainesville Florida), Box 23.
586. Ibid.

CHAPTER 8: OPPOSING THE WEST INDIES FEDERATION

Early Critique against Federation

In the aftermath of the Second World War, the Colonial Office launched plans to federate the British West Indies and declared that, in the long run, the newly created political entity should be granted self-government. The idea was initially endorsed by the political leaders of both political parties in Jamaica, the PNP and the JLP. Without much public discussion, Jamaica joined the other colonies in the British Caribbean in the slow and tedious process of creating a federation.

The idea of merging the British Caribbean possessions into a federation had existed for some time in the Colonial Office as a means of streamlining administrative duties. While it was often rejected as impractical, the idea gained much popularity among officials from 1943 onwards. They regarded it as a means to meet the increased demands for self-government, both in the region as well as in the US, and to safeguard continued British political and economic influence in the Caribbean.[1] As Jason Parker puts it: 'Race, reform, security, and the minuet of British reassertion and U.S. deferral did, however, begin to coalesce around one issue in the mid-1940s, the idea of a regional federation....'[2]

The idea was especially attractive because not only strategists in the US and in England sympathized with the idea, but it was also popular in the Eastern Caribbean as a vision of black emancipation and nationhood in the region in the early twentieth century.[3] Furthermore, as Eric D. Duke's study on the diasporic dimensions of federation convincingly shows, the idea was endorsed in the Caribbean diaspora, where many Caribbean immigrants eventually adopted a regional identity.[4] In these circles, the idea of federation was often embedded in broader anti-racist and anti-colonial frameworks of black liberation and nation-building, as promoted by many of the early activists like Robert Love, Hubert H. Harrison, S.A.G. Cox and Marcus Garvey. These early activists exerted a profound influence on Harlem's young radicals during the 1920s.

Indeed, many of Domingo's friends from the old networks in New York were outspoken proponents of federation.[5] However, the Jamaica Progressive League, which had helped to initiate the nationalist struggle in Jamaica and had financially and ideologically supported it for years, was divided over the question of whether Jamaica should join the federation or continue its march toward independence alone. Instead of intuitively believing in the mutual benefits of federation with the other islands, a faction around Adolphe Roberts and Wilfred Domingo was strongly convinced that joining the federation would hamper Jamaica's economic and political development and impede the decolonization process. Further, the nationalists argued that contrary to the islands in the east, Jamaicans had very little contact with the other islands and never shared feelings of West Indian communality.

In the 1950s, Roberts and Domingo started a radical campaign against the federation and were among the earliest and most outspoken critics.

Roberts' ideal of Jamaican nationhood developed from a decidedly regional perspective, inspired by the free republics in the Americas that had successfully cut their ties with their colonial rulers. Yet, he was never keen about Jamaica entering a federation with the other British colonies in the region. In 1934, Roberts welcomed the 'profound impulse towards self-government'[6] in the Eastern Caribbean that was spearheaded by the agitation of T.A. Marryshow of Grenada and A.A. Cipriani of Trinidad and Tobago, who advocated a federation of the islands in the British Caribbean with dominion status as the final goal. At this time, Roberts sympathized with the idea of a federation of the eastern islands, of which he felt the majority was too small to stand alone as independent states. After considering various ideas for different forms of federation, Roberts emphasized that the bigger islands, Trinidad and Tobago and Jamaica were 'in every way equipped either to stand alone politically or to become the cornerstone of a federation'. Yet, he rejected the claim that all West Indian colonies needed to federate in order to achieve Dominion status and asserted that both islands would be ready for self-government. In contrast to a recent statement of Sir Algernon Aspignall, Secretary of the West India Committee in London, that the colonies in the Caribbean were not yet ready to rule themselves, Roberts claimed: 'Thoughtful persons in Jamaica and Trinidad, however, assert that they are conscious of no unreadiness or incapacity, and that they are merely waiting for a favorable moment to press their claims with the Colonial Office'.

Roberts preferred Jamaica to become independent on its own. In 1936, he felt the right moment had arrived to press the demand for self-government, when Roberts successfully created a suitable instrument by launching the Progressive League in New York, demanding that Jamaica should become a full-fledged Dominion within the British Commonwealth of Nations.

When Roberts was in Jamaica during his propaganda campaign for self-government in 1937, Ken Hill explicitly asked in an interview for his opinion in regards to a British West Indian federation. Roberts answered that while federation was 'an excellent idea', he felt that 'it would be a mistake on the part of Jamaicans or the people of any other colony to pin their hope on this as the first thing to be obtained'.[7] He warned that England never yet agreed to 'an advanced form of government for a federation of colonies' when none of the parts had been granted self-government before. At this early point, he warned that Great Britain might use futile discussions about federation to delay self-government for the single units. He therefore claimed that it would be a 'foolish dream for people as advanced as the people of Jamaica to be deluded by a federation of colonies'.[8]

In front of a large audience at Ward Theatre, the Progressive League founder reaffirmed his objection to federation. Although Roberts held that the idea of a federation with Dominion status was 'attractive in theory', he claimed that it was not 'within the realm of practical politics'.[9] Roberts was convinced that:

> Jamaica, on account of her size, population, material resources and past political history can reasonably ask Westminster to be allowed to emerge as a nation. If Jamaica is successful, she may win the fight for others as well as herself. Then the federation of some, or all, of the self-governing units may be achieved.[10]

The young Progressive League branch in Kingston agreed that self-government must precede any possible federation, as McFarlane pointed out in a letter to the *Gleaner*.[11] At a big welcome meeting for Roberts and Domingo on a visit to Jamaica in 1939, Roberts repeated his arguments and claimed that federation would postpone the granting of self-government.[12]

Domingo also opposed the idea of a federation from early on. At a Progressive League meeting in 1937, he claimed: '…self-government must precede federation. Jamaica…is fit for self-government now. Let us work for it'.[13] In a letter to Campbell in 1940, Domingo commented on an article in *Public Opinion* that favourably discussed federation and explained why he rejected the idea:

> This is impractical for all the colonies. The distances are too great and the economic interests of many of them will clash, not omitting the insular, and other jealousies, that are bound to militate against efficient administration and equal development of all.[14]

The points Domingo mentioned would indeed be some of the greatest obstacles toward the successful development of the federation. Since Domingo realized that some PNP members had started to think about federation, he tried to lend his advice. In a letter to PNP secretary Arnett, he complained about the practice of the Colonial Office to 'lump the British West Indies and British Guiana mor [sic] or less together' and stated:

> I am personally not an advocate of Federation of the Colonies. I believe such a forced union should not be thrust upon them, but it is my view that there should be some degree of united action and pressure emanated from the Colonies…without committing Jamaica to any program for Federation.[15]

In another letter to Arnett, Domingo expressed his fears that joining a federation with the other islands could mean a 'retardment of our progress' and compared the federation to 'a three-legged race', in which 'the speed of the faster runner is limited to that of the slower person whose leg is tied to his'.[16]

In the 1940s, Roberts still rejected the idea of an all-island federation. However, in contrast to Domingo, he was open to the idea of forming two federations in the British Caribbean. In his eyes, one federation of the islands could be centred on Trinidad and Tobago in the east. Jamaica and the mainland colony, British Honduras, could tie up their destinies in the west. Roberts explicated this idea at a conference on 'The Economic Future of the Caribbean'[17] at Howard University. In his lecture, Roberts revisited Jamaica's special importance as a role model for the region in the face of the planned constitutional advancement that was to be reviewed after five years. Roberts expected: 'If all goes well, Jamaica will soon have achieved real autonomy'.[18] He did not see any similar development in the other islands, with the exception of Trinidad and Tobago where he expected similar changes over time. He was aware of the significant macro-political changes, namely the combination of Great Britain's decreased interest in the region and an increased interest of the US. While Roberts did not believe that both powers would advocate an all-island federation, he was convinced that some form of unification was in the air to achieve more efficient administration of the colonies. Roberts believed that one eastern and one western federation would soon be created and speculated: 'When these are self-governing they may, of course, agree to merge. Singly or separately their goal under the British flag is Dominion status'.[19]

Roberts misinterpreted the attitudes of Great Britain and the US. In 1940, the Moyne Commission presented its report on the reasons for the disturbances in the 1930s. It suggested far-reaching constitutional changes including universal suffrage and indicated that a federation of all British territories in the Caribbean would be desirable: 'Political federation is not of itself an appropriate means of meeting the pressing needs of West Indians. Nevertheless, it is the end to which policy should be directed'.[20] In the US, the idea also had supporters. Charles W. Taussig, for instance, regarded federation as a significant step toward economic and political development and stability in what strategists regarded as the superpower's most important backyard.[21] In the wake of macro-political changes which had placed the impoverished but politically and socially awakened Caribbean in the centre of US strategic interests, the Empire was forced to consider steps toward decolonization. Upon the granting of Jamaica's new constitution in 1944, Secretary of State, Oliver Stanley, had declared: 'It is the policy of His Majesty's Government...to foster the practical development of self-government throughout the Colonial Empire'.[22]

At the same time, public discussions about a possible federation flared up in the PNP.[23] Hart suspected that the subject was brought by Secretary of State for the Colonies, Oliver Stanley, who circulated a draft of a dispatch suggesting federation in order to investigate the attitude of leaders in the Caribbean. However, interest for federation, and more generally, in the affairs of the other English-speaking islands was low in Jamaica. Apart from the Jamaican migrant Louis S. Meikle, who had advocated the idea in 1912 to prevent US annexation, the subject was never widely discussed.[24] According to Richard Hart: 'Prior to 1944, the issue of federation had not been considered in Jamaica, the only Jamaican organizations with Caribbean wide connections being the cricketers and the sugar manufacturers'.[25]

Yet, Jamaica's political elite supported the idea. In the Legislative Council a resolution to further investigate the practicability and desirability of a federation was passed.[26] Manley wholeheartedly endorsed the idea and the PNP officially approved it on its annual conference of the same year, although Hart recalled that it was passed without considerable interest or discussion.[27] However, Ken Hill points to Domingo's important influence on the PNP's position that was based on the prerequisite that the federation should be granted Dominion status. He remembered:

> For several years after his release from detention in 1943 he remained here holding a frontline position in the national movement. In the first federal stirrings here in 1944, Domingo set his face firmly against any projected union until independence was first secured for Jamaica. More than most PNP policymakers, he influenced the party to the compromise line of Federation with Dominion status.[28]

Richard Hart commented on Domingo's position toward federation and vividly recalled one occasion when the party executives chose Domingo as the party's representative at a conference of the Caribbean Labour Congress (CLC) in 1945, an all-island trade union meeting, to discuss federation.[29] Hart was still amused when he recalled the incident:

> That was so funny....I heard that we have decided to accept [the invitation to the CLC conference] and that we had chosen Domingo to go. I said: 'Comrades, Domingo is the only member we have in the

PNP who has any ideas about Federation and he is strongly against it'. So Domingo said: 'Hart is perfectly right, if I go down there, I am going to oppose Federation'. But who the hell is to go? Nobody was particularly interested, 'Well, Hart, would you go?', 'Yes, yes, I'm in favour of federation, I will go'. So this was quite amicably settled, because Domingo understood completely, he agreed completely.[30]

This statement not only reflects how isolated Domingo's position was in the PNP, but also how low the general interest in the federation was within the PNP executive.

In contrast to Domingo, many of his friends and co-workers in New York, among them Richard B. Moore, Hope Stevens and Reginald Pierrepoint with whom he cooperated in the WINC, were strong advocates of federation.[31] Especially among migrants from the eastern Caribbean, the agitation for federation fell on fertile grounds. In the US, many islanders had adopted a regional perspective, inspired by the way they were lumped together in the eyes of Americans. Domingo remembered from his own personal experience:

For instance, it was in Boston that I discovered that I was a West Indian. Until then I was a Jamaican. But pressure from Americans, who did not differentiate between Jamaicans and other English-speaking Negroes from the Caribbean area, drove all of us to this: [to think] of ourselves as West Indians. In other words, we were forced to adopt the regional name and acquire something of a regional outlook.[32]

However, Domingo did not put such a regional identity above his identification with Jamaica. As seen in the run-up to the founding of the WINEC, the idea of cooperating with his radical friends from other islands was a mere stopgap for Domingo, as he could not find enough radical Jamaicans for his emergency plans. Domingo then explained in a letter to Roberts: 'I felt that in this matter a joint West Indian call could be useful, although there is no intention on my part to go off into futile discussions about Federation'.[33] In another letter Domingo declared: 'Jamaica's case is strong and I keep it clear of all encumbrances about confederation, etc., although I work with the Committee'.[34] The special attention given to Jamaica was further reflected in two separate documents that WINC delegate Hope Stevens had in hand when he arrived in Havana; one WINC document claiming the right to self-government of the British colonies in general and the other document prepared by the Progressive League specifically demanding self-government for Jamaica.

During his forced stay in Jamaica, Domingo observed that in contrast to the immigrants in New York, people on the island were largely indifferent or hostile toward federation. When PNP member William Seivreight returned from a trip to New York in 1944 and reported about the positive attitude toward federation in the immigrant community overseas, Domingo offered an explanation for the diametrically opposed perceptions:

> The truth is that Jamaica is in sentiment isolated from the other islands. Great distances separate Jamaica from her British neighbours and there is little contact between the peoples. In New York they are thrown willy nilly together and come to regard themselves as one. Federation may be a lively political issue in Barbados, Trinidad, British Guiana, and the Leeward and Windward Islands but it is a misreading of the facts for anyone to believe that Jamaicans have the slightest interest in it. And there are good reasons for it.[35]

Domingo objected to the idea not only because there was no interest in federation in Jamaica, but also because he was convinced that 'any attempt to work up such a sentiment is doomed to failure and likely to injure the movement in Jamaica for National freedom'.[36]

In face of such fears, Domingo felt it was about time to publicly express his concerns. At the end of January 1945, a few weeks before Stanley would present his dispatch that affirmed federation as official colonial policy, Domingo published a lengthy article, in which he explicated his arguments against a federation. He pointed to the great distances between the islands, the lack of contact and communication and the absence of any feeling of unity. He claimed that although many migrants developed a regional identity through their experiences abroad, 'West Indian' was merely a geographic or regional term and that would not signify 'nationality or oneness'.[37] Jamaicans had virtually no contact with the people of the eastern islands and rather migrated to the US, Cuba or Panama. Further, Domingo argued that there was no economic benefit in federation or a customs union because the islands basically produced the same export goods and competed for the same markets. Domingo's major concern, however, was the unequal political development.[38]

The Colonial Office obviously had a different opinion. In March 1945, Stanley released his dispatch in which he affirmed that it was the declared aim of British colonial policy to quicken the process of decolonization which also pertained to the islands in the British Caribbean. Yet, he urged to '…keep in view the larger project of their political federation, as being the end to which, in the view of the Royal Commission, policy should be directed'.[39] The dispatch, nonetheless, expressed concerns as to whether the technical difficulties brought on by geographic separation would allow for a speedy development toward federation. Stanley further questioned whether the general attitude in the islands was favourable enough to accept a federal constitution and carefully declared that such a movement for federation must 'come from within and not from outside the area'. He further declared that 'full internal self-government within the British

Commonwealth' was the final aim of the federation, but qualified the statement by demanding that, as a prerequisite, the federal government must be able to maintain itself without financial support from outside.

Just as Roberts had presumed, Stanley felt that the creation of two federations, one in the east and one in the west, might prove useful. In every case, the Secretary of State for the Colonies concluded that it was necessary that 'British policy should aim at the fostering of a sense of West Indian unity and a removal of the present obstacles in the way of federation'. To help bring about such a sense of unity and to popularize the idea, Stanley suggested publishing the dispatch in all colonies to inspire discussions in the respective Legislative Councils. He planned to convene a conference to bring all leaders in the region on one table to discuss proposals for the formation of a closer union that could be established in the near future.

Stanley's dispatch stimulated some discussions about federation among the politicians, not only in the other islands but also in Jamaica. In the following months, Domingo observed that Jamaicans were blamed for their low interest in federation. Jamaicans were not 'consciously isolationists', Domingo countered and claimed: 'Our attitude is due to our physical or geographical isolation from the other islands. It is not the result of any snobbishness on our part'.[40]

Domingo continued to occasionally voice his concern in public and tried to influence the position of the PNP. However, being a guest at Norman Manley's house, it was difficult for Domingo to openly oppose his policy. In a letter to Roberts in 1952, he explained his dilemma: 'I do not understand why a man of Manley's intellect allows himself to be seduced by the idea. I tried to discuss it with him once – only once – in Jamaica, but I saw that he approached the subject a priori, so I did not press the argument he being my host'.[41]

For the time he was in Jamaica, Domingo chose a mild approach. Only after his return to the US, when the federal plans took concrete shape, he started a relentless campaign against the proposed federation. For the remaining time in Jamaica, he employed the strategy of focusing on nationalist agitation, rather than openly opposing the PNP by harshly criticizing the idea of federation.

Back in New York, Domingo observed with great worries that federation was about to develop from the status of an idea to the embodiment of reality quite soon and tried to influence the Progressive League to adopt an anti-federalist position. In September 1947, the first concrete step toward federation was taken at a conference in Montego Bay, Jamaica, shortly after Domingo's return to the US in August.[42] With the exception of the Bahamas, all British colonies in the area sent their representatives to the conference to discuss the possibility of federation. Although major concerns had been voiced by a number of participants, among them Bustamante, the conference agreed that a federation would be desirable and a Standing Closer Association Committee was formed. While the conference is often interpreted as the starting point of the federation and the climax of positive expectations, Michele A. Johnson argues that a close examination of the proceedings exposes the main challenges that eventually contributed to its break-up, caused by Jamaica's secession.[43] Vital questions raised, such as which advantages the federation would have for the individual units, how to handle the differential stages of development and how to stem the costs of the federation remained unanswered until the end. Finally, Johnson argues, the omission of finding answers to these questions 'made the federal enterprise a difficult product to sell'.[44]

One day after the conference, Norman Manley wrote to Brown, and stated: 'On the whole, I think it has been a success, and has carried the Federation idea as far forward as it could for the time being'.[45] Manley went on: 'I am very grateful to you for your promised help in getting the Progressive League to continue its support as from October this year. I sincerely hope that something comes out of it and need hardly tell you how much I appreciate the unfailing zeal of your services'.[46] Although there is not much material available on the Progressive League in the 1940s and 1950s, the few sources suggest that the Progressive League was divided over the question of federation and apparently, some members, including Brown, were in support of the idea and continued to support the PNP in its course.[47] Together with the American Committee for West Indian Federation, the Progressive League and the WINC helped to sponsor a US tour conducted by Manley to raise funds and to promote federation.[48] Apparently, Brown played an instrumental role and had developed into one of Manley's reliable confidants in New York. Brown's position is further evidenced by a statement of Manley in a letter to Brown, in which he expressed disappointment over the lack of support from abroad for the second Caribbean Labour Conference:

> I am sorry to learn that because of lukewarm attitudes all the burden is being cast on your shoulders again. I should have thought that after all the agitation in America for Federation the news of what was about to happen would have caused very wide-spread interest.[49]

However, the close cooperation was disturbed when difficulties arose between the Progressive League and the PNP after Domingo's return. It is more than likely that Domingo's decided stand against federation was responsible for the problems. In a letter from PNP Secretary Arnett to Progressive League Secretary Brooks-Johnson, he mentioned misunderstandings in regards to the federation and feared that the Progressive League might stop its financial support.[50] Although the letter contained no more details, the speculation that the tensions between the groups resulted from differences over the proposed federation is not far-fetched. In order to calm the storm, the PNP sent one of their long-time members, Edith

Dalton James, to New York. In a letter to her, Manley explained the nature of the problems with the Progressive League and emphasized the importance of the funds from New York:

> I hope you are able to clear up the many doubts and queries that constantly arise in the Progressive League. We are in desperate straits financially and the continuance of their help will mean such a lot to us today facing as we do a deficit of £50. ...There has been some confusion about the supposed conflict between Federation as a goal and local Self-Government. It is easiest to explain that the two logically go hand in hand side by side.[51]

Local self-government, contrary to Manley's position, had never been enough for the Progressive League. Some members, therefore, were deeply concerned about the idea of joining the proposed federation and felt that their goals had been betrayed. Manley really seemed to believe that there was no contradiction in the PNP's strategy to promote federation as a patriotic aim. In a letter to Brown in 1951, he affirmed on his return from another successful speaking tour in the US that he saw no reason for conflict:

> I trust that the League appreciates that we are always mindful in the party of their historical connection with our move and of the valued importance of their continued support. As I understand it the purpose of the League is to see that we press forward in the fight for Self Government and West Indian Federation.[52]

Thanking the Progressive League for its continued and much needed support, Manley hoped that their 'close, valuable co-operation...will forever be continued until our efforts are crowned with success'.[53] Manley's words unquestionably show how much the PNP depended on the Progressive League's financial support.

In the meantime, federation plans went on in a tedious and tiresome process of reports, negotiations and conferences during which grave differences occasionally threatened to frustrate the venture. Yet, the leaders of the two parties in Jamaica, where the parallel process of constitutional development continued, saw no reason to worry too much about federation. They were united in a general positive commitment, without paying much attention to the problems in party meetings or election campaigns. Such unanimity had the effect that both parties saw no need to discuss the issue on a broad level or to start expensive educational campaigns to create interest and support at the grass-roots level.[54] The initial affirmation of the federal project was limited to the political elite. Trevor Munroe is therefore right when he emphasizes: '...though the Jamaicans for other reasons were far from united in their anxiety for self-government, they were even less concerned with Federation. Isolated from the other islands, they felt no emotional impetus to unite with them'.[55]

In the atmosphere of the Cold War, the conditions for an accelerated course of decolonization deteriorated as a result of the conservative administrations that had taken over in the US and in Great Britain. The result was a lessened attention of both countries to the region as a whole, while other world areas more urgently demanded attention.[56]

In the course of the 1950s, the plans for the federation slowly became more concrete and at the same time less committed to the granting of Dominion status. In March 1950, the report of the Rance Committee that was formed in Montego Bay was published and suggested a weak federal structure with internal self-government of the individual units.[57] By accepting the proposals, it was clear that the PNP had left the compromise course that Domingo had helped to bring about, that of demanding self-government as a prerequisite of federation. The developments affirmed Domingo and Roberts' worries that federation would prolong the colonial status. Frank Hill later recalled that the PNP's new course aggravated Domingo: 'Domingo felt betrayed. From New York he kept up a barrage of letters and articles against the changed political objective'.[58]

When Domingo's letters to influential PNP members like Manley, Nethersole, Ken Hill and Allan remained unanswered, Domingo contacted Roberts in Jamaica, hoping that he would have similar objections against Jamaica joining the federation.[59] Domingo shared his fear with Roberts '...that the PNP with its incomprehensible adherence to federation may, without sufficient thought or patriotism allow federation to delay <u>our own</u> political progress'.[60] He told Roberts that he observed with greatest concern how the PNP was willing to make far-reaching compromises in vitally important questions as the representation in the federal legislature by accepting fewer seats than what he felt would be appropriate in regard to Jamaica's population. Domingo listed a number of arguments against the federation and concluded that federation could only be of value in a different world, in a 'socialist world',[61] but since this was not likely to happen, his stand was uncompromisingly against federation.

Domingo's letter is important because it marks the first step in what would become a fiery nationalist campaign against federation. Roberts answered that he was happy to hear from Domingo and assured:

> I am no more in favor of Federation than I was when I last talked with you on the subject. The British want to establish a federated colony of the West Indies, not a federated dominion. They will promise eventual Dominion status but be infinitely slow about granting it. Jamaican participation would simply hold us back, for standing alone we are close to Dominion status and can obtain it.[62]

In another letter, Roberts mentioned that he could sympathize with the idea of two federations; an idea which he still felt could be beneficial to Jamaica. In any case he preferred independence for Jamaica as the next step, at the same time, he regarded the idea of an all-island federation as so impractical that he doubted that it could become reality.

> However, should the unexpected happen and the formula for an all British Caribbean federation be adopted, I shall oppose it tooth and nail unless Dominion status is given from the start. I'd accept any federation, no matter how impractical, if it were on the basis of Dominion status, because that would mean independence and Jamaica could secede from a Dominion.[63]

'Opposing It Tooth and Nail': The Campaign against Federation

The 'unexpected' happened quite soon. At a conference in April 1953 in London, the representatives of the Caribbean colonies adopted the proposal for a weak federation without Dominion status, with limited powers over the individual entities and a strong influence of a Governor and the Colonial Office.[64] In both mainland colonies, British Honduras and British Guiana, strong nationalist tendencies had become dominant and their respective leaders abstained from joining the proposed Federation. In British Guiana, the fortified nationalism was embodied in the radical, multi-ethnic and radical left-wing People's Progressive Party (PPP) under Cheddi Jagan.[65] This shift to the left was a source of great concern to Great Britain and the US alike, and they renewed their efforts to achieve a moderate, slow and guided development toward federation, without any haste to grant Dominion status.[66]

Roberts lived up to his word, and joined Domingo in a vigorous campaign, fighting federation. While the conference in London was still underway, Roberts decided to intervene and published a lengthy article in the *Gleaner* that served as a prelude to the campaign. Roberts expressed his grave concerns:

> A combination of all the British possessions in the Caribbean looms from one standpoint as a snare, and from another as a mirage. I speak as a Jamaican who wants complete self-government for this Island as quickly as possible. The brand of federation debated is a snare, because the scheme calls for prolonged colonial status. The implication that growth into a Dominion would soon follow is not to be taken too seriously. How soon is soon?[67]

Roberts suspected that the different stages of development in the islands would be used 'as an argument to delay autonomy for the whole' and that this was 'what the advocates of the plan desire'. Roberts went on discussing the details why he felt that the federation was doomed to failure. In his eyes, the decision by British Honduras and British Guiana to abstain from joining was a major shortcoming of the proposed federation that now lacked the territory to help compensate the challenge of overpopulation in the islands. He pointed to difficulties in the negotiations that displayed the existing antagonism between the islands, namely Trinidad and Tobago's demand to curtail immigration, the bickering over the federal capital, the quarrel about representation as Jamaica's size and population required that Jamaicans would have a majority voice. Therefore Roberts was convinced: 'An all-island federation simply would not hold together except as a British-sponsored colony'. Roberts repeated his idea that a possible solution would be to form two federations with Dominion status and concluded: 'There can never be only one [federation], as a lasting proposition. Jamaica's statesmen who preach the contrary are deluding their supporters and delaying the achievement of full self-government. Some few have seen it clearly'. As one of those few positive examples, Roberts favourably quoted the prominent JLP member Sir Harold Allen, the party's specialist on foreign affairs, who had stated that he would not be willing to place federation ahead of self-government. With this implicit closing of ranks with the JLP, Roberts signalled the start of a new era of relations between the Progressive League and the PNP. Roberts and Domingo's decision to openly oppose the PNP's position reminds again on the fact that the cooperation was always based on tactical considerations.

Domingo followed suit with a letter to the *Gleaner* in which he agreed with Roberts' arguments and lauded his patriotic approach. He recalled how he unsuccessfully tried persuading Jamaicans to examine the risks of the federation:

> The leaders were convinced, without any genuine examination of the question, that Jamaica should subordinate some of her own national interests to what they were pleased to call West Indian unity...I am still convinced that Jamaica's real interest is to march forward to full self-government in whatever shape it may take.[68]

Domingo complained that Jamaica was about to accept a disproportional representation in the federal government and stressed: '...by tying our country to the more backward areas especially when we are unfairly given minority representation we will retard our own progress towards autonomy'. Instead, Domingo highlighted the benefits that independence would mean for Jamaica, including a seat in the United Nations, control of Jamaica's judiciary, its finances, trade agreements and the civil service and a non-quota status for immigration to the United States. In reference to the strong nationalist demand in British Guiana, Domingo claimed: '... our success, and perhaps that of British Guiana, will spur the other colonies of the Caribbean to make realistic and democratic demands leading up to gains similar to those made by the leaders'. This statement shows that Domingo's nationalist position was still embedded in a wider project of anti-colonialism, although Jamaica clearly took precedence.

While the opponents of federation were able to present serious arguments against the federation and for national independence, Domingo criticized the lack of arguments on the side of the advocates:

> A strange feature about the case for Federation, as expounded in Jamaica, has been the reluctance of those who advocate federation to invite full dressed discussion of the subject from Jamaica's point of view. They talk a lot about West Indian unity and progress, but what Jamaicans should want to hear is clear argument, pro and con, not self-serving speculations unrelated to reality.

The intervention of Domingo and Roberts had the desired effect of stirring up a discussion. Subsequently, several letters appeared in the *Gleaner* repudiating their arguments and arguing in favour of federation.[69] In an editorial, the *Gleaner* supported federation, but gave credit for the inspirational effect of their utterances: 'We do not agree with the views on Federation of Mr. Adolphe Roberts and Mr. W.A. Domingo: but they have had the merit of drawing fire'.[70] In another editorial, the *Gleaner* pointed out: 'Mr. W.A. Domingo's forthright denunciation of Federation should at any rate rouse politicians in Jamaica to do what they have never tried to do before – to sell the idea of Federation to the country'.[71] Such reactions demonstrate that hitherto federation was neither actively promoted nor substantially questioned in society.

The outspoken manner in which the two Progressive League founders opposed federation raised concerns within the PNP about the continuation of financial support from overseas. Manley sent a statement of the PNP to the Progressive League, explaining the position of the party. After paying tribute to the Progressive League as the 'pioneer of the self-government movement in Jamaica',[72] Manley admitted that the PNP was not satisfied with the results of the London conference, but that they had decided to accept it as a starting point for further advancement. He blamed some of the leaders of the other colonies for being afraid of the responsibility of self-government:

> To them we owe what must surely be one of the strangest and most ironic happening in the history of Colonialism. For here we have an Imperial Power, England, offering almost any degree of political freedom that the subject peoples may demand and they in turn with timid shrinking reluctance asking to be spared and modestly insisting that the half-loaf will suffice.

Manley explained that he would therefore work toward a situation in which Jamaica could have full internal self-government but still be part of a federation without Dominion status. Assuring the Progressive League that the PNP would continue to press for self-government, Manley begged: 'Meantime sustain us in our labours with your face [sic!] and your help. In all humility but with great confidence I pledge we will not fail you nor our own people in the task that lies before us'. However, such explanations were not satisfactory to Roberts and Domingo, who were not willing to sacrifice Jamaica's independence for a federation of colonies. Accordingly, they intensified their campaign.

In the middle of the 1950s, Bustamante and the JLP still agreed to federation in principle, although the JLP leader frequently emphasized that he would not support a federation with negative impact for Jamaica. But for now, the basic acceptance of the plans for a federation within the political elite resulted in public silence about the matter as the masses had little knowledge and understanding of what was decided above their heads in regards to their political future.[73] Even during the election campaign of 1955, federation was not yet a popular issue. The PNP won the elections, but with a campaign that was primarily concerned with getting Bustamante out of office, not with federation.[74]

After the London conference in 1953, the federation moved on only slowly, while the different interests and expectations of the participating units became increasingly visible. Shortly before the Legislative Council was about to decide to accept the proposals in 1955, Roberts published another article to inspire a critical debate, at least about the form of the federation, as he now expected that federation was to become a reality. The widespread indifference toward this important decision worried Roberts: 'The apathy with which the tentative plans have been received makes me fear that most Jamaicans care little about independence. But I care'.[75]

He rejected the federation without Dominion status and pointed to the advantages of a federation which would include the mainland colonies and which he would have supported. Without British Honduras and British Guiana, he doubted that the federation had a realistic chance for success. Roberts continued to criticize the design of the federation and offered his opinion on what he felt were the major shortcomings. One main argument was the 'irrational structure' of the Legislative, in which Jamaica was to have 17 of 45 elected members in the House of Representatives and two representatives in a Senate of 19 members, appointed by the Governor. Roberts admitted that Jamaica, with slightly more than half of the territory and population, could not expect to have a majority in both organs, as that would contradict the idea of federation. However, he felt that the proposed representation was far too low: 'I regard it as sure that if Jamaica accepts a foolish structure, she will someday secede from the Federation in disgust....The interests of the friends of the project require that they build intelligently'.[76] This comment made by Roberts in 1955, before the federation was even formally ratified, would prove to be of a prophetic nature.

Although both men rejected the present design of the federation, the outline of their positions shows that a difference existed between Domingo's uncompromising objection to federation and Roberts' more constructive position. But even Roberts' practical criticism did not result in a considerable public discussion about the form of the federation, although he continued to address his concerns in articles and in public lectures for the extra-mural department of the University.[77]

The Legislative Council agreed that Jamaica should join the proposed federation and the Jamaican delegation arrived with a positive mandate at another conference in London in 1956. Despite severe disagreements reflecting the diverging interests of the units on vital matters like the site of the capital, taxation and the establishment of a customs union or the political status of the whole body, the conference formally agreed on the formation of a federation. Although Manley had strongly advocated for Dominion status, the delegates finally agreed on a constitution that was less developed than Jamaica's own.[78] A few months later, the British government ratified the 'British Caribbean Federation Act'. Finally, Trinidad and Tobago was chosen to host the federal capital and the first federal elections were scheduled for March 1958.[79] The federation, although remaining behind all expectations of creating a self-governed unit, was now to become a reality.

Roberts was deeply disappointed. Before the conference, he had again put the idea of two federations on the table and complained that the idea had not been further debated, although Stanley had mentioned such a possibility in 1945 and leaders in British Honduras indicated some interest in a federation with Jamaica on the basis of Dominion status. In a *Gleaner* article he claimed, 'British Honduras is our natural partner'.[80] He pointed out that the two colonies had been governed together from Spanish Town until 1884, the population shared a similar ethnic composition speaking the same idiom, a similar climate and would ideally complement each other. Roberts claimed that while Jamaica was overpopulated and lacked employment for its population, British Honduras lacked capital and population to develop the country. Together the landmass would be big enough to form a new American nation that could sustain itself. In favour of this idea, Roberts even accepted a definition of the nation that stood in contradiction to his original definition which was based on a shared territory.

Such flexibility marked an essential difference in comparison with Domingo's more rigid position. Domingo clearly rejected federation without making constructive proposals. In a letter to the *Gleaner* he tried to arouse the interest of the masses by complaining that Kingston would not be chosen to become the capital and deplored the unjust representation in the federal government:

> If Jamaicans realized that their country, the most advanced politically of the unit, with approximately 59 per cent of the area and 53 per cent of the people will have ONLY 34 per cent of the representation I am

sure they would rise up and reject the whole scheme that has been foisted on them by their leaders.[81]

Yet, no one cared for the critique presented by the two pioneers of the national movement. In February 1956, *Gleaner* columnist Thomas Wright[82] stated with some resignation: 'I agree...with W. Adolphe Roberts that the whole of the present proposals are unworkable nonsense, but you need pay no attention to us, for not a soul is listening anyway'.[83] Although Jamaican politicians discussed the results of the London conference, a majority in the JLP and the PNP still agreed on the general desirability of federation, without a public discussion taking place.[84] Only Bustamante's concern that Jamaica was not chosen as the site to host the federal capital and his strong objection to a customs union indicated that the unity among the parties would not last forever.[85]

Domingo was eager to challenge the widespread apathy. In July 1956, he published a pamphlet, 'British West Indian Federation: A Critique', which marked one of the cornerstones of the campaign. It contained a foreword by Roberts, in which he urged: 'It is not too late to reject federation on the terms proposed'.[86] Domingo presented his main arguments against federation, hoping to convince some of the legislators to give the matter a second thought before they would ratify the agreement. He complained about the lack of a public discussion, and referred to a statement by Norman Manley's son, Michael Manley, who had crticized in the *Gleaner* that the masses knew little about the federal project and had never been asked whether they agreed.

Domingo pointed out that no connections existed between the islands other than 'the fact that the colonies have been tied to Britain, their political "motherland", for a long period of time'. He rejected the federalists' main thesis that federation and self-government would go hand in hand and countered it with the argument that from the perspective of Jamaica, federation meant sacrificing self-government by subjugation under a federal government. Now, Domingo even took up Roberts' point of the idea of two federations, to demonstrate the absurdity of one all-island federation. He referred to Stanley's dispatch and indicated:

> England's policy, motivated by intelligent self-interest, most naturally is to make concessions, when they are inevitable, with the objective of reducing as much of her financial responsibility as possible, while retaining the maximum economic and political advantages.

But the local politicians, obsessed with an emotional 'the bigger the better' scheme of an all-island federation, completely ignored the idea. Domingo criticized Manley's appeal to emotions when the latter complained about a 'lack of faith' and rejected the assumption that 'unity is strength' with the argument that a 'chain...is as weak as its weakest link'.

Domingo claimed that the naive belief in the economic benefits of federation was not justified and emphasized that the islands were in fact competitors for the same markets. He elaborated on the argument that while in New York, many West Indians started to adopt a regional identity and increasingly became indifferent in regard to the political future of their own islands. He pointed out that 'apart from the Jamaica Progressive League of New York there is no organization of West Indians in the metropolis dedicated solely to the task of securing self-government for any section of the British Caribbean'.

Domingo credited the Progressive League with the achievement that Jamaica was politically more advanced than the rest of the islands and pointed out his own role:

> History, honestly written, will show what part the writer played in the political drama in shaping policies, suggesting the raising of badly-needed organizational and campaign funds in the United States (funds without which as leaders of the People's National Party have frequently publicly testified, victory would have been impossible or long-delayed); besides speaking and writing for years in Jamaica and the United States for the cause nearest to his heart – the extension of democracy in the British West Indies through winning complete autonomy for Jamaica.

The quote contains an important aspect regarding the financial support that he further explicated. Domingo quoted at length from the Progressive League declaration and emphasized that self-government was the sole objective behind its donations to the party, 'unconnected with anything not contained in the declaration'. By using this argument as a blow against the PNP, Domingo took the anti-federation campaign to another next level, openly disclosing the rift between the PNP and the Progressive League.

Domingo repudiated allegations that he was promoting a 'narrow, insular chauvinism' by arguing that Jamaica's achievement of Dominion status was a catalyst for the demands for self-government in the region, whereas federation would be misused by the British officials to delay this development. He was not willing to sacrifice Jamaica's achievements, which he claimed had even inspired anti-colonial movements in Africa. In his eyes, independence necessarily had to precede any plan for federation and was an 'indefeasible right of all peoples', no matter the size of the territory they inhabited. Achieving self-government was not only in Jamaica's best interest he argued, but would finally benefit the rest of the colonies in the region and pointed again to the fact that as independent countries, the islands would enjoy less restriction for immigration to the US.

Domingo was convinced that Jamaica would already enjoy Dominion status, had it not diverged from the ideals outlined by the Progressive League and become distracted by involvement in the federation. He pointed to the newly created nations in Asia and Africa and claimed that the colonies in the Caribbean could have also reached that point because the colonies were a financial liability and 'England would be more than happy to rid herself of the burden'.

Domingo recurred on the particular colonial mentality he regarded as the main reason for the lack of a desire for independence:

> West Indians have no traditions or ideal of independence. Their histories, which begin with slavery or more precisely since Emancipation a little over 100 years ago, are not calculated to inspire them with the strong desire for colonial liberation. Long colonial subjection and indoctrination have developed in them a feeling of dependency on outsiders. In the main, they seldom look to themselves for leadership and representation in their relations with the world. This is so because of no innate reason. It is the result of their conditioning.

The pamphlet has been presented in length, because it contains the central arguments Domingo brought forward against the federation. Moreover, it signalled that Domingo was prepared to openly criticize the PNP by exposing the contradiction between the party's original goal for self-government for Jamaica and the advocacy of a federation. The fundamental critique of the PNP's support of a federation with colonial status from an acknowledged pioneer of the demand for self-government, a respected and valued personality in the PNP, must have stirred discussions in the party. The allusion that the important monetary contribution from the Progressive League was always tied to the aim of reaching self-government for Jamaica in the shortest possible time was a bitter pill to swallow for the PNP.

While Domingo intensified his critique, the Progressive League now accepted federation as a given fact. In a general statement, the group declared: 'Federation, although deliberately excluded from among the objectives of the League, which are clearly and unequivocally stated in its Declaration of Principles of 1936, will be a reality in 1958'.[87] The recommendations that followed contained some general advice, for example, that the federation should be granted self-government, that its citizens enjoyed universal human rights and that discrimination should not prevent upward mobility. Although the document also contained references to the crucial role of the Progressive League in launching and financing the movement for self-government, it lacked any criticism of the question of representation, the site of the capital, the customs union or any other of the most controversial aspects of the design of the federation.

Meanwhile, the Colonial Office continued the course of parallel development of the federation and constitutional advancements in the single units. This led to the paradoxical situation that in January 1958, Jamaica became part of a federation with inferior constitutional status.[88]

In Jamaica, the general attitude toward federation changed. Fears increased that the newly achieved economic prosperity from the flourishing bauxite and tourism industries could be endangered. Especially in the JLP, voices against federation became more articulate, but concerns also grew in the ranks of the PNP. In this atmosphere, Domingo launched a second anti-federation pamphlet, 'Federation: Jamaica's Folly'. In the preface, Domingo expressed his regret that his arguments openly offended Manley:

> I find it especially painful to challenge the Federation views of Mr. N. W. Manley, whose great ability, devotion and sacrifices contributed much to the political awakening of Jamaicans. But principle and conviction count most with me. They come first and friendship can never, the far as I am concerned, supersede principles.[89]

Therefore, he felt obliged to encourage all Jamaicans to rethink their attitude, to express their concerns and to correct their country's mistake.

Domingo described an atmosphere of disillusionment in the region, in which the populations of the islands were starting to see the negative effects federation could have. For instance, he mentioned a statement by the *New York Times*' foreign correspondent from December 1957, who stated that 'the average citizen of Trinidad feels he has much to lose and nothing to gain from the federation'. He complained that an educational campaign only began after Jamaica had already joined the federation, when the leaders recognized that the general sentiment among Jamaicans was one of hostility or indifference. Hence, a 'team of influential federalists' sent on an educational tour throughout the island had done nothing more than to promote federation on the grounds of alleged benefits.

In his pamphlet, Domingo discussed four of the main arguments of the advocates of federation and rejected all assumptions as false and misleading. The first one was the claim that Jamaica could only achieve full nationhood in the context of the federation. Domingo responded by quoting from official British policy statements that had unmistakably argued in favour of self-government for the colonies no matter how small, without any requirement of federation. He further pointed to recent examples, such as Ghana, which recently had been granted independence, and pointed to other African examples he expected to follow soon.

Similar to his critique in the first pamphlet, Domingo reminded that the Progressive League's tremendous support for the PNP was meant to bring about Jamaican freedom, not federation. He remarked that the granting of universal suffrage, 'the greatest political revolution in the British West Indies since emancipation in 1834', had been achieved by the self-government movement before plans to form a federation had been discussed. Therefore, Domingo concluded, 'the assertion that Jamaican nationhood was possibly only through federation was self-evidently false'.

Domingo also denied the claim that Jamaica would benefit politically from federating with the other islands and argued that the contrary was true. Jamaica could be overridden by the federal legislature at any time, while the federation would not have more political rights than Jamaica would have as a sovereign nation. The third point addressed the alleged economic benefits. Domingo argued that this assumption was unrealistic and wishful thinking that lacked economic foundation. Because all of the islands produced similar products and dreamt of their own industrialization, there was nothing to gain from such a union. He further rejected the claim that federation would attract more foreign capital than the individual islands could on their own and pointed to Jamaica's example that showed that the island was able to draw investment.

Finally, Domingo discussed the argument that the federation would gain international recognition and prestige. He countered that as individual nations, the Caribbean islands would have more voices in the United Nations (UN) and thus receive more recognition. He alleged that Great Britain, with the same self-interest with which it had ruled the islands for centuries, now tried to impose a federation on them that was serving first and foremost British interests. Race played a major role in Domingo's argument. He challenged the widespread belief that racial harmony was a characteristic feature of the societies in the West Indies and favourably mentioned the analysis of some observers who argued that '...the existing state of affairs in the West Indies is due to the fact that the black majority unprotestingly accepts a status of social inferiority based on colour'.

Again, he pointed to the imperial identity and exposed the subtle methods with which the British had instilled the feeling of inferiority:

> Colonies occupy an inferior position in the world. Most colonial peoples of modern times have been non-Europeans. Their status of political inferiority vis-á-vis their so-called 'mother country' engendered a deep sense of racial self-deprecation. This feeling is deliberately cultivated and strengthened in colonials by the metropolitan country. It is instilled through educational systems, religion, historical laudation of the ruling nation, social seduction, and by more subtle means.

Furthermore, Domingo alleged that Great Britain acted in pure self-interest when it now attempted to decolonize the Empire. He asked provocatively:

> May it not be that the British gave their powerful support to Federation as a means of relieving themselves of further financial responsibility for the Caribbean colonies? May it not be, also, that the British, noted for their far-sightedness, realizing that colonialism is doomed and looking into the future that makes U.N. membership almost obligatory for new nations, cunningly encourage West Indians, a coloured people, to federate into one nation, thereby sharply limiting the political influence of coloured people in the world?

While the first speculation certainly contained a grain of truth, the second one seems to be a bit far-fetched; however, it shows the deep suspicion with which decided anti-colonialists like Domingo viewed Great Britain. He concluded: 'The inescapable logic of anti-colonialism is the attainment of independence. Any compromise with this objective serves the perpetuation of colonialism'.

Roberts also continued his agitation, although on a less radical level. In an article in the *Gleaner*, he presented his concept of 'Nationalist Liberalism'. Roberts deplored that federation was impeding the development toward self-government and blamed the PNP that it had allowed its nationalism to become dimmed by adopting Socialism. Both parties, he argued, were much too concerned with class interests, while they all lacked a decided nationalist approach. While he opposed a federation of the British islands, he was more open to regional conceptualizations: 'A closer association with other Caribbean lands, including free Cuba and Haiti, a league, a confederation, would be desirable'.[90] Like Domingo, Roberts blamed the long period of colonialism for the ready acceptance of Jamaicans to let others dictate their affairs. He warned: 'We are in danger of stolidly regarding for too long the Red House, Port of Spain, as a sort of replacement of the Colonial Office'.[91]

The statements of Roberts and Domingo show the continuity of their respective thinking. While Domingo emphasized racial and anti-colonial arguments, Roberts argued from a decidedly nationalist but still regional perspective that already had inspired his early thinking. Despite differences in argumentation, both of them could agree on one crucial point, a fiery nationalism that dictated an anti-colonial course to reach the objective of independence at the earliest time possible.

With their arguments against Jamaica's remaining in the federation, Roberts and Domingo indirectly played into the hands of Bustamante. Now that he found himself in the opposition, Bustamante discovered the benefits of opposing federation with a strong nationalist agitation, while the difficulties in the negotiations about the federal constitution provoked serious questions whether or not the project was able to succeed. In the wake of the federal elections to be held in March 1958 and the general elections in Jamaica in 1959, federation promised to be a suitable topic for Bustamante to regain popularity.[92] Voices against federation became more powerful, not only in the JLP. In the PNP, an increasing number of members voiced their concerns, among them Wills O. Isaacs, the party's popular vice president.[93]

In this situation, Manley decided not to run for the office of the Prime Minister of the federation, but to stay in Jamaica to safeguard that national feeling would not turn against the federation. Trevor Munroe emphasizes two important effects of the disagreement between the two parties in the run-up to the federal elections. It provoked the first public debate about federation and evinced the 'overwhelming apathy which the previous unanimity on the issue had both disguised and helped to perpetuate'.[94] The fact that the PNP lost the federal elections with 46 per cent of the votes, while Bustamante's campaign with the slogan 'if you vote for Manley he is going to sell you out to the small islands' found support of 54 per cent of the population was a first sign of the increased scepticism toward federation. However, with only 53.6 per cent the voter turnout was low and, in Munroe's words, 'evidence for popular unconcern'. Hugh W. Springer cames to a similar conclusion when he summarized: 'West Indian sentiment in Jamaica was a young and tender plant, at an early stage of growth and not well nourished'.[95]

In Jamaica, disinterest increasingly developed into grave concerns regarding the federal project. This trend was fortified when a statement by federal Prime Minister Grantley Adams demonstrated how federation might impact Jamaican affairs.[96] In October 1958, Adams announced that the federal government considered retroactive taxation for the period of the first five years, during which taxation was not included in the list of federal responsibility. Such statements further alienated the population and strengthened the position of critics in both parties. Shortly after the PNP lost the federal elections, Roberts felt sure: 'Both the established parties in Jamaica are shot through with sentiment for the reality of nationalist liberalism. Watch it grow. Secession, one way or another, is the sure climax'.[97] Roberts would eventually be right. However, Manley was not willing to accept that he and his pro-federation course were losing ground.

Roberts and Domingo continued their agitation, especially Domingo who wrote frequent letters to the press. Commenting on a radio broadcast by Manley in which he admitted that the country was undergoing a deep crisis over the question of the federation, Domingo deplored that Manley had not foreseen that the federation was 'on the verge…of disintegration'.[98] Domingo warned the PNP:

> Jamaicans are now awake to the menace that federation is to their future. The advisors of Sir Bustamante see the vote-catching value of organizing and responding to this Jamaican attitude. If Mr. Manley is to win the coming elections he had better take heed and show himself no less a good Jamaican than his rival. He may use more subtle methods and more dignified language but he cannot, if he hopes to win, give the impression that he is opposed to what is today the seemingly unanimous feeling of Jamaicans. That feeling is, I think, that Jamaica should get out of the Federation as soon as possible.[99]

In the run-up to the Jamaican general elections in summer 1959, Manley increasingly argued from a decidedly Jamaican perspective and criticized the practical developments in the federation.[100] For Domingo, this development was reason to hope that Federation could be stopped and Jamaica finally become independent on its own. In view of an upcoming conference scheduled for summer 1959 at which the constitution of the federation was to be revised, Domingo wrote optimistically:

> Now that the two leaders of the two political parties and, I presume, all other patriotic Jamaicans are united in their opposition to Jamaica being in the federation as it has revealed itself, I think it is high time that certain fateful decision be made.[101]

He felt it was a good sign, that Wills O. Isaacs, the 'well-known anti-federationist', was placed 'in the close council of Mr. Manley'. Jamaicans at home and abroad would now 'pray and hope that their island home will move on to the fulfilment of its national destiny and become an independent nation – not part of a glorified colony composed of irreconcilable elements'.

Finally, Domingo and Roberts ceased to stand alone with their critique on federation, with their complaints about the unfavourable representation and their fears that Jamaica and Trinidad and Tobago were meant to assume the Colonial Office's financial responsibility for the smaller islands. The general atmosphere turned increasingly hostile toward regional union. The advocates of federation were finally pressured to rethink their position and to provide good arguments why they believed in the advantages for Jamaica to remain in the federation. In this atmosphere, Ken Hill recommended consulting Domingo's second pamphlet. He emphasized that although it would not be necessary to agree with Domingo's judgment, '…his essential integrity and sincerity shine through brilliantly. In the current "re-check on Federation" it is worth careful reading'.[102]

The campaign for the general elections in 1959 showed that Domingo was right with his prediction that Manley needed to prove himself as a patriot. When Bustamante boasted that Jamaica would secede from the federation if the country's rights would not be safeguarded by a constitution to be agreed upon at a conference scheduled in September 1959, Manley made a similar statement.[103] Both parties had significantly radicalized their positions and now demanded equal representation in the federal legislature. Although the PNP won the general elections in July 1959, Manley was under pressure.

Commenting on the election campaign, Domingo claimed that because both parties now had similar positions regarding federation, the voters had decided on the basis of domestic issues and preferred the social programme of the PNP over the reactionary course of the JLP.[104] Indeed, at the Inter-Governmental Conference in Port of Spain in September and October 1959, which aimed to ratify revisions of the constitution, both parties' representatives formed a bloc defending Jamaica's national interests. As a result of the radically changed approach of the Jamaican delegation, which now demanded more adequate representation in the legislature, the conference turned into a bitter confrontation.[105] It ended prematurely, with the sudden departure of the Jamaican delegation.[106] After the island had achieved full internal self-government in 1959, Jamaica was even less prepared to withstand the increasing pressure of those who opposed federation in the fear that it would curtail the recently granted freedom. Munroe is therefore right when he surmises: 'This was one sign that the parallel lines of decolonization – regionalization on the one level and territorial advance on the other – were heading towards each other and threatening political deadlock'.[107]

'At the Crossroads of Destiny': The Referendum

At the end of the 1950s, the Federation was in a deep crisis, even before it developed any stability. The leadership style of Federal Prime Minister Grantley Adams did not help the Federation to gain popularity. Domingo reported on a meeting in New York, at which Adams made awkward statements that further exacerbated the tensions, such as claiming that Trinidadians loved Calypso more than work or that Jamaica's illiteracy rate was so high that adequate numerical representation was not desirable. Such inept leadership alienated even strong advocates of federation, like the Barbadian Richard B. Moore, and delivered more arguments for the critics of federation.[108]

Domingo was convinced that the time was ripe to launch a campaign for a referendum in Jamaica that should decide whether Jamaica should remain in the federation. At the end of October 1959, he shared his idea in a letter to Roberts: 'I am asking for a Referendum, using the demand as propaganda against the leadership that insists on our remaining in the artificial union'.[109] He pointed to how Adams' blundering statements played into the hands of the anti-federationists:

> Last Sunday I had the League pass tendentious resolutions I had written denouncing Adams insults to Jamaica....Even the pro-federationists in the League had to support the resolution or stand revealed as being more for the Federation than for their country.

Domingo gathered from his sources in Jamaica that his exposure of Adams's statements 'occasioned considerable interest and discussion' on the island. He assured Roberts that he was prepared to turn against his friends and former co-workers and insisted: 'For my part, I have no friends where principle is concerned and the matter of Jamaica becoming free is to me the greatest principle conceivable and I have dedicated myself to do my best to bring that result about'. Especially in the PNP, Domingo's critique had a considerable impact. He recalled: 'I have begun to train my guns on Manley, not as a person, but as a politician. When his son Michael was here he made a couple of remarks to me that made me realise that they feel the effects of my constant hammering away at the Federation issue'. Yet, Domingo felt it would be of advantage to detach the question from party loyalties and suggested that a non-partisan movement should be formed to lobby for secession from the federation.

Two days later, Domingo placed a big advertisement in the *Gleaner* under the headline: 'Do You Want Jamaica To Remain in the Federation? Now is the time for a Referendum' and insisted: 'Our country is at the crossroads of its destiny'.[110] He pointed to the evident difficulties in the federal negotiations and alleged that the other units in the federation followed their 'undisguised aim of using the Federation as a means of exploiting Jamaican resources for their benefit'. He blamed the Jamaican leaders for having ignored the warnings against the 'unnatural' and 'unholy alliance' of islands, which shared little more commonalities than the fact that they were British colonies. He legitimized the call for a referendum with the argument: 'Jamaica joined the federation at the dictation of its political leaders who did not consult the people. They acted without study or understanding and solely because of sentiment. Responsible statesmen do not allow their emotions to dominate them'. Although it was true that the people had not been asked, such a statement was in fact an insult to both parties' leaders.

Domingo claimed that without federation, the country had been able to achieve internal self-government. Provocatively, he asked: 'Are we inferior people that we should be satisfied with partial control of our destiny, or should we not prove ourselves to be real men and women and move on to COMPLETE NATIONAL FREEDOM?' Domingo referred to the time he spent in detention and urged in an emotional ply: 'My fellow countrymen, I appeal to you as one who fought and sacrificed 20 months of his freedom for his country and countrymen, to agitate for a REFERENDUM'. Domingo was optimistic that a referendum would have the desired effect: 'I firmly believe that Jamaica's best interest will be served by our country voting to LEAVE THE FEDERATION. Such a vote will be a MANDATE for Jamaica to continue its fight for FULL FREEDOM'.

This advertisement was the most radical and populist piece in Domingo and Roberts' campaign. It provoked harsh critique from pro-federationists and instigated a public debate in the *Gleaner* between Domingo and Christopher B. Hills, a wealthy and renowned gallerist and author. On the very next day, the *Gleaner* carried a letter from Hills, in which he outlined that federation was the only practical way forward and asked Domingo:

> Why don't you stop theorising up there in New York and come and do some hard work in your own country. This country needs builders and pioneers to do the work. It has enough people theorizing for it already.[111]

A long and detailed debate followed, in which Hills appealed to feelings of 'unity and Christian brotherhood' and accused Domingo of 'selfish nationalism'.[112]

Domingo was not the only one who opposed federation and demanded that the people should decide. Three days before Domingo's advertisement appeared, James Gore, entrepreneur and past president of the Jamaican Manufacturers Association, wrote a lengthy letter to the *Gleaner* editor in which he demanded: 'Put the federal issue to the vote'.[113]

The strong and emotional nationalist appeal of ex-PNP activist Domingo was grist on the mills of the JLP and caused further friction in the PNP. In a review of the year 1959, *Gleaner* columnist 'Scrutator' commented on the situation of the PNP and pointed to strengthening anti-federation sentiments within the party. He commented that Isaacs' increasing popularity helped the party to win the recent elections despite the fact that he made no secret that he opposed federation, although he officially conformed to the party line. 'Scrutator' claimed that Isaacs was backed by a number of influential businessmen who were eager to prevent any form of customs union to protect Jamaica's trading interests. Due to Isaacs' rising power, Manley had decided against leaving Jamaica for joining federal politics. He pointed to the potentially deteriorating effect to the PNP of Domingo's agitation: when 'anybody inside it makes a stand on principles, particularly if the principle can be recognized by any large number of party supporters as the 'good old cause', the very thing they started out to do'.[114] In regard to Domingo's advertisement for a referendum, Scrutator remarked:

> From this point of view the most startling event of the year was something which the public scarcely realised as an event at all. Mr. W. A. Domingo, who has always opposed Federation from New York, as something at variance with the whole idea of Jamaican nationalism, suddenly published an advertisement here calling on all Jamaicans to rally against Federation. Would a man like Domingo take such a step unless he meant to take others? Does he intend to return to Jamaica and take an active part in organizing a secession movement on the grounds of principle?[115]

A few days after the advertisement appeared in the *Gleaner*, Roberts congratulated Domingo and assured him: 'I am with you in every aspect of this fight. The majority of Jamaicans is disillusioned with the Federation, if not yet actively hostile' and agreed that 'the referendum would be the fair and logical step to take now'.[116]

Roberts felt that Manley tried to employ a tactic of small steps and commented: 'This is not altogether visionary on his part, because national sentiment here is not strong. The job is to arouse it again, even as the self-government-movement aroused it at the start in 1936–1939.'[117]

This quote demonstrates the significance that Roberts and Domingo attached to their campaign against federation by putting it in direct line with their early campaign for self-government. Moreover, Roberts' diagnosis of a lack of nationalism is important for our analysis. Nationalism was still not deeply rooted and was not easily aroused by a campaign against federation, although the federation was not altogether popular. The widespread indifference regarding political questions had seemingly not changed much after a short-lived surge before the Second World War.

Roberts blamed Manley that he 'is no longer a nationalist leader. He is what was called in the Irish struggle a "Home Ruler"'[118] and complained that Manley was still attached to British ideals. In another letter to Domingo, he confided:

> My confidence in Manley as a statesman has been ebbing for some time. He is an honest and efficient administrator, primarily interested in social welfare, but as a leader he is disappointing, being too much of a Socialist at heart to care greatly about national patriotism.[119]

The evidence presented throughout this work supports Roberts' claim that Manley's nationalism was dominated by moderate views, except for short and limited radicalized periods, for example, after Domingo's detention. This attitude was a source of frequent disappointments to the Progressive League leaders, who continued to feel isolated with their anti-colonial demands. Now, they started to feel optimistic that the question of federation was able to inflame nationalist feelings. Roberts shared Domingo's optimism regarding the outcome of a desirable referendum. He recognized that Manley's stand was weakening and gladly noted that with Arnett and Isaacs, Manley had appointed two anti-federalists in his cabinet.[120]

Like 'Scrutator', Roberts interpreted the advertisement as Domingo's decision to return to Jamaica.[121] Domingo's skills as a mass orator would probably have been helpful in the anti-federal campaign. Yet, Domingo did not return to Jamaica and the sources do not provide information as to whether or not he considered this step.

However, the future development shows that his return was not necessary to bring about the desired referendum. An increasing number of JLP members and prominent businessmen started to call for a revision of the decision to stay in the federation. In November, JLP member Linden Newland, pressed in the Legislative Council for a referendum to decide whether Jamaica should stay in the federation.[122] At this point in time, Manley opted to avoid the risk and also Bustamante and other leading members in the JLP decided to continue negotiating a constitution for the federation that would not be harmful to Jamaica's interests.[123]

Slowly, Bustamante's tactic to style himself as the guardian of Jamaica's interest was challenged by Manley, who had taken up a similar pro-Jamaican stand in the federal negotiations.[124] Manley's stiffened attitude provoked further alienation between him and the rest of the leaders in the federation. Domingo recognized with satisfaction:

> Mr. Manley, heeding the voice of his country and recognizing the blundering tactics of the leaders of the Eastern Caribbean, found it comparatively easy to outsmart them. It must have been a difficult personal task for Mr. Manley to change the opinions he held on Federation twelve years ago, but he proved his Jamaican patriotism and his willingness to face facts.[125]

In January 1960, Manley went to London to discuss the way forward and to prevent that Dominion status was granted before the federal government had agreed on the final structure of the federation and ratified its constitution.[126] During informal conversations with the Colonial Office, Manley was given the assurance that the British government would not object to the granting of Dominion status for the island, should Jamaica find it necessary to secede from the federation.[127] While this knowledge strengthened Manley's efforts to impose his positions on the set-up of the federation on the other leaders, Bustamante destroyed Manley's plan with a new coup. On May 30, when the JLP should have nominated a candidate for a by-election in the federal parliament, Bustamante suddenly announced that his party abstained from replacing the vacant seat and that the JLP was committed to achieve Jamaica's secession from the federation as soon possible. Immediately, Manley decided to suggest to his cabinet to take up the challenge and to hold a referendum as soon as the federal constitution was accepted in its final terms.

Roberts informed Domingo about the recent developments and wrote: 'Yes, we may surely take some of the credit – and you in particular – for Manley having been forced to concede a referendum on Federation'.[128] Although the immediate trigger for Manley's decision was Bustamante's spontaneous withdrawal of his party's support for the federation, the internal conflicts in the PNP that Domingo had helped to aggravate demanded a radical reaction.

In the following federal negotiations, the referendum was a powerful weapon for Manley that forced the leaders to let Jamaica's proposals through on the nod. Supported by Eric Williams who understood Jamaica's situation and was willing to concede considerable compromises to save the federation, Manley was able to succeed with most of his demands. However, the victory had a make-believe character, because the most controversial questions of taxation and self-determination of the units over industrial development was referred to another conference in London. British officials and many of the other leaders were disappointed with the result and the displayed lack of enthusiasm for the federal project.[129] However, on his return to Jamaica, Manley announced: 'We have succeeded in getting all the changes and safeguards we had promised Jamaica to

Opposing the West Indies Federation

secure – Jamaica can go forward in safety'.[130] Finally, Jamaica was granted a de facto veto on matters of taxation and industrial development for Jamaica included in the constitution, so Manley was optimistic that the referendum should be won. Nevertheless, the JLP now waged a furious fight against the federation.

The conflict over federation was fought out on party lines and the rivalry overshadowed earnest considerations of the subject. Domingo's suggestion to detach the question from being a matter of party loyalty, as mentioned in the above quoted letter to Roberts, was therefore only logical. Roberts took up the idea and launched an eye-catching advertisement in the *Gleaner* on July 20, in which he recommended to vote against the federation in the upcoming referendum and declared: 'As a historian I have repeatedly warned against the dangers of the proposed weak, deceptive and paralysing so-called union. An attack on a broader front is now needed'.[131] He summarized why the federation was negative for Jamaica and announced a series of broadcasts, sponsored by the 'Save Jamaica Volunteer Non-Partisan Group', in which he would further elaborate his position.

In a column in the *Gleaner*, the 'Political Reporter' remarked: 'Two new groups joined the general melee as the battle for the Referendum grows apace, one spearheaded by that doyen of Jamaican writers W. Adolphe Roberts and the other by adopted son Christopher Hills'.[132] The same Christopher B. Hills who had taken up his pen against Domingo after he had called for the referendum now countered Roberts' effort with the launch of a pro-federation group, 'The Atlantic Federal Union – A Non-Partisan Group'.[133] He answered Roberts' advertisement by publishing one himself in which he declared that 'Nationalism is dead for all time'[134] and pleaded for unity and brotherly love in a world which he saw developing toward a world government.

However, the allegedly non-partisan approach was rather wishful thinking than reality, as Roberts admits in his autobiography. He recalled:

> A representative of Bustamante's Labour Party approached me and asked me to speak on their side, in opposition. I answered that I would not support Bustamante directly, but if any one wished to arrange radio time for me as an independent it would not matter to me who paid for it. This was finally agreed upon.[135]

Hills, on the other hand, was a close friend of the Manley family and sympathized with the PNP.[136]

In six radio broadcasts that were heavily advertised in the *Gleaner*, Roberts aimed to reach out to broader sections of the society and presented his arguments why Jamaica should vote against the federation in detail. Explaining the 'non-partisan' nature of the campaign, Roberts said:

> I wish to emphasize the point that I am neither a member of an existing Jamaican political party nor affiliated with any one of them. I am a native born Jamaican, having the interest of the Island passionately at heart, and these interests can best be served by an absolutely non-partisan attitude.[137]

In the announcement to the broadcasts, Roberts emphasized the original purpose of the nationalist movement he pioneered had always been national independence, and not for Jamaica to become an underrepresented member of a 'burlesque Federation'. He suspected that the federation would not be able to sustain itself, so that Jamaica would have to carry the financial burden of the bankrupt small islands.[138]

In the first broadcast, Roberts remembered how the founders of the Progressive League discussed whether federation was a suitable way to bring about self-government, but had abandoned the idea as visionary. Roberts criticized that when the plan to form a federation was introduced after the Second World War, 'It was inspired largely by the Colonial Office itself, backed by various English interests as well as by certain Jamaican and regional leaders'.[139] Roberts then went into the details of the particular design of the federation and why it was opposed to the interests of Jamaica. He repeated all his arguments against federation: the disproportionate representation, the great distances between the islands, overpopulation of the islands without territories included to provide an outlet, and the slowdown that federation meant for Jamaica's independence. Roberts pointed to the fact that the special needs and demands of Jamaica and Trinidad and Tobago as the two powerful players would weaken the whole federation; no matter how justified they may be for the single countries.

Roberts felt that in the future, a Caribbean League under the umbrella of the Organization of American States (OAS), a voluntarily association of various independent states in the region, including not only English-speaking countries, was in the realm of possibilities. However, first he encouraged Jamaicans to reject the proposed federation and 'to proceed to the building of their own national home'.

The main argument Roberts presented in this broadcast displayed the continuity with Roberts' long-held principles, particularly his nationalism that was framed by the expectation of regional cooperation transcending the limitations of the British Empire. Further continuity was embodied in Roberts' lengthy anti-Communist remarks. Against voices who saw in the federation a safeguard against Communist tendencies in the region, for example, in Cuba and in British Guiana, Roberts argued:

> A people that is on its own, conscious of shaping itself into a new nation, and taking pride in the achievement would be far less likely to

Opposing the West Indies Federation 407

go 'red' that a state that had already surrendered part of its individuality in a toy union.

In the second broadcast, Roberts pointed to geographical factors like the different size of the units, the distances between them and the lack of hinterlands that could be developed to meet the challenge of overpopulation, pointing again to the two-federation solution that he would have preferred.[140] In the third broadcast, Roberts explicated the economic aspects of federation and pointed to the disastrous financial situation of the smaller islands and complained that Jamaica and Trinidad and Tobago would have to carry the burden that the crown's exchequer had tired of carrying.[141] This was a legitimate argument. The financial sustainability of the federal union constantly worried the Colonial Office, and many reports, memos and assessments addressed this problem.[142]

In the fourth broadcast, Roberts explicated the argument that the expected economic benefits from federation were an illusion, and argued that the islands were in fact competitors with similar products for similar markets.[143] The fifth broadcast countered the argument presented by the PNP that federation was 'the cheapest and quickest way to become independent'.[144] Roberts contended: 'I deny that Jamaica is offered full and true independence. She is being asked to sink her identity to a large extent, and to diminish the inspirational value of her name'. In another broadcast, Roberts laid down the argument that from the earliest ideas of federation in the Colonial Office, they were always designed to relieve 'the British taxpayer of the necessity of aiding distressed colonies'.[145] Further, he quoted at length from critical remarks of British officials, who were sceptical about the possible success of the West Indian Federation. In the last broadcast, Roberts showed his optimism that Domingo's and his own campaign helped to inspire nationalist feelings in Jamaica and to swell the ranks of those who opposed federation: 'The pioneers continue their fight, and are backed by tens of thousands of the young generation'. He conjured up this feeling and asserted:

> There is a tendency nowadays to give nationalism a bad name, especially in circles where Socialist ideas are dominant. But the fact remains eternally true that nationalism embodies the power to stir men and women to the depths of their beings, as no other political doctrine can do.[146]

In this final instalment, Roberts pointed to the complications of the racial composition of the population in the islands. He claimed that the large groups of East Indians in the Eastern Caribbean feared large waves of Afro-Caribbean settlers from islands like Jamaica. While the eastern islands were likely to federate, Roberts demanded, 'Jamaica must stand alone in the West'. Concluding, Roberts stated: 'I have consistently advised you to vote "No", and in this I have had the support of thousands. If my arguments have convinced many others who were hesitating, I shall be grateful'.[147]

With his broadcasts, Roberts had found a means to reach out to larger audiences and to explain his arguments in detail, although the accessibility was still limited to the wealthier Jamaicans. In addition to Roberts, Domingo also made use of the opportunity and spoke in a radio broadcast from New York, sponsored by the same non-partisan group. In the announcement, Domingo was described as the 'most active in the building of the independence movement which at first took the form of the founding of the People's National Party'.[148] The fiery opposition toward the PNP was especially delicate for Domingo. He and Roberts frequently emphasized that the PNP had left the common course toward national liberation. They stressed their stand on principles and their own pioneer role for the movement, knowing quite well how much impact this would have, especially on the members of the PNP. It was nevertheless uncomfortable for Domingo to turn his back on his former co-workers. In a letter to the *Gleaner* in August 1961, in which he disproved the argument of a PNP pamphlet that argued for federation he stated:

> I know the leaders of the PNP very well. I consider them my friends, but I am opposed, as a Jamaican, to the course they are pursuing for our country. I worked hard for the PNP when I was in Jamaica. I worked hard for it in New York, helping to raise thousands of dollars for self-government. I did not sacrifice for Federation, which I regard as unnecessary for Jamaica even though it might be necessary for other peoples.[149]

Domingo pointed out that before 1945, the PNP and the Progressive League had been united in the demand for national independence, and that he only learned recently that Manley claimed that he had favoured federation since 1938. Despite his regret for the need to oppose the PNP, Domingo welcomed the effect of his propaganda on the position of the federation critics within the party. However, the sources do not reveal how Domingo felt when Bustamante explicitly capitalized on this effect in an anti-federation advertisement in the *Gleaner* that appeared before the referendum, in which the JLP leader claimed:

> The person who has changed is Mr. Manley. He fought for years, night and day, to get independence for Jamaica on his own – not in Federation. His party received thousands of Progressive League of New York [sic!], and other sources, to back his party's stand for complete independence for Jamaica. But lo! and behold, the greed for more power has darkened his eyes, and today he does not want independence for Jamaica, instead he wants to enslave us in a farcical Federation to be ruled by the small islands.[150]

Although employing another tone, Bustamante used similar arguments as Roberts and Domingo and benefited from their anti-federation campaign. Finally, Bustamante, the old reliable opponent of self-government, had fully grasped the value of a decided national stand with which he could challenge the PNP, defeating it with its own nationalist arguments of the old days.

In the days before the referendum, Domingo and Roberts repeated their arguments in numerous letters and articles in the press.[151] On September 19, 1961, the people of Jamaica decided whether they wished to remain in the federation. Of the eligible voters 61.6 per cent casted their ballot; 54.1 per cent voted against remaining in the federation, while 45.9 per cent wished to stay.[152] A majority of the pro-federal votes was collected in traditionally PNP-dominated areas Kingston, St Andrew and Port Royal, whereas the majority of the voters in the countryside, where the JLP was traditionally strong, had voted against federation.[153]

After hearing about the outcome of the referendum over the radio, Domingo exclaimed in a letter to Roberts: 'Jamaica can now march forward to achieve the independence that you, O'Meally, Burrell and myself dreamt of and worked for'.[154]

Although they had reached their goal, Domingo felt sorry for Manley and reflected on their own contribution to bring about the desired result of the referendum:

> He [Manley] has spoiled a brilliant career with his obsession for Federation. Of course, I firmly believe that latterly he allowed his ambition to get the better of his judgment and patriotism. I have received many congratulations over the phone. Many people know of my uncompromising stand, also of yours. I may over-rate our contribution, but I believe your articles and broadcasts had a lot to do with the outcome.[155]

Domingo felt confirmed in his tactic 'to wean away some PNP members who, no matter how much they admire Manley, would not follow him into destruction'.[156] It is difficult to judge which impact Domingo and Roberts' agitation in fact exerted on the decision against the referendum. However, Domingo's agitation certainly helped to encourage a number of PNP members and voters to oppose the party line when he argued that their position was not in contrast to the PNP's original aims.

Were Domingo and Roberts right in their suspicions that federation was primarily a means for Great Britain to get rid of the responsibility for the unprofitable islands? Minutes prepared in the Colonial Office by Lord Perth, shortly before the referendum, suggests that this was indeed a strong motive. Lord Perth stated that a possible withdrawal of Jamaica from the federation would signify 'a major failure of our colonial policy', while he called the Caribbean a 'constant and considerable drain'.[157] A draft memorandum of April 1941 contains further illuminating comments on the British colonial policy in the region:

> The Caribbean is an area of the world where there are no vital United Kingdom interests and few strategic considerations, and where our fundamental aim in the area since 1945 has been political disengagement. This being so our principal objective following secession by Jamaica must be to avoid any situation which results in our being left with any of the of the present federated territories on our hands for which we can see no obvious future except as colonies.[158]

David Killingray comes to a similar conclusion when he reflects on the situation of the Empire in the early 1960s: 'Colonies were increasingly a political and international embarrassment and in the economic climate of 1961 a heavier financial burden; London was anxious to rid itself of both'.[159]

In the eyes of Ian Macleod, Secretary of State for the Colonies, the outcome of the referendum was simply a 'most grievous blow to the Federal ideal for which we and enlightened West Indian opinion have striven for so many years. It is certain that the Federation cannot continue in its present form and it is doubtful whether it can survive it all'.[160] Macleod was right in his suspicion. After Jamaica was granted independence, Trinidad and Tobago followed suit. Eric Williams expressed his disappointment with the form of the federation enforced by Jamaica's uncompromising stand in face of the referendum and was not willing to let Trinidad and Tobago carry the burden.[161] All efforts to federate the remaining eight colonies around Barbados as a centre likewise failed. While most of the islands became independent, a few small islands remained part of Great Britain, still depending on financial support.[162]

In preparation for Jamaica's independence, a new constitution was hastily put together by a committee consisting of representatives of the political elites of the colony. The constitution represented continuity of the established political order rather than radical change and was implemented without consultation of the populace. In Munroe's eyes, this practice had the effect that the widespread indifference and the attitude of accepting to be ruled by strong leaders were not questioned by the masses.[163]

A few months before the country would be granted independence, the PNP lost the general elections. Of the 72 per cent voter turn out, the PNP received 48.6 per cent and the JLP 50 per cent. This meant in fact that Bustamante, who had opposed the demands for self-government for the longest time, was elected to become the first Prime Minister of independent Jamaica. In a letter to the press Domingo commented on the reasons for the PNP's defeat. He saw the main reason in the party's support for federation and the contradiction this attitude meant in regards to the party's tradition. Not only had the majority of the populace rejected this stand, but also a considerable number of PNP members, Domingo attested. He complimented the

> ...large number of members of the PNP [who] refused to follow their leaders and either stayed home or voted with their conscience in the referendum which placed them squarely in the ranks of anti-federationists. These people were not disloyal to their convictions or to their highest party ideals. They were loyal to Jamaica. Indeed, the party for years had preached Jamaican nationalism and made great sacrifices for it.[164]

Some of the previous co-workers of Roberts and Domingo felt that Domingo's position was a detour from an emancipatory, internationally inspired anti-colonialism. Many of Domingo's close friends in New York were surprised to learn that he bitterly opposed federation. One of them was his good friend Richard B. Moore, with whom he had already disagreed on the question of participation in the Second World War. Back then, mutual respect ensured that the disagreement did not affect their friendship; in the course of events, Moore and others even changed their minds and adopted Domingo's position. Now, the disagreement would last and leave Moore perplexed about Domingo's stand. In 1962, shortly after the independence celebrations in Jamaica, Moore wrote an essay in which he explained that he could not fully rejoice over Jamaica's independence, because it had been achieved at the cost of destroying the federation, and thus, so he believed, a formerly shared vision of the WINC members including Domingo. We saw earlier, that Domingo might have obscured his true feelings about federation in the early 1940s, while in the letters to Roberts and Campbell he had always been frank about the motives behind forming the Committee and had distanced himself from any plans for a federation. Probably this was the reason why Moore now felt that Domingo had changed his mind. Moore claimed that Domingo's opposition played an important role in breaking up the federation:

> One of the worst things that happened was the distribution in Jamaica of two pamphlets written and sent from here by W. A. Domingo. In these pamphlets this former progressive advocate of Federation now opposed it by appealing to the worst reactionary narrow, insular, and base passions of the most backward of the people of Jamaica. Unfortunately, no counter action was taken by any Jamaica-born supporter of federation here to mitigate the effect of Domingo's harmful propaganda.[165]

Similar accusations that Domingo advocated an insular and narrow nationalism were frequently raised in the press. Another example is Jamaican-born author Jervis Anderson, who also belonged to the Caribbean migrant scene in Harlem. He wrote in the *Gleaner* in January 1961:

> How unkind is time to some of our liberal socialists! Take Mr. Domingo, a man, who…was brought up in the nurture and admonition of liberal politics. By refusing to budge from the kind of narrow nationalism that was eminently suited to the Jamaican circumstances of his time he is now almost creaking with conservatism.…he would call the country's leadership away from its new liberal regional spirit. Mr. Domingo's nationalism…was the kind that sought the end of British imperialism and the beginning of local pride. Pride has come and imperialism for all practical purposes in Jamaica is dead. So should be the old Domingo nationalism.[166]

Anderson admitted that nationalism was a useful and legitimate instrument against imperialism, yet, he felt that turning it against a 'new West Indianism' was regressive at a time in which the world was allegedly 'turning once and for all to internationalism, to daring innovations of thought designed to meet the new challenges and the new people of a new time' and concluded: 'Old insular pride is also dead'.[167]

To Domingo's fellow migrants in New York, it was surprising that he had chosen the nationalist road, although his radicalism was rooted in the very same milieu of West Indian and African American anti-colonial thought in which they all had common political roots. However, for Domingo, the striving for Jamaica's independence was part of the same broader goal of putting an end to colonialism like the federation was for its advocates. He frequently stressed the inspiring effect which creating a nation of predominately black inhabitants in the Caribbean would have on the other islands. From a Jamaican perspective, the advantages of federation were not self-evident. A federation with the distant, comparably small and poor islands in the eastern Caribbean with possible negative effects on Jamaica's economic and political development was not particularly attractive. Thus, the nationalists Domingo and Roberts put in a last strong and finally successful effort to prevent their goal of an independent Jamaica being sacrificed for a federation with uncertain benefit for the country.

The open opposition to the PNP's stand on the question of federation and the acceptance that the Progressive League's nationalist stand had played into the hands of Bustamante and the JLP provide a last and very powerful demonstration of the fact that for Roberts and Domingo, nationalism was the one and only guiding principle behind all political activities, behind every alliance and behind all tactical considerations. For them, it overshadowed all individual political inclinations, demanded high personal sacrifices and justified all measures to make Jamaica an independent nation.

Nationalist Stance

That neither Roberts nor Domingo expressed any interest in starting a new party or running for public office in Jamaica testifies to their disappointment in the local scene. Still, they were drawn out for one last and highly political campaign to ensure that their long-time goal of Jamaica's independence was finally achieved. Both men fiercely rejected the Colonial Office's post-war policy that planned to bundle the British possessions in the Caribbean into one political entity. This opposition characterizes a coherent development of the nationalist position of the two main Progressive League leaders and can be regarded as the high-water mark of their nationalist activities. At the same time, it provoked the break with many previous political co-workers and close friends that once more showed that Jamaican anti-colonial nationalism was not yet deeply rooted in the leadership of the PNP.

Although the Progressive League leaders were not the only opponents, their powerful campaign was one of the earliest and most powerful stands against the Federation. From early on, Roberts and Domingo repudiated the Colonial Office's plans as a cunning effort to slow the movement toward self-government, to satisfy US and local pressure by offering the prospect of eventual Dominion status for the Federation, and at the same time, to rid itself of the financial burden of the less profitable colonies. It is proof that nationalism was stronger outside of the colony than in Jamaica. The PNP, and initially Bustamante and the JLP as well, decided to accept the plans of the Colonial Office. The decision reflected the political leaders' strong attachment to Great Britain and the will to believe in Britain's unselfish motives. In the long tradition of political apathy of the masses, both parties did not attempt to actively involve the populace in the process of deciding about the political future of the island. Such a behaviour indicates how strong mentalities and traditions were, among both the local leaders and the masses.

Even shortly before Jamaica was granted independence, neither West Indian nor insular Jamaican nationalism had become deeply rooted in Jamaica. In accordance with the thesis that the migration experience predisposed the emigrants for nationalist ideas, both nationalist concepts had rather taken particularly strong roots in the migrant communities in New York. In Jamaica, the reactions to, or, more precisely, the ignorance toward the federal plans is remarkable. Despite the heavy nationalist propaganda of the Progressive League, nationalism was not a strong force in the shaping of the events. Manley withdrew from nationalist demands, and Bustamante adopted a strong nationalist position only when it promised to increase his popularity after the negotiations revealed the grave difficulties the federation would face, the potential disadvantages for

Jamaica and increasing doubts in the population as to whether federation would be of advantage to their economic situation.

Contrary to the Progressive League's hope, the masses had not yet started to regard nationalist demands as a means to achieve improved living conditions. Although anti-federal sentiment was increasing in the late 1950s, nationalist feeling was not particularly strong. Trying once more to reinforce nationalism in Jamaica, Roberts and Domingo knew that they were engaged in a difficult task. Similar to the situation in the early days of the movement, their propaganda influenced some of the politically active intellectuals more than it reached out to the masses. Even by the time the referendum was called on whether Jamaica should remain in the federation or become independent on its own, no strong nationalist mass movement had developed and the masses were largely indifferent to both forms of nationalism. This indifference revealed the general apathy of the masses, but also showed how much Jamaicans still adhered to British colonial designs.

Historians draw different conclusions from the episode of federation. While Springer claims that the federation had provoked a 'clash of nationalisms',[168] Munroe rejects such an interpretation. The observations in this work affirm Munroe's claims that the masses were largely indifferent to both forms of nationalism. Munroe is therefore right when he concludes that the referendum showed that '[i]ndifference to Federation was greater than an indifference to Jamaican nationhood....'[169] Analysing the reasons for the general indifference toward the country's political fate, Munroe points to the long tradition of non-participation of the masses under colonialism. In his eyes, middle-class political leadership had done little to change this fact. The personality-cult dominated politics of Bustamante and Manley inhibited the development of more democratic involvement. While this is surely one aspect of the explanation, the powerful legacy of colonialism that had been indoctrinated into the minds of many Jamaicans and resulted in a deep identification with and loyalty to the Empire needs to be taken into account in explaining why both forms of nationalism did not attract and stimulate a mass-based movement. In Roberts' words: 'Federation arouses no enthusiasm on its own account, but at least causes Jamaicans to think about an exterior question as affecting their interests as a country, not a colony'.[170]

It is therefore no surprise that agitation against a colonial mindset was a constantly recurring feature of the propaganda of the Progressive League, and that it also played an important role in Roberts and Domingo's final nationalist campaign. Shortly before independence was achieved, the emigrants still seemed to be ahead of local feeling. Nevertheless, the Progressive League leaders once again influenced the course of affairs and contributed to the fact that their dream was finally fulfilled when Jamaicans thwarted the British plans and voted to leave the Federation, so that the country eventually became independent in August 1962.

Notes

1. S.R. Ashton and David Killingray, eds., *British Documents on the End of Empire: The West Indies*, Series B, Vol. 6 (London: Stationery Office, 1999), xliv.
2. Parker, 'Remapping the Cold War', 324.
3. For a detailed account on the development of the idea of federation in the Eastern Caribbean see, Alomar, *Revisiting the Transatlantic Triangle*; Hugh W. Springer, *Reflections on the Failure of the First West Indian Federation*. Reprint ed. (New York, 1973), 1–11.
4. Eric E. Duke, 'The Diasporic Dimensions of British Caribbean Federation.' *New West Indian Guide* 83 (2009): 219–48.
5. Joyce Moore Turner, and W. Burghardt Turner, *Richard B. Moore, Caribbean Militant in Harlem: Collected Writings 1920-1972* (Bloomington: Indiana University Press, 1988), 69–91.
6. W. Adolphe Roberts, 'British West Indian Aspirations.' *Current History* 40 (1934): 552–56.
7. *Daily Gleaner*, December 7, 1937.
8. Ibid.
9. Ibid., December 31, 1937.
10. Ibid.
11. Ibid., September 14, 1938.
12. Ibid., January 9, 1939.
13. Ibid., September 23, 1937.
14. Domingo to Campbell, August 15, 1940, JA, NMP, 4/60/2A/2.
15. Domingo to Arnett, December 2, 1940, JA, NMP, 4/60/2A/2.
16. Domingo to Arnett, January 24, 1941, JA, NMP, 4/60/2A/2.
17. Tony Martin republished Eric Williams's publication of the lectures and discussion at the conference, see Tony Martin, ed. *The Economic Future of the Caribbean* (Dover: The Majority Press, 2004).
18. Roberts, 'The Future of Colonialism in the Caribbean: The British West Indies', *Economic Future*, 37.
19. Roberts, 'Future of Colonialism', 39.
20. Extract Royal Commission Report, undated [early 1940], PRO, CO, 137/843/1.
21. Jason C. Parker, *Brother's Keeper: The United States, Race, and Empire in the British Caribbean, 1937-1962* (Oxford: Oxford University Press, 2008), 65.
22. *Public Opinion*, January 5, 1945.
23. Richard Hart, *Time for a Change: Constitutional, Political and Labour Developments in Jamaica and Other Colonies in the Caribbean Region, 1944-1955* (Kingston: Arawak Publications, 2004) 22. Although Hart and Manley were both not exactly sure how the subject came up, Manley stated in a letter to Hart '…I was very nearly the first to have ideas about Federation just as I remained almost the last to support it wholeheartedly'.
24. For a more detailed discussion of Meikle's ideas see Duke, 'Diasporic Dimensions', 227f.
25. Hart, *Time for a Change*, 22. *Public Opinion*, June 2, 1944.
26. Hart, *Time for a Change*, 22; Hart, *Towards Decolonisation*, 295.
27. *Daily Gleaner*, February 8, 1959.

28. For a detailed account of the CLC conference, see Hart, *Time for a Change*, 24.
29. Interview by the author with Richard Hart, Brighton, July 2, 2007.
30. Moore Turner and Turner, eds., *Richard B. Moore*, 69–91.
31. *Public Opinion*, October 29, 1945.
32. Domingo to Roberts, May 27, 1940, NLJ, WAR, MS 353, Box 2b.
33. Domingo to Roberts, August 2, 1940, NLJ, WAR, MS 353, Box 2b.
34. *Public Opinion*, November 10, 1944.
35. Ibid.
36. Ibid., January 29, 1945.
37. Ibid.
38. Stanley to Huggins, March 14, 1945, NARA, RG 84, Classified General Records, UD 2822, 1946, Box 6.
39. *Daily Gleaner*, October 29, 1945.
40. Domingo to Roberts, September 16, 1952, NLJ, WAR, MS 353, Box 2b (emphasis in original).
41. *Daily Gleaner*, August 7, 1947.
42. Michele A. Johnson, 'The Beginning and the End: The Montego Bay Conference and the Jamaican Referendum on West Indian Federation', *Social and Economic Studies* 48 (1999): 117–49.
43. Johnson, 'The Beginning and the End', 149.
44. Manley to Brown, September 20, 1947, Louis Moyston Private Archive.
45. Ibid.
46. Additionally, Brown was reported to advocate federation at a conference where he appeared as a main speaker alongside Eric Williams. See *Pittsburgh Courier*, June 12, 1943. He further was a member of the West Indian Conference Committee that promoted the slogan: 'For a Federated, Free and Independent West Indies'. See Osborne to Manley, July 31, 1947, JA, NMP, 4/60/2B/12.
47. *Daily Gleaner*, October 11, 1945; *Public Opinion*, October 12, 1945. Still in Jamaica, Domingo commented only carefully on Manley's trip. Although he criticized a tendency to minimize or ignore the role of the JPL in the decolonization process, he did not openly criticize Manley. See *Public Opinion*, October 15, 1945.
48. Manley to Brown, May 29, 1947, Louis Moyston Private Archive.
49. Arnett to Brooks Johnson, May 10, 1948, Louis Moyston Private Archive.
50. Manley to Dalton James, September 30, 1948, JA, NMP, 4/60/2B/13.
51. Manley to Brown, March 1, 1951, Louis Moyston Private Archive.
52. Ibid.
53. Trevor Munroe, *The Politics of Constitutional Decolonization, Jamaica 1944–1962* (Kingston: ISER, University of the West Indies, 1972), 120f.
54. Ibid., 120.
55. Cary Fraser, *Ambivalent Anti-Colonialism: The United States and the Genesis of West Indian Independence, 1940–1964* (Westport, Conn: Greenwood Press, 1994), 124ff.
56. Ibid., 108ff.
57. *Daily Gleaner*, February 8, 1959.
58. Domingo to Roberts, August 21, 1952, NLJ, WAR, MS 353, Box 2b.
59. Ibid.
60. Ibid.

Opposing the West Indies Federation

61. Roberts to Domingo, September 10, 1952, NLJ, WAR, MS 353, Box 2b.
62. Roberts to Domingo, September 23, 1952, NLJ, WAR, MS 353, Box 2b.
63. Hart, *Time for a Change*, 194ff.
64. Fraser, *Ambivalent Anti-Colonialism*, 123ff.
65. In 1952, the British Government had recognized with satisfaction that internal conflicts in the PNP led to the ousting of four prominent leaders of the radical left wing. The victory of the PPP in 1953 alarmed the officials and reminded them again, that the alignment of the colonies with the Western powers was not a given fact; see Hart, *Time for a Change*, 199ff.
66. *Daily Gleaner*, April 29, 1953.
67. Ibid., May 7, 1953.
68. Ibid., May 8, 1953; May 14, 1953.
69. Ibid., May 16, 1953.
70. Ibid., June 5, 1953.
71. Norman Manley, 'Statement to the Jamaica Progressive League New York', June 3, 1959, Louis Moyston Private Archive.
72. Munroe, *Constitutional Decolonization*, 122ff.
73. Hart, *Time for a Change*, 337ff.
74. *Daily Gleaner*, September 7, 1955.
75. Ibid.
76. Ibid., October 8, 1955; October 14, 1955.
77. Munroe, *Constitutional Decolonization*, 126f.
78. Ibid., 127.
79. *Daily Gleaner*, February 20, 1956.
80. Ibid., July 21, 1956 (emphasis in original).
81. Thomas Wright was the pen name of Morris Cargill, a high-ranking JLP member. In 1958, he became one of the JLP's representatives in the federal government. For decades he contributed a column to the *Gleaner*. See *Daily Gleaner*, April 19, 2000.
82. *Daily Gleaner*, February 29, 1956.
83. Maynard to Department of State, May 2, 1956, NARA, RG 84, Classified General Records, NND 959049, 1956–1958, Box 1.
84. George E. Eaton, *Alexander Bustamante and Modern Jamaica* (Kingston: Kingston Publishers, 1995), 174.
85. W.A. Domingo, *British West Indian Federation: A Critique* (New York, 1956), 1–16.
86. Jamaica Progressive League, 'Statement on Federation', Louis Moyston Private Archive.
87. Munroe, *Constitutional Decolonization*, 127ff.
88. Domingo, 'Federation: Jamaica's Folly', (New York, 1958), 1–25.
89. *Daily Gleaner*, May 4, 1958.
90. Ibid.
91. Eaton, *Alexander Bustamante*, 176; Munroe, *Constitutional Decolonization*, 127.
92. *Daily Gleaner*, February 5, 1959.
93. Munroe, *Constitutional Decolonization*, 128.
94. Hugh W. Springer, *Reflections on the Failure of the First West Indian Federation*. Reprint ed. (New York: AMS Press, 1973), 19.

95. Richard Hart, *The End of Empire: Transition to Independence in Jamaica and Other Caribbean Region Colonies* (Kingston: Arawak Publications, 2006), 146ff.
96. *Daily Gleaner*, May 4, 1958.
97. Ibid., December 29, 1958.
98. Ibid.
99. Munroe, *Constitutional Decolonization*, 130.
100. *Daily Gleaner*, February 5, 1959.
101. Ibid., February 8, 1959.
102. Munroe, *Constitutional Decolonization*, 130.
103. *Daily Gleaner*, August 10, 1959
104. Munroe, *Constitutional Decolonization*, 130.
105. Hart, *End of Empire*, 157ff.
106. Munroe, *Constitutional Decolonization*, 130.
107. *Daily Gleaner*, October 26, 1959.
108. Domingo to Roberts, October 27, 1959, NLJ, WAR, MS 353, Box 2b.
109. *Daily Gleaner*, October 29, 1959 (all emphases in original).
110. Ibid., October 30, 1959.
111. Ibid., December 21, 1959. The voluminous debate was waged rather on the basis of personal attacks than on rational arguments and will therefore not be further examined.
112. Ibid., October 26, 1959.
113. Ibid., December 18, 1959.
114. Ibid.
115. Roberts to Domingo, November 2, 1959, NLJ, WAR, MS 353, Box 2b.
116. Ibid.
117. Ibid.
118. Roberts to Domingo, June 11, 1960, NLJ, WAR, MS 353, Box 2b.
119. Ibid.
120. Roberts to Domingo, November 2, 1959, NLJ, WAR, MS 353, Box 2b.
121. *Daily Gleaner*, November 4, 1959.
122. Ibid.
123. Munroe, *Constitutional Decolonization*, 131.
124. *Daily Gleaner*, February 16, 1960.
125. Hart, *End of Empire*, 265ff.
126. Hart, *End of Empire*, 269.
127. Roberts to Domingo, June 11, 1960, NLJ, WAR, MS 353, Box 2b.
128. See Ashton and Killingray, eds., *West Indies*, lxxii.
129. *Daily Gleaner*, May 27, 1961.
130. Ibid., July 20, 1961.
131. Ibid., July 30, 1961.
132. Ibid., July 22, 1961.
133. Ibid.
134. Roberts, 'Autobiography', 92.
135. Hills cooperated closely with Edna Manley in the art scene and Christopher B. Hills' wife was given in marriage by Norman Manley. See *Daily Gleaner*, July 31, 1950; August 2, 1950.

136. *Daily Gleaner*, July 20, 1961.
137. Ibid.
138. Roberts, 'Radiobroadcast No. 1', NLJ, WAR, MS 353, Box 23.
139. Roberts, 'Radiobroadcast No. 2', NLJ, WAR, MS 353, Box 23.
140. Roberts, 'Radiobroadcast No. 3', NLJ, WAR, MS 353, Box 23.
141. Ashton Killingray, 'Introduction', *West Indies*.
142. Roberts, 'Radiobroadcast No. 4', NLJ, WAR, MS 353, Box 23.
143. Roberts, 'Radiobroadcast No. 5', NLJ, WAR, MS 353, Box 23.
144. Ibid.
145. Roberts, 'Radiobroadcast No. 6', NLJ, WAR, MS 353, Box 23.
146. Ibid.
147. *Daily Gleaner*, August 21, 1961.
148. Ibid., August 22, 1961.
149. Ibid., September 17, 1961.
150. Ibid., September 2, 1961; September 5, 1961; September 12, 1961; September 18, 1961.
151. Hart, *End of Empire*, 292.
152. *Daily Gleaner*, September 20, 1961.
153. Domingo to Roberts, September 20, 1961, NLJ, WAR, MS 353, Box 2b.
154. Ibid.
155. Ibid.
156. Minutes by Lord Perth, November 22, 1961, PRO, CO 1031/3278, no 147, in *West Indies*, ed. Ashton and Killingray, 469.
157. Colonial Office, Draft Memorandum, April 1961, PRO, CO 1031/4274, no 5, in. *West Indies*, ed. Ashton and Killingray, 398.
158. David Killingray, 'The West Indian Federation and Decolonization in the British Caribbean', *The Journal of Caribbean History* 34 (2000): 82.
159. Macleod to Macmillan, September 22, 1961, CO 1031/3270, no 43A, in *West Indies*, ed. Ashton and Killingray, 438.
160. Hart, *End of Empire*, 293.
161. Killingray, 'West Indian Federation', 82.
162. Munroe, *Constitutional Decolonization*, 147ff.
163. *Daily Gleaner*, April 25, 1962.
164. Richard B. Moore, 'Independent Caribbean Nationhood', 1962; in *Richard B. Moore*, 298.
165. *Daily Gleaner*, January 9, 1961.
166. Ibid.
167. Springer, *Reflections*, 18.
168. Munroe, *Constitutional Decolonization*, 138.
169. Roberts, 'National Consciousness', undated [after 1959], NLJ, WAR, MS 353, Box 9.

CONCLUSION

At midnight, on August 6, 1962, the Union Jack was lowered, and the black, green and gold Jamaican flag was hoisted for the first time, the national anthem played, while fireworks lit up the night sky over the National Stadium. As invited guests of the newly formed independent government, the two prime leaders of the Progressive League, W. Adolphe Roberts and Wilfred Domingo proudly witnessed the historical occasion from the tribunes of the stadium.[1] Their vision of an independent Jamaica, to which they had both dedicated their lives and accepted great challenges and sacrifices, had finally come true. On the evening of Jamaica's first day as an independent nation state, the two pioneers were amongst the statesmen and celebrities at a great State Ball in the Forum of the Sheraton Hotel.

On the day of Jamaica's independence, the *New York Times* highlighted the Progressive League's pioneering role in a historical sketch: 'Jamaica's voyage toward nationhood began in 1936 when the Jamaica Progressive League, a group of islanders living in New York, issued a demand for self-government'.[2] Ironically, the two senior leaders of the Progressive League celebrated Jamaica's independence as guests of a JLP government led by Alexander Bustamante – the man who had placed so many obstacles in their way in the early struggle for self-government and who had only recently converted into an advocate of independence when he had called for a referendum for Jamaica to leave the West Indies Federation in 1961. Although the Progressive League finally achieved its declared aim, Domingo's joy was dulled by the fact that victory was won in open opposition to the Progressive League's closest partner in Jamaica. In a letter to Roberts, he confided that this was not only unfortunate because of the break in the long-term collaboration between the Progressive League and the PNP, and in his personal friendship with Manley, but also because it shattered his personal career plans:

> I am sorry that Manley and I disagreed about Federation. Had he been on the winning side I would angle for appointment to the Jamaican Delegation to the UN or to being attached to our N.Y. Consulate. That is about my only ambition for what I did for Jamaica. But such are the

Conclusion

fortunes of war, especially when, like you and me, we put principle above all else.³

Domingo ended his letter to Roberts as follows: 'Jamaica owes you and the founders of the League a great debt of gratitude, even though many of them don't realize it'.⁴

In an article in the *Gleaner* in October 1962, Domingo worried:

> My great fear is that Jamaicans, especially their 'historians' will fail to see history in its proper perspective. So many people imbue their thinking with their ego and prejudices that the great contribution of Roberts and his brainchild the Jamaica Progressive League to the freedom of Jamaica may be obscured, even ignored.⁵

Domingo's concern was justified. Today, more than 50 years after independence, hardly anyone remembers the important contribution of the Jamaica Progressive League. A year before Jamaica celebrated its 50th anniversary as a nation state, Journalist Ken Jones called attention to the undue neglect of the contribution of the Progressive League and published a series of three articles on the founders of the Progressive League, on Roberts, Domingo and Brown in the *Daily Gleaner*, expressing the hope that this would be the occasion where the contribution of the Progressive League would be recognized.⁶ However, Jamaica's jubilee passed by in 2012 without public recognition of the role of the Jamaica Progressive League.

In contrast, the influence of the Progressive League was initially acknowledged by many politicians of their generation. Not only during the time of their common struggle, but also in the years after independence, contemporaries who witnessed Roberts and Domingo's activities in Jamaica clearly acknowledged their important contribution to Jamaica's political development. Manley and other PNP-members of the first generation initially acknowledged the Progressive League's pioneer role and its monetary contribution, which provided crucial support for the party's educational and propaganda campaigns.

Roberts died only a few weeks after independence, during a visit to London to find a publisher for his memoirs. In his eulogy, H.P. Jacobs, co-founder of *Public Opinion*, co-founder and vice president of the NRA and founding member of the PNP, clearly remembered when Roberts first approached his countrymen with the demand for independence: 'People laughed at his vision a quarter of a century ago, yet a few weeks before his death Jamaica became an independent nation'.⁷ This Englishman who had made Jamaica his home emphasized the originality of Roberts' ideas and asserted that his decision not to enter politics but to focus on cultural nationalism was no retreat from political activism and concluded that there was a 'uniform patriotic motive in these activities'.

Despite Roberts' objection to federation, Jacobs rejected the notion that his nationalism was in any sense narrow:

> The concept of Federation...always seemed to him a digression, a turning aside from the path. This was not my view, but I found that his opposition to Federation was neither due to any narrowness of outlook nor the result of any pique because his own idea was being abandoned. He considered that the goals of nationhood could not be reached by watering down the concept of country and nation to include lands and peoples that most Jamaicans had never seen.

Statements like these clearly display Jacobs' respect for Roberts' ideas.

Another influential figure in Jamaican cultural affairs, J.E. Clare McFarlane, Jamaican poet, literary critic and Roberts' colleague in the Board of Governors of the Institute of Jamaica, also testified to Roberts' pioneering influence in an obituary in the *Jamaica Times*: 'In the late 1930s he had brought from New York the flame of the Jamaica Progressive League which set us afire with the idea of nationhood'.[8] However, C.B. Lewis, a colleague as Director of the Institute of Jamaica, was unfortunately wrong when he prophesied, in a letter to Vincent Johnston, President of the Progressive League in New York: 'Indeed he was a great Jamaican, whose works and contributions will probably be far better appreciated in the years to come'.[9] On the contrary, Roberts contribution is nearly forgotten today.

Initially, Domingo's role was similarly recognized. When he died on February 14, 1968, his death was announced on the front page of the *Gleaner*.[10] A few days later, Manley published a lengthy tribute to Domingo, in which he emphasized:

> ...no one, and I repeat, no one in the world made greater sacrifices or suffered more for the cause he believed in – the cause of freedom for Jamaica and our escape from the bonds and fetters of British Imperialism.[11]

Without mentioning his own reservations towards the Progressive League's demands for immediate self-government, Manley testified to the influence of the Progressive League on the policy of the PNP. Manley affirmed the significant influence of Domingo at the first party conference regarding the position the PNP adopted toward self-government:

> I best remember my first encounter with the quality of the man when in 1939 he came from New York to the first P.N.P. annual conference and led with vigour and success a move to commit the party to full Self-Government as our positive and determined and immediate goal.

As it had led to Domingo's detention for more than two and a half years, Manley recalled with a guilty conscience his 'Macedonian cry' for Domingo's help in the 'political field where the Self Government struggle was reaching a climax', so that he, Manley, could focus on the work for the Trade Unions. Manley omitted the fact that the PNP had immediately retreated from political action when the war broke out, and that the activities of the WINEC at the Havana Conference and Domingo's numerous letters to Jamaica had helped to shake the PNP out of its apathy.

Regarding the Governor's motive for detaining Domingo aboard the ship before he even set foot on Jamaica, Manley pointed out: 'It was of Domingo's implacable hatred of Imperialism and his dislike and contempt for England in that field and because as well of our then Governor's determination to crush the Self Government movement'. He remembered Domingo's forced stay in Jamaica, during which he had stayed at Manley's private residence, *Drumblair*. He commended his oratory and writing skills, his sense for the development of the future, his sharpness in exchanges with political opponents and described him as a lovable and modest man. He concluded his accolades by assuring: 'Those of us who knew him well and worked with him will never forget this unforgettable man'.

It is also striking that Manley did not mention their disagreement over federation with a single word. This was to become a continuous line in the PNP's propaganda, which was faced with the difficulty of integrating their advocacy of federation into a coherent narrative of portraying the party as the pioneer of independence.

As a sign of appreciation and respect for the party, the PNP's General Secretary S.O. Veitch attended Domingo's funeral in New York in 1968. A cable from Manley, as well as Veitch's tribute, clearly recognized Domingo's contribution to the independence movement as well as to the party. The *Gleaner* reported that Veitch mentioned the sacrifices of Domingo, especially during his detention, and expected that one day he would be 'enshrined as one of Jamaica's National Hero's [sic]'.[12]

Domingo's funeral was attended by representatives from various organizations with which he had been affiliated at some point in his life. The Governor General of Jamaica sent a cable, and Keith Johnson, Jamaica's Ambassador to the United Nations, presented the eulogy, in which he claimed: 'History will record that Wilfred Domingo was in the forefront of Jamaica's fight for nationhood. ...It was he who was called in 1941 to help wage war for nationhood, and to help in the partisan, political institutions'. He further credited Domingo with successfully lobbying for amendments to the McCarran Immigration Act, which allowed skilled and unskilled labourers from Jamaica to enter the US opening up an important emigration route for the young nation plagued by high unemployment rates. In contrast to Manley and Veitch, Keith Johnson, appointed as Jamaica's representative to the UN by a JLP government did mention Domingo's opposition to the Federation, albeit indirectly, when he recalled how Domingo had pointed to the advantage of having several voices of Caribbean nations in the UN instead of one federated nation.

In the 1970s, the Progressive League and its founders could still attract a fair amount of recognition. Prime Minister Michael Manley, who had succeeded his father in the leadership of the PNP, referred to the importance of the Progressive League. At a banquet which the Progressive League held in honour of Norman Manley, he emphasized the Progressive League's 'decisive role in the founding of the PNP and the country's attainment of self-government'.[13]

On the occasion of the 40th anniversary of the Progressive League in New York in 1976, Dudley Thompson, Minister of Foreign Affairs in the PNP cabinet, emphasized the importance of the Progressive League, in particular in lending financial support to the party. The *New York Amsterdam News* reported him saying:

> ...the Jamaica Progressive League emerged as a response to the political, intellectual and cultural ferment in the Jamaica of the 1930s. He says the League was one of the sponsors of the P.N.P., the first political party to be formed in Jamaica, and that the party relied heavily on the firm and unwavering support which the League has continued to give it. The People's National Party is a vanguard of the movement to achieve independence for Jamaica and to make it a reality.[14]

In 1977, the Jamaican government under Michael Manley officially recognized the contribution of the Progressive League by honouring Roberts and Domingo posthumously with the Order of Distinction (Commander Class) for their 'contribution to Jamaica's Political Development'.[15] One year later, Brown also received the Order of Distinction (Officer Class) for his 'distinguished service in the cause of Jamaican Nationalism, his efforts towards the attainment of Independence and his unselfish work among Jamaicans in the U.S.A.'[16]

However, this official recognition had no further effect in keeping the memory alive. With the death of the activists and their contemporaries, the contribution of the Progressive League slowly sank into oblivion. Under the JLP government of Edward Seaga in the 1980s, there is no indication that the Progressive League was especially recognized in public.

One series of articles on the history of Jamaica, prepared by H.P. Jacobs, who had praised the contributions of Roberts in the graveside eulogy quoted above, did not even acknowledge the Progressive League, although he pointed out that the island's political history did not start in 1938 and mentioned organizations like the National Reform Association, the Federation of Citizens Associations and the *Public Opinion*.[17] Addressing the founding of the PNP, Jacobs now declared without naming Roberts and Domingo:

> In the preliminary discussions it was agreed that self-government and adult suffrage should be the objectives of the new organization and

claims that the PNP chose its name because it feared that calling the party 'Labour Party', as some suggested, would have hampered the movement for self-government.[18]

Out of the mouth of someone who definitely knew better, such a statement twists history in favour of the PNP. To promote a version of history that credited the party as the pioneer of the demand for self-government seemed to have taken precedence, probably in light of the upcoming elections in October 1980.

In the early 1990s, the late surviving founder of the Progressive League's branch in Kingston, W.G. McFarlane, joined with Jimmy Tucker and tried reviving the Jamaica Progressive League in Jamaica, demanding constitutional changes that would cut ties with England and turn the constitutional monarchy into a republic.[19] In a letter to the *Gleaner*, McFarlane tried to challenge the widespread notion that depicted Manley as Jamaica's founding father while neglecting the Progressive League's contribution:

> Mr. Manley is not the founder of the Jamaican nation. The founder is Mr. Walter Adolphe Roberts, a Jamaican who emigrated to the United States of America as a young man and there created a distinguished career for himself and others as a Jamaican immigrant. He decided that Jamaicans at home and abroad were fit and ready to govern themselves as a nation.[20]

Journalist Terry Smith followed up on that claim and interviewed McFarlane. Afterwards, he published a series of articles in the *Daily Gleaner*, in which he recalled the history of the Progressive League in New York and in Kingston.[21] Smith's explanation for the neglect points to the common practice of nations constructing their own national legacies, which are linked to political power, influence and purpose: 'For politics, which is, among other things, about power and the pecking order, has consequently a very dark and vengeful side, and recall is sometimes painful, almost bitter and in conflict with unquestioned views which have become traditional'.[22] Smith claims that the history of the Progressive League and its founders should be more adequately recognized. He referred to a letter to the *Gleaner* written by Domingo upon Roberts' death, in which he had professed:

> Many persons are hailed as the 'Father' of Jamaican self-government, but if we are to measure accomplishment rightly we should concede that the first practical effort, after Cox, aimed at gaining for Jamaicans control of their government must go to the man who ORGANISED that effort. Roberts did not dream dreams and remain in an ivory tower, at his own expense he returned to Jamaica from New York in 1937 and so spread the seeds of his liberal ideas on Jamaica, which seed developed into the mighty tree that became the Dominion of Jamaica on August 6, 1962.[23]

Smith reaffirmed Domingo's views and portrayed Roberts as '...undoubtedly the great and uncompromising Conceptualizer of (if not admittedly a 'Father of') self-government for Jamaica'.[24] He makes an important point when he referred to the difficulties in judging how the idea of self-government was received in the wider population. Drawing a similar conclusion to this book, Smith states:

> What is definitely recorded is that the then establishment opinion expressed on behalf of the entire country was very conservative, and such opinion-makers and defenders saw the call for self-government as a reckless mixture of lunacy, ingratitude and treason.[25]

After the futile efforts of the renewed Progressive League in Kingston to lobby for Jamaica to become a republic, nearly two decades of silence passed – without even obituaries for the Progressive League's remaining members prompting any further recollections – and with little interest in the contribution of the Progressive League, although calls for turning Jamaica into a republic occur in the political discussions from time to time. Most Jamaicans today are not familiar with the names of W. Adolphe Roberts, Wilfred A. Domingo or Ethelred Brown; and many have never heard of the Progressive League. Only a few elderly citizens recall the existence of a group of that name and some remember the role it played in the struggle for Jamaican self-government. For instance, Frank Gordon, who was a member of the Progressive League in Kingston and the PNP, beside playing a prominent role in the UNIA in Jamaica, was aware of the influence the Progressive League exerted on shaping modern Jamaica.[26]

The evidence presented throughout this book, supported by the testimony of well-informed contemporaries like Manley, Jacobs, Veitch, Thompson, Gordon and others confirms the relevance of the Progressive League and its important influence on the political developments, and on the PNP in particular. Why then is the history of the Progressive League neglected today?

One important reason is the effort of both political parties to portray themselves as the pioneers of self-government. Politicized versions of history contributed to the erasure of the legacy of the Progressive League and its pioneer role as a catalyst for anti-colonial nationalism in Jamaica. Increasingly, that legacy got overshadowed by a standardized and widely accepted narrative that privileges the year 1938, in particular the labour rebellions of May and June, as a watershed in Jamaica's history. While the events across the Anglphone Caribbean in the early summer of 1938 were undoubtedly of great relevance and served as a wakeup call, especially for the middle class – and, indeed, for the colonial administration in London – the subsequent political developments in Jamaica could not have taken place in the same form and speed without the work of the Progressive League and the discussions its propaganda had sparked since 1936; the constant call for a nationalist party, the demand for immediate self-government, and the critique of political inertia and loyalty with Great Britain.

Conclusion

The two Jamaican leaders who emerged from the events of 1938, Norman W. Manley and Alexander Bustamante, heading those organizations that would rise to channel the labour and the political movement, would dominate the developments of the following generation. In the quest for national identity in post-colonial Jamaica, the two cousins became larger than life figures. In 1969, they were officially elevated into the status of officially declared National Heroes. Ever since, they overshadow all other activists of the pre-independence period. On the occasion of a public forum in the National Arena on the crisis of the two-party system, one discussant questioned the practice of appointing National Heroes from above and demanded that the populace should participate in the discussion about who should be declared a National Hero. Frank Hill, *Public Opinion* co-founder and PNP founding member, deplored the tendency to glorify certain individuals and reminded his readers that they had all relied heavily on the work of colleagues who were no less important to the course of events. He named a few that were crucial, among them Domingo as 'one of the earliest fighters for self-government.'[27]

The apotheosis of individuals as national heroes clearly serves the individual parties in carving and legitimizing their own legacy. Moreover, it reflects the internal logic of nation-building processes. National heroes and glorious founding myths belong to the standard repertoire of most, if not all, nations. In post-colonial nation states, the figures who challenged colonial rule are usually given prominent places in the nation-state's politics of memory.

In the two-party system of Jamaica, both PNP and JLP were keen to show their own contribution in the best light. The website of the PNP, for instance, omits the important contribution of the Progressive League on the party's position toward self-government and ignores the role of the Progressive League activists.[28] In the subsection on the 'Forerunners', the website incorrectly claims that the Progressive League was founded in 1937, the same year as *Public Opinion*, and does not mention the important influence of the Progressive League on the positions of the developing nationalist scene. The PNP generously credited the moderate National Reform Association (NRA) to be 'another group agitating for self-government', in which many of the PNP founders were previously organized. The way the PNP credits the local scene while obscuring the contribution of the emigrants highlights the fact that in order to serve the production of national legacies, 'the Jamaican people' needed to be the source that inspired the change. Finally, the PNP apotheosized Manley's contribution to self-government when it claimed: 'Manley, early in his speech, put forward what was to become the central theme in the PNP's demand for self-government'.

Clearly, the PNP had foregrounded its own contribution, which eventually become canonized, while the Progressive League was only mentioned *en passant*, along with the NRA and the launch of *Public Opinion*. The story continues that all groups together called for self-government and prepared the founding of the PNP, which from then on consistently embodied the institutional expression of the demand for self-government. From the time of independence, the PNP, now in the opposition in Parliament, played an important part in constructing this account, crediting the PNP with the pioneer role in the nationalist struggle. Another example is a political programme published by the PNP after independence, in which the party was singled out as the pioneer of the movement toward independence.[29] This pattern is also evident in a debate about the independence constitution in the Legislative Council, in which the PNP's long-time secretary V.L. Arnett recalled the history of the independence movement. Repeating the version presented on the PNP website, he dated the founding of *Public Opinion* and Progressive League to 1937, omitting the significant role in shaping the PNP's position on self-government, and instead claimed that the party had declared self-government to be its goal.[30]

Another important factor was the disagreements over the question of federation between the Progressive League and the PNP during the last stage on the road to independence, which had deeply disturbed the relationship between the two close allies. The Progressive League's open opposition to Manley and the policies of the PNP under his leadership seriously impaired the largely harmonious cooperation between the organizations. After independence, the PNP faced the double challenge of establishing itself and its local precursors as the pioneers of the independence movement, and of defending itself against the political opposition's allegations that the party had not acted in Jamaica's best interests by sacrificing its nationalist demands in favour of a Federation without immediate Dominion status. Under these circumstances any official commemoration of the Progressive League would only have served as a reminder that the party had initially rejected the Progressive League's efforts to convince it to include nationalist demands in the party platform, and that Norman Manley had continually refused to reverse its course regarding federation.

The JLP, the first ruling party in independent Jamaica, was also not anxious to acknowledge the contribution of the Progressive League and to risk reminding voters that it had harshly opposed the idea of independence for many years. Party leader Bustamante had been highly outspoken against the Progressive League leaders and their ideas, and likewise, Progressive League leaders had never made a secret of their low opinion of Bustamante. The canonization of the Progressive League would have been highly inconvenient for the first Prime Minister of independent Jamaica and his attempts to style himself as a great patriot who had single-handedly saved Jamaica from the disastrous consequences of remaining in the Federation.

Conclusion

In addition to the partisan versions of historical memory, the outsider status of the Progressive League has not particularly qualified its migrant leaders for integration into the newly forged national legend of a people that always aspired to nationhood, as it points to uncomfortable realities about the great obstacles with which the demand for self-government was initially received. While the experience of migration was integral in shaping radical anti-colonial positions, the existence of grave doubts about independence and resistance to the demand for self-government would not serve the development of the young nation state's legitimizing myth. The glorification of local activists in Jamaica was much more suitable for this purpose. Both political parties in post-independence Jamaica were interested in highlighting their own contributions, and neither was particularly keen about emphasizing the role of outsiders and exposing their own timidity toward the idea of self-government.

Hence, neither of the two political parties or the conservative elite were interested in giving prominence to the visions of the early nationalists, which included firm demands for fundamental changes in the country's social order, challenging the privileges of the elite and the light-skinned middle class, racial equality, and drastically improved living standards. In accordance with the notion of post-colonial theorists' claims that decolonization often was a 'false decolonization'[31] that left many features of the colonial order intact and enabled the continued hegemony of the political and economic elite without fundamentally challenging the status quo, it was more opportune for the ruling political elite to portray nationalism as a continuity, and let the most radical claims, associated with the Progressive League's vision of independence, fall by the wayside.

Those individuals who had started to fundamentally question the social order in post-colonial Jamaica in the late 1960s and 1970s, among them several radical Marxist groups, Black Power organizations, Rastafarians, intellectuals, artists, poets and critical scholars, were also not particularly interested in the Progressive League, because it embodied what many reject as 'creole nationalism' and blame for the continuity of racist and oppressive structures in modern Jamaica.[32] Roberts' skin colour and his adoption of US citizenship are also now probably detrimental to his recognition, reversing the fact that his status as a white Jamaican had helped to attract recognition for the nationalist cause in the pre-independence era.

Indeed, racial and cultural discrimination and an ever increasing cleavage between rich and poor, uptown and downtown still exists in post-colonial Jamaica. The ambivalence of the category of 'race' in Jamaican society, in ideals as well as in everyday reality, blatantly exposes the deep scars which colonial rule, slavery, racism and oppression have left. The arguments of the nation's Afrocentric critics therefore resonate with a post-colonial critique on false or unfinished decolonization.

In this situation, what is the merit of deploring the lack of recognition of the Progressive League, other than saving its contribution from oblivion? Does its contribution still matter? The two journalists, Louis Moyston and Ken Jones, seem to be the lone voices expressing concern about the forgotten legacy of the Progressive League and the partisan version of Jamaican history that has become the widely accepted national narrative. Jones emphasizes that the members of the Progressive League had to put in keen efforts to convince the PNP to include the demand for self-government in the party programme and directly mentions Manley's hesitations. He also refers to Bustamante's opposition to demands for immediate self-government. In general, Jones points to the objections Roberts' ideas met and claims:

> Bustamante and Norman Manley deserve their places in the history of our Independence; but we should also raise a memorial to Adolphe Roberts whose focus was unwaveringly on self-government for Jamaica. There were times when others argued, with some justification, that the country and its people were not ready for political independence. There were suggestions that Jamaica could not go it alone. Roberts never relented, although he acknowledged that the road to self-determination would be long, but exciting.[33]

In regard to his views on federation, Jones calls Roberts 'prophetic'. Apart from Roberts' political activities, Jones emphasized his important scholarship and his many contributions to the civil society of Jamaica, among them the Jamaica Historical Society, the Jamaica Library Association, the Poetry League of Jamaica, the Natural History Society and the Board of Governors of the Institute of Jamaica. Like PNP Secretary Veitch, Jones deplored the lack of recognition of the contribution of the Progressive League's founders, and hoped that this omission would have been corrected at Jamaica's 50th anniversary. He suggested: 'The names of these pioneers should be inscribed on some prominent monument mounted in National Heroes Park. They deserve no less.'[34]

However, the overemphasis on the seven officially declared National Heroes who have been canonized in the historiography of modern Jamaica tends to overshadow other important historical actors while supporting the creation of national myths. For a more indepth analysis of the pre-independence period, it is important that all forces that shaped the society receive more attention. Only a candid look into various types of sources can help to put historical events into perspective and to reduce uncritical apotheosis of the National Heroes. By offering insight into the visions of those who have not been incorporated into the national narrative we gain a more complex understanding of the run-up to independence. Moreover, it is relevant to see the political developments in Jamaica in the broader context of decolonization in the twentieth century and to recognize their transnational dimension.

Conclusion

The examination of the Progressive League might provide a useful tool in contrasting the Jamaica of today with the dreams of the nationalist pioneers, with the visions of equal opportunities for all citizens regardless of colour, class, or creed, and with the idea of a unified society in which social differences between rich and poor would diminish rather than increase. This is not to say that the protagonists of the Progressive League would have been able to live up to their own expectations or that they would necessarily have been able to move the country in another direction had they become more directly involved in local politics. On the contrary, their attitude toward minorities, their narrow focus on Jamaica in the question of Federation and their occasional belittling of other countries and the tendency to follow European models of progress unquestionably testify to the shortcomings of their vision of nationalism, if not to the shortcomings of nationalist ideology per se. Nevertheless, the contribution of the Progressive League to the decolonization process exemplifies the power of nationalism as a weapon against colonialism and testifies to the importance of transnational actors, whose experiences transcended traditional ways of colonial thinking. Prepared to take high personal risks, they played an instrumental role in the history of Jamaica's decolonization that deserves to be both recognized and acknowledged. The material presented in this book illustrates the interplay of power between those actors before, during and after the Second World War, which resulted in a substantial power shift in the region. This constellation opened up new space for anti-colonial activities, which the Progressive League leaders readily utilized.

The Progressive League's impact not only demonstrates that Caribbean immigrants played a crucial role in the vibrant black transnational political space that Harlem offered in the early twentieth century, but also highlights that this interplay influenced political developments in their home country as well. It exemplifies how anti-colonial activists capitalized on the shifting international power relations, how they utilized the transnational network of Caribbean and African American activists and how they played an active role in the process of decolonization. In times where the role of Jamaicans living abroad or living transnational lives across the borders of nation states is once again increasingly important to Jamaica's development, the acknowledgement of the diaspora's role in the origination of nationalist thought is important and illuminates the role of wider diasporic networks in the decolonization process.

The examination of the local scene as well as the routes that the protagonists of the Progressive League followed makes it possible to see why and how anti-colonialist thought developed outside of Jamaica. The migration experience played a key role in overcoming colonial ways of thinking and imperial loyalties predisposed the migrants to anti-colonial thought. Tracing the activities of the migrants in the US showed that they were exposed to a variety of influences that inspired them to look at their country of origin with different eyes and led many to fundamentally challenge all forms of colonial rule and racist discrimination. The experience of a different conception of race in the US and contacts with other black people from all over the world allowed them to see racism as an instrument of rule and power that took a different shape in various societies. Anti-imperialist elements and Socialist ideas, particularly the affirmation of the right to self-determination, contributed substantially to put the protagonists in opposition to colonialism and leading them to regard capitalism and colonialism as two sides of one coin. The disappointment that derived from futile attempts to merge race- and class-based approaches to fight oppression and exploitation played an instrumental role. The examination of the protagonists' backgrounds showed that a mixture of these experiences prepared the fertile ground on which an organization demanding self-government for Jamaica could flourish. The Progressive League's Harlem-based founders did not perceive nationalism to be in any sense contradictory to the internationalist foundations of their thinking, but rather saw it as an expression of a transnational anti-imperialist vision of the black diaspora that had earlier attracted them to Black Nationalism and Socialism, both of which had profoundly shaped their thinking.

The transnational research perspective applied throughout this work, following the activists on their movements across the Atlantic, helped to deconstruct some of the powerful national legacies that often cast deep shadows across the analysis of the decolonization process and underexpose important actors. Re-integrating the Progressive League's leaders into the account enabled a shift in focus from local protagonists to Jamaican emigrants and the roles they played, which were more important in the interplay of forces leading up to Jamaica's independence than has hitherto been acknowledged. Thus, the study of the Progressive League offers further evidence reaffirming the observation of scholars that anti-colonial movements often have strong roots outside of the colony, as in the cases of Ireland, India, or colonies on the African continent, all of which had also inspired the strategists of the Progressive League. Many anti-colonial movements originated outside the firm grip of the colonial power, or at least received strong support from expatriates in the inspiring atmosphere of intellectual circles in metropolises like New York, London, or Paris. These circles of transnational activists often provided anti-colonial movements with political connections, an international audience and the capacity to raise much-needed funds to publicize the ideas in the home country. This was also true for the Progressive League, which benefited from the tight-knit networks of Caribbean and African American radicals in Harlem and in turn, was able to support the political struggle significantly. More than 50 years after Jamaica's Independence, as we seek to understand the development of post-imperial nationalisms,

Conclusion

highlighting unduly neglected protagonists of the anti-colonial struggle and its transnational dimension, this work offers a contribution to the ongoing debate on the process of decolonization in Jamaica.

Notes

1. *Daily Gleaner*, June 14, 1962.
2. *New York Times*, August 6, 1962.
3. Domingo to Roberts, November 30, 1961, NLJ, WAR, MS 353, Box 2b.
4. Ibid.
5. *Daily Gleaner*, October 10, 1962.
6. Ibid., July 31, 2011; August 21, 2011; September 4, 2011.
7. H.P. Jacobs, 'Funeral Eulogy for W. Adolphe Roberts', November 18, 1962, NLJ, WAR, MS 353, Box 12.
8. The *Jamaica Times*, September 22, 1962.
9. Lewis to Johnston, October 9, 1962, NLJ, WAR, MS 353, Box 12.
10. *Daily Gleaner*, February 16, 1968.
11. Ibid., February 22, 1968.
12. Ibid., January 23, 1968.
13. Ibid., October 22, 1968.
14. *New York Amsterdam News*, October 30, 1976.
15. *Daily Gleaner*, October 18, 1977. The Order of Distinction is the lowest of six ranks of orders from the Jamaican government; the highest is the Order of a National Hero.
16. Ibid., August 4, 1980.
17. Ibid., February 3, 1980; February 10, 1980; February 17, 1980; February 24, 1980; March 2, 1980; March 9, 1980; March 16, 1980; March 23, 1980; March 30, 1980; April 6, 1980.
18. Ibid., February 24, 1980.
19. Interview by the author with Jimmy Tucker, December 12, 2006. See also *Daily Gleaner*, July 30, 1993; Tucker, *Developments in the Renewed Jamaica Progressive League* (Kingston: Jamaica Progressive League, 1992).
20. *Daily Gleaner*, July 30, 1993.
21. Ibid., November 21, 1993; November 28, 1993; December 12, 1993.
22. Ibid., November 28, 1993
23. Ibid., October 10, 1962.
24. Ibid., November, 1993.
25. Ibid., December 12, 1993.
26. See the interview by the author with Frank Gordon, Kingston, April 9, 2008.
27. *Daily Gleaner*, October 26, 1969.
28. For this and the following quotes see PNP-Website, http://www.pnpjamaica.com/index.php/who-we-are/our-history (last viewed October 24, 2011).
29. PNP, 'Independence and the People of Jamaica'.
30. *Daily Gleaner*, January 25, 1962.
31. Reiland Rabaka, *Africana Critical Theory: Reconstructing the Black Radical Tradition, from W.E.B. DuBois and C.L.R. James to Franz Fanon and Amilcar Cabral* (Lanham, MD: Lexington Books, 2009); for Jamaica, see Loius Lindsay, *The Myth of Independence:*

Middle Class Politics and Non-Mobilization in Jamaica (Mona: Institute of Social and Economic Research, University of the West Indies), 1981.
32. Bogues, 'Nationalism and Jamaican Political Thought', in *Jamaica in Slavery and Freedom*, ed. Kathleen E.A. Monteith and Glen Richards (Kingston: University of the West Indies Press, 2002).
33. *Daily Gleaner*, July 31, 2011.
34. Ibid.

BIBLIOGRAPHY

Primary Sources
Manuscript Collections

Jamaica

National Library of Jamaica, Kingston (NLJ)
W. Adolphe Roberts Papers (WAR)
W.G. McFarlane Papers (WGMcF)

Jamaica Archives and Records Department, Spanish Town (JA)
Norman Manley Papers

Louis Moyston Private Archive
Jamaica Progressive League Collection

United States of America

National Archives and Record Administration (II), College Park, Maryland (NARA)
Record Group 59: Records of the Department of State
Record Group 84: Records of the Foreign Service Posts, Jamaica US Consulate Kingston, Classified General Records 1936–62.

Elmer Holmes Bobst Library, New York University, New York
The Tamiment Library & Robert F. Wagner Labor Archives
Mark Solomon and Robert Kaufman Papers: Research Files on African Americans and Communism

Schomburg Center for Research in Black Culture, New York Public Library (SCRB)
E. Ethelred Brown Papers (EEB)
Richard B. Moore Papers (RBM)
West Indies National Council Papers (WINC)

Library of Congress, Manuscript Division, Washington DC (LOC)
Records of the NAACP
A. Philip Randolph Papers

Great Britain

Public Record Office, Kew (PRO)
Colonial Office Records

Institute of Commonwealth Studies, London (IOCS)
RG 84, Records of the Foreign Service Posts, Jamaica US Consulate Kingston, Classified General Records 1936–62, (1936–41 All Files) Box 1.

Newspapers and Magazines

Jamaica Labour Weekly
Negro Word
Our Own
Public Opinion
The Chicago Defender (National Edition)
The Crisis
The Daily Gleaner/The Gleaner
The Jamaica Labor Weekly
The Jamaica Times
The Emancipator
The Messenger
The New York Amsterdam News/New York Amsterdam Star News
The New York Times
The Opportunity
The Pittsburgh Courier
The Washington Post

Published Sources

Ashton, S. R. and David Killingray, eds. *The West Indies: British Documents on the End of Empire.* Series B, vol. 6. London: Stationery Office, 1999.

Bryan, Patrick E., and Karl Watson, eds. *Not for Wages Alone: Eyewitness Summaries of the 1938 Labour Rebellion in Jamaica.* Kingston: Department of History, University of the West Indies, 2003.

Garvey, Marcus. *The Marcus Garvey and Universal Negro Improvement Association Papers.* Edited by Robert A. Hill. 10 vols. Berkeley: University of California Press, 1983.

Parascandola, Louis J., ed. *Look for Me All Around You: Anglophone Caribbeans in the Harlem Renaissance.* Detroit: Wayne State University Press, 2005.

Turner, Joyce Moore, and W. Burghardt Turner, *Richard B. Moore, Caribbean Militant in Harlem: Collected Writings 1920–1972.* Bloomington: Indiana University Press, 1988.

Books and Articles

Brown, E. Ethelred. 'Labour Conditions in Jamaica Prior to 1917.' *The Journal of Negro History* 9 (1919): 349–60.

McFarlane, Walter G. *The Birth of Self-Government for Jamaica and the Jamaica Progressive League 1937–1944.* Kingston: 1957.

Moore, Richard B. 'Independent Caribbean Nationhood.' In *Richard B. Moore*, edited by Turner and Turner. Bloomington: Indiana University Press, 1962.

Roberts, W. Adolphe. 'British West Indian Aspirations.' *Current History* 40 (1934): 552–56.

———. *The Caribbean: The Story of Our Sea of Destiny.* Indianapolis: Bobbs-Merrill, 1940.

———. 'Great Men of the Caribbean 1: Toussaint L'Ouverture.' *Caribbean Quarterly* 1 (1949): 4–8.

———. 'Great Men of the Caribbean 2: Simón Bolívar.' *Caribbean Quarterly* 1 (1949/50): 4–8.

———. 'Great Men of the Caribbean 3: José Martí.' *Caribbean Quarterly* 1 (1949/50): 4–6.

———. *Havana: The Portrait of a City.* New York: Coward-McCann, 1953.

———. *Sir Henry Morgan: Buccaneer and Governor.* London: Covici, Friede, 1933.

———. *Six Great Jamaicans: Biographical Sketches.* Kingston: Pioneer Press, 1951.

———. *The Single Star.* Kingston: Pioneer Press, 1956.

Young, John S. *Lest We Forget.* New York: Isidor Books, 1981.

Pamphlets

Brown, Ethelred. *Injustices in the Civil Service of Jamaica.* New York: Jamaica Progressive League, 1937.

Domingo, Wilfred A. *The British West Indian Federation: A Critique.* New York, 1956.

———. *Federation: Jamaica's Folly.* New York, 1958.

Jamaica Progressive League New York. *Onward, Jamaica!* New York, 1937.

O'Meally, Jaime. *Why We Demand Self-Government.* New York: Jamaica Progressive League, 1938.

PNP. *Forward March.* Kingston, undated [1941].
——. *The Case of Domingo.* Kingston, undated.
Roberts, W. Adolphe. *The Patriot.* Kingston, 1939.
——. *Self-Government for Jamaica.* New York, 1936.
Tucker, Jimmy. *Developments in the Renewed Jamaica Progressive League.* Kingston: Jamaica Progressive League, 1992.

Unpublished Thesis

Lumsden, Joy. 'Robert Love and Jamaican Politics.' Unpublished PhD thesis, University of the West Indies, Mona, 1987.

Internet

Bender, Thomas. 'Internationalizing the Study of American History: A Joint Project of the Organization of American Historians and New York University: Report on Planning Conference, Villa La Pietra, New York University in Florence, Italy, July 6–9, 1997. http://www.oah.org/activities/lapietra/report1.html (last viewed October 15, 2011).
PNP website, http://www.pnpjamaica.com/index.php/who-we-are/our-history (last viewed, November 29, 2011).

Interviews, conducted by the Author

Interview with Frank Gordon, Kingston, April 9, 2008.
Interview with Richard Hart, Brighton, July 3, 2007.
Interview with Jimmy Tucker, December 12, 2006.

Secondary Literature

Aarons, John A. 'W. Adolphe Roberts and the Movement for Self-Government.' *Jamaica Journal* 16 (1983): 58–63.
Allen, Theodore W. *The Invention of the White Race: The Origin of Racial Oppression in Anglo-America.* Vol. 2. London: Verso, 1997.
Anderson, Benedict. *Imagined Communities.* 2nd ed. London: Verso, 2006.
Anderson, Benedict R. O'Gorman. *Long-Distance Nationalism: World-Capitalism and the Rise of Identity Politics.* Berkeley: Center for German and European Studies, University of California, 1992.
Appadurai, Arjun. 'The Production of Locality.' In *Counterworks: Managing the Diversity of Knowledge,* edited by Richard Fardon, 208–29. Oxon: Routledge, 1995.

Bibliography

Ashcroft, Bill, Gareth Griffiths and Helen Tiffin, eds. *The Post-Colonial Studies Reader*. London, New York: Routledge, 1995.

Augier, Roy. 'Before and After 1865.' *New World Quarterly* 2 (1966): 21–40.

Ayearst, Morley. *The British West Indies*. New York: New York University Press, 1960.

Baptiste, Fitzroy. *War, Cooperation, and Conflict: The European Possessions in the Caribbean 1939–1945*. Westport: Greenwood Publishing, 1988.

Barkan, Elazar. 'Introduction: Historians and Historical Reconciliation.' *The American Historical Review* 114 (2009): 899–913.

Bay, Mia. 'Race.' In *Encyclopedia of American Cultural and Intellectual History*. Vol 3. Edited by Mary Kupiec Cayton and Peter W. Williams, 121–29. New York: Scribner, 2001.

Beckford, George L. *Persistent Poverty: Underdevelopment in Plantation Economies of the Third World*. Morant Bay: George L. Beckford, 1983.

Bender, Thomas. *A Nation among Nations: America's Place in World History*. New York: Hill and Wang, 2006.

——, ed. *Rethinking American History in a Global Age*. Berkeley, Los Angeles: University of California Press, 2002.

Benn, Denis M. *The Caribbean: An Intellectual History, 1774–2003*. Kingston: Ian Randle Publishers, 2004.

——. 'The Theory of Plantation Economy and Society: A Methodological Critique.' *The Journal of Commonwealth & Comparative Politics* 12 (1974): 249–60.

Bennet, Wycliffe: 'W. Adolphe Roberts: A Personal Recollection.' *Jamaica Journal* 16 (1983): 54–64.

Black, Clinton V. *History of Jamaica*. London: Longman, 1979.

Bogues, Anthony. 'Nationalism and Jamaican Political Thought.' In *Jamaica in Slavery and Freedom*, edited by Kathleen E.A. Monteith and Glen Richards, 363–87. Kingston: University of the West Indies Press, 2002.

——. 'Politics, Nation and PostColony: Caribbean Inflections.' *Small Axe* 6.1 (2002): 1–30.

Bolland, O. Nigel. *The Politics of Labour in the British Caribbean: The Social Origins of Authoritarianism and Democracy in the Labour Movement*. Kingston: Ian Randle Publishers, 2001.

Brereton, Bridget, ed. *General History of the Caribbean: The Caribbean in the 20th Century*. Vol. 5. Paris: UNESCO, 2004.

Brown, Aggrey. *Colour, Class and Politics in Jamaica*. New Brunswick: Transaction, 1979.

Bryan, Patrick. *Inside Out & Outside In: Factors in the Creation of Contemporary Jamaica*. Kingston: Grace Kennedy Foundation, 2000.

——. *The Jamaican People, 1880–1902: Race, Class and Social Control.* Kingston: University of the West Indies Press, 2000.

Bryce-Laporte, Roy S. 'Black Immigrants: The Experience of Invisibility and Inequality.' *Journal of Black Studies* 3 (1972).

Budde, Gunilla-Friederike, Sebastian Conrad and Oliver Janz, eds. *Transnationale Geschichte: Themen Tendenzen und Theorien.* Göttingen, 2006.

Carnegie, James. *Some Aspects of Jamaica's Politics 1918–1938.* Kingston: Institute of Jamaica, 1973.

Chatterjee, Partha. *Nationalist Thought and the Colonial World: A Derivative Discourse.* London: Zed Books, 1986.

——. 'Whose Imagined Community.' *Millennium: Journal of International Studies* 20 (1991): 521–25.

Chivallon, Christine. *The Black Diaspora of the Americas.* Kingston: Ian Randle Publishers, 2011.

Clarke, John Henrik, ed. *Marcus Garvey and the Vision of Africa.* New York: Black Classic Press, 1974.

Collier, Simon. 'Nationality, Nationalism, and Supranationalism in the Writings of Simón Bolívar.' *The Hispanic American Historical Review* 63 (1983): 37–64.

Cronon, E. David, ed. *Marcus Garvey.* Englewood Cliffs, NJ: Prentice-Hall, 1973.

Dagnini, Jérémie Kroubo. 'Marcus Garvey: A Controversial Figure in the History of Pan-Africanism.' *The Journal of Pan African Studies* 2 (2008): 198–208.

Dalleo, Raphael. 'The Public Sphere and Jamaican Anticolonial Politics: Public Opinion, Focus, and the Place of the Literary.' *Small Axe* 14.2, no. 32 (2010): 56–82

David, E.J.R. *Filipino-/American Postcolonial-Psychology: Oppression, Colonial Mentality and Decolonization.* Bloomington: AuthorHouse, 2011.

Davis, F. James. *Who is Black?* 2nd ed. University Park: Pennsylvania State University Press, 2001.

Derrick, Jonathan. *Africa's 'Agitators:' Militant Anti-Colonialism in Africa and the West, 1918–1939.* New York: Columbia University Press, 2008.

Duke, Eric E. 'The Diasporic Dimensions of British Caribbean Federation.' *New West Indian Guide* 83 (2009): 219–48.

Eaton, George E. *Alexander Bustamante and Modern Jamaica.* Kingston: Kingston Publishers, 1995.

Eschen, Penny M. von. *Race against Empire: Black Americans and Anticolonialism, 1937–1957.* Ithaca: Cornell University Press, 1997.

Fanon, Franz. *Black Skin, White Masks.* New York: Grove Press, 1991.

——. *The Wretched of the Earth.* New York: Grove Press, 2004.

Fardon, Richard, ed. *Counterworks: Managing the Diversity of Knowledge.* Oxon: Routledge, 1995.

Fisher Fishkin, Shelly. 'Crossroads of Cultures: The Transnational Turn in American Studies: Presidential Address to the American Studies Association November 12, 2004.' *American Quarterly* 57 (2005): 17–57.

Floyd-Thomas, Juan M. *The Origins of Black Humanism in America: Reverend Ethelred Brown and the Unitarian Church.* New York: Palgrave Macmillan, 2008.

Foner, Nancy. 'What's New About Transnationalism?: New York Immigrants Today and at the Turn of the Century.' *Diaspora: A Journal of Transnational Studies* 6.3 (1977): 355–75.

Fraser, Cary, *Ambivalent Anti-Colonialism: The United States and the Genesis of West Indian Independence, 1940–196.* Westport, Conn: Greenwood Press, 1994.

Füllberg-Stollberg, Claus. 'The Caribbean in the Second World War.' In *General History of the Caribbean: The Caribbean in the 20th Century*, edited by Bridget Brereton. Vol. 5. Paris: UNESCO Publishing; London: Macmillan Publishers, 2004.

Garvey, Amy J. *Garvey and Garveyism.* Kingston: A. Jacques Garvey, 1963.

Gellner, Ernest. *Nations and Nationalism.* 2nd ed. Oxford: Blackwell Publishing, 2006.

Gilroy, Paul. *The Black Atlantic: Modernity and Double Consciousness.* London: Verso, 2002.

Glick Schiller, Nina, Linda Basch and Christina Szanton-Blanc. 'From Immigrant to Transmigrant: Theorizing Transnational Migration.' *Anthropological Quarterly* 68 (1995): 48–63.

Greene, Julie. *The Canal Builders: Making America's Empire at the Panama Canal.* London: Penguin, 2009.

Hall, Stuart. 'Old and New Identities, Old and New Ethnicities.' In *Culture, Globalization and the World System: Contemporary Conditions for the Representation of Identity*, edited by Anthony D. King, 41–68. Minnesota: University of Minnesota Press, 1997.

Hart, Richard. *The End of Empire: Transition to Independence in Jamaica and Other Caribbean Region Colonies.* Kingston: Arawak Publications, 2006.

——. 'Jamaica and Self-Determination, 1660–1970.' *Race* XIII (1972): 271–79.

——. *Rise and Organise: The Birth of the Workers and National Movements in Jamaica 1936–1939.* London: Karia Press, 1989.

——. *Time for a Change: Constitutional, Political and Labour Developments in Jamaica and Other Colonies in the Caribbean Region, 1944–1955.* Kingston: Arawak Publications, 2004.

——. *Towards Decolonisation: Political, Labour and Economic Developments in Jamaica 1938–1945.* Barbados: Canoe Press, 1999.

Heuman, Gad. *The Killing Time: The Morant Bay Rebellion in Jamaica.* Knoxville: University of Tennessee, 1994.

Hill, Robert A., ed. *The Marcus Garvey and Universal Negro Improvement Association Papers. Vol. I. 1826–1919.* Berkeley: University of California Press, 1983.

Hobsbawm, Eric J. *Nations and Nationalism Since 1780: Programme, Myth, Reality.* 2nd ed. Cambridge: Cambridge University Press, 2000.

——, and Terence Ranger, eds. *The Invention of Tradition.* Canto ed. Cambridge: Cambridge University Press, 1992.

Horne, Gerald. 'Toward a Transnational Research Agenda for African American History in the 21st Century.' *The Journal of African American History* 91 (2006): 288–303.

Horne, Gerald. *Cold War in a Hot Zone: The United States Confronts Labor and Independence Struggles in the British West Indies.* Philadelphia: Temple University Press, 2007.

Hulme, Peter. 'W. Adolphe Roberts and Jamaica.' *Jamaica Journal* 34.3 (2013): 14–23

James, Winston. *Holding Aloft the Banner of Ethiopia: Caribbean Radicalism in Early Twentieth-Century America.* London, New York: Verso, 1998.

Johnson, Anthony. *JAG Smith.* Kingston: Kingston Publishers, 1991.

Johnson, Howard B.D. 'The Politics of the Past: National Heroes in Post-Colonial Jamaica.' *The Elsa Goveia Memorial Lecture 2003.* Kingston: University of the West Indies, 2004.

Johnson, James W. *Black Manhattan.* New York: Da Capo Press, 1930.

Johnson, Michele A. 'The Beginning and the End: The Montego Bay Conference and the Jamaican Referendum on West Indian Federation.' *Social and Economic Studies* 48 (1999): 117–49.

Kasinitz, Philip. *Caribbean New York: Black Immigrants and the Politics of Race.* Ithaca: Cornell University Press, 1992.

Kedourie, Elie. *Nationalism in Asia and Africa.* New York: New American Library, 1970.

Killingray, David. 'The West Indian Federation and Decolonization in the British Caribbean.' *The Journal of Caribbean History* 34 (2000): 71–88.

Khan, Aisha. 'Journey to the Center of the Earth: The Caribbean as Master Symbol.' *Cultural Anthropology* 16 (2001): 271–302.

Kornweibel, Theodore. *No Crystal Stair: Black Life and the Messenger, 1917–1928.* Westport: Greenwood Press, 1975.

LaGuerre, John G. 'The Moyne Commission and the Jamaican Left.' *Social and Economic Studies* 31 (1982): 59–94.

Lazarus, Neil. *Nationalism and Practice in the Postcolonial World.* Cambridge: Cambridge University Press, 1999.

Leoussi, Athena S., and Steven Grosby, eds. *Nationalism and Ethnosymbolism: History, Culture and Ethnicity in the Formation of Nations.* Edinburgh: Edinburgh University Press, 2006.

Levitt, Peggy, Josh DeWind and Steven Vertovec. 'International Perspectives on Transnational Migration: An Introduction.' *International Migration Review* 37 (2003): 565–75.

Lewis, Gordon K. *Growth of the Modern West Indies.* Kingston: Ian Randle Publishers, 2004.

Lewis, Rupert, and Patrick E. Bryan, eds. *Garvey: His Work and Impact.* Trenton, NJ: Africa World Press, 1991.

Lewis, Rupert, Garvey in Jamaica. In *Marcus Garvey*, edited by E. David Cronon, 154–60. Englewood Cliffs, NJ: Prentice-Hall, 1973.

Lewis, Rupert. *Marcus Garvey: Anti-Colonial Champion.* Trenton, NJ: Africa World Press, 1988.

Lindsay, Louis. *The Myth of Independence: Middle Class Politics and Non-Mobilization in Jamaica.* Mona: Institute of Social and Economic Research, University of the West Indies, 1981.

Locke, Alain. *The New Negro.* New York: Albert & Charles Boni, 1925.

Louis, Wm. Roger. *Ends of British Imperialism: The Scrumble for Empire, Suez and Decolonization.* London: I.B. Tauris, 2006.

Manela, Erez. *The Wilsonian Moment.* Oxford: Oxford University Press, 2007.

Maingot, Anthony P., and Wilfredo Lozano. *The United States and the Caribbean: Transforming Hegemony and Sovereignty.* New York: Routledge, 2005.

Mars, Perry, 'Caribbean Influences in African-American Political Struggles.' *Ethnic and Racial Studies*, 27 (2004): 565-583.

Martin, Tony. *Race First: The Ideological and Organizational Struggle of Marcus Garvey and the Universal Negro Improvement Association.* Westport: Greenwood Press, 1976.

———, ed. *The Economic Future of the Caribbean.* Dover, MA: The Majority Press, 2004.

———. *The Pan-African Connection: From Slavery to Garvey and Beyond.* Dover, MA: The Majority Press, 1984.

Mills, Charles W. *Radical Theory and Caribbean Reality.* Kingston: University of the West Indies Press, 2010.

Monteith, Kathleen E. A., and Glen Richards, eds. *Jamaica in Slavery and Freedom: History, Heritage and Culture.* Kingston: University of the West Indies Press, 2002.

Moore, Brian L., and Michele Johnson. *Neither Led nor Driven: Contesting British Cultural Imperialism in Jamaica, 1865–1920.* Kingston: University of the West Indies Press, 2004.

Moore Turner, Joyce. *Caribbean Crusaders in the Harlem Renaissance.* Chicago: University of Illinois Press, 2005.

———, W. Burghardt Turner and Richard B. Moore. *Caribbean Militant in Harlem: Collected Writings 1920-1972 (Blacks in the Diaspora)*. Bloomington: Indiana University Press, 1988.

Morrison-Reed, Mark D. *Black Pioneers in a White Denomination*. Boston: Skinner House Books, 1980.

Moses, Wilson Jeremiah. *The Golden Age of Black Nationalism, 1850-1925*. Oxford: Oxford University Press, 1988.

Munroe, Trevor. *The Politics of Constitutional Decolonization: Jamaica 1944-1962*. Kingston: ISER, University of the West Indies, 1972.

Nnam, Michael Nkuzi. *Colonial Mentality in Africa*. Lanham: Hamilton Books, 2007.

Nouzeilles, Gabriela. 'Beyond Imagined Communities: Reading and Writing the Nation in Nineteenth-Century Latin America.' *Hispanic Review* 73 (2005): 514-17.

Norris, Katrin, Jamaica. *The Search for an Identity*. Oxford: Oxford University Press, 1962.

Osofsky, Gilbert. *Harlem: The Making of a Ghetto*. 2nd ed Chicago: Ivan R. Dee, 1966.

Palmer, Colin. *Freedom's Children: The 1938 Labor Rebellion and the Birth of Modern Jamaica*. Chapel Hill: UNC Press, 2014.

Parker, Jason C. *Brother's Keeper: The United States, Race, and Empire in the British Caribbean, 1937-1962*. Oxford: Oxford University Press, 2008.

Parker, Jason C. '"Capital of the Caribbean": The African American-West Indian "Harlem Nexus" and the Transnational Drive for Black Freedom, 1940-1948.' *The Journal of African American History* 89 (2004): 98-117.

Parker, Jason C. 'Remapping the Cold War in the Tropics: Race, Communism, and National Security in the West Indies.' *The International History Review* 24 (2002): 318-47.

Parascandola, Louis J., ed. *Look for Me All Around You: Anglophone Caribbeans in the Harlem Renaissance*. Detroit: Wayne State University Press, 2005.

Patsides, Nicholas. 'Marcus Garvey: Race Idealism and His Vision of Jamaican Self-Government.' *Caribbean Quarterly* 51 (2005): 37-52.

Phelps, O. W. 'Rise of the Labour Movement in Jamaica.' *Social and Economic Studies* 4 (1960): 417-86.

Philogène, Gina. *From Black to African American: A New Social Representation*. Westport: Praeger Publishers/Greenwood Publishing Group, 1999.

Post, Ken. *Arise Ye Starvelings: The Jamaican Labour Rebellion of 1938 and its Aftermath*. The Hague: Martinus Nijhoff Publishers, 1978.

———. *Strike the Iron: A Colony at War, Jamaica 1939-1945*. 2 vols. London: Humanities Press, 1981.

Rabaka, Reiland. *Africana Critical Theory: Reconstructing the Black Radical Tradition, from W.E.B. DuBois and C.L.R. James to Franz Fanon and Amilcar Cabral.* Lanham: Lexington Books, 2009.

Richards, Glen. 'Race, Class, and Labour Politics in Colonial Jamaica, 1900–1934.' In *Jamaica in Slavery and Freedom,* edited by Monteith and Richards, 340–62. Kingston: University of the West Indies Press, 2002.

——. 'Race, Labour, and Politics in Jamaica and St Kitts, 1909–1940: A Comparative Survey of the Roles of the National Club of Jamaica and the Workers League of St Kitts.' In *Working Slavery, Pricing Freedom: Perspectives from the Caribbean, Africa and the African Diaspora,* edited by Verene A. Shepherd, 502–532. New York: Palgrave, 2001.

Rinke, Stefan, H. *Der letzte freie Kontinent: Deutsche Lateinamerikapolitik im Zeichen Transnationaler Beziehungen, 1918–1933.* Stuttgart: Heinz, 1996.

Robotham, Don. 'The Development of a Black Ethnicity in Jamaica.' In *Garvey: His Work and Impact,* edited by Rupert Lewis and Patrick E. Bryan, 23–38. Trenton, NJ: Africa World Press, 1991.

Samuels, Wilfred D. *Five Afro-Caribbean Voices in American Culture, 1917–1929: Hubert H. Harrison, Wilfred A. Domingo, Richard B. Moore, Cyril V. Briggs, and Claude McKay.* Boulder: Belmont Books, 1977.

Scheiner, Seth M. *Negro Mecca: A History of the Negro in New York City.* New York: New York University Press, 1965.

Schirmer, Daniel B., and Stephen Rosskamm Shalom. *The Philippines Reader: A History of Colonialism, Neocolonialism, Dictatorship and Resistance.* Cambridge: South End Press, 1987.

Shepherd, Verene A. *Working Slavery, Pricing Freedom: Perspectives from the Caribbean, Africa and the African Diaspora.* New York: Palgrave, 2001.

Sherlock, Philip, and Hazel Bennett. *The Story of the Jamaican People.* Kingston: Ian Randle Publishers, 1998.

Showers Johnson, Violet. 'Racial Frontiers in Jamaica's Nonracial Nationhood.' In *Race and Nation, Ethnic Systems in the Modern World,* edited by Paul Spickard, 155–70. New York: Routlege, 2005.

Sires, Ronald V. 'The Experience of Jamaica With Modified Crown Colony Government.' *Social and Economic Studies* 4 (1955): 150–67.

Slocum, Karla, and Deborah Thomas. 'Rethinking Global and Area Studies: Insights from Caribbeanist Anthropology.' *American Anthropologist* 105 (2003): 553–65.

Smith, Anthony D. *Nationalism: Theory, Ideology, History.* Hoboken: Wiley, 2001.

——. *National Identity.* Reno: University of Nevada Press, 1991.

Smith, Michael Garfield. *Culture, Race, and Class in the Commonwealth Caribbean.* Kingston: University of the West Indies, 1984.

Smith, Richard. *Jamaican Volunteers in the First World War: Race, Masculinity and the Development of National Consciousness.* Manchester: Manchester University Press, 2004.

Solomon, Mark. *The Cry Was Unity: Communists and African Americans, 1917–1936.* Jackson: University Press of Mississippi, 1998.

Spickard, Paul R., ed. *Race and Nation, Ethnic Systems in the Modern World.* New York: Routledge, 2005.

Springer, Hugh W. *Reflections on the Failure of the First West Indian Federation.* Reprint. New York: AMS Press, 1973.

Spry Rush, Anne. *Bonds of Empire: West Indians and Britishness from Victoria to Decolonization.* Oxford: Oxford University Press, 2011.

Spry Rush, Anne. 'Imperial Identities in Colonial Minds: Harold Moody and the League of Coloured Peoples, 1931–1950.' *Twentieth Century British History* 13, no. 4 (2002): 356–83.

Stein, Judith. *The World of Marcus Garvey: Race and Class in Modern Society.* Baton Rouge: Louisiana State University Press, 1986.

Stone, Carl. 'Decolonization and the Caribbean State System: The Case of Jamaica.' In *The Newer Caribbean: Decolonization, Democracy and Development*, edited by Carl Stone and Henry Paget. Philadelphia: Institute for the Study of Human Issues, 1983.

——, and Henry Paget, eds. *The Newer Caribbean: Decolonization, Democracy and Development.* Philadelphia: Institute for the Study of Human Issues, 1983.

Thelen, David. 'Of Audiences, Borderlands, and Comparisons: Toward the Internationalization of American History.' *Journal of American History* 79 (1992): 432–26.

Thelen, David. 'The Nation and Beyond: Transnational Perspectives on United States History.' *Journal of American History* 86 (1999): 965–75.

Timm, Birte. 'Caribbean Leaven in the American Loaf: Wilfred A. Domingo, the Jamaica Progressive League, and the Founding of a Decolonization Movement for Jamaica.' In *Beyond the Nation: United States History in Transnational Perspective*, edited by Thomas Adam and Uwe Leubken, 81–89. Bulletin of the German Historical Institute, Supplement 5, 2008.

Trouillot, Michel-Rolph. 'The Caribbean Region: An Open Frontier in Anthropological Theory.' *Annual Review of Anthropology* 21 (1992): 19–42.

Tyrell, Ian. 'Reflections on the Transnational Turn in United States History: Theory and Practice.' *Journal of Global History* 4 (2009): 453–74.

Volkov, Shulamit. 'Jewish History: The Nationalism of Transnationalism.' In *Transnationale Geschichte*, edited by Budde et al., 190–201. Göttingen: Vandenhoeck and Ruprecht, 2011.

Wade, Peter. *Race and Ethnicity in Latin America.* 2nd ed. London: Pluto Press, 2010.

Watkins-Owens, Irma. *Blood Relations: Caribbean Immigrants and the Harlem Community 1900–1930.* Bloomington: Indiana University Press, 1996.

Wehler, Hans-Ulrich.'Transnationale Geschichte – der neue Königsweg historischer Forschung?' In *Transnationale Geschichte: Themen Tendenzen und Theorien,* edited by Gunilla Budde and others, 161–74. Göttingen: Vandenhoeck und Ruprecht, 2006.

Williams, Eric. *Capitalism and Slavery.* Chapel Hill: UNC Press, 1944.

Wimmer, Andreas, and Nina Glick Schiller. 'Methodological Nationalism and Beyond: Nation State Building, Migration and the Social Sciences.' *Global Networks* 2, no. 4 (2002): 301–334.

Witham, Charlie. *'Bitter Rehearsal: British and American Planning for a Post-War West Indies.'* Westport: Praeger Publishers, 2002.

Zeidenfelt, Alex. 'Political and Constitutional Developments in Jamaica.' *Journal of Politics* 14 (1952): 512–40.

INDEX OF NAMES AND ORGANIZATIONS

A
Aarons, John, 37
Adams, David, 285
Adams, Grantley, 398, 400
Aiken, Percy A., 84, 118, 132, 171, 199, 309, 342, 344
Aiken, DeMena, 84, 118
Abyssinian Baptist Church, 55, 117
Acheson, Dean, 334
Afro-American Liberty League, 46, 50
African Blood Brotherhood (ABB), 46, 48, 50, 55ff.
African Orthodox Catholic Church, 199
Aguilera, Francisco, 374
Alcantara, Theo J., 263
Allen, E. V., 84
Allen, Harold, 388
America First Committee, 284f.
American Civil Liberties Union (ACLU), 285
American Committee for West Indian Federation, 384
American West Indian Association on Caribbean Affairs, 263, 289
Anderson, Benedict, xiii–xv, 103, 316,
Anderson, Jervis, 411f.
Anderson, Oswald E., 25, 90f., 127, 132, 167, 200, 204, 249, 266
Anglo-American Caribbean Commission (AACC), 296, 313, 362
Arnett, V. L., 180, 236, 238, 241, 251, 268, 278, 342, 347, 362, 378f., 384, 403, 428

Ashenheim, Leslie E., 272, 276f.
Aspignall, Algernon, 377
Atherton, G. C., 181
Atlantic Federal Union – A Non-Partisan Group, 405

B
Bailey, Amy, 59, 84, 113, 118, 182, 190, 192, 265, 267f., 268, 308
Bailey-Essien, Ivy, 33, 59, 70, 228, 261, 275, 300
Bailey, M. G., 89, 127f.,
Bailey, Victor A., 182, 198, 305
Bain-Alves, Alexander, 25
Barclay, A. A., 25
Batista, Fulgencio, 353
Beckford, George, ix, 4, 22
Bell, R. O., 198
Benn, Denis M., xxii, 21f., 91, 239
Betánoes, Ramón Emeterio, 374
Bethune, D., 203
Bernard, Agnes, 118, 120, 132
Bertram, Arnold, xix
Blackman, Peter, 203
Blackwood, James, 26
Black Panther Party, 44
Blanshard, Paul, 299f., 307–12, 332, 338f., 363
Bogle, Paul, 3
Bogues, Anthony, 5, 7, 24
Bolívar, Simón, xiv, 36, 232, 351f., 353
Bolivarian Society of Jamaica, 350, 351ff., 353f., 374
Boulin, Herbert Simeon, 289

Bowen, George R., 84, 128, 201
Bowen, Thomas, 59
Boyer, Dominic, xiv
Bradshaw, E. A., 132
Bradey, E., 132
Braithwaite, S. R., 84
Brandon, Karl, 132
Bridgeman, Reginald, 203
Brierre, John-Ferdinand, 353
Brinton, Henry, 255, 265, 277
Briggs, Cyril V., 46, 48, 50, 56ff., 62ff, 282
Brooke, S. E., 182,
Brooks-Johnson, Daisy, 384
Brown, Egbert Ethelred, vii, xix, xxiv, 9, 28, 32, 35, 40, 51–55, 58f., 63ff., 70, 73ff., 78, 80, 84, 87, 112, 117, 119ff., 127, 138, 150–60, 163, 200, 212, 223, 226, 234, 258f., 262f., 275, 286–89, 343, 347, 356, 361, 384f., 416, 421, 424, 426
Brown, Ella Matilda, 65
Brown, Lucien M., 131, 263, 289
Brown, S., 128,
British Commonwealth of Nations, 2f., 12, 14, 19, 22, 30, 33, 39, 70, 79, 88, 92, 103, 110, 119, 142, 151, 153, 162, 182f., 223, 253, 316f., 329, 336, 377, 382f.
British Council, 292
British Labour Party (BLP), 104, 129, 139, 147, 237, 244, 286, 297, 317, 327, 345, 363
British West India Regiment, xv, 202
Bryan, Patrick, xii, 6
Bryant, Robert William, 25
Buchanan, Hugh C., 84, 88ff., 93, 98f., 103, 105f., 113, 120, 122f., 127ff., 172, 204, 261
Burrell, Ben 35, 48, 50, 52, 199, 409

Burrell, Theodore, 32, 35, 48, 50, 59, 409
Bustamante, Alexander, vii–ix, xi, xxv, 15, 20, 88f., 116ff., 122f., 132, 157, 159, 174–77, 204, 248, 272, 274, 284, 290–95, 298, 306–12, 319, 326, 328, 337, 339, 342f., 345f., 362, 371, 383, 390, 392, 397ff., 403ff., 408, 410, 412ff., 420, 427f., 430
Bustamante Industrial Trade Union (BITU) 122, 176f., 272, 277, 290–93

C
Cameron, O. H., 182, 198
Campbell, C. C., 202
Campbell, E. E. A., 133, 165ff., 168, 171, 174f., 202, 204, 249, 278, 306, 359
Campbell, Grace, 55, 57, 62f., 65
Campbell, Martin L., 55, 63, 65, 230, 235, 241, 245, 256f., 272, 278–83, 287, 296, 378, 411
Campbell, W. F., 87
Cargill, Morris, 417
Caribbean Labour Congress (CLC), 380
Carnegie, James, xxii, 4, 11, 14, 21, 77
Cawley, A., 175
Cawley, T. J., 93, 182
Chalwell, T. E., 264,
Chapman, Esther, 168f., 306, 318
Chatterjee, Partha, xiv
Chisholm, J. C., 267
Churchill, Winston, 239f., 284, 299, 326
Cipriani, Arthur A., 39, 377
Citrine, Walter, 154, 156, 174, 199

Index of Names and Organizations

Civil Liberties Council 277, 296, 337, 359
Clarke, A. J., 128
Clarke, C. B., 203
Clerk's Union, 167
Cooke, H. F., 180, 198,
Collard, Dudley, 203
Colonial Office, Great Britain, xii, xxv, 7, 10, 27, 32, 91, 96, 148f, 166, 174, 218, 254, 256, 258, 271, 286, 293, 295ff., 299f., 303, 324, 335, 352f., 356, 363, 376f, 379, 382, 387, 394, 397, 399, 404, 406f., 409, 412f.
Coombs, A. G. S., 175f., 204
Cooper, D. A., 131, 267
Cox, Samuel A. G., xi, xv, 8f., 11, 58, 144, 304, 376, 425
Comintern, 56
Committee for West Indian Affairs, 174
Communist Party USA, 56f., 334, 358
Council of Pan-American Democracy, 259
Creech Jones, Arthur, 203, 286, 297, 363
Cripps, Stafford, 139–42, 203
Cromwell, Oliver, 81
Crosswaith, Frank, 62, 64f.
Curran, Eileen, 69

D

DaCosta, G. M., 84
DaCosta, L. A., 359
DaCosta, V. P., 84, 182
Dalton James, Edith, 385
Davidson, G. L., 128
Davidson, S., 181
Davis, E. C., 128
Davis, I. E., 203

D'Aguilar, Tessie A., 59
de Hostos, Eugenio Mariá, 352
de Lisser, Herbert George, 18, 37, 91, 94f., 114, 120, 128, 137f., 168ff., 187, 192, 195f., 215, 234f., 247, 303f., 311, 338, 359
Denham, Edward Brandis, 96, 116
Derrick, Jonathan, xxi
Diego, Juan, 553
Dixon, Alexander, 6ff.
Dixon, Edward T., 10
Domingo Manherz, Eulalie, 51, 64, 75, 84
Domingo, Karl Marx, 64, 301
Domingo, Wilfred A., viii, ix, xv, xix, xxii–xxv, 8, 13, 21, 29–32, 35, 40–51, 53–57, 62–65, 70, 73ff., 78, 80f., 83f., 88, 92, 98, 102–106, 109, 113f., 120f., 123ff., 131f., 135f., 140–48, 150, 152, 158–65, 169f., 172–82, 184ff., 189f., 193ff., 197, 201–204, 207–46, 248–60, 262ff., 268, 271–302, 304–35, 337f., 340f., 345, 352, 356–62, 364, 372, 377–84, 386–405, 408–14, 416, 420–27
Domingo, Yolanda, 64
Douglass, Frederick, 81
Draper, Theodore, 56
Draughon, Donald A., 223
Dreyfus, Alfred, 284
Duhaney, W. S., 87, 112, 118, 127f, 131, 199, 202f, 212, 342, 344
Duke, Eric D., 376
Durant, E. Elliott, 263
Durham, B., 199

E

East Indian Progressive Society, 321, 324
Eastwood, E., 128
Edwards, J. A. G., 174, 204
Ehrenstein, Rudolph, 90, 110, 115, 127, 130
Elected Members Association, 15, 237, 304
Ernest, William, 199, 262
Evans, E. R. Dudley, 117f., 120, 131f., 157, 165–68, 170f., 192, 199ff., 203, 206, 309, 371
Eyre, Edward, 349

F

Fairclough, O. T., 77f., 84, 106, 135f., 142ff., 180, 198, 206
Farquharson, May, 155, 359
Fanon, Frantz xiv, 147, 317
Federation of Citizen's Associations (FCA) 79, 91, 171f., 192, 198, 202, 249, 266, 304, 309, 424
Firmin, Amténor (acc), 374
Floyd-Thomas, Juan M., 53
Ford, James, 58
Fort-Whiteman, Lovett, 63
Foster-Davis, W. E., 133
Fraser, Carry, 297
Fraser, I. A., 59
Friends of Negro Freedom, 57
Füllberg-Stollberg, Claus, 208
Fyzullah, I. N., 323f.

G

Garvey, Amy Jacques, 19, 330
Garvey, Marcus Mosiah, xi, xiv, xxi, 8, 15–21, 27, 40, 44, 47ff., 51, 57, 62f., 98f, 124, 189f., 304, 376
Gellner, Ernest, xiii

George V, King, 284
Ghandi, Mahatma, xiv, 143, 327, 329
Gilroy, Paul, xvii
Glasspole, Florizel, 28, 109, 337, 347
Glick-Schiller, Nina, xvi
Gossip, Alex, 203
Gordon, Frank, xix, 426
Gordon, George William, 3, 284
Grant, St William, 116ff., 132,
Grant, Ulysses S., 246
Gulley, C. A. (sometimes spelled Gully), 87, 127f., 131

H

Halifax, Edward Frederick Lindley Wood, 274
Hall, George, 286
Hall, Stuart, 3
Hall, Otto, 63
Hanson, T. E., 59, 263, 289
Harlem Unitarian Church (HUC), 51, 53–56
Harper, Lucius C., 298
Harrison, Hubert H., 45ff., 49f., 53, 62, 376
Harrods, Jeffrey, xx
Harry, V. R., 108
Haywood, Harry, 63
Henriques, C. G. X., 76, 84
Henry, A. E. T., 28
Henry, Arthur, 295
Hart, Ansell, 276f., 298, 395
Hart, Richard, xix, xx, 15, 21, 77, 98f., 102–105, 117, 120–25, 127ff., 132f, 135, 150, 172, 174, 184, 204, 216, 256, 261, 272f., 276, 293ff., 299, 331, 346, 358, 362, 380f., 415
Hendrickson, Elizabeth, 62

Index of Names and Organizations

Hill, Frank, 77, 84, 85, 135, 181, 295, 386, 427
Hill, Ken, 74–79, 84, 85, 88f., 93, 106, 108f., 122f., 128, 139, 144, 174, 181, 206, 295, 328, 343, 378, 380, 386, 399
Hill, Robert A., ix, 8
Hillquit, Morris, 46
Hills, Christopher B., 401, 405, 418
Holness, Andrew, vii, viiii
Hopwood, H. Vincent, 10
Horne, Gerald, xxi
Houston, Charles, 231
Huggins, John, 297, 336
Huiswoud, Otto, 46, 54, 56, 63, 282
Hull, Cordell, 223, 226f., 230, 236, 242f., 284, 287, 328
Hulme, Peter, xxi
Huxley, Aldous, 359

I

Independent Political Council, 46
Institute of Jamaica, 128, 318, 344, 354, 422, 430
International African Service Bureau, 155
International Labor Defense, 131
International Union of American Republics, 352
International Uplift League, 57
Irish Progressive League, 69
Isaac-Henry, C. A., 26, 82, 93
Isaacs, Edith, 107,
Isaacs, Wills O., 28, 292, 298, 305, 397, 399, 402f.
Issa, Abe, 305

J

Jacobs, H. P., 77, 84, 106, 128, 143, 155, 196, 198, 206, 246f., 356, 421f., 424, 426
Jagan, Cheddi, 387
Jagger, John, 203
Jamaica Benevolent Association, 30, 32, 47
Jamaica Conservative Party (JCP), 305f.
Jamaica Democratic Party (JDP), 305, 309
Jamaica Deputation Committee (JDC), 152–55, 158, 200
Jamaica Federation of Labour, 25
Jamaica Indian Conference, 323
Jamaica Imperial Association (JIA), 12, 135
Jamaica Historical Society, 340, 350, 430
Jamaica Labour Party (JLP), vii, viii–x, xx, xxv, 167, 176, 202, 307–10, 337, 341f., 346, 371, 376, 388, 390, 392, 395, 397, 399, 402–405, 408ff., 412f., 417, 420, 423f., 427f.
Jamaica League, 9f., 13, 53
Jamaica Library Association, 354, 430
Jamaica National League, 13, 78
Jamaica Political Constitution Reform Association, 11
Jamaica Press Club, 340
Jamaica Progressive League, passim
Jamaica Reform Club, 12
Jamaica Representative Government Association, 11
Jamaica Union of Teachers (JUT), 13, 318
Jamaica Welfare Ltd., 155

Jamaica Workers and Tradesmen's Union (JWTU), 116, 123
Jamaican Council for Civic Liberties (JCCL), 276
James, Winston, 32, 42–45
Johnson, Keith, 423
Johnson, Michele, xi, xii, 5, 384
Johnson, S. O. G., 128, 199, 201, 203, 206
Johnson, W. S., 267
Johnston, Vincent, 422
Jones, Ken, x, xi, 421, 430
Jones, Morgan, 156, 199
Jones, S. M., 25
Jordon, Edward, 189f., 205, 318

K
Kasinitz, Phillip, xxiii, xxvi, 44
Kelly, George F., 334f.
Kemp, Edwin C., 313f.,
Kerr-Coombs, Stennett, 128, 172, 174
Killingray, David, 410
King, Arthur, E., 262, 264, 287
King, Charles D. B., 48
Kingston and St Andrew Voters League, 13
Kingston and St Andrew Corporation (KSAC), 18, 88, 171, 203, 343
Kingston and St Andrew Literary and Debating Society, 86
Kirkpatrick, R. J., 59
Knuckles, C. J. , 199
Ku Klux Klan, 61

L
League for Coloured People, 155
League of Nations, 18, 48
Lee, Algernon, 49
Left Book Club, 28, 129, 164

Legislative Council of Jamaica, 4, 6, 8–15, 17f., 30, 36, 78, 88, 90, 92f., 99, 106, 111, 115, 135, 153f., 156, 160, 162, 165f., 181, 191, 193f., 214f., 249, 256–59, 266, 277, 291, 299, 301, 380, 383, 390f., 403, 428
Lenin, Vladimir I., xiv, xxi, 45, 51, 56, 358
Lecesne, Arnold J., 13, 89, 93, 102
Lewis, Alfred Baker, 285, 289
Lewis, C. B., 422
Lewis, Gordon K., xi, xxii, 5, 356f.
Lewis, Rupert ix, 7, 15, 20
Lewis, Walter, 306
Liberal Association, 28, 52
Lightbody, P., 25
Lindsay, Louis, ix, 208
Livingston, R. C., 132
Lloyd, Ivan, 337
Lloyd, T. K., 298
Lochard, Metz T. P., 284
Locke, Alain, 61
Lomnitz, Claudio, xiv
Louis, Roger Wm., xx
Luperón, Gregorio, 374
L' Ouverture, Toussaint, 36, 81, 232, 351
Love, Robert, 6ff., 24, 304, 376
Lyle, Leonard, 286

M
Maceo, Antonio, 353
Malliet, A. M. Wendell, 29f., 32, 218, 222, 226, 232, 263, 305
Manela, Erez, xxi
Manley, Edna, 118, 209, 219, 239, 247–51, 278, 288, 354f., 418

Index of Names and Organizations

Manley, Michael, 392, 424
Manley, Norman Washington, vii, viii, x, xi, xix, xxv, 15, 21, 28, 95f., 106, 117, 122f., 129, 135–44, 146f., 155ff., 159, 162–65, 170f., 174–77, 179–86, 190, 192, 198, 200f., 208, 214f., 219, 222, 236–41, 243–48, 250–54, 257, 259, 265f., 268, 273f., 277ff., 284, 287–306, 308, 310f., 313f., 329, 334, 336f., 340ff., 344–47, 364, 380, 383–86, 389, 391f., 395, 397–400, 402–405, 408f., 413–18, 420–28, 430
Maragh, Winston, vii, viii, x
Marquis, Samuel S., 272, 359
Marryshow, T. A., 39, 377

Marson, Una, 84, 128
Martí, José, 36, 351
Martin, Tony, 415
Maxwell, J. W., 84
MacDonald, Malcolm, 149
McBean, W. A., 97f., 105f., 113, 127ff., 172, 174, 189, 197, 201, 203, 261, 267
McCulloch, D. W. E., 155, 200
McFarlane, Clare J. I., 354), 190, 206, 354, 422
McFarlane, Walter G., viii, xxii, xxiv, 28, 86–90, 94, 97, 109–12, 116, 118f., 121, 126ff., 131f., 135–38, 140, 158, 167f., 178ff., 184, 186, 189f., 194, 198f., 201, 203, 206, 212f., 234f., 255f., 258, 298, 308, 340–44, 354, 378, 425
McKay, Claude, 12, 62f.
McKay, U. Theo, 12
Macleod, Ian, 410
McNeil, P., 128

McPherson, C. A., 84, 154, 158, 171, 180, 200, 203, 249, 267f.
Meikle, Louis S., 380
Meikle, Rupert E., 13f., 28, 39, 72f., 82, 108
Melo, Leopoldo, 227f., 234f.
Mends, Alfred R., 12f., 25, 202,
Messam, Don, 87, 128, 131, 267, 344
Millbourne, J. W., 64
Miller, P. L., 181
Millner, Lucille B., 285
Milne, A. A., 359
Montego Bay Literary and Debating Society, 52
Moore, Brian L., xi, xii, 5,
Moore, Richard B., xxiii, 46, 54, 56ff., 62–65, 117, 131, 193, 218, 221, 262ff., 282, 308, 360, 381, 400, 411
Moore Turner, Joyce, xxiii, 46, 50, 54f., 61, 65, 262
Morgan, Henry, 37
Morgan, H. B., 203, 286
Morris-Knibb, Mary, 84, 118, 171f., 190, 200, 203
Moyne, Lord Walter Guinness, 149, 153–56, 256, 274ff.
Moyston, Louis, x, xi, 111, 430
Moyston, Mr., 308
Munroe, O., 181
Munroe, Trevor, ix, 385, 397f., 400, 410, 414
Mussolini, Benito, 276

N

Nash, A. G., 25
National Association for the Advancement of Colored People (NAACP), 57, 231, 243, 274, 284, 289, 313

Nation of Islam, 44
National Club, xi, xv, 8f., 24, 47, 58
National Equal Rights League, 57
National Race Congress, 57
National Reform Association (NRA), x, xxii, 74–80, 82–85, 89ff., 93, 98f., 103, 105–109, 120, 136, 138, 152, 183, 195, 304, 421, 424, 427
Natural History Society, 430
Nelson, Cecil, 261
Negro Welfare Association, 155
Negro Workers Education League (NWEL), 261
Negroes against the War Committee, 281,
Nehru, Jawaharlal, 289, 327
Nethersole, Noel N., 76, 84, 133, 143, 155, 175, 198, 200, 204, 249, 254, 265f., 278, 284, 291, 305, 310, 334, 340, 386
Nevinson, Henry, 359
Newland, Linden, 403
Norris, Katrin, 5
Nuckle, C. G., 203

O

Olivier, Sir Sydney, 7f.
Osborne, H. P., 228, 253, 262, 289, 292
O'Meally, Jaime, 32, 35, 40, 48, 52, 59, 70f., 73, 78, 98, 100–106, 109, 113, 117, 120–23, 125, 132, 135, 165, 172, 194, 211, 226, 409
O'Meally, Walter, 88
Organization of American States (OAS), 374, 406
Owen, Chandler, 46, 48, 56f., 62ff.

P

Padgett, John F., xviii
Padmore, George, 231, 297f.
Paget, Hugh, 340, 357
Palache, Jack, 9f.
Pan-African Association, 7
Parascandola, Louis J., xxiii
Parker, Jason, xx, xxi, 207, 228, 296, 330f., 362, 376
Parker, Natty, 215
Patterson, Orlando, xvii, 44
Pen Club Jamaica, 354f., 374
Penso, O. G., 25, 198
People's Convention, 6
Peoples Educational Forum, 55
People's National Party (PNP), vii–xi, xviii–xx, xxii– xxv, 32, 59, 85, 95, 97ff., 129, 133f., 139, 141–48, 155–68, 170f., 174f., 177ff., 182, 183–88, 190–97, 202, 207–10, 213, 219, 229, 231, 236–39, 241–45, 248–60, 266, 268, 272–79, 290–98, 300–10, 312, 314, 321, 331, 334, 336f., 339–47, 356, 359, 364, 372, 376, 378, 380f., 383–86, 388ff., 392–95, 397–400, 402, 404f, 407–10, 412f. 417, 420–28, 430
People's Political Party (PPP), xi, 18f.
Peoples Progressive Party (PPP) (British Guiana), 387, 417
Petioni, Charles A., 262ff.
Pierrepoint, Reginald, 262f., 285, 381
Pixley, Frank A., 175, 337
Poetry League of Jamaica, 430
"Political Reporter" (Gleaner columnist), 405
Post, Ken, xxii, 77, 97f., 105, 115, 149, 156, 172, 174, 180, 228f., 297f., 299, 310

Index of Names and Organizations

Potter, Thomas A., 64f.
Powell, Jr, Adam Clayton, 55, 117, 231, 263, 308
Powell, Sr, Adam Clayton, 55
Probyn, Leslie, 10
Progressive Negro Association, 52
Putnam, Lara, xvii

Q
Quill and Ink Club, 13f., 28, 39
Queen Victoria I, xii, 5f.

R
Radway, S. P., 12f.
Rae, Clifford, 202, 267
Rance Committee, 386
Rand School of Social Science, 46
Randolph, A. Philip, 46, 48, 56f, 62ff., 281
Ranger, Terence, xiii
Readers and Writers Club, 28, 94, 128
Reid, C. A., 14, 88, 90, 110, 127, 211, 291
Reid, F. Theo, 262
Richards, Glen, 3, 122
Richards, Arthur Frederick, 175, 191, 214f., 252f., 271f., 274ff., 283–86, 290, 293, 295–98, 312, 334, 362
Roberts, W. Adolphe, ix, xi, xix, xxi, xxii, xxiv, xxv, 14, 29–41, 50f., 58ff., 69–74, 77–84, 89–99, 106–13, 118f., 125ff., 130, 135, 137–41, 143f., 146ff., 150, 152, 158–65, 168–71, 173–89, 191–97, 199, 201ff., 207–22, 224–30, 232–39, 242–52, 255, 257ff., 262, 271ff., 275f., 281, 286, 288ff., 292, 294, 300–303, 308, 311, 313, 315, 318, 330, 335–41, 344–57, 371f., 374, 377ff., 381, 383, 386–92, 397–409, 411–14, 420ff., 424ff., 429f.
Robotham, Don, 15
Rodney, Walter, ix
Rogers, Joel A., 45
Roosevelt, Franklin D., 41, 232, 240, 242, 245, 284, 297, 299, 313f., 331f., 338
Ross, C. A., 180
Roy, Manabendra Naht, 327
Russell, Bertrand, 359

S
Sassen, Saskia, xviii
Save Jamaica Volunteer Non-Partisan Group, 405
Savory, P. M. H., 131, 263
Schomburg, Arthur, 69
Schuyler, George S., 281, 289
Scotter, G. St C., 272, 276, 359
"Scrutator" (Gleaner columnist), 402f.
Seaga, Edward, 424
Sealy, Theodore E., 290, 340
Seivreight, William, 268, 337, 381
Sharp, T. H., 105
Shipping Association, 176
Shovington, Hayward, 65
Simpson, H. A. L., 8–11, 25
Simpson Miller, Portia, vii, viii
Scarlett-Munroe, Z., 192
Shirley, H. M., 265, 277, 290f.
Sherlock, Philip, 128, 340, 351, 373
Skinner, S. A., 131
Slater, Alexander, 14
Smith, J. A. G., 10, 14f., 191f., 359
Smith, Terry, 79, 88f., 425f.
Socialist Party of America, 45f., 49f., 54, 56, 65, 243
Soulette, John, 25
Somers, T. Gordon, 7, 9
Springer, Hugh W., 398, 414

Spry Rush, Anne, xi
Stalin, Joseph V., 276
Standing Closer Association Committee, 384
Stanley, Oliver, 297, 311, 380, 382f., 391
Stannard, Harold, 292, 294
St Mary Debating Association, 13
St Mary Citizens Association, 13, 142
Stevens, Hope, 193, 226, 232, 261, 263, 381
Stevens, D. Stockton, 285
Stone, Carl, 6
Stubbs, Reginald E., 11f., 14
Society for the Americas, 285

T

Taussig, Charles, 266, 284, 313, 363, 379
Thomas, A. A., 128
Thomas, Norman, 243, 285
Thompson, Dorcas, 59
Thompson, Dudley, 424, 426
Thompson, Herman, xix
Tomlinson, W. J., 198
Trade Union Advisory Council (TUAC), 174–77, 206
Trade Union Council (TUC), 174, 176f., 199, 290, 292
Trew, R. Samuel, 59, 262
Trinidad Benevolent Association, 131
Tucker, Jimmy, xix, 344, 372, 425
Turner, W. Burghardt, xxiii, 262
Twenty-First Assembly District Socialist Club, 46

U

United Aid for Persons of African Descent, 131
United Aid Society, 108f

United Nations (UNO), 328f., 388, 396, 420, 423f.
United Negro Improvement Association (UNIA), 12, 15–18, 20, 25, 44, 47f., 52, 57, 64, 426
U.S. Department of State, xii, 276, 285, 296, 301, 312ff., 334, 356

V

Valentine, G. E., 204
Varma, V. L., 86, 118, 120, 132, 189f., 192, 198, 201, 203, 249, 298, 321ff., 374
Veitch, S. O., 423, 426, 430
Villard, Oswald Garrison, 285

W

Walker, Cleveland G., 26, 79, 85, 198
Wallace, C. A., 59
Walstrom, Milton C., 335
Waison, L. P., 175
Ward, Lucille E., 65
Washington, George, 81, 232
Waters, Mary, xxiii
Watkins-Owens, Irma, 42f., 46, 53f., 62
Watson, Hugh H., 96, 254, 285
Watson, James S., 30, 131
Waugh, D. A., 64
Welles, Sumner, 285
Wells, H. G., 359
Wesley, Charles, 231
West India Committee, 377
West Indies National Emergency Council (WINEC), xxiv, 216ff., 220f., 224–28, 230ff., 234, 236ff., 241f., 244f., 249, 262f., 272f., 381, 423
West Indies National Council (WINC), 245, 250, 253, 258ff.,

Index of Names and Organizations

262, 264, 274ff., 278, 283, 287–90, 292, 312, 381, 384, 411
White, Walter, 231, 243, 284f., 289, 313, 333
Williams, Bonita, 131
Williams, Eric, 320, 404, 410, 416
Williams, Henry Sylvester, 7, 26
Williams, Vernal G., 59, 131
Williams, W. A., 272
Wilkens, Roy, 289
Wilson, Woodrow, xxi
Wilson, Benjamin B., 128, 201, 291
Wint, D. T., 25
Women's International League for Progress and Freedom (WILPF), 240, 259
Wood, Edward F. L., 11, 31
Woolley, Charles Campbell, 149
Workers Alliance, 131
Workers Party of America, 56f.
Wright, Thomas (Morris Cargill), 356, 417

Y

Yergan, Max, 193, 231
Young Men's Christian Association (YMCA), 131, 193, 259
Young, John S., xxix, 74, 127

Z

Zeidenfelt, Alex, xxii, xxiii, 184

www.ingramcontent.com/pod-product-compliance
Lightning Source LLC
Chambersburg PA
CBHW020832020526
44114CB00040B/596